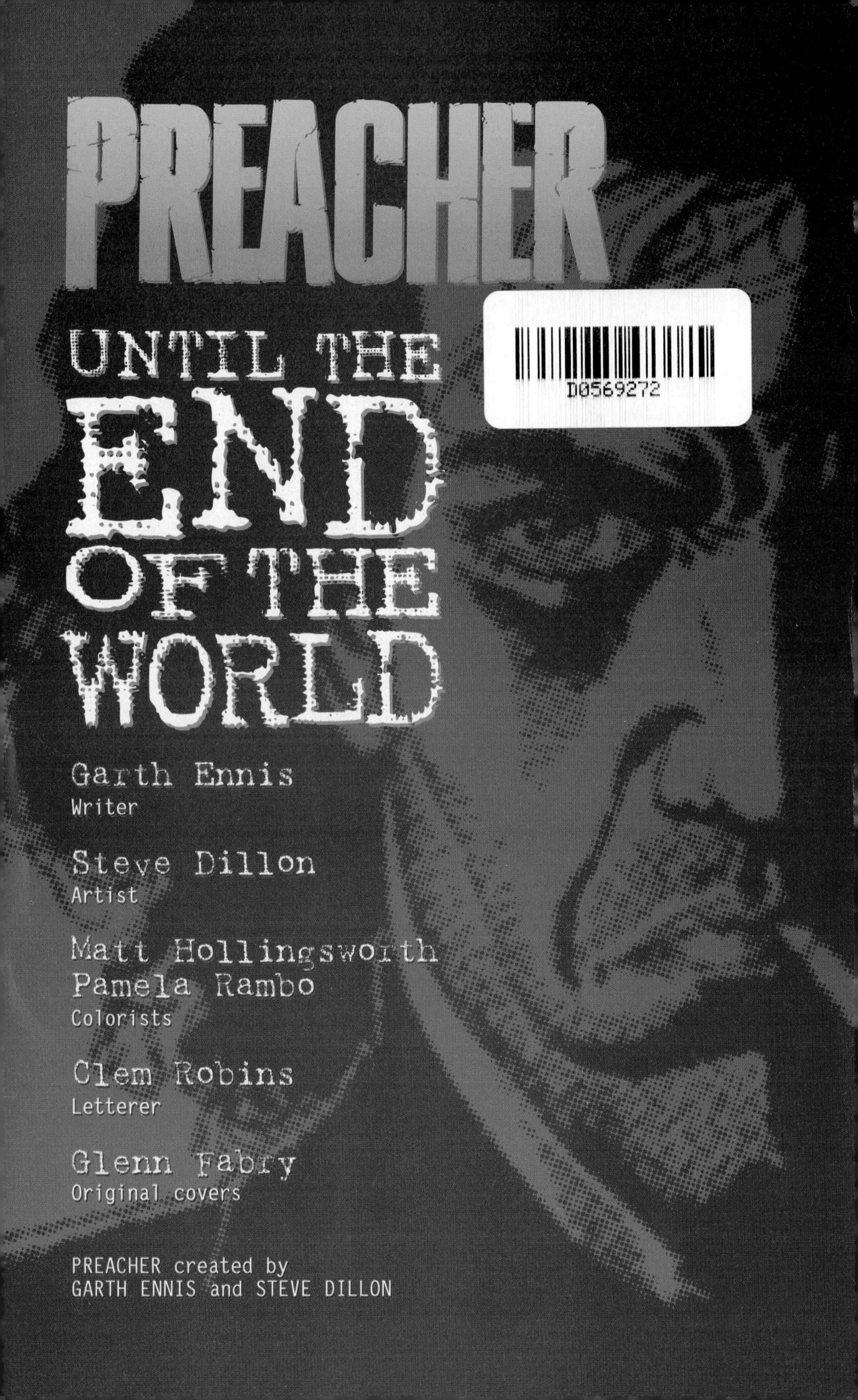

PREACHER

UNTIL THE END OF THE WORLD

Garth Ennis
Writer

Steve Dillon
Artist

Matt Hollingsworth
Pamela Rambo
Colorists

Clem Robins
Letterer

Glenn Fabry
Original covers

PREACHER created by
GARTH ENNIS and STEVE DILLON

PREACHER: UNTIL THE END OF THE WORLD

Published by DC Comics. Cover, introduction and compilation
copyright © 1997 DC Comics. All Rights Reserved.
Originally published in single magazine form as PREACHER 8-17.
Copyright © 1995, 1996 Garth Ennis and Steve Dillon.
All Rights Reserved. All characters, their distinctive likenesses and related indicia
featured in this publication are trademarks of Garth Ennis and Steve Dillon.
Vertigo is a trademark of DC Comics.
The stories, characters, and incidents featured in this publication are entirely fictional.
DC Comics, 1700 Broadway, New York, NY 10019
A division of Warner Bros. - An AOL Time Warner Company
Printed in Canada. Fourth Printing.
ISBN:1-56389-312-6

Cover painting by Glenn Fabry.
Publication design by Jim Chadwick/Suddenly Chadwick!

INTRODUCTION
by Kevin Smith

This is sort of a story about how you can't please everybody (or in some cases, anybody).

The last time I said something nice about PREACHER, the good folks who compile the trade paperbacks at DC pulled a quote from my gushing praise of the parties involved in bringing this fierce new book to life, and they printed it on the cover — along the top and above the title.

That *really* put a smile on my face. Not only was my name finally on a comic book (sort of) — but it was on a compilation of a fantastic comic book that I wish anybody (or in some cases, everybody) would give a try. I was honored that any sort of connection would forever be made between this brave, original entry into the art form called comics, and myself.

For the record, the pull quote was "More fun than going to the movies!," complete with my name and then-filmography printed underneath.

Then it dawned on me: I was suddenly a very easy target.

And — as with all easy targets — some zero took perhaps the easiest shot in the world at me.

Hiding within a then-current issue of The Comics Journal, at the bottom of the 'Viva la Comics!' section, was my quote and credits — over which was the oh-so-damn-witty headline "Well, maybe one of *yours* ..."

Everyone's a comedian...

It was my fault, however — if you hang your balls out like that, there's always at least one person who wants to introduce them to a swift kick (a routine occurrence in my line of work, actually).

So you can imagine my trepidation when Garth asked me to write an intro for this collection...

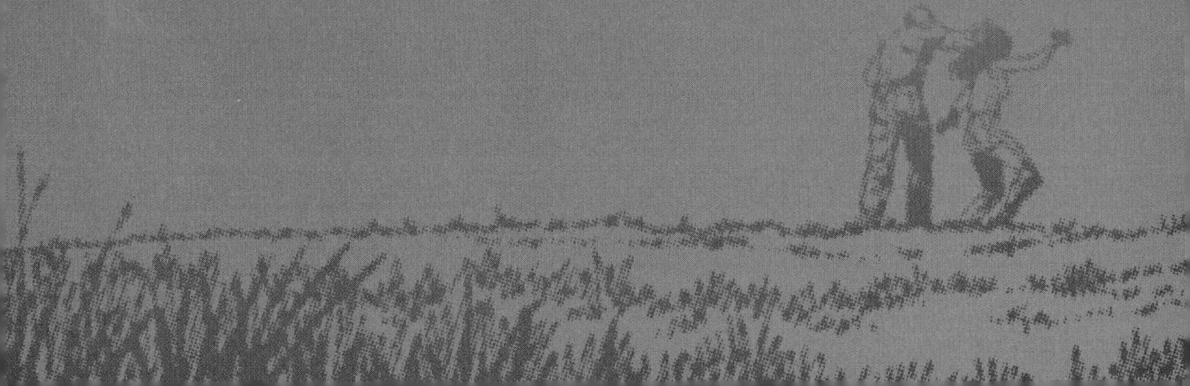

...Actually, you can't.

Because there was none.

See, I'd risk getting kicked in the balls again to gush over PREACHER. And why? Because Garth hangs a great deal more than his balls out with every issue, and risks far more than just a kick by fashioning an ongoing tale that's packed wall-to-wall with thought-provoking commentary on religion and spirituality (fave-rave topics of mine).

We're instructed from an early age that discussion of religion is a social faux pas - that to talk about God is to possibly offend someone. Garth must have been absent when they taught that lesson, or perhaps chose to ignore it. And thank God he did - because in the pages of PREACHER, Mister Ennis talks about faith, spirituality, religion, and hypocrisy in a fashion that any publisher responsible for putting out the monthly antics of flying, invulnerable and magic-ring-bearing men would have to be near-crazy (or perhaps just plain smart) to mass-market. Usually such work is cited as "too controversial."

"Controversial," as we all know, is often a euphemism for "interesting and intelligent." Although the pages of PREACHER are filled with avant garde takes on the nature of God and the questionable manner in which religion is followed by the masses without thought (not to mention renderings of brutal bloodletting and graphic, often disturbingly funny violence), this is not a book full of sensationalistic crap writing or drawing. To me, sensationalistic crap writing is lopping off the hand of a time-honored character to give him a "new direction," and sensationalistic crap drawing is page after page of uber-nimrods penned with little regard for proper proportions, set against background-deficient splash pages.

Garth and Steve fall prey to none of that - they tell straightforward stories with the enviable skill often found only possessed by those who've spent years honing their craft. And while both have achieved respectability and kudos prior to their current endeavor (see Garth and Steve's run on HELLBLAZER, not to mention Garth's Fleetway-published *True Faith*), it is on PREACHER that both have hit their to-date creative zenith - a synergism that has produced the most scintillating and - I'll say it - *brilliant* piece of comics literature to come down the pike since DC landed Moore, Gaiman, and Morrison (why are non-Americans so much better at this than most?).

In the Angelville saga, Garth has basically told us something that we've known all along - family can be a scary thing. Whether it's the gotta-have-a-member-of-the-cloth-in-the-family-demanding Gran'ma, the chicken-fucking T.C., or the ready-to-make-a-man-out-of-ya Jody, the reader has to see some uncomfortable similarities (albeit distant ones, I'd hope) to his or her own dysfunctional family tree.

Not that it's all evil in this tale of woe. Garth gives us two powerful tastes of star-cros't love in the poignant flashbacks to both the gob-in-the-face introduction of Jesse's parents, and the knew-it-when-Ilaid-eyes-on-him/her romance of Jesse and Tulip. And from the more orally amorous interpretation of "star-gazing," to Jesse's declaration of "Until the end of the world," Garth and Steve flesh out a relationship both credible and familiar.

But at the same time, if one looks closely, the true malevolent fuck of the story isn't Jody - although his cold proclamation of "You come with us quiet and make no fuss, or I'll shoot her through the fuckin' head," would certainly make him a candidate for the title. No - the real black soul is the Ennis/Dillon team who actually make good on Jody's threat - albeit temporarily - with the last panel of "How I Learned to Love the Lord" (I can't remember another piece of graphic art leaving me as speechless or as manically anxious to get my hands on the next installment).

The "Hunters" storyline introduces yet another wicked pair of Ennis and Dillon creations. In The Grail, we find a bunch who know something about Christ himself that would send Christians the world over first to the nearest bar, and subsequently to collect every donated cent back from Holy Mother Church. And in Jesus de Sade, we meet the ultimate in debauchery, whose casual aside of "Ah, Demi - I do hope I'll have the pleasure of urinating into your cleavage later?" and fistful of chocolate (...or is it?) make for the most delightfully decadent and evil arsehole this side of the Moore-scripted Anton Arcane.

Throw in an Irish vampire, a couple of titty-shots, some marathon, catch-up in-and-out sessions, and the best dialogue being written in comics today, and you've got some damned exquisite and thought-provoking entertainment. And for those who missed it the first time, I'll say it again - this book *is* more fun than going to the movies...

...even mine.

Garth and Steve have accomplished nothing short of a miracle in PREACHER - producing a hot new title that actually *surpasses* its hype. They are to be congratulated, envied, marveled at, and well paid.

And if this book offends the delicate sensibilities of some people due to their religious convictions - well, that saddens me. Because, as a man who has an unflappable, fervent, and devout faith in God, let me assure those who find this book spiritually questionable that I know - in my heart and soul - the Lord to be mighty, just, loving, and righteous...

...and a huge fan of PREACHER.

Kevin Smith

Kevin Smith has made three movies to date. The first one was set in a convenience store and received huge praise and awards at the Sundance and Cannes Film Festivals (Clerks). The second was set in an indoor shopping center, got trashed by critics and tanked at the box office... but was still kind of funny (Mallrats). The third one - set in the comic-book industry - isn't out yet, though people who've seen it seem to like it (Chasing Amy).

His next assignment is putting words in the mouth of Clark Kent and his Kryptonian alter ego in the new Superman movie from Warner Bros.

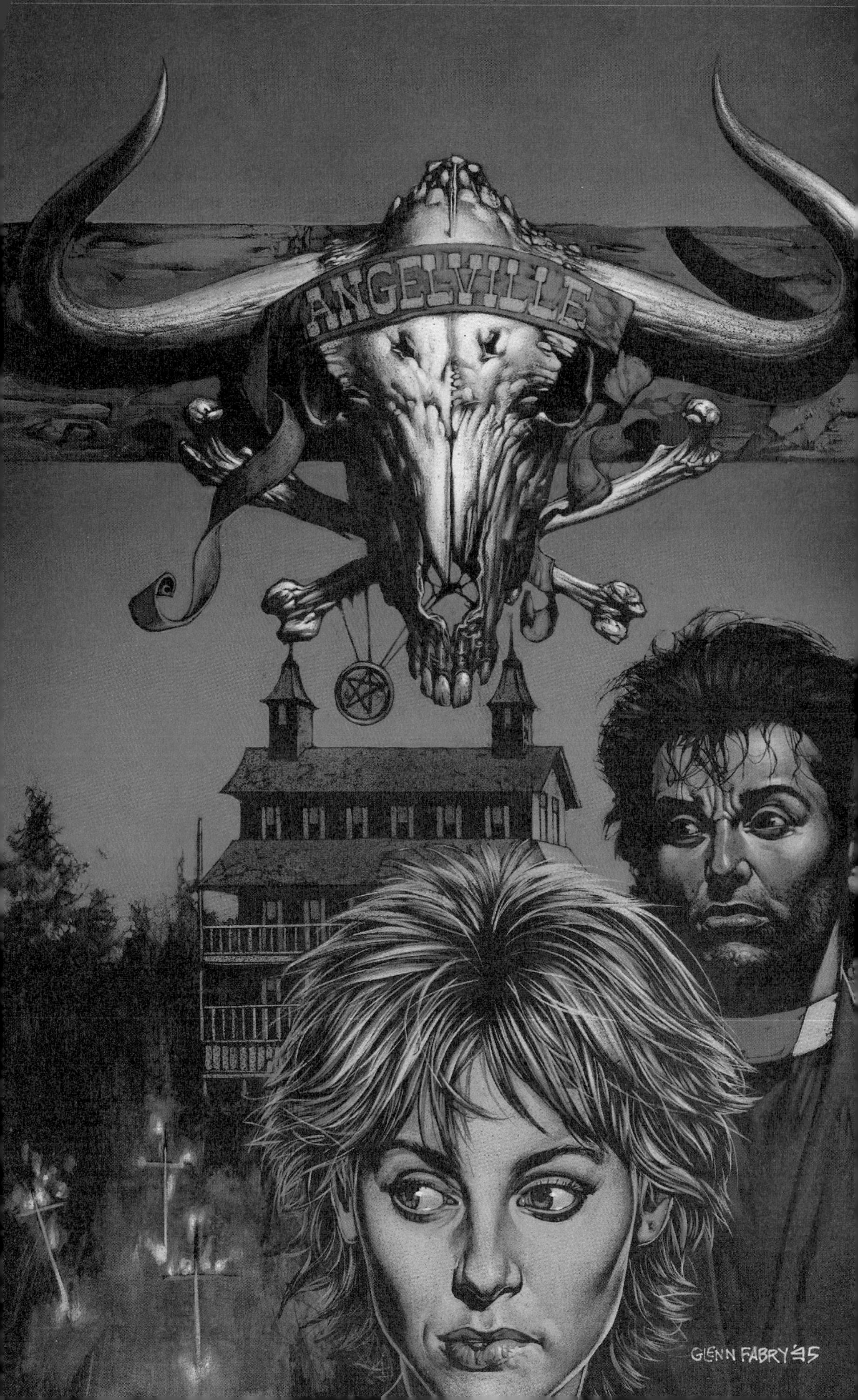
ANGELVILLE
GLENN FABRY '95

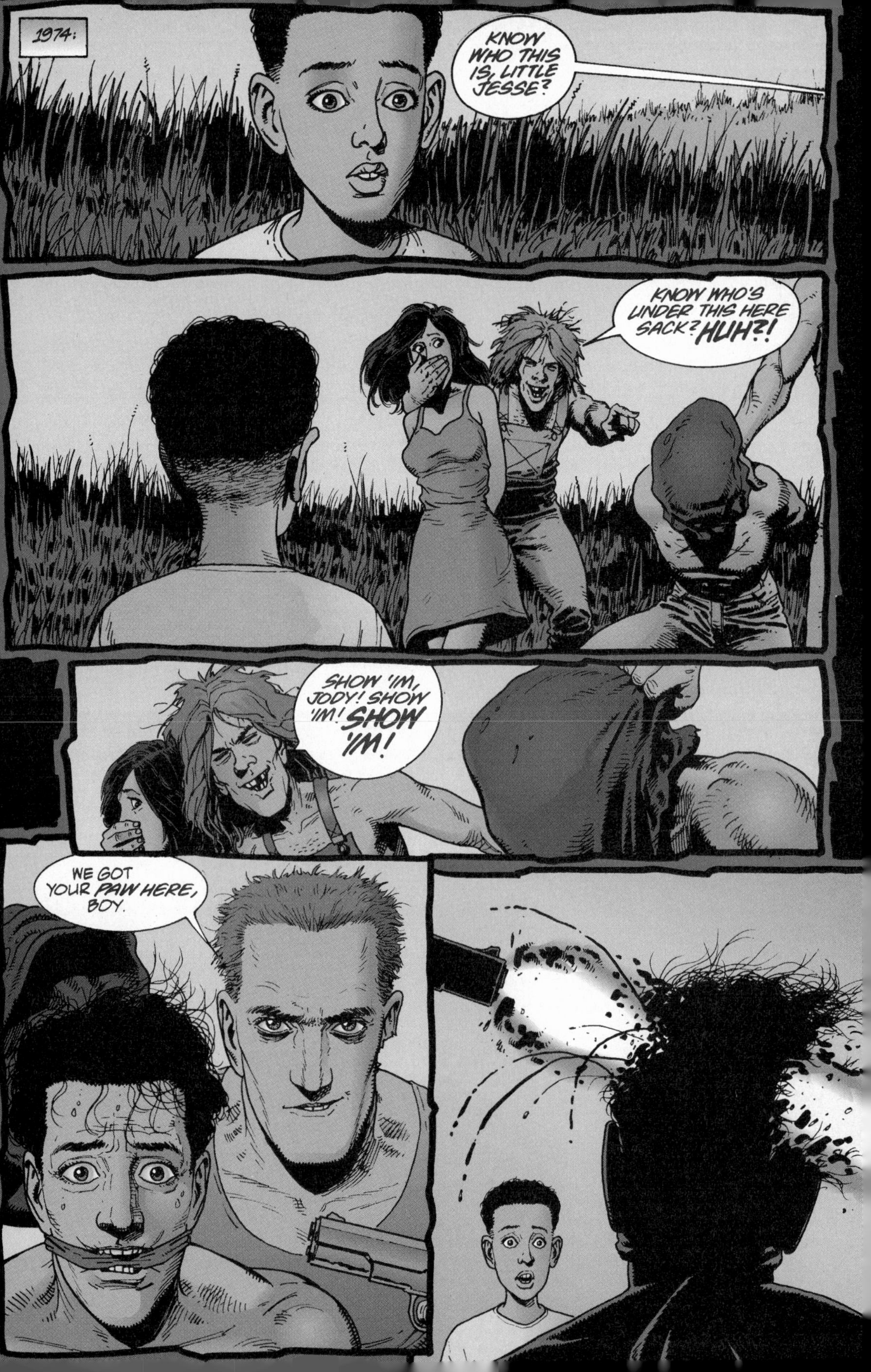
1974:
KNOW WHO THIS IS, LITTLE JESSE?
KNOW WHO'S UNDER THIS HERE SACK? HUH?!
SHOW 'IM, JODY! SHOW 'IM! SHOW 'IM!
WE GOT YOUR PAW HERE, BOY.

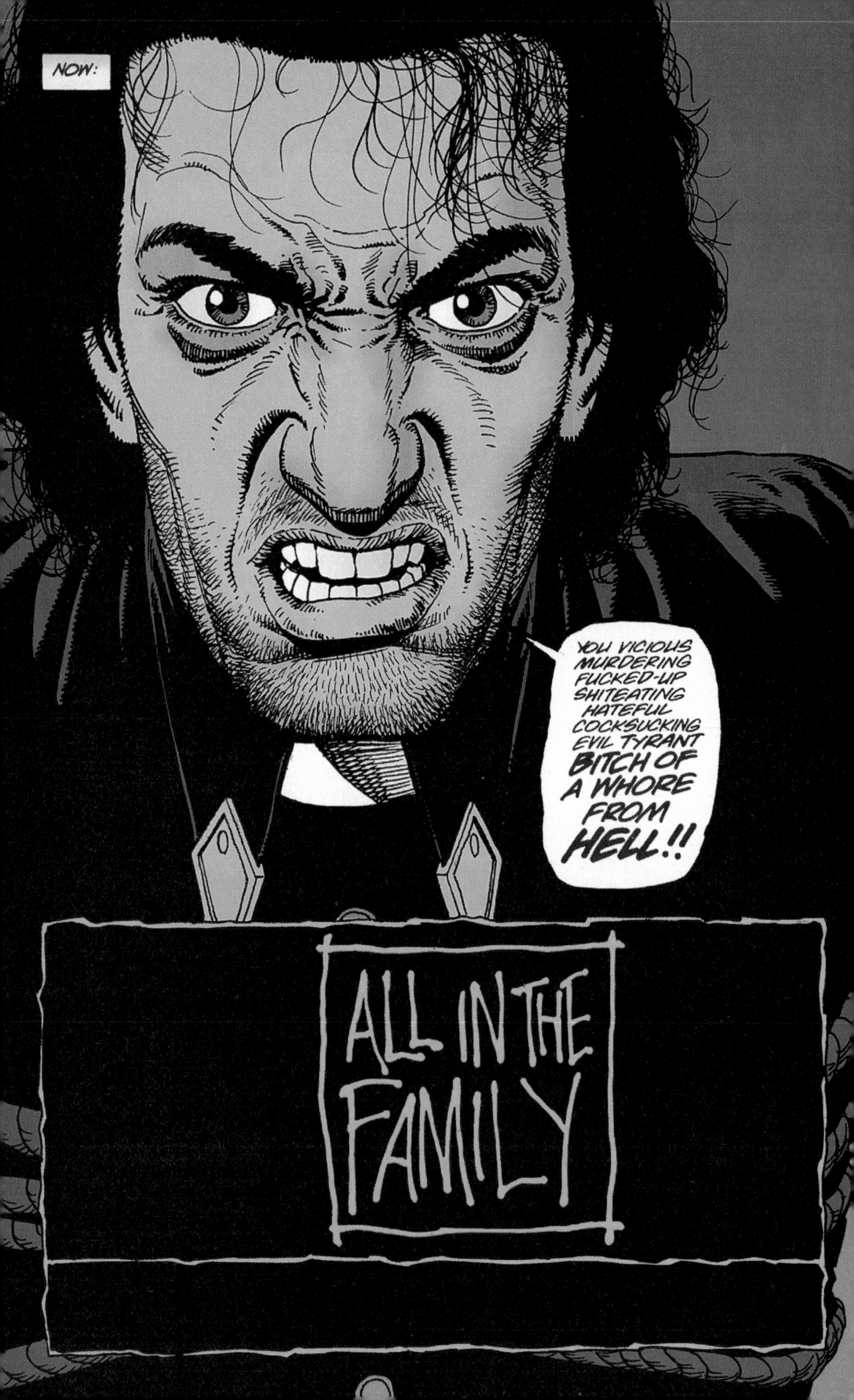
NOW:
YOU VICIOUS MURDERING FUCKED-UP SHITEATING HATEFUL COCKSUCKING EVIL TYRANT BITCH OF A WHORE FROM HELL!!
ALL IN THE FAMILY

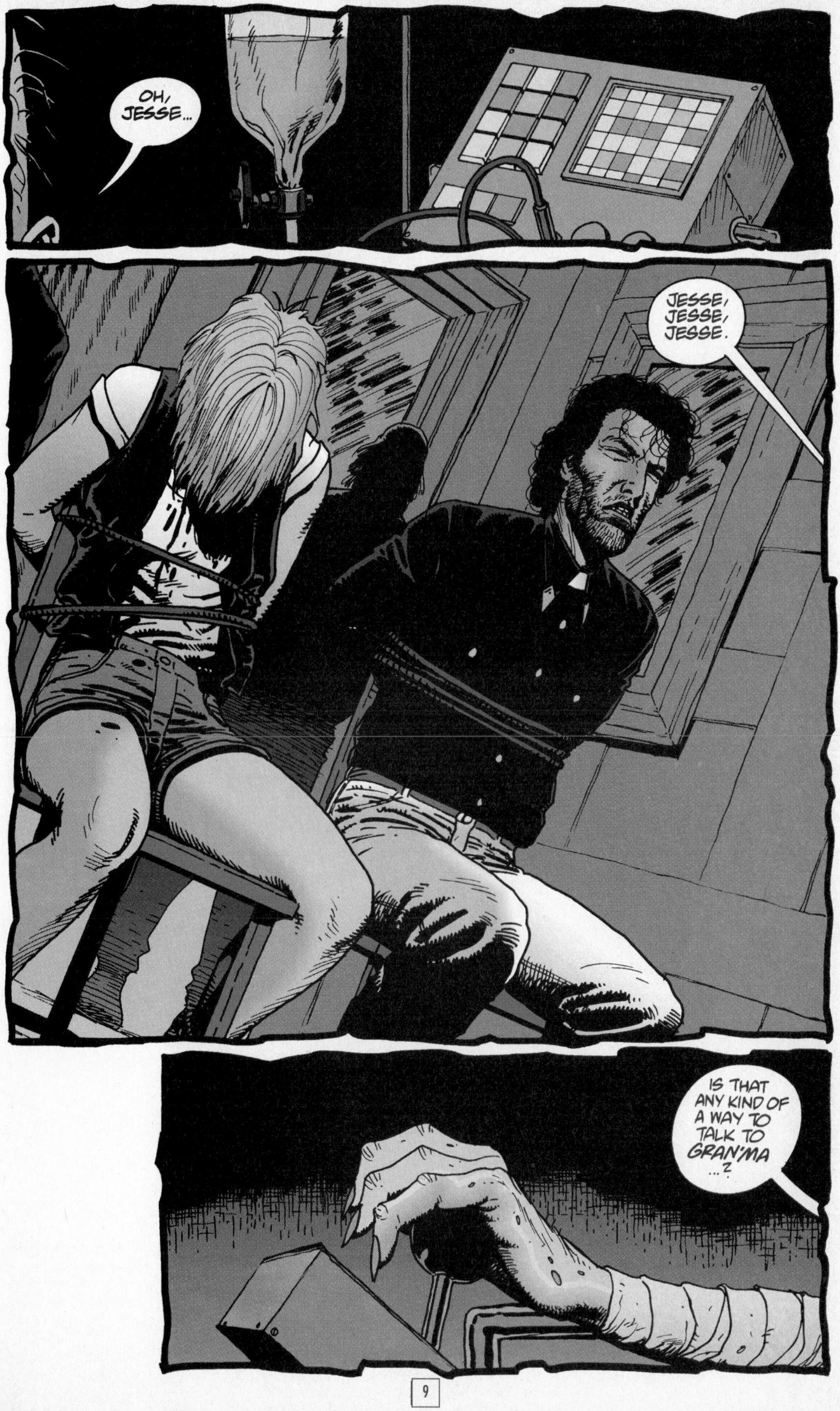
OH, JESSE...
JESSE, JESSE, JESSE.
IS THAT ANY KIND OF A WAY TO TALK TO GRAN'MA ...?

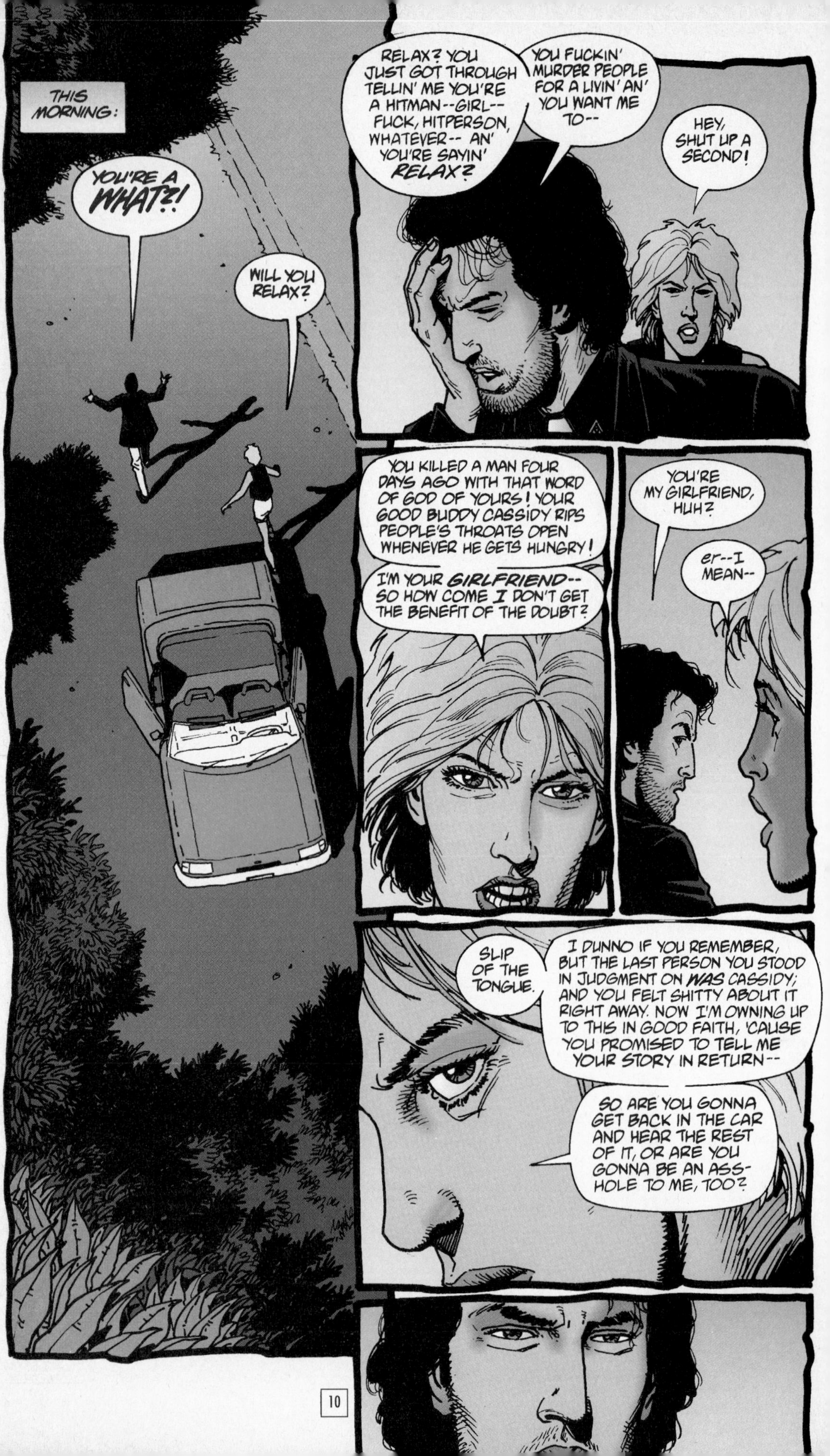
THIS MORNING:
YOU'RE A WHAT?!
WILL YOU RELAX?
RELAX? YOU JUST GOT THROUGH TELLIN' ME YOU'RE A HITMAN--GIRL--FUCK, HITPERSON, WHATEVER-- AN' YOU'RE SAYIN' RELAX?
YOU FUCKIN' MURDER PEOPLE FOR A LIVIN' AN' YOU WANT ME TO--
HEY, SHUT UP A SECOND!
YOU KILLED A MAN FOUR DAYS AGO WITH THAT WORD OF GOD OF YOURS! YOUR GOOD BUDDY CASSIDY RIPS PEOPLE'S THROATS OPEN WHENEVER HE GETS HUNGRY!
I'M YOUR GIRLFRIEND-- SO HOW COME I DON'T GET THE BENEFIT OF THE DOUBT?
YOU'RE MY GIRLFRIEND, HUH?
er--I MEAN--
SLIP OF THE TONGUE.
I DUNNO IF YOU REMEMBER, BUT THE LAST PERSON YOU STOOD IN JUDGMENT ON WAS CASSIDY; AND YOU FELT SHITTY ABOUT IT RIGHT AWAY. NOW I'M OWNING UP TO THIS IN GOOD FAITH, 'CAUSE YOU PROMISED TO TELL ME YOUR STORY IN RETURN--
SO ARE YOU GONNA GET BACK IN THE CAR AND HEAR THE REST OF IT, OR ARE YOU GONNA BE AN ASS-HOLE TO ME, TOO?

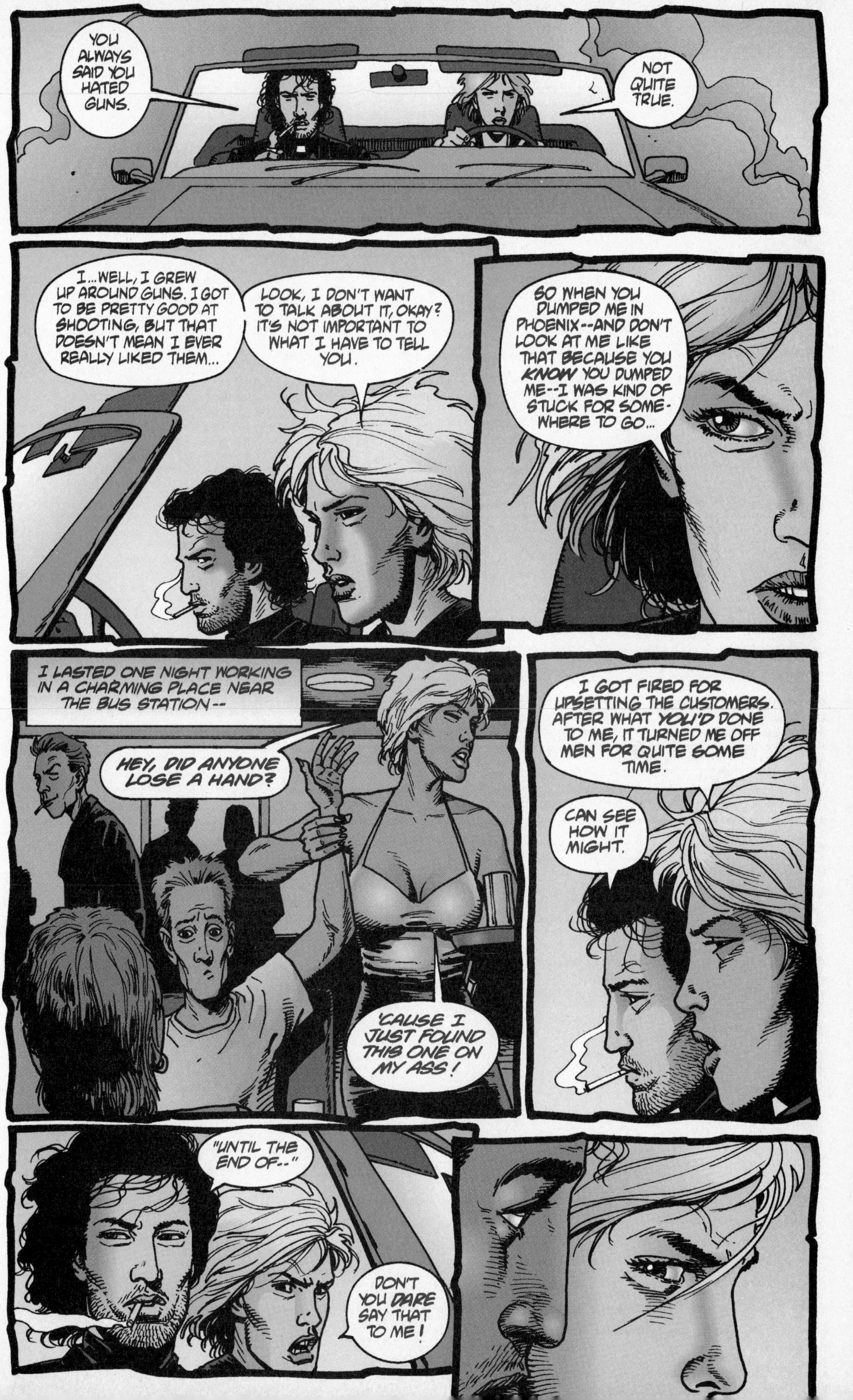

YOU ALWAYS SAID YOU HATED GUNS.
NOT QUITE TRUE.
I...WELL, I GREW UP AROUND GUNS. I GOT TO BE PRETTY GOOD AT SHOOTING, BUT THAT DOESN'T MEAN I EVER REALLY LIKED THEM...
LOOK, I DON'T WANT TO TALK ABOUT IT, OKAY? IT'S NOT IMPORTANT TO WHAT I HAVE TO TELL YOU.
SO WHEN YOU DUMPED ME IN PHOENIX--AND DON'T LOOK AT ME LIKE THAT BECAUSE YOU KNOW YOU DUMPED ME--I WAS KIND OF STUCK FOR SOME-WHERE TO GO...
I LASTED ONE NIGHT WORKING IN A CHARMING PLACE NEAR THE BUS STATION--
HEY, DID ANYONE LOSE A HAND?
'CAUSE I JUST FOUND THIS ONE ON MY ASS!
I GOT FIRED FOR UPSETTING THE CUSTOMERS. AFTER WHAT YOU'D DONE TO ME, IT TURNED ME OFF MEN FOR QUITE SOME TIME.
CAN SEE HOW IT MIGHT.
"UNTIL THE END OF--"
DON'T YOU DARE SAY THAT TO ME!

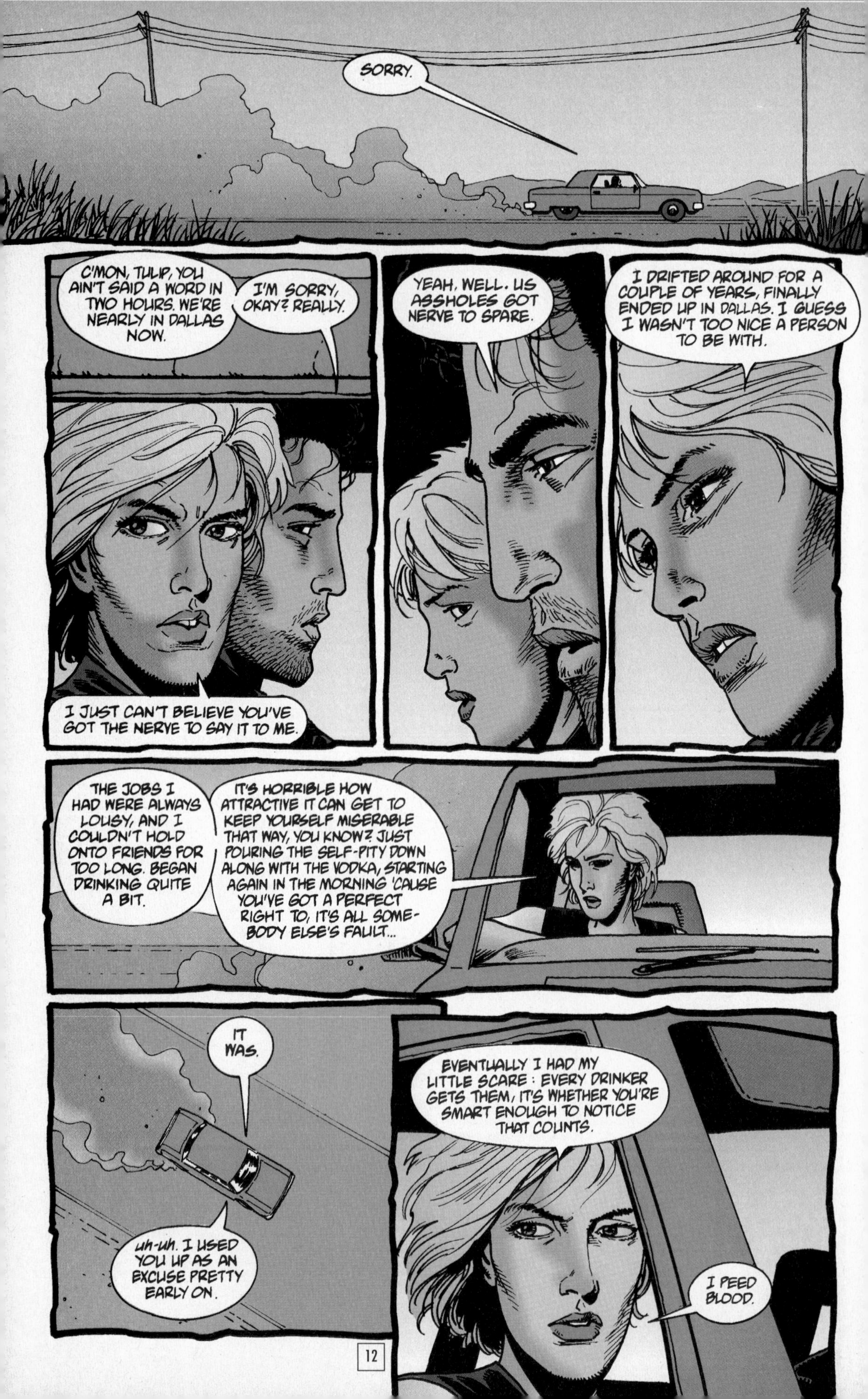
SORRY.
C'MON, TULIP, YOU AIN'T SAID A WORD IN TWO HOURS. WE'RE NEARLY IN DALLAS NOW.
I'M SORRY, OKAY? REALLY.
I JUST CAN'T BELIEVE YOU'VE GOT THE NERVE TO SAY IT TO ME.
YEAH, WELL. US ASSHOLES GOT NERVE TO SPARE.
I DRIFTED AROUND FOR A COUPLE OF YEARS, FINALLY ENDED UP IN DALLAS. I GUESS I WASN'T TOO NICE A PERSON TO BE WITH.
THE JOBS I HAD WERE ALWAYS LOUSY, AND I COULDN'T HOLD ONTO FRIENDS FOR TOO LONG. BEGAN DRINKING QUITE A BIT.
IT'S HORRIBLE HOW ATTRACTIVE IT CAN GET TO KEEP YOURSELF MISERABLE THAT WAY, YOU KNOW? JUST POURING THE SELF-PITY DOWN ALONG WITH THE VODKA, STARTING AGAIN IN THE MORNING 'CAUSE YOU'VE GOT A PERFECT RIGHT TO, IT'S ALL SOMEBODY ELSE'S FAULT...
IT WAS.
uh-uh. I USED YOU UP AS AN EXCUSE PRETTY EARLY ON.
EVENTUALLY I HAD MY LITTLE SCARE : EVERY DRINKER GETS THEM, IT'S WHETHER YOU'RE SMART ENOUGH TO NOTICE THAT COUNTS.
I PEED BLOOD.

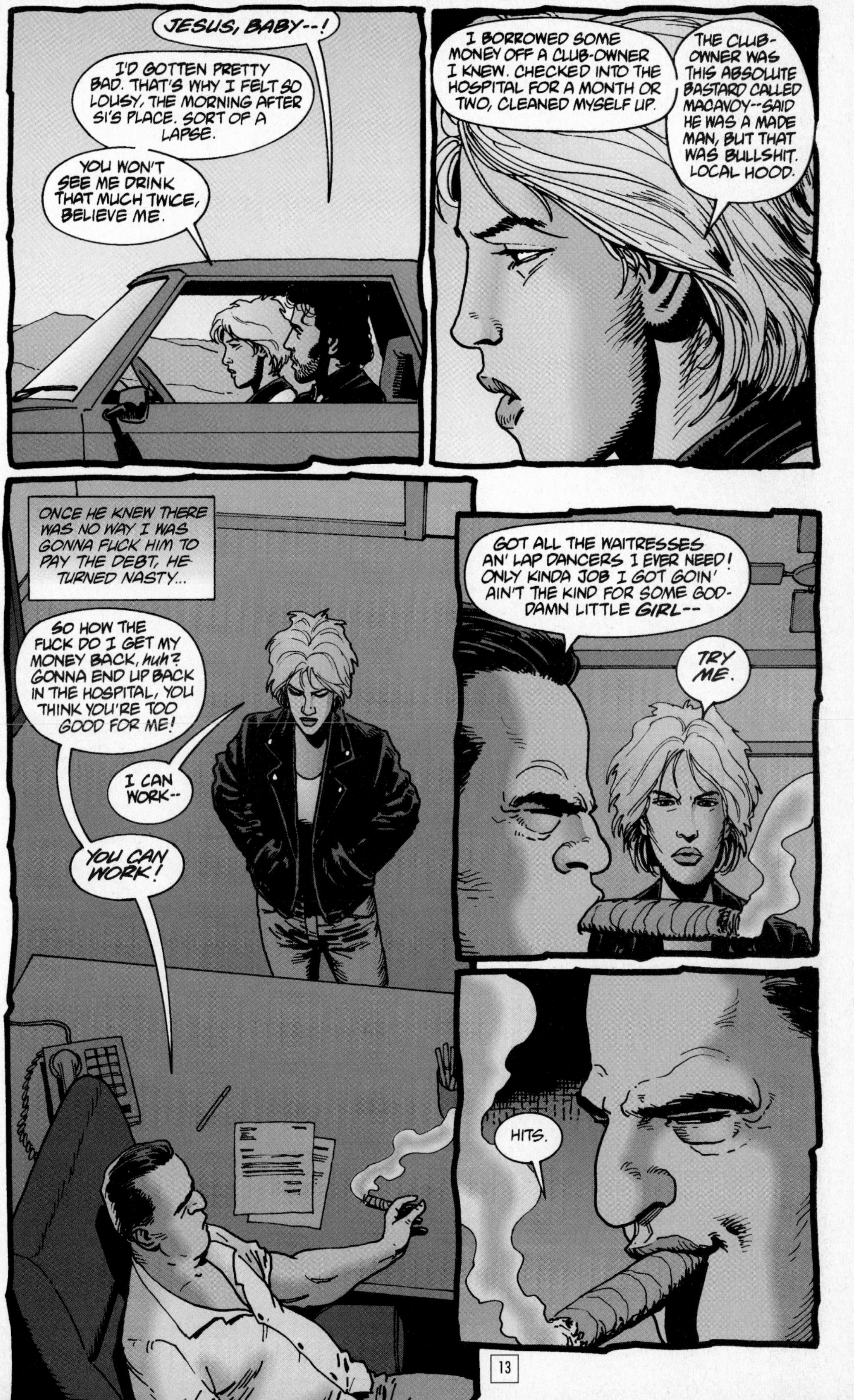
JESUS, BABY--!
I'D GOTTEN PRETTY BAD. THAT'S WHY I FELT SO LOUSY, THE MORNING AFTER SI'S PLACE. SORT OF A LAPSE.
YOU WON'T SEE ME DRINK THAT MUCH TWICE, BELIEVE ME.
I BORROWED SOME MONEY OFF A CLUB-OWNER I KNEW. CHECKED INTO THE HOSPITAL FOR A MONTH OR TWO, CLEANED MYSELF UP.
THE CLUB-OWNER WAS THIS ABSOLUTE BASTARD CALLED MACAVOY--SAID HE WAS A MADE MAN, BUT THAT WAS BULLSHIT. LOCAL HOOD.
ONCE HE KNEW THERE WAS NO WAY I WAS GONNA FUCK HIM TO PAY THE DEBT, HE TURNED NASTY...
SO HOW THE FUCK DO I GET MY MONEY BACK, huh? GONNA END UP BACK IN THE HOSPITAL, YOU THINK YOU'RE TOO GOOD FOR ME!
I CAN WORK--
YOU CAN WORK!
GOT ALL THE WAITRESSES AN' LAP DANCERS I EVER NEED! ONLY KINDA JOB I GOT GOIN' AIN'T THE KIND FOR SOME GOD-DAMN LITTLE GIRL--
TRY ME.
HITS.

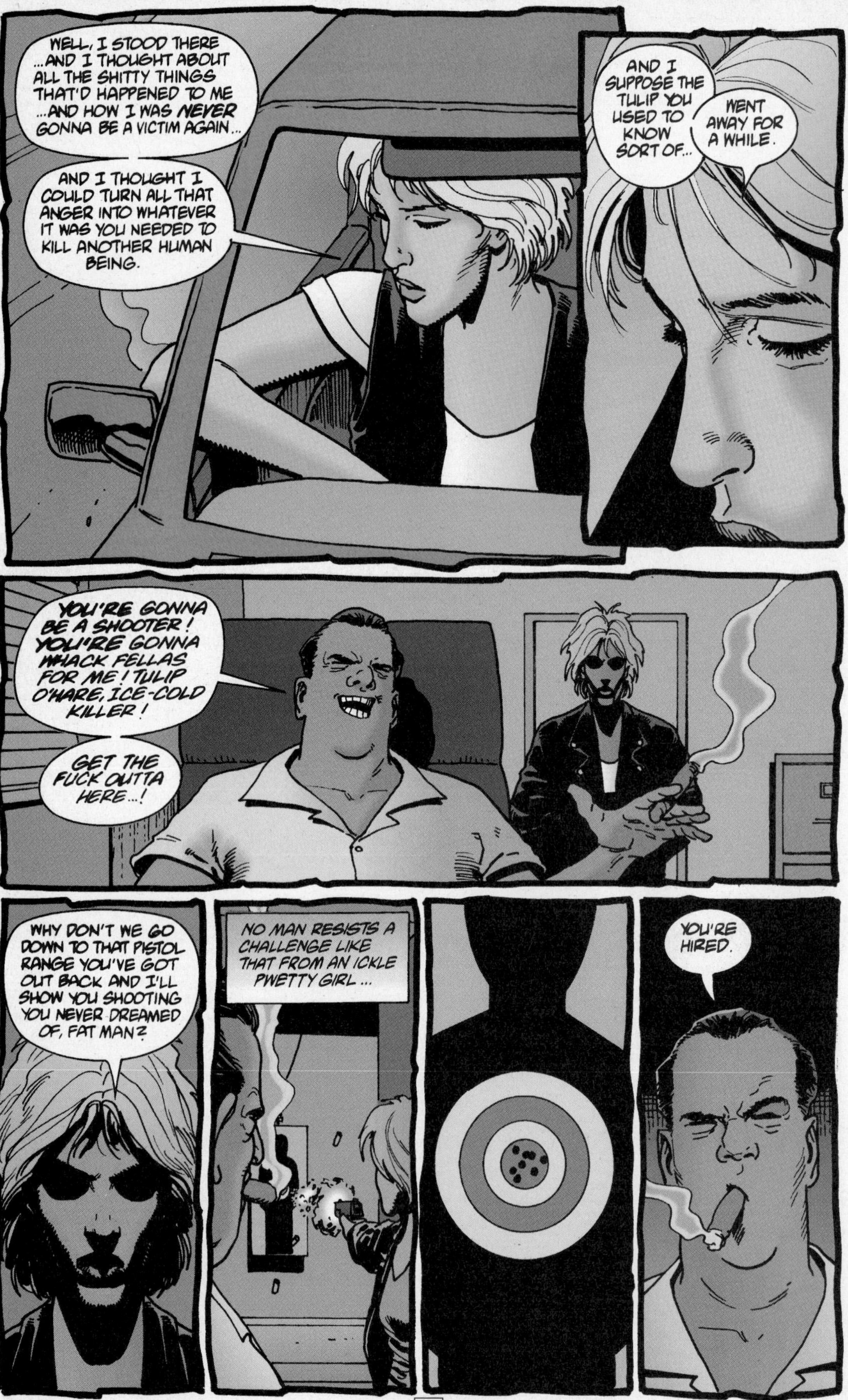
WELL, I STOOD THERE ...AND I THOUGHT ABOUT ALL THE SHITTY THINGS THAT'D HAPPENED TO ME ...AND HOW I WAS NEVER GONNA BE A VICTIM AGAIN...
AND I THOUGHT I COULD TURN ALL THAT ANGER INTO WHATEVER IT WAS YOU NEEDED TO KILL ANOTHER HUMAN BEING.
AND I SUPPOSE THE TULIP YOU USED TO KNOW SORT OF...
WENT AWAY FOR A WHILE.
YOU'RE GONNA BE A SHOOTER! YOU'RE GONNA WHACK FELLAS FOR ME! TULIP O'HARE, ICE-COLD KILLER!
GET THE FUCK OUTTA HERE...!
WHY DON'T WE GO DOWN TO THAT PISTOL RANGE YOU'VE GOT OUT BACK AND I'LL SHOW YOU SHOOTING YOU NEVER DREAMED OF, FAT MAN?
NO MAN RESISTS A CHALLENGE LIKE THAT FROM AN ICKLE PWETTY GIRL...
YOU'RE HIRED.

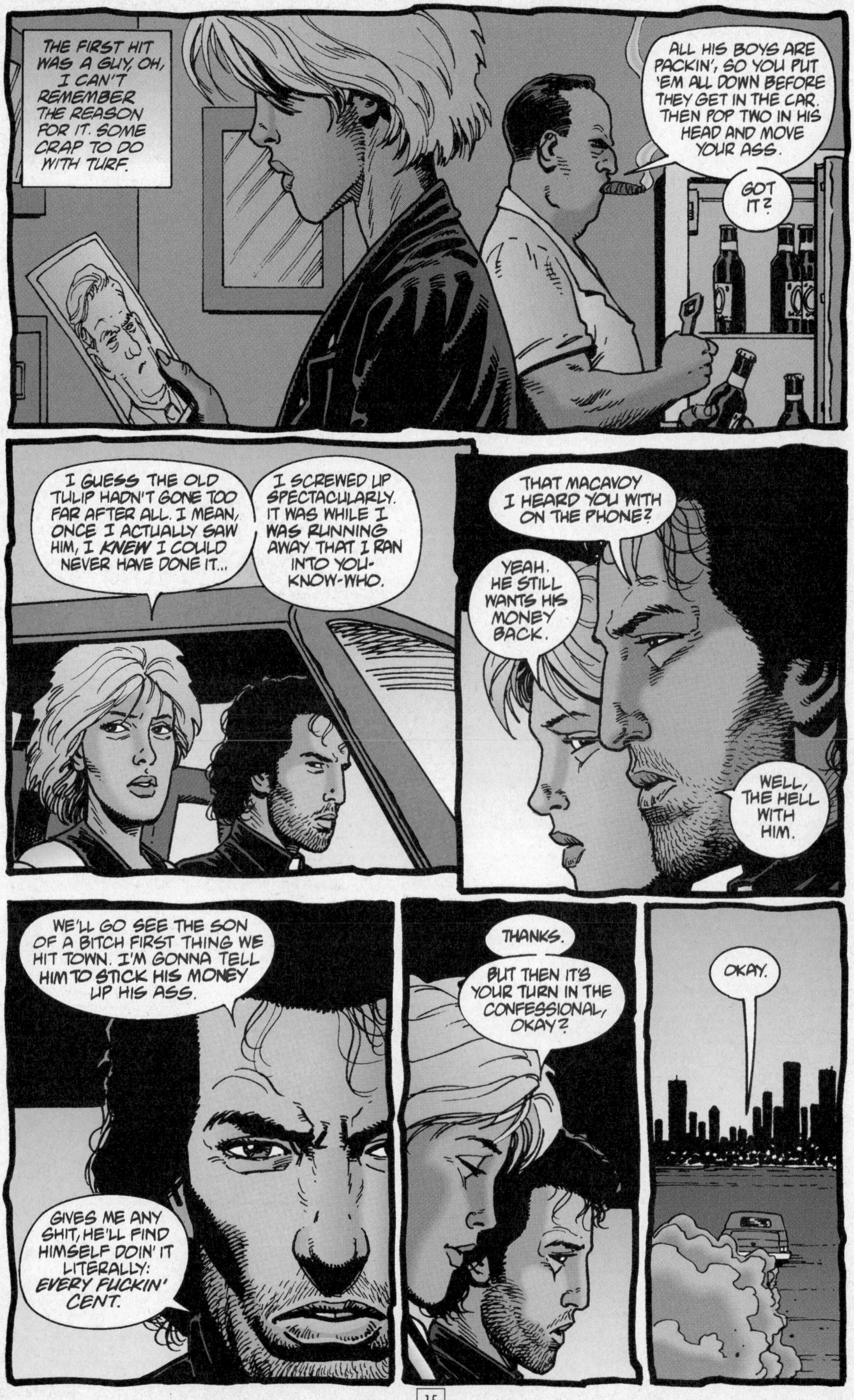
THE FIRST HIT WAS A GUY, OH, I CAN'T REMEMBER THE REASON FOR IT. SOME CRAP TO DO WITH TURF.
ALL HIS BOYS ARE PACKIN', SO YOU PUT 'EM ALL DOWN BEFORE THEY GET IN THE CAR. THEN POP TWO IN HIS HEAD AND MOVE YOUR ASS.
GOT IT?
I GUESS THE OLD TULIP HADN'T GONE TOO FAR AFTER ALL. I MEAN, ONCE I ACTUALLY SAW HIM, I *KNEW* I COULD NEVER HAVE DONE IT...
I SCREWED UP SPECTACULARLY. IT WAS WHILE I WAS RUNNING AWAY THAT I RAN INTO YOU-KNOW-WHO.
THAT MACAVOY I HEARD YOU WITH ON THE PHONE?
YEAH. HE STILL WANTS HIS MONEY BACK.
WELL, THE HELL WITH HIM.
WE'LL GO SEE THE SON OF A BITCH FIRST THING WE HIT TOWN. I'M GONNA TELL HIM TO STICK HIS MONEY UP HIS ASS.
GIVES ME ANY SHIT, HE'LL FIND HIMSELF DOIN' IT LITERALLY: *EVERY FUCKIN' CENT.*
THANKS.
BUT THEN IT'S YOUR TURN IN THE CONFESSIONAL, OKAY?
OKAY.

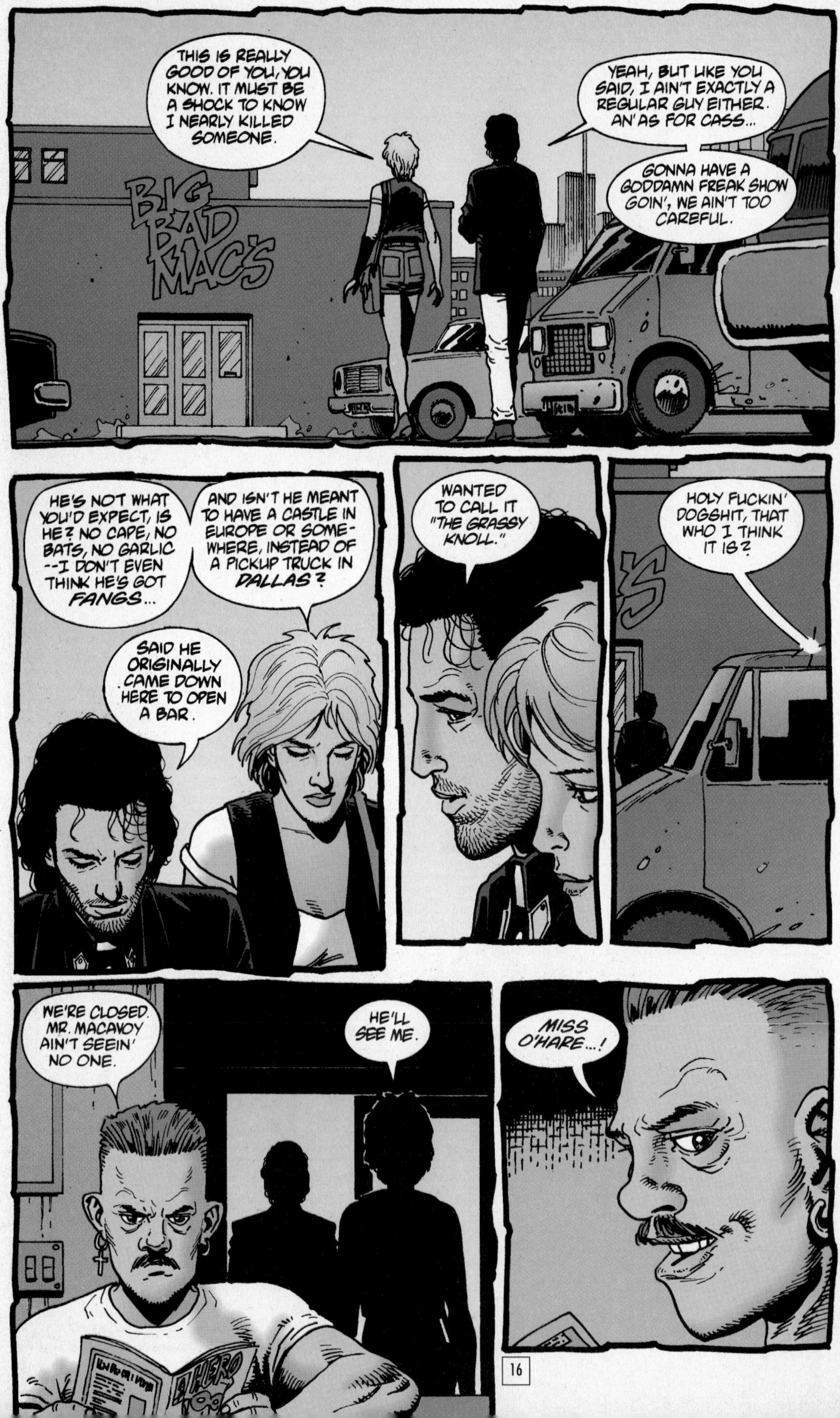
THIS IS REALLY GOOD OF YOU, YOU KNOW. IT MUST BE A SHOCK TO KNOW I NEARLY KILLED SOMEONE.
YEAH, BUT LIKE YOU SAID, I AIN'T EXACTLY A REGULAR GUY EITHER. AN' AS FOR CASS...
GONNA HAVE A GODDAMN FREAK SHOW GOIN', WE AIN'T TOO CAREFUL.
BIG BAD MAC'S
HE'S NOT WHAT YOU'D EXPECT, IS HE? NO CAPE, NO BATS, NO GARLIC --I DON'T EVEN THINK HE'S GOT FANGS...
AND ISN'T HE MEANT TO HAVE A CASTLE IN EUROPE OR SOMEWHERE, INSTEAD OF A PICKUP TRUCK IN DALLAS?
SAID HE ORIGINALLY CAME DOWN HERE TO OPEN A BAR.
WANTED TO CALL IT "THE GRASSY KNOLL."
HOLY FUCKIN' DOGSHIT, THAT WHO I THINK IT IS?
WE'RE CLOSED. MR. MACAVOY AIN'T SEEIN' NO ONE.
HE'LL SEE ME.
MISS O'HARE...!

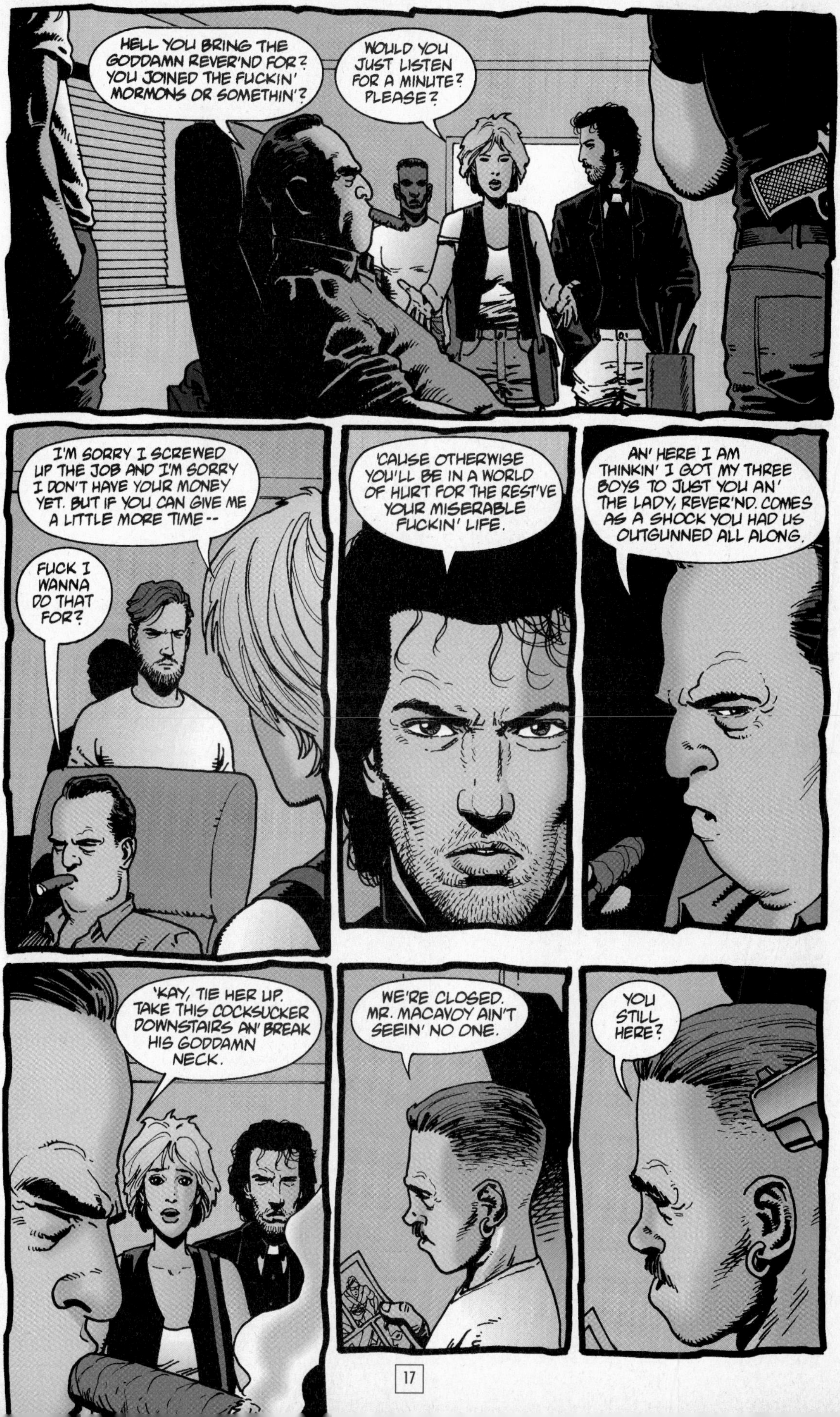
HELL YOU BRING THE GODDAMN REVER'ND FOR? YOU JOINED THE FUCKIN' MORMONS OR SOMETHIN'?
WOULD YOU JUST LISTEN FOR A MINUTE? PLEASE?
I'M SORRY I SCREWED UP THE JOB AND I'M SORRY I DON'T HAVE YOUR MONEY YET. BUT IF YOU CAN GIVE ME A LITTLE MORE TIME--
FUCK I WANNA DO THAT FOR?
'CAUSE OTHERWISE YOU'LL BE IN A WORLD OF HURT FOR THE REST'VE YOUR MISERABLE FUCKIN' LIFE.
AN' HERE I AM THINKIN' I GOT MY THREE BOYS TO JUST YOU AN' THE LADY, REVER'ND. COMES AS A SHOCK YOU HAD US OUTGUNNED ALL ALONG.
'KAY, TIE HER UP. TAKE THIS COCKSUCKER DOWNSTAIRS AN' BREAK HIS GODDAMN NECK.
WE'RE CLOSED. MR. MACAVOY AIN'T SEEIN' NO ONE.
YOU STILL HERE?

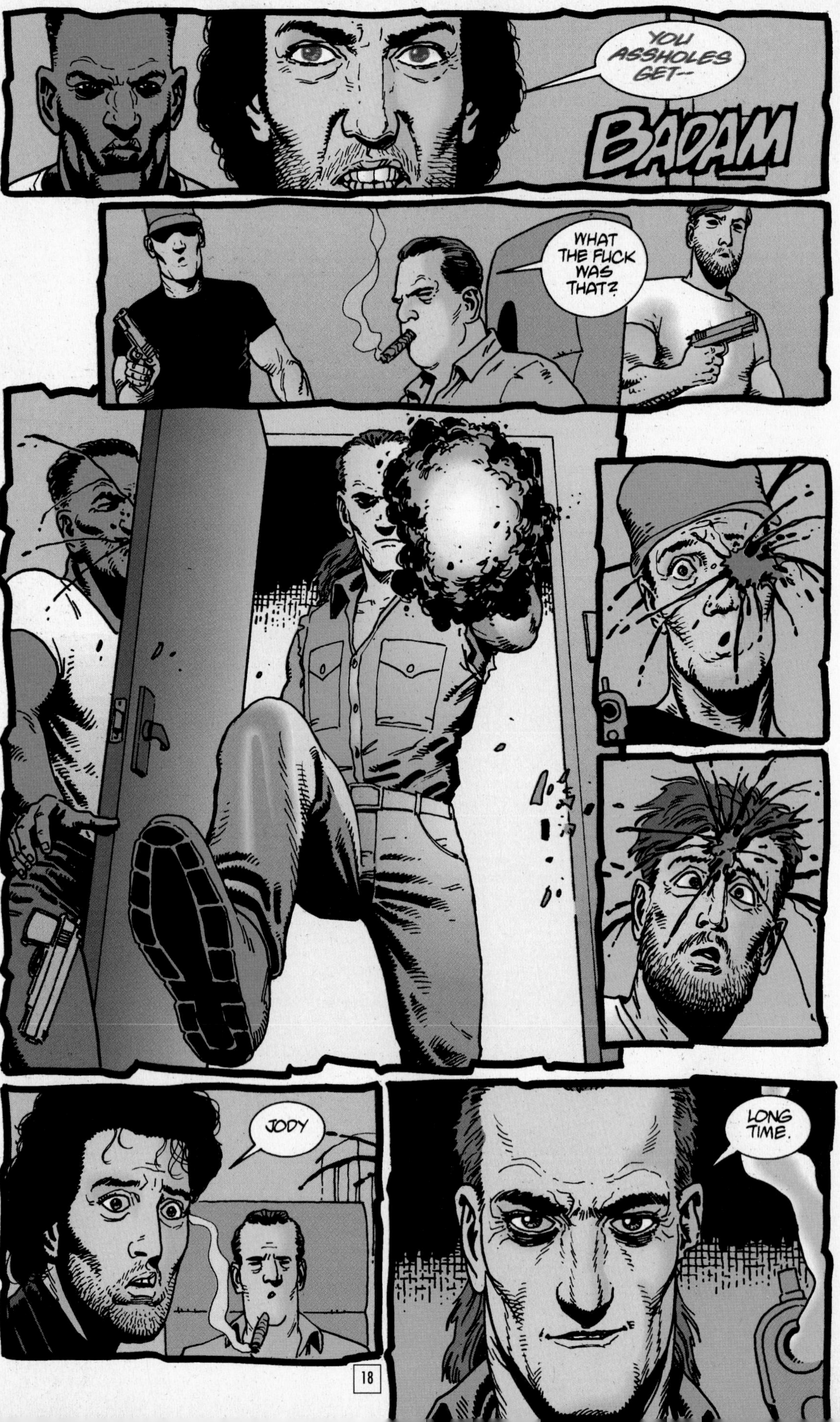
YOU ASSHOLES GET--
BADAM
WHAT THE FUCK WAS THAT?
JODY
LONG TIME.

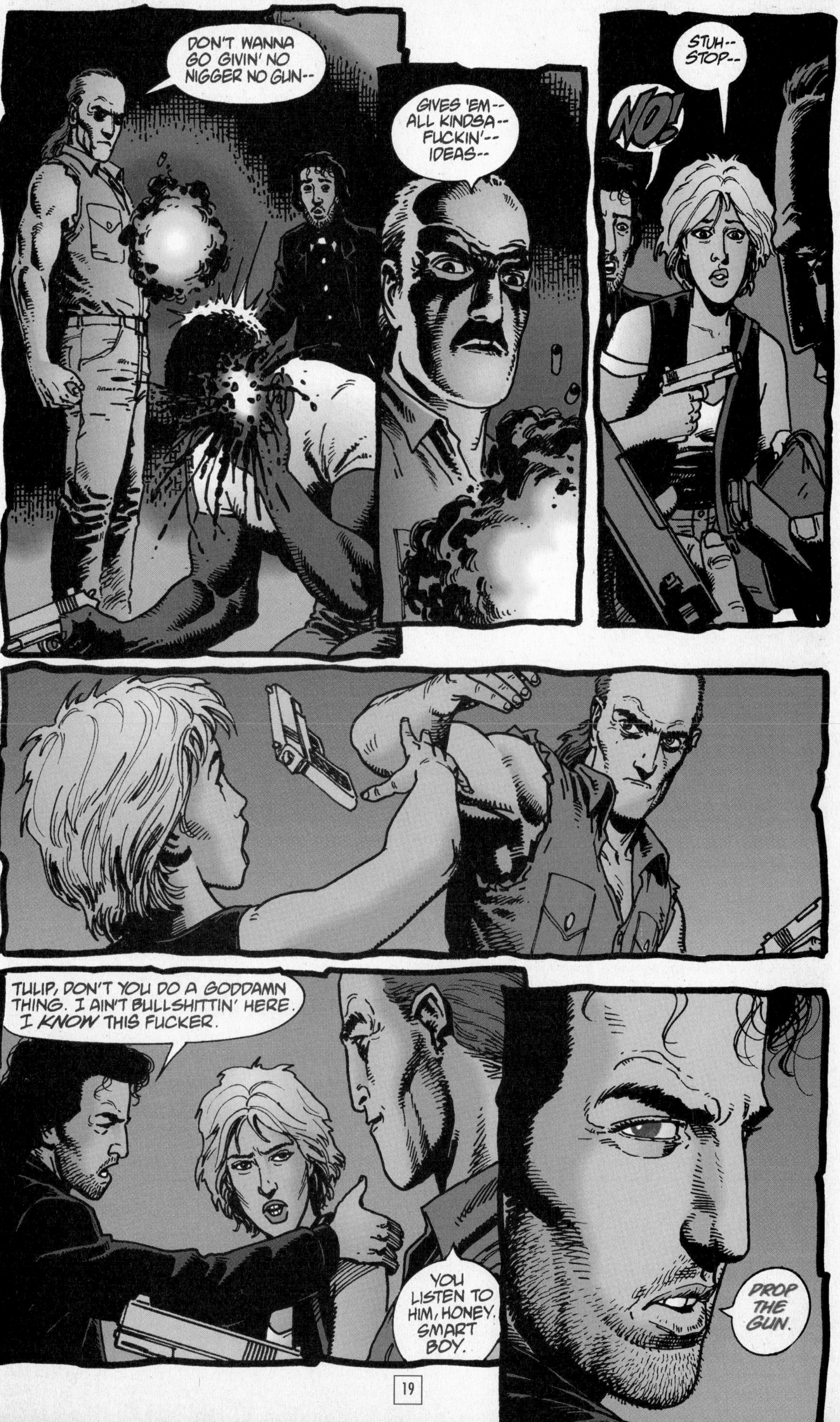
DON'T WANNA GO GIVIN' NO NIGGER NO GUN--
GIVES 'EM-- ALL KINDSA-- FUCKIN'-- IDEAS--
STUH-- STOP--
NO!
TULIP, DON'T YOU DO A GODDAMN THING. I AIN'T BULLSHITTIN' HERE. I *KNOW* THIS FUCKER.
YOU LISTEN TO HIM, HONEY. SMART BOY.
DROP THE GUN.

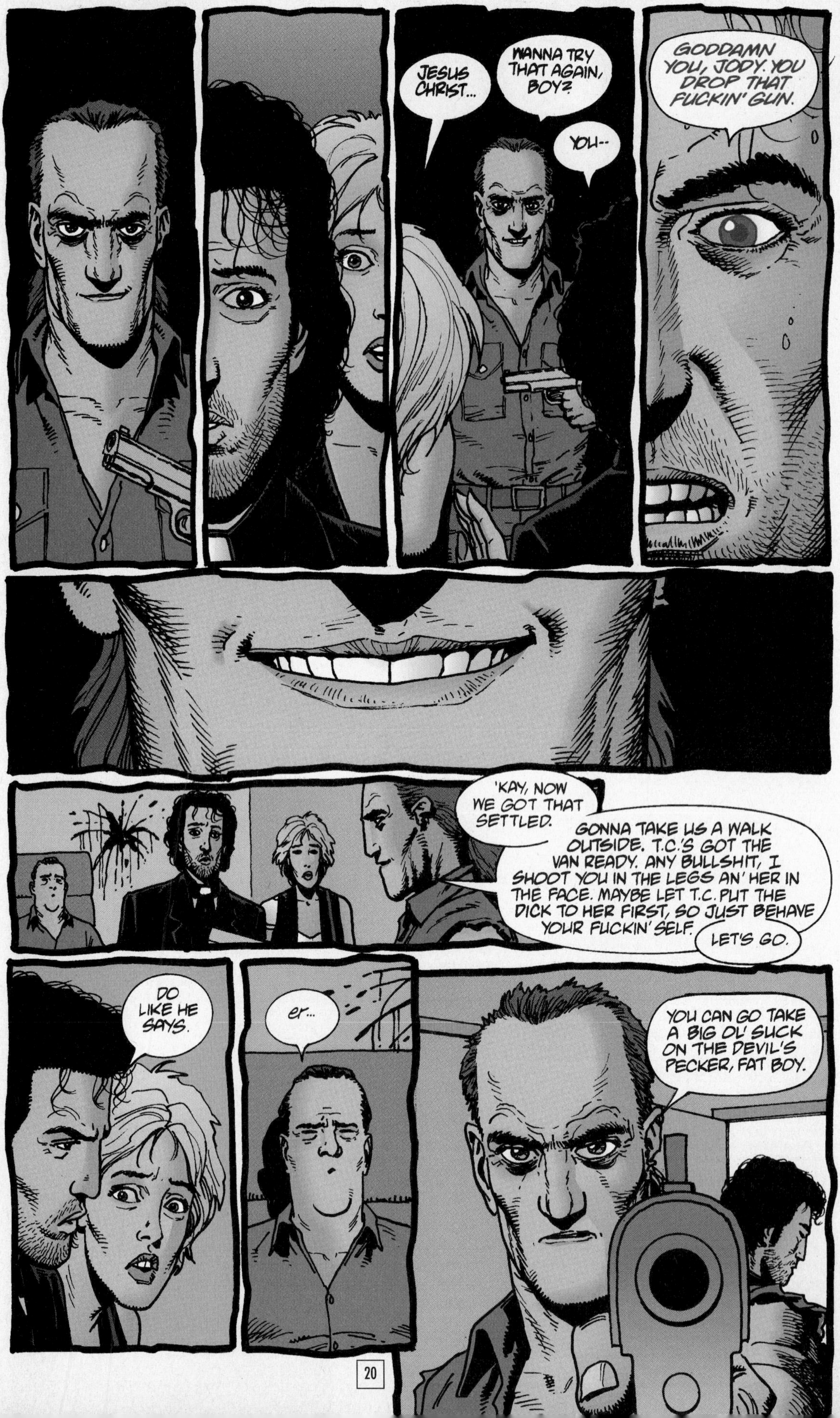
JESUS CHRIST...
WANNA TRY THAT AGAIN, BOY?
YOU--
GODDAMN YOU, JODY. YOU DROP THAT FUCKIN' GUN.
'KAY, NOW WE GOT THAT SETTLED.
GONNA TAKE US A WALK OUTSIDE. T.C.'S GOT THE VAN READY. ANY BULLSHIT, I SHOOT YOU IN THE LEGS AN' HER IN THE FACE. MAYBE LET T.C. PUT THE DICK TO HER FIRST, SO JUST BEHAVE YOUR FUCKIN' SELF.
LET'S GO.
DO LIKE HE SAYS.
er...
YOU CAN GO TAKE A BIG OL' SUCK ON THE DEVIL'S PECKER, FAT BOY.

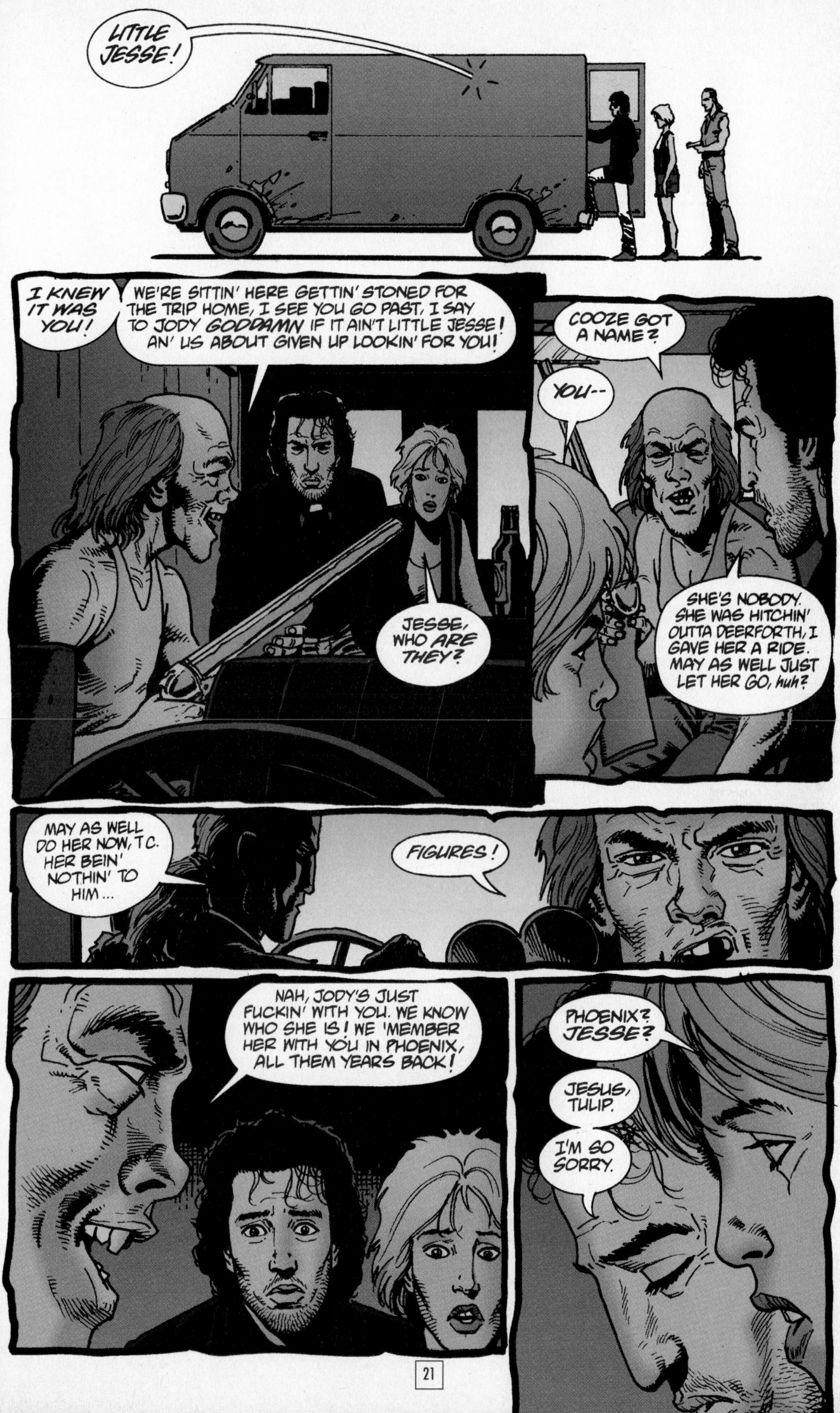

LITTLE JESSE!
I KNEW IT WAS YOU!
WE'RE SITTIN' HERE GETTIN' STONED FOR THE TRIP HOME, I SEE YOU GO PAST, I SAY TO JODY *GODDAMN* IF IT AIN'T LITTLE JESSE! AN' US ABOUT GIVEN UP LOOKIN' FOR YOU!
JESSE, WHO *ARE* THEY?
COOZE GOT A NAME?
YOU--
SHE'S NOBODY. SHE WAS HITCHIN' OUTTA DEERFORTH, I GAVE HER A RIDE. MAY AS WELL JUST LET HER GO, *huh?*
MAY AS WELL DO HER NOW, T.C. HER BEIN' NOTHIN' TO HIM...
FIGURES!
NAH, JODY'S JUST FUCKIN' WITH YOU. WE KNOW WHO SHE IS! WE 'MEMBER HER WITH YOU IN PHOENIX, ALL THEM YEARS BACK!
PHOENIX? JESSE?
JESUS, TULIP.
I'M SO SORRY.

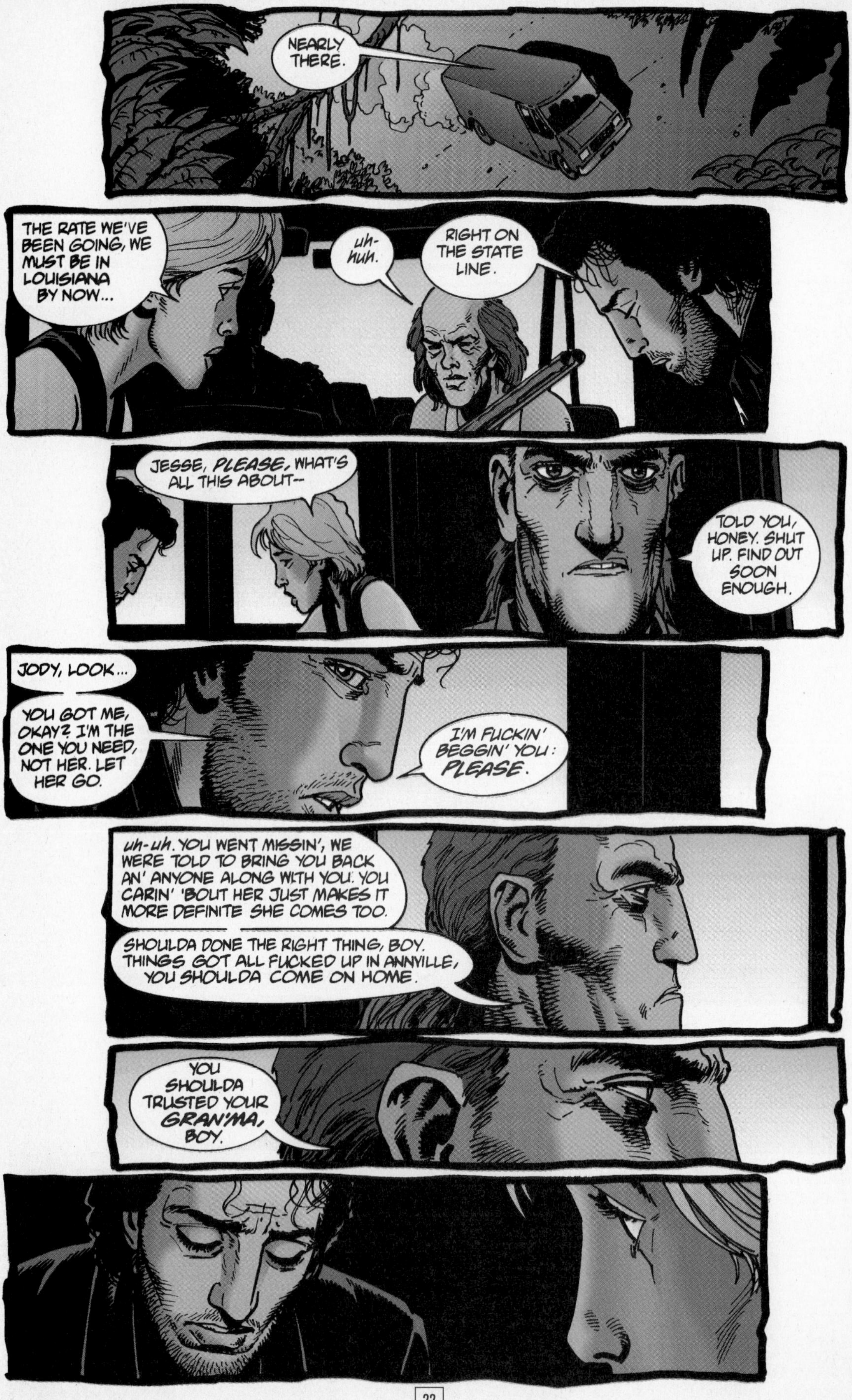
NEARLY THERE.
THE RATE WE'VE BEEN GOING, WE MUST BE IN LOUISIANA BY NOW...
uh-huh.
RIGHT ON THE STATE LINE.
JESSE, PLEASE, WHAT'S ALL THIS ABOUT--
TOLD YOU, HONEY. SHUT UP. FIND OUT SOON ENOUGH.
JODY, LOOK...
YOU GOT ME, OKAY? I'M THE ONE YOU NEED, NOT HER. LET HER GO.
I'M FUCKIN' BEGGIN' YOU: PLEASE.
uh-uh. YOU WENT MISSIN', WE WERE TOLD TO BRING YOU BACK AN' ANYONE ALONG WITH YOU. YOU CARIN' 'BOUT HER JUST MAKES IT MORE DEFINITE SHE COMES TOO.
SHOULDA DONE THE RIGHT THING, BOY. THINGS GOT ALL FUCKED UP IN ANNVILLE, YOU SHOULDA COME ON HOME.
YOU SHOULDA TRUSTED YOUR GRAN'MA, BOY.

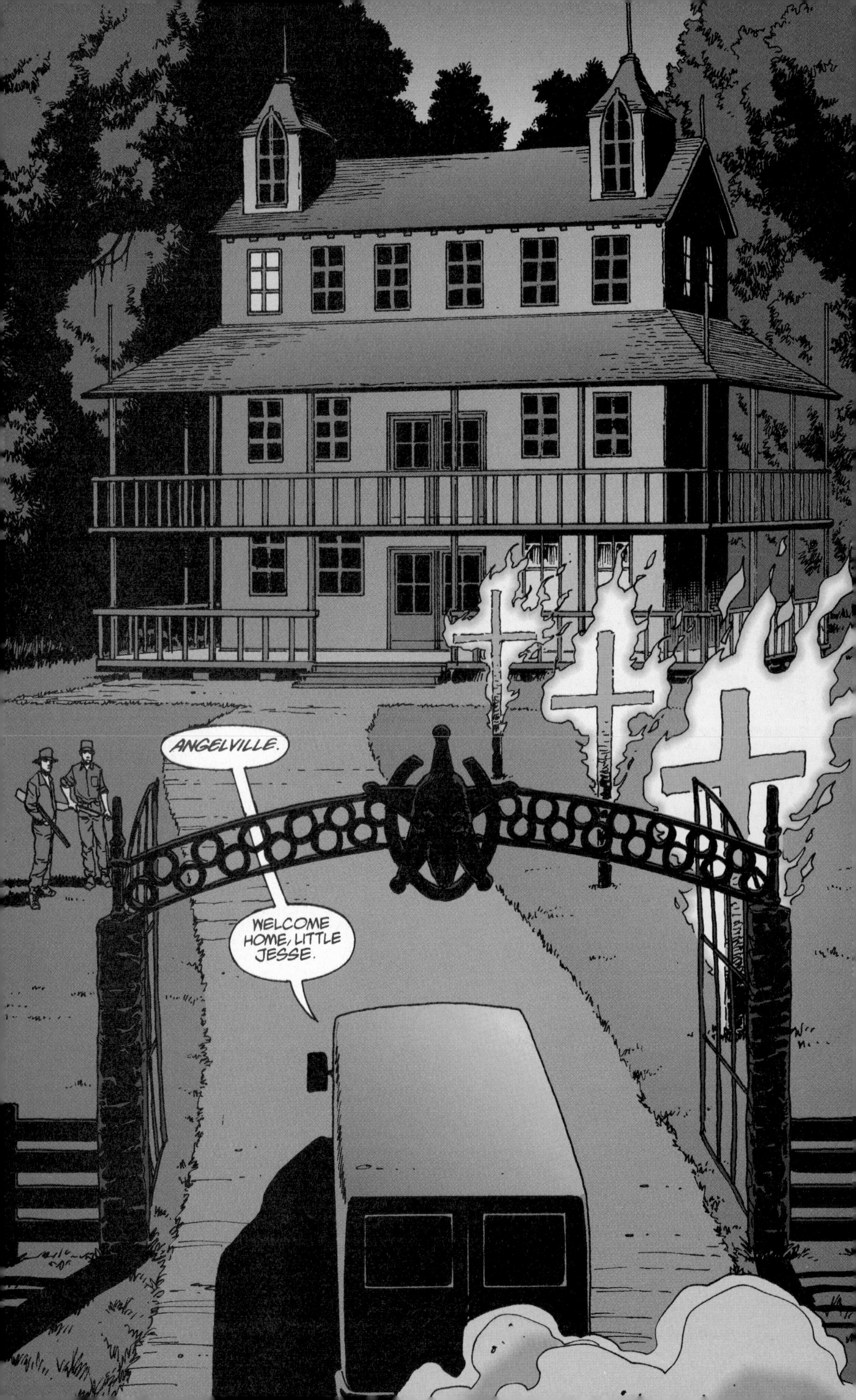
ANGELVILLE.
WELCOME HOME, LITTLE JESSE.

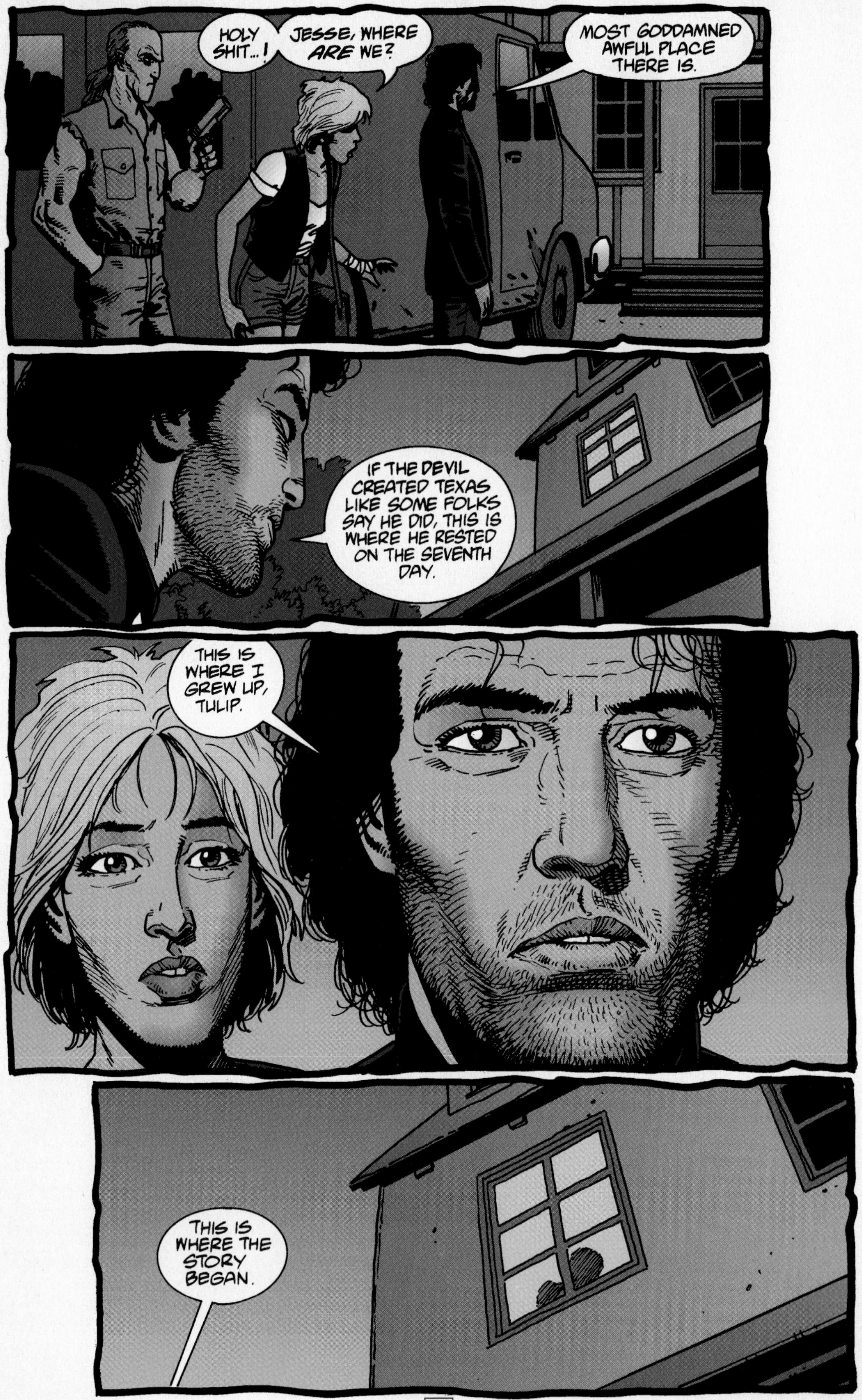
HOLY SHIT...!
JESSE, WHERE ARE WE?
MOST GODDAMNED AWFUL PLACE THERE IS.
IF THE DEVIL CREATED TEXAS LIKE SOME FOLKS SAY HE DID, THIS IS WHERE HE RESTED ON THE SEVENTH DAY.
THIS IS WHERE I GREW UP, TULIP.
THIS IS WHERE THE STORY BEGAN.

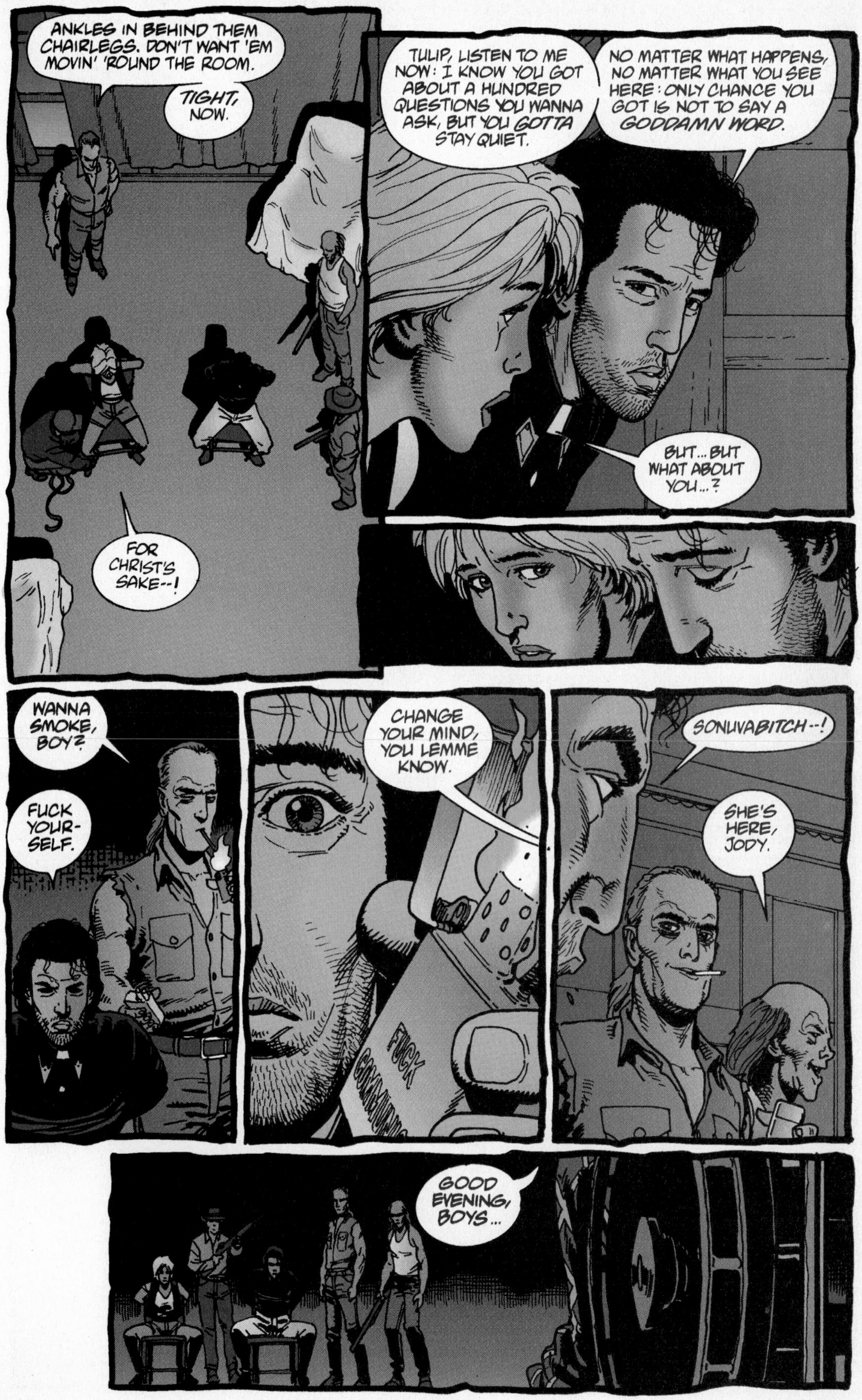
ANKLES IN BEHIND THEM CHAIRLEGS. DON'T WANT 'EM MOVIN' 'ROUND THE ROOM.
TIGHT, NOW.
FOR CHRIST'S SAKE--!
TULIP, LISTEN TO ME NOW: I KNOW YOU GOT ABOUT A HUNDRED QUESTIONS YOU WANNA ASK, BUT YOU GOTTA STAY QUIET.
NO MATTER WHAT HAPPENS, NO MATTER WHAT YOU SEE HERE: ONLY CHANCE YOU GOT IS NOT TO SAY A GODDAMN WORD.
BUT... BUT WHAT ABOUT YOU...?
WANNA SMOKE, BOY?
FUCK YOURSELF.
CHANGE YOUR MIND, YOU LEMME KNOW.
SONUVABITCH--!
SHE'S HERE, JODY.
GOOD EVENING, BOYS...

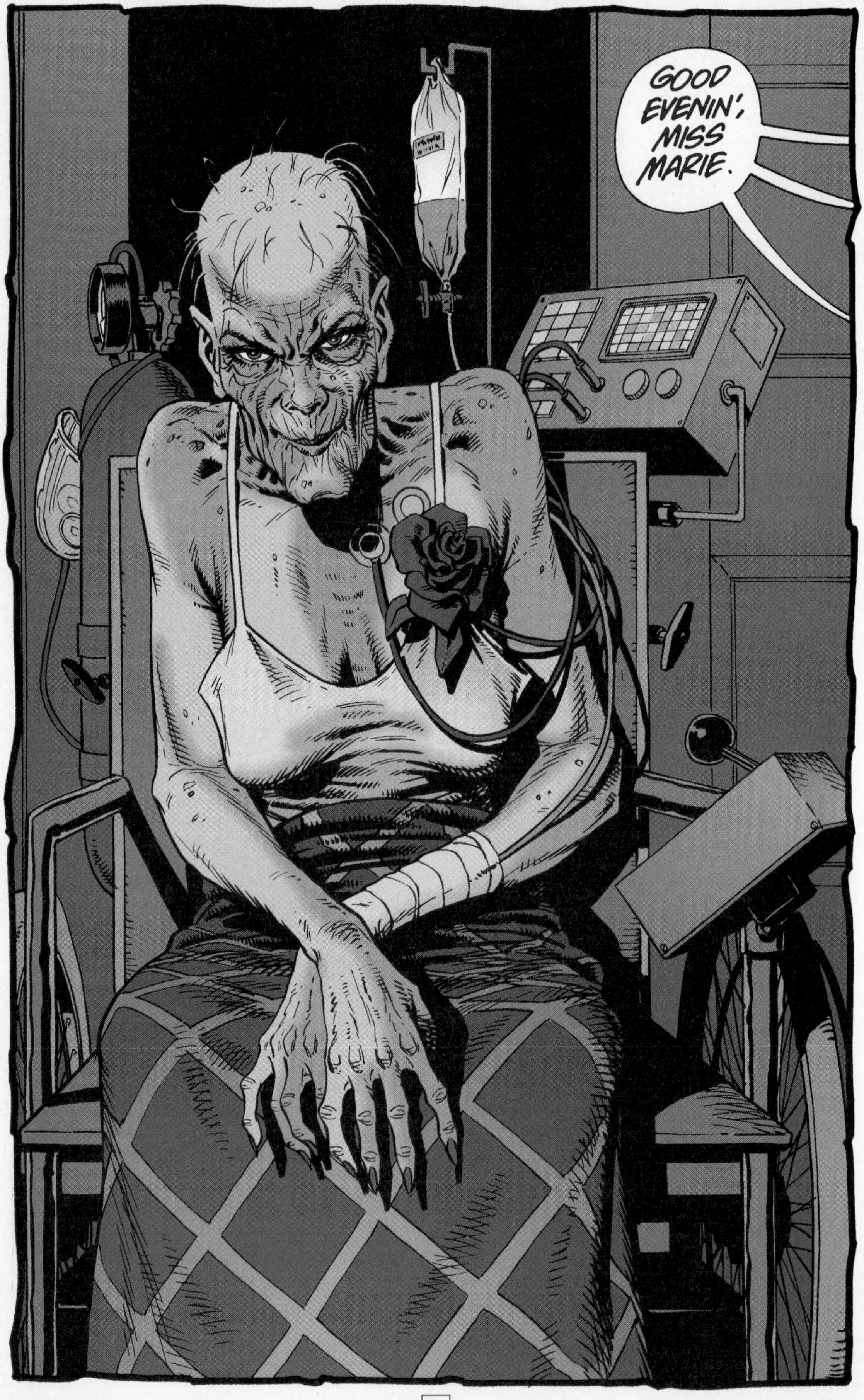
GOOD EVENIN', MISS MARIE.

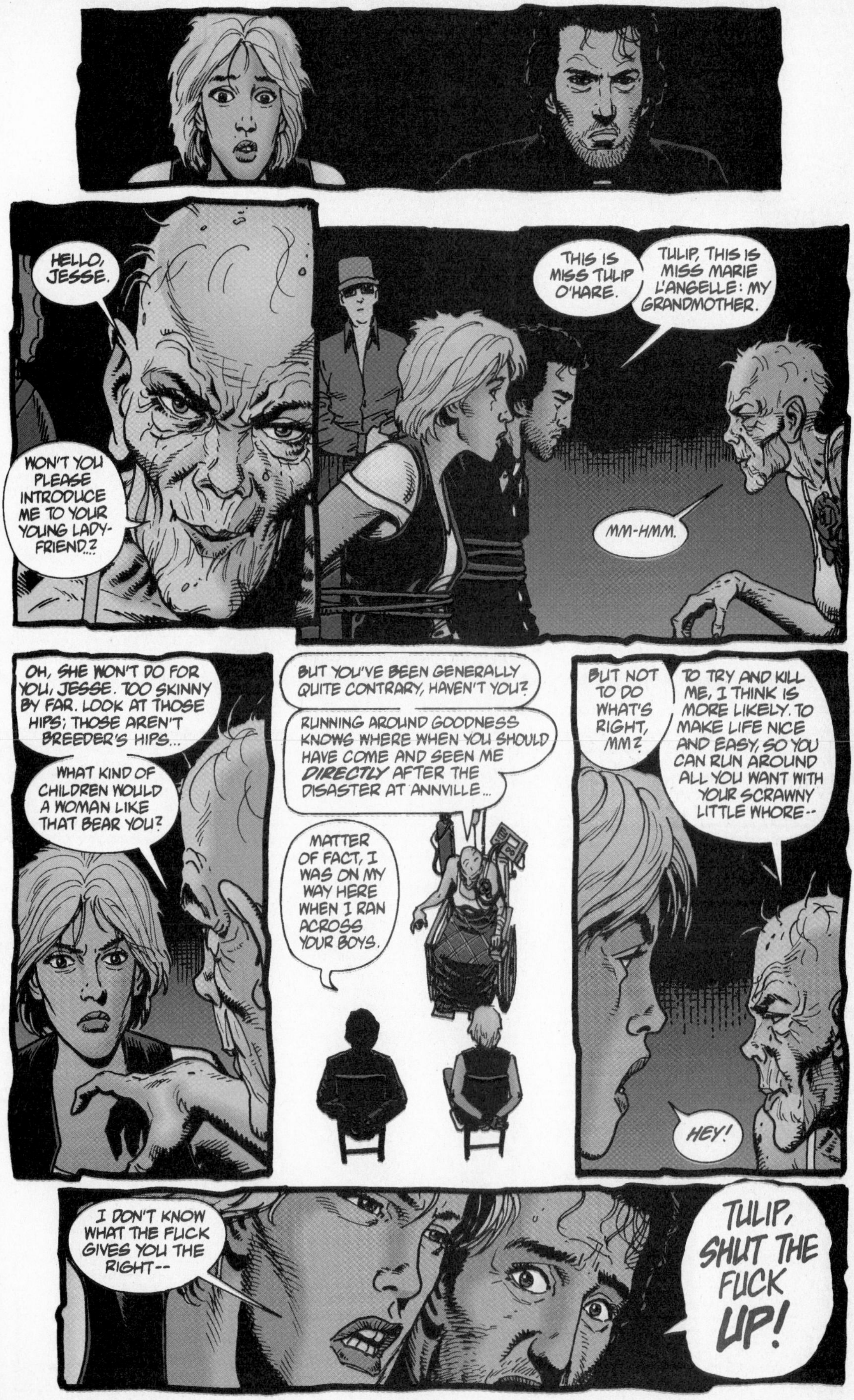
HELLO, JESSE.
WON'T YOU PLEASE INTRODUCE ME TO YOUR YOUNG LADY-FRIEND?...
THIS IS MISS TULIP O'HARE.
TULIP, THIS IS MISS MARIE L'ANGELLE: MY GRANDMOTHER.
MM-HMM.
OH, SHE WON'T DO FOR YOU, JESSE. TOO SKINNY BY FAR. LOOK AT THOSE HIPS; THOSE AREN'T BREEDER'S HIPS...
WHAT KIND OF CHILDREN WOULD A WOMAN LIKE THAT BEAR YOU?
BUT YOU'VE BEEN GENERALLY QUITE CONTRARY, HAVEN'T YOU?
RUNNING AROUND GOODNESS KNOWS WHERE WHEN YOU SHOULD HAVE COME AND SEEN ME DIRECTLY AFTER THE DISASTER AT ANNVILLE...
MATTER OF FACT, I WAS ON MY WAY HERE WHEN I RAN ACROSS YOUR BOYS.
BUT NOT TO DO WHAT'S RIGHT, MM?
TO TRY AND KILL ME, I THINK IS MORE LIKELY. TO MAKE LIFE NICE AND EASY, SO YOU CAN RUN AROUND ALL YOU WANT WITH YOUR SCRAWNY LITTLE WHORE--
HEY!
I DON'T KNOW WHAT THE FUCK GIVES YOU THE RIGHT--
TULIP, SHUT THE FUCK UP!

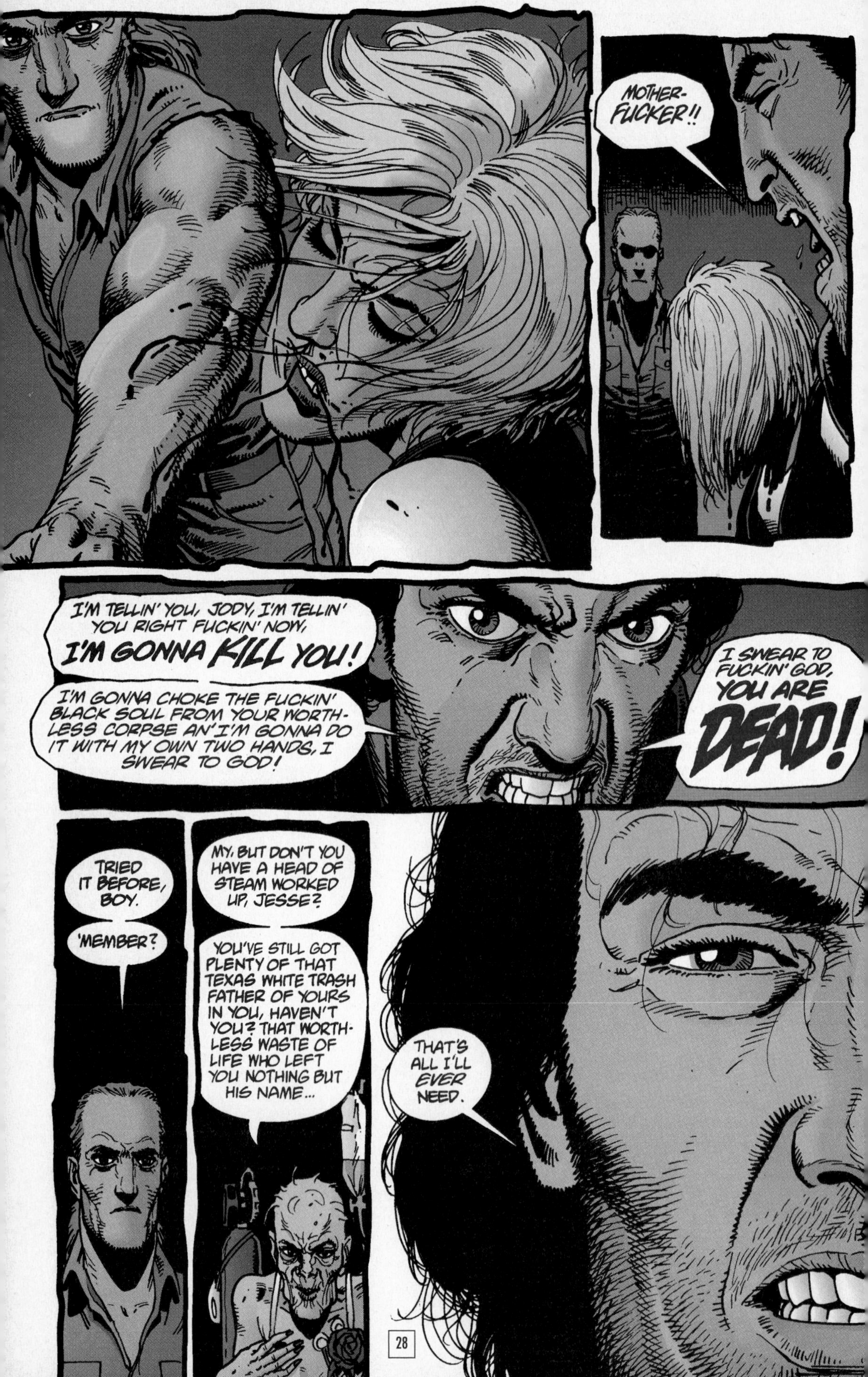
MOTHER-FUCKER!!
I'M TELLIN' YOU, JODY, I'M TELLIN' YOU RIGHT FUCKIN' NOW, I'M GONNA KILL YOU!
I'M GONNA CHOKE THE FUCKIN' BLACK SOUL FROM YOUR WORTHLESS CORPSE AN' I'M GONNA DO IT WITH MY OWN TWO HANDS, I SWEAR TO GOD!
I SWEAR TO FUCKIN' GOD, YOU ARE DEAD!
TRIED IT BEFORE, BOY.
'MEMBER?
MY, BUT DON'T YOU HAVE A HEAD OF STEAM WORKED UP, JESSE?
YOU'VE STILL GOT PLENTY OF THAT TEXAS WHITE TRASH FATHER OF YOURS IN YOU, HAVEN'T YOU? THAT WORTHLESS WASTE OF LIFE WHO LEFT YOU NOTHING BUT HIS NAME...
THAT'S ALL I'LL EVER NEED.

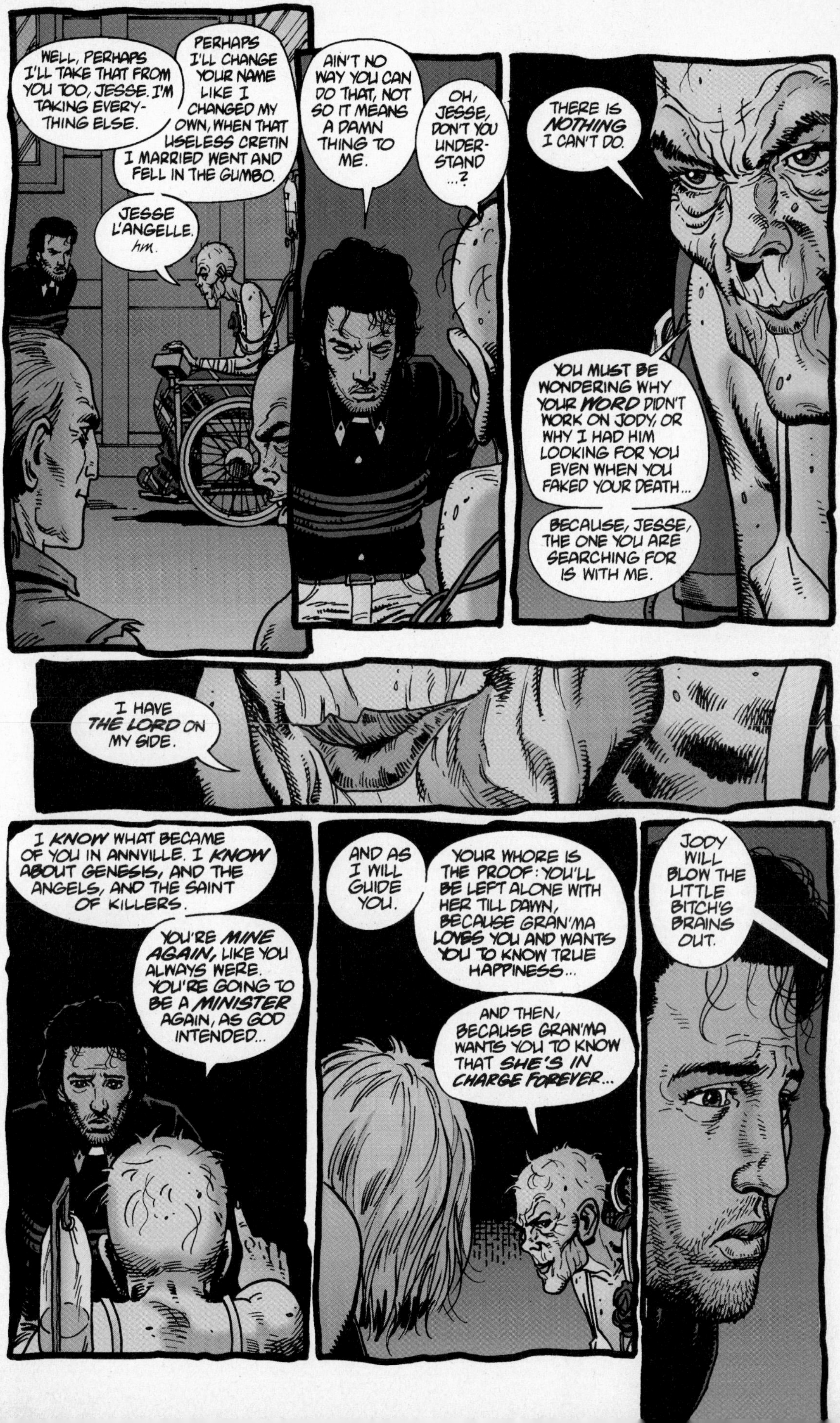
WELL, PERHAPS I'LL TAKE THAT FROM YOU TOO, JESSE. I'M TAKING EVERY-THING ELSE.
PERHAPS I'LL CHANGE YOUR NAME LIKE I CHANGED MY OWN, WHEN THAT USELESS CRETIN I MARRIED WENT AND FELL IN THE GUMBO.
JESSE L'ANGELLE. hm.
AIN'T NO WAY YOU CAN DO THAT, NOT SO IT MEANS A DAMN THING TO ME.
OH, JESSE, DON'T YOU UNDER-STAND ...?
THERE IS NOTHING I CAN'T DO.
YOU MUST BE WONDERING WHY YOUR WORD DIDN'T WORK ON JODY, OR WHY I HAD HIM LOOKING FOR YOU EVEN WHEN YOU FAKED YOUR DEATH...
BECAUSE, JESSE, THE ONE YOU ARE SEARCHING FOR IS WITH ME.
I HAVE THE LORD ON MY SIDE.
I KNOW WHAT BECAME OF YOU IN ANNVILLE. I KNOW ABOUT GENESIS, AND THE ANGELS, AND THE SAINT OF KILLERS.
YOU'RE MINE AGAIN, LIKE YOU ALWAYS WERE. YOU'RE GOING TO BE A MINISTER AGAIN, AS GOD INTENDED...
AND AS I WILL GUIDE YOU.
YOUR WHORE IS THE PROOF: YOU'LL BE LEFT ALONE WITH HER TILL DAWN, BECAUSE GRAN'MA LOVES YOU AND WANTS YOU TO KNOW TRUE HAPPINESS...
AND THEN, BECAUSE GRAN'MA WANTS YOU TO KNOW THAT SHE'S IN CHARGE FOREVER...
JODY WILL BLOW THE LITTLE BITCH'S BRAINS OUT.

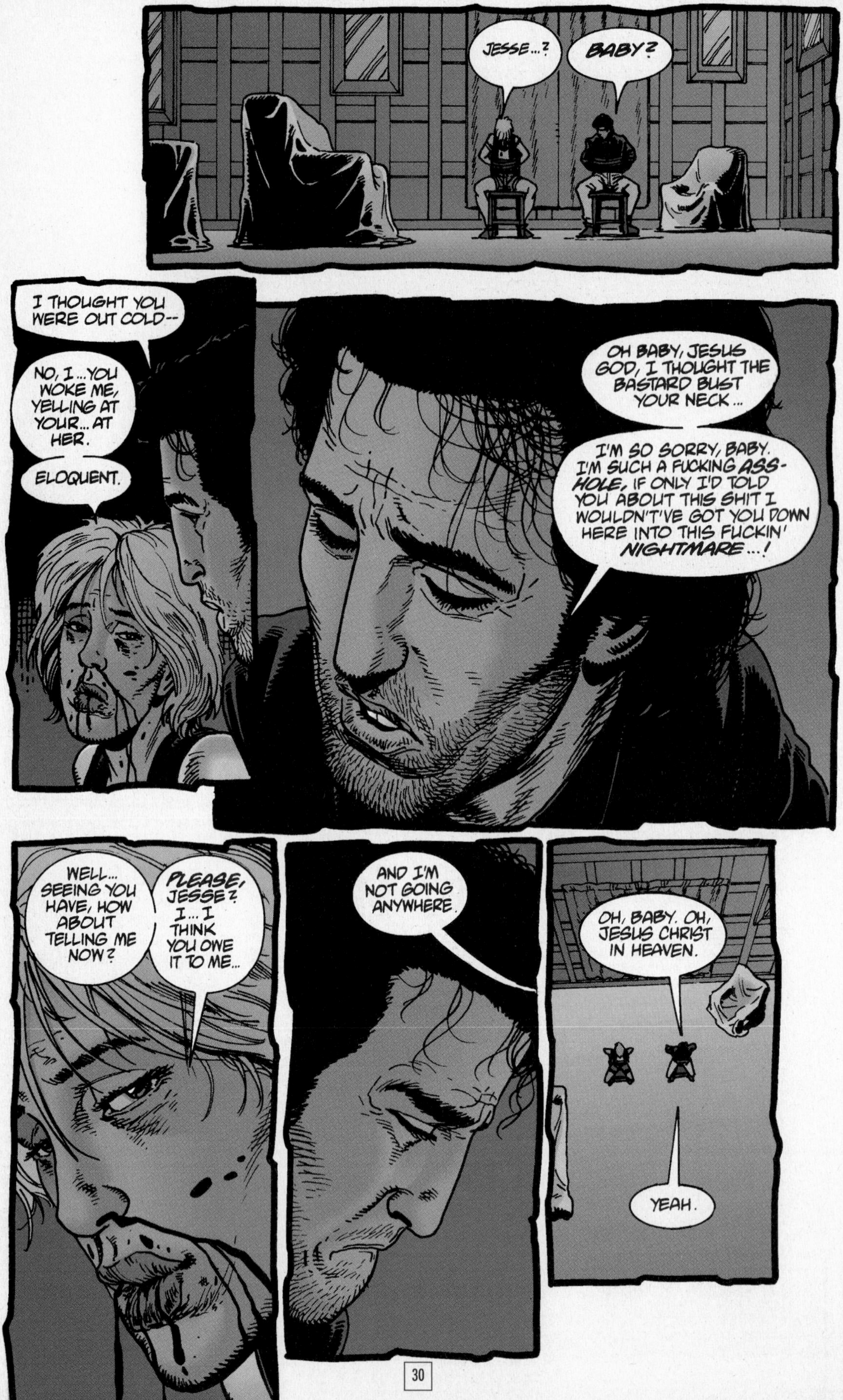
JESSE...?
BABY?
I THOUGHT YOU WERE OUT COLD--
NO, I...YOU WOKE ME, YELLING AT YOUR...AT HER.
ELOQUENT.
OH BABY, JESUS GOD, I THOUGHT THE BASTARD BUST YOUR NECK...
I'M SO SORRY, BABY. I'M SUCH A FUCKING ASS-HOLE, IF ONLY I'D TOLD YOU ABOUT THIS SHIT I WOULDN'T'VE GOT YOU DOWN HERE INTO THIS FUCKIN' NIGHTMARE...!
WELL... SEEING YOU HAVE, HOW ABOUT TELLING ME NOW?
PLEASE, JESSE? I... I THINK YOU OWE IT TO ME...
AND I'M NOT GOING ANYWHERE.
OH, BABY. OH, JESUS CHRIST IN HEAVEN.
YEAH.

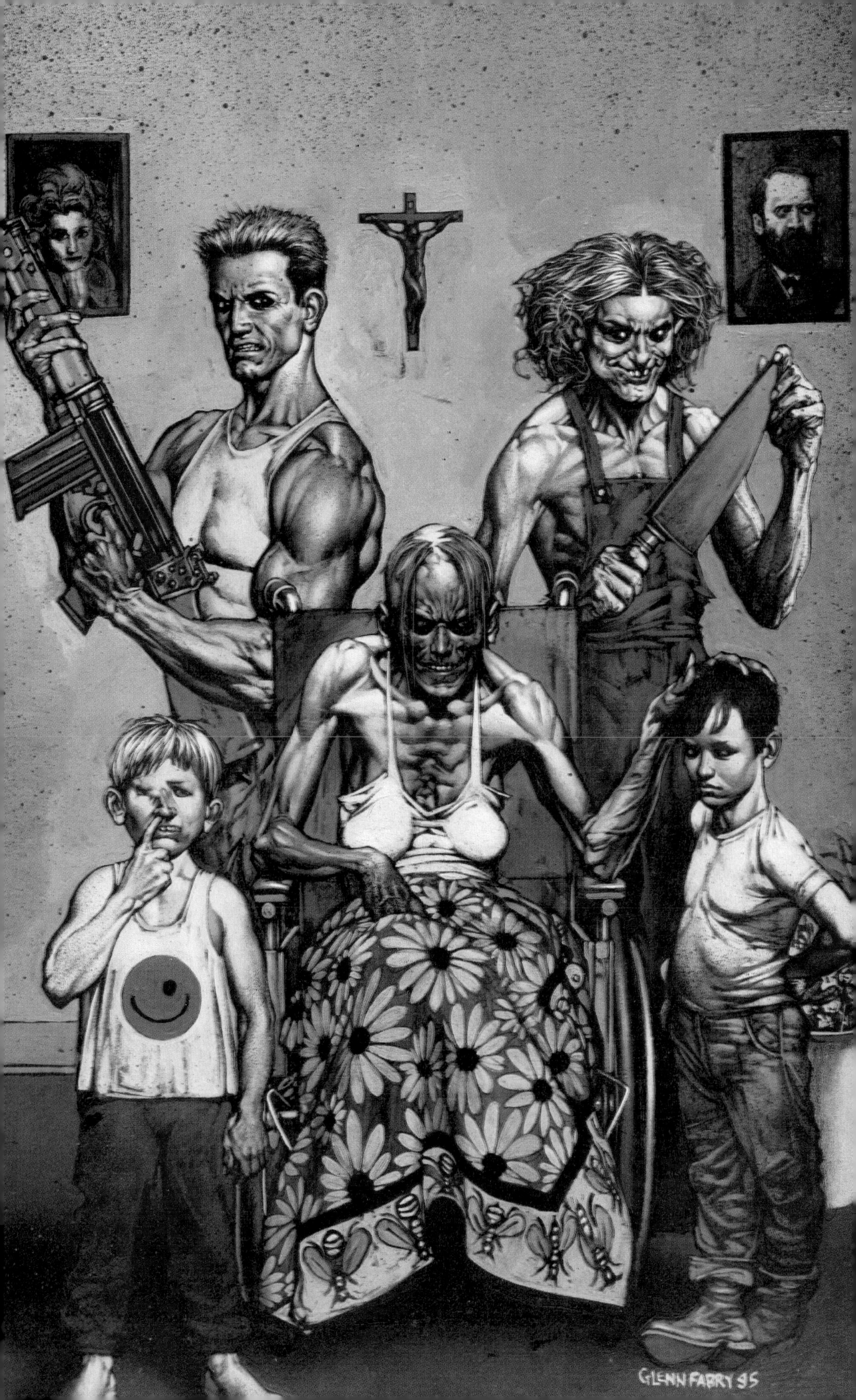
GLENN FABRY 95

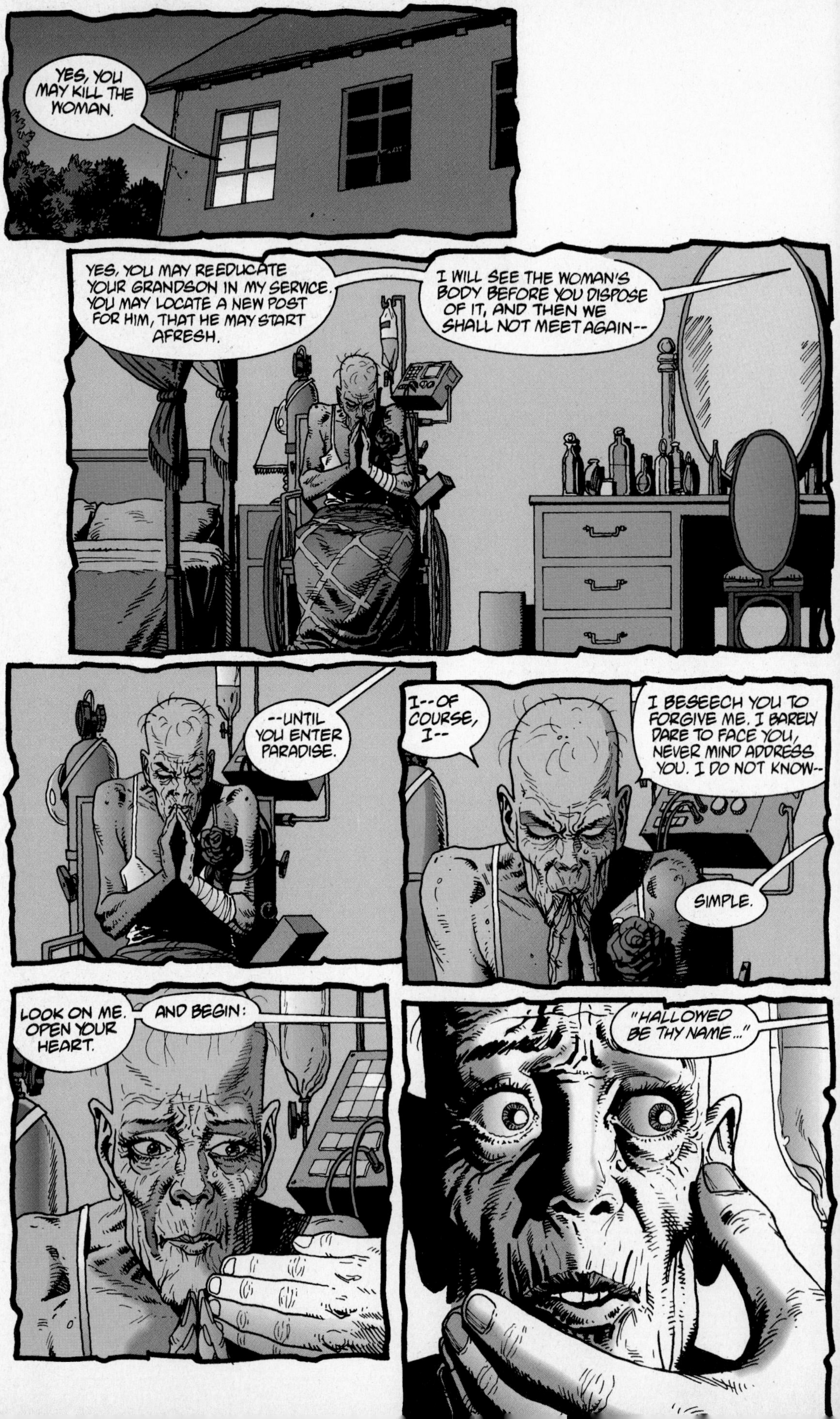
YES, YOU MAY KILL THE WOMAN.
YES, YOU MAY REEDUCATE YOUR GRANDSON IN MY SERVICE. YOU MAY LOCATE A NEW POST FOR HIM, THAT HE MAY START AFRESH.
I WILL SEE THE WOMAN'S BODY BEFORE YOU DISPOSE OF IT, AND THEN WE SHALL NOT MEET AGAIN--
--UNTIL YOU ENTER PARADISE.
I--OF COURSE, I--
I BESEECH YOU TO FORGIVE ME. I BARELY DARE TO FACE YOU, NEVER MIND ADDRESS YOU. I DO NOT KNOW--
SIMPLE.
LOOK ON ME. OPEN YOUR HEART.
AND BEGIN:
"HALLOWED BE THY NAME..."

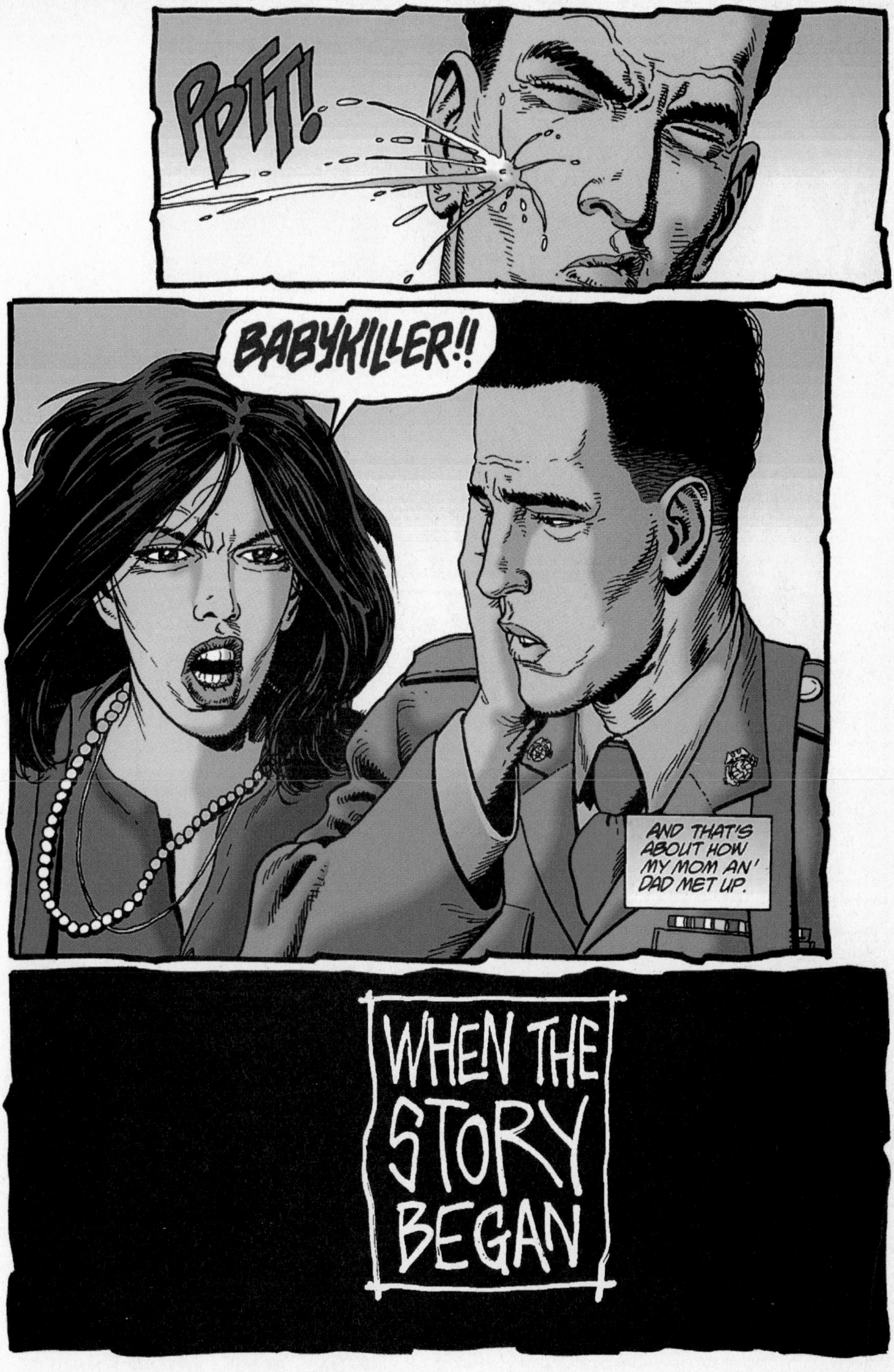
PPTT!
BABYKILLER!!
AND THAT'S ABOUT HOW MY MOM AN' DAD MET UP.
WHEN THE STORY BEGAN

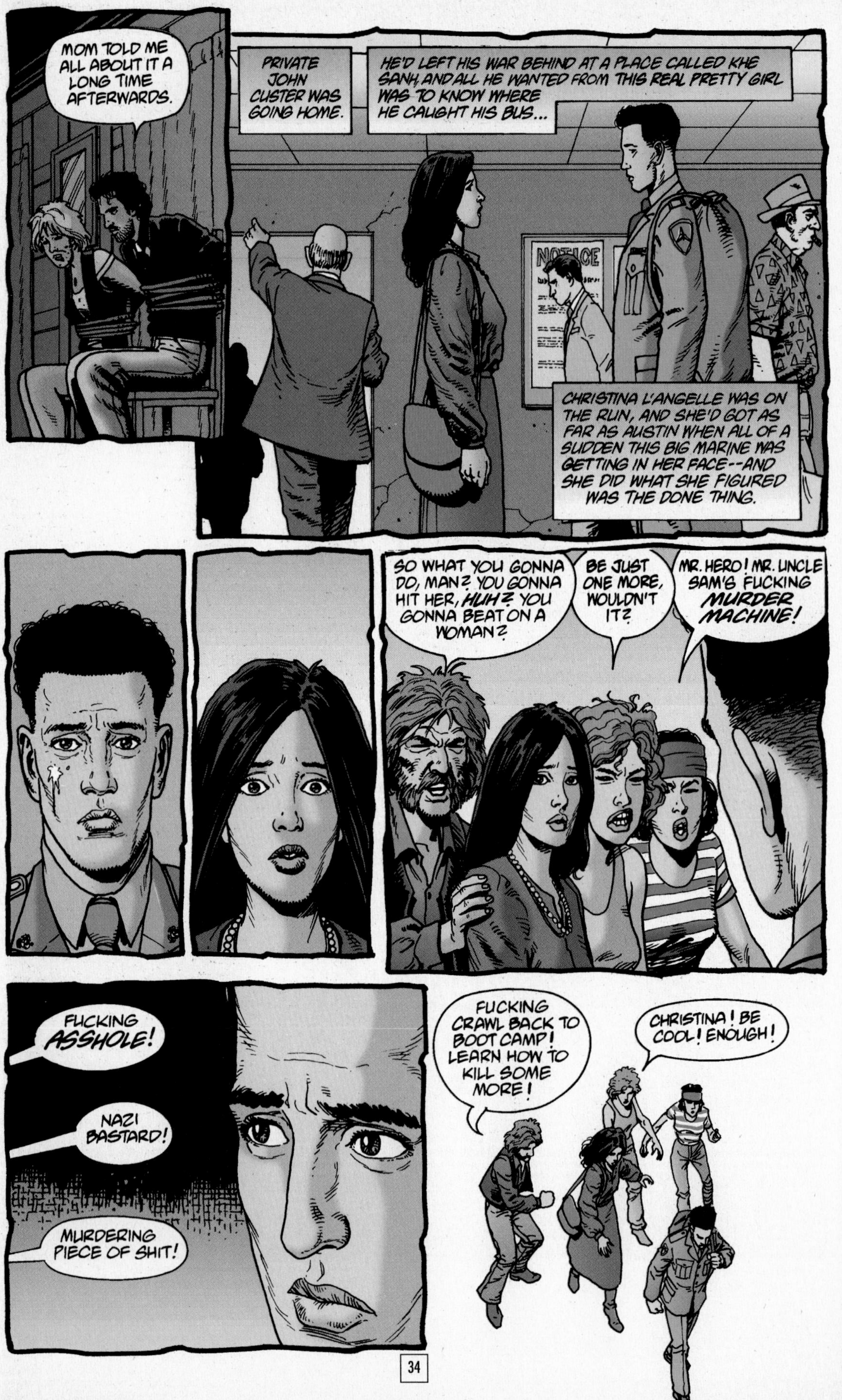
MOM TOLD ME ALL ABOUT IT A LONG TIME AFTERWARDS.
PRIVATE JOHN CUSTER WAS GOING HOME.
HE'D LEFT HIS WAR BEHIND AT A PLACE CALLED KHE SANH, AND ALL HE WANTED FROM THIS REAL PRETTY GIRL WAS TO KNOW WHERE HE CAUGHT HIS BUS...
NOTICE
CHRISTINA L'ANGELLE WAS ON THE RUN, AND SHE'D GOT AS FAR AS AUSTIN WHEN ALL OF A SUDDEN THIS BIG MARINE WAS GETTING IN HER FACE--AND SHE DID WHAT SHE FIGURED WAS THE DONE THING.
SO WHAT YOU GONNA DO, MAN? YOU GONNA HIT HER, HUH? YOU GONNA BEAT ON A WOMAN?
BE JUST ONE MORE, WOULDN'T IT?
MR. HERO! MR. UNCLE SAM'S FUCKING MURDER MACHINE!
FUCKING ASSHOLE!
NAZI BASTARD!
MURDERING PIECE OF SHIT!
FUCKING CRAWL BACK TO BOOT CAMP! LEARN HOW TO KILL SOME MORE!
CHRISTINA! BE COOL! ENOUGH!

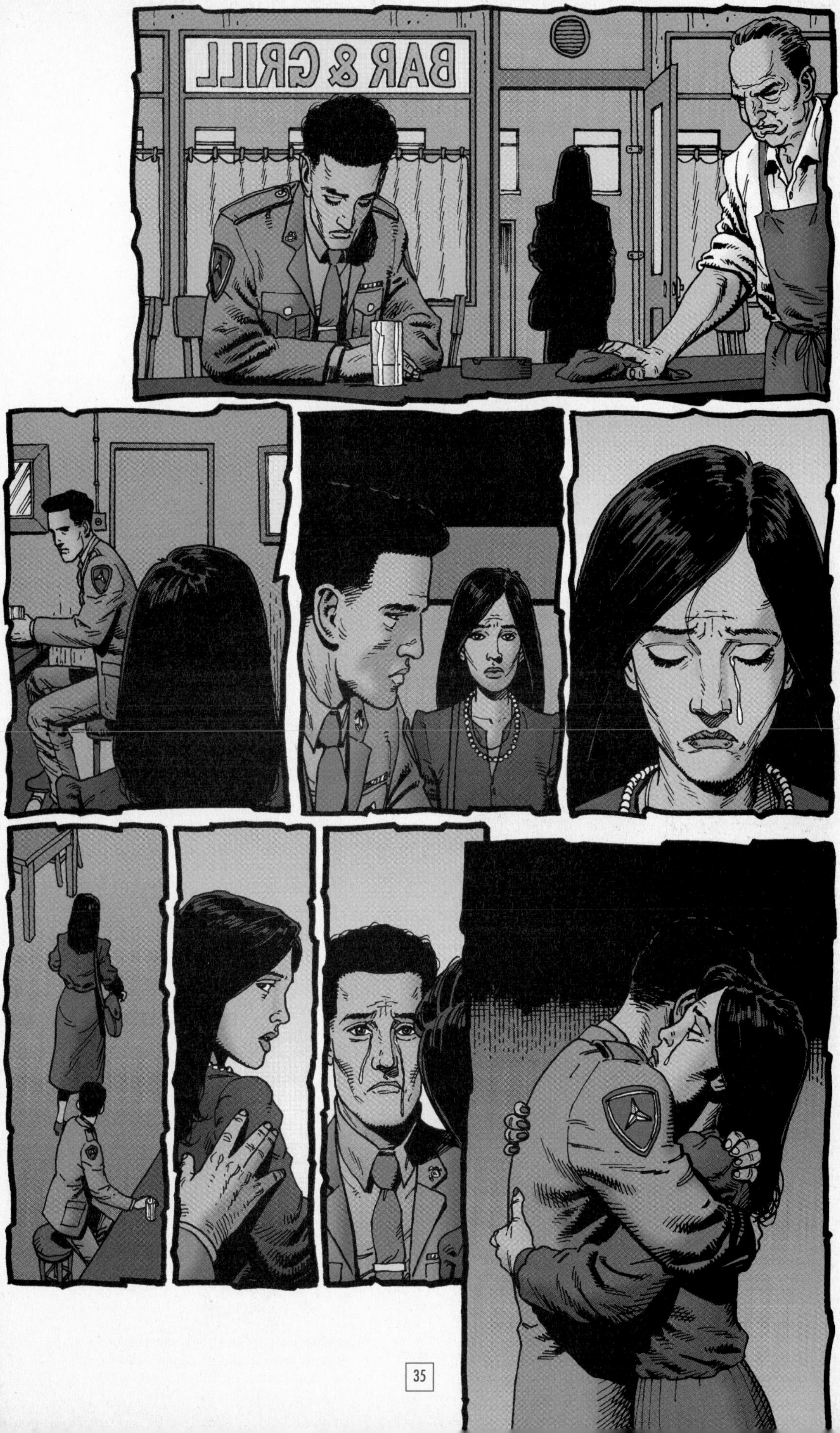
BAR & GRILL

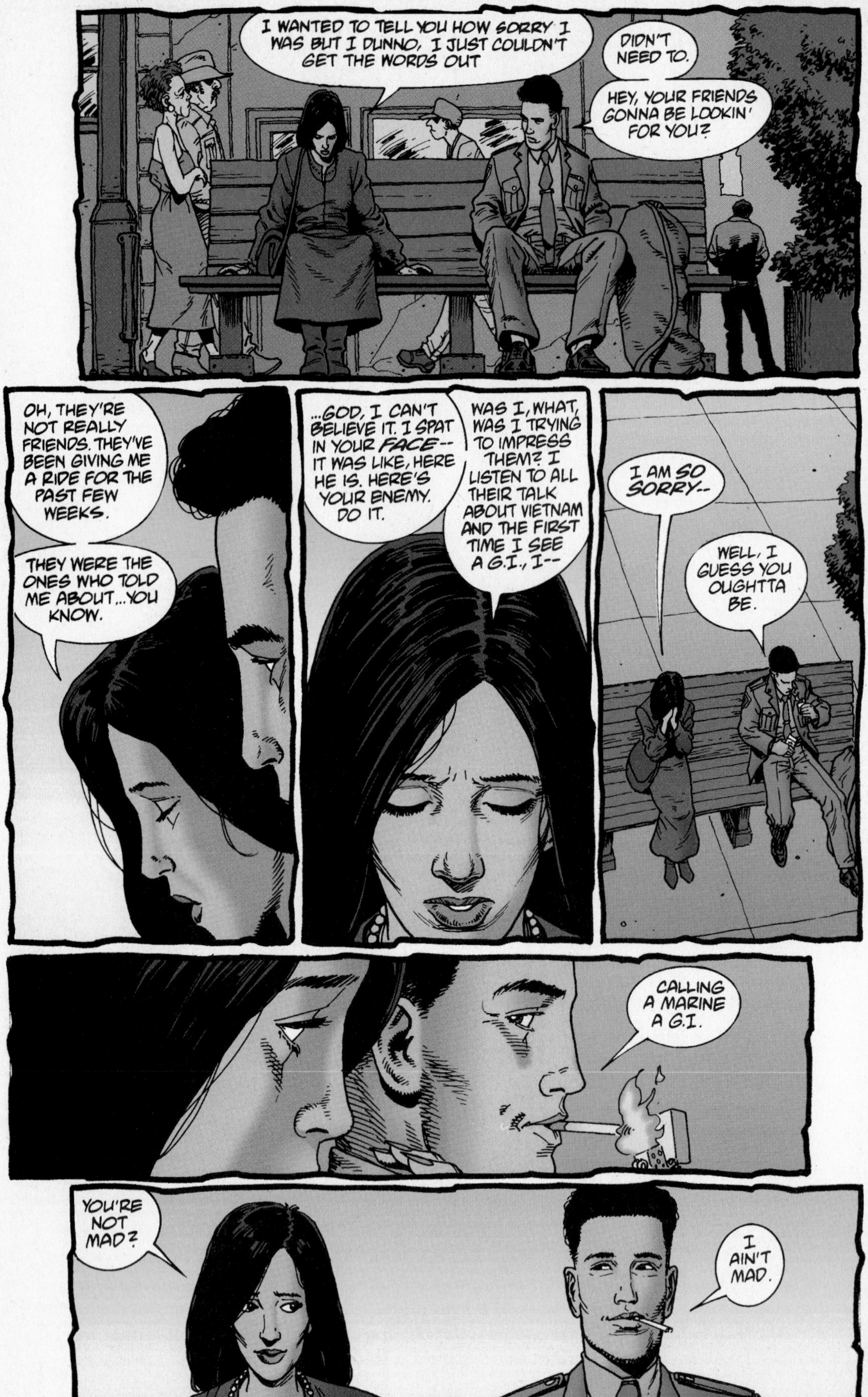
I WANTED TO TELL YOU HOW SORRY I WAS BUT I DUNNO, I JUST COULDN'T GET THE WORDS OUT
DIDN'T NEED TO.
HEY, YOUR FRIENDS GONNA BE LOOKIN' FOR YOU?
OH, THEY'RE NOT REALLY FRIENDS. THEY'VE BEEN GIVING ME A RIDE FOR THE PAST FEW WEEKS.
THEY WERE THE ONES WHO TOLD ME ABOUT...YOU KNOW.
...GOD, I CAN'T BELIEVE IT. I SPAT IN YOUR FACE-- IT WAS LIKE, HERE HE IS. HERE'S YOUR ENEMY. DO IT.
WAS I, WHAT, WAS I TRYING TO IMPRESS THEM? I LISTEN TO ALL THEIR TALK ABOUT VIETNAM AND THE FIRST TIME I SEE A G.I., I--
I AM SO SORRY--
WELL, I GUESS YOU OUGHTTA BE.
CALLING A MARINE A G.I.
YOU'RE NOT MAD?
I AIN'T MAD.

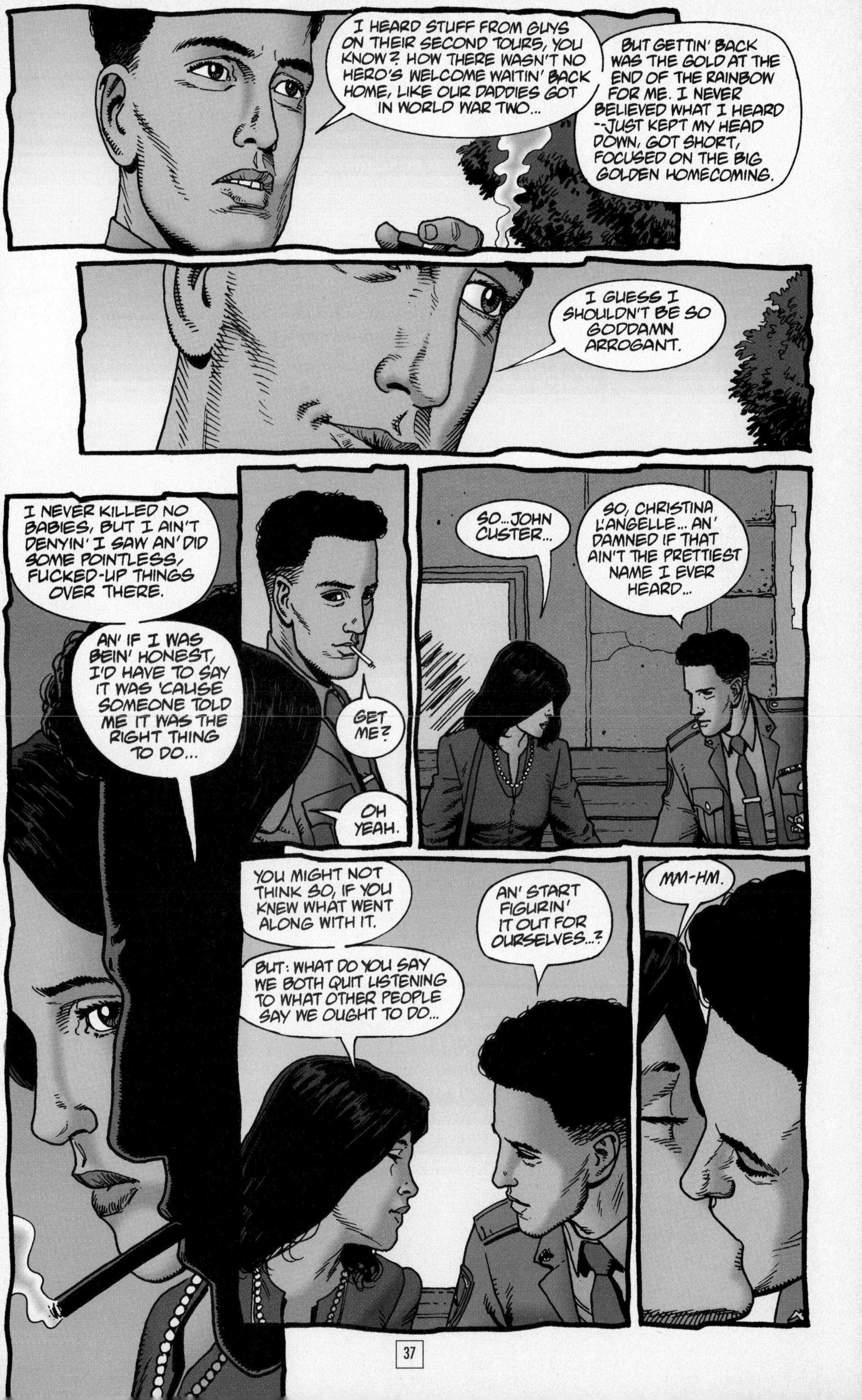
I HEARD STUFF FROM GUYS ON THEIR SECOND TOURS, YOU KNOW? HOW THERE WASN'T NO HERO'S WELCOME WAITIN' BACK HOME, LIKE OUR DADDIES GOT IN WORLD WAR TWO...
BUT GETTIN' BACK WAS THE GOLD AT THE END OF THE RAINBOW FOR ME. I NEVER BELIEVED WHAT I HEARD --JUST KEPT MY HEAD DOWN, GOT SHORT, FOCUSED ON THE BIG GOLDEN HOMECOMING.
I GUESS I SHOULDN'T BE SO GODDAMN ARROGANT.
I NEVER KILLED NO BABIES, BUT I AIN'T DENYIN' I SAW AN' DID SOME POINTLESS, FUCKED-UP THINGS OVER THERE.
AN' IF I WAS BEIN' HONEST, I'D HAVE TO SAY IT WAS 'CAUSE SOMEONE TOLD ME IT WAS THE RIGHT THING TO DO...
GET ME?
OH YEAH.
SO...JOHN CUSTER...
SO, CHRISTINA L'ANGELLE... AN' DAMNED IF THAT AIN'T THE PRETTIEST NAME I EVER HEARD...
YOU MIGHT NOT THINK SO, IF YOU KNEW WHAT WENT ALONG WITH IT.
BUT: WHAT DO YOU SAY WE BOTH QUIT LISTENING TO WHAT OTHER PEOPLE SAY WE OUGHT TO DO...
AN' START FIGURIN' IT OUT FOR OURSELVES...?
MM-HM.

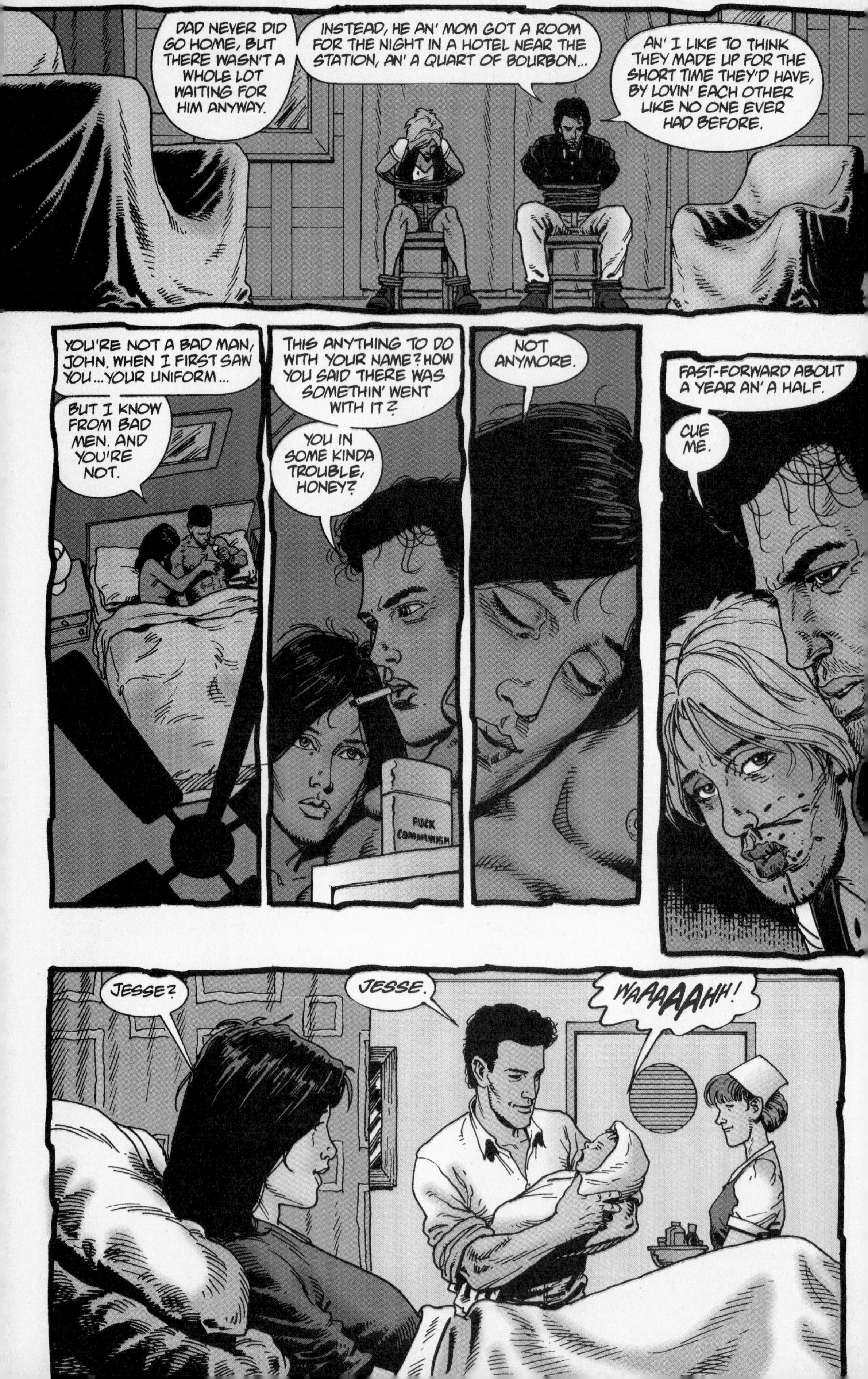
DAD NEVER DID GO HOME, BUT THERE WASN'T A WHOLE LOT WAITING FOR HIM ANYWAY.
INSTEAD, HE AN' MOM GOT A ROOM FOR THE NIGHT IN A HOTEL NEAR THE STATION, AN' A QUART OF BOURBON...
AN' I LIKE TO THINK THEY MADE UP FOR THE SHORT TIME THEY'D HAVE, BY LOVIN' EACH OTHER LIKE NO ONE EVER HAD BEFORE.
YOU'RE NOT A BAD MAN, JOHN. WHEN I FIRST SAW YOU...YOUR UNIFORM...
BUT I KNOW FROM BAD MEN. AND YOU'RE NOT.
THIS ANYTHING TO DO WITH YOUR NAME? HOW YOU SAID THERE WAS SOMETHIN' WENT WITH IT?
YOU IN SOME KINDA TROUBLE, HONEY?
FUCK COMMUNISM
NOT ANYMORE.
FAST-FORWARD ABOUT A YEAR AN' A HALF.
CUE ME.
JESSE?
JESSE.
WAAAAAHH!

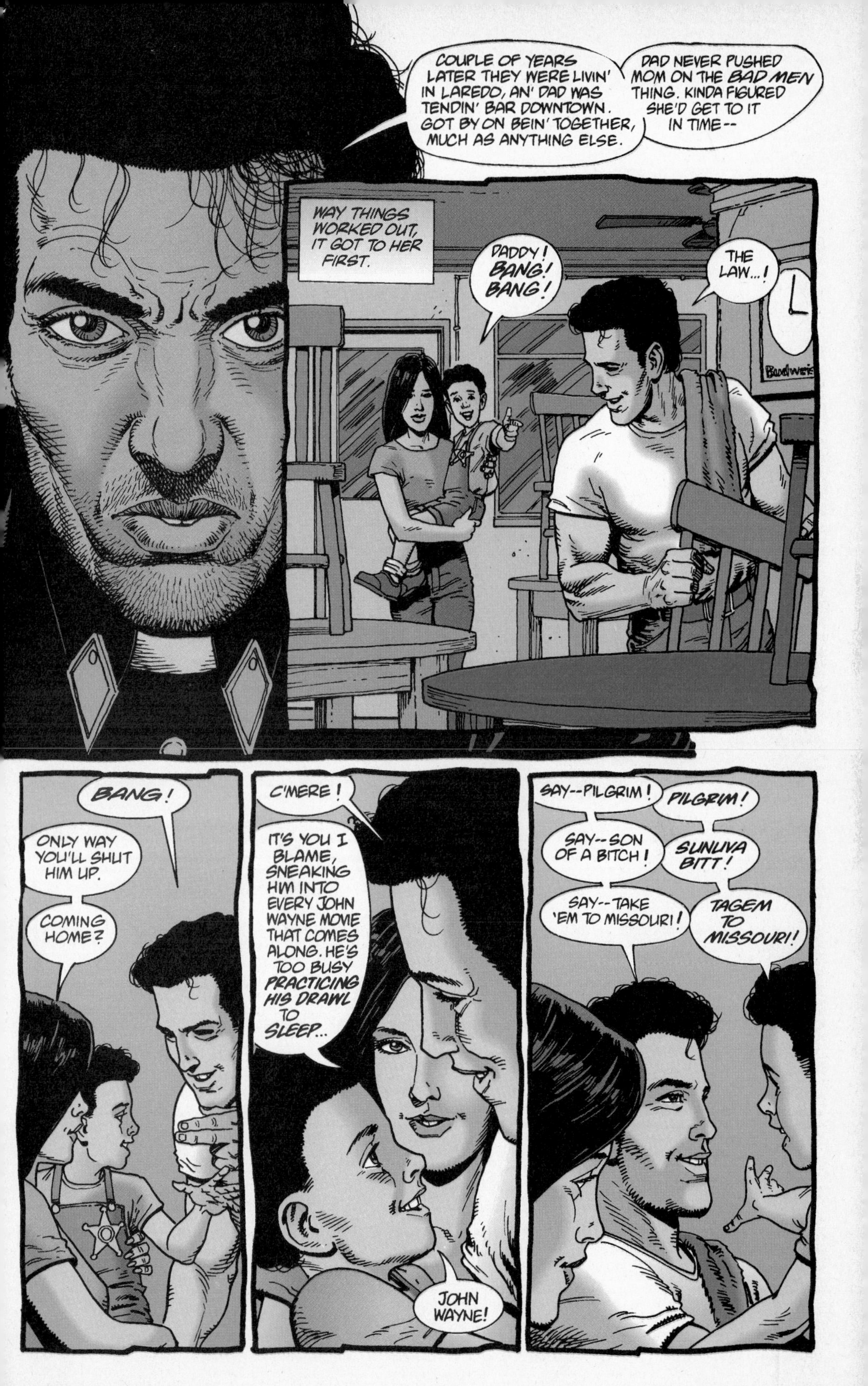

COUPLE OF YEARS LATER THEY WERE LIVIN' IN LAREDO, AN' DAD WAS TENDIN' BAR DOWNTOWN. GOT BY ON BEIN' TOGETHER, MUCH AS ANYTHING ELSE.
DAD NEVER PUSHED MOM ON THE *BAD MEN* THING. KINDA FIGURED SHE'D GET TO IT IN TIME--
WAY THINGS WORKED OUT, IT GOT TO HER FIRST.
DADDY! *BANG! BANG!*
THE LAW...!
BANG!
ONLY WAY YOU'LL SHUT HIM UP.
COMING HOME?
C'MERE!
IT'S YOU I BLAME, SNEAKING HIM INTO EVERY JOHN WAYNE MOVIE THAT COMES ALONG. HE'S TOO BUSY *PRACTICING HIS DRAWL* TO *SLEEP*...
JOHN WAYNE!
SAY--PILGRIM!
PILGRIM!
SAY--SON OF A BITCH!
SUNUVA BITT!
SAY--TAKE 'EM TO MISSOURI!
TAGEM TO MISSOURI!

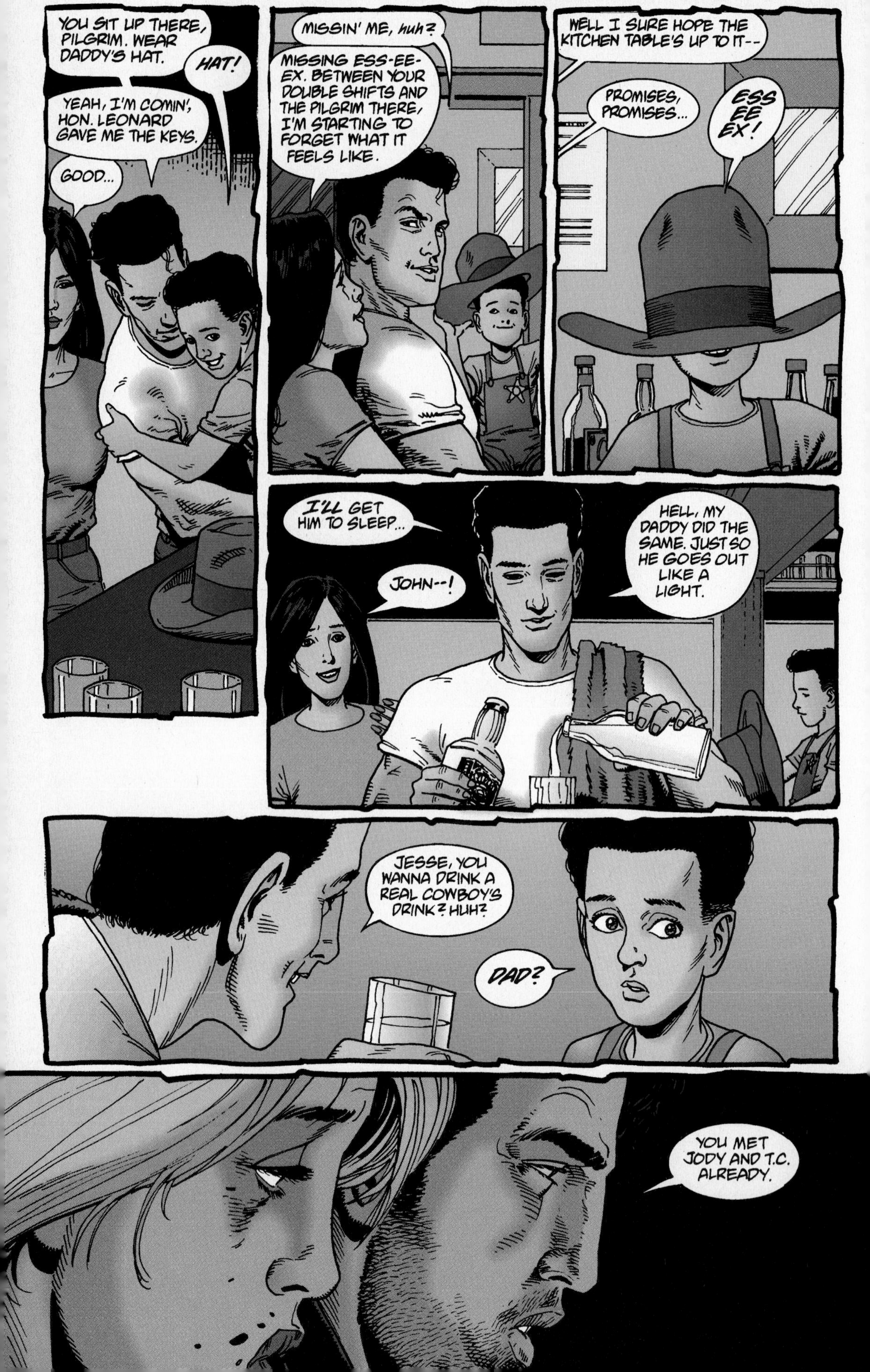
YOU SIT UP THERE, PILGRIM. WEAR DADDY'S HAT.
HAT!
YEAH, I'M COMIN', HON. LEONARD GAVE ME THE KEYS.
GOOD...
MISSIN' ME, huh?
MISSING ESS-EE-EX. BETWEEN YOUR DOUBLE SHIFTS AND THE PILGRIM THERE, I'M STARTING TO FORGET WHAT IT FEELS LIKE.
WELL I SURE HOPE THE KITCHEN TABLE'S UP TO IT--
PROMISES, PROMISES...
ESS EE EX!
I'LL GET HIM TO SLEEP...
JOHN--!
HELL, MY DADDY DID THE SAME. JUST SO HE GOES OUT LIKE A LIGHT.
JESSE, YOU WANNA DRINK A REAL COWBOY'S DRINK? HUH?
DAD?
YOU MET JODY AND T.C. ALREADY.

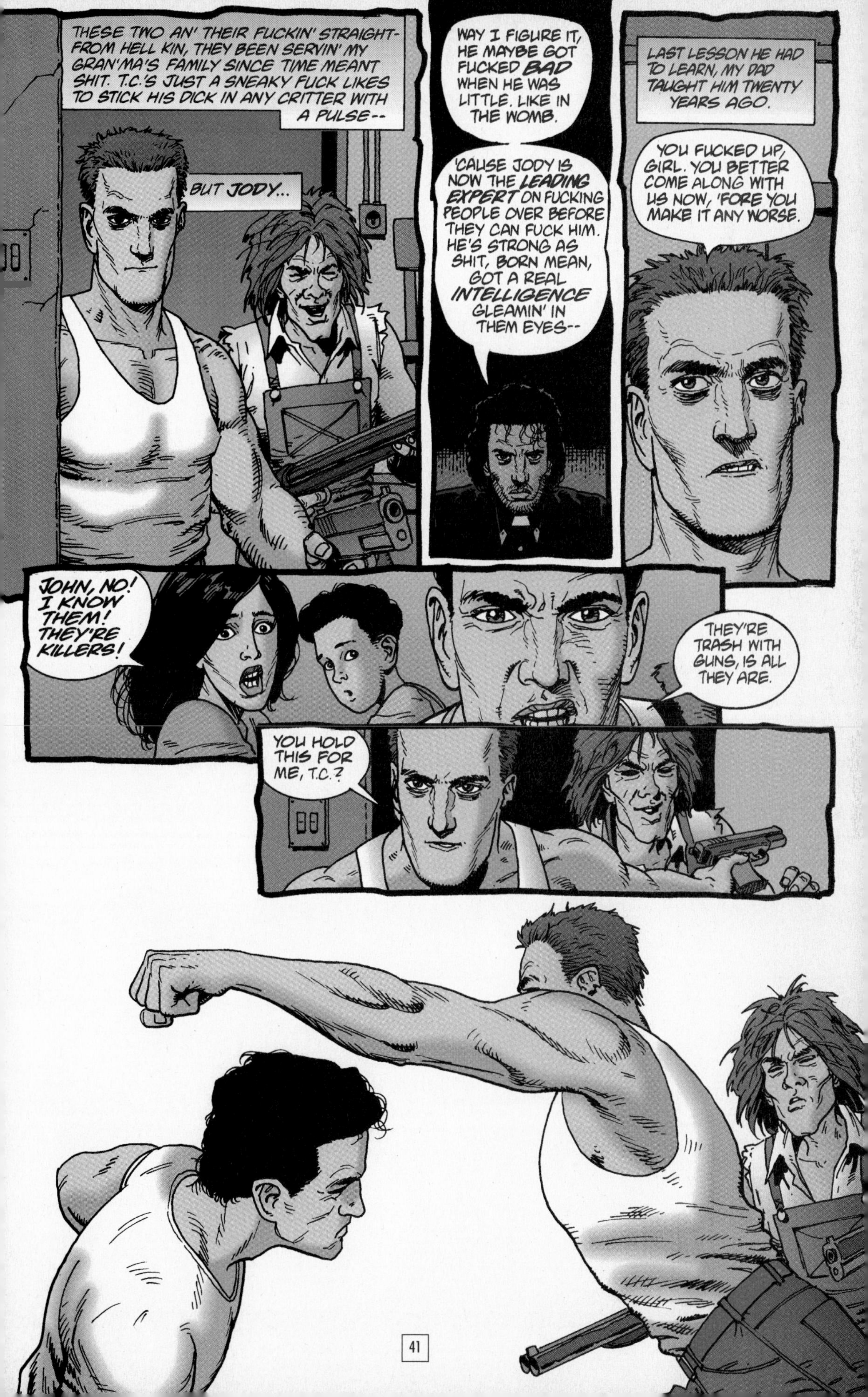
THESE TWO AN' THEIR FUCKIN' STRAIGHT-FROM HELL KIN, THEY BEEN SERVIN' MY GRAN'MA'S FAMILY SINCE TIME MEANT SHIT. T.C.'S JUST A SNEAKY FUCK LIKES TO STICK HIS DICK IN ANY CRITTER WITH A PULSE--
BUT JODY...
WAY I FIGURE IT, HE MAYBE GOT FUCKED BAD WHEN HE WAS LITTLE. LIKE IN THE WOMB.
'CAUSE JODY IS NOW THE LEADING EXPERT ON FUCKING PEOPLE OVER BEFORE THEY CAN FUCK HIM. HE'S STRONG AS SHIT, BORN MEAN, GOT A REAL INTELLIGENCE GLEAMIN' IN THEM EYES--
LAST LESSON HE HAD TO LEARN, MY DAD TAUGHT HIM TWENTY YEARS AGO.
YOU FUCKED UP, GIRL. YOU BETTER COME ALONG WITH US NOW, 'FORE YOU MAKE IT ANY WORSE.
JOHN, NO! I KNOW THEM! THEY'RE KILLERS!
THEY'RE TRASH WITH GUNS, IS ALL THEY ARE.
YOU HOLD THIS FOR ME, T.C.?

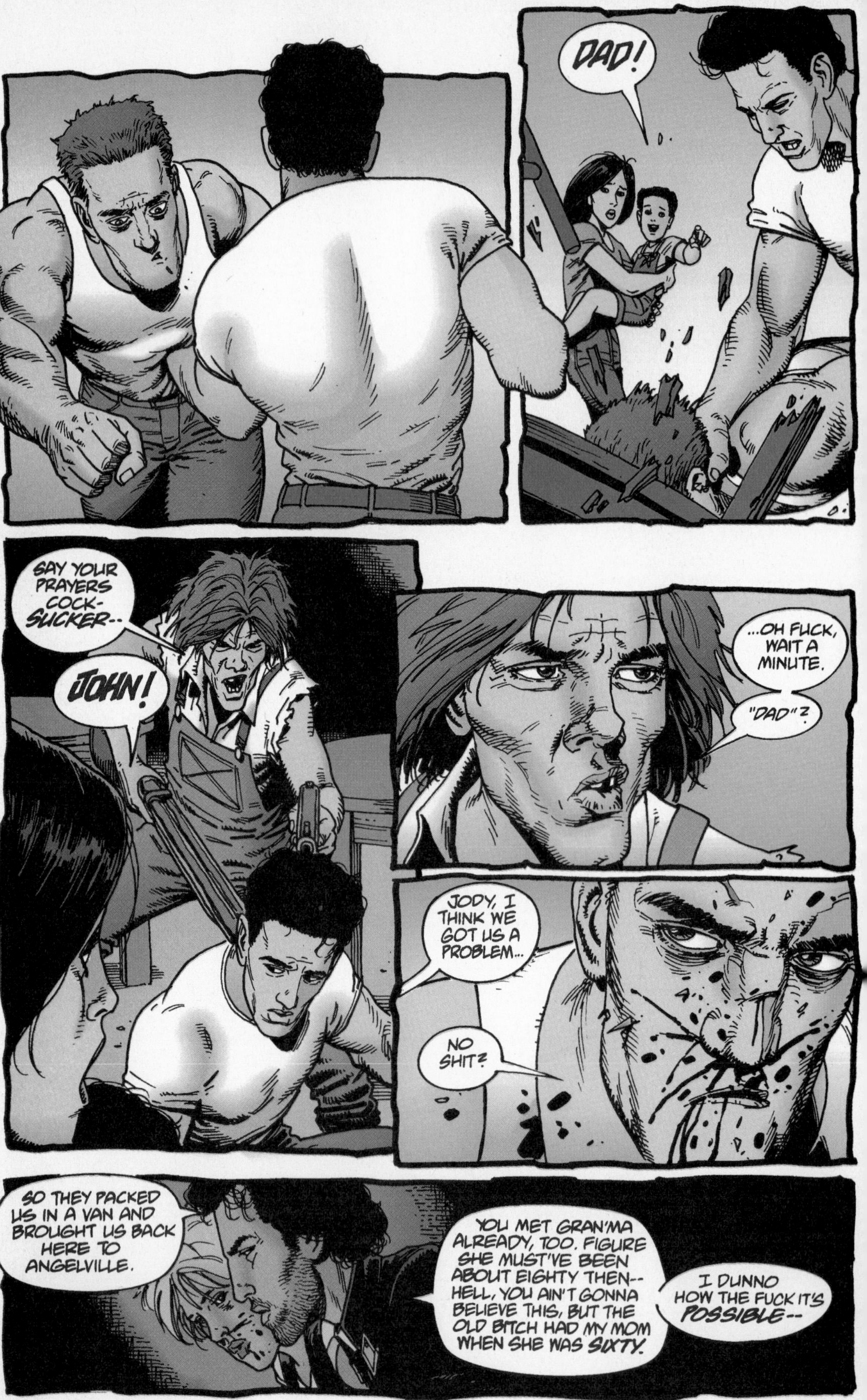

DAD!
SAY YOUR PRAYERS COCK-SUCKER--
JOHN!
...OH FUCK, WAIT A MINUTE.
"DAD"?
JODY, I THINK WE GOT US A PROBLEM...
NO SHIT?
SO THEY PACKED US IN A VAN AND BROUGHT US BACK HERE TO ANGELVILLE.
YOU MET GRAN'MA ALREADY, TOO. FIGURE SHE MUST'VE BEEN ABOUT EIGHTY THEN--HELL, YOU AIN'T GONNA BELIEVE THIS, BUT THE OLD BITCH HAD MY MOM WHEN SHE WAS SIXTY.
I DUNNO HOW THE FUCK IT'S POSSIBLE--

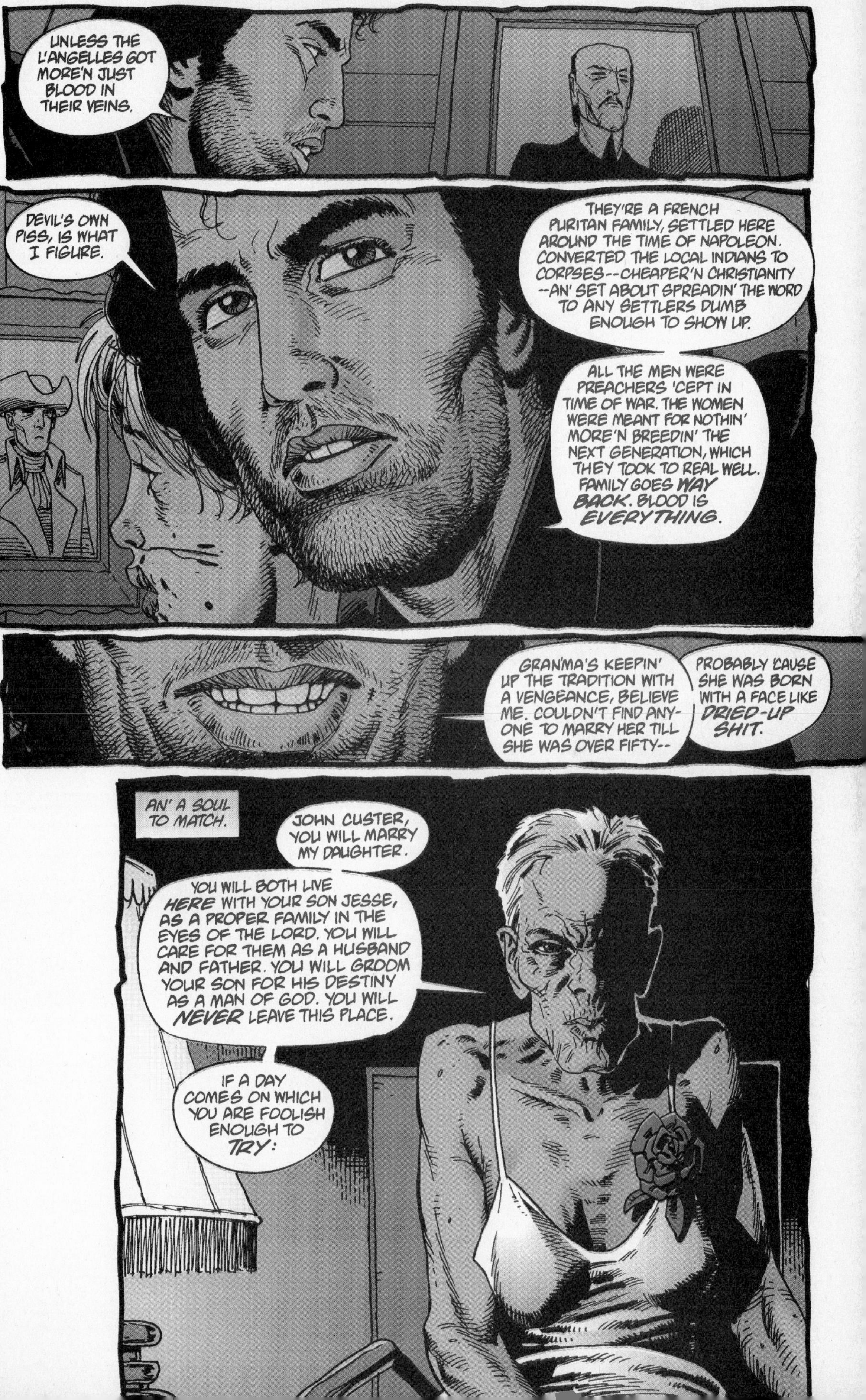
UNLESS THE L'ANGELLES GOT MORE'N JUST BLOOD IN THEIR VEINS.
DEVIL'S OWN PISS, IS WHAT I FIGURE.
THEY'RE A FRENCH PURITAN FAMILY, SETTLED HERE AROUND THE TIME OF NAPOLEON. CONVERTED THE LOCAL INDIANS TO CORPSES--CHEAPER'N CHRISTIANITY --AN' SET ABOUT SPREADIN' THE WORD TO ANY SETTLERS DUMB ENOUGH TO SHOW UP.
ALL THE MEN WERE PREACHERS 'CEPT IN TIME OF WAR. THE WOMEN WERE MEANT FOR NOTHIN' MORE'N BREEDIN' THE NEXT GENERATION, WHICH THEY TOOK TO REAL WELL. FAMILY GOES WAY BACK. BLOOD IS EVERYTHING.
GRAN'MA'S KEEPIN' UP THE TRADITION WITH A VENGEANCE, BELIEVE ME. COULDN'T FIND ANY-ONE TO MARRY HER TILL SHE WAS OVER FIFTY--
PROBABLY 'CAUSE SHE WAS BORN WITH A FACE LIKE DRIED-UP SHIT.
AN' A SOUL TO MATCH.
JOHN CUSTER, YOU WILL MARRY MY DAUGHTER.
YOU WILL BOTH LIVE HERE WITH YOUR SON JESSE, AS A PROPER FAMILY IN THE EYES OF THE LORD. YOU WILL CARE FOR THEM AS A HUSBAND AND FATHER. YOU WILL GROOM YOUR SON FOR HIS DESTINY AS A MAN OF GOD. YOU WILL NEVER LEAVE THIS PLACE.
IF A DAY COMES ON WHICH YOU ARE FOOLISH ENOUGH TO TRY:

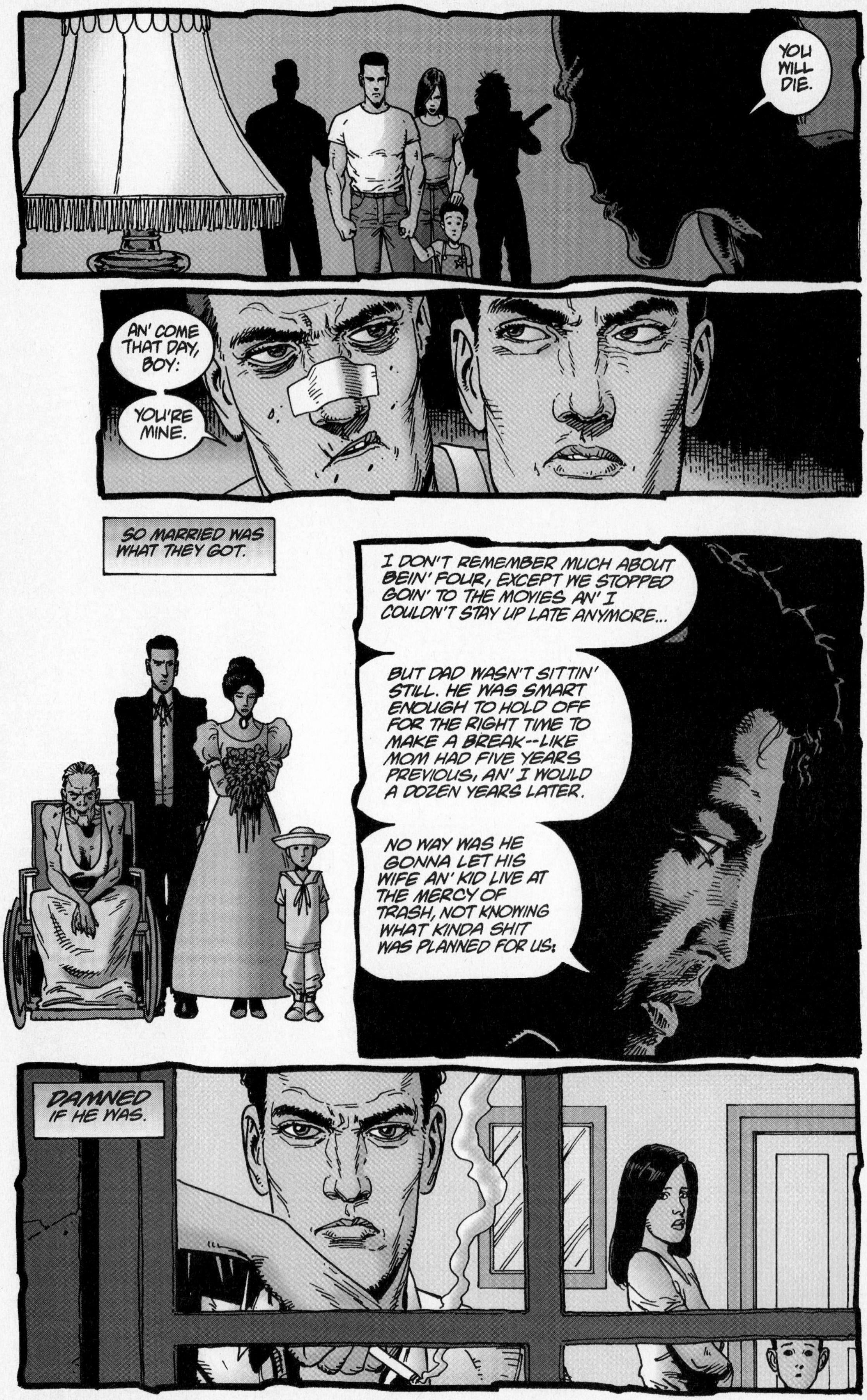
YOU WILL DIE.
AN' COME THAT DAY, BOY:
YOU'RE MINE.
SO MARRIED WAS WHAT THEY GOT.
I DON'T REMEMBER MUCH ABOUT BEIN' FOUR, EXCEPT WE STOPPED GOIN' TO THE MOVIES AN' I COULDN'T STAY UP LATE ANYMORE...
BUT DAD WASN'T SITTIN' STILL. HE WAS SMART ENOUGH TO HOLD OFF FOR THE RIGHT TIME TO MAKE A BREAK--LIKE MOM HAD FIVE YEARS PREVIOUS, AN' I WOULD A DOZEN YEARS LATER.
NO WAY WAS HE GONNA LET HIS WIFE AN' KID LIVE AT THE MERCY OF TRASH, NOT KNOWING WHAT KINDA SHIT WAS PLANNED FOR US:
DAMNED IF HE WAS.

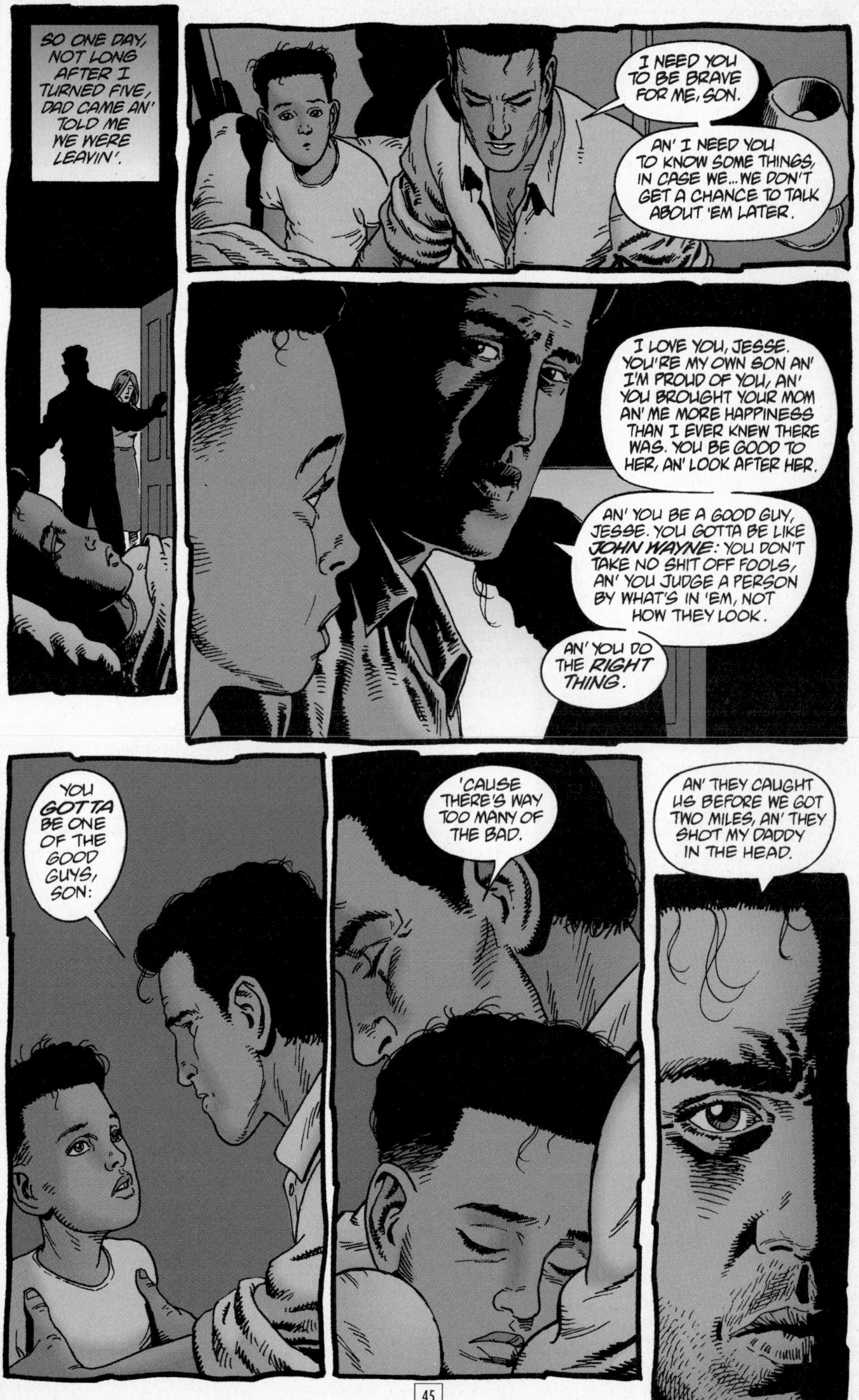
SO ONE DAY, NOT LONG AFTER I TURNED FIVE, DAD CAME AN' TOLD ME WE WERE LEAVIN'.
I NEED YOU TO BE BRAVE FOR ME, SON.
AN' I NEED YOU TO KNOW SOME THINGS, IN CASE WE...WE DON'T GET A CHANCE TO TALK ABOUT 'EM LATER.
I LOVE YOU, JESSE. YOU'RE MY OWN SON AN' I'M PROUD OF YOU, AN' YOU BROUGHT YOUR MOM AN' ME MORE HAPPINESS THAN I EVER KNEW THERE WAS. YOU BE GOOD TO HER, AN' LOOK AFTER HER.
AN' YOU BE A GOOD GUY, JESSE. YOU GOTTA BE LIKE JOHN WAYNE: YOU DON'T TAKE NO SHIT OFF FOOLS, AN' YOU JUDGE A PERSON BY WHAT'S IN 'EM, NOT HOW THEY LOOK.
AN' YOU DO THE RIGHT THING.
YOU GOTTA BE ONE OF THE GOOD GUYS, SON:
'CAUSE THERE'S WAY TOO MANY OF THE BAD.
AN' THEY CAUGHT US BEFORE WE GOT TWO MILES, AN' THEY SHOT MY DADDY IN THE HEAD.

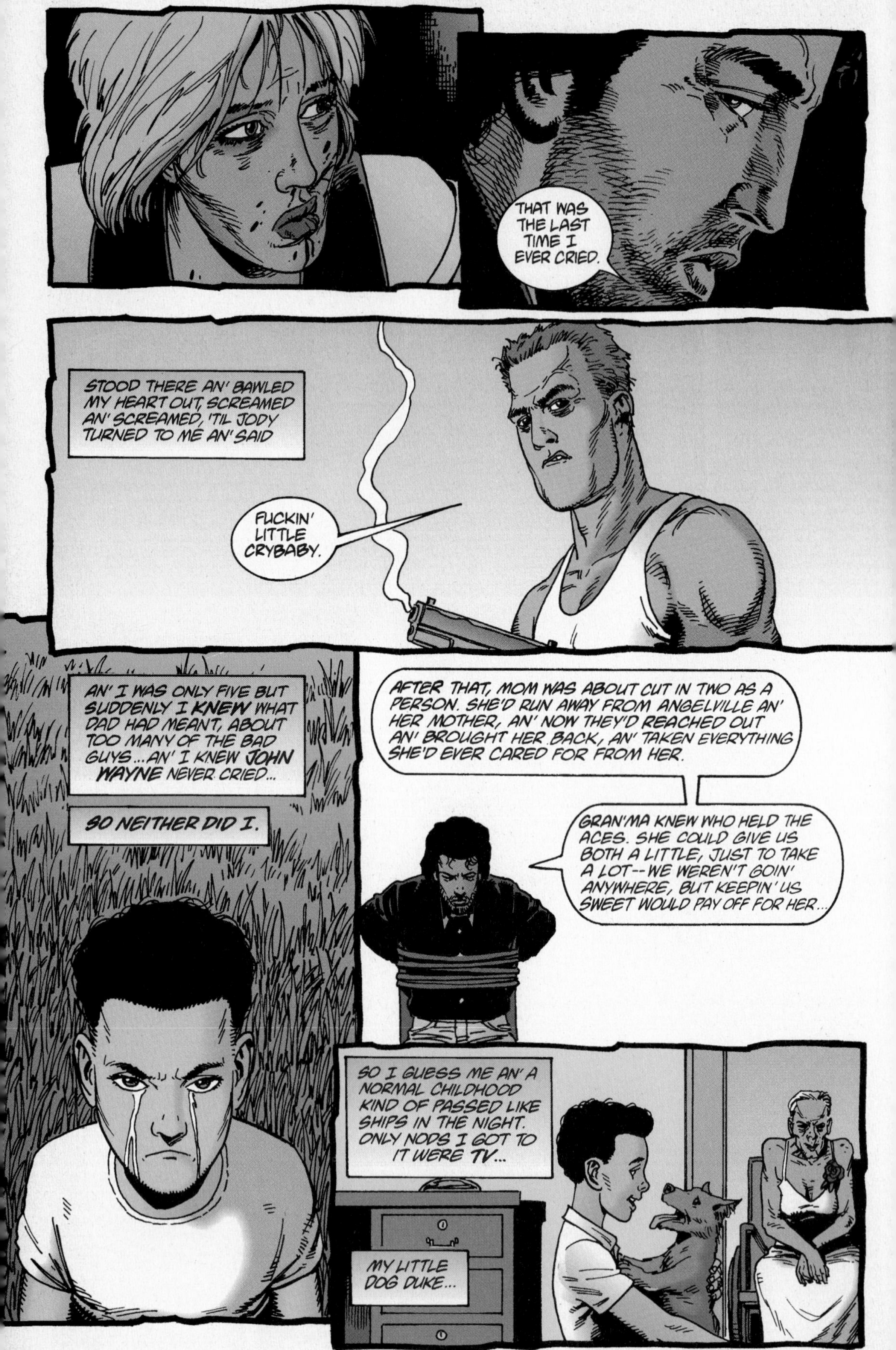
THAT WAS THE LAST TIME I EVER CRIED.
STOOD THERE AN' BAWLED MY HEART OUT, SCREAMED AN' SCREAMED, 'TIL JODY TURNED TO ME AN' SAID
FUCKIN' LITTLE CRYBABY.
AN' I WAS ONLY FIVE BUT SUDDENLY I KNEW WHAT DAD HAD MEANT, ABOUT TOO MANY OF THE BAD GUYS... AN' I KNEW JOHN WAYNE NEVER CRIED...
SO NEITHER DID I.
AFTER THAT, MOM WAS ABOUT CUT IN TWO AS A PERSON. SHE'D RUN AWAY FROM ANGELVILLE AN' HER MOTHER, AN' NOW THEY'D REACHED OUT AN' BROUGHT HER BACK, AN' TAKEN EVERYTHING SHE'D EVER CARED FOR FROM HER.
GRAN'MA KNEW WHO HELD THE ACES. SHE COULD GIVE US BOTH A LITTLE, JUST TO TAKE A LOT--WE WEREN'T GOIN' ANYWHERE, BUT KEEPIN' US SWEET WOULD PAY OFF FOR HER...
SO I GUESS ME AN' A NORMAL CHILDHOOD KIND OF PASSED LIKE SHIPS IN THE NIGHT. ONLY NODS I GOT TO IT WERE TV...
MY LITTLE DOG DUKE...

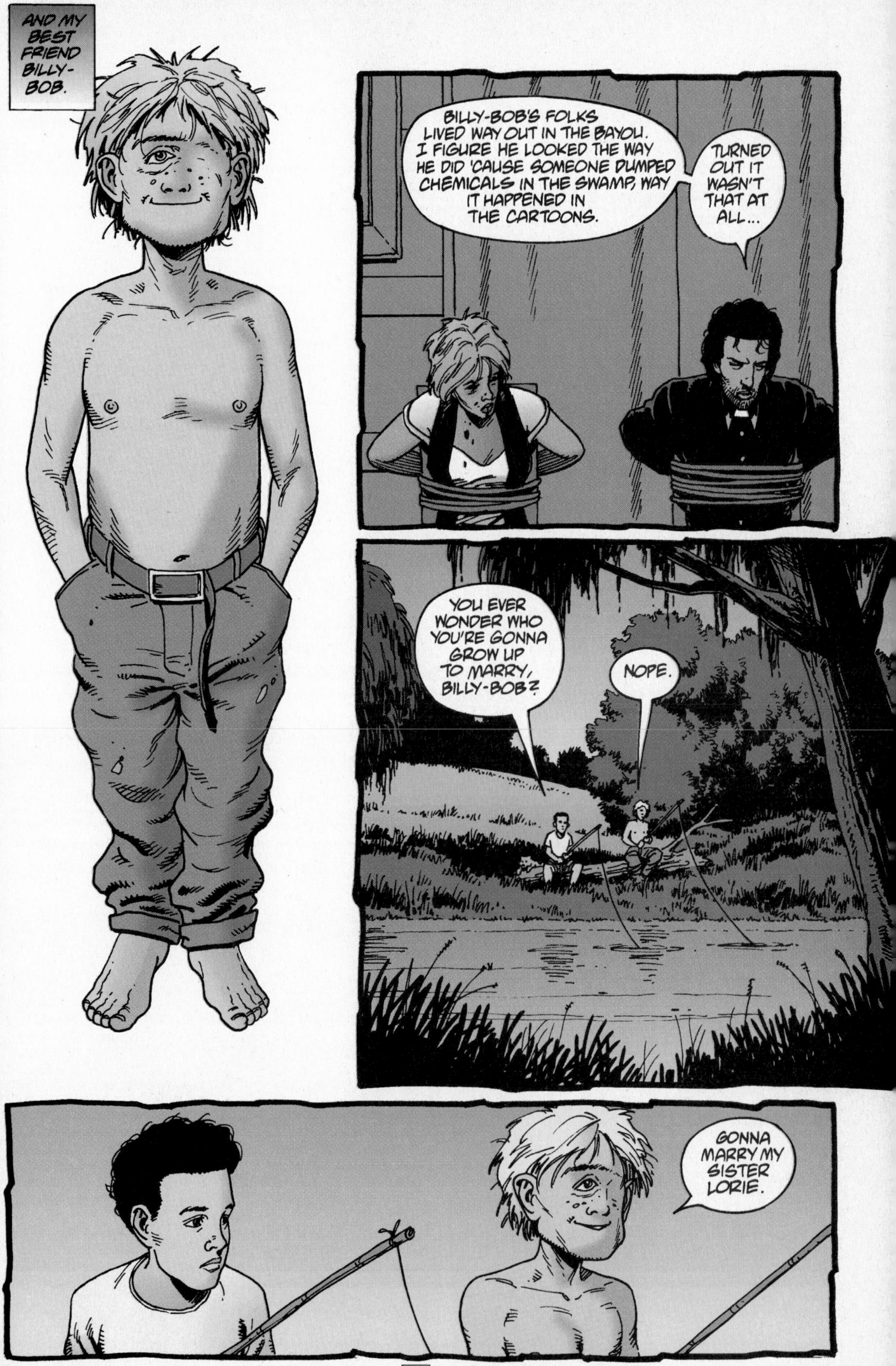
AND MY BEST FRIEND BILLY-BOB.
BILLY-BOB'S FOLKS LIVED WAY OUT IN THE BAYOU. I FIGURE HE LOOKED THE WAY HE DID 'CAUSE SOMEONE DUMPED CHEMICALS IN THE SWAMP, WAY IT HAPPENED IN THE CARTOONS.
TURNED OUT IT WASN'T THAT AT ALL...
YOU EVER WONDER WHO YOU'RE GONNA GROW UP TO MARRY, BILLY-BOB?
NOPE.
GONNA MARRY MY SISTER LORIE.

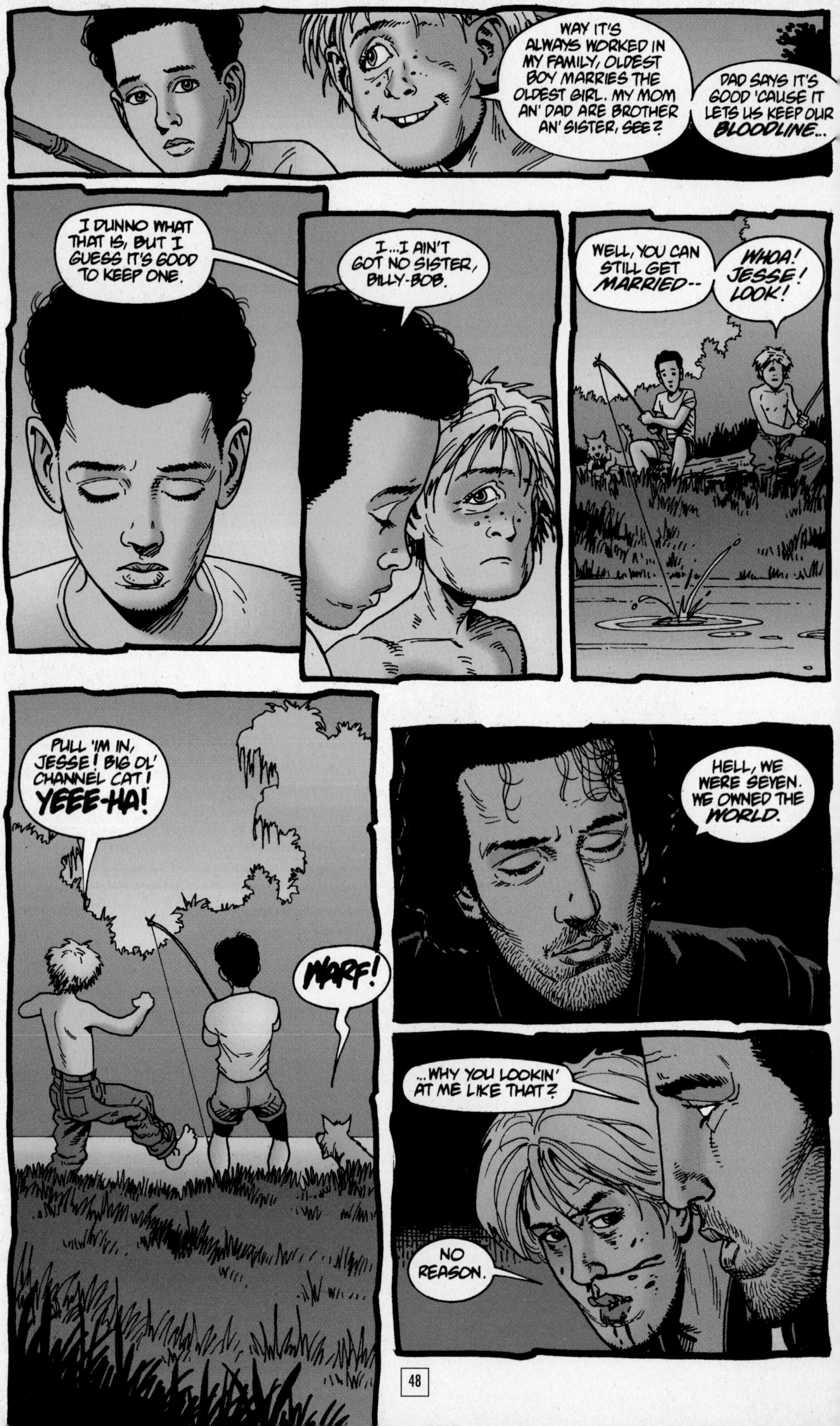
WAY IT'S ALWAYS WORKED IN MY FAMILY, OLDEST BOY MARRIES THE OLDEST GIRL. MY MOM AN' DAD ARE BROTHER AN' SISTER, SEE?
DAD SAYS IT'S GOOD 'CAUSE IT LETS US KEEP OUR BLOODLINE...
I DUNNO WHAT THAT IS, BUT I GUESS IT'S GOOD TO KEEP ONE.
I...I AIN'T GOT NO SISTER, BILLY-BOB.
WELL, YOU CAN STILL GET MARRIED--
WHOA! JESSE! LOOK!
PULL 'IM IN, JESSE! BIG OL' CHANNEL CAT! YEEE-HA!
WARF!
HELL, WE WERE SEVEN. WE OWNED THE WORLD.
...WHY YOU LOOKIN' AT ME LIKE THAT?
NO REASON.

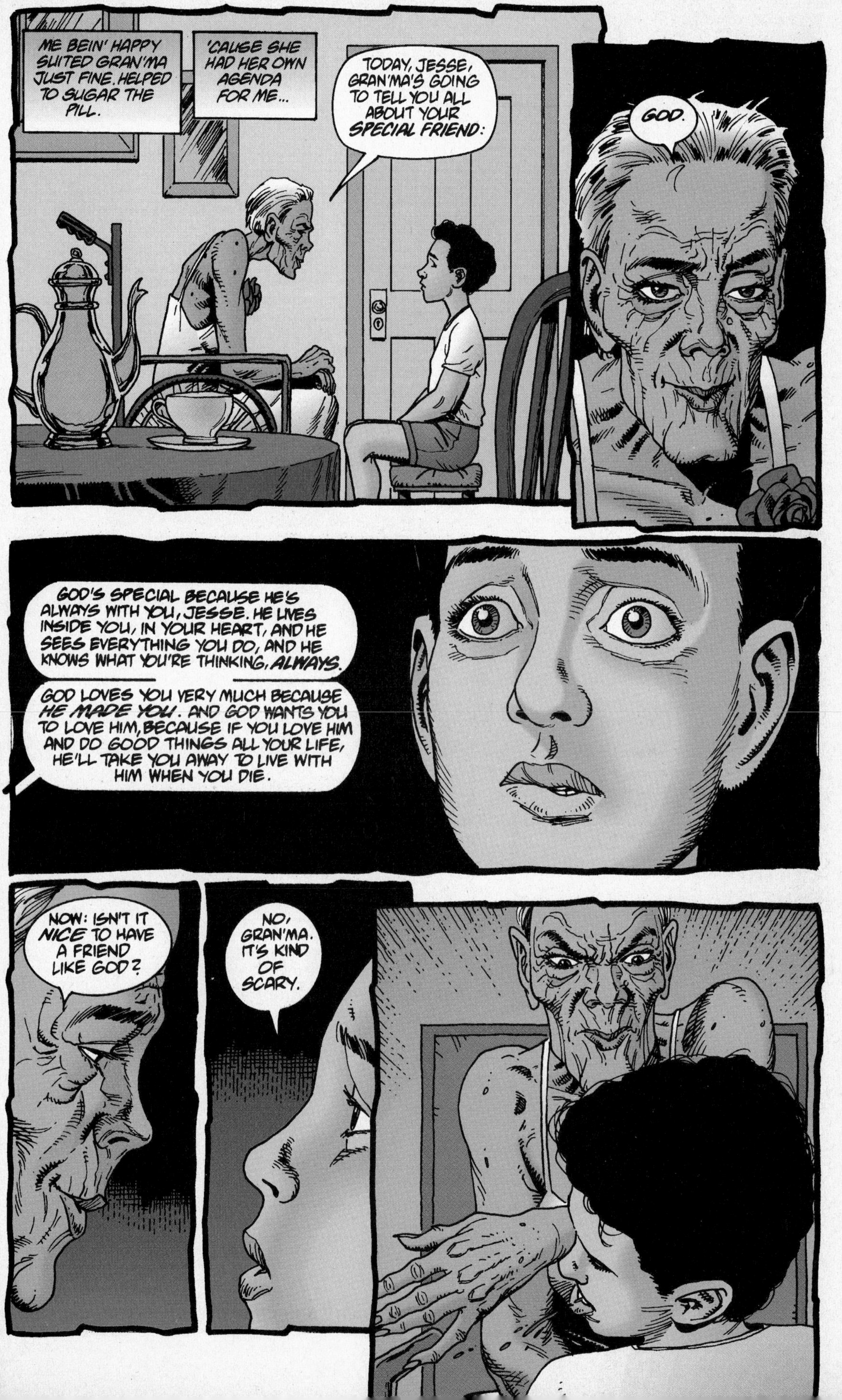
ME BEIN' HAPPY SUITED GRAN'MA JUST FINE. HELPED TO SUGAR THE PILL.
'CAUSE SHE HAD HER OWN AGENDA FOR ME...
TODAY, JESSE, GRAN'MA'S GOING TO TELL YOU ALL ABOUT YOUR SPECIAL FRIEND:
GOD.
GOD'S SPECIAL BECAUSE HE'S ALWAYS WITH YOU, JESSE. HE LIVES INSIDE YOU, IN YOUR HEART, AND HE SEES EVERYTHING YOU DO, AND HE KNOWS WHAT YOU'RE THINKING, ALWAYS.
GOD LOVES YOU VERY MUCH BECAUSE HE MADE YOU. AND GOD WANTS YOU TO LOVE HIM, BECAUSE IF YOU LOVE HIM AND DO GOOD THINGS ALL YOUR LIFE, HE'LL TAKE YOU AWAY TO LIVE WITH HIM WHEN YOU DIE.
NOW: ISN'T IT NICE TO HAVE A FRIEND LIKE GOD?
NO, GRAN'MA. IT'S KIND OF SCARY.

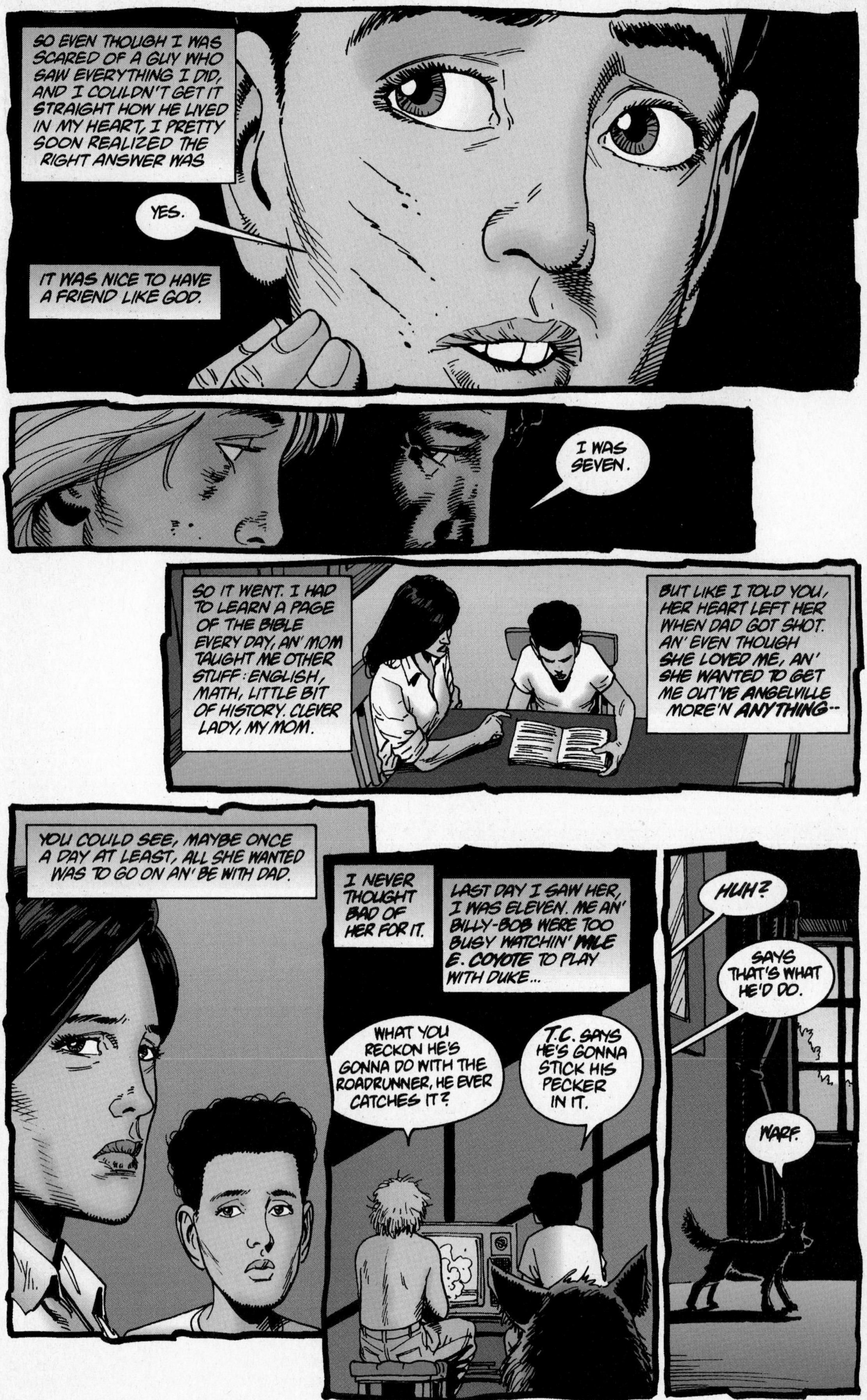
SO EVEN THOUGH I WAS SCARED OF A GUY WHO SAW EVERYTHING I DID, AND I COULDN'T GET IT STRAIGHT HOW HE LIVED IN MY HEART, I PRETTY SOON REALIZED THE RIGHT ANSWER WAS
YES.
IT WAS NICE TO HAVE A FRIEND LIKE GOD.
I WAS SEVEN.
SO IT WENT. I HAD TO LEARN A PAGE OF THE BIBLE EVERY DAY, AN' MOM TAUGHT ME OTHER STUFF: ENGLISH, MATH, LITTLE BIT OF HISTORY. CLEVER LADY, MY MOM.
BUT LIKE I TOLD YOU, HER HEART LEFT HER WHEN DAD GOT SHOT. AN' EVEN THOUGH SHE LOVED ME, AN' SHE WANTED TO GET ME OUT'VE ANGELVILLE MORE'N ANYTHING--
YOU COULD SEE, MAYBE ONCE A DAY AT LEAST, ALL SHE WANTED WAS TO GO ON AN' BE WITH DAD.
I NEVER THOUGHT BAD OF HER FOR IT.
LAST DAY I SAW HER, I WAS ELEVEN. ME AN' BILLY-BOB WERE TOO BUSY WATCHIN' WILE E. COYOTE TO PLAY WITH DUKE...
WHAT YOU RECKON HE'S GONNA DO WITH THE ROADRUNNER, HE EVER CATCHES IT?
T.C. SAYS HE'S GONNA STICK HIS PECKER IN IT.
HUH?
SAYS THAT'S WHAT HE'D DO.
WARF.

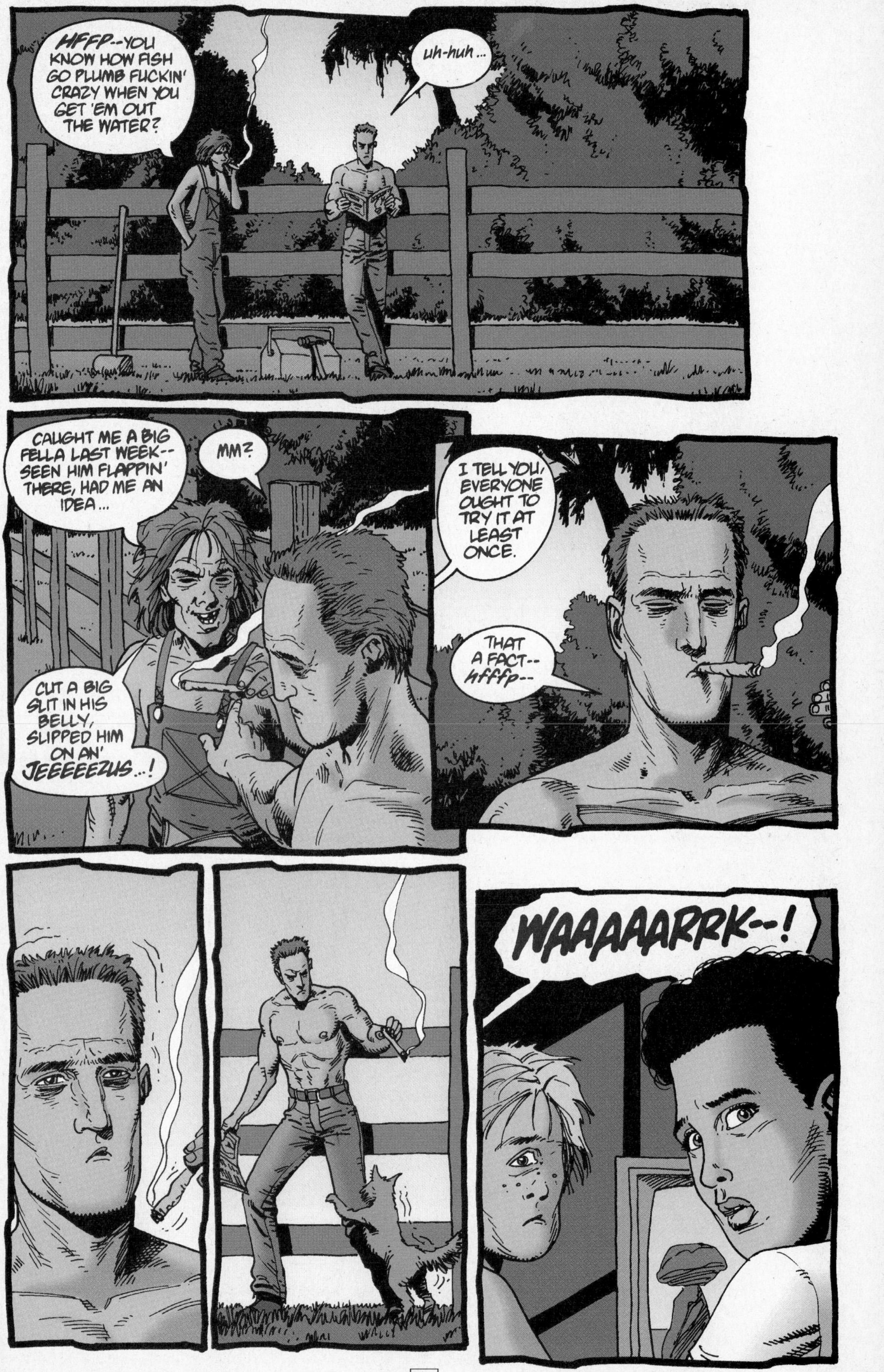
HFFP--YOU KNOW HOW FISH GO PLUMB FUCKIN' CRAZY WHEN YOU GET 'EM OUT THE WATER?
uh-huh...
CAUGHT ME A BIG FELLA LAST WEEK--SEEN HIM FLAPPIN' THERE, HAD ME AN IDEA...
MM?
CUT A BIG SLIT IN HIS BELLY, SLIPPED HIM ON AN' JEEEEEZUS...!
I TELL YOU, EVERYONE OUGHT TO TRY IT AT LEAST ONCE.
THAT A FACT--hfffp--
WAAAAARRK--!

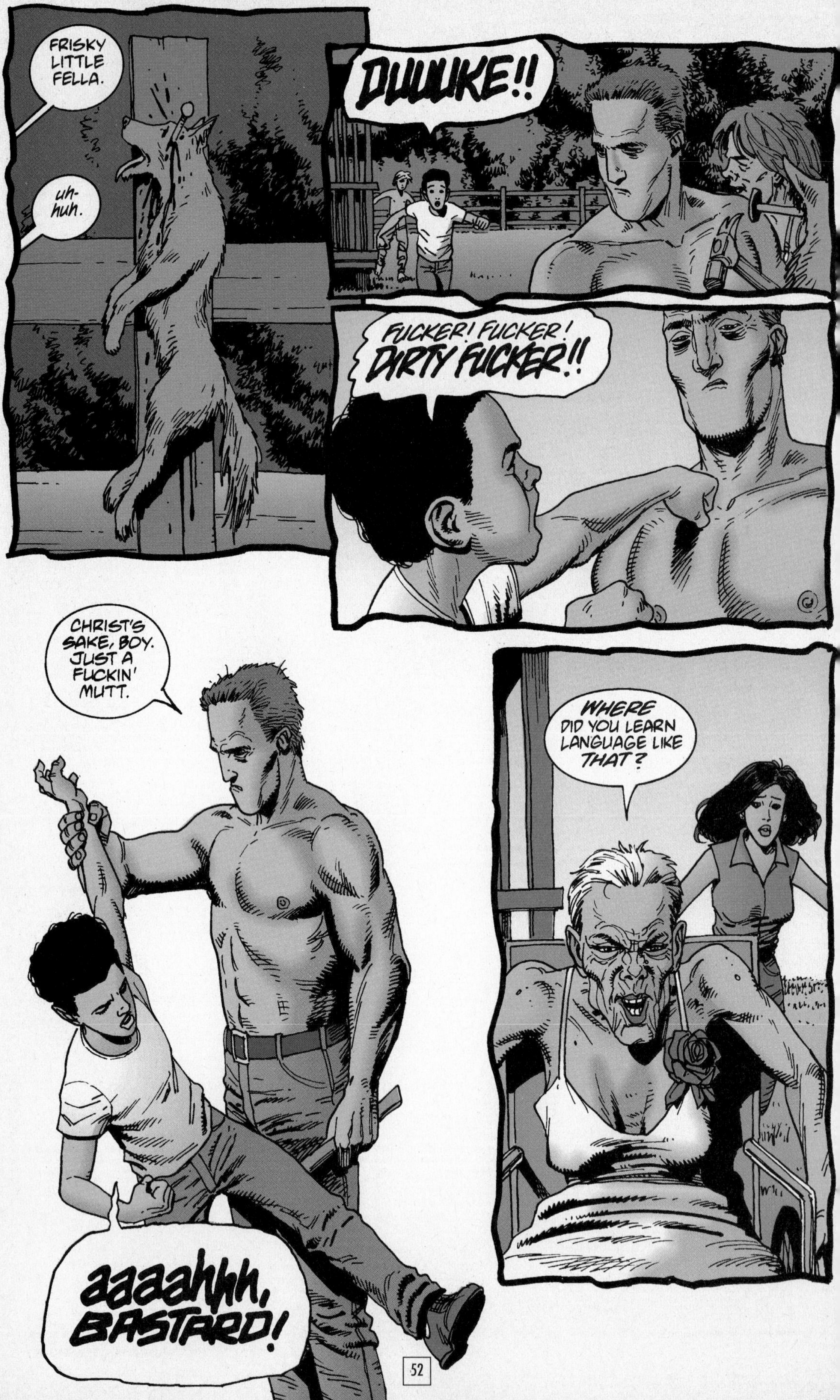
FRISKY LITTLE FELLA.
uh-huh.
DUUUKE!!
FUCKER! FUCKER! DIRTY FUCKER!!
CHRIST'S SAKE, BOY. JUST A FUCKIN' MUTT.
aaaahhh, BASTARD!
WHERE DID YOU LEARN LANGUAGE LIKE THAT?

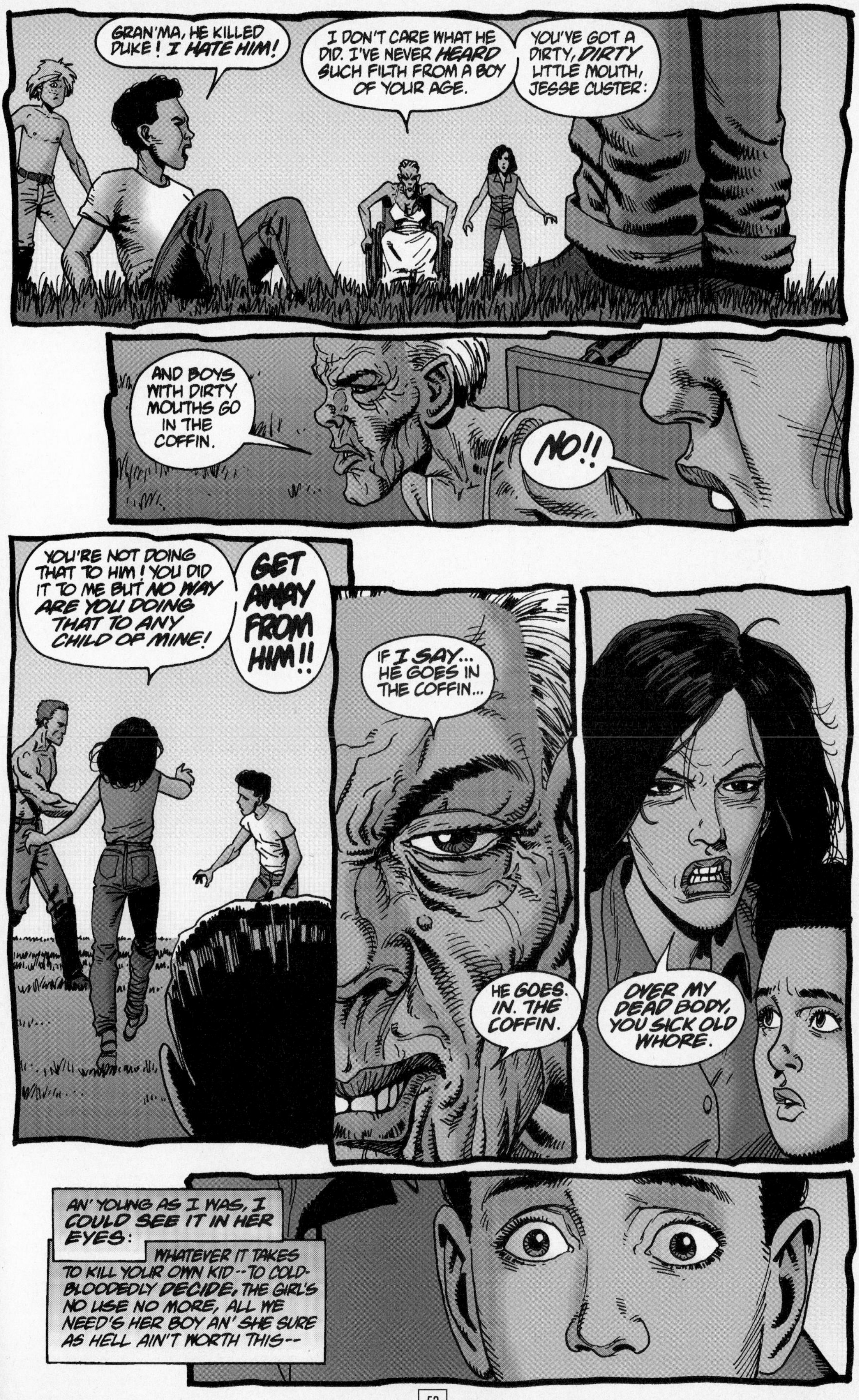
GRAN'MA, HE KILLED DUKE! I HATE HIM!
I DON'T CARE WHAT HE DID. I'VE NEVER HEARD SUCH FILTH FROM A BOY OF YOUR AGE.
YOU'VE GOT A DIRTY, DIRTY LITTLE MOUTH, JESSE CUSTER:
AND BOYS WITH DIRTY MOUTHS GO IN THE COFFIN.
NO!!
YOU'RE NOT DOING THAT TO HIM! YOU DID IT TO ME BUT NO WAY ARE YOU DOING THAT TO ANY CHILD OF MINE!
GET AWAY FROM HIM!!
IF I SAY... HE GOES IN THE COFFIN...
HE GOES. IN. THE COFFIN.
OVER MY DEAD BODY, YOU SICK OLD WHORE.
AN' YOUNG AS I WAS, I COULD SEE IT IN HER EYES:
WHATEVER IT TAKES TO KILL YOUR OWN KID--TO COLD-BLOODEDLY DECIDE, THE GIRL'S NO USE NO MORE, ALL WE NEED'S HER BOY AN' SHE SURE AS HELL AIN'T WORTH THIS--

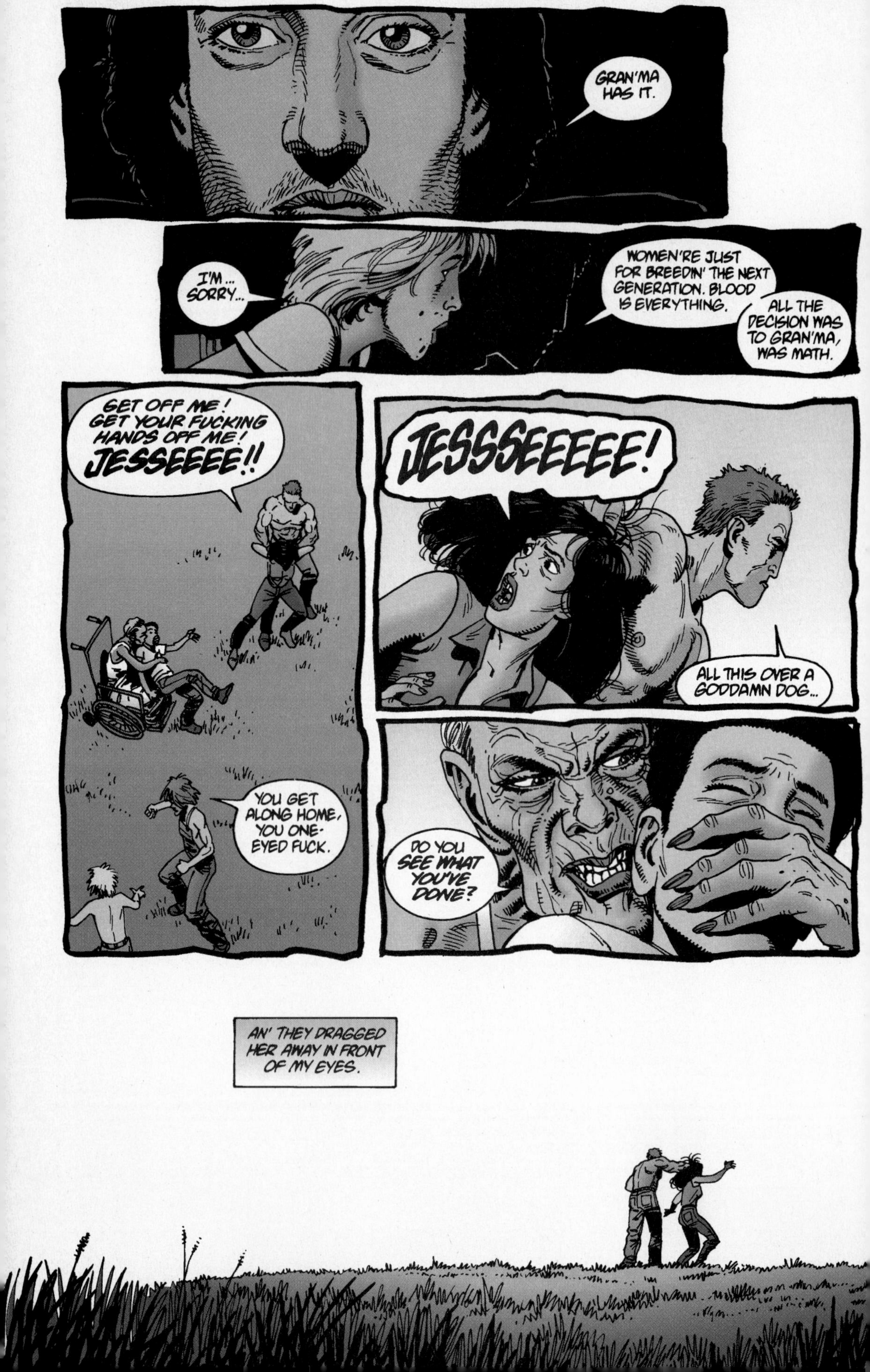
GRAN'MA HAS IT.
I'M ... SORRY...
WOMEN'RE JUST FOR BREEDIN' THE NEXT GENERATION. BLOOD IS EVERYTHING.
ALL THE DECISION WAS TO GRAN'MA, WAS MATH.
GET OFF ME! GET YOUR FUCKING HANDS OFF ME! JESSEEEE!!
YOU GET ALONG HOME, YOU ONE-EYED FUCK.
JESSSEEEEE!
ALL THIS OVER A GODDAMN DOG...
DO YOU SEE WHAT YOU'VE DONE?
AN' THEY DRAGGED HER AWAY IN FRONT OF MY EYES.

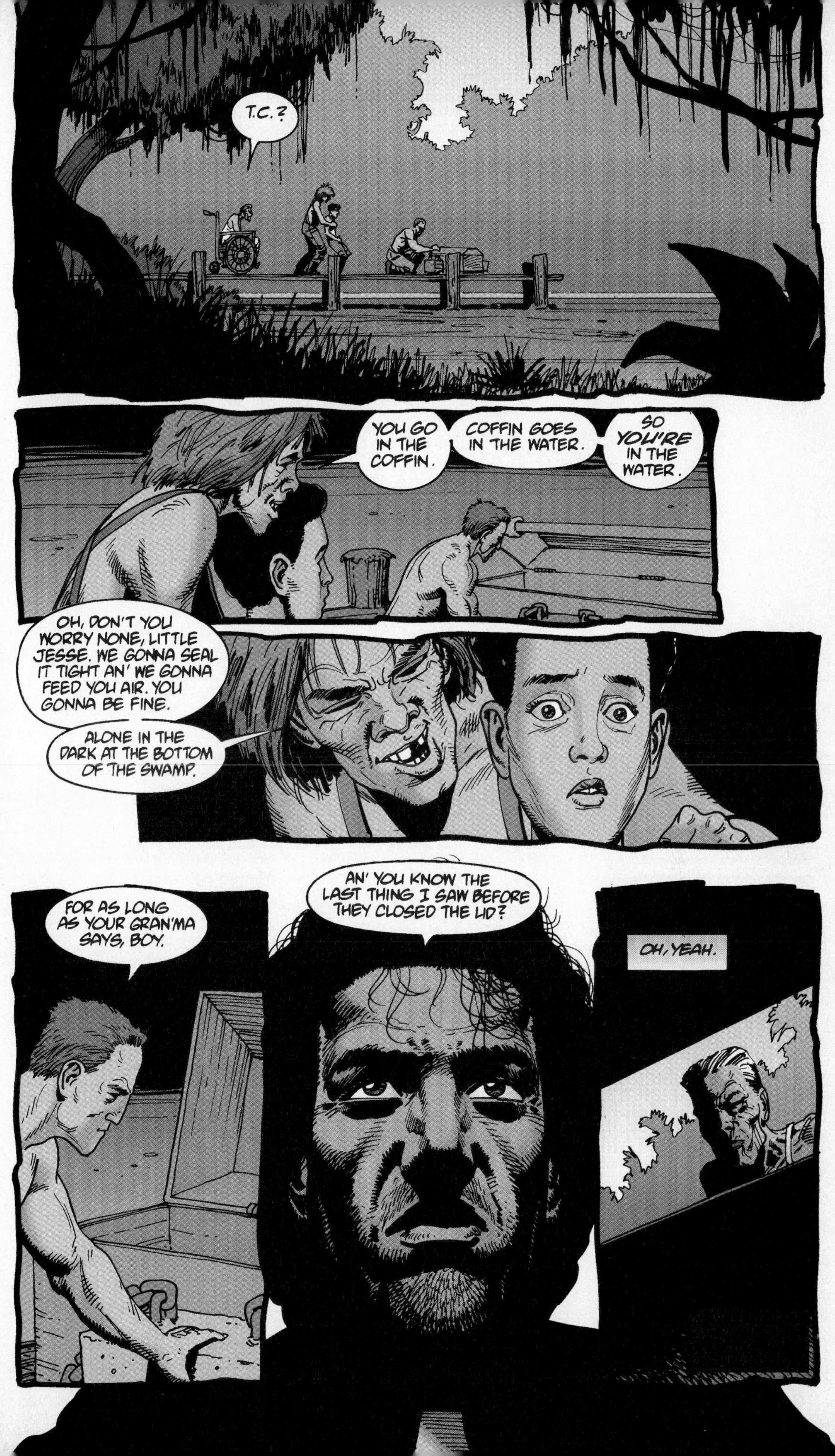
T.C.?
YOU GO IN THE COFFIN.
COFFIN GOES IN THE WATER.
SO YOU'RE IN THE WATER.
OH, DON'T YOU WORRY NONE, LITTLE JESSE. WE GONNA SEAL IT TIGHT AN' WE GONNA FEED YOU AIR. YOU GONNA BE FINE.
ALONE IN THE DARK AT THE BOTTOM OF THE SWAMP.
FOR AS LONG AS YOUR GRAN'MA SAYS, BOY.
AN' YOU KNOW THE LAST THING I SAW BEFORE THEY CLOSED THE LID?
OH, YEAH.

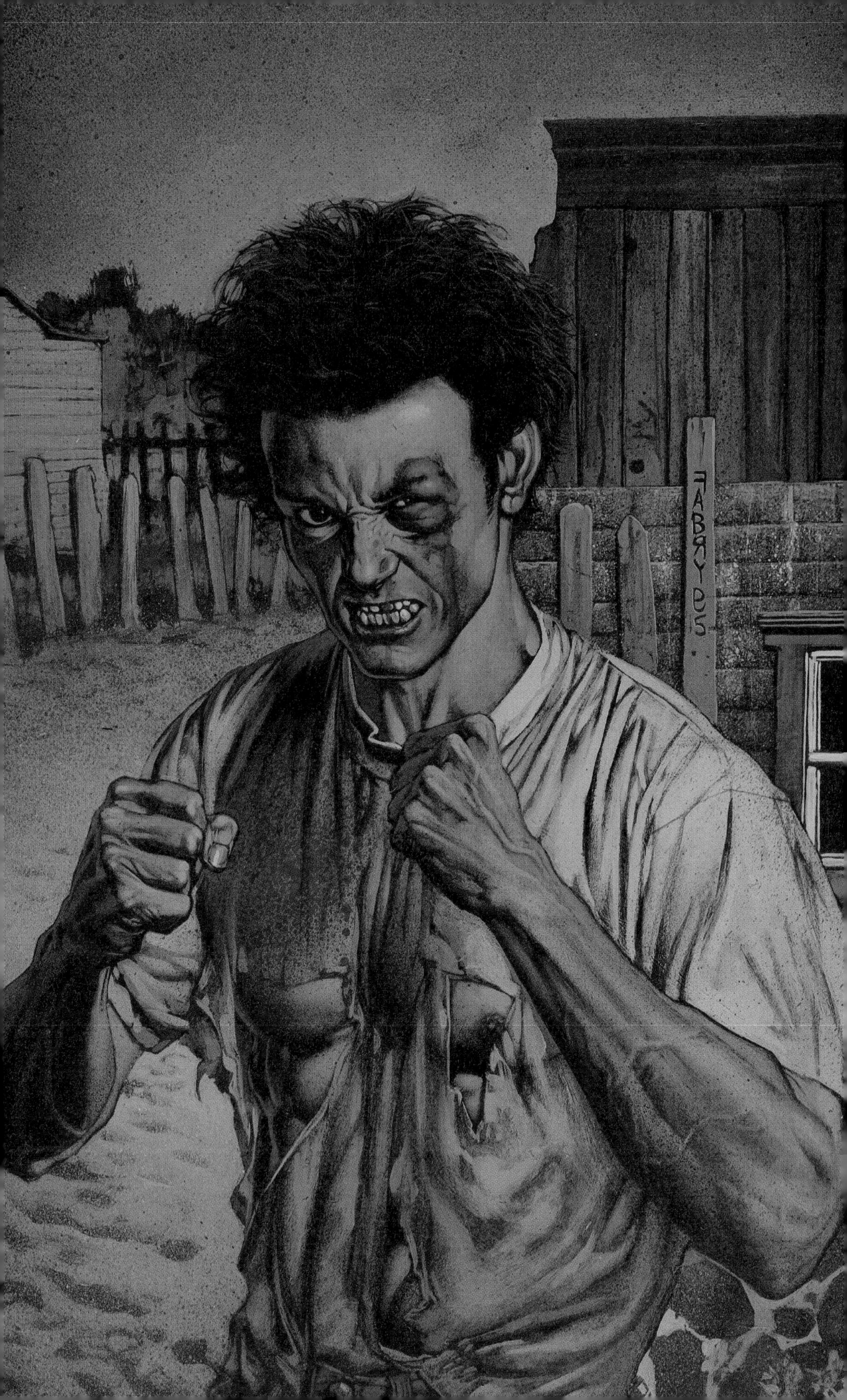
FABRY 05

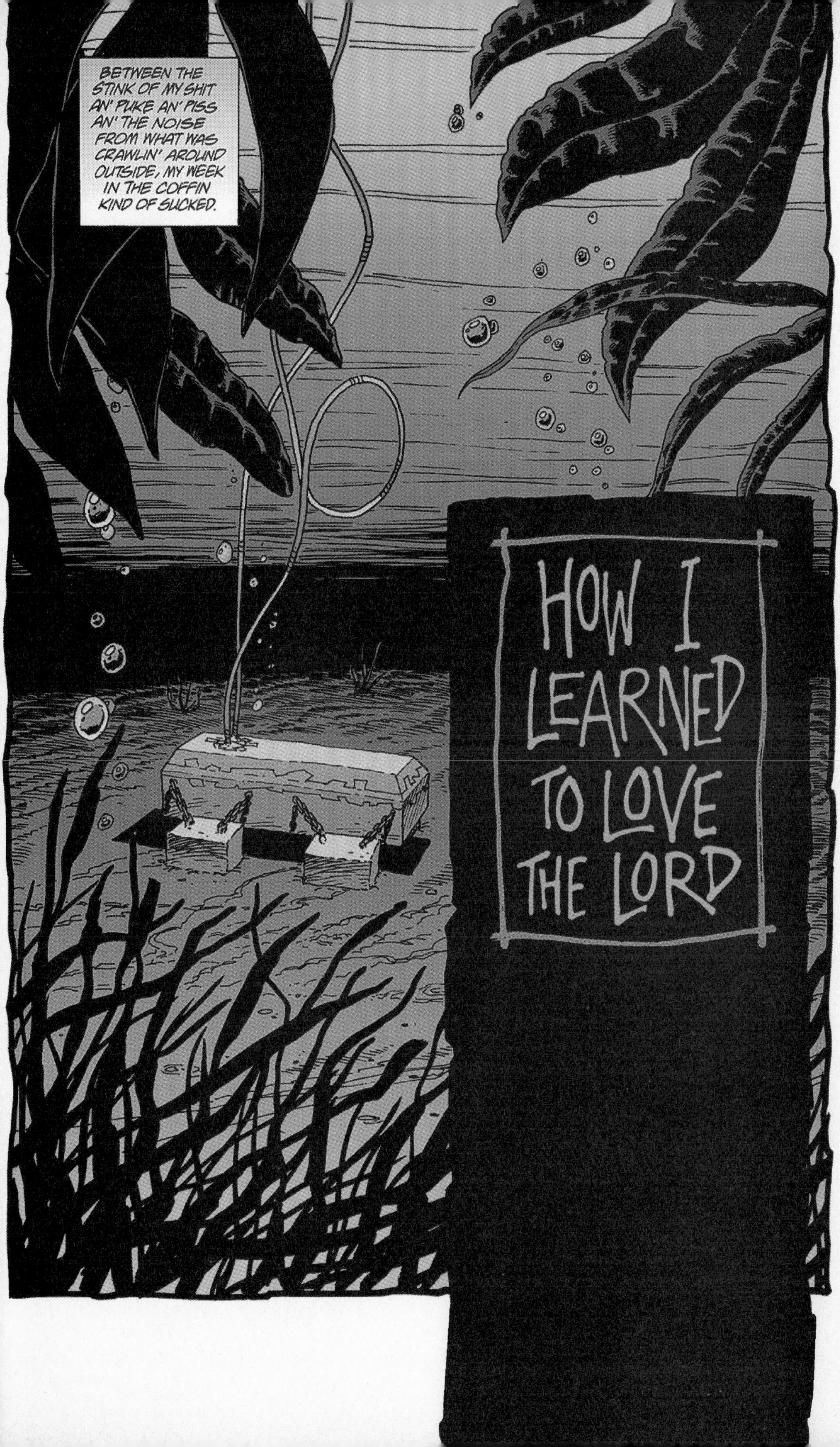
BETWEEN THE STINK OF MY SHIT AN' PUKE AN' PISS AN' THE NOISE FROM WHAT WAS CRAWLIN' AROUND OUTSIDE, MY WEEK IN THE COFFIN KIND OF SUCKED.
HOW I LEARNED TO LOVE THE LORD

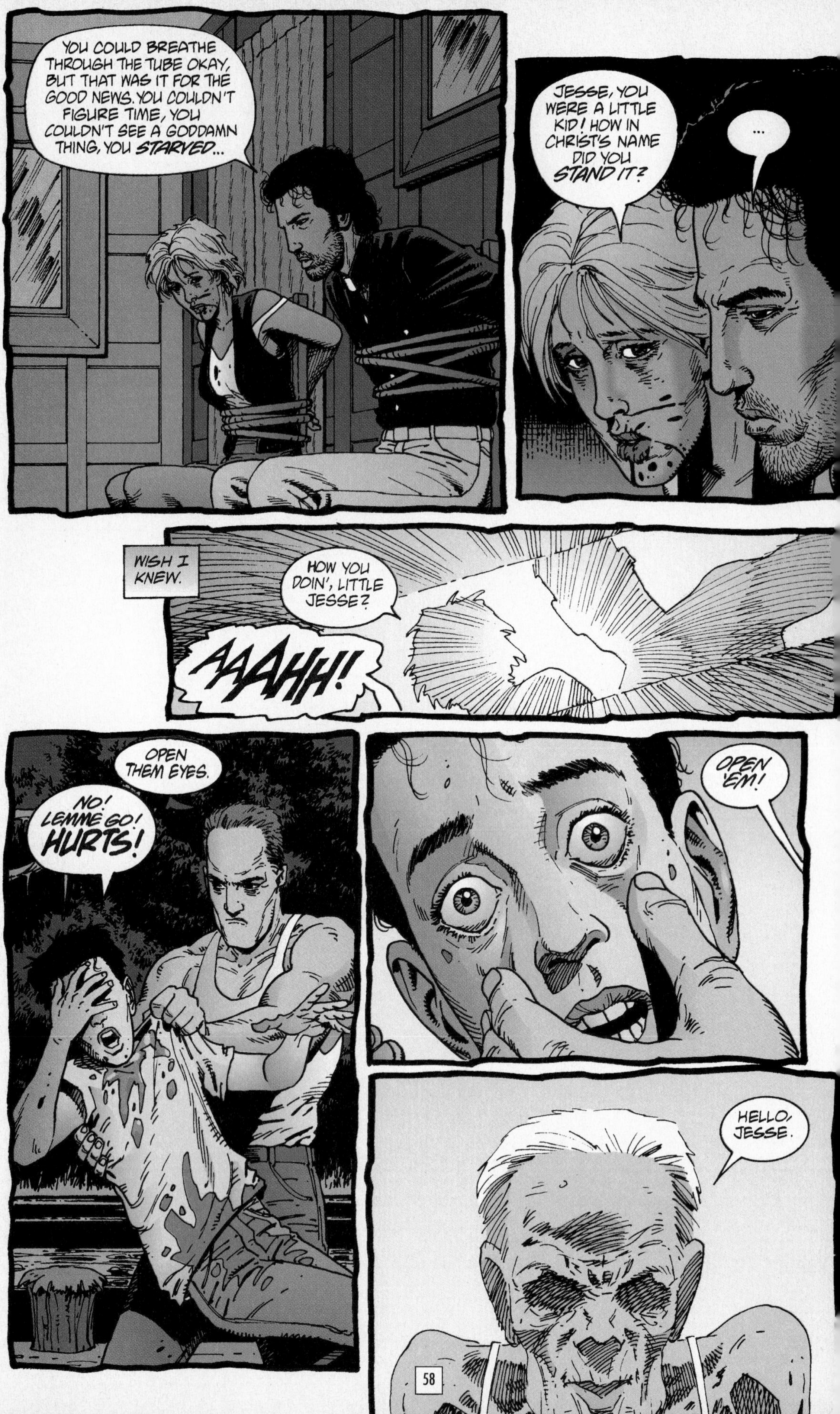
YOU COULD BREATHE THROUGH THE TUBE OKAY, BUT THAT WAS IT FOR THE GOOD NEWS. YOU COULDN'T FIGURE TIME, YOU COULDN'T SEE A GODDAMN THING, YOU STARVED...
JESSE, YOU WERE A LITTLE KID! HOW IN CHRIST'S NAME DID YOU STAND IT?
...
WISH I KNEW.
HOW YOU DOIN', LITTLE JESSE?
AAAHH!
OPEN THEM EYES.
NO! LEMME GO! HURTS!
OPEN 'EM!
HELLO, JESSE.

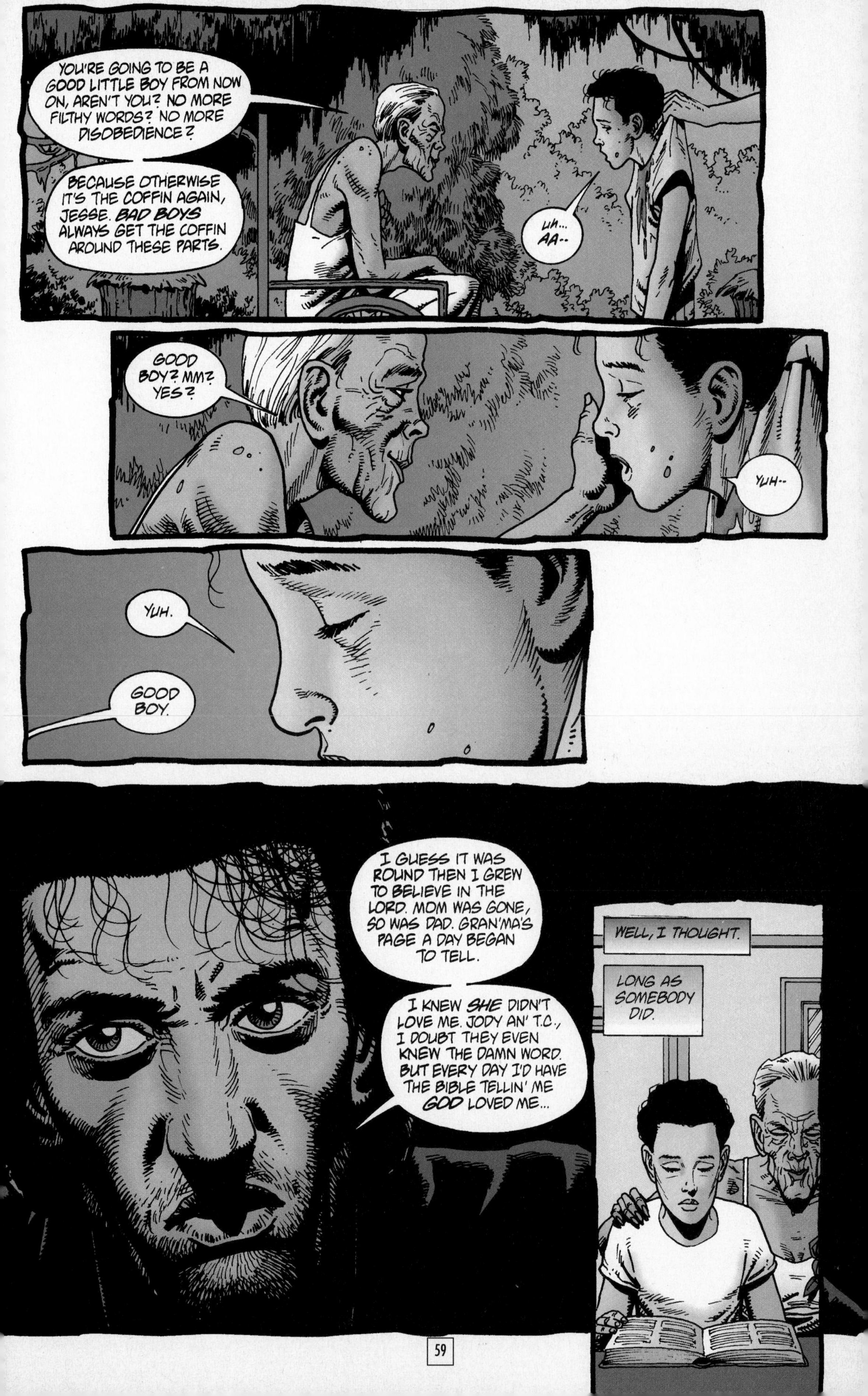
YOU'RE GOING TO BE A GOOD LITTLE BOY FROM NOW ON, AREN'T YOU? NO MORE FILTHY WORDS? NO MORE DISOBEDIENCE?
BECAUSE OTHERWISE IT'S THE COFFIN AGAIN, JESSE. BAD BOYS ALWAYS GET THE COFFIN AROUND THESE PARTS.
UH... AA--
GOOD BOY? MM? YES?
YUH--
YUH.
GOOD BOY.
I GUESS IT WAS ROUND THEN I GREW TO BELIEVE IN THE LORD. MOM WAS GONE, SO WAS DAD. GRAN'MA'S PAGE A DAY BEGAN TO TELL.
I KNEW SHE DIDN'T LOVE ME. JODY AN' T.C., I DOUBT THEY EVEN KNEW THE DAMN WORD. BUT EVERY DAY I'D HAVE THE BIBLE TELLIN' ME GOD LOVED ME...
WELL, I THOUGHT.
LONG AS SOMEBODY DID.

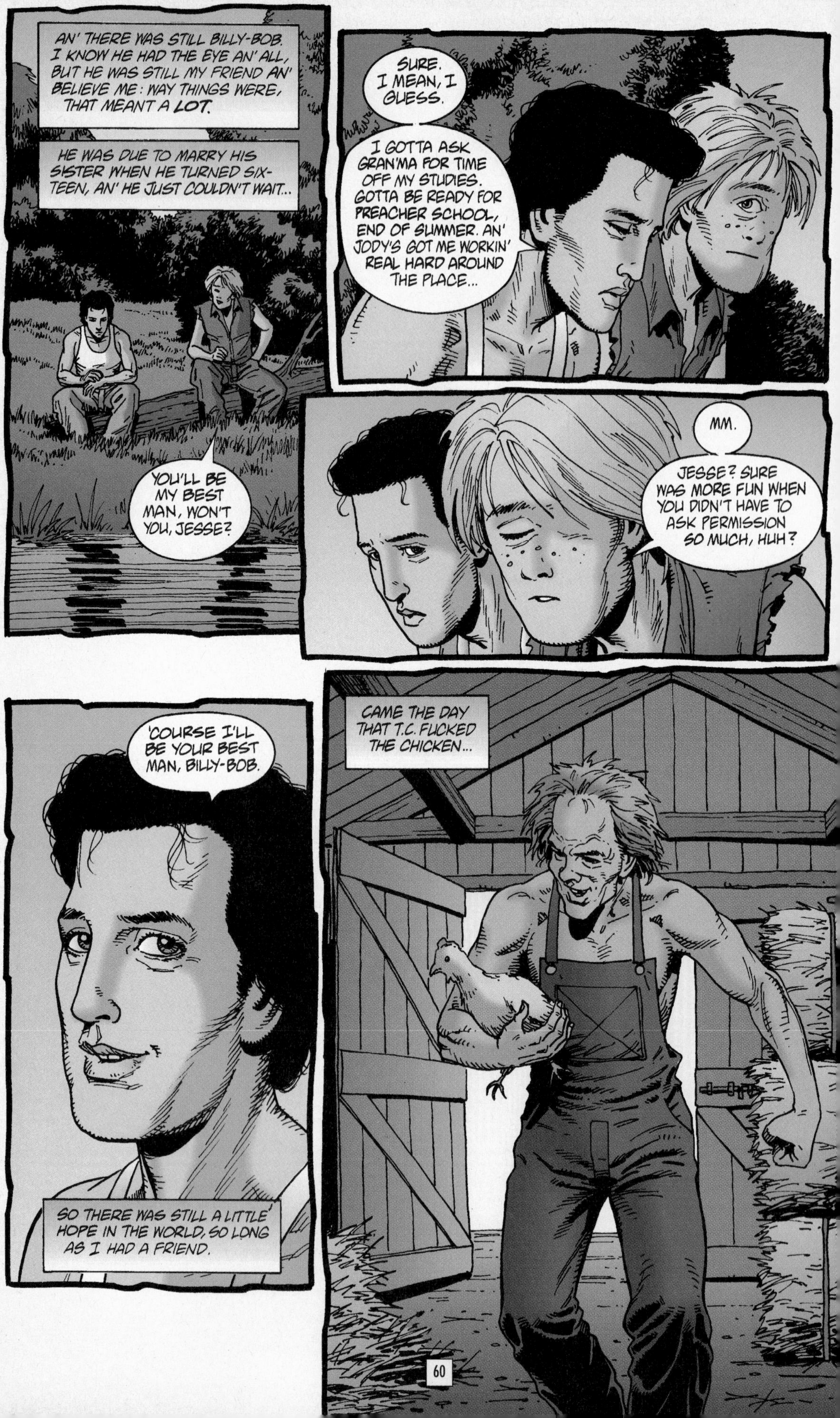
AN' THERE WAS STILL BILLY-BOB. I KNOW HE HAD THE EYE AN' ALL, BUT HE WAS STILL MY FRIEND AN' BELIEVE ME: WAY THINGS WERE, THAT MEANT A LOT.
HE WAS DUE TO MARRY HIS SISTER WHEN HE TURNED SIX-TEEN, AN' HE JUST COULDN'T WAIT...
YOU'LL BE MY BEST MAN, WON'T YOU, JESSE?
SURE. I MEAN, I GUESS.
I GOTTA ASK GRAN'MA FOR TIME OFF MY STUDIES. GOTTA BE READY FOR PREACHER SCHOOL, END OF SUMMER. AN' JODY'S GOT ME WORKIN' REAL HARD AROUND THE PLACE...
MM.
JESSE? SURE WAS MORE FUN WHEN YOU DIDN'T HAVE TO ASK PERMISSION SO MUCH, HUH?
'COURSE I'LL BE YOUR BEST MAN, BILLY-BOB.
SO THERE WAS STILL A LITTLE HOPE IN THE WORLD, SO LONG AS I HAD A FRIEND.
CAME THE DAY THAT T.C. FUCKED THE CHICKEN...

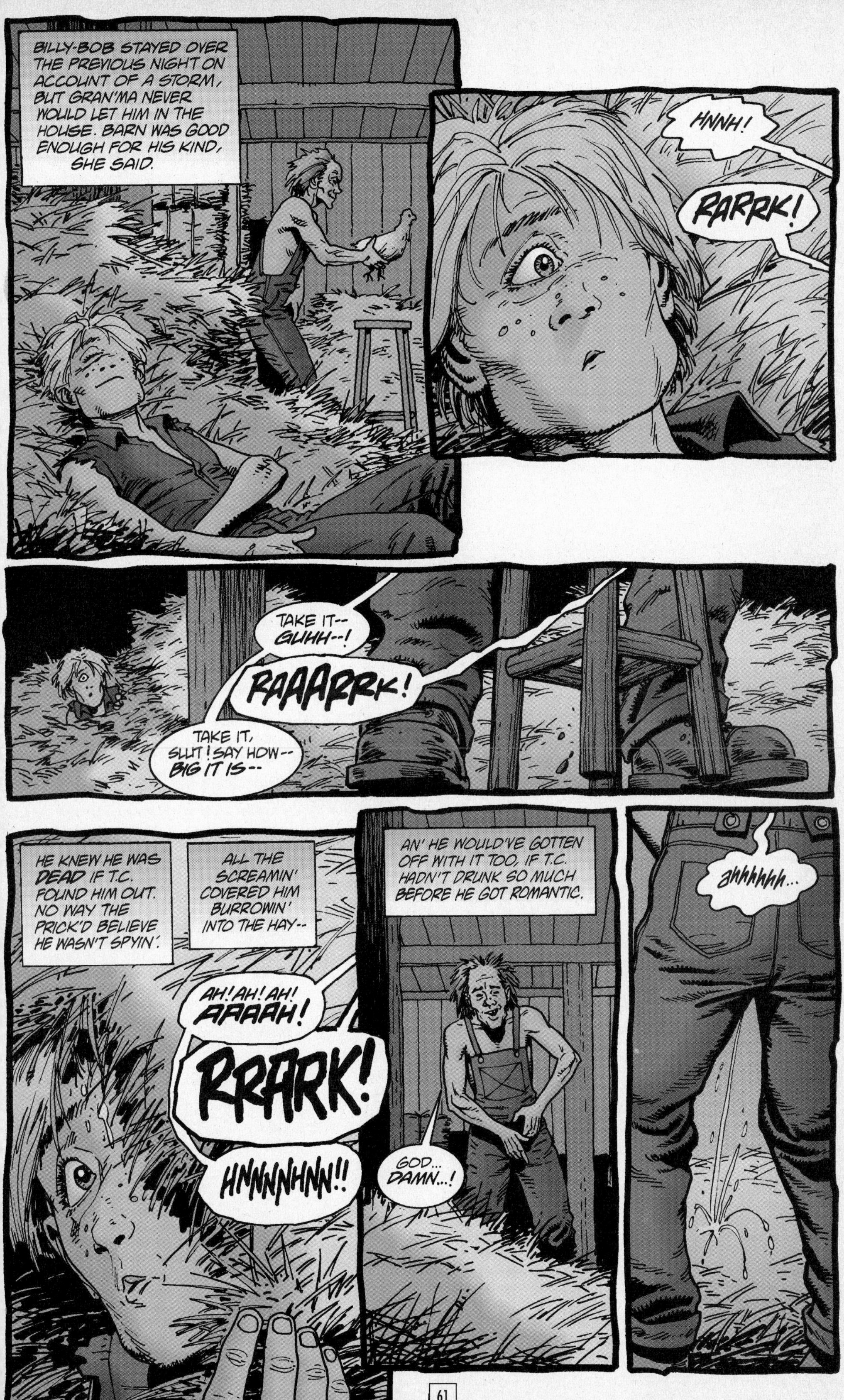
BILLY-BOB STAYED OVER THE PREVIOUS NIGHT ON ACCOUNT OF A STORM, BUT GRAN'MA NEVER WOULD LET HIM IN THE HOUSE. BARN WAS GOOD ENOUGH FOR HIS KIND, SHE SAID.
HNNH!
RARRK!
TAKE IT-- GUHH--!
RAAARRK!
TAKE IT, SLUT! SAY HOW-- BIG IT IS--
HE KNEW HE WAS DEAD IF T.C. FOUND HIM OUT. NO WAY THE PRICK'D BELIEVE HE WASN'T SPYIN'.
ALL THE SCREAMIN' COVERED HIM BURROWIN' INTO THE HAY--
AH! AH! AH! AAAAH!
RRARK!
HNNNHNN!!
AN' HE WOULD'VE GOTTEN OFF WITH IT TOO, IF T.C. HADN'T DRUNK SO MUCH BEFORE HE GOT ROMANTIC.
GOD... DAMN...!
ahhhhhh...

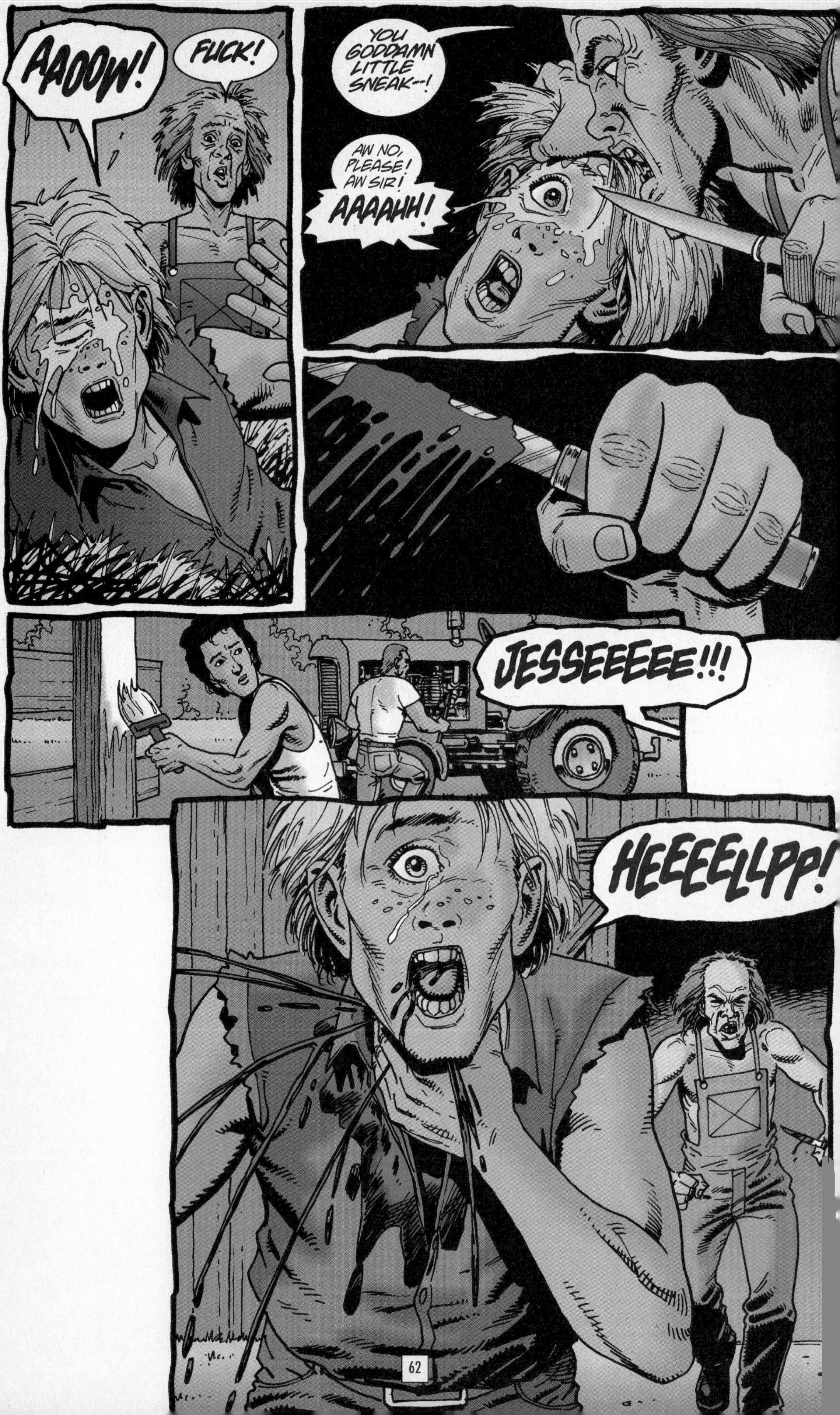
AAOOW!
FUCK!
YOU GODDAMN LITTLE SNEAK--!
AW NO, PLEASE! AW SIR! AAAAHH!
JESSEEEEEE!!!
HEEEELLPP!

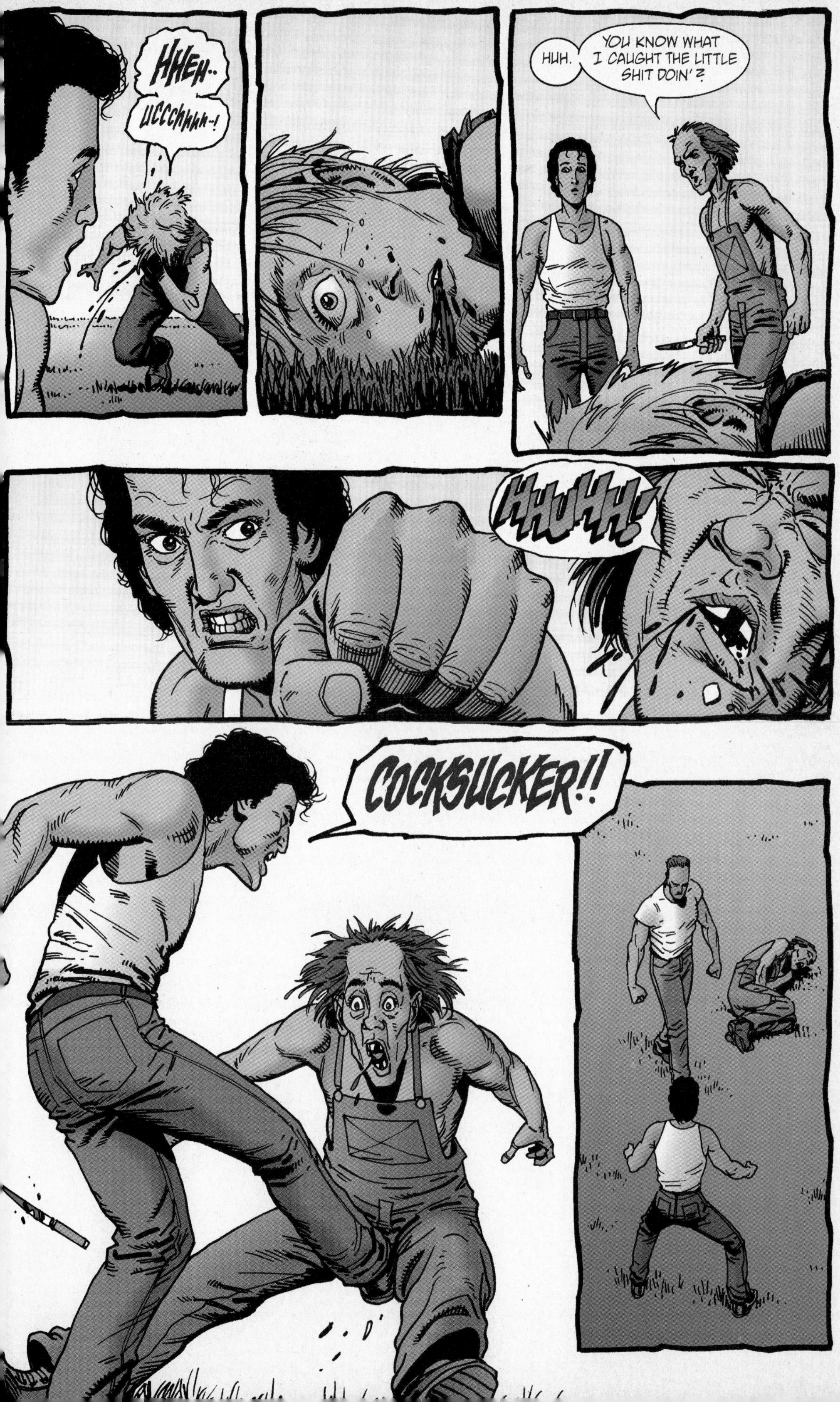
HHEH..
UCCChhhh--!
HUH.
YOU KNOW WHAT I CAUGHT THE LITTLE SHIT DOIN'?
HHUHH!
COCKSUCKER!!

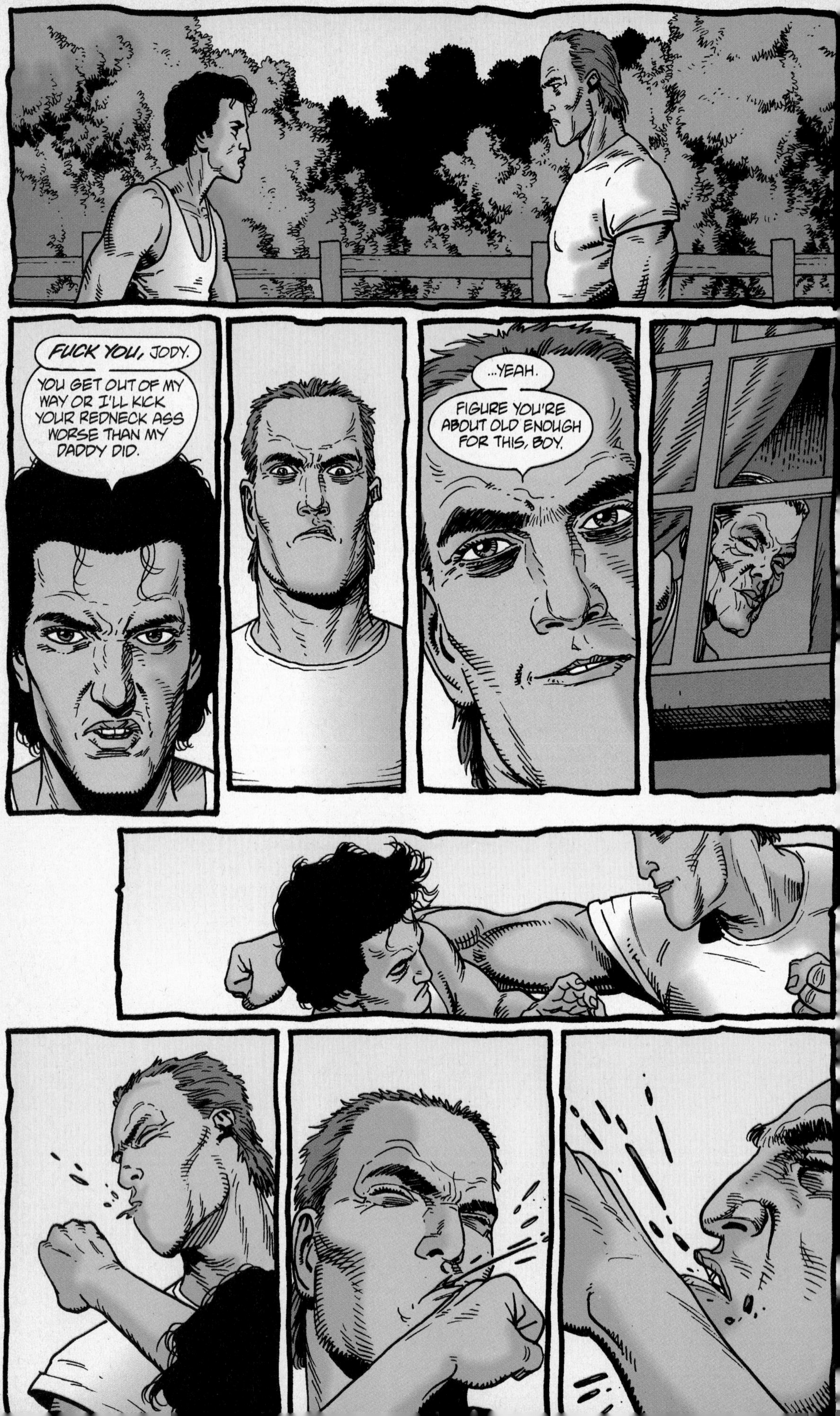
FUCK YOU, JODY.
YOU GET OUT OF MY WAY OR I'LL KICK YOUR REDNECK ASS WORSE THAN MY DADDY DID.
...YEAH.
FIGURE YOU'RE ABOUT OLD ENOUGH FOR THIS, BOY.

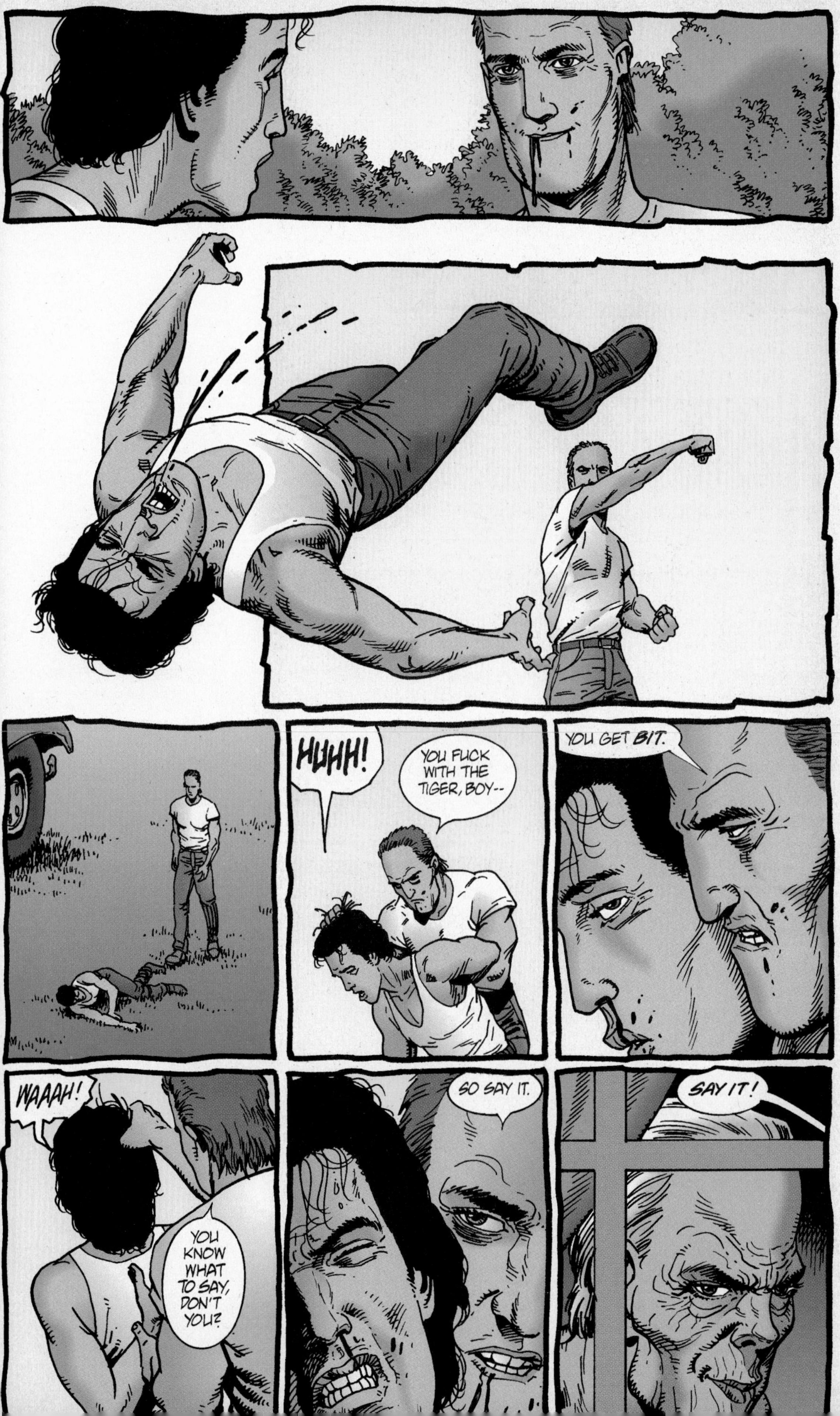
HUHH!
YOU FUCK WITH THE TIGER, BOY--
YOU GET BIT.
WAAAH!
YOU KNOW WHAT TO SAY, DON'T YOU?
SO SAY IT.
SAY IT!

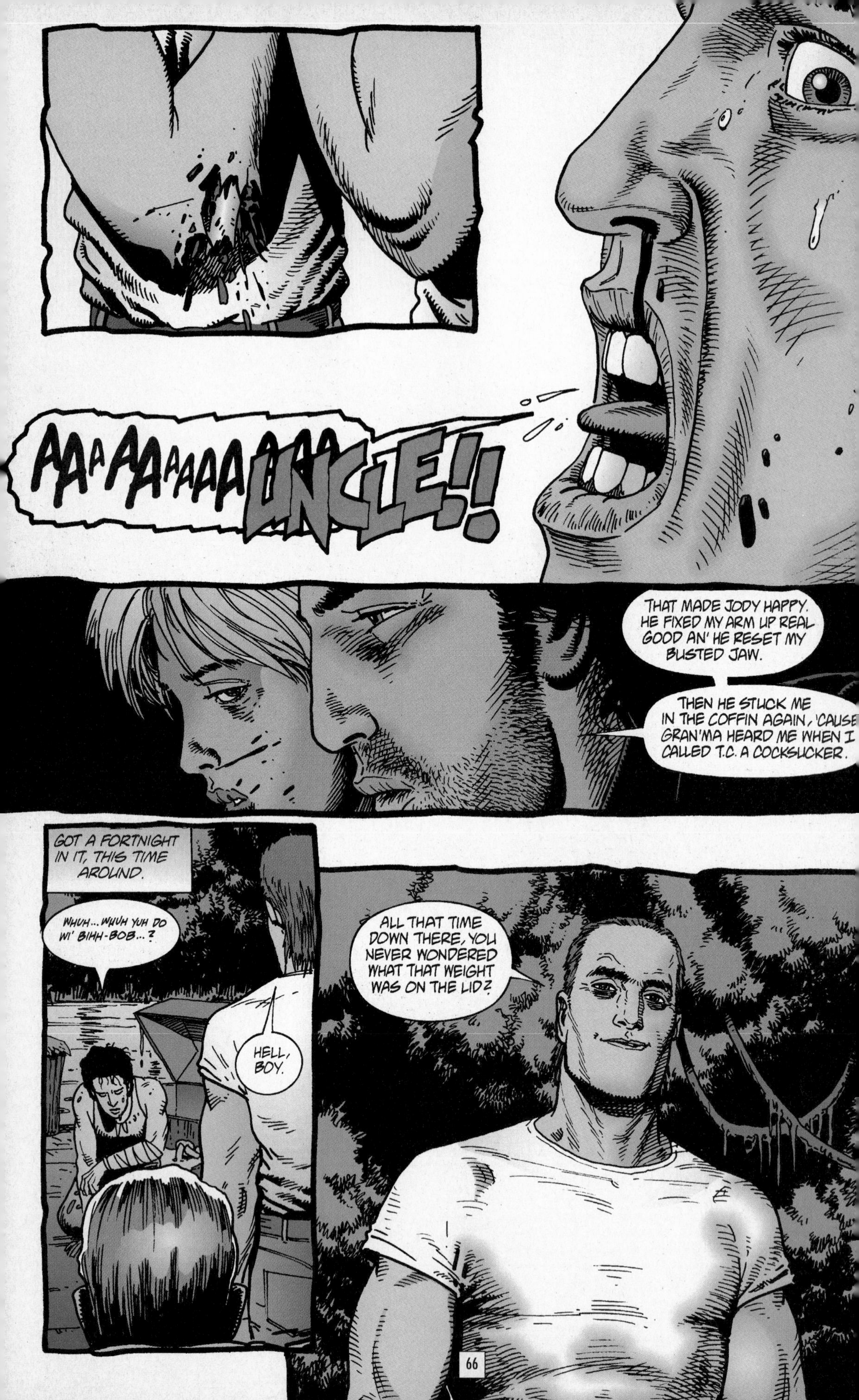
AAaAAaaaaAaaa UNCLE!!
THAT MADE JODY HAPPY. HE FIXED MY ARM UP REAL GOOD AN' HE RESET MY BUSTED JAW.
THEN HE STUCK ME IN THE COFFIN AGAIN, 'CAUSE GRAN'MA HEARD ME WHEN I CALLED T.C. A COCKSUCKER.
GOT A FORTNIGHT IN IT, THIS TIME AROUND.
WHUH... WHUH YUH DO WI' BIHH-BOB...?
HELL, BOY.
ALL THAT TIME DOWN THERE, YOU NEVER WONDERED WHAT THAT WEIGHT WAS ON THE LID?

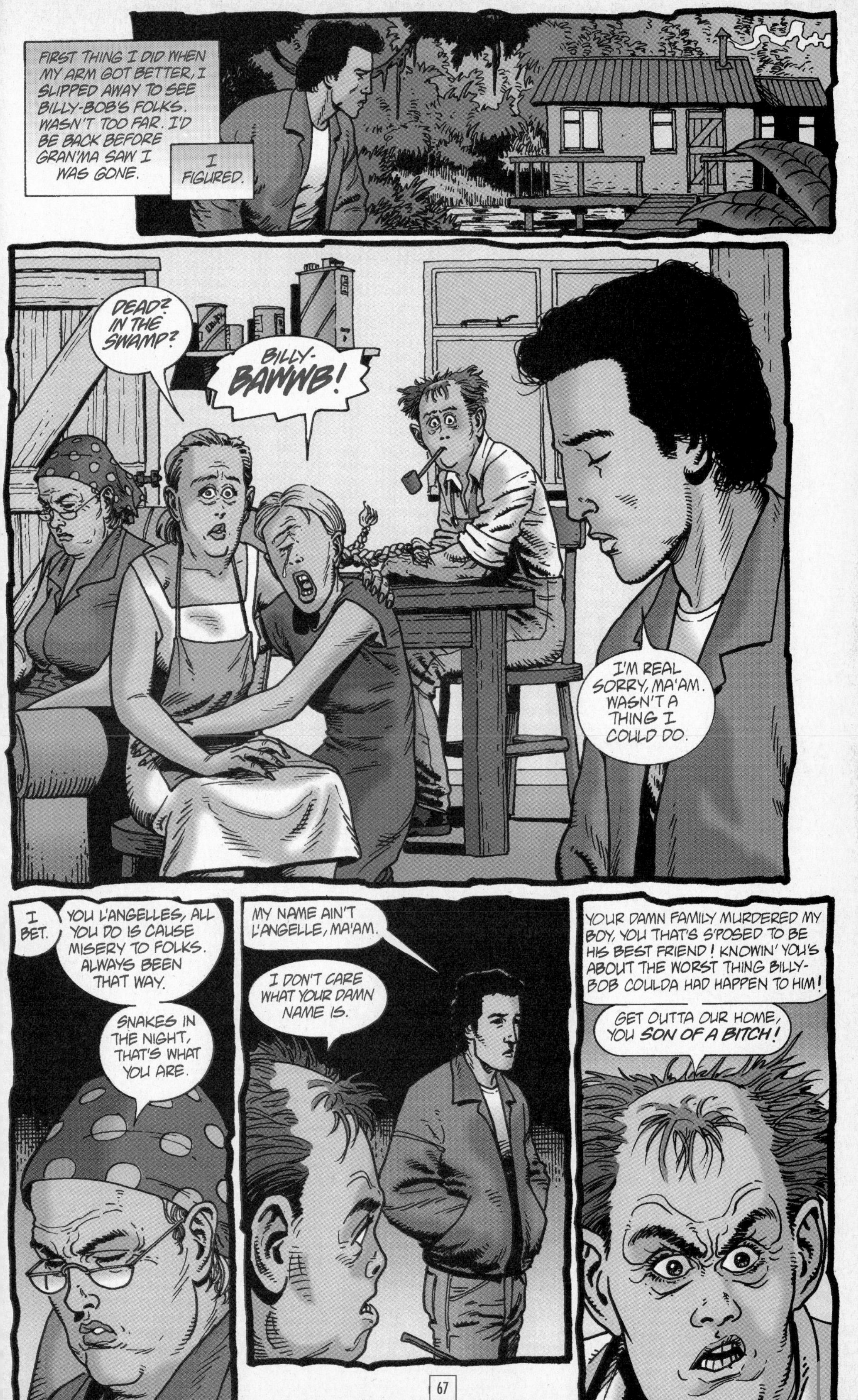
FIRST THING I DID WHEN MY ARM GOT BETTER, I SLIPPED AWAY TO SEE BILLY-BOB'S FOLKS. WASN'T TOO FAR. I'D BE BACK BEFORE GRAN'MA SAW I WAS GONE.
I FIGURED.
DEAD? IN THE SWAMP?
BILLY-BAWWB!
I'M REAL SORRY, MA'AM. WASN'T A THING I COULD DO.
I BET.
YOU L'ANGELLES, ALL YOU DO IS CAUSE MISERY TO FOLKS. ALWAYS BEEN THAT WAY.
SNAKES IN THE NIGHT, THAT'S WHAT YOU ARE.
MY NAME AIN'T L'ANGELLE, MA'AM.
I DON'T CARE WHAT YOUR DAMN NAME IS.
YOUR DAMN FAMILY MURDERED MY BOY, YOU THAT'S S'POSED TO BE HIS BEST FRIEND! KNOWIN' YOU'S ABOUT THE WORST THING BILLY-BOB COULDA HAD HAPPEN TO HIM!
GET OUTTA OUR HOME, YOU SON OF A BITCH!

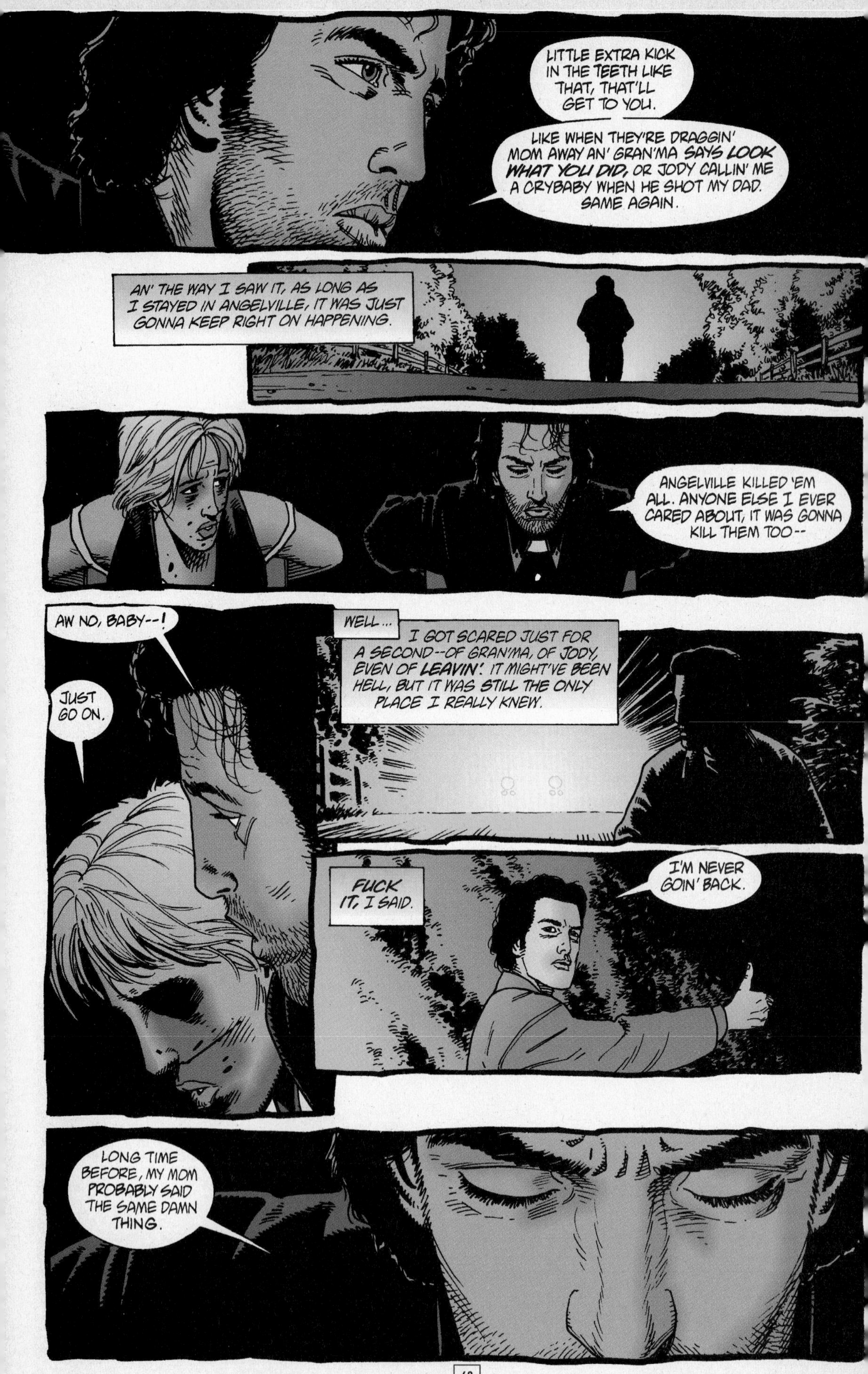
LITTLE EXTRA KICK IN THE TEETH LIKE THAT, THAT'LL GET TO YOU.
LIKE WHEN THEY'RE DRAGGIN' MOM AWAY AN' GRAN'MA SAYS LOOK WHAT YOU DID, OR JODY CALLIN' ME A CRYBABY WHEN HE SHOT MY DAD. SAME AGAIN.
AN' THE WAY I SAW IT, AS LONG AS I STAYED IN ANGELVILLE, IT WAS JUST GONNA KEEP RIGHT ON HAPPENING.
ANGELVILLE KILLED 'EM ALL. ANYONE ELSE I EVER CARED ABOUT, IT WAS GONNA KILL THEM TOO--
AW NO, BABY--!
JUST GO ON.
WELL...
I GOT SCARED JUST FOR A SECOND--OF GRAN'MA, OF JODY, EVEN OF LEAVIN'. IT MIGHT'VE BEEN HELL, BUT IT WAS STILL THE ONLY PLACE I REALLY KNEW.
FUCK IT, I SAID.
I'M NEVER GOIN' BACK.
LONG TIME BEFORE, MY MOM PROBABLY SAID THE SAME DAMN THING.

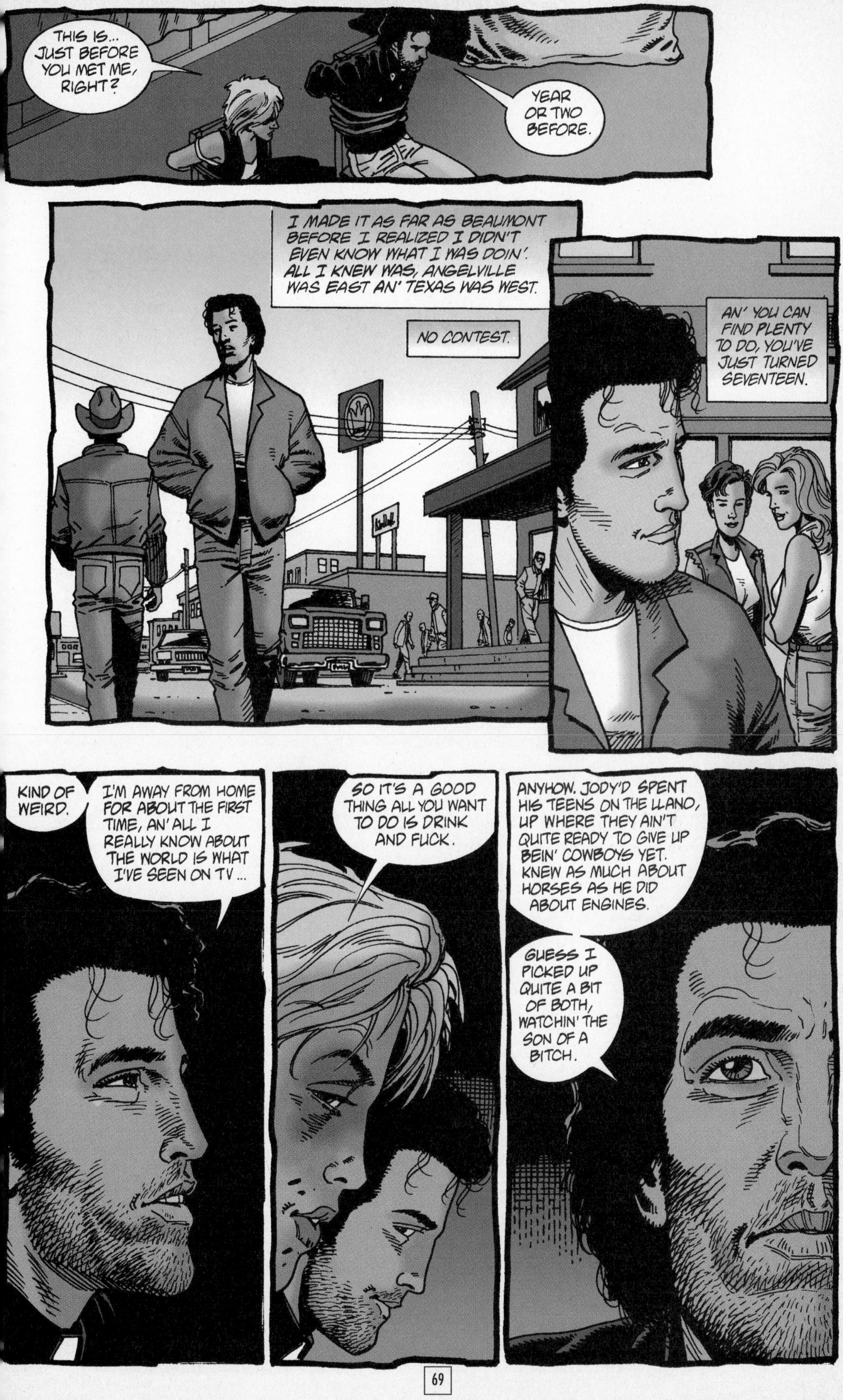
THIS IS... JUST BEFORE YOU MET ME, RIGHT?
YEAR OR TWO BEFORE.
I MADE IT AS FAR AS BEAUMONT BEFORE I REALIZED I DIDN'T EVEN KNOW WHAT I WAS DOIN'. ALL I KNEW WAS, ANGELVILLE WAS EAST AN' TEXAS WAS WEST.
NO CONTEST.
AN' YOU CAN FIND PLENTY TO DO, YOU'VE JUST TURNED SEVENTEEN.
KIND OF WEIRD.
I'M AWAY FROM HOME FOR ABOUT THE FIRST TIME, AN' ALL I REALLY KNOW ABOUT THE WORLD IS WHAT I'VE SEEN ON TV...
SO IT'S A GOOD THING ALL YOU WANT TO DO IS DRINK AND FUCK.
ANYHOW. JODY'D SPENT HIS TEENS ON THE LLANO, UP WHERE THEY AIN'T QUITE READY TO GIVE UP BEIN' COWBOYS YET. KNEW AS MUCH ABOUT HORSES AS HE DID ABOUT ENGINES.
GUESS I PICKED UP QUITE A BIT OF BOTH, WATCHIN' THE SON OF A BITCH.

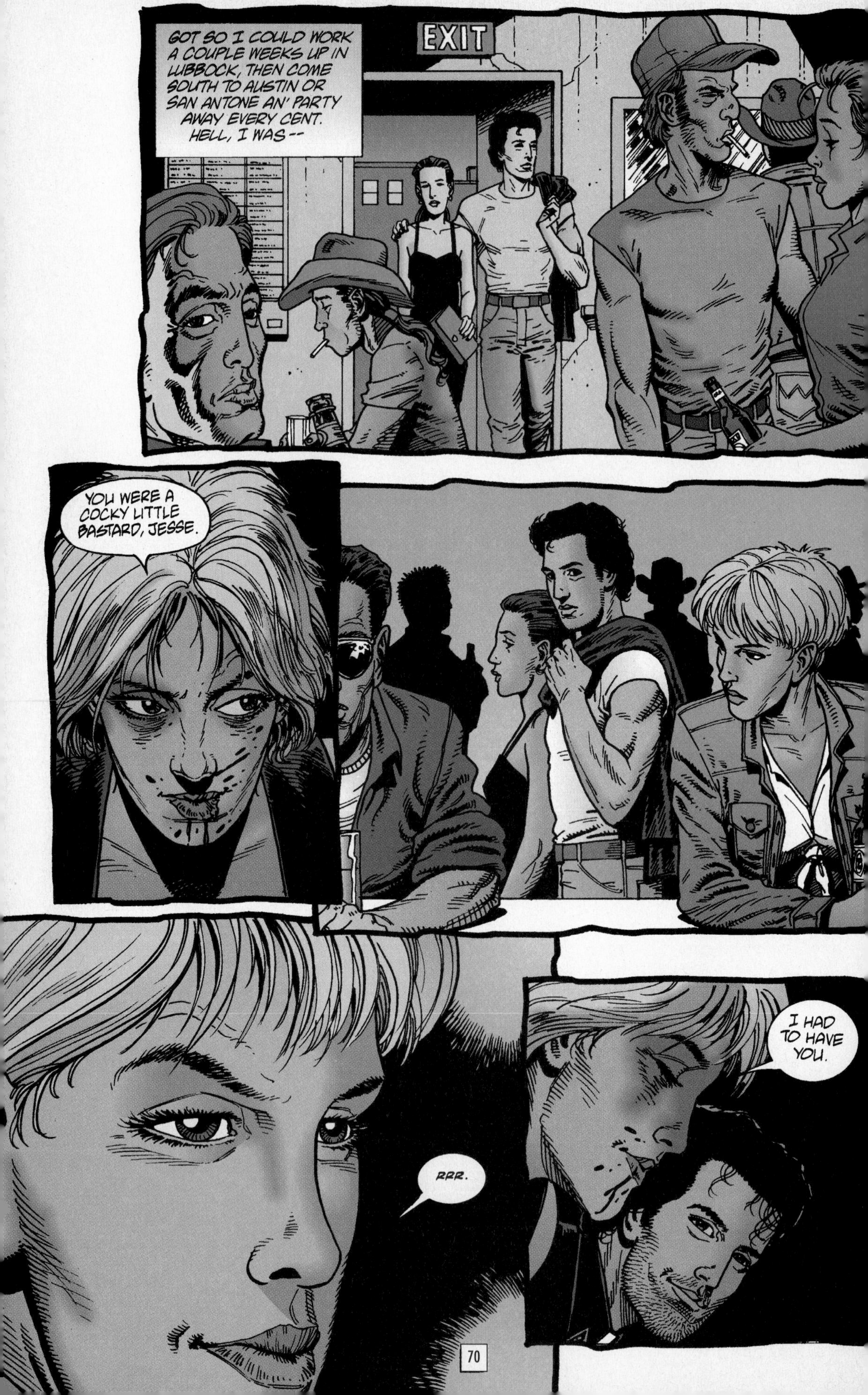
GOT SO I COULD WORK A COUPLE WEEKS UP IN LUBBOCK, THEN COME SOUTH TO AUSTIN OR SAN ANTONE AN' PARTY AWAY EVERY CENT. HELL, I WAS --
EXIT
YOU WERE A COCKY LITTLE BASTARD, JESSE.
RRR.
I HAD TO HAVE YOU.

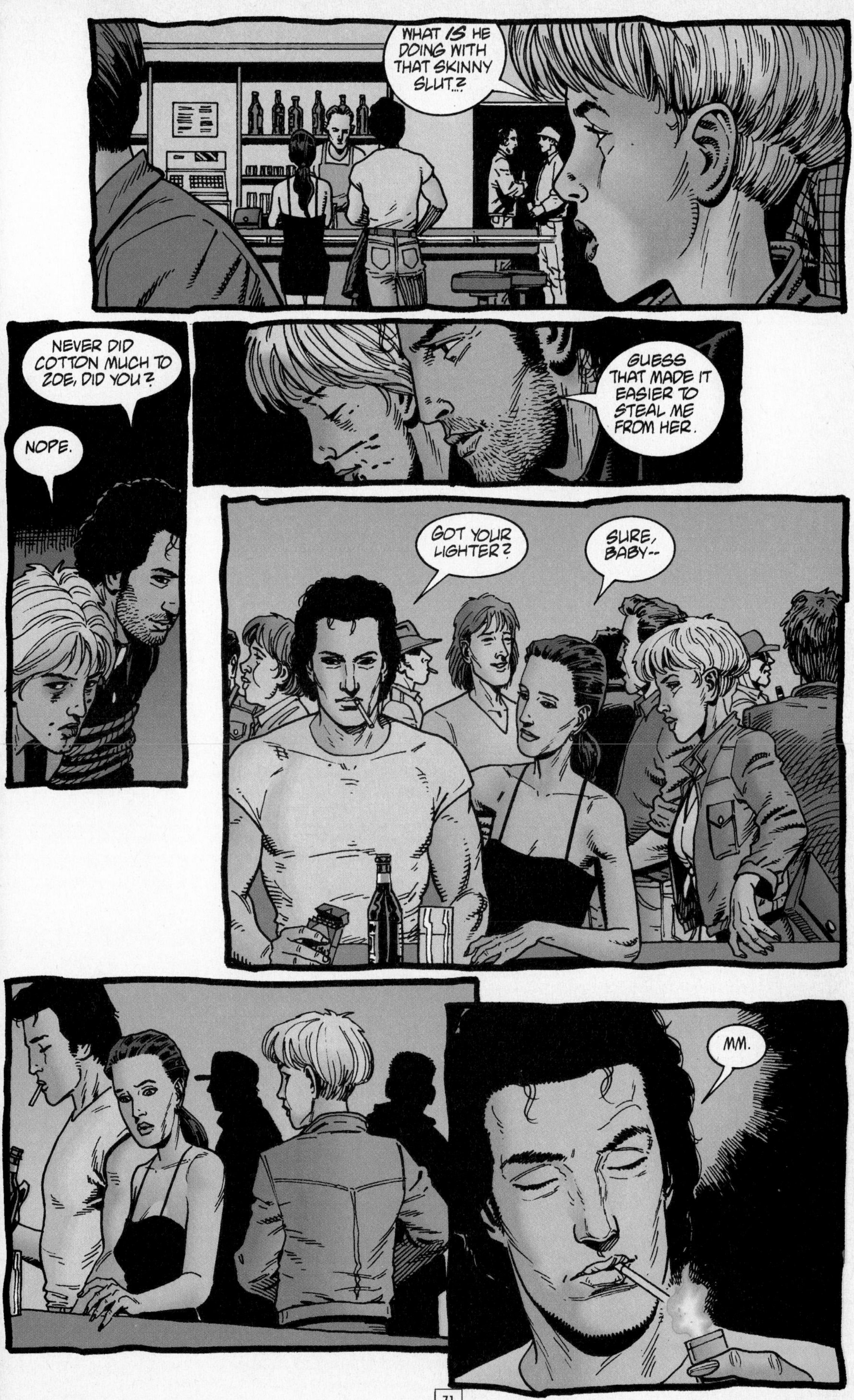
WHAT IS HE DOING WITH THAT SKINNY SLUT..?
NEVER DID COTTON MUCH TO ZOE, DID YOU?
NOPE.
GUESS THAT MADE IT EASIER TO STEAL ME FROM HER.
GOT YOUR LIGHTER?
SURE, BABY--
MM.

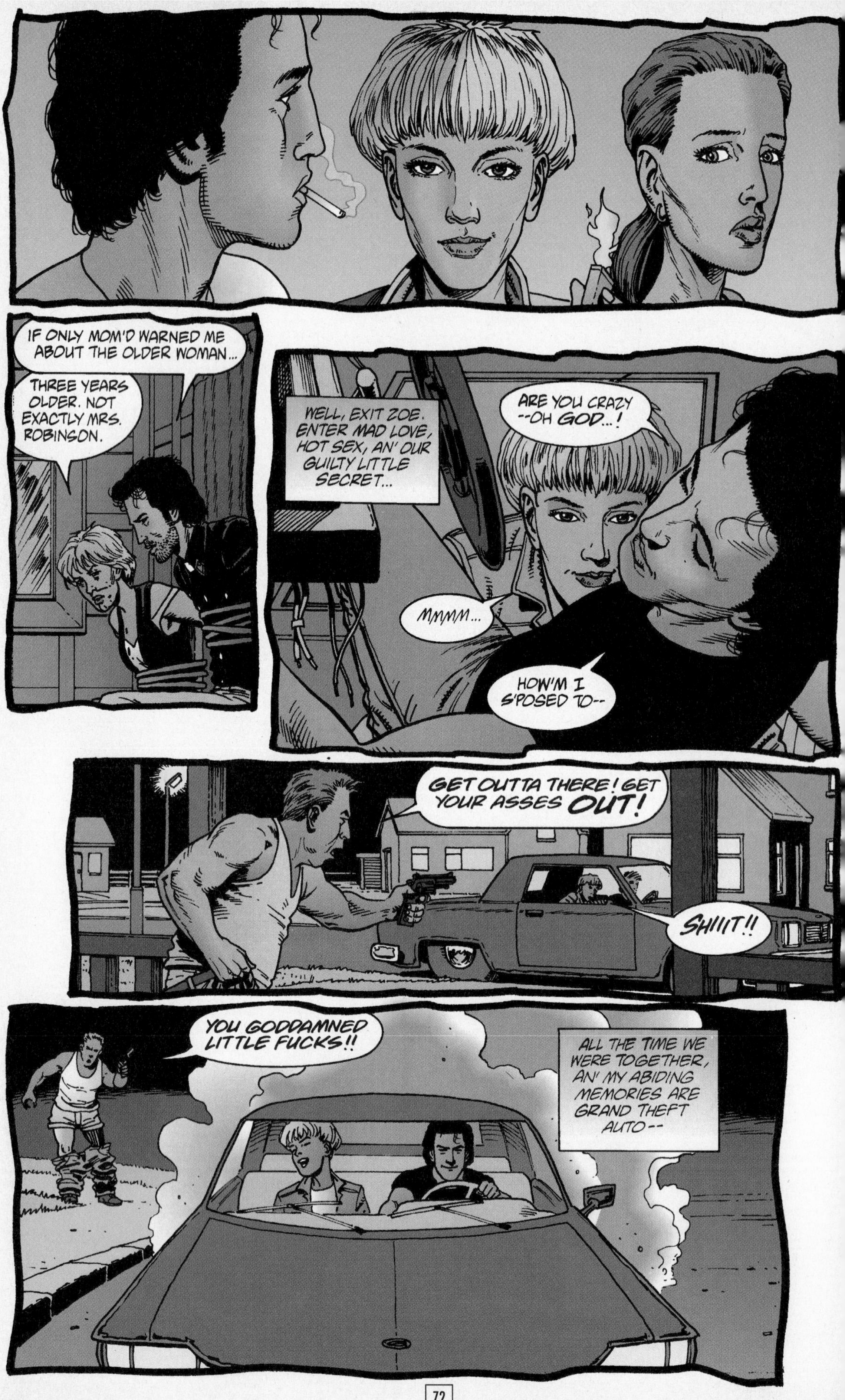
IF ONLY MOM'D WARNED ME ABOUT THE OLDER WOMAN...
THREE YEARS OLDER. NOT EXACTLY MRS. ROBINSON.
WELL, EXIT ZOE. ENTER MAD LOVE, HOT SEX, AN' OUR GUILTY LITTLE SECRET...
ARE YOU CRAZY --OH GOD...!
MMMM...
HOW'M I S'POSED TO--
GET OUTTA THERE! GET YOUR ASSES OUT!
SHIIIT!!
YOU GODDAMNED LITTLE FUCKS!!
ALL THE TIME WE WERE TOGETHER, AN' MY ABIDING MEMORIES ARE GRAND THEFT AUTO--

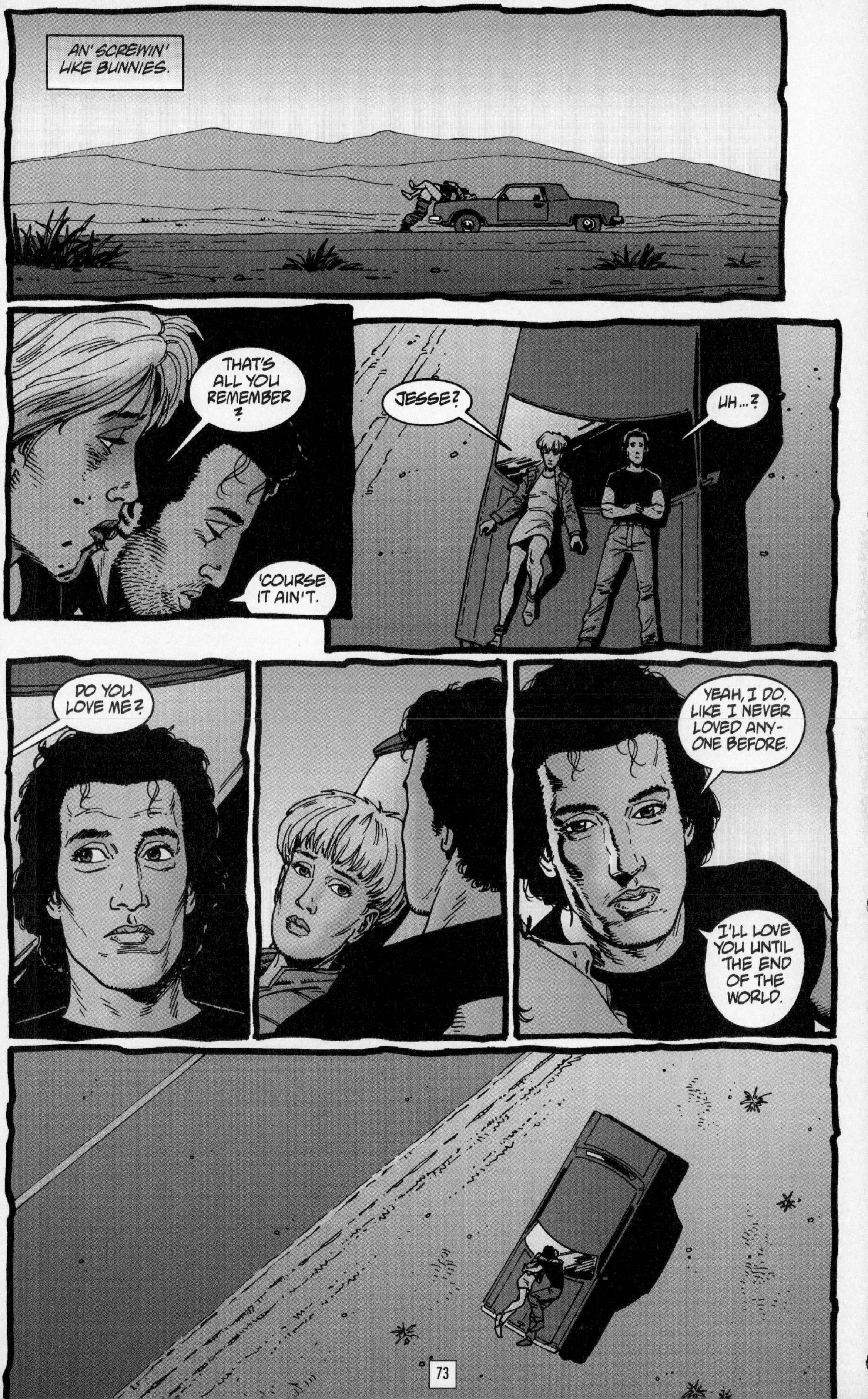
AN' SCREWIN' LIKE BUNNIES.
THAT'S ALL YOU REMEMBER?
'COURSE IT AIN'T.
JESSE?
UH...?
DO YOU LOVE ME?
YEAH, I DO. LIKE I NEVER LOVED ANY-ONE BEFORE.
I'LL LOVE YOU UNTIL THE END OF THE WORLD.

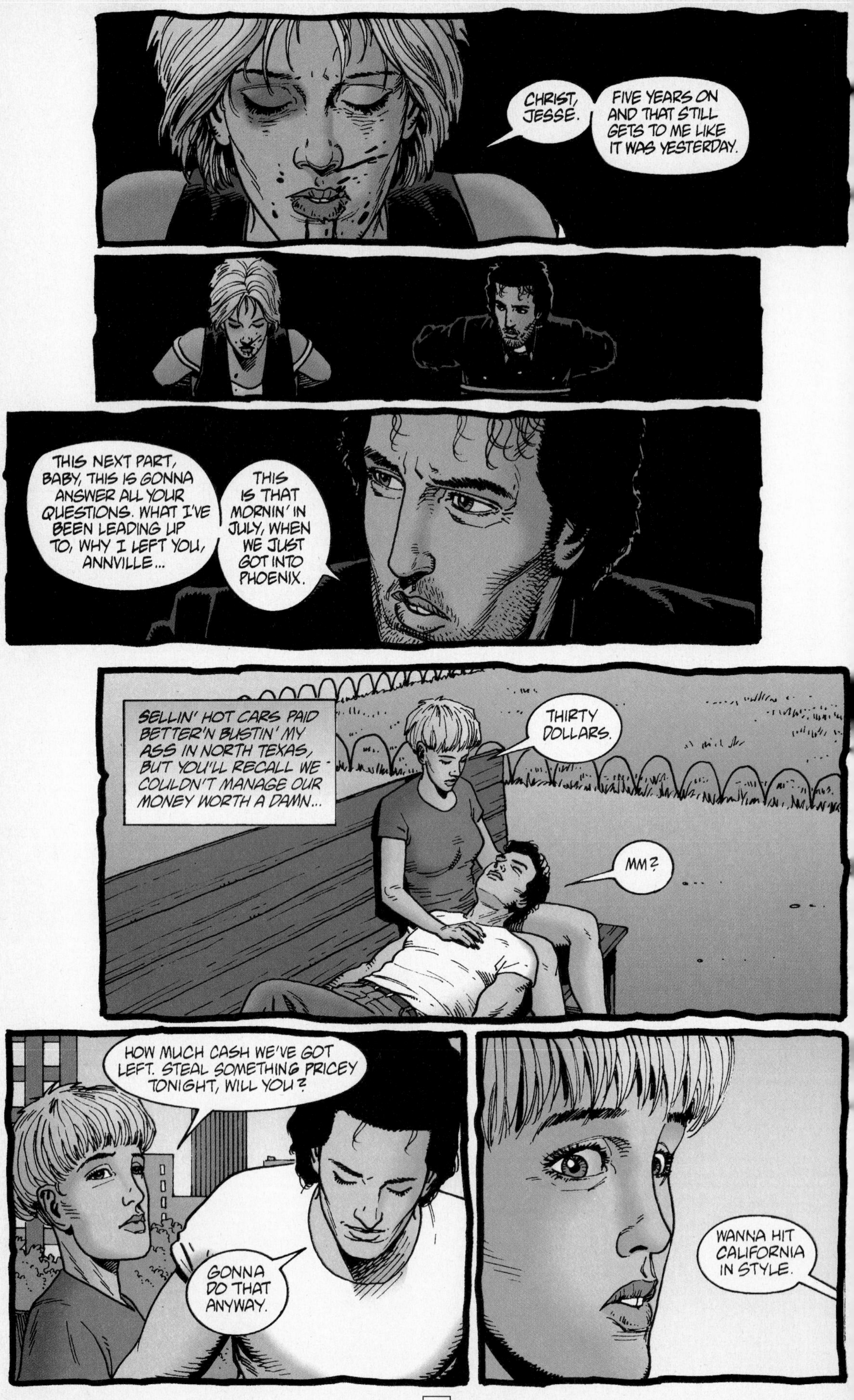
CHRIST, JESSE.
FIVE YEARS ON AND THAT STILL GETS TO ME LIKE IT WAS YESTERDAY.
THIS NEXT PART, BABY, THIS IS GONNA ANSWER ALL YOUR QUESTIONS. WHAT I'VE BEEN LEADING UP TO, WHY I LEFT YOU, ANNVILLE...
THIS IS THAT MORNIN' IN JULY, WHEN WE JUST GOT INTO PHOENIX.
SELLIN' HOT CARS PAID BETTER'N BUSTIN' MY ASS IN NORTH TEXAS, BUT YOU'LL RECALL WE COULDN'T MANAGE OUR MONEY WORTH A DAMN...
THIRTY DOLLARS.
MM?
HOW MUCH CASH WE'VE GOT LEFT. STEAL SOMETHING PRICEY TONIGHT, WILL YOU?
GONNA DO THAT ANYWAY.
WANNA HIT CALIFORNIA IN STYLE.

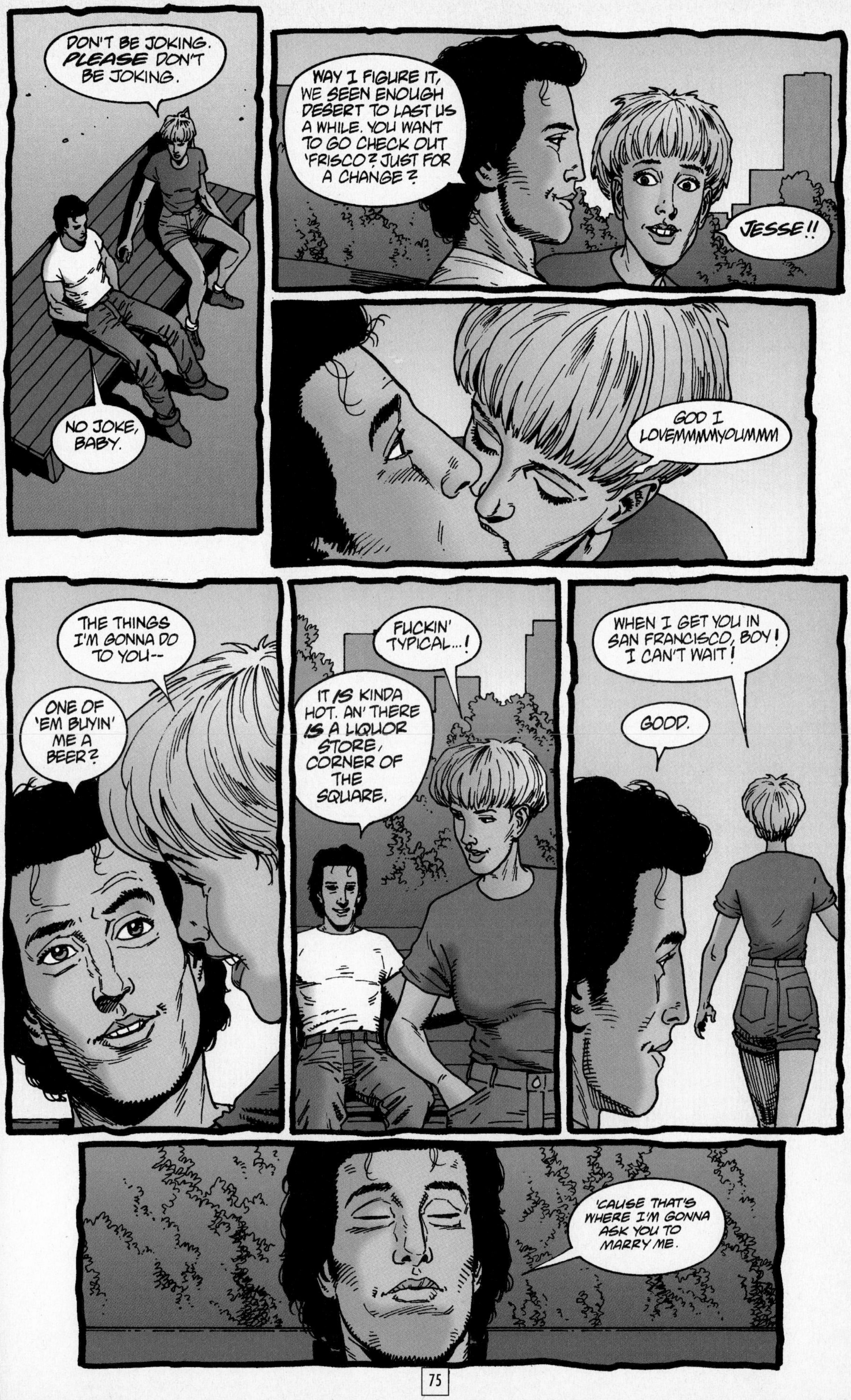
DON'T BE JOKING. PLEASE DON'T BE JOKING.
NO JOKE, BABY.
WAY I FIGURE IT, WE SEEN ENOUGH DESERT TO LAST US A WHILE. YOU WANT TO GO CHECK OUT 'FRISCO? JUST FOR A CHANGE?
JESSE!!
GOD I LOVEMMMYOUMMM
THE THINGS I'M GONNA DO TO YOU--
ONE OF 'EM BUYIN' ME A BEER?
FUCKIN' TYPICAL...!
IT IS KINDA HOT. AN' THERE IS A LIQUOR STORE, CORNER OF THE SQUARE.
WHEN I GET YOU IN SAN FRANCISCO, BOY! I CAN'T WAIT!
GOOD.
'CAUSE THAT'S WHERE I'M GONNA ASK YOU TO MARRY ME.

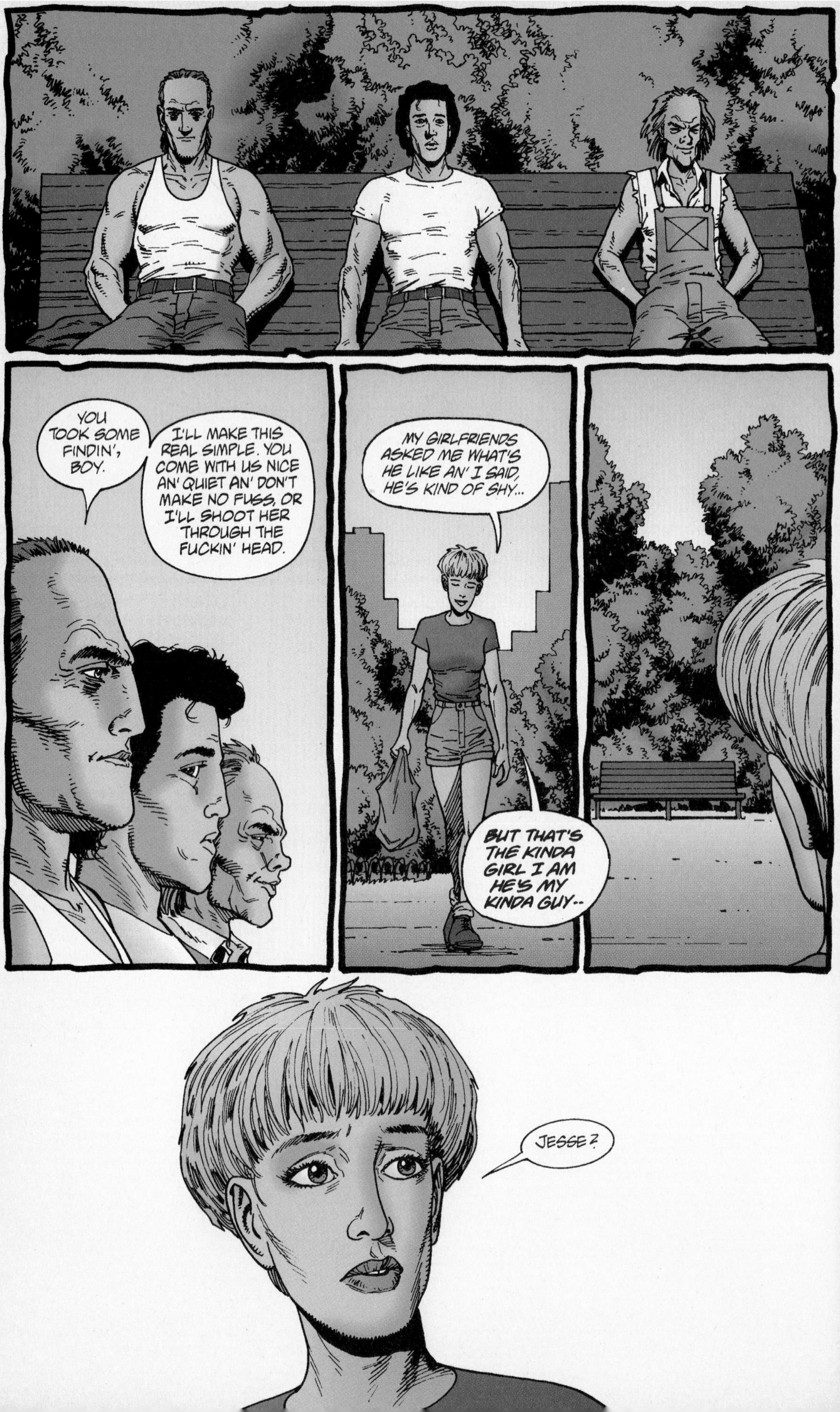
YOU TOOK SOME FINDIN', BOY.
I'LL MAKE THIS REAL SIMPLE. YOU COME WITH US NICE AN' QUIET AN' DON'T MAKE NO FUSS, OR I'LL SHOOT HER THROUGH THE FUCKIN' HEAD.
MY GIRLFRIENDS ASKED ME WHAT'S HE LIKE AN' I SAID, HE'S KIND OF SHY...
BUT THAT'S THE KINDA GIRL I AM HE'S MY KINDA GUY..
JESSE?

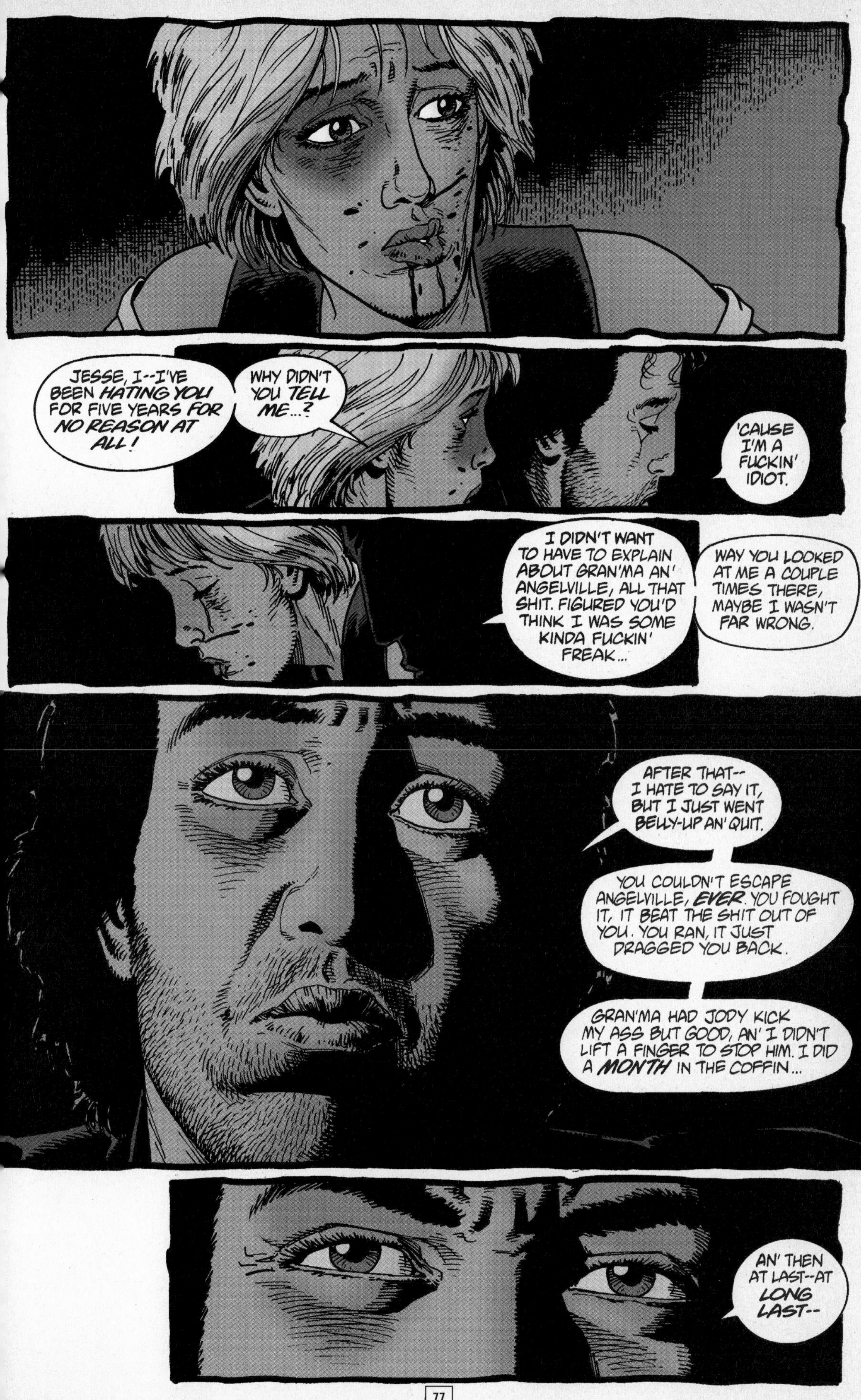

JESSE, I--I'VE BEEN HATING YOU FOR FIVE YEARS FOR NO REASON AT ALL!
WHY DIDN'T YOU TELL ME...?
'CAUSE I'M A FUCKIN' IDIOT.
I DIDN'T WANT TO HAVE TO EXPLAIN ABOUT GRAN'MA AN' ANGELVILLE, ALL THAT SHIT. FIGURED YOU'D THINK I WAS SOME KINDA FUCKIN' FREAK...
WAY YOU LOOKED AT ME A COUPLE TIMES THERE, MAYBE I WASN'T FAR WRONG.
AFTER THAT-- I HATE TO SAY IT, BUT I JUST WENT BELLY-UP AN' QUIT.
YOU COULDN'T ESCAPE ANGELVILLE, EVER. YOU FOUGHT IT, IT BEAT THE SHIT OUT OF YOU. YOU RAN, IT JUST DRAGGED YOU BACK.
GRAN'MA HAD JODY KICK MY ASS BUT GOOD, AN' I DIDN'T LIFT A FINGER TO STOP HIM. I DID A MONTH IN THE COFFIN...
AN' THEN AT LAST--AT LONG LAST--

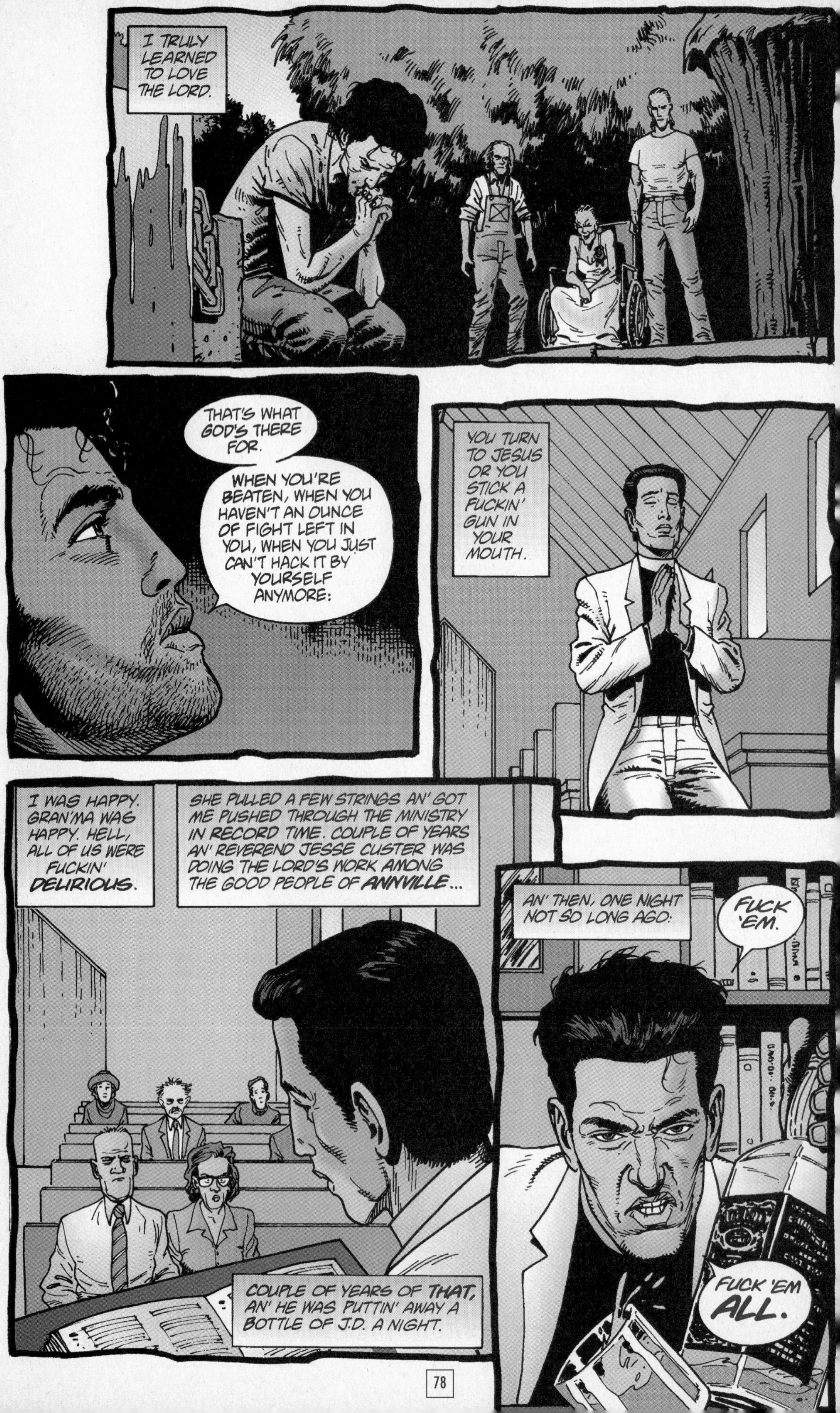
I TRULY LEARNED TO LOVE THE LORD.
THAT'S WHAT GOD'S THERE FOR.
WHEN YOU'RE BEATEN, WHEN YOU HAVEN'T AN OUNCE OF FIGHT LEFT IN YOU, WHEN YOU JUST CAN'T HACK IT BY YOURSELF ANYMORE:
YOU TURN TO JESUS OR YOU STICK A FUCKIN' GUN IN YOUR MOUTH.
I WAS HAPPY. GRAN'MA WAS HAPPY. HELL, ALL OF US WERE FUCKIN' DELIRIOUS.
SHE PULLED A FEW STRINGS AN' GOT ME PUSHED THROUGH THE MINISTRY IN RECORD TIME. COUPLE OF YEARS AN' REVEREND JESSE CUSTER WAS DOING THE LORD'S WORK AMONG THE GOOD PEOPLE OF ANNVILLE...
COUPLE OF YEARS OF THAT, AN' HE WAS PUTTIN' AWAY A BOTTLE OF J.D. A NIGHT.
AN' THEN, ONE NIGHT NOT SO LONG AGO:
FUCK 'EM.
FUCK 'EM ALL.

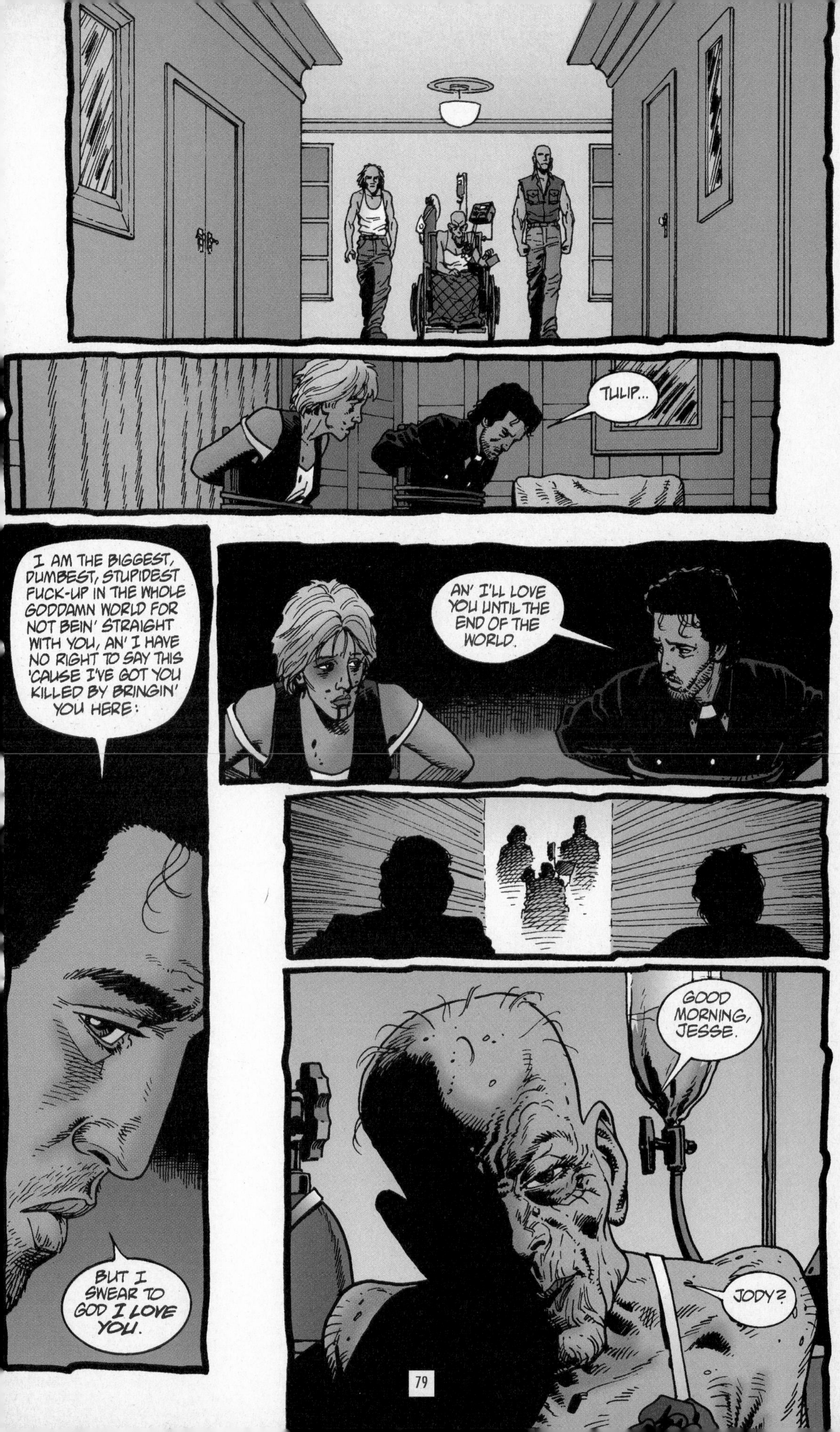
TULIP...
I AM THE BIGGEST, DUMBEST, STUPIDEST FUCK-UP IN THE WHOLE GODDAMN WORLD FOR NOT BEIN' STRAIGHT WITH YOU, AN' I HAVE NO RIGHT TO SAY THIS 'CAUSE I'VE GOT YOU KILLED BY BRINGIN' YOU HERE:
BUT I SWEAR TO GOD I LOVE YOU.
AN' I'LL LOVE YOU UNTIL THE END OF THE WORLD.
GOOD MORNING, JESSE.
JODY?

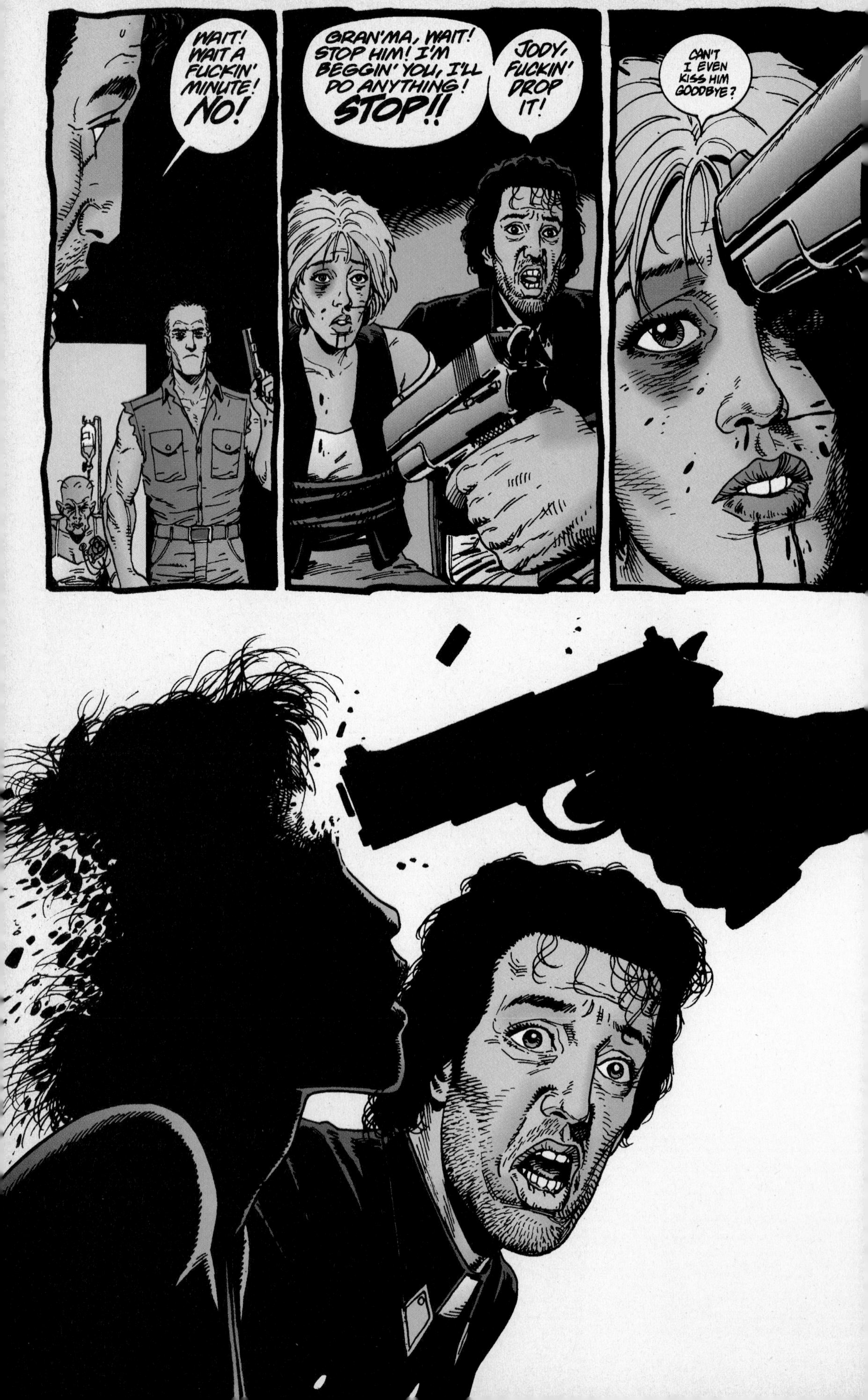
WAIT! WAIT A FUCKIN' MINUTE! NO!
GRAN'MA, WAIT! STOP HIM! I'M BEGGIN' YOU, I'LL DO ANYTHING! STOP!!
JODY, FUCKIN' DROP IT!
CAN'T I EVEN KISS HIM GOODBYE?

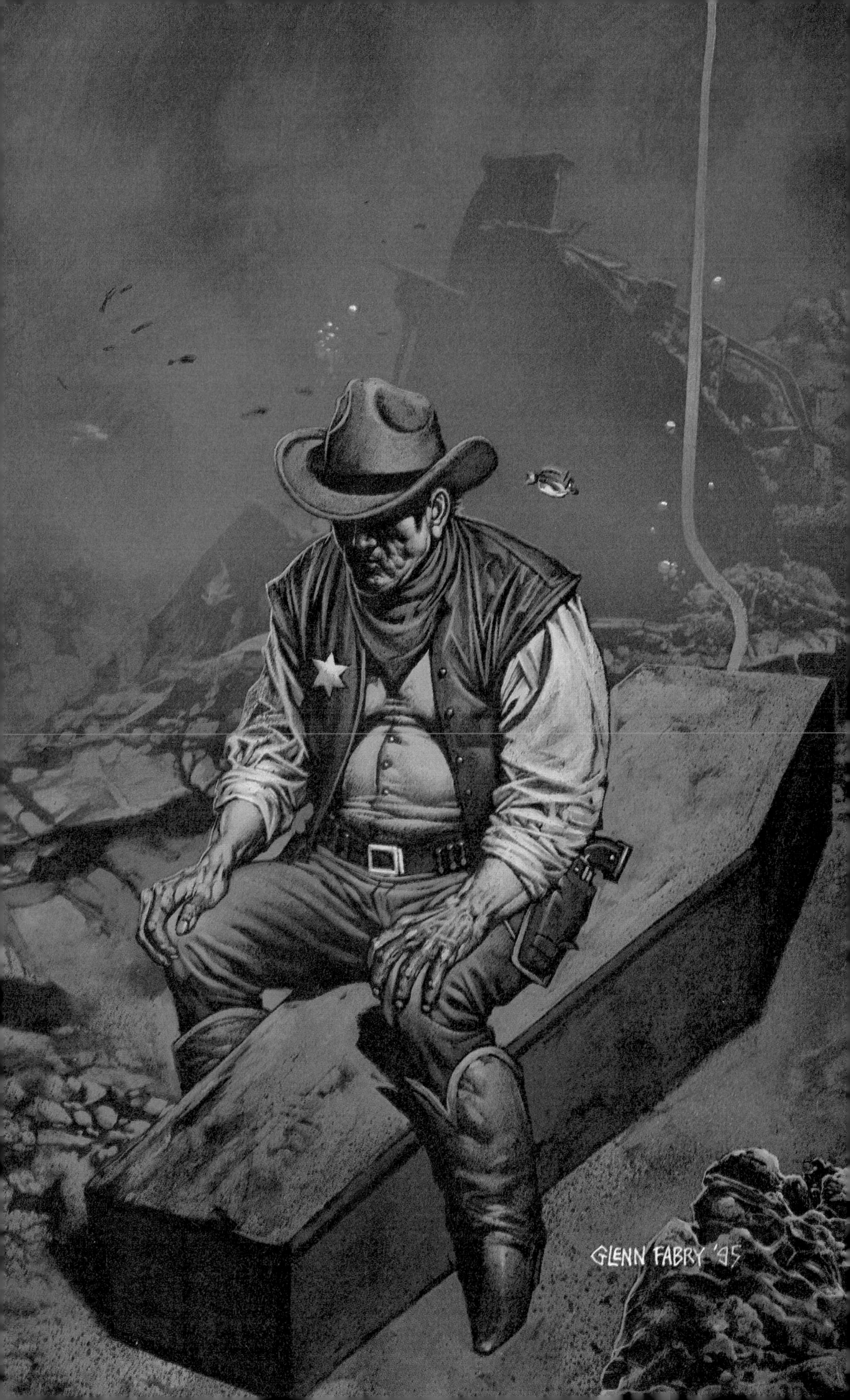
GLENN FABRY '95

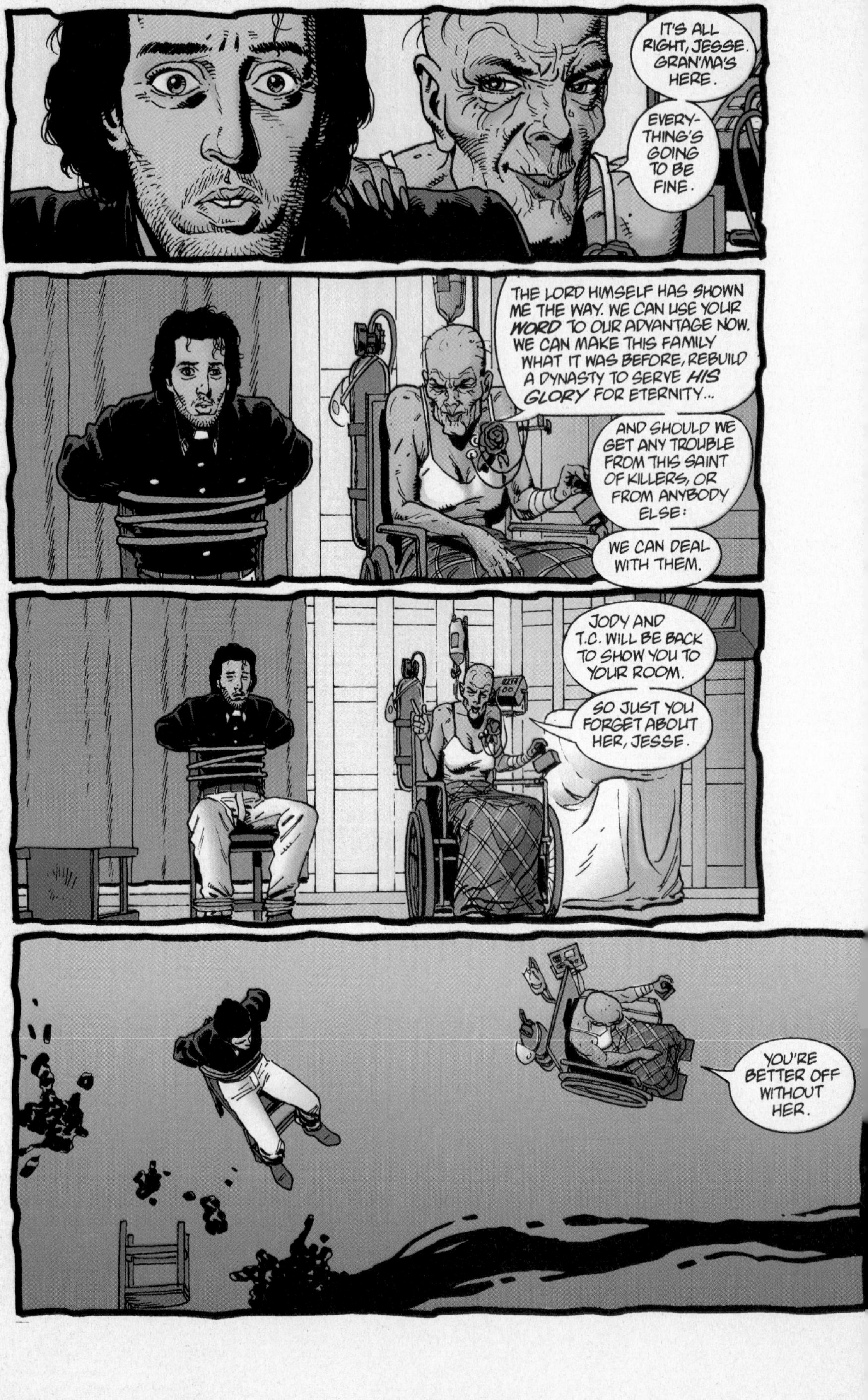
IT'S ALL RIGHT, JESSE. GRAN'MA'S HERE.
EVERY-THING'S GOING TO BE FINE.
THE LORD HIMSELF HAS SHOWN ME THE WAY. WE CAN USE YOUR WORD TO OUR ADVANTAGE NOW. WE CAN MAKE THIS FAMILY WHAT IT WAS BEFORE, REBUILD A DYNASTY TO SERVE HIS GLORY FOR ETERNITY...
AND SHOULD WE GET ANY TROUBLE FROM THIS SAINT OF KILLERS, OR FROM ANYBODY ELSE:
WE CAN DEAL WITH THEM.
JODY AND T.C. WILL BE BACK TO SHOW YOU TO YOUR ROOM.
SO JUST YOU FORGET ABOUT HER, JESSE.
YOU'RE BETTER OFF WITHOUT HER.

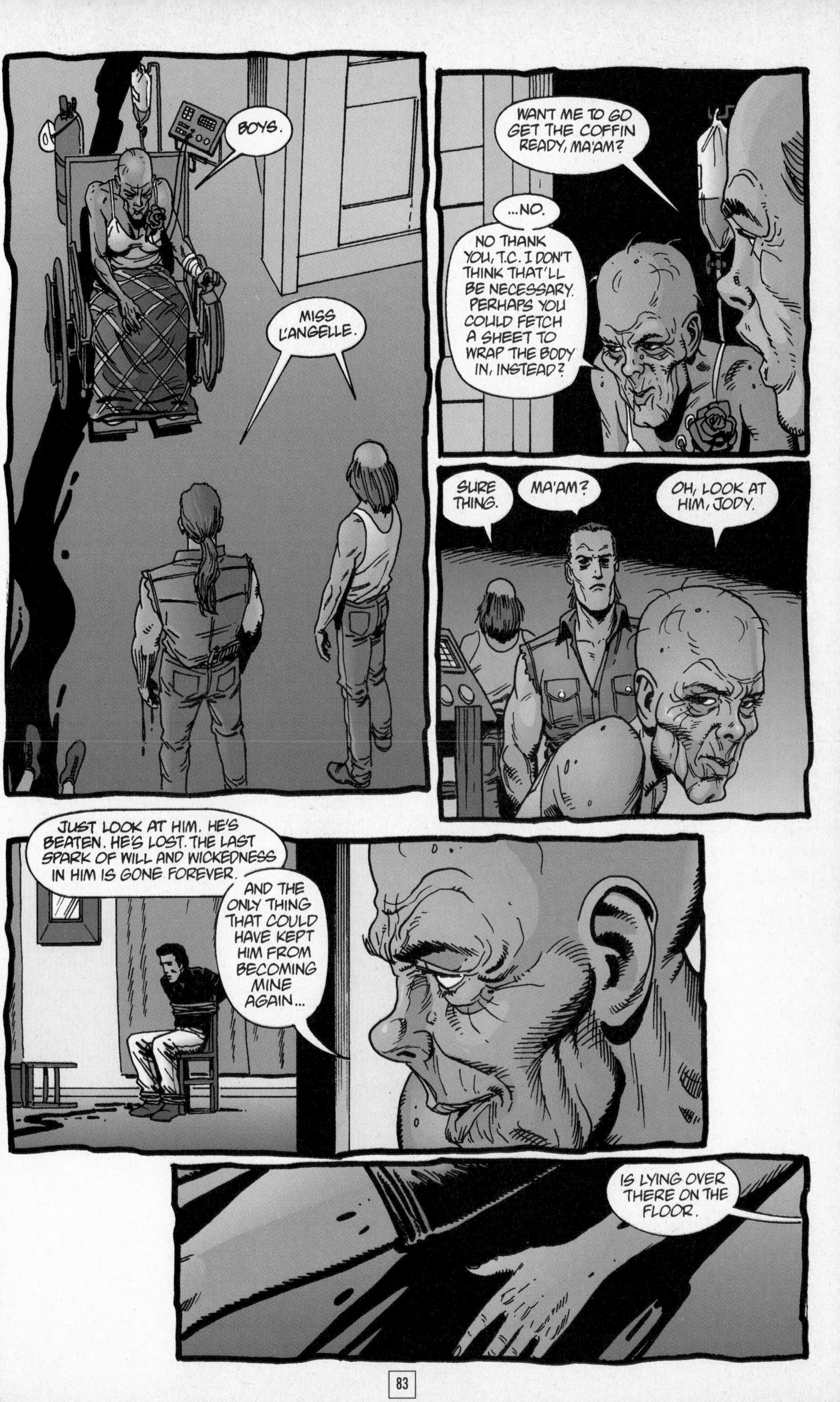
BOYS.
MISS L'ANGELLE.
WANT ME TO GO GET THE COFFIN READY, MA'AM?
...NO.
NO THANK YOU, T.C. I DON'T THINK THAT'LL BE NECESSARY. PERHAPS YOU COULD FETCH A SHEET TO WRAP THE BODY IN, INSTEAD?
SURE THING.
MA'AM?
OH, LOOK AT HIM, JODY.
JUST LOOK AT HIM. HE'S BEATEN. HE'S LOST. THE LAST SPARK OF WILL AND WICKEDNESS IN HIM IS GONE FOREVER.
AND THE ONLY THING THAT COULD HAVE KEPT HIM FROM BECOMING MINE AGAIN...
IS LYING OVER THERE ON THE FLOOR.

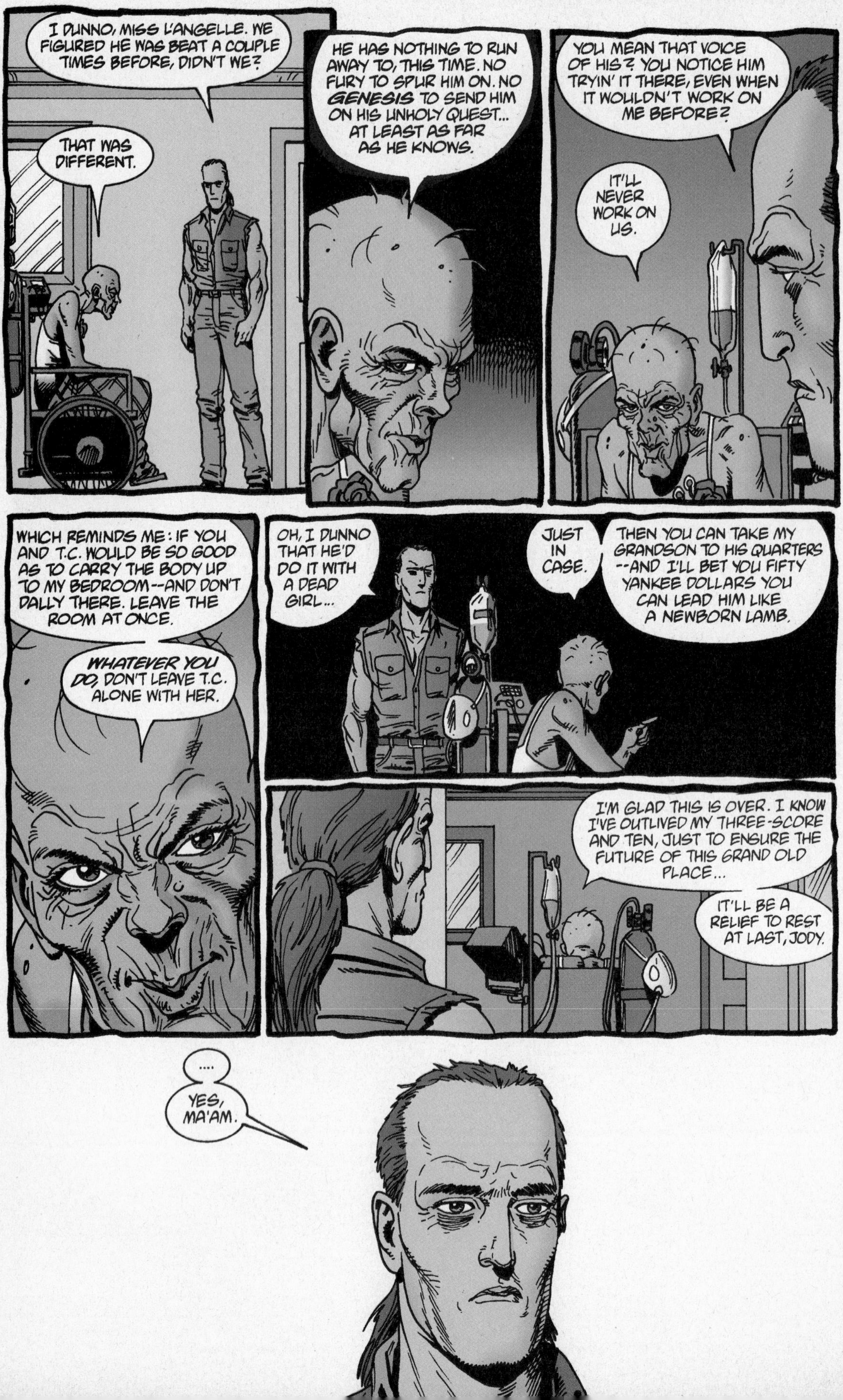
I DUNNO, MISS L'ANGELLE. WE FIGURED HE WAS BEAT A COUPLE TIMES BEFORE, DIDN'T WE?
THAT WAS DIFFERENT.
HE HAS NOTHING TO RUN AWAY TO, THIS TIME. NO FURY TO SPUR HIM ON. NO GENESIS TO SEND HIM ON HIS UNHOLY QUEST... AT LEAST AS FAR AS HE KNOWS.
YOU MEAN THAT VOICE OF HIS? YOU NOTICE HIM TRYIN' IT THERE, EVEN WHEN IT WOULDN'T WORK ON ME BEFORE?
IT'LL NEVER WORK ON US.
WHICH REMINDS ME: IF YOU AND T.C. WOULD BE SO GOOD AS TO CARRY THE BODY UP TO MY BEDROOM--AND DON'T DALLY THERE. LEAVE THE ROOM AT ONCE.
WHATEVER YOU DO, DON'T LEAVE T.C. ALONE WITH HER.
OH, I DUNNO THAT HE'D DO IT WITH A DEAD GIRL...
JUST IN CASE.
THEN YOU CAN TAKE MY GRANDSON TO HIS QUARTERS --AND I'LL BET YOU FIFTY YANKEE DOLLARS YOU CAN LEAD HIM LIKE A NEWBORN LAMB.
I'M GLAD THIS IS OVER. I KNOW I'VE OUTLIVED MY THREE-SCORE AND TEN, JUST TO ENSURE THE FUTURE OF THIS GRAND OLD PLACE...
IT'LL BE A RELIEF TO REST AT LAST, JODY.
....
YES, MA'AM.

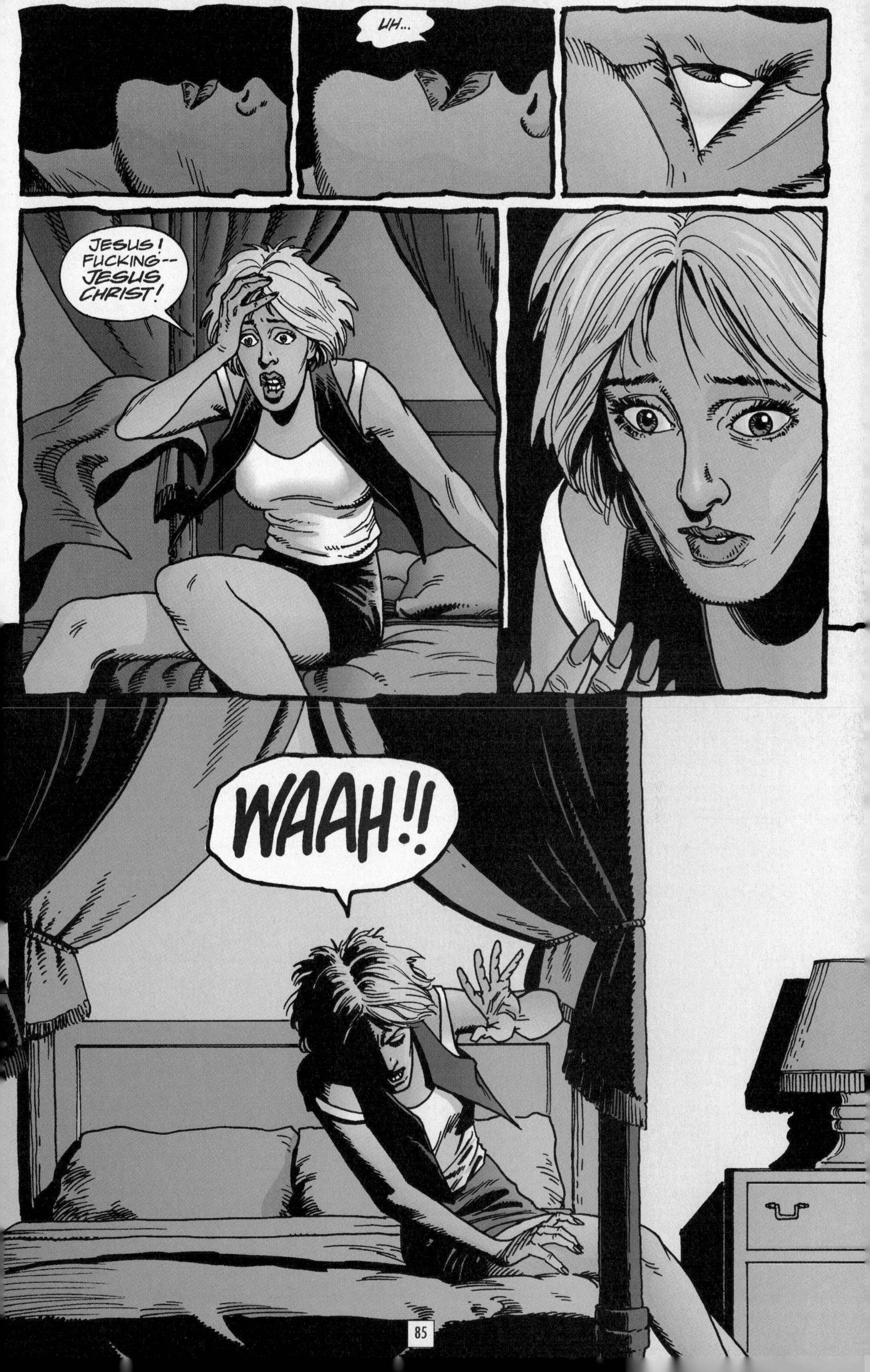
UH...
JESUS! FUCKING--JESUS CHRIST!
WAAH!!

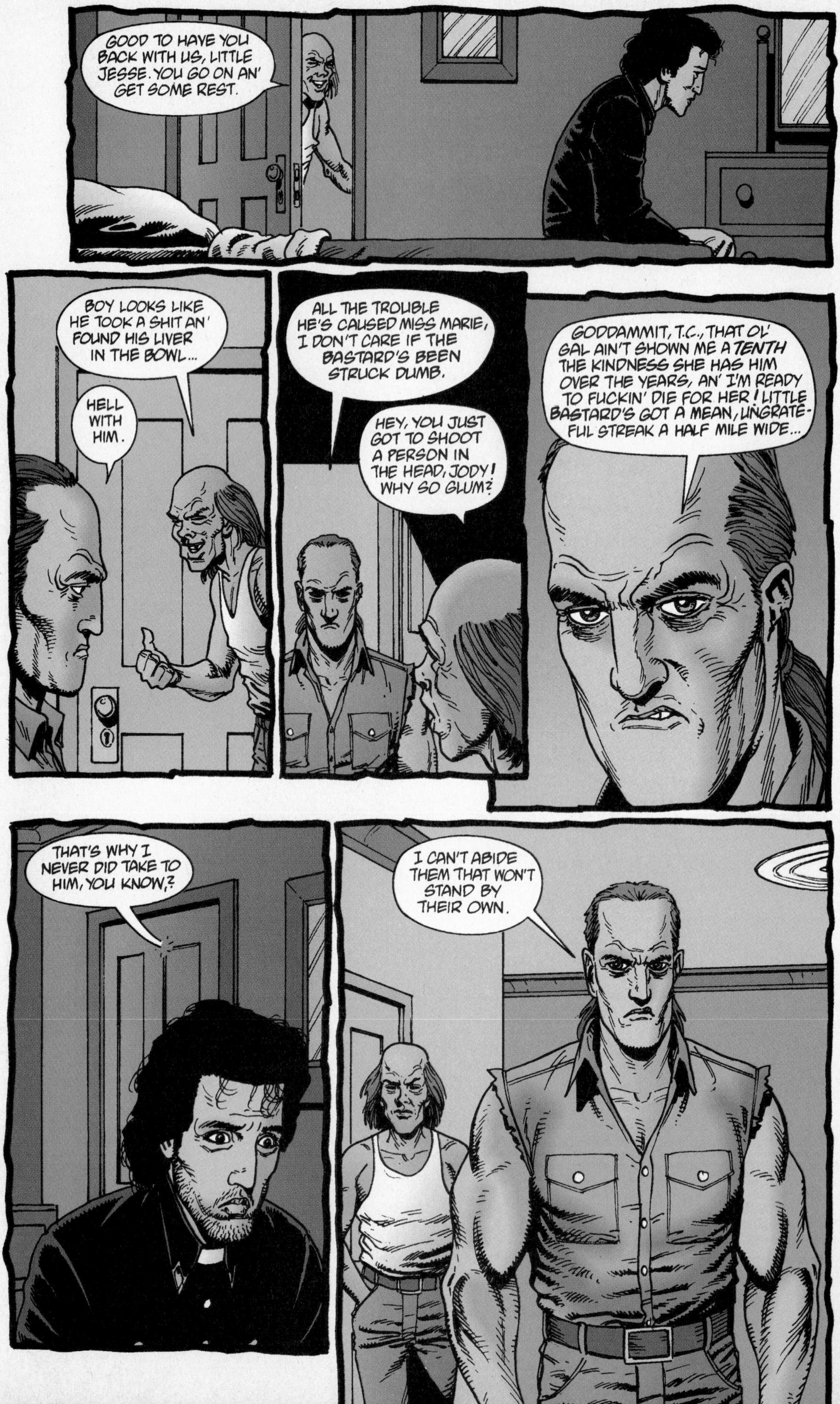
GOOD TO HAVE YOU BACK WITH US, LITTLE JESSE. YOU GO ON AN' GET SOME REST.
BOY LOOKS LIKE HE TOOK A SHIT AN' FOUND HIS LIVER IN THE BOWL...
HELL WITH HIM.
ALL THE TROUBLE HE'S CAUSED MISS MARIE, I DON'T CARE IF THE BASTARD'S BEEN STRUCK DUMB.
HEY, YOU JUST GOT TO SHOOT A PERSON IN THE HEAD, JODY! WHY SO GLUM?
GODDAMMIT, T.C., THAT OL' GAL AIN'T SHOWN ME A TENTH THE KINDNESS SHE HAS HIM OVER THE YEARS, AN' I'M READY TO FUCKIN' DIE FOR HER! LITTLE BASTARD'S GOT A MEAN, UNGRATEFUL STREAK A HALF MILE WIDE...
THAT'S WHY I NEVER DID TAKE TO HIM, YOU KNOW,?
I CAN'T ABIDE THEM THAT WON'T STAND BY THEIR OWN.

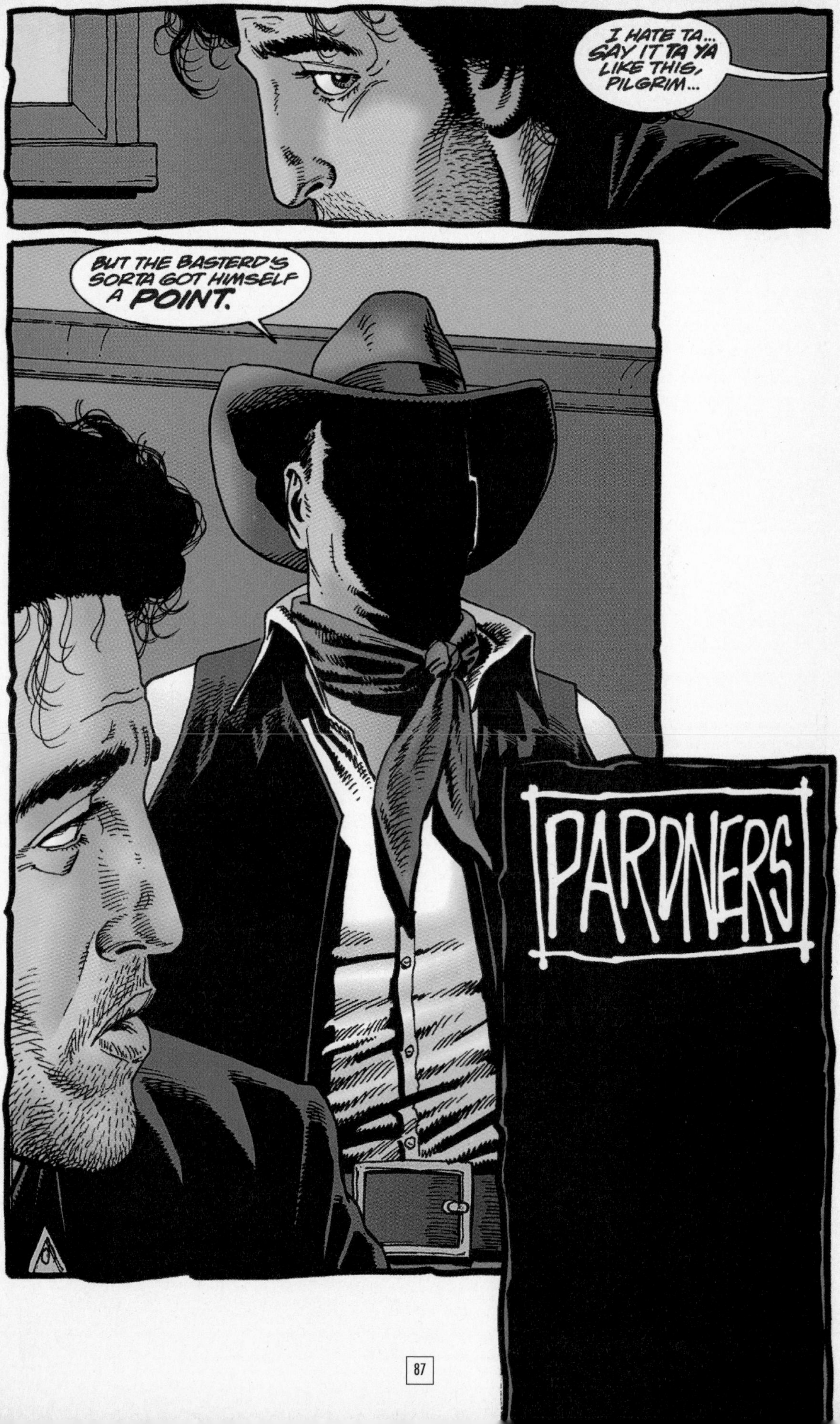
I HATE TA... SAY IT TA YA LIKE THIS, PILGRIM...
BUT THE BASTERD'S SORTA GOT HIMSELF A POINT.
PARDNERS

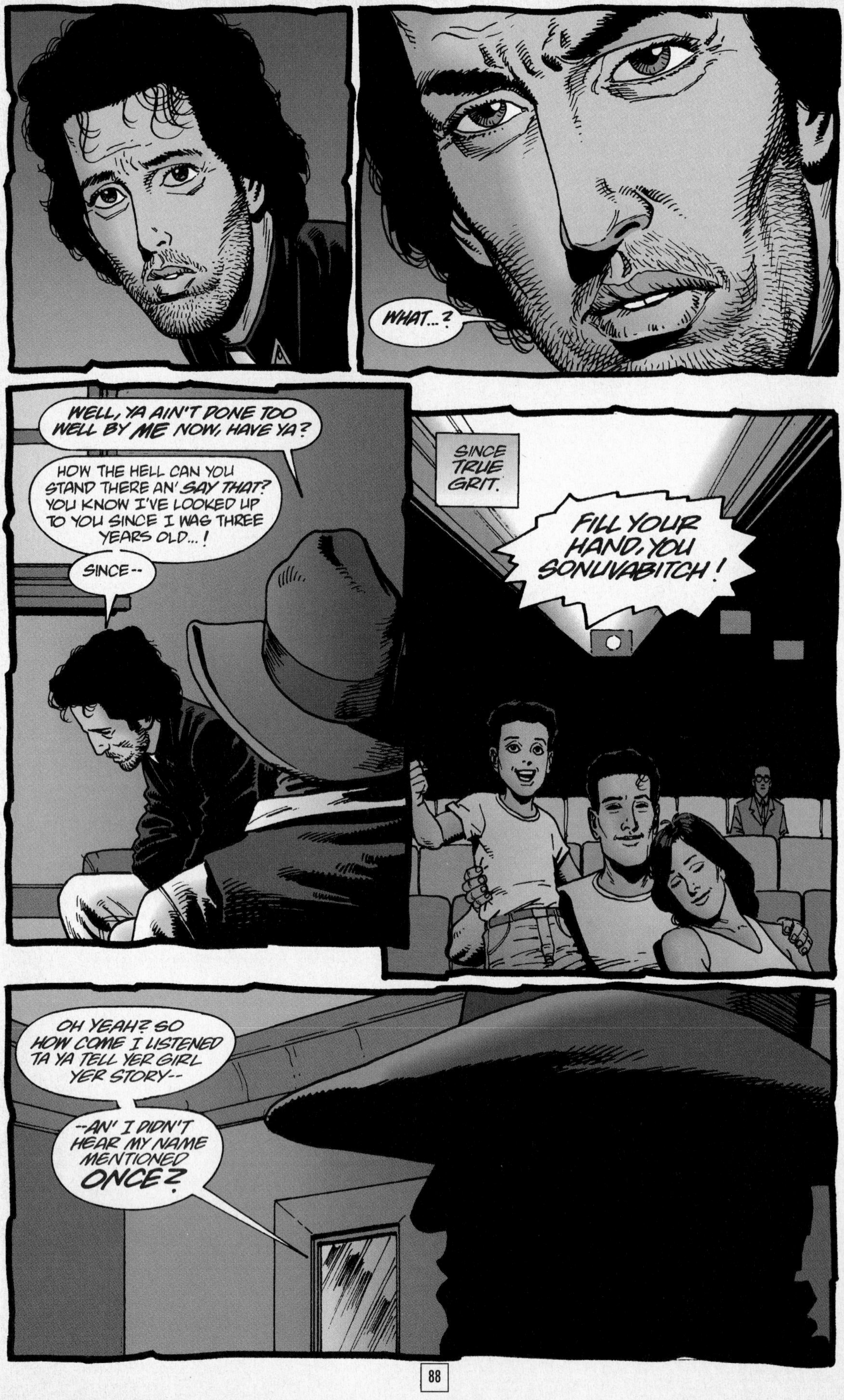
WHAT...?
WELL, YA AIN'T DONE TOO WELL BY ME NOW, HAVE YA?
HOW THE HELL CAN YOU STAND THERE AN' SAY THAT? YOU KNOW I'VE LOOKED UP TO YOU SINCE I WAS THREE YEARS OLD...!
SINCE--
SINCE TRUE GRIT.
FILL YOUR HAND, YOU SONUVABITCH!
OH YEAH? SO HOW COME I LISTENED TA YA TELL YER GIRL YER STORY--
--AN' I DIDN'T HEAR MY NAME MENTIONED ONCE?

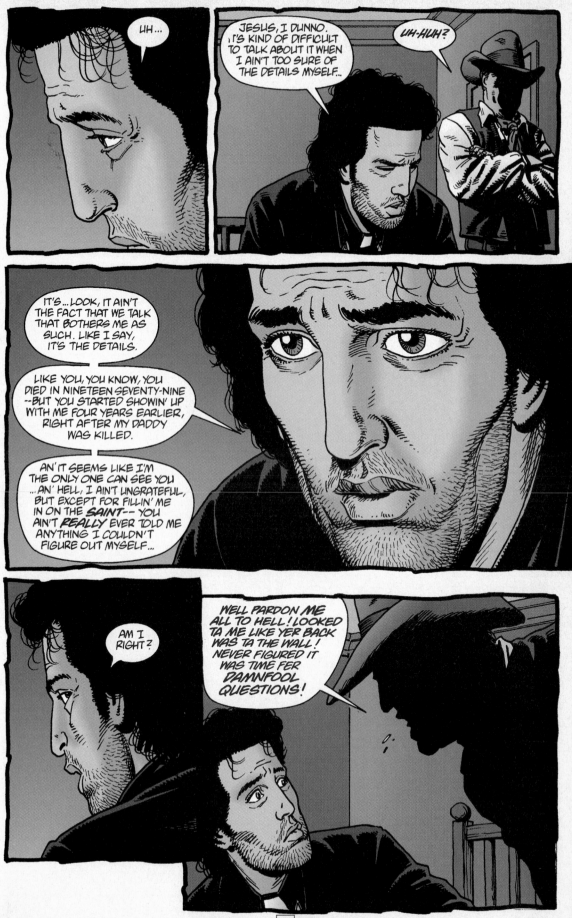

UH...

JESUS, I DUNNO. IT'S KIND OF DIFFICULT TO TALK ABOUT IT WHEN I AIN'T TOO SURE OF THE DETAILS MYSELF...

UH-HUH?

IT'S ... LOOK, IT AIN'T THE FACT THAT WE TALK THAT BOTHERS ME AS SUCH. LIKE I SAY, IT'S THE DETAILS.

LIKE YOU, YOU KNOW, YOU DIED IN NINETEEN SEVENTY-NINE -- BUT YOU STARTED SHOWIN' UP WITH ME FOUR YEARS EARLIER, RIGHT AFTER MY DADDY WAS KILLED.

AN' IT SEEMS LIKE I'M THE ONLY ONE CAN SEE YOU ... AN' HELL, I AIN'T UNGRATEFUL, BUT EXCEPT FOR FILLIN' ME IN ON THE *SAINT* -- YOU AIN'T *REALLY* EVER TOLD ME ANYTHING I COULDN'T FIGURE OUT MYSELF...

AM I RIGHT?

WELL PARDON *ME* ALL TO HELL! LOOKED TA ME LIKE YER BACK WAS TA THE WALL! NEVER FIGURED IT WAS TIME FER *DAMNFOOL* QUESTIONS!

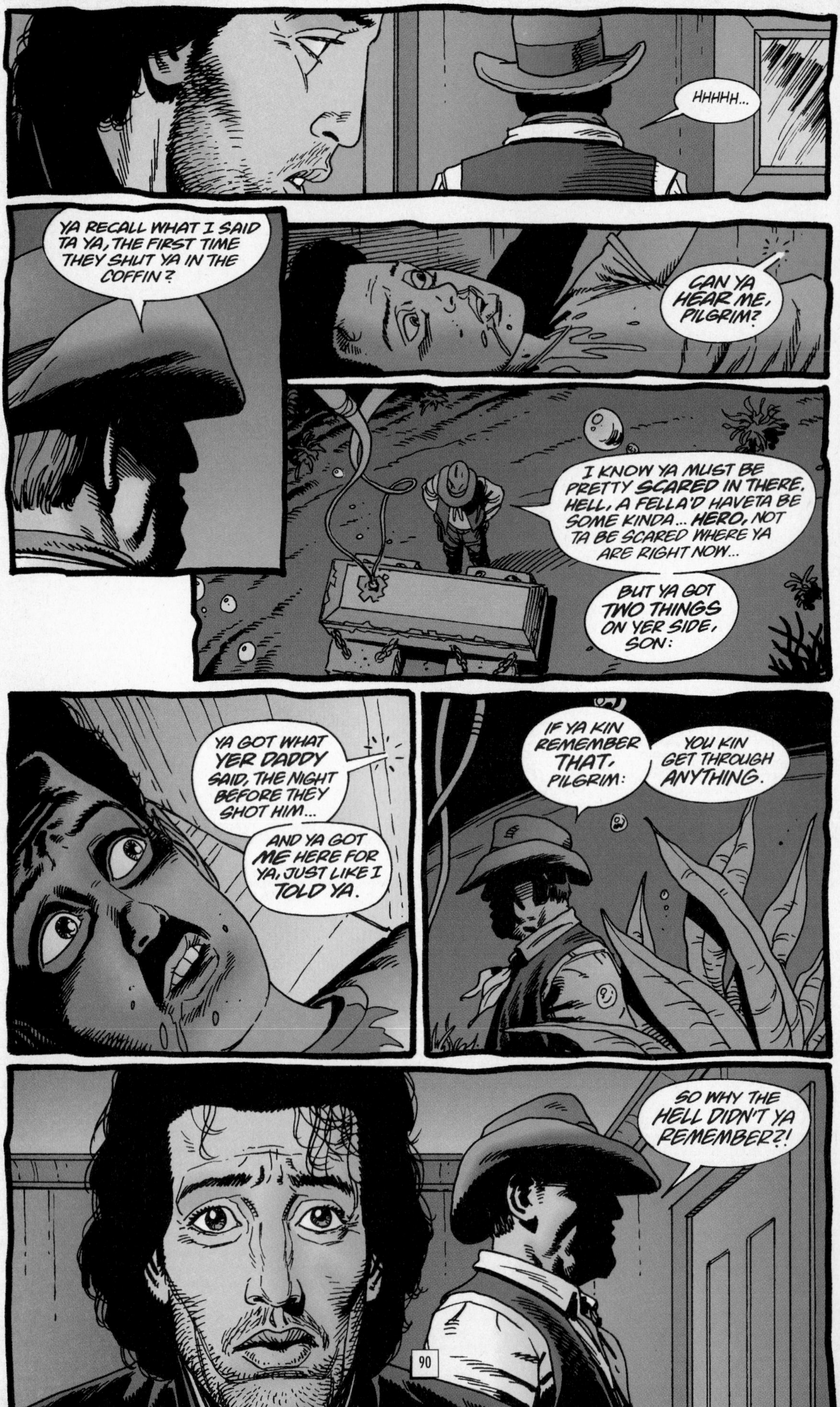
HHHHH...
YA RECALL WHAT I SAID TA YA, THE FIRST TIME THEY SHUT YA IN THE COFFIN?
CAN YA HEAR ME, PILGRIM?
I KNOW YA MUST BE PRETTY SCARED IN THERE. HELL, A FELLA'D HAVETA BE SOME KINDA... HERO, NOT TA BE SCARED WHERE YA ARE RIGHT NOW...
BUT YA GOT TWO THINGS ON YER SIDE, SON:
YA GOT WHAT YER DADDY SAID, THE NIGHT BEFORE THEY SHOT HIM...
AND YA GOT ME HERE FOR YA, JUST LIKE I TOLD YA.
IF YA KIN REMEMBER THAT, PILGRIM:
YOU KIN GET THROUGH ANYTHING.
SO WHY THE HELL DIDN'T YA REMEMBER?!

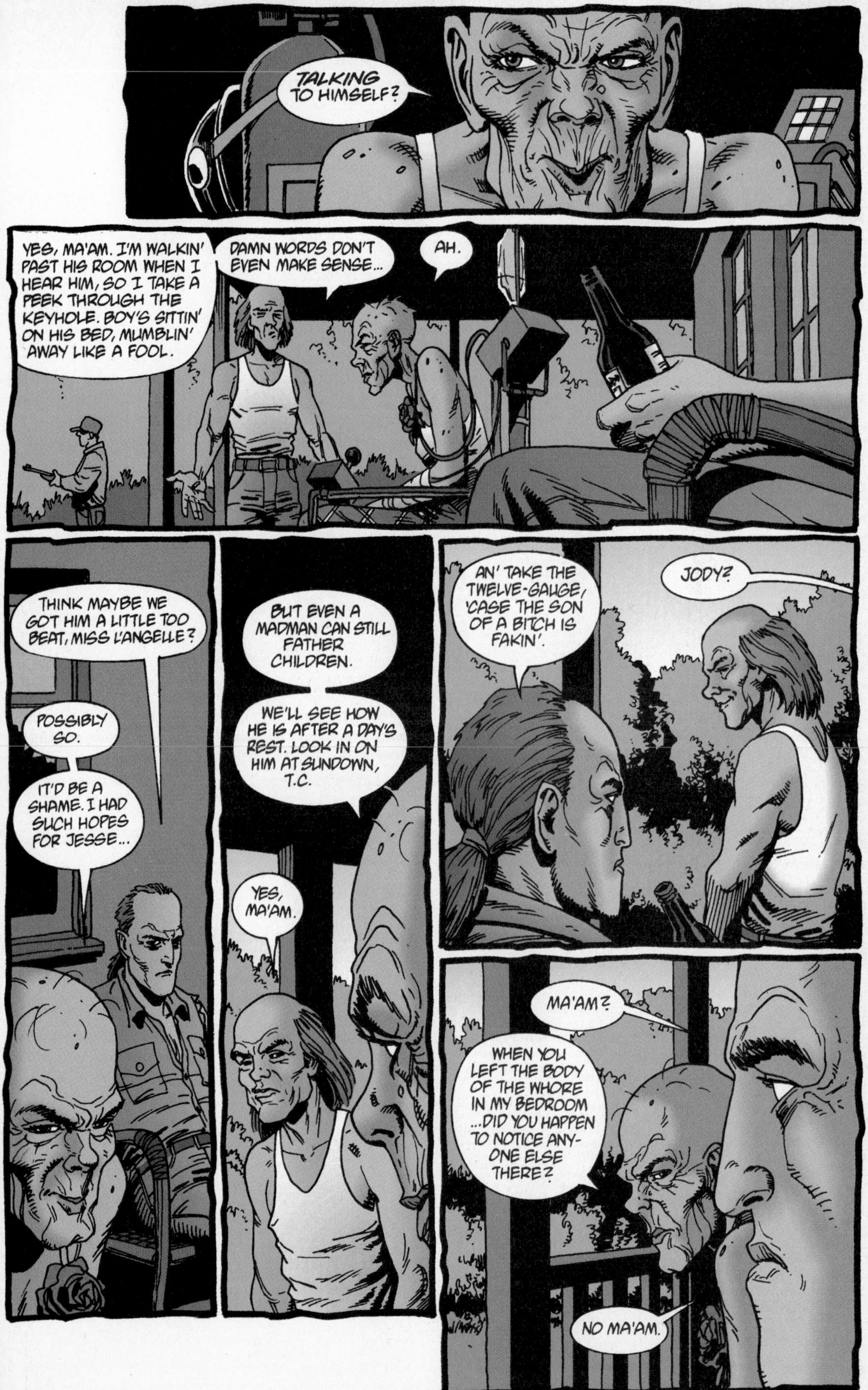

TALKING TO HIMSELF?
YES, MA'AM. I'M WALKIN' PAST HIS ROOM WHEN I HEAR HIM, SO I TAKE A PEEK THROUGH THE KEYHOLE. BOY'S SITTIN' ON HIS BED, MUMBLIN' AWAY LIKE A FOOL.
DAMN WORDS DON'T EVEN MAKE SENSE...
AH.
THINK MAYBE WE GOT HIM A LITTLE TOO BEAT, MISS L'ANGELLE?
POSSIBLY SO.
IT'D BE A SHAME. I HAD SUCH HOPES FOR JESSE...
BUT EVEN A MADMAN CAN STILL FATHER CHILDREN.
WE'LL SEE HOW HE IS AFTER A DAY'S REST. LOOK IN ON HIM AT SUNDOWN, T.C.
YES, MA'AM.
AN' TAKE THE TWELVE-GAUGE, 'CASE THE SON OF A BITCH IS FAKIN'.
JODY?
MA'AM?
WHEN YOU LEFT THE BODY OF THE WHORE IN MY BEDROOM ...DID YOU HAPPEN TO NOTICE ANY-ONE ELSE THERE?
NO MA'AM.

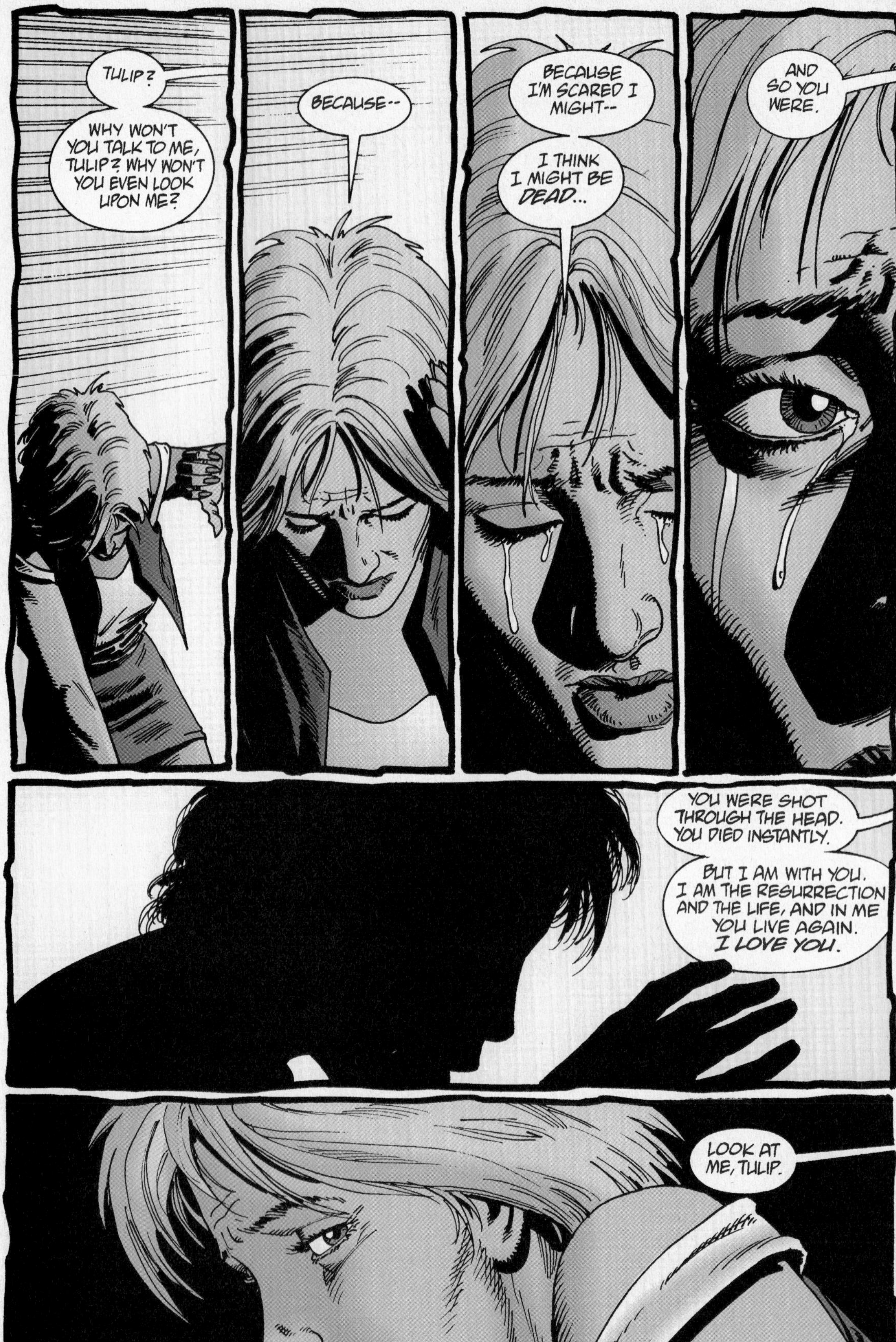

TULIP?
WHY WON'T YOU TALK TO ME, TULIP? WHY WON'T YOU EVEN LOOK UPON ME?
BECAUSE--
BECAUSE I'M SCARED I MIGHT--
I THINK I MIGHT BE DEAD...
AND SO YOU WERE.
YOU WERE SHOT THROUGH THE HEAD. YOU DIED INSTANTLY.
BUT I AM WITH YOU. I AM THE RESURRECTION AND THE LIFE, AND IN ME YOU LIVE AGAIN. I LOVE YOU.
LOOK AT ME, TULIP.

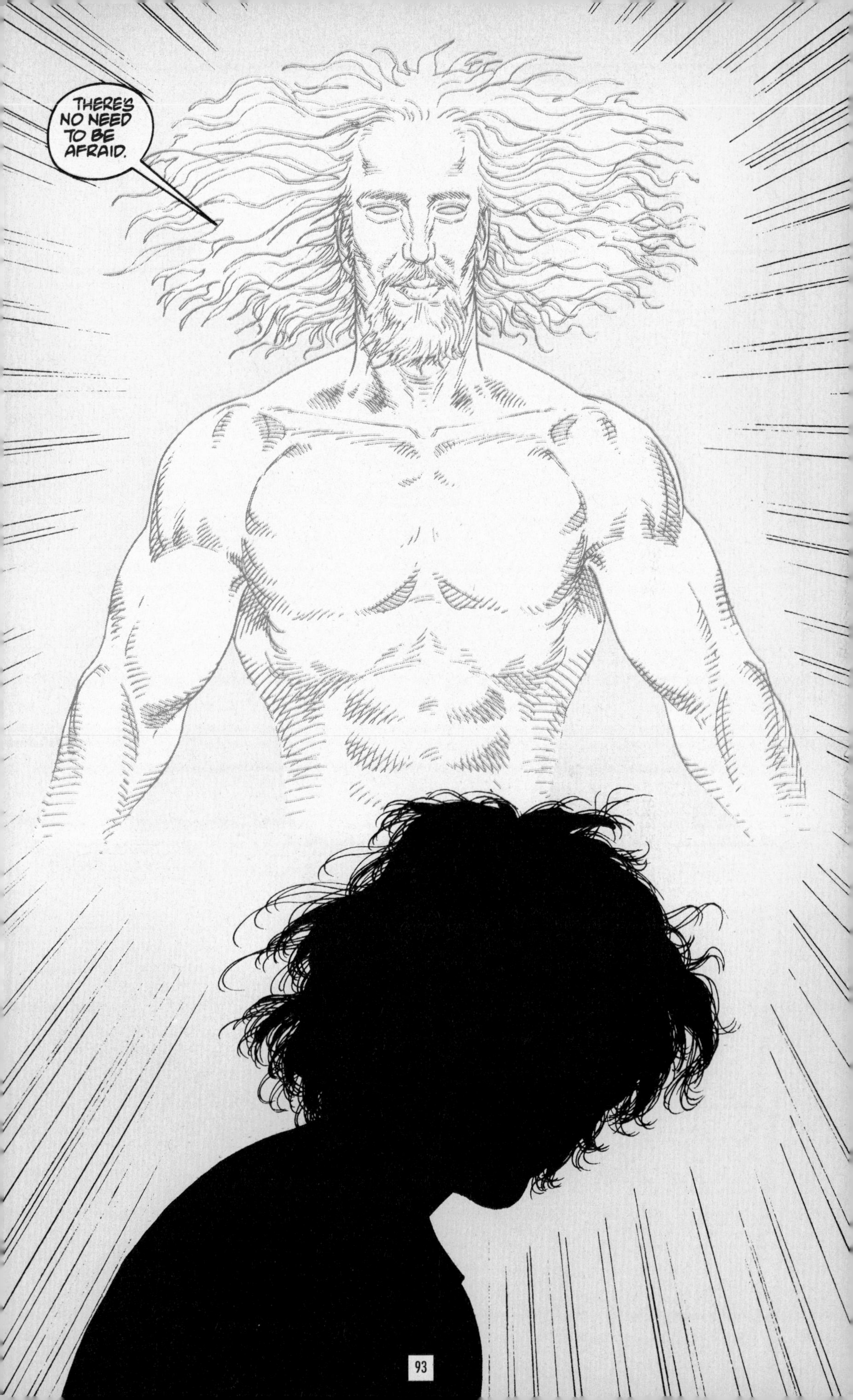
THERE'S NO NEED TO BE AFRAID.

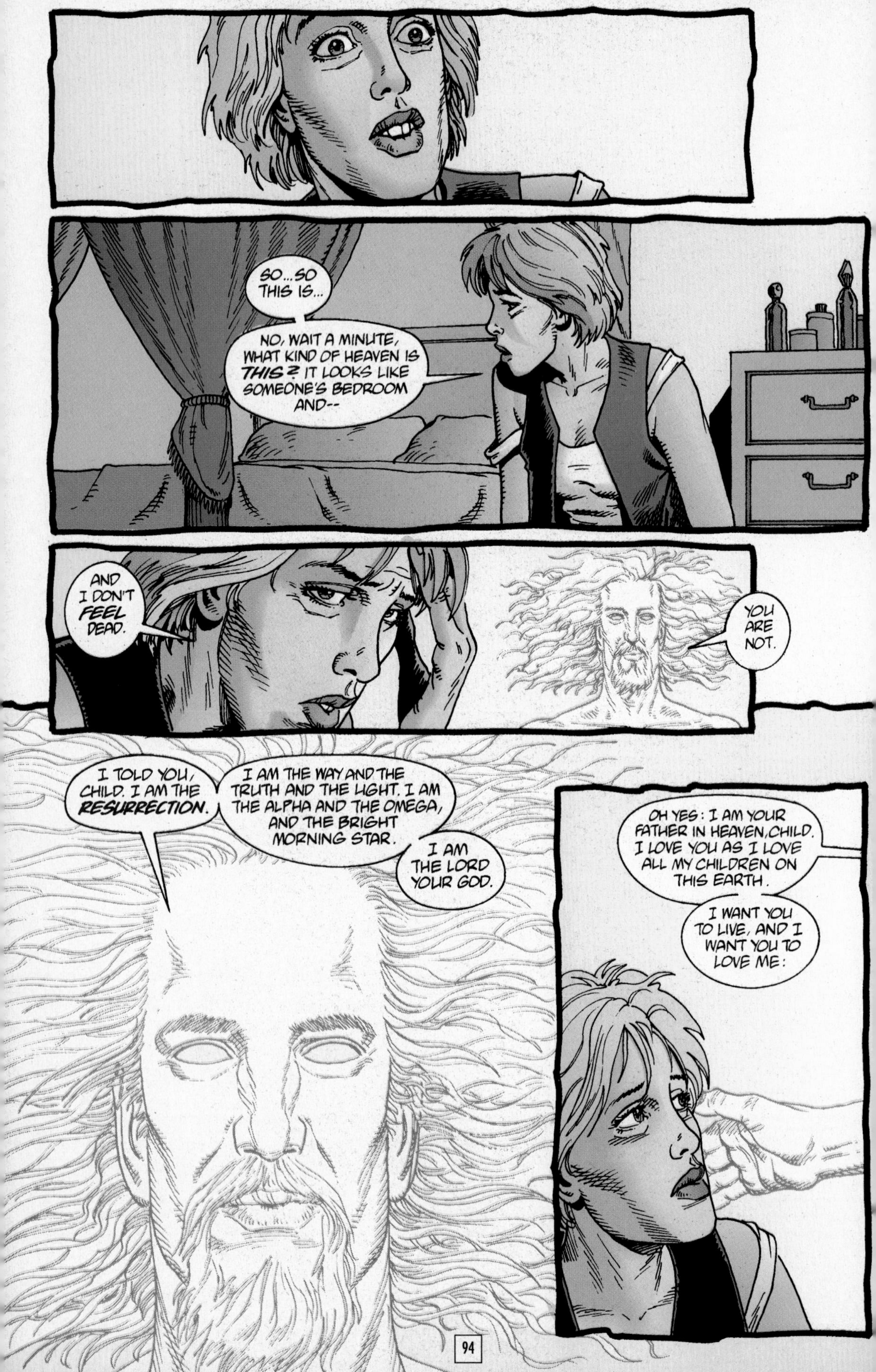
SO...SO THIS IS...
NO, WAIT A MINUTE, WHAT KIND OF HEAVEN IS THIS? IT LOOKS LIKE SOMEONE'S BEDROOM AND--
AND I DON'T FEEL DEAD.
YOU ARE NOT.
I TOLD YOU, CHILD. I AM THE RESURRECTION.
I AM THE WAY AND THE TRUTH AND THE LIGHT. I AM THE ALPHA AND THE OMEGA, AND THE BRIGHT MORNING STAR.
I AM THE LORD YOUR GOD.
OH YES: I AM YOUR FATHER IN HEAVEN, CHILD. I LOVE YOU AS I LOVE ALL MY CHILDREN ON THIS EARTH.
I WANT YOU TO LIVE, AND I WANT YOU TO LOVE ME:

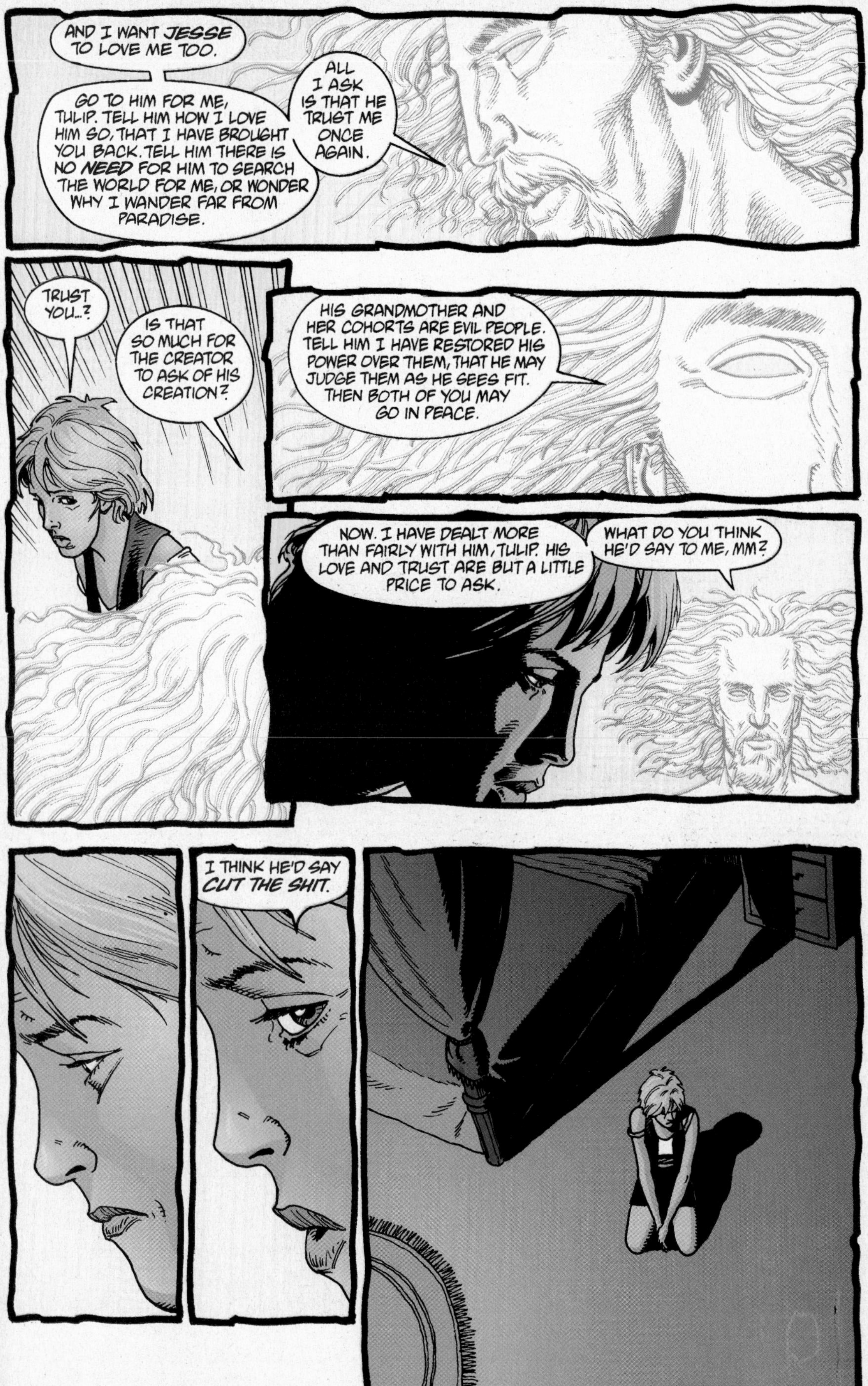
AND I WANT JESSE TO LOVE ME TOO.
GO TO HIM FOR ME, TULIP. TELL HIM HOW I LOVE HIM SO, THAT I HAVE BROUGHT YOU BACK. TELL HIM THERE IS NO NEED FOR HIM TO SEARCH THE WORLD FOR ME, OR WONDER WHY I WANDER FAR FROM PARADISE.
ALL I ASK IS THAT HE TRUST ME ONCE AGAIN.
TRUST YOU..?
IS THAT SO MUCH FOR THE CREATOR TO ASK OF HIS CREATION?
HIS GRANDMOTHER AND HER COHORTS ARE EVIL PEOPLE. TELL HIM I HAVE RESTORED HIS POWER OVER THEM, THAT HE MAY JUDGE THEM AS HE SEES FIT. THEN BOTH OF YOU MAY GO IN PEACE.
NOW. I HAVE DEALT MORE THAN FAIRLY WITH HIM, TULIP. HIS LOVE AND TRUST ARE BUT A LITTLE PRICE TO ASK.
WHAT DO YOU THINK HE'D SAY TO ME, MM?
I THINK HE'D SAY CUT THE SHIT.

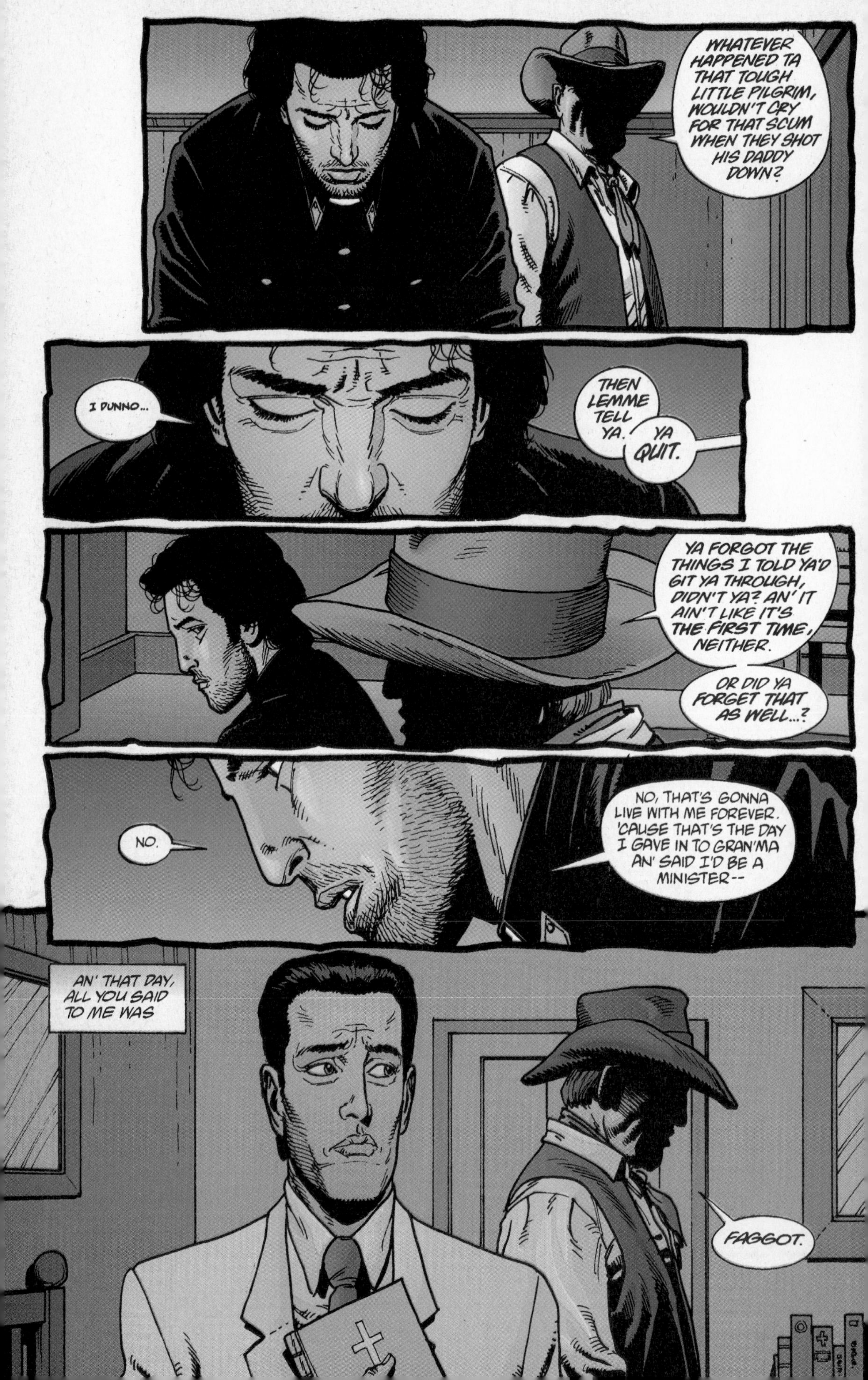
WHATEVER HAPPENED TA THAT TOUGH LITTLE PILGRIM, WOULDN'T CRY FOR THAT SCUM WHEN THEY SHOT HIS DADDY DOWN?
I DUNNO...
THEN LEMME TELL YA.
YA QUIT.
YA FORGOT THE THINGS I TOLD YA'D GIT YA THROUGH, DIDN'T YA? AN' IT AIN'T LIKE IT'S THE FIRST TIME, NEITHER.
OR DID YA FORGET THAT AS WELL...?
NO.
NO, THAT'S GONNA LIVE WITH ME FOREVER. 'CAUSE THAT'S THE DAY I GAVE IN TO GRAN'MA AN' SAID I'D BE A MINISTER--
AN' THAT DAY, ALL YOU SAID TO ME WAS
FAGGOT.

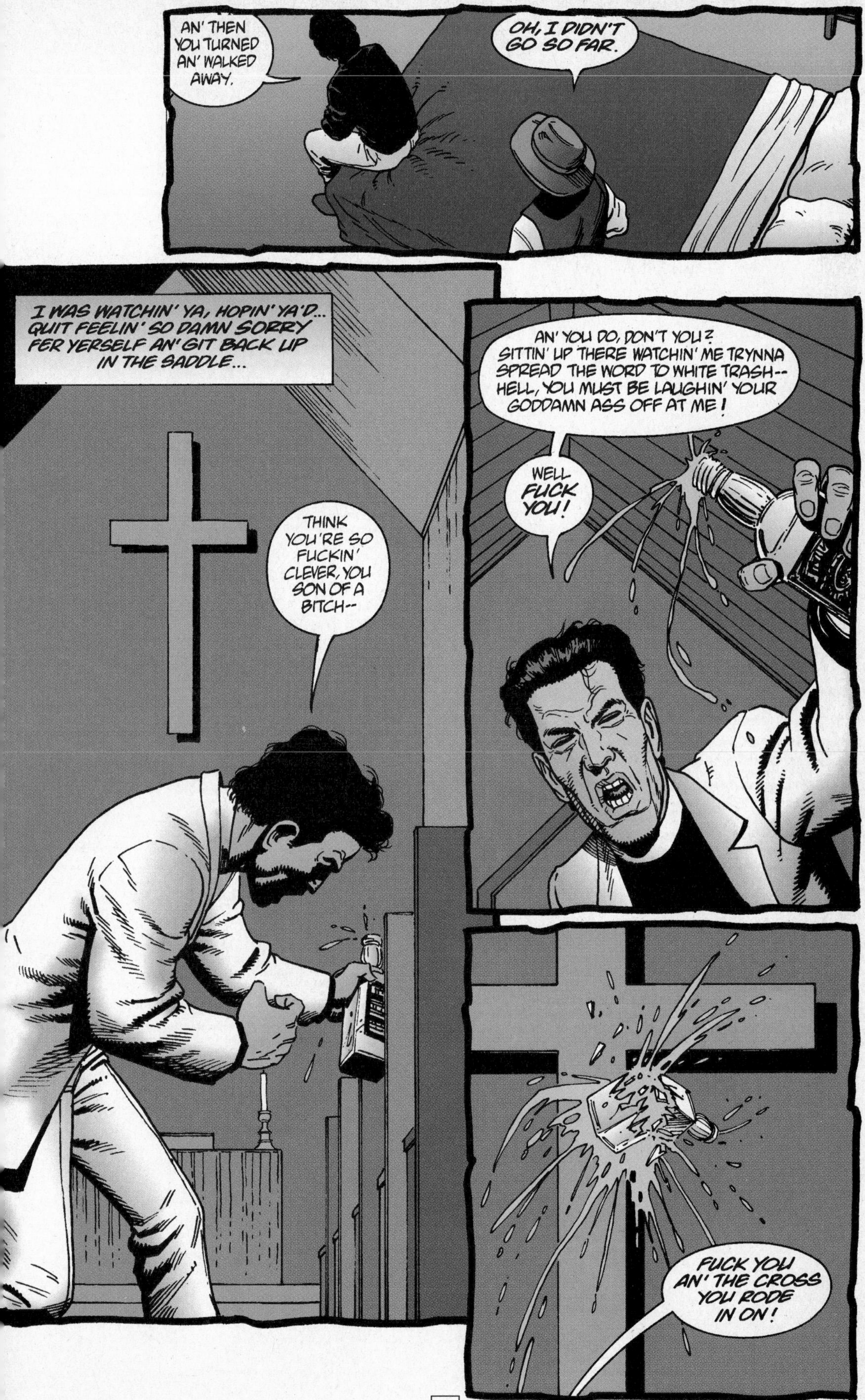
AN' THEN YOU TURNED AN' WALKED AWAY.
OH, I DIDN'T GO SO FAR.
I WAS WATCHIN' YA, HOPIN' YA'D... QUIT FEELIN' SO DAMN SORRY FER YERSELF AN' GIT BACK UP IN THE SADDLE...
THINK YOU'RE SO FUCKIN' CLEVER, YOU SON OF A BITCH--
AN' YOU DO, DON'T YOU? SITTIN' UP THERE WATCHIN' ME TRYNNA SPREAD THE WORD TO WHITE TRASH-- HELL, YOU MUST BE LAUGHIN' YOUR GODDAMN ASS OFF AT ME!
WELL FUCK YOU!
FUCK YOU AN' THE CROSS YOU RODE IN ON!

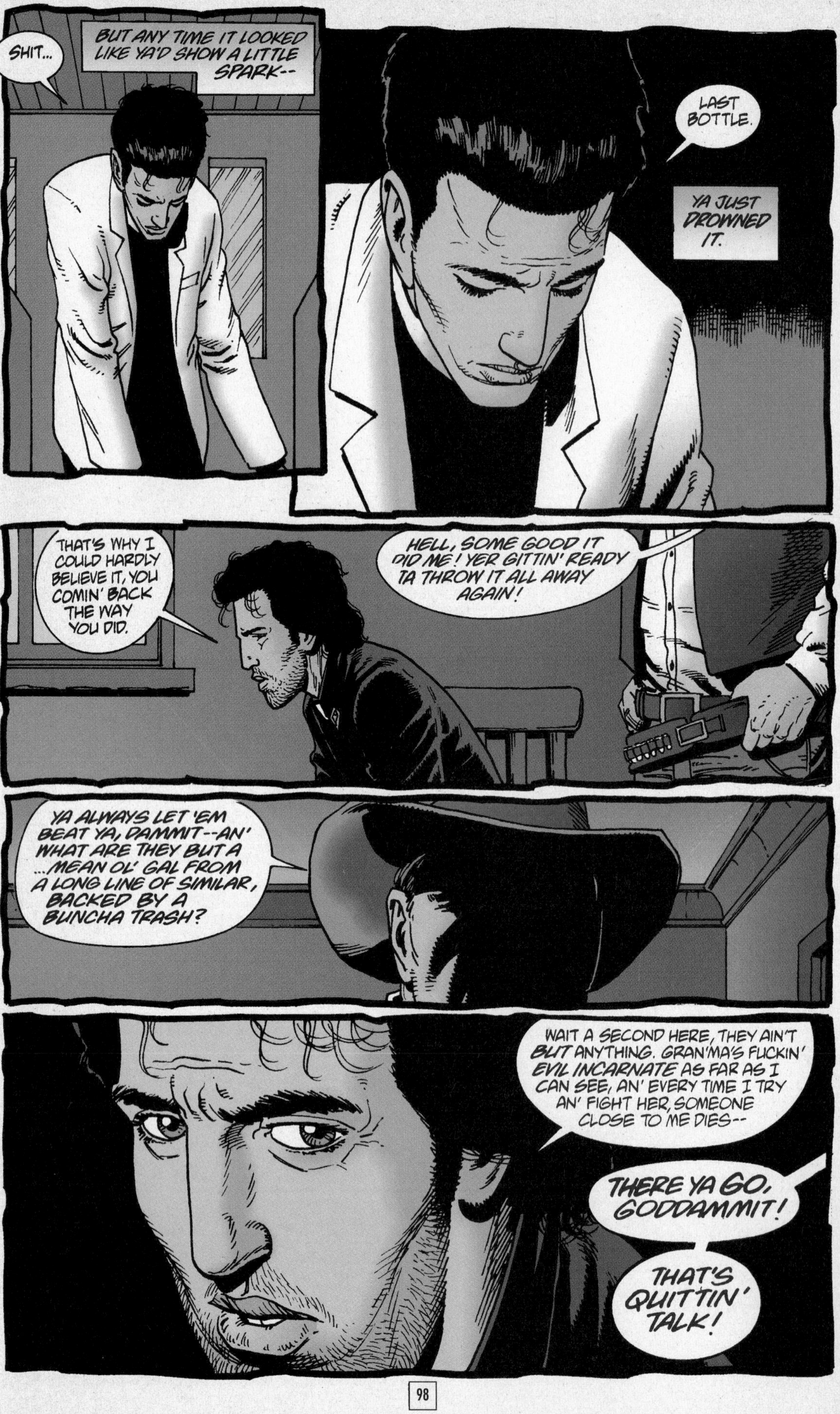
BUT ANY TIME IT LOOKED LIKE YA'D SHOW A LITTLE SPARK--
SHIT...
LAST BOTTLE.
YA JUST DROWNED IT.
THAT'S WHY I COULD HARDLY BELIEVE IT, YOU COMIN' BACK THE WAY YOU DID.
HELL, SOME GOOD IT DID ME! YER GITTIN' READY TA THROW IT ALL AWAY AGAIN!
YA ALWAYS LET 'EM BEAT YA, DAMMIT--AN' WHAT ARE THEY BUT A ...MEAN OL' GAL FROM A LONG LINE OF SIMILAR, BACKED BY A BUNCHA TRASH?
WAIT A SECOND HERE, THEY AIN'T BUT ANYTHING. GRAN'MA'S FUCKIN' EVIL INCARNATE AS FAR AS I CAN SEE, AN' EVERY TIME I TRY AN' FIGHT HER, SOMEONE CLOSE TO ME DIES--
THERE YA GO, GODDAMMIT!
THAT'S QUITTIN' TALK!

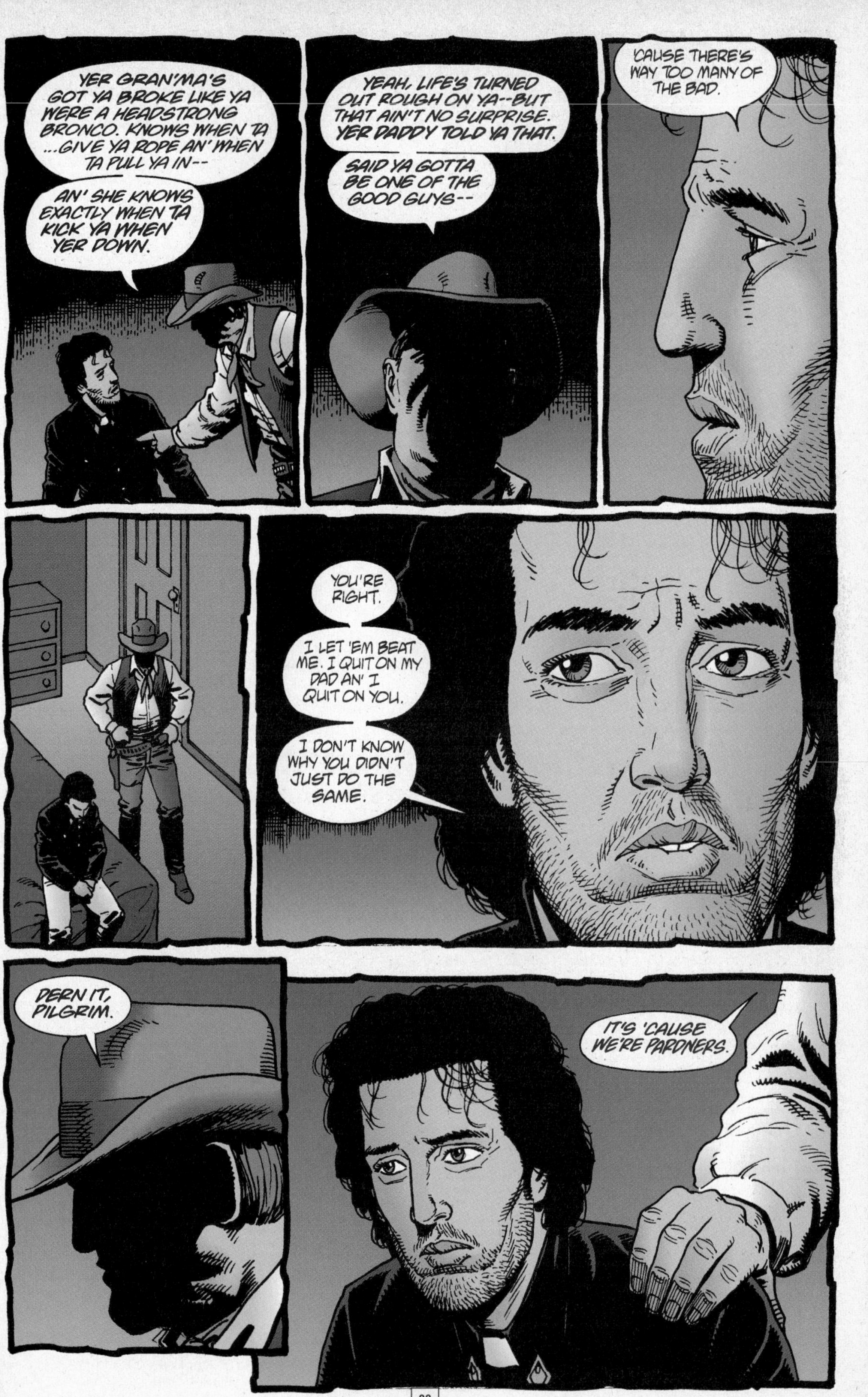
YER GRAN'MA'S GOT YA BROKE LIKE YA WERE A HEADSTRONG BRONCO. KNOWS WHEN TA ...GIVE YA ROPE AN' WHEN TA PULL YA IN--
AN' SHE KNOWS EXACTLY WHEN TA KICK YA WHEN YER DOWN.
YEAH, LIFE'S TURNED OUT ROUGH ON YA--BUT THAT AIN'T NO SURPRISE. YER DADDY TOLD YA THAT.
SAID YA GOTTA BE ONE OF THE GOOD GUYS--
'CAUSE THERE'S WAY TOO MANY OF THE BAD.
YOU'RE RIGHT.
I LET 'EM BEAT ME. I QUIT ON MY DAD AN' I QUIT ON YOU.
I DON'T KNOW WHY YOU DIDN'T JUST DO THE SAME.
DERN IT, PILGRIM.
IT'S 'CAUSE WE'RE PARDNERS.

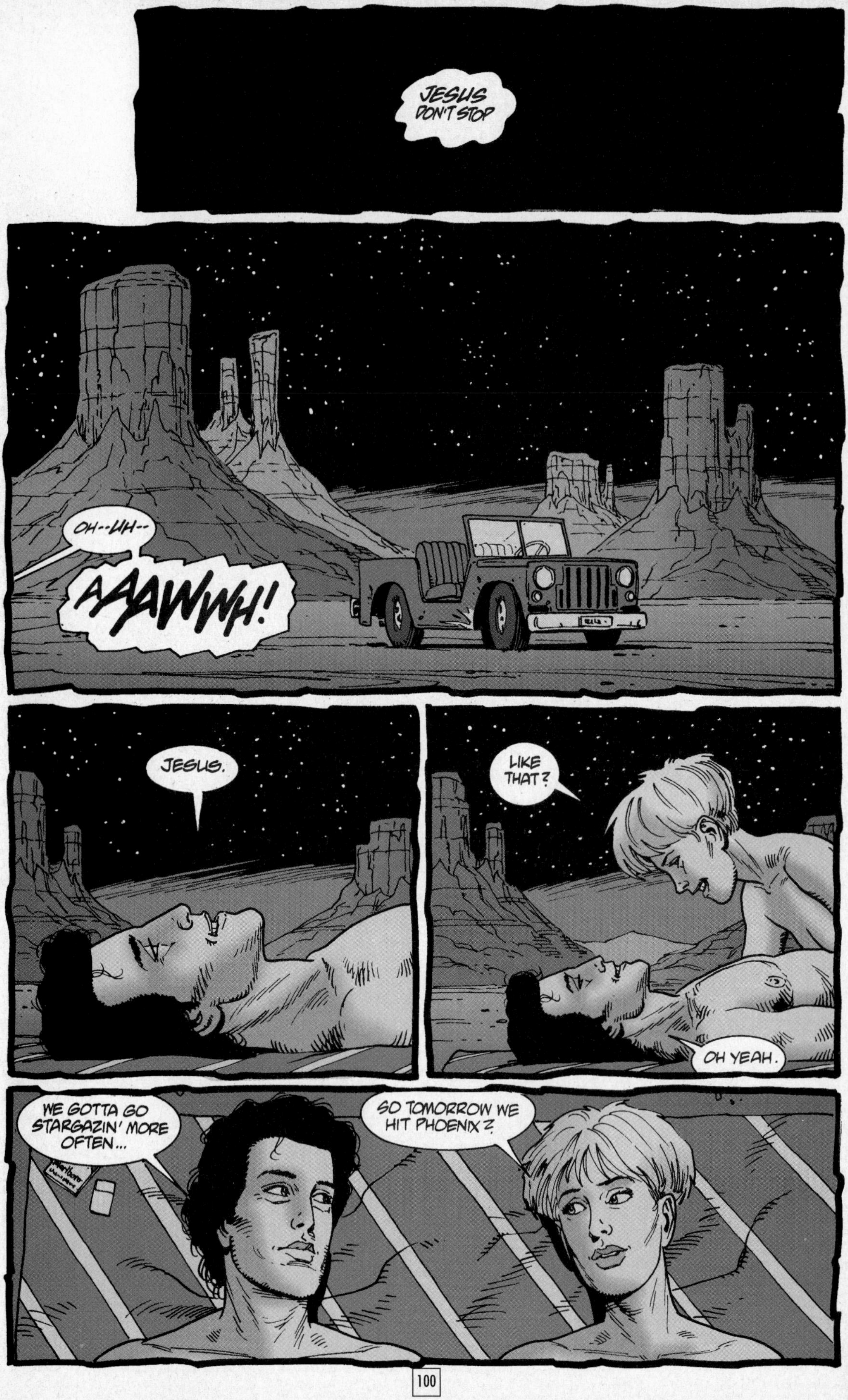

JESUS DON'T STOP
OH--UH--
AAAWWH!
JESUS.
LIKE THAT?
OH YEAH.
WE GOTTA GO STARGAZIN' MORE OFTEN...
SO TOMORROW WE HIT PHOENIX?

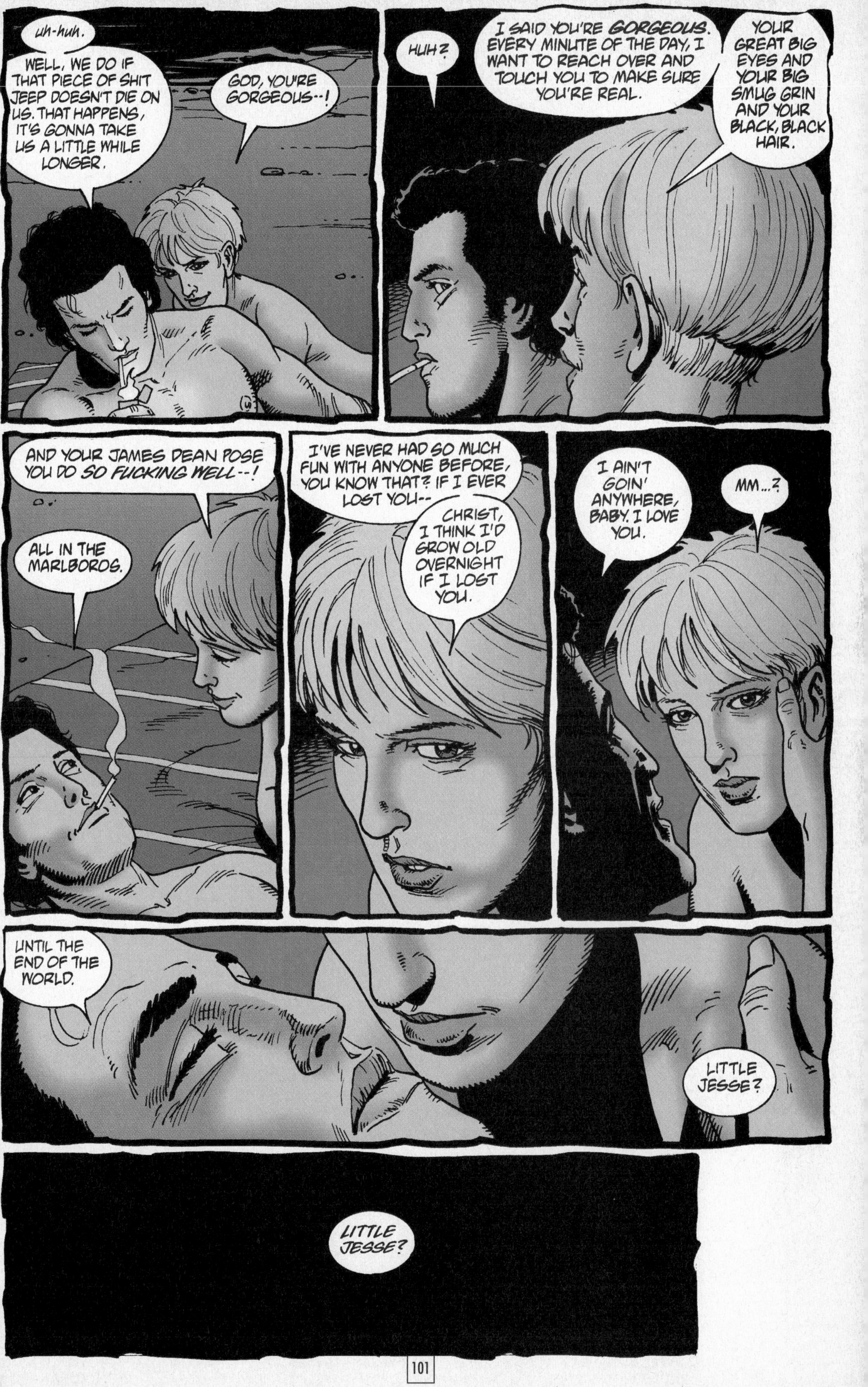
uh-huh.
WELL, WE DO IF THAT PIECE OF SHIT JEEP DOESN'T DIE ON US. THAT HAPPENS, IT'S GONNA TAKE US A LITTLE WHILE LONGER.
GOD, YOU'RE GORGEOUS--!
HUH?
I SAID YOU'RE GORGEOUS. EVERY MINUTE OF THE DAY, I WANT TO REACH OVER AND TOUCH YOU TO MAKE SURE YOU'RE REAL.
YOUR GREAT BIG EYES AND YOUR BIG SMUG GRIN AND YOUR BLACK, BLACK HAIR.
AND YOUR JAMES DEAN POSE YOU DO SO FUCKING WELL--!
ALL IN THE MARLBOROS.
I'VE NEVER HAD SO MUCH FUN WITH ANYONE BEFORE, YOU KNOW THAT? IF I EVER LOST YOU--
CHRIST, I THINK I'D GROW OLD OVERNIGHT IF I LOST YOU.
I AIN'T GOIN' ANYWHERE, BABY. I LOVE YOU.
MM...?
UNTIL THE END OF THE WORLD.
LITTLE JESSE?
LITTLE JESSE?

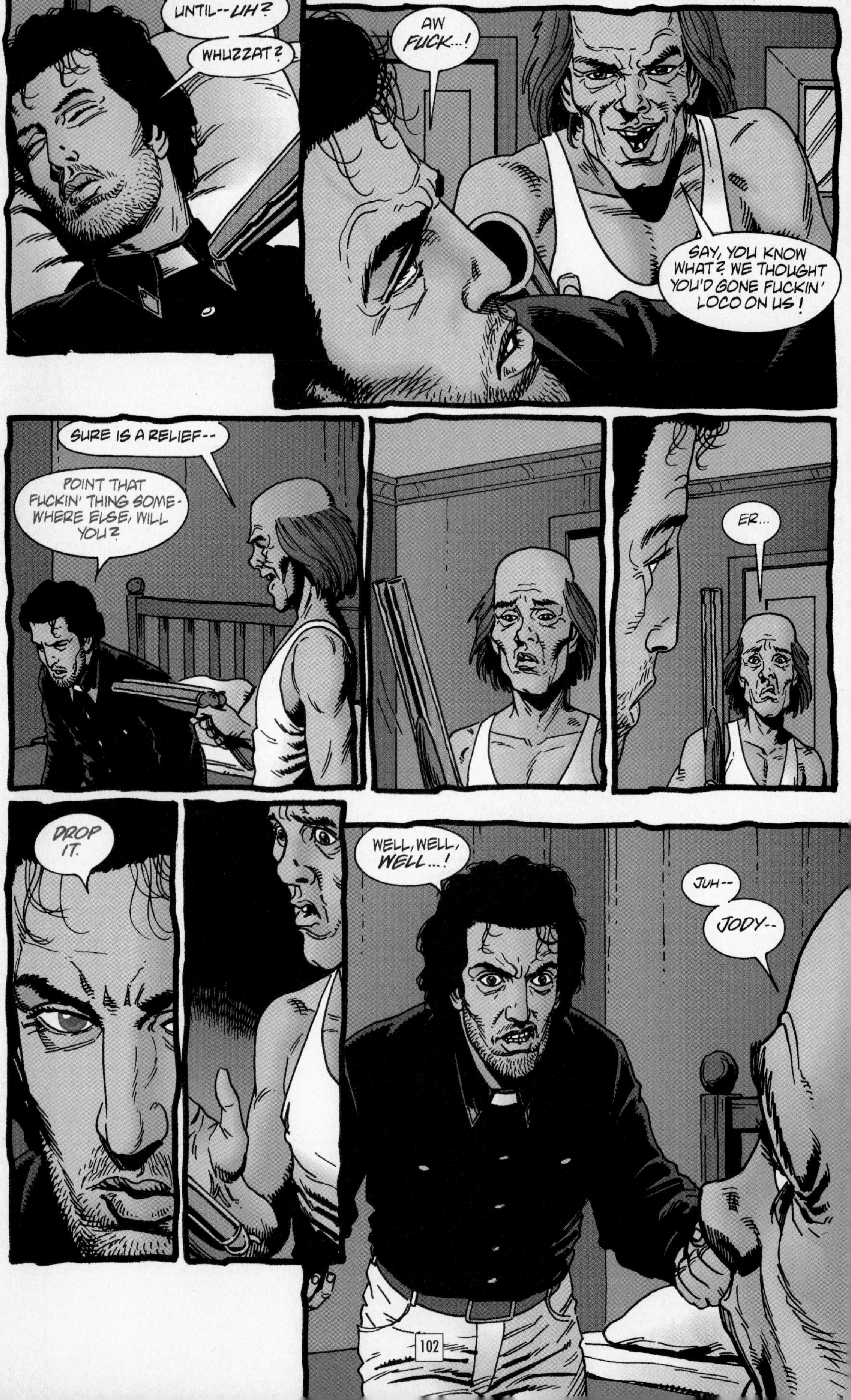
UNTIL--UH?
WHUZZAT?
AW FUCK...!
SAY, YOU KNOW WHAT? WE THOUGHT YOU'D GONE FUCKIN' LOCO ON US!
SURE IS A RELIEF--
POINT THAT FUCKIN' THING SOME-WHERE ELSE, WILL YOU?
ER...
DROP IT.
WELL, WELL, WELL...!
JUH--
JODY--

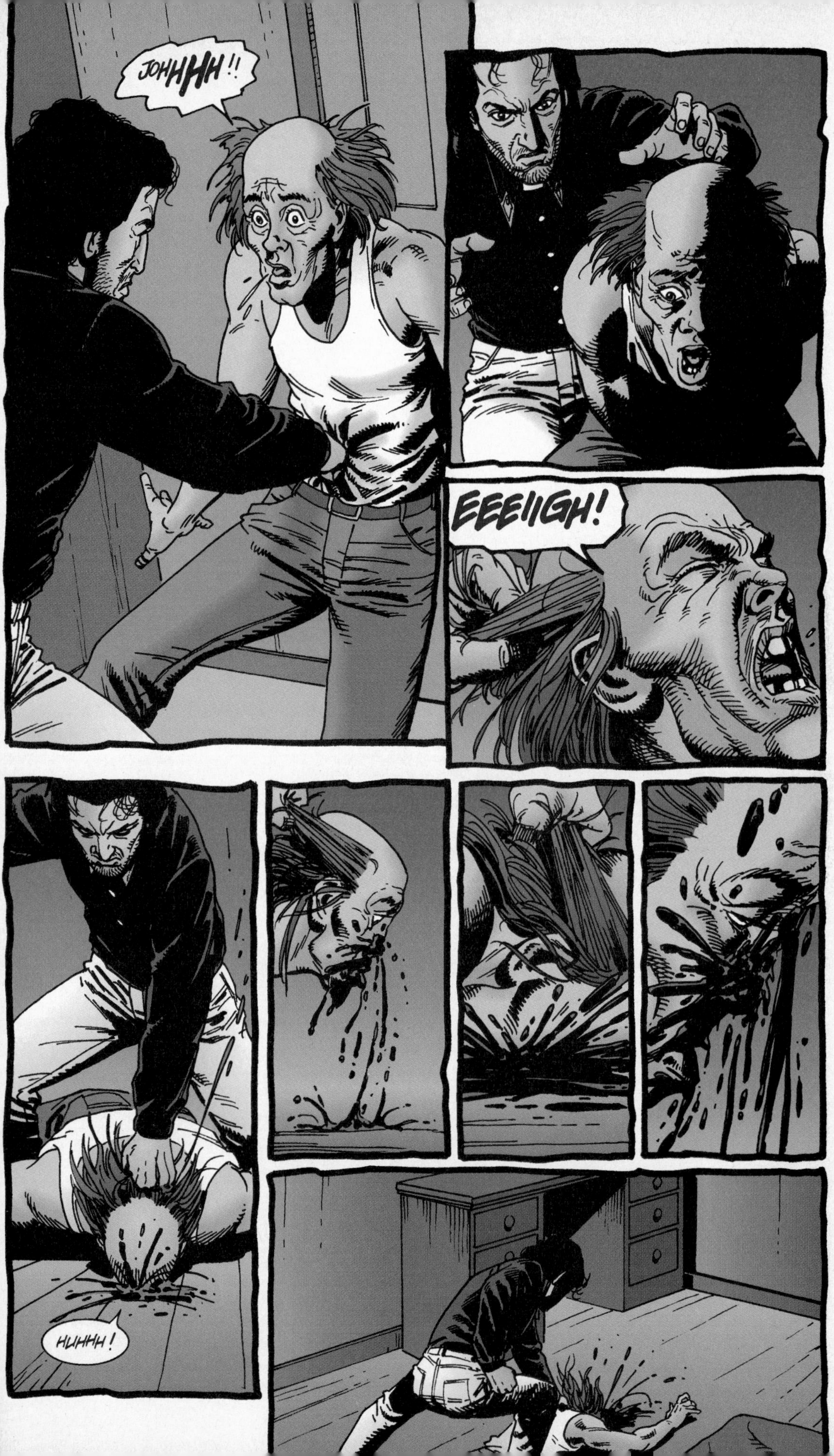
JOHHHH!!
EEEIIGH!
HUHHH!

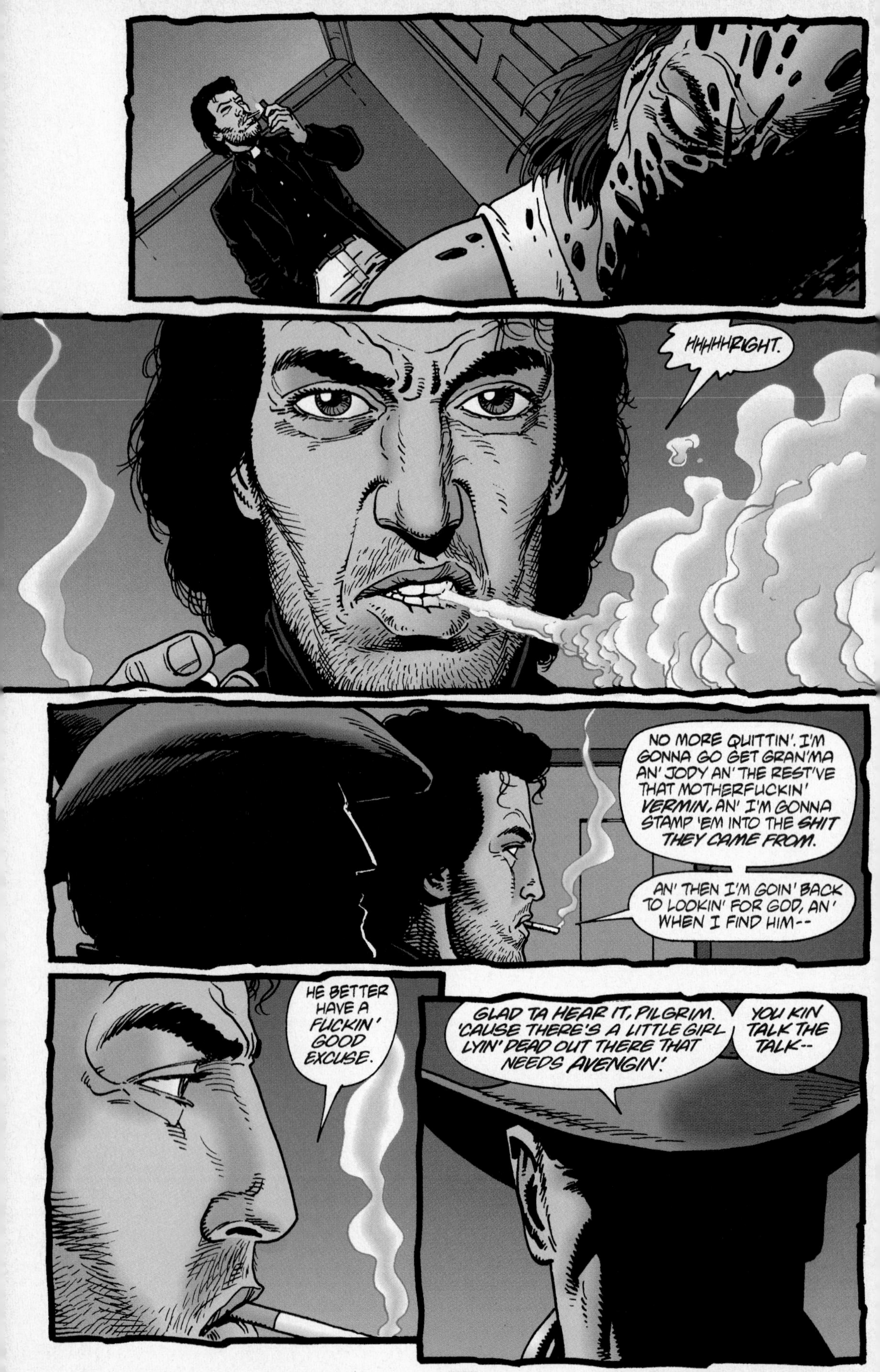
HHHHHRIGHT.
NO MORE QUITTIN'. I'M GONNA GO GET GRAN'MA AN' JODY AN' THE REST'VE THAT MOTHERFUCKIN' VERMIN, AN' I'M GONNA STAMP 'EM INTO THE SHIT THEY CAME FROM.
AN' THEN I'M GOIN' BACK TO LOOKIN' FOR GOD, AN' WHEN I FIND HIM--
HE BETTER HAVE A FUCKIN' GOOD EXCUSE.
GLAD TA HEAR IT, PILGRIM. 'CAUSE THERE'S A LITTLE GIRL LYIN' DEAD OUT THERE THAT NEEDS AVENGIN'.
YOU KIN TALK THE TALK--

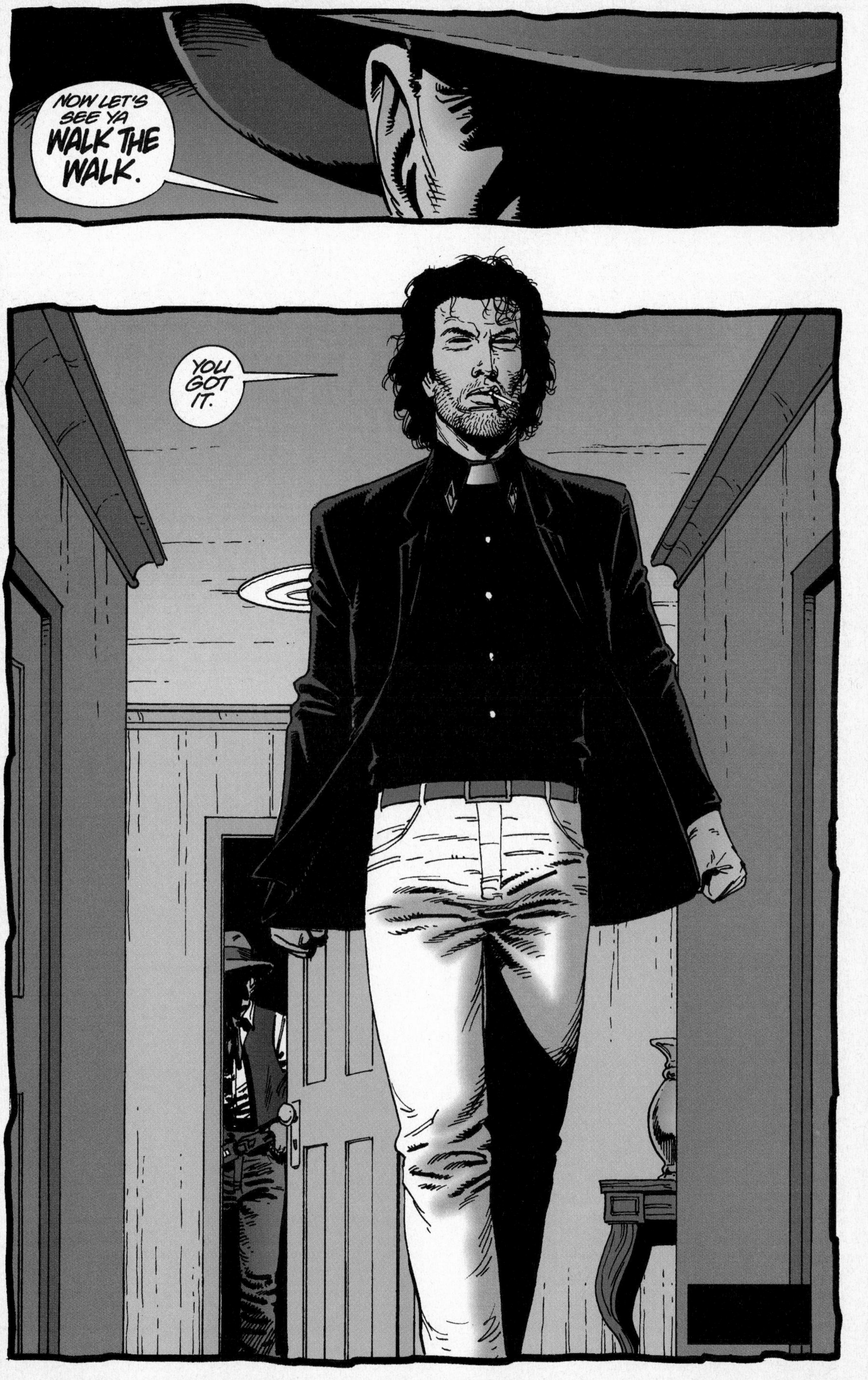

NOW LET'S SEE YA WALK THE WALK.
YOU GOT IT.

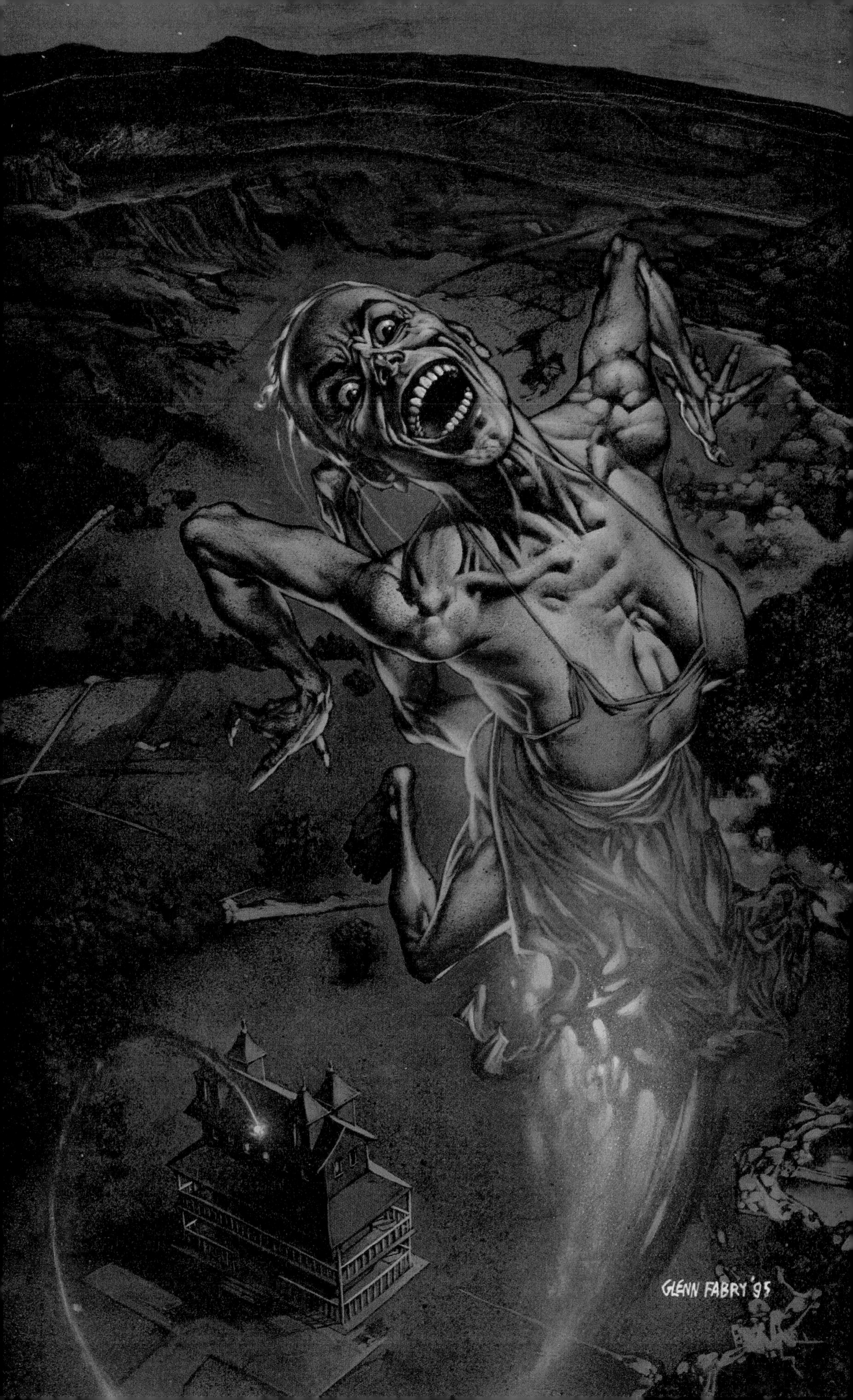
GLENN FABRY '95

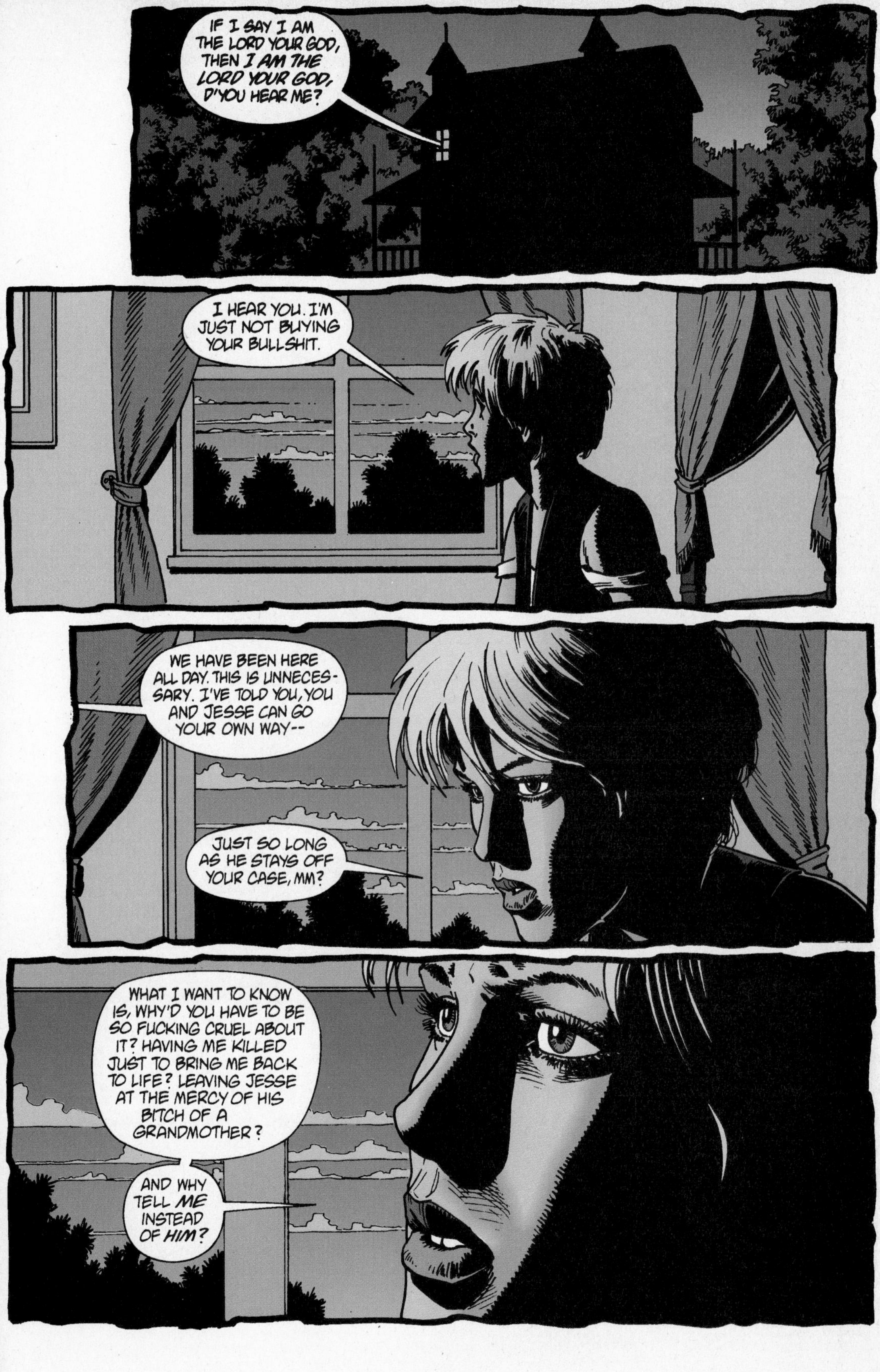
IF I SAY I AM THE LORD YOUR GOD, THEN I AM THE LORD YOUR GOD, D'YOU HEAR ME?
I HEAR YOU. I'M JUST NOT BUYING YOUR BULLSHIT.
WE HAVE BEEN HERE ALL DAY. THIS IS UNNECES-SARY. I'VE TOLD YOU, YOU AND JESSE CAN GO YOUR OWN WAY--
JUST SO LONG AS HE STAYS OFF YOUR CASE, MM?
WHAT I WANT TO KNOW IS, WHY'D YOU HAVE TO BE SO FUCKING CRUEL ABOUT IT? HAVING ME KILLED JUST TO BRING ME BACK TO LIFE? LEAVING JESSE AT THE MERCY OF HIS BITCH OF A GRANDMOTHER?
AND WHY TELL ME INSTEAD OF HIM?

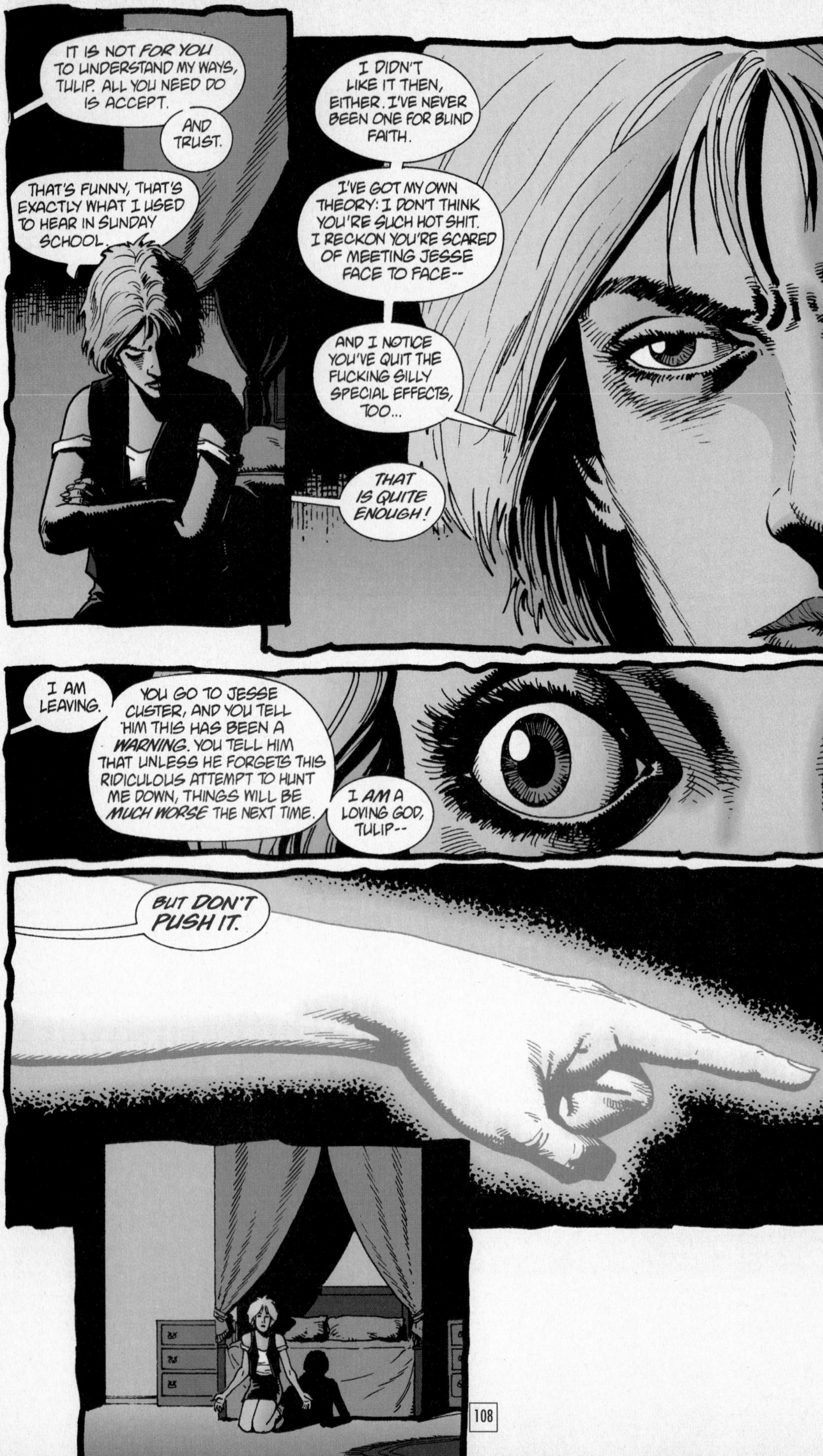
IT IS NOT FOR YOU TO UNDERSTAND MY WAYS, TULIP. ALL YOU NEED DO IS ACCEPT.
AND TRUST.
THAT'S FUNNY, THAT'S EXACTLY WHAT I USED TO HEAR IN SUNDAY SCHOOL.
I DIDN'T LIKE IT THEN, EITHER. I'VE NEVER BEEN ONE FOR BLIND FAITH.
I'VE GOT MY OWN THEORY: I DON'T THINK YOU'RE SUCH HOT SHIT. I RECKON YOU'RE SCARED OF MEETING JESSE FACE TO FACE--
AND I NOTICE YOU'VE QUIT THE FUCKING SILLY SPECIAL EFFECTS, TOO...
THAT IS QUITE ENOUGH!
I AM LEAVING.
YOU GO TO JESSE CUSTER, AND YOU TELL HIM THIS HAS BEEN A WARNING. YOU TELL HIM THAT UNLESS HE FORGETS THIS RIDICULOUS ATTEMPT TO HUNT ME DOWN, THINGS WILL BE MUCH WORSE THE NEXT TIME.
I AM A LOVING GOD, TULIP--
BUT DON'T PUSH IT.

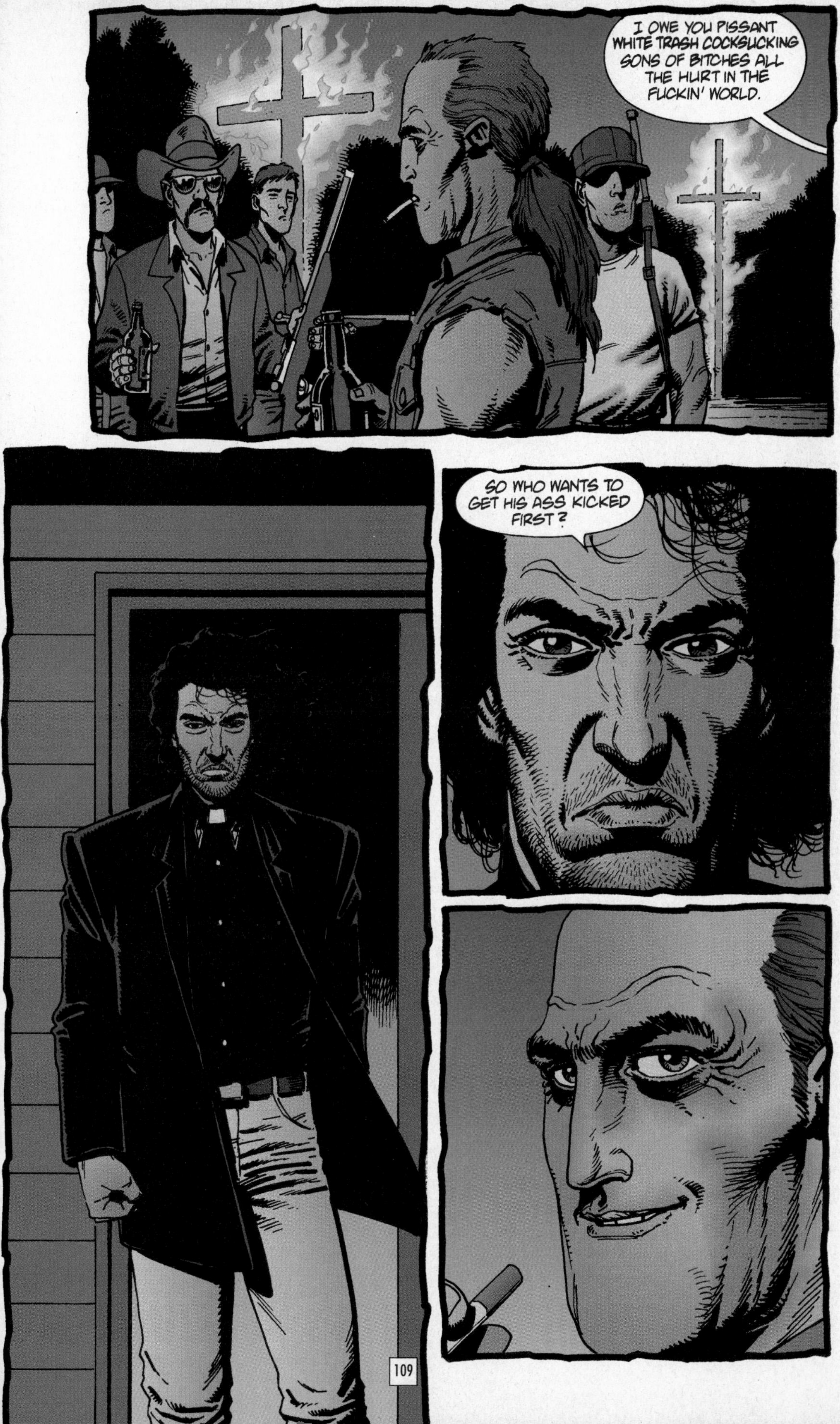
I OWE YOU PISSANT WHITE TRASH COCKSUCKING SONS OF BITCHES ALL THE HURT IN THE FUCKIN' WORLD.
SO WHO WANTS TO GET HIS ASS KICKED FIRST?

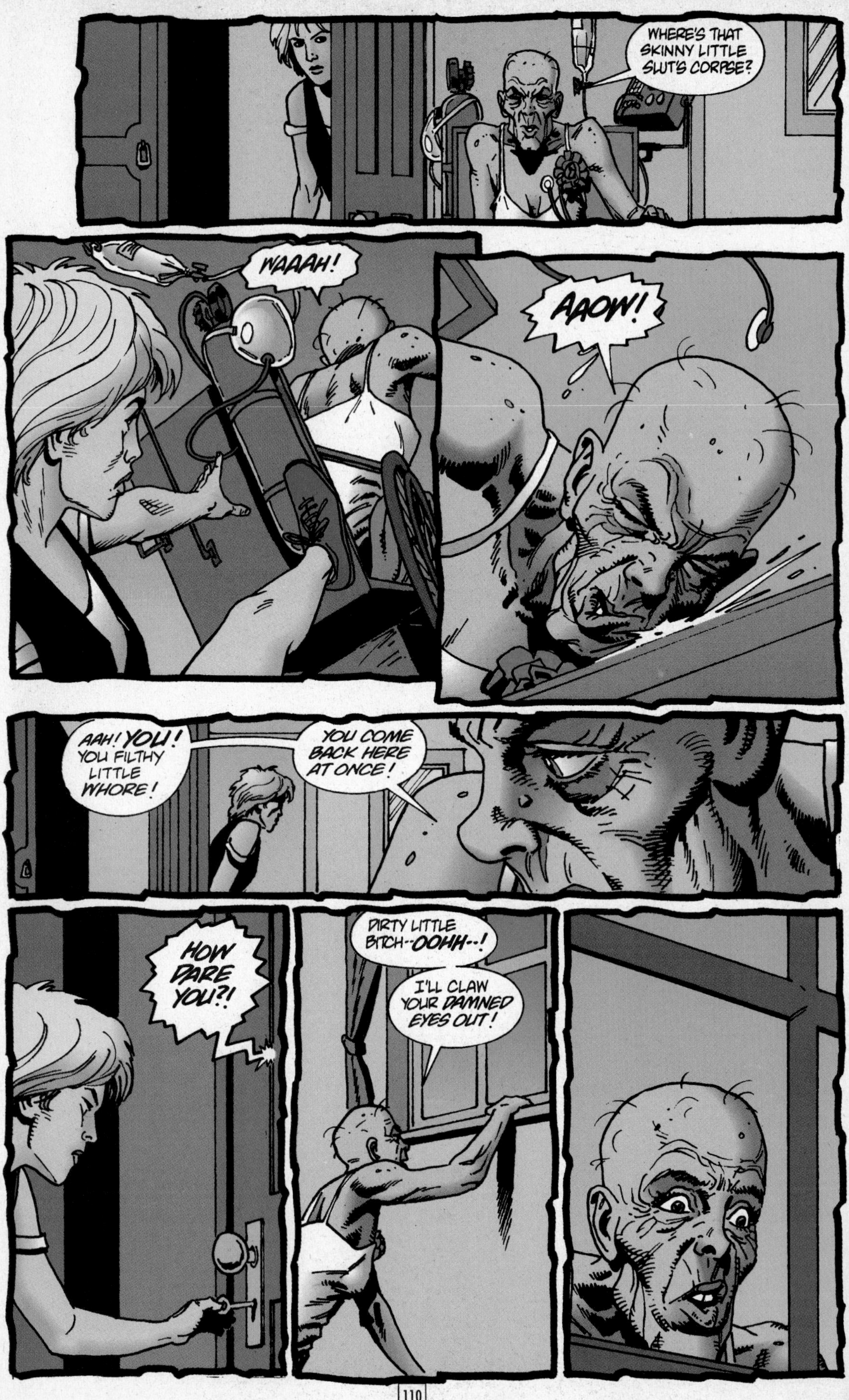
WHERE'S THAT SKINNY LITTLE SLUT'S CORPSE?
WAAAH!
AAOW!
AAH! YOU! YOU FILTHY LITTLE WHORE!
YOU COME BACK HERE AT ONCE!
HOW DARE YOU?!
DIRTY LITTLE BITCH--OOHH--!
I'LL CLAW YOUR DAMNED EYES OUT!

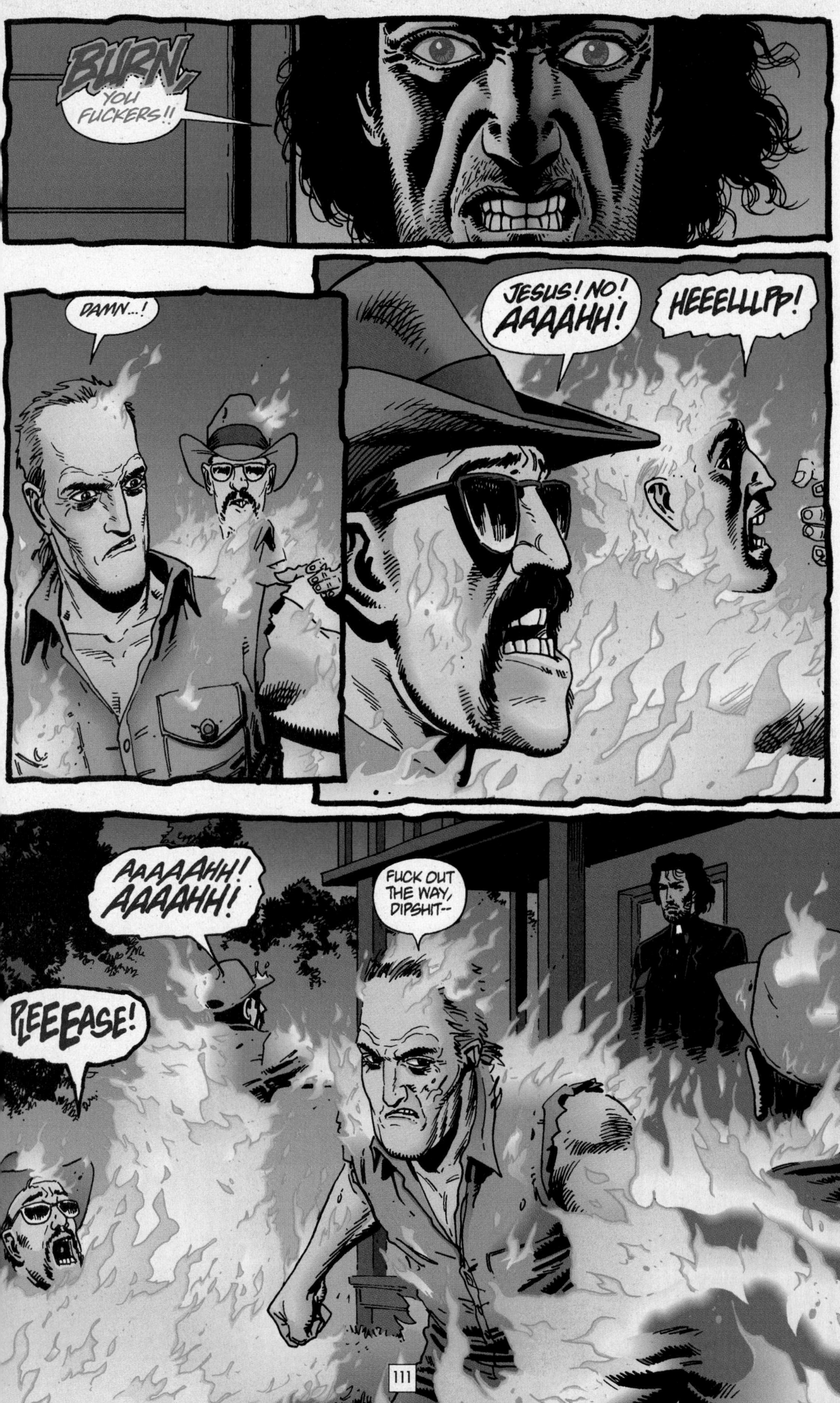
BURN, YOU FUCKERS!!
DAMN...!
JESUS! NO! AAAAHH!
HEEELLLPP!
AAAAAHH! AAAAHH!
FUCK OUT THE WAY, DIPSHIT--
PLEEEASE!

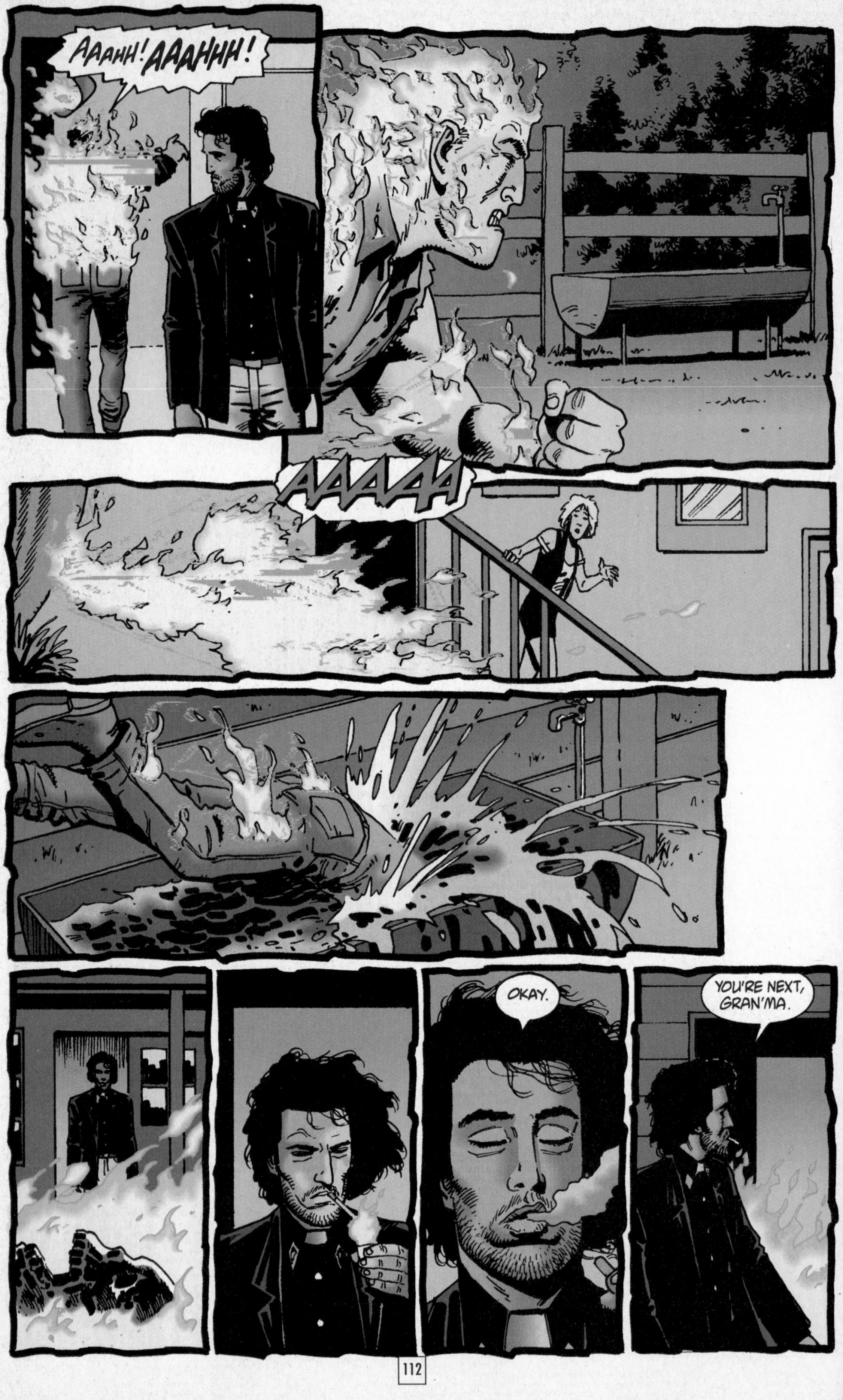
AAAHH! AAAHHH!
AAAAA
OKAY.
YOU'RE NEXT, GRAN'MA.

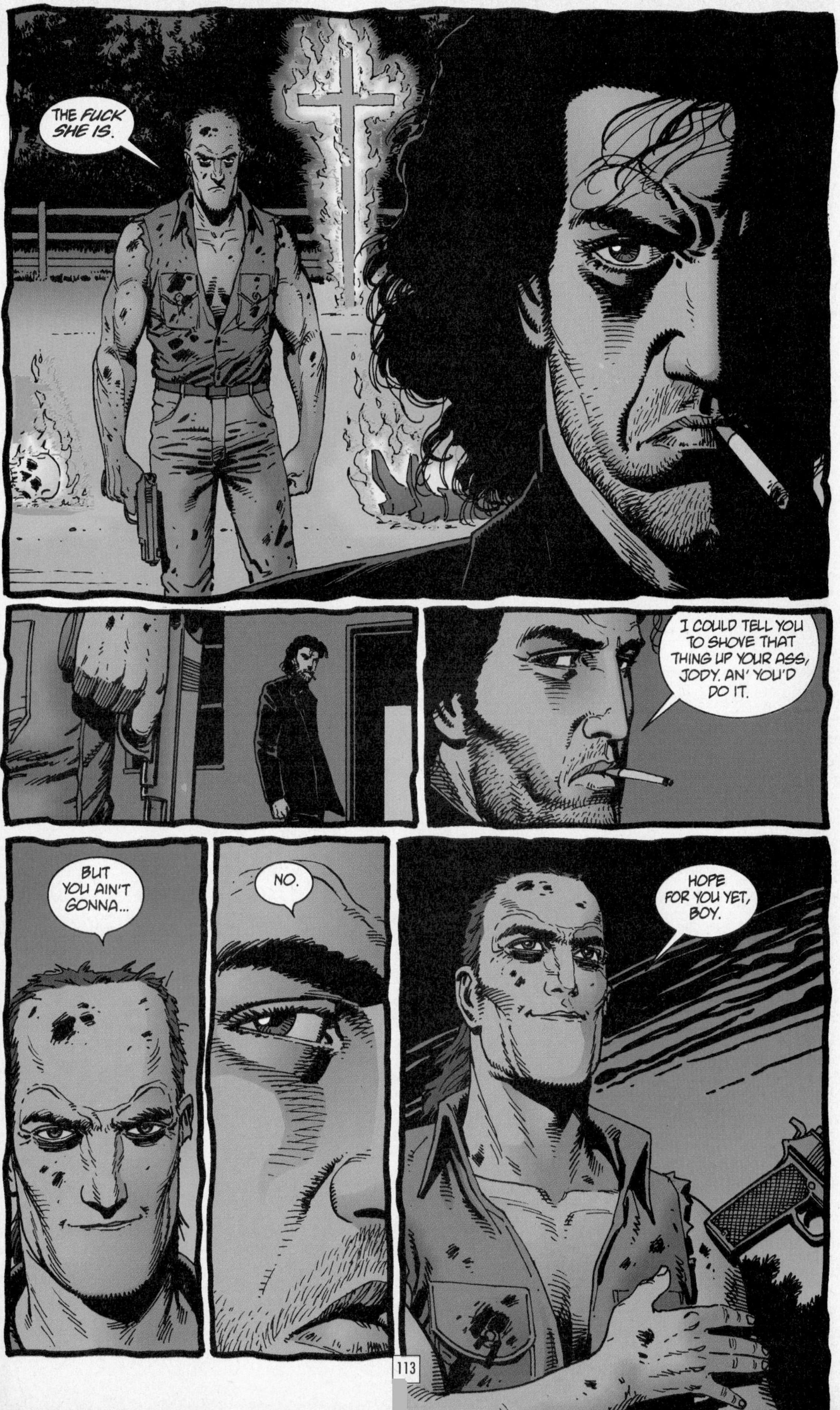
THE FUCK SHE IS.
I COULD TELL YOU TO SHOVE THAT THING UP YOUR ASS, JODY. AN' YOU'D DO IT.
BUT YOU AIN'T GONNA...
NO.
HOPE FOR YOU YET, BOY.

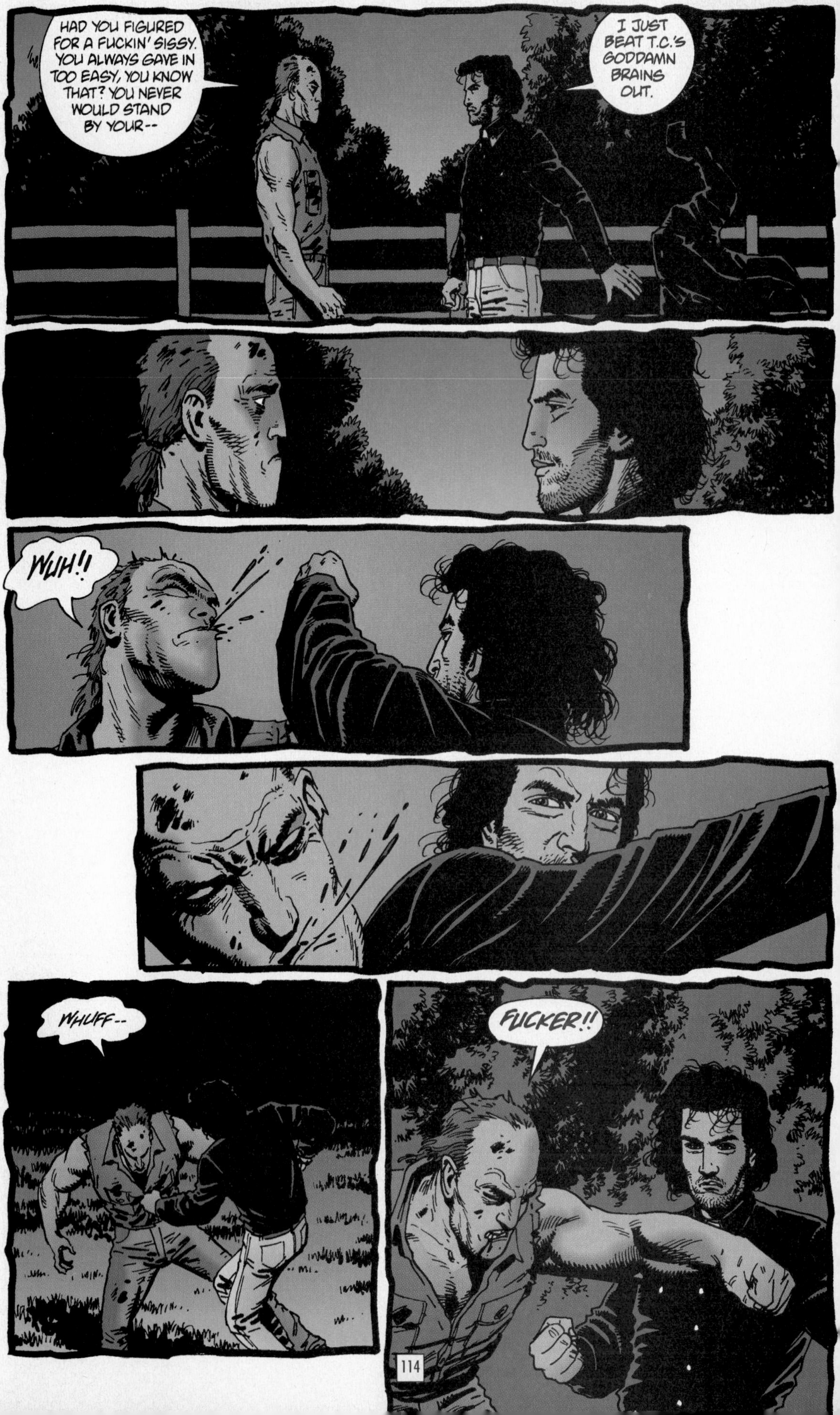
HAD YOU FIGURED FOR A FUCKIN' SISSY. YOU ALWAYS GAVE IN TOO EASY, YOU KNOW THAT? YOU NEVER WOULD STAND BY YOUR--
I JUST BEAT T.C.'S GODDAMN BRAINS OUT.
WUH!!
WHUFF--
FUCKER!!

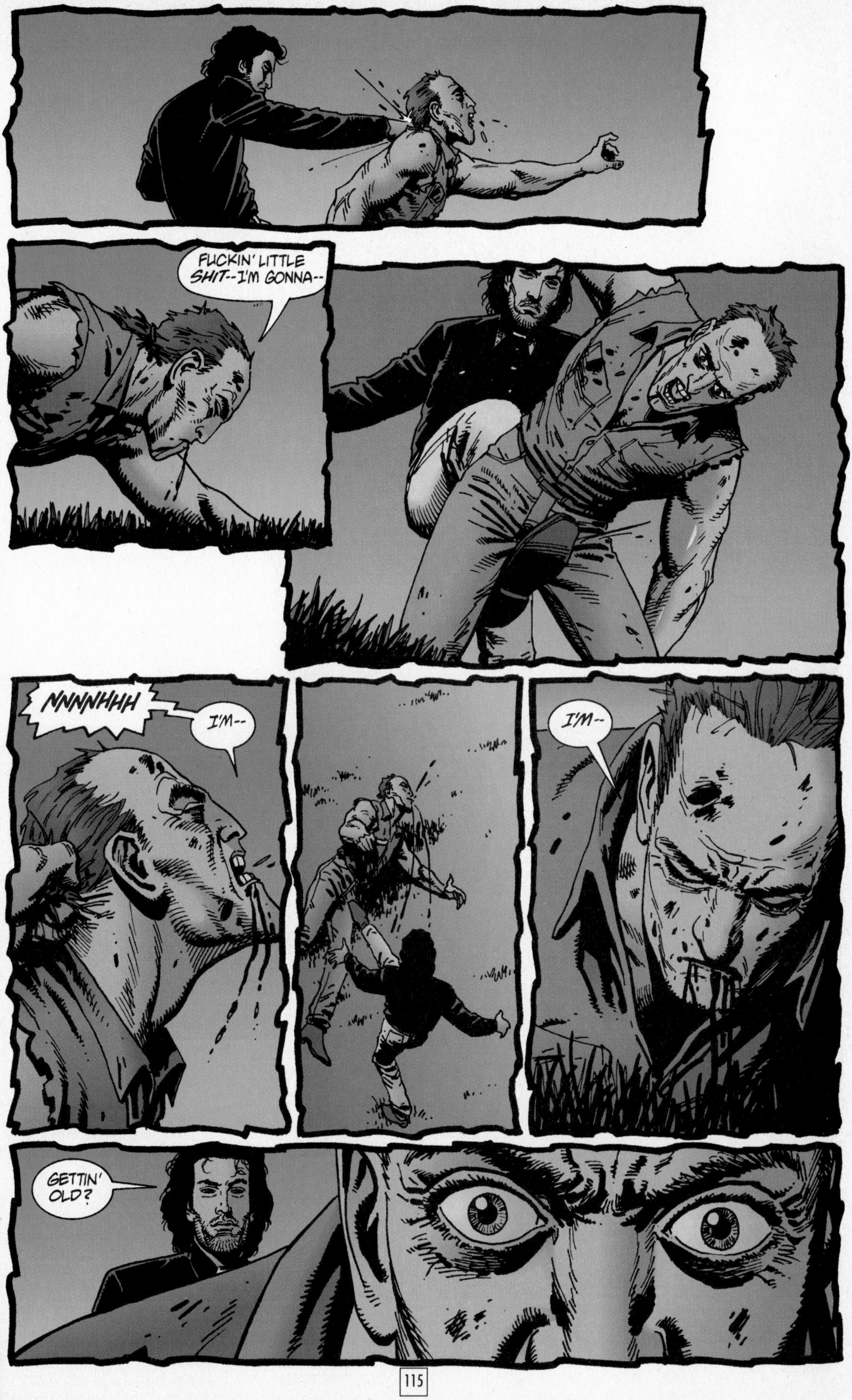
FUCKIN' LITTLE SHIT--I'M GONNA--
NNNNHHH
I'M--
I'M--
GETTIN' OLD?

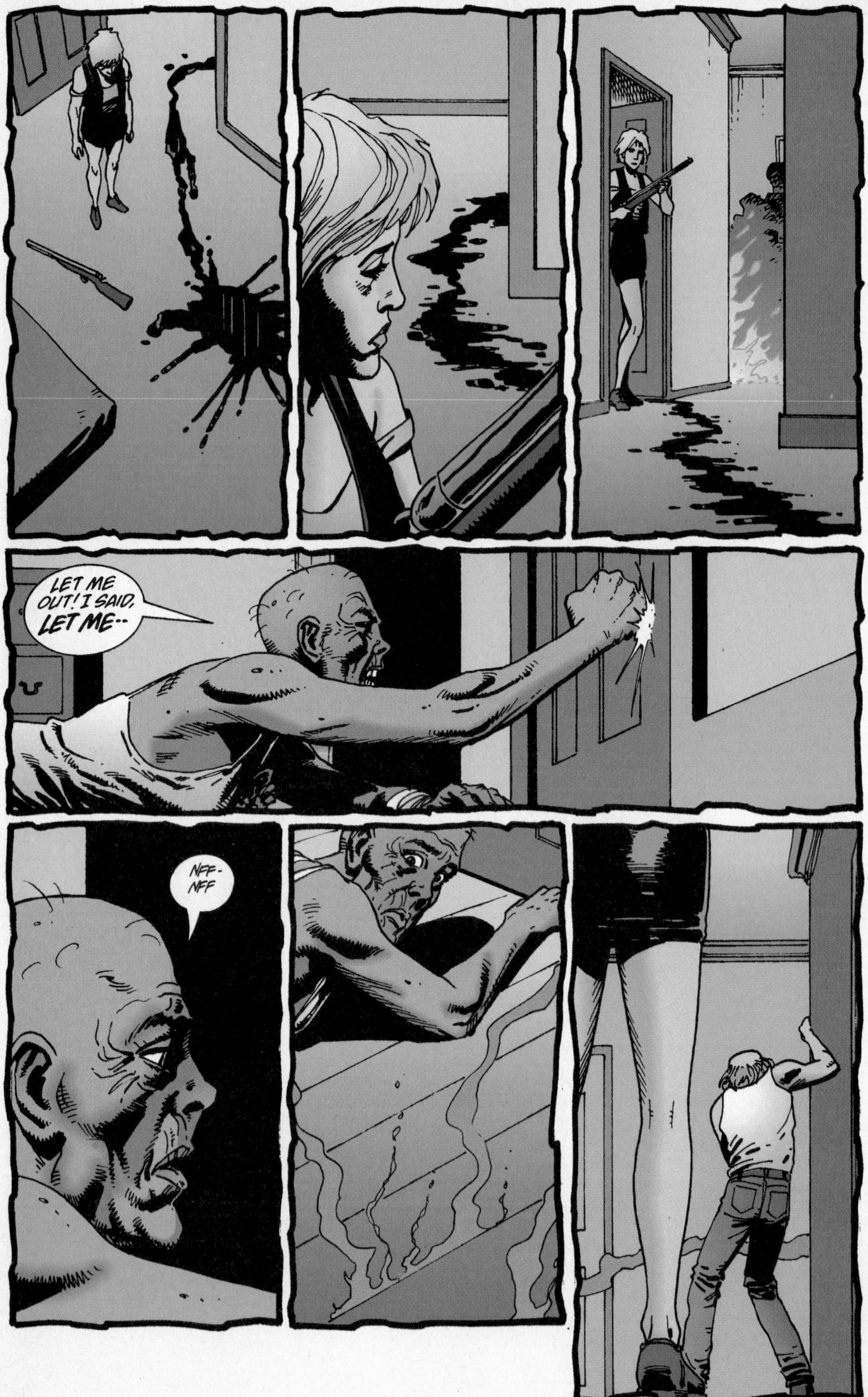
LET ME OUT! I SAID, LET ME--
NFF-NFF

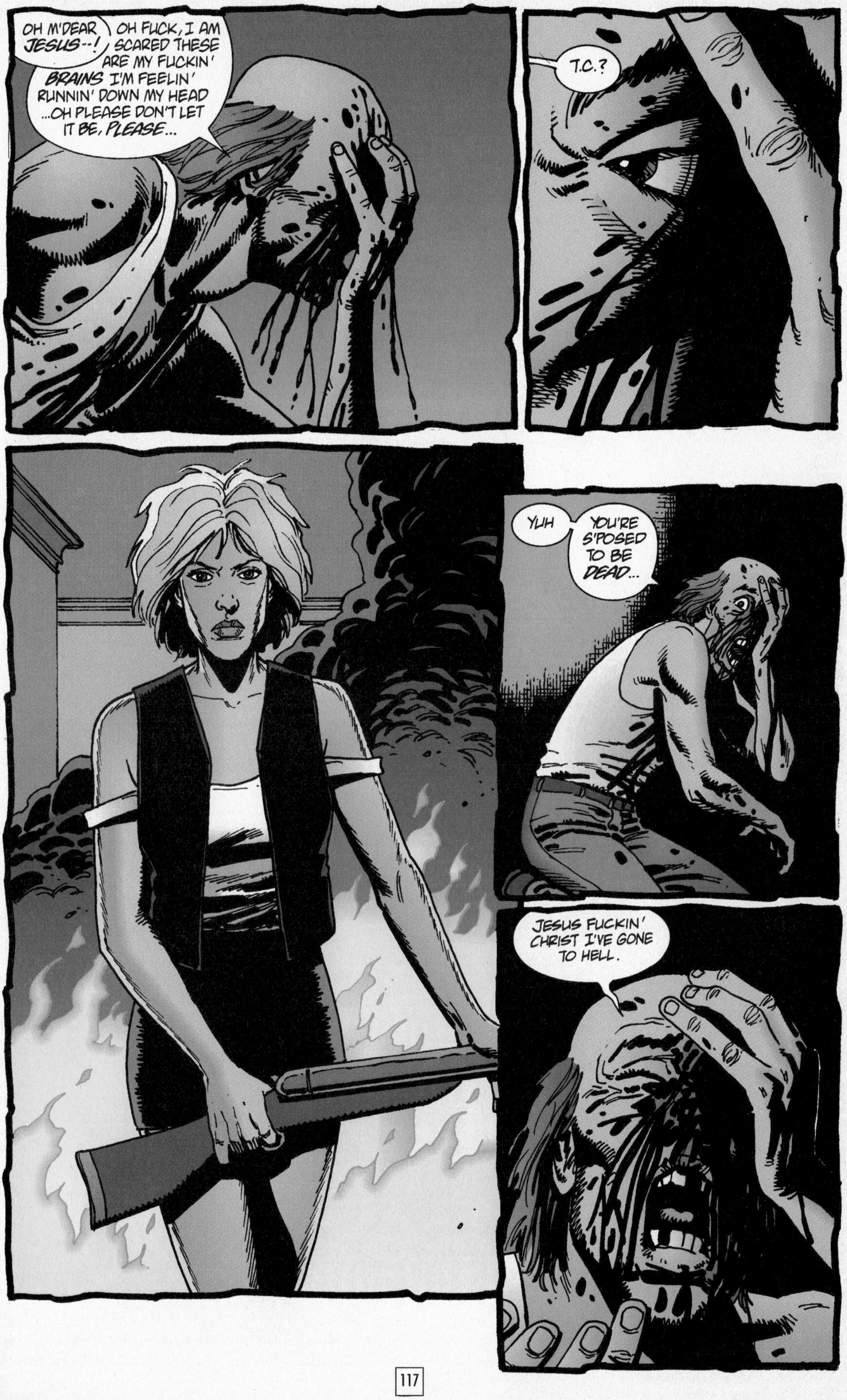
OH M'DEAR JESUS--!
OH FUCK, I AM SCARED THESE ARE MY FUCKIN' BRAINS I'M FEELIN' RUNNIN' DOWN MY HEAD ...OH PLEASE DON'T LET IT BE, PLEASE...
T.C.?
YUH
YOU'RE S'POSED TO BE DEAD...
JESUS FUCKIN' CHRIST I'VE GONE TO HELL.

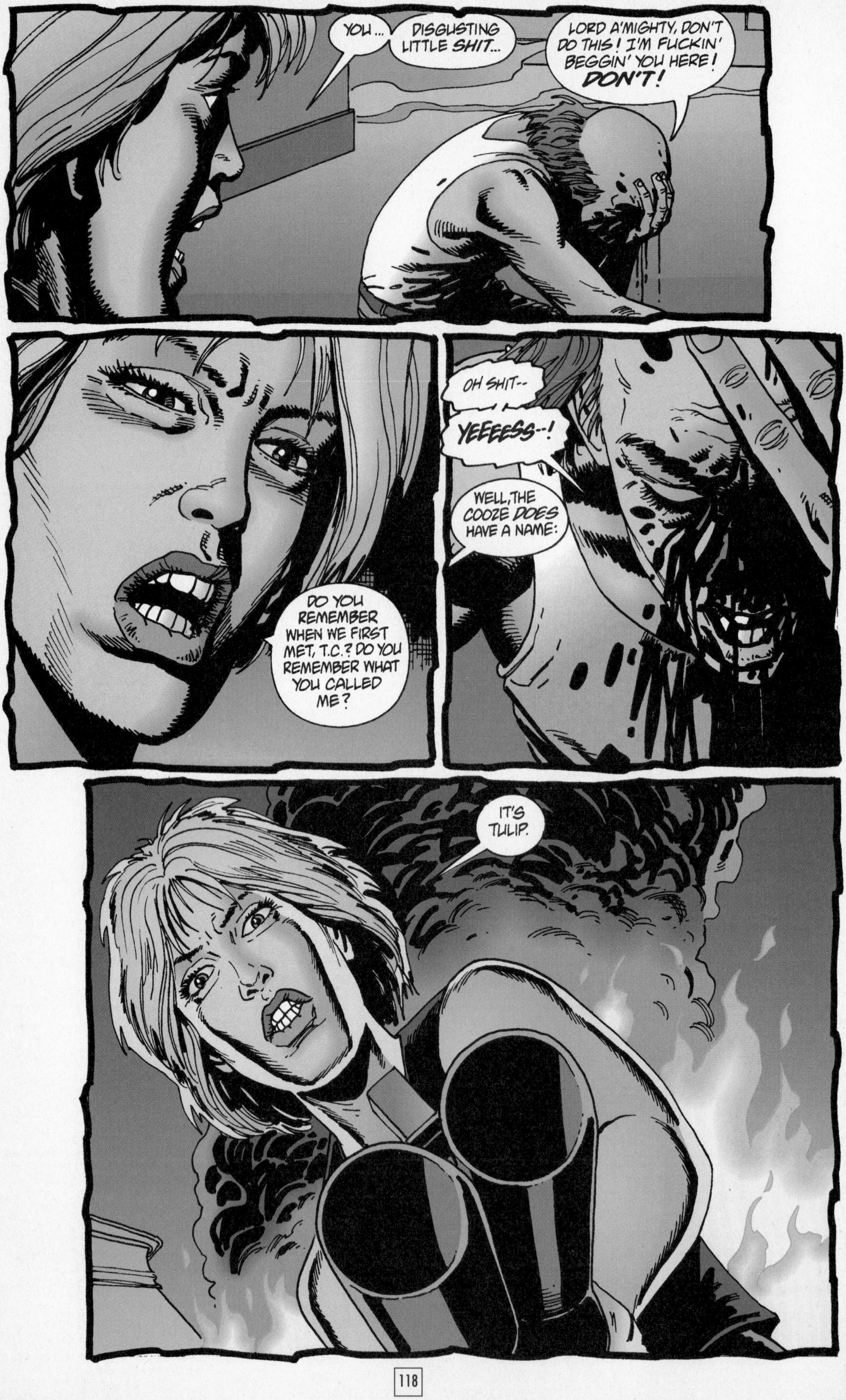
YOU...
DISGUSTING LITTLE SHIT...
LORD A'MIGHTY, DON'T DO THIS! I'M FUCKIN' BEGGIN' YOU HERE! DON'T!
DO YOU REMEMBER WHEN WE FIRST MET, T.C.? DO YOU REMEMBER WHAT YOU CALLED ME?
OH SHIT--
YEEEESS--!
WELL, THE COOZE DOES HAVE A NAME:
IT'S TULIP.

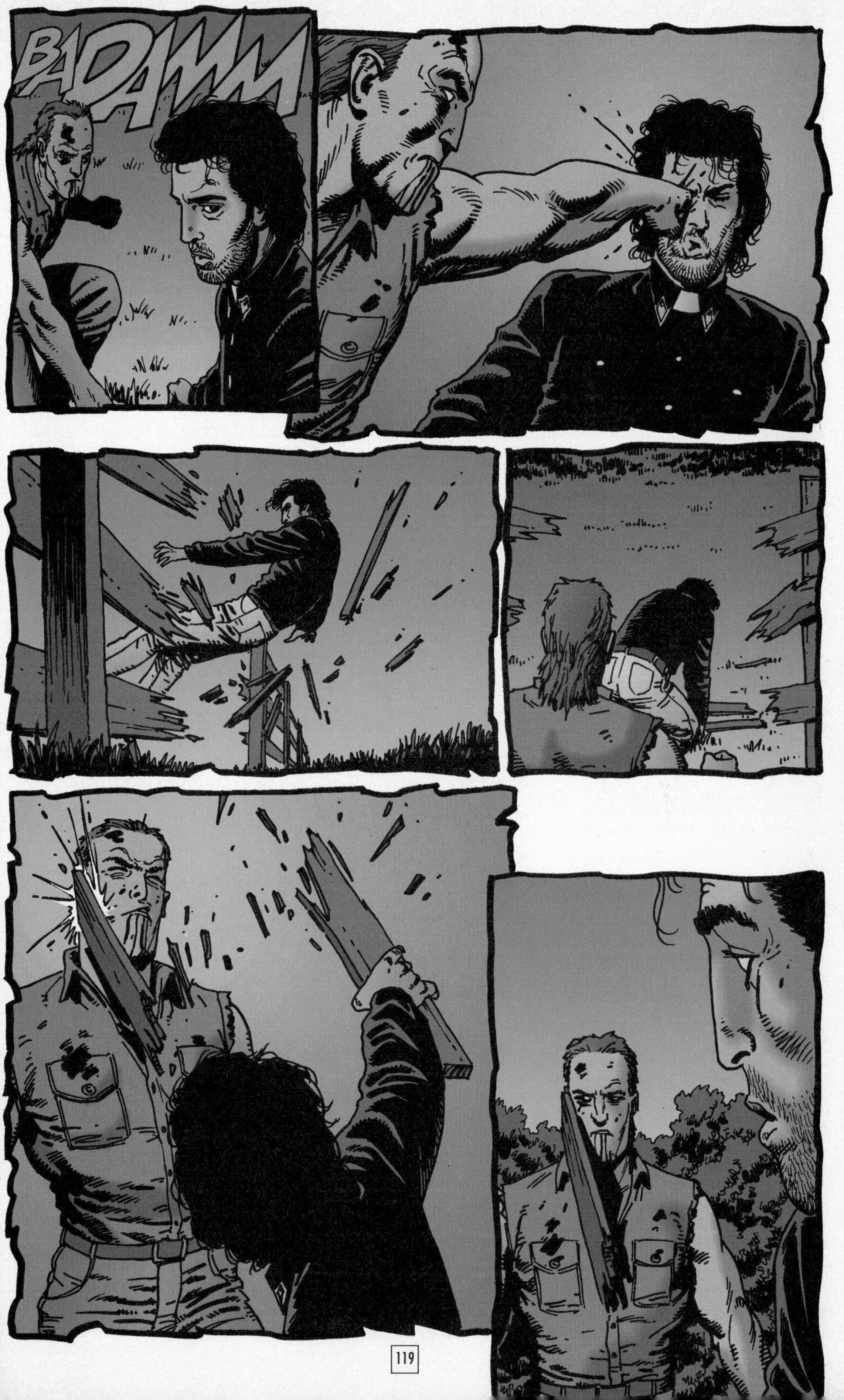
BADAMM

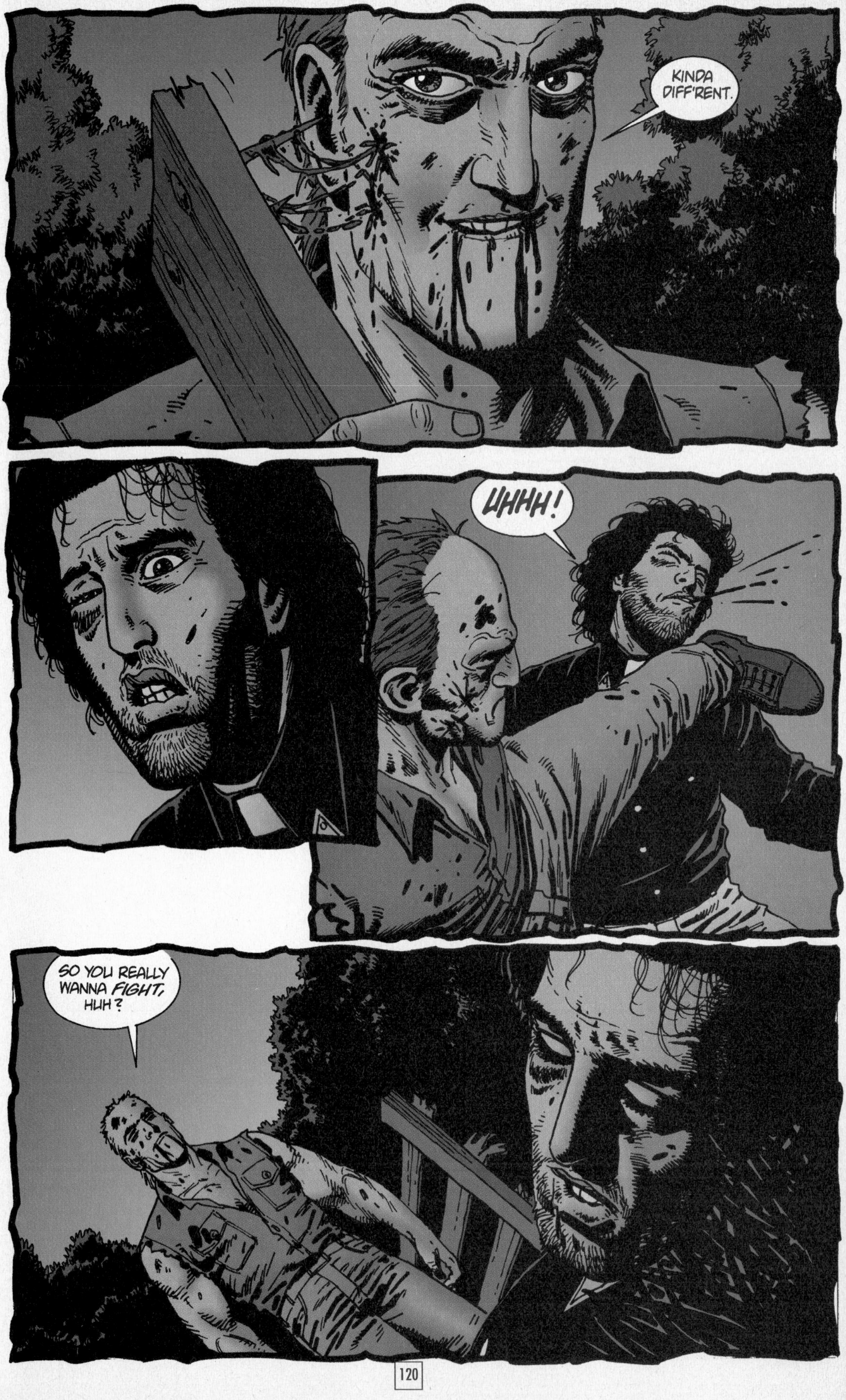
KINDA DIFF'RENT.
UHHH!
SO YOU REALLY WANNA *FIGHT*, HUH?

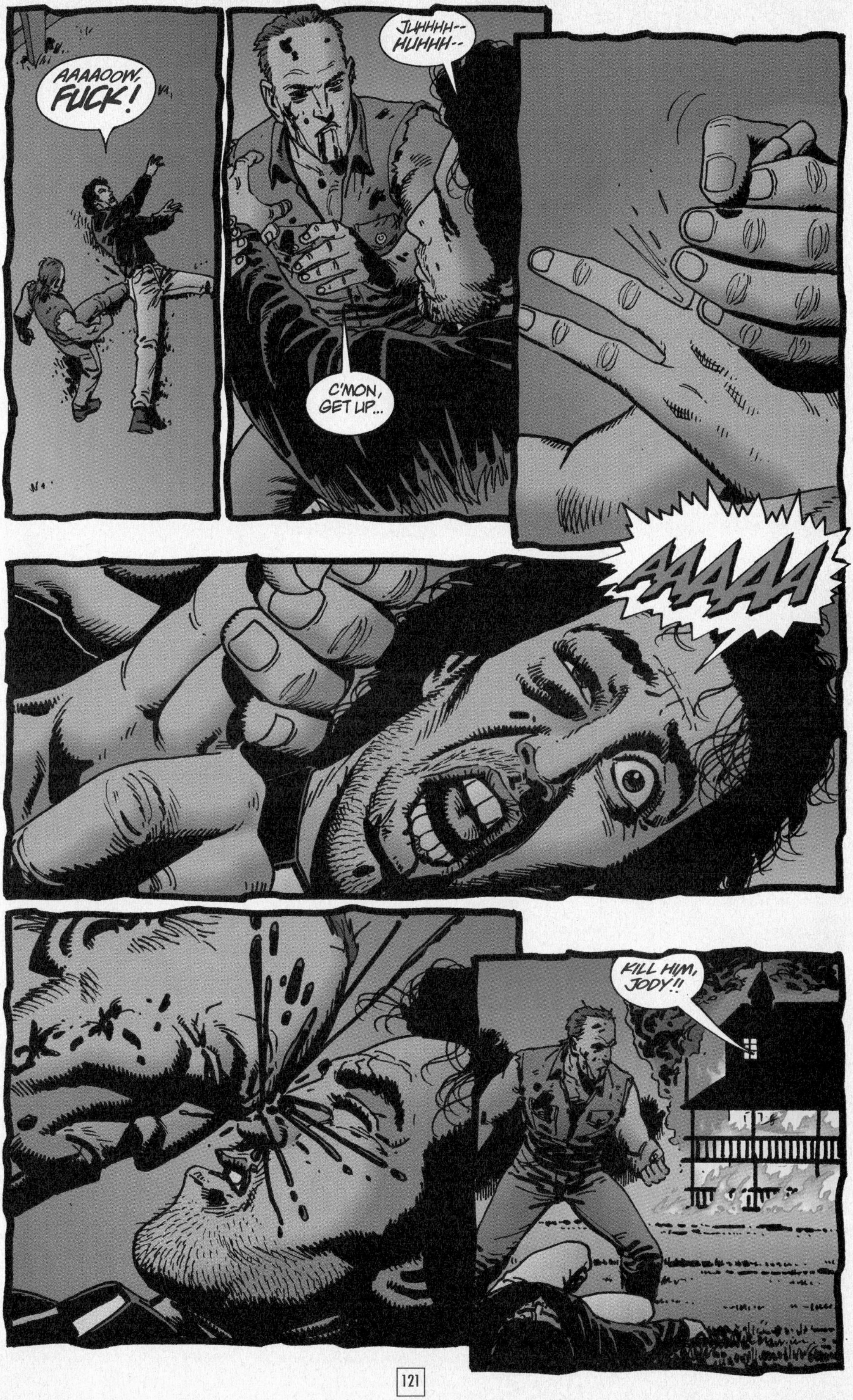
AAAAOOW, FUCK!
JUHHHH-- HUHHH--
C'MON, GET UP...
AAAAA
KILL HIM, JODY!!

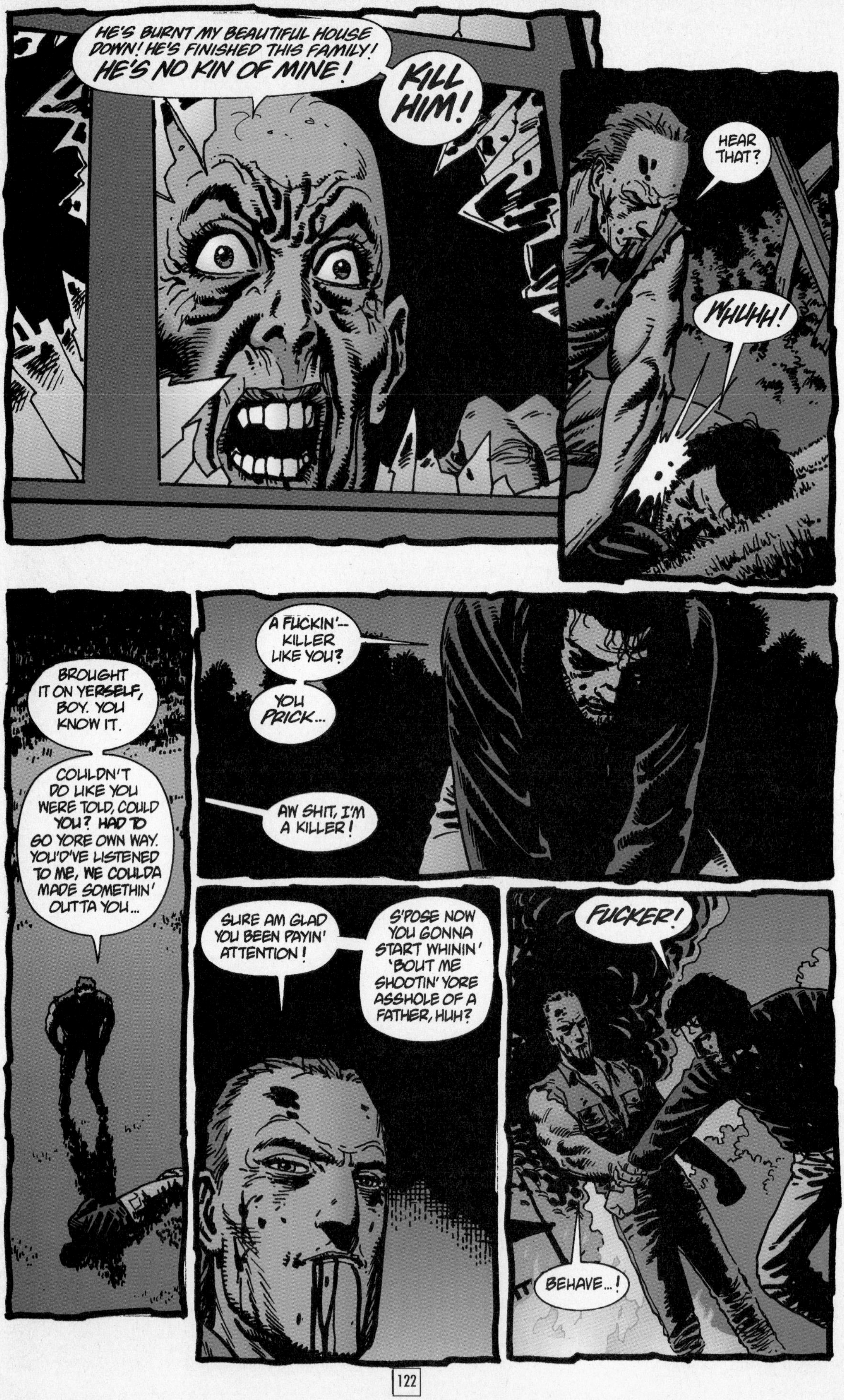
HE'S BURNT MY BEAUTIFUL HOUSE DOWN! HE'S FINISHED THIS FAMILY! HE'S NO KIN OF MINE!
KILL HIM!
HEAR THAT?
WHUHH!
BROUGHT IT ON YERSELF, BOY. YOU KNOW IT.
COULDN'T DO LIKE YOU WERE TOLD, COULD YOU? HAD TO GO YORE OWN WAY. YOU'D'VE LISTENED TO ME, WE COULDA MADE SOMETHIN' OUTTA YOU...
A FUCKIN'-- KILLER LIKE YOU?
YOU PRICK...
AW SHIT, I'M A KILLER!
SURE AM GLAD YOU BEEN PAYIN' ATTENTION!
S'POSE NOW YOU GONNA START WHININ' 'BOUT ME SHOOTIN' YORE ASSHOLE OF A FATHER, HUH?
FUCKER!
BEHAVE...!

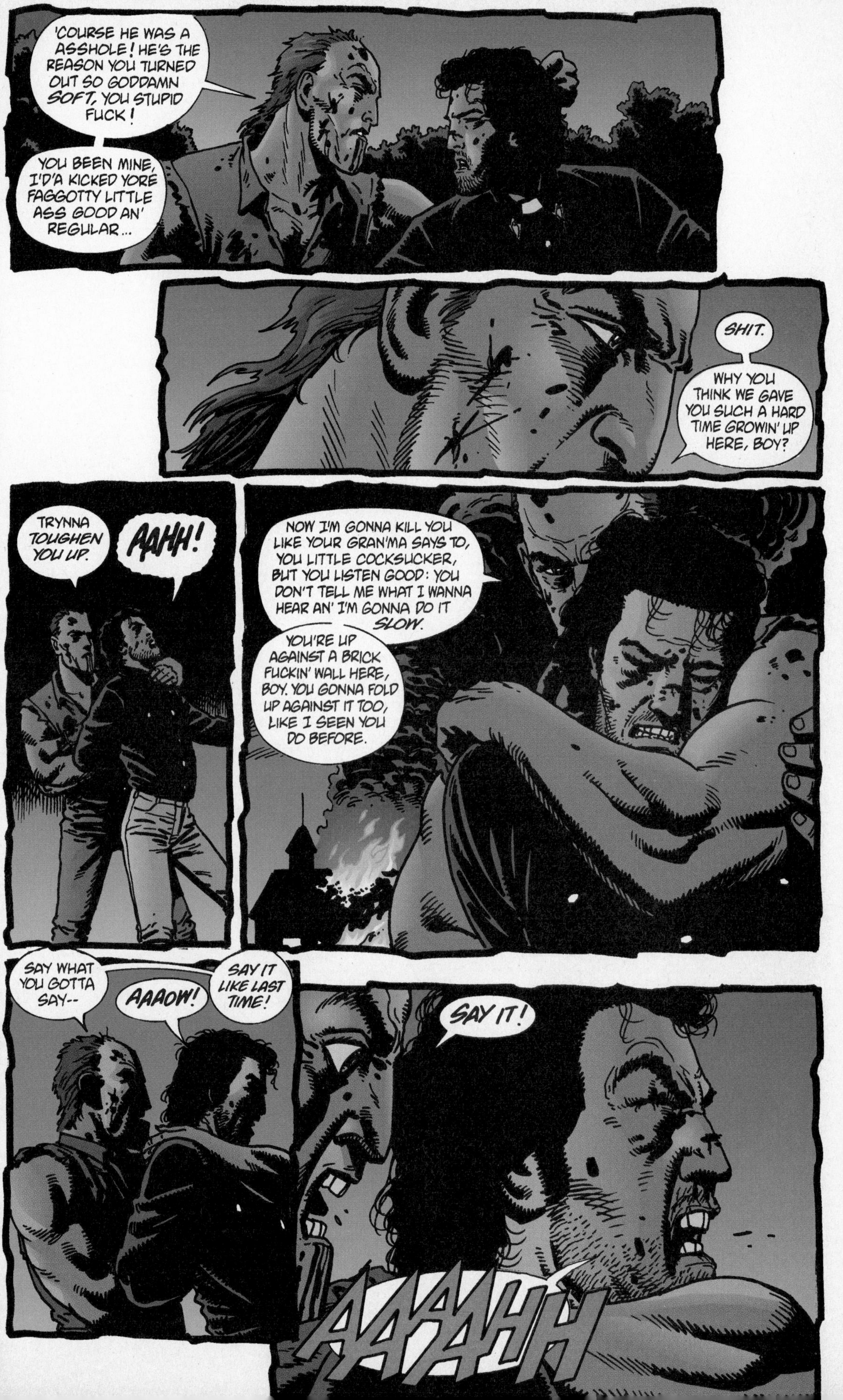
'COURSE HE WAS A ASSHOLE! HE'S THE REASON YOU TURNED OUT SO GODDAMN SOFT, YOU STUPID FUCK!
YOU BEEN MINE, I'D'A KICKED YORE FAGGOTTY LITTLE ASS GOOD AN' REGULAR...
SHIT.
WHY YOU THINK WE GAVE YOU SUCH A HARD TIME GROWIN' UP HERE, BOY?
TRYNNA TOUGHEN YOU UP.
AAHH!
NOW I'M GONNA KILL YOU LIKE YOUR GRAN'MA SAYS TO, YOU LITTLE COCKSUCKER, BUT YOU LISTEN GOOD: YOU DON'T TELL ME WHAT I WANNA HEAR AN' I'M GONNA DO IT SLOW.
YOU'RE UP AGAINST A BRICK FUCKIN' WALL HERE, BOY. YOU GONNA FOLD UP AGAINST IT TOO, LIKE I SEEN YOU DO BEFORE.
SAY WHAT YOU GOTTA SAY--
AAAOW!
SAY IT LIKE LAST TIME!
SAY IT!
AAAAHH

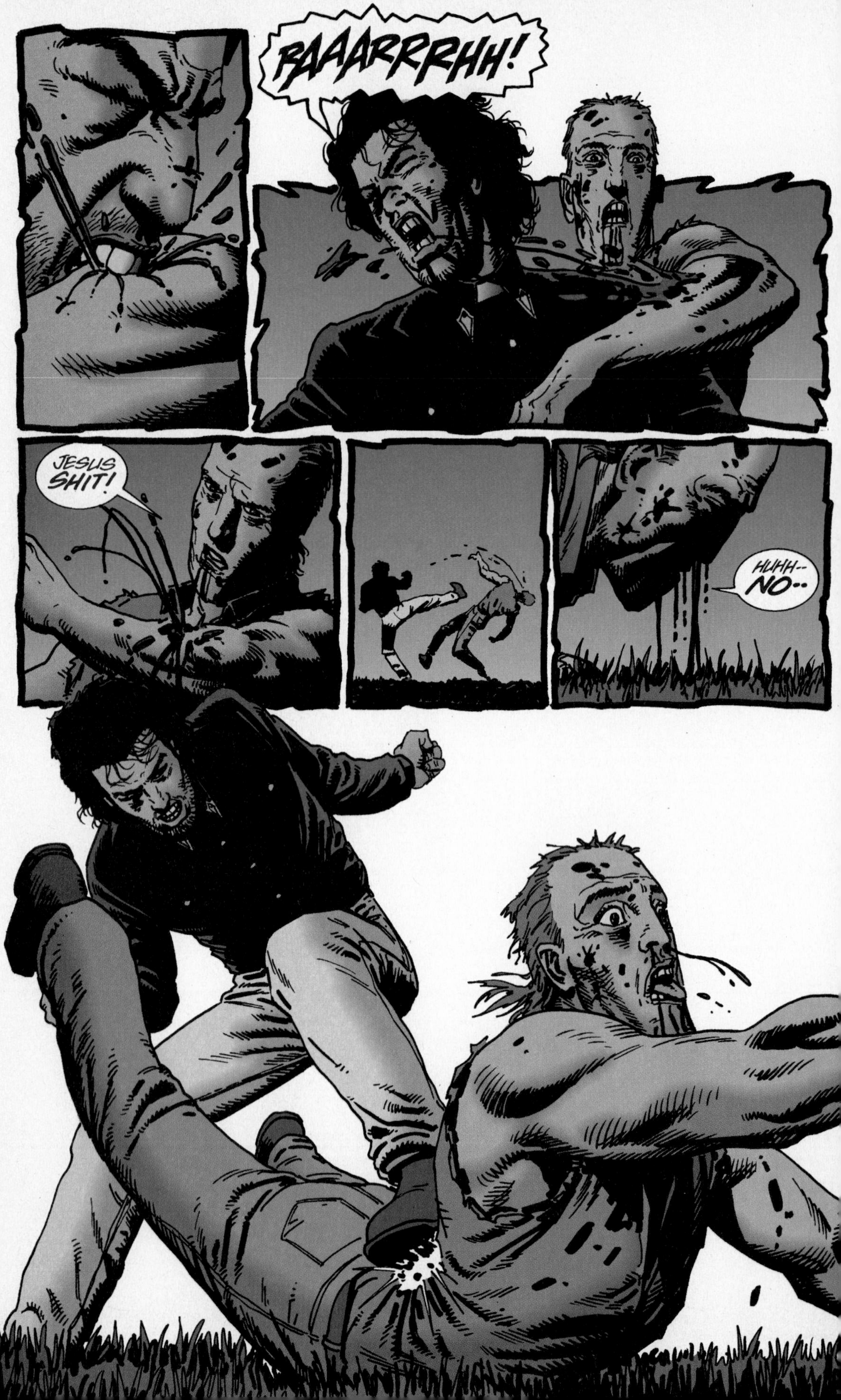
RAAARRRHH!
JESUS SHIT!
HUHH-- NO--

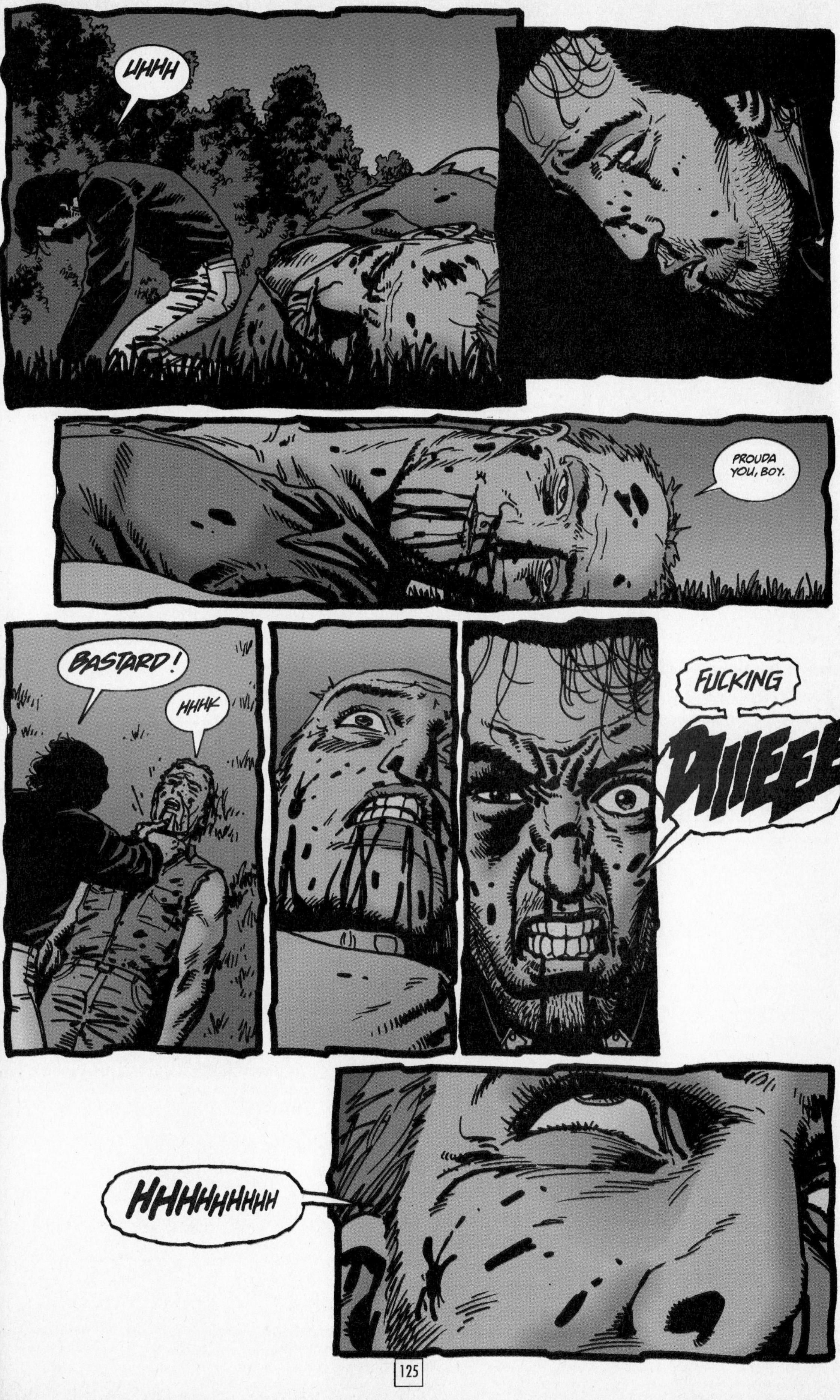
UHHH
PROUDA YOU, BOY.
BASTARD!
HHHK
FUCKING
DIIEEE
HHHHHHHHH

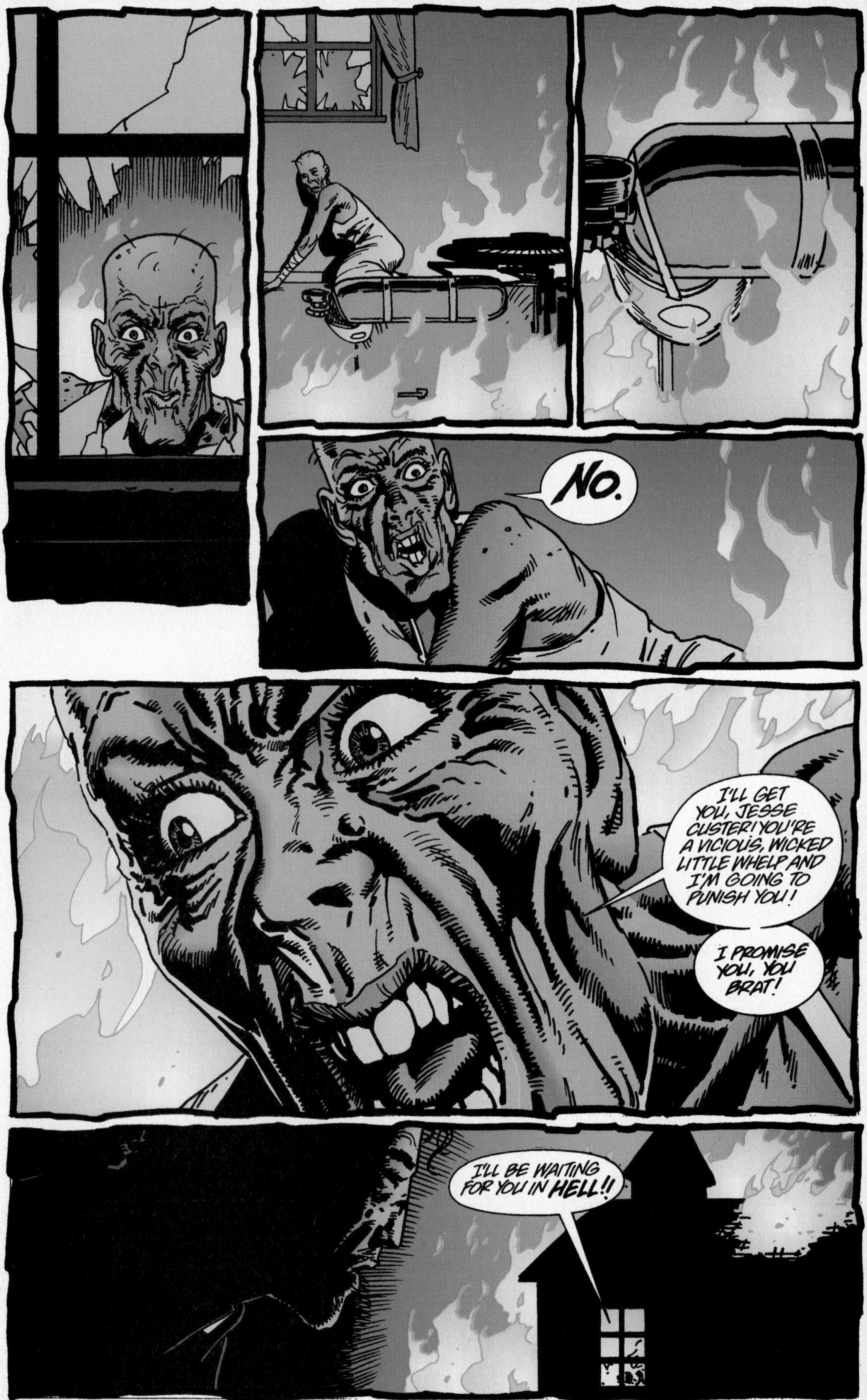
NO.
I'LL GET YOU, JESSE CUSTER! YOU'RE A VICIOUS, WICKED LITTLE WHELP AND I'M GOING TO PUNISH YOU!
I PROMISE YOU, YOU BRAT!
I'LL BE WAITING FOR YOU IN HELL!!

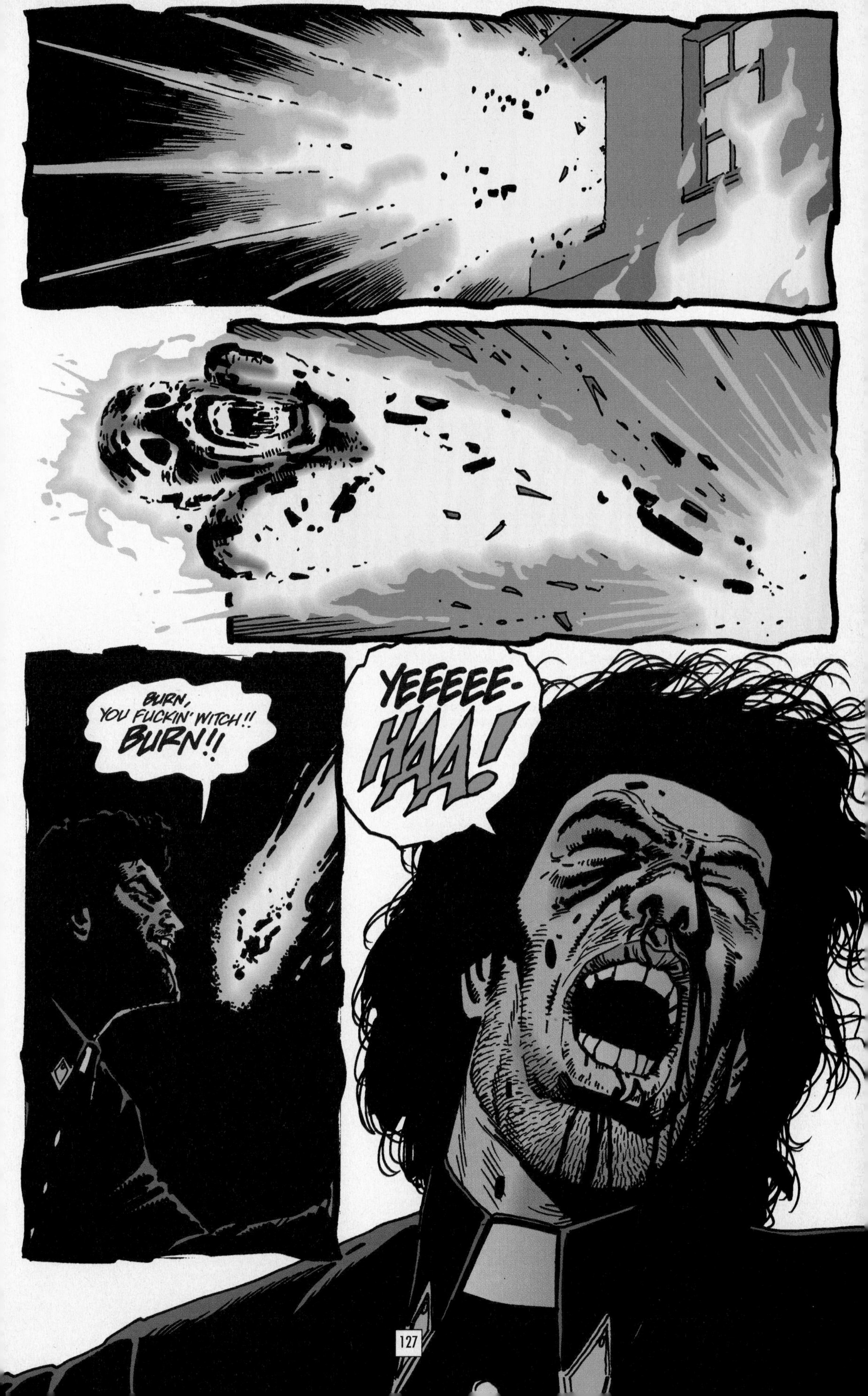
BURN, YOU FUCKIN' WITCH!! BURN!!
YEEEEE-HAA!

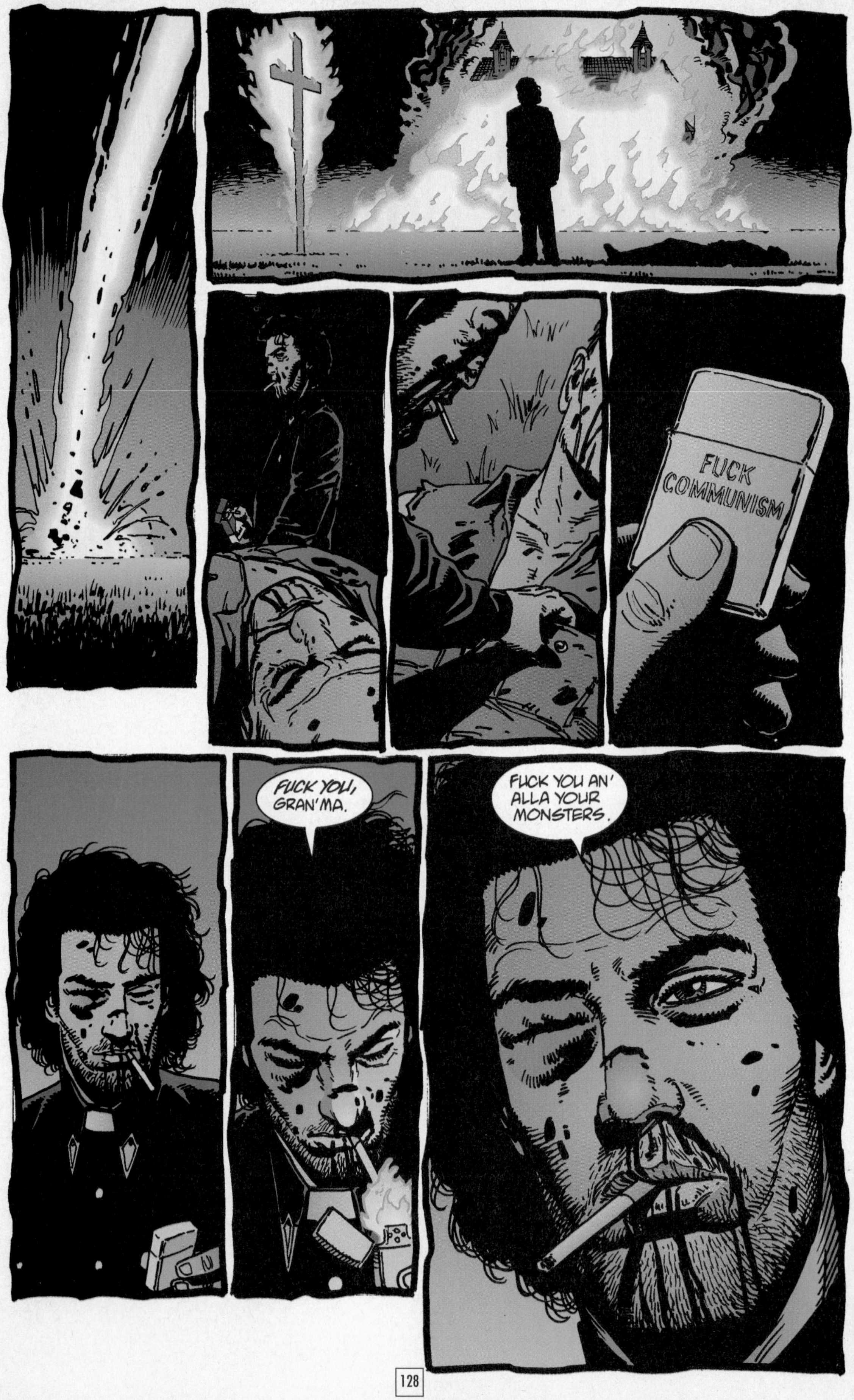
FUCK COMMUNISM
FUCK YOU, GRAN'MA.
FUCK YOU AN' ALLA YOUR MONSTERS.

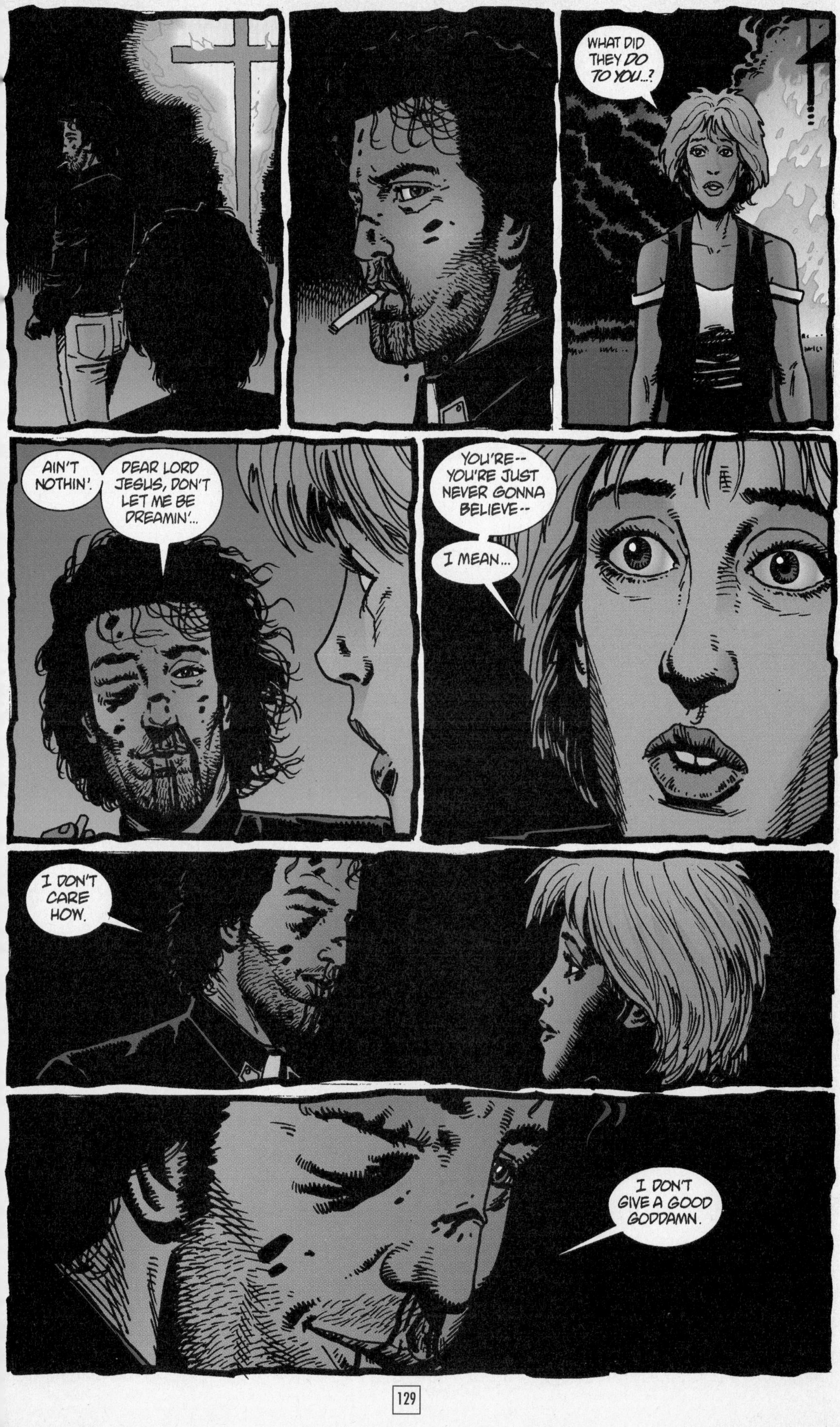
WHAT DID THEY DO TO YOU..?
AIN'T NOTHIN'.
DEAR LORD JESUS, DON'T LET ME BE DREAMIN'...
YOU'RE-- YOU'RE JUST NEVER GONNA BELIEVE--
I MEAN...
I DON'T CARE HOW.
I DON'T GIVE A GOOD GODDAMN.

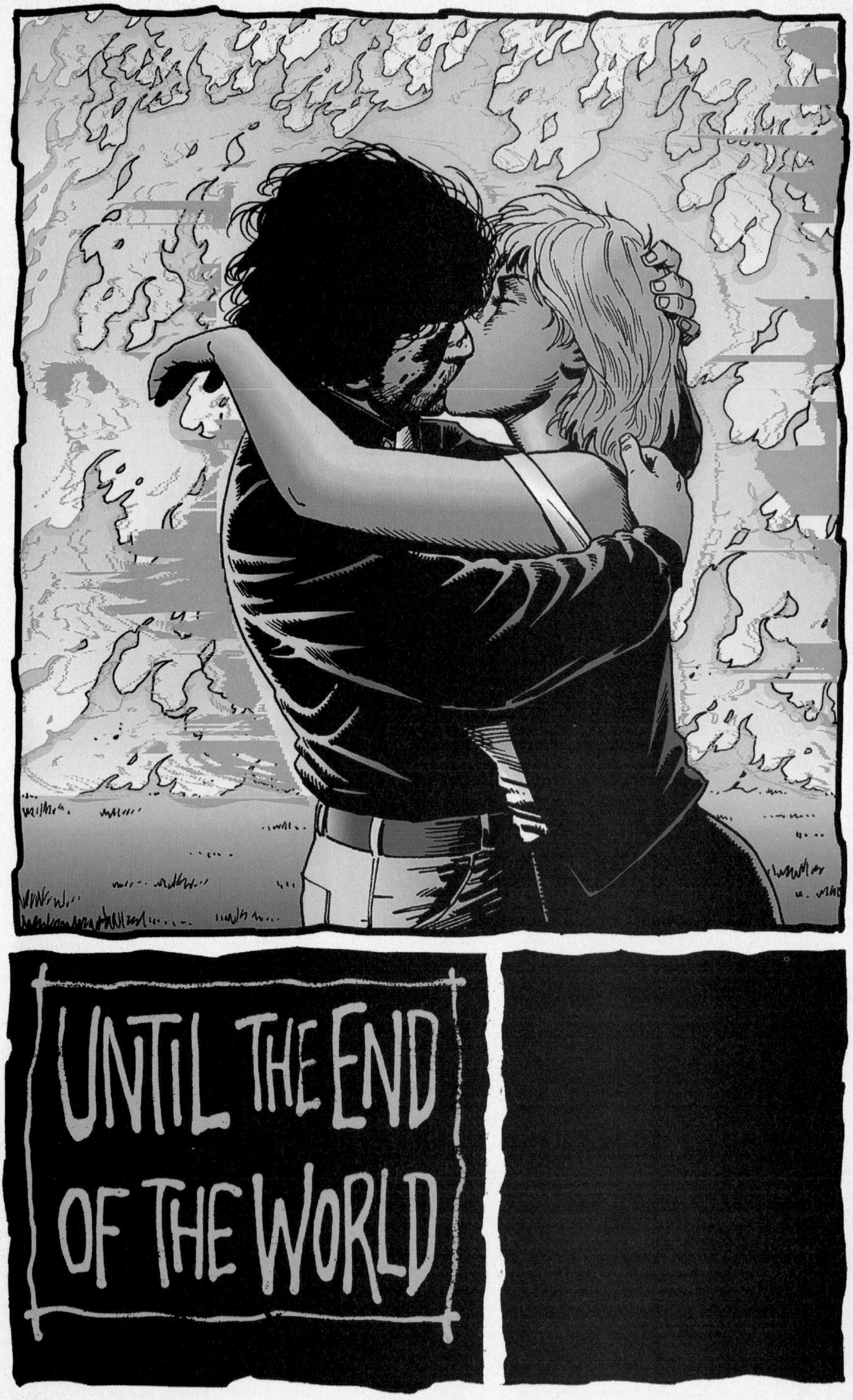
UNTIL THE END OF THE WORLD

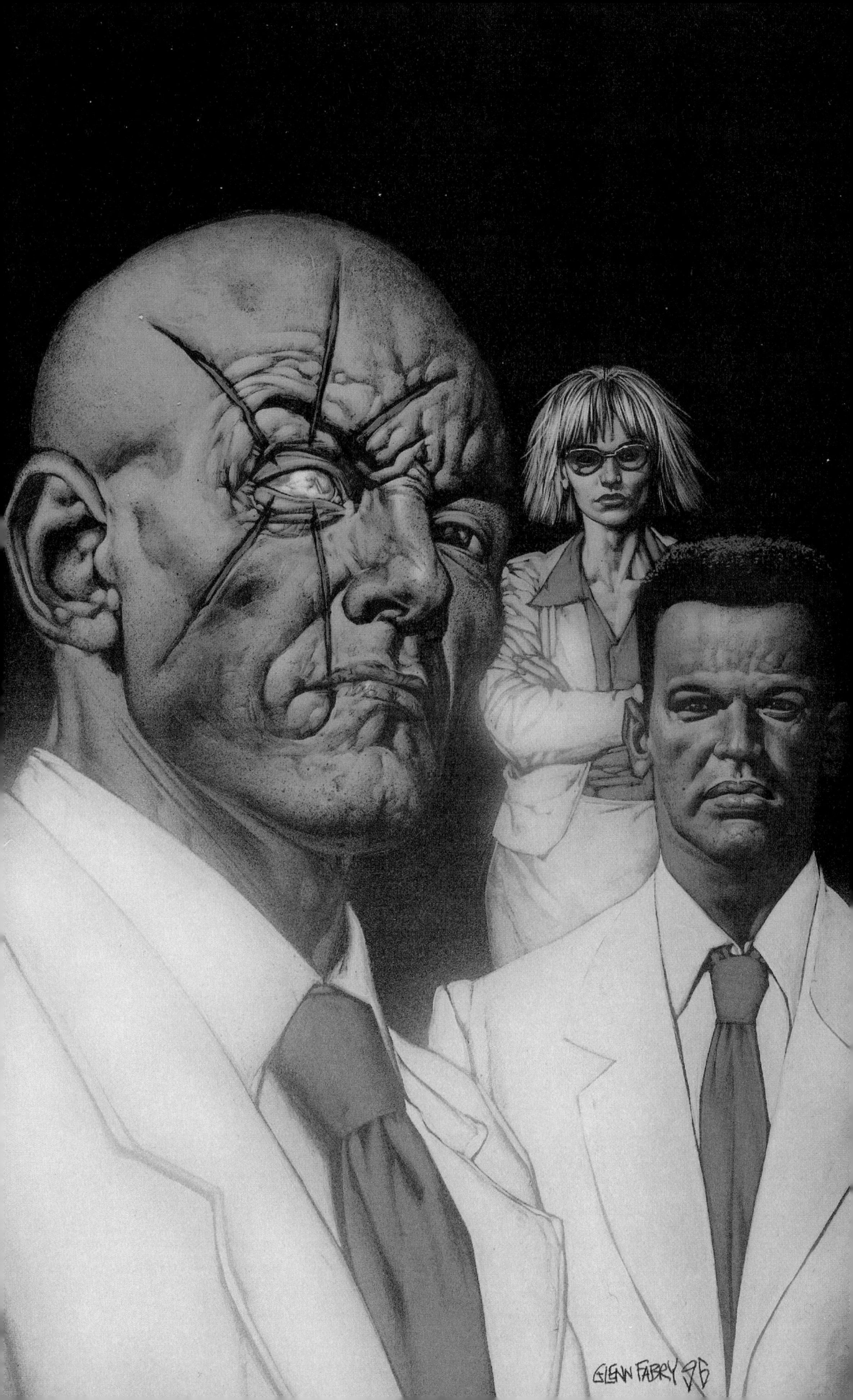
GLENN FABRY 86

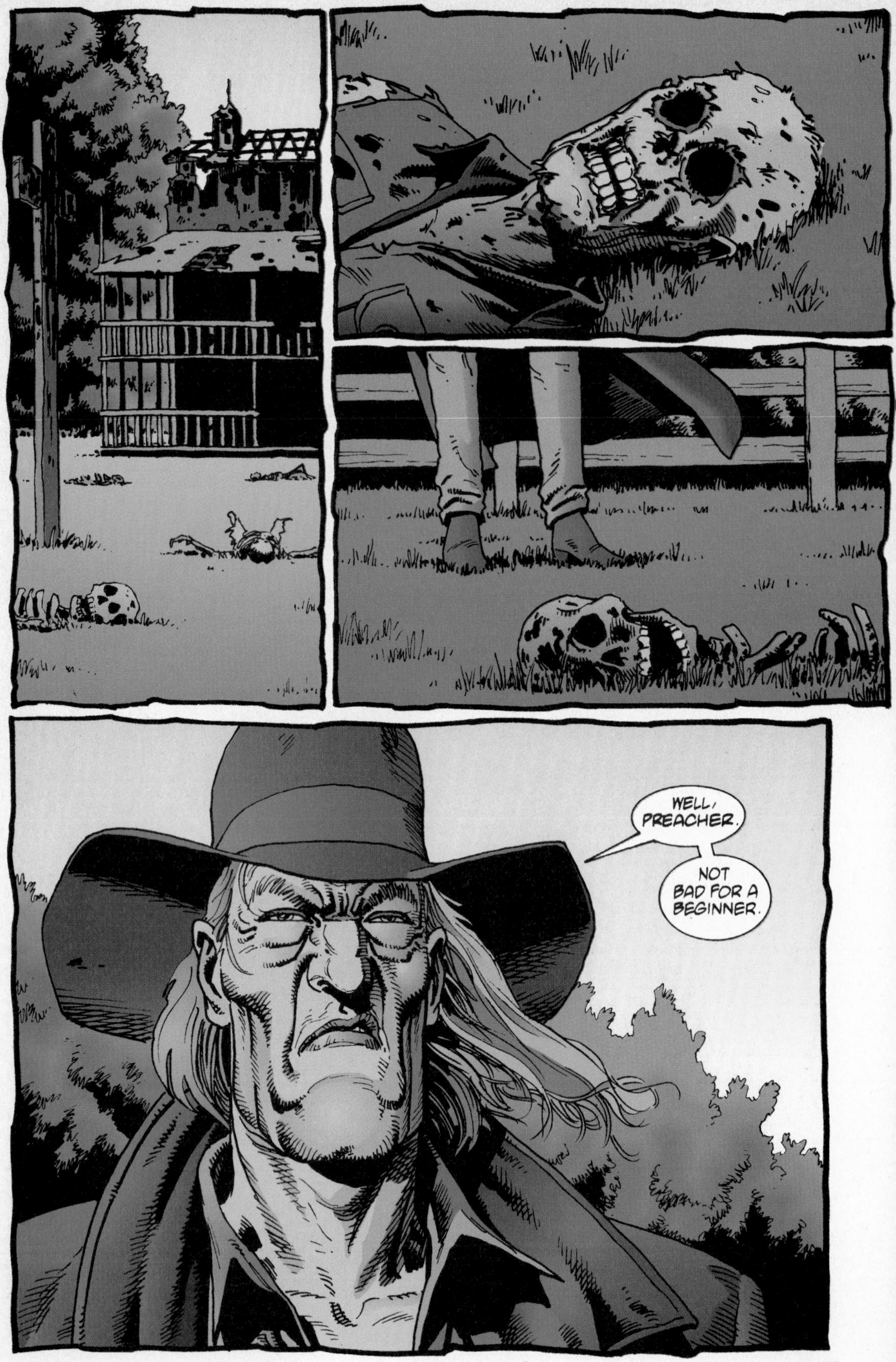
WELL, PREACHER.
NOT BAD FOR A BEGINNER.

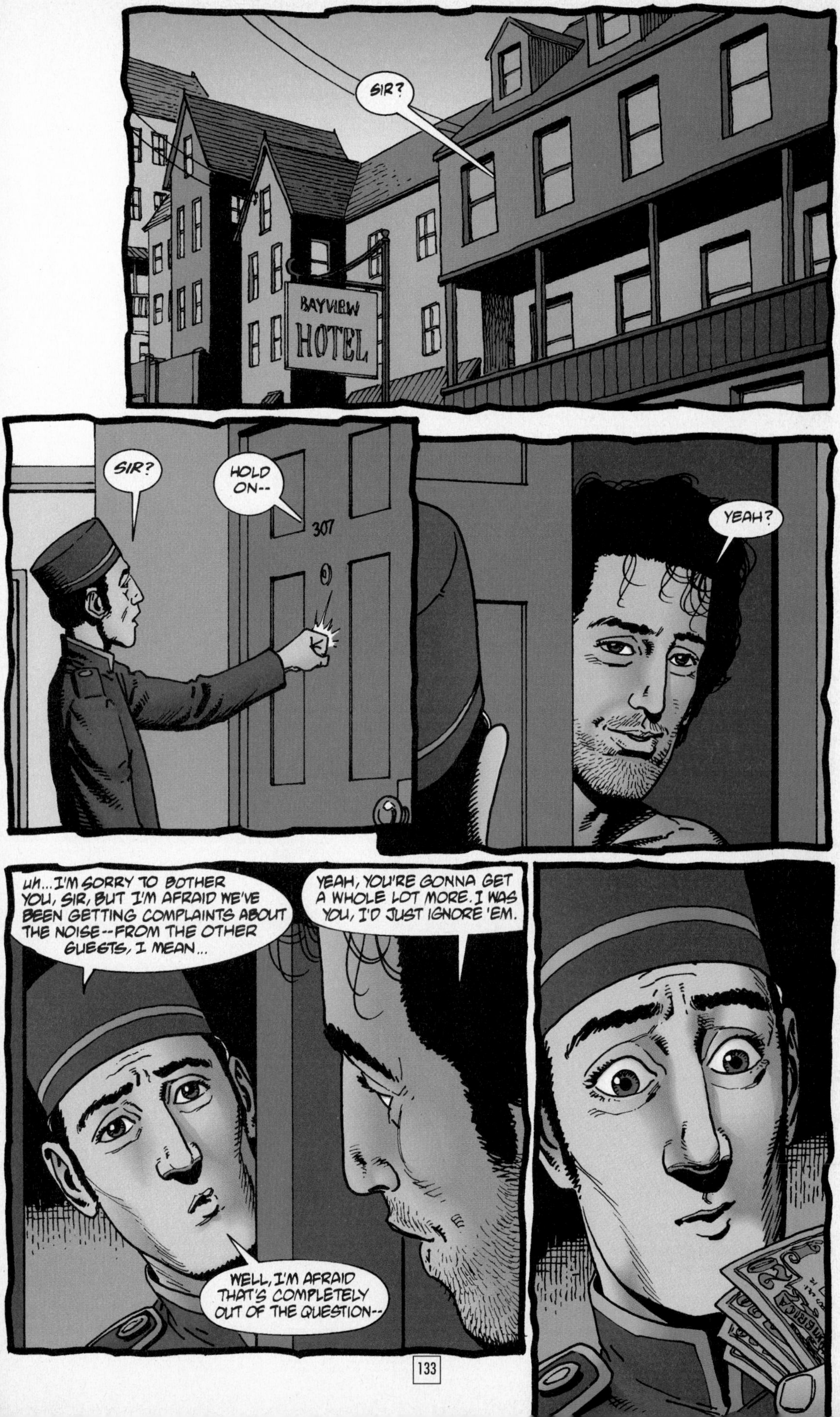
SIR?
BAYVIEW HOTEL
SIR?
HOLD ON--
307
YEAH?
UH... I'M SORRY TO BOTHER YOU, SIR, BUT I'M AFRAID WE'VE BEEN GETTING COMPLAINTS ABOUT THE NOISE--FROM THE OTHER GUESTS, I MEAN...
YEAH, YOU'RE GONNA GET A WHOLE LOT MORE. I WAS YOU, I'D JUST IGNORE 'EM.
WELL, I'M AFRAID THAT'S COMPLETELY OUT OF THE QUESTION--

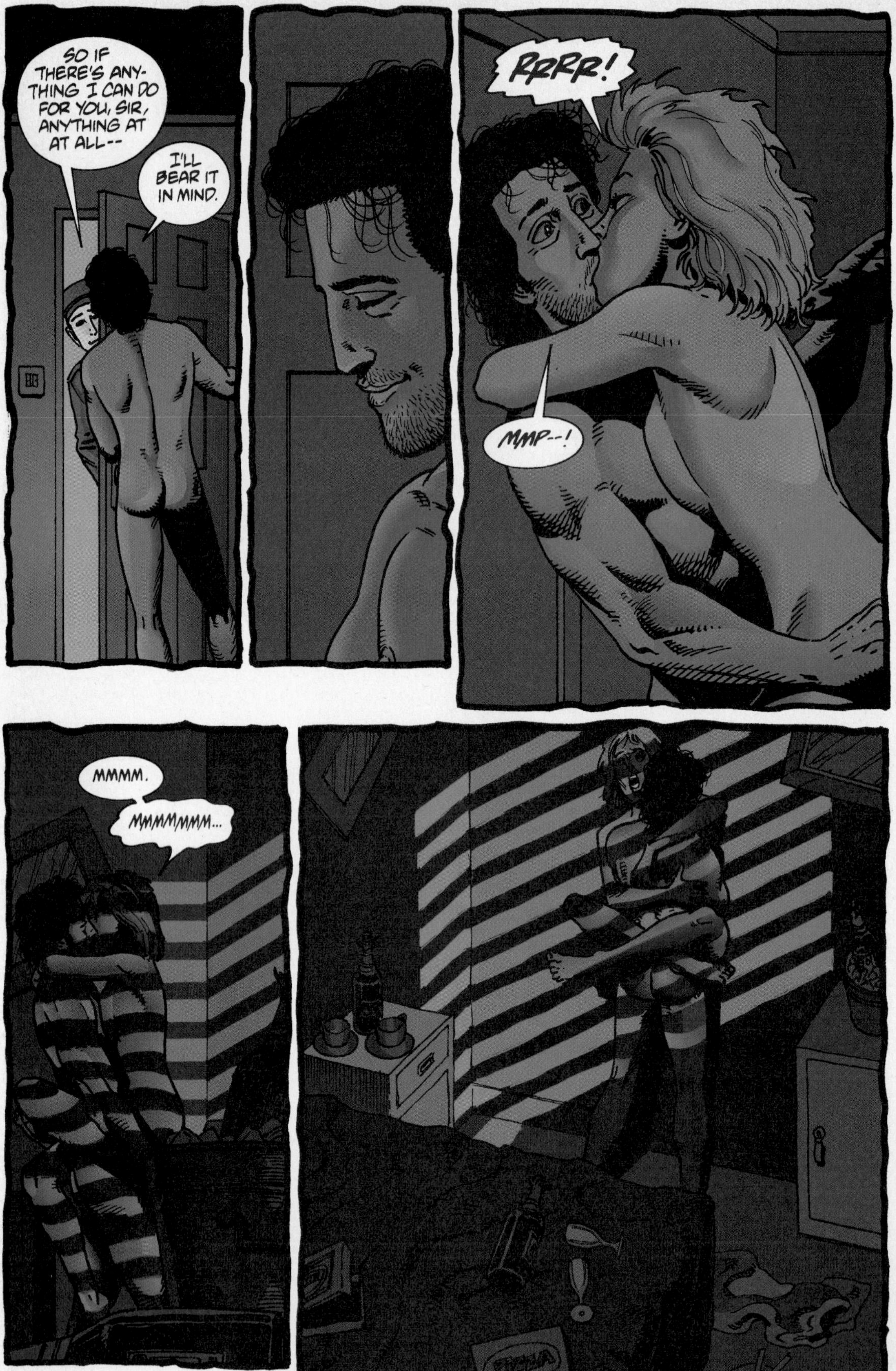
SO IF THERE'S ANYTHING I CAN DO FOR YOU, SIR, ANYTHING AT AT ALL--
I'LL BEAR IT IN MIND.
RRRR!
MMP--!
MMMM.
MMMMMMM...
PIZZA

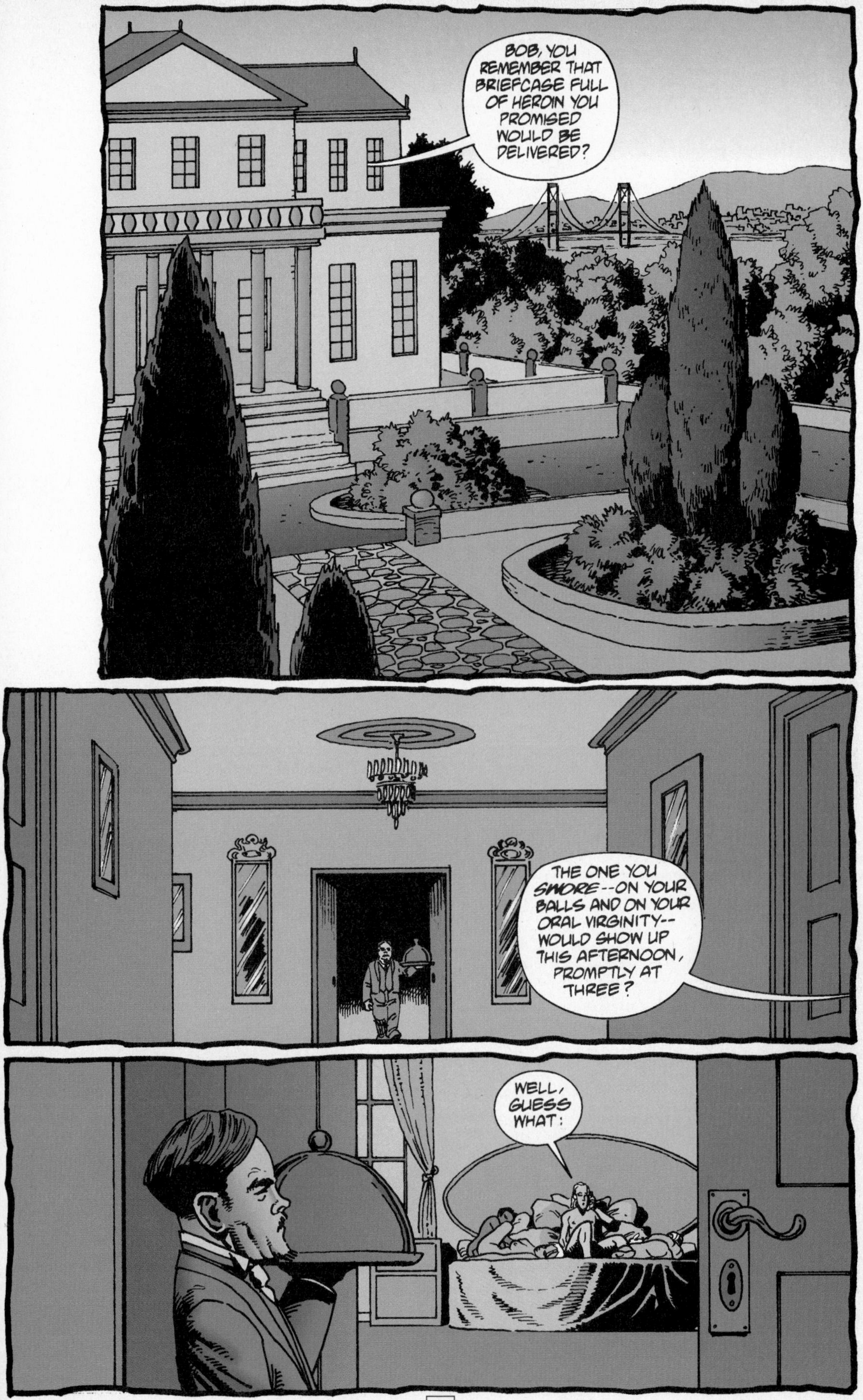
BOB, YOU REMEMBER THAT BRIEFCASE FULL OF HEROIN YOU PROMISED WOULD BE DELIVERED?
THE ONE YOU SWORE--ON YOUR BALLS AND ON YOUR ORAL VIRGINITY--WOULD SHOW UP THIS AFTERNOON, PROMPTLY AT THREE?
WELL, GUESS WHAT:

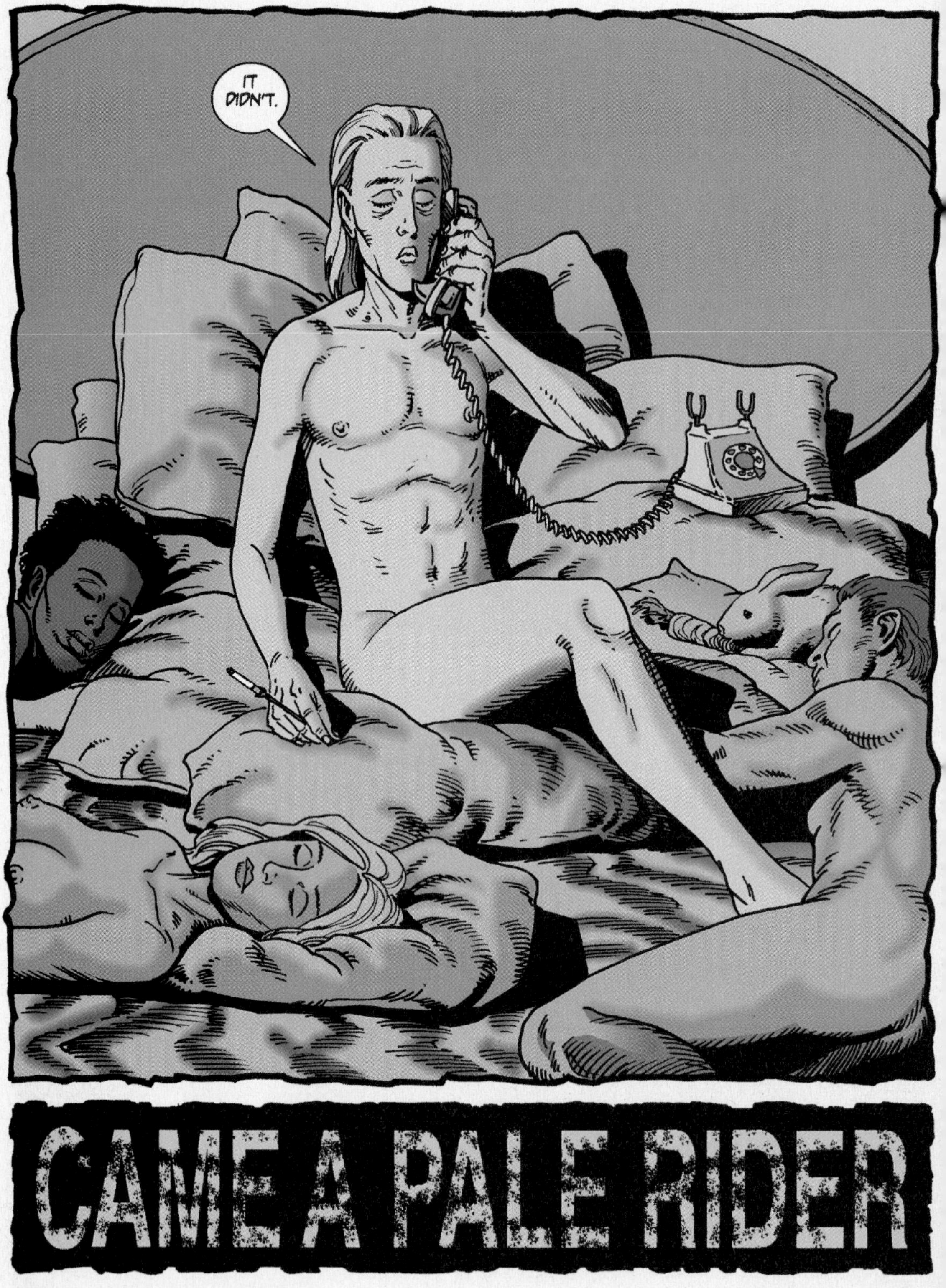
IT DIDN'T.

CAME A PALE RIDER

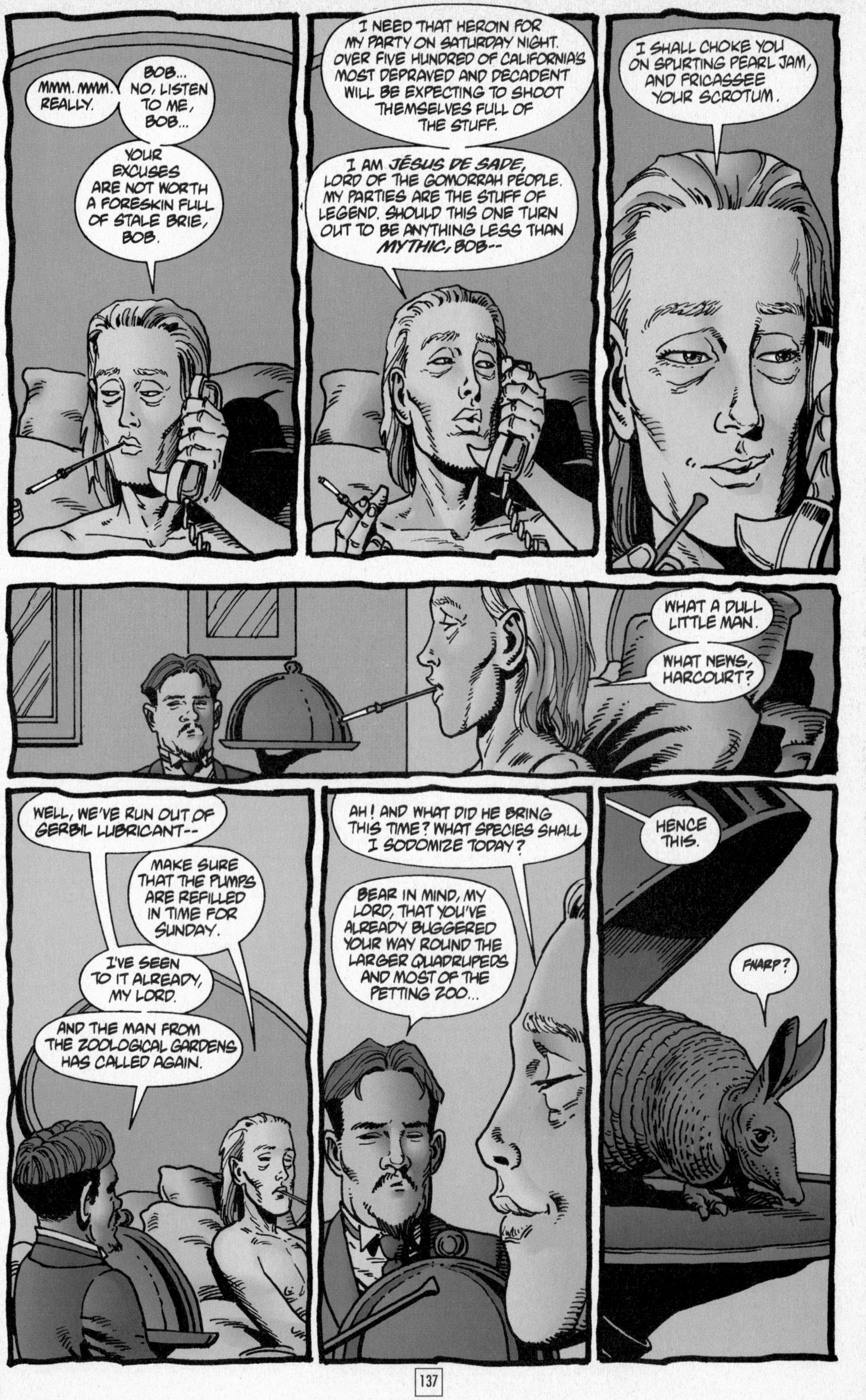
MMM. MMM. REALLY.
BOB... NO, LISTEN TO ME, BOB...
YOUR EXCUSES ARE NOT WORTH A FORESKIN FULL OF STALE BRIE, BOB.
I NEED THAT HEROIN FOR MY PARTY ON SATURDAY NIGHT. OVER FIVE HUNDRED OF CALIFORNIA'S MOST DEPRAVED AND DECADENT WILL BE EXPECTING TO SHOOT THEMSELVES FULL OF THE STUFF.
I AM *JÉSUS DE SADE*, LORD OF THE GOMORRAH PEOPLE. MY PARTIES ARE THE STUFF OF LEGEND. SHOULD THIS ONE TURN OUT TO BE ANYTHING LESS THAN *MYTHIC*, BOB--
I SHALL CHOKE YOU ON SPURTING PEARL JAM, AND FRICASSEE YOUR SCROTUM.
WHAT A DULL LITTLE MAN.
WHAT NEWS, HARCOURT?
WELL, WE'VE RUN OUT OF GERBIL LUBRICANT--
MAKE SURE THAT THE PUMPS ARE REFILLED IN TIME FOR SUNDAY.
I'VE SEEN TO IT ALREADY, MY LORD.
AND THE MAN FROM THE ZOOLOGICAL GARDENS HAS CALLED AGAIN.
AH! AND WHAT DID HE BRING THIS TIME? WHAT SPECIES SHALL I SODOMIZE TODAY?
BEAR IN MIND, MY LORD, THAT YOU'VE ALREADY BUGGERED YOUR WAY ROUND THE LARGER QUADRUPEDS AND MOST OF THE PETTING ZOO...
HENCE THIS.
FNARP?

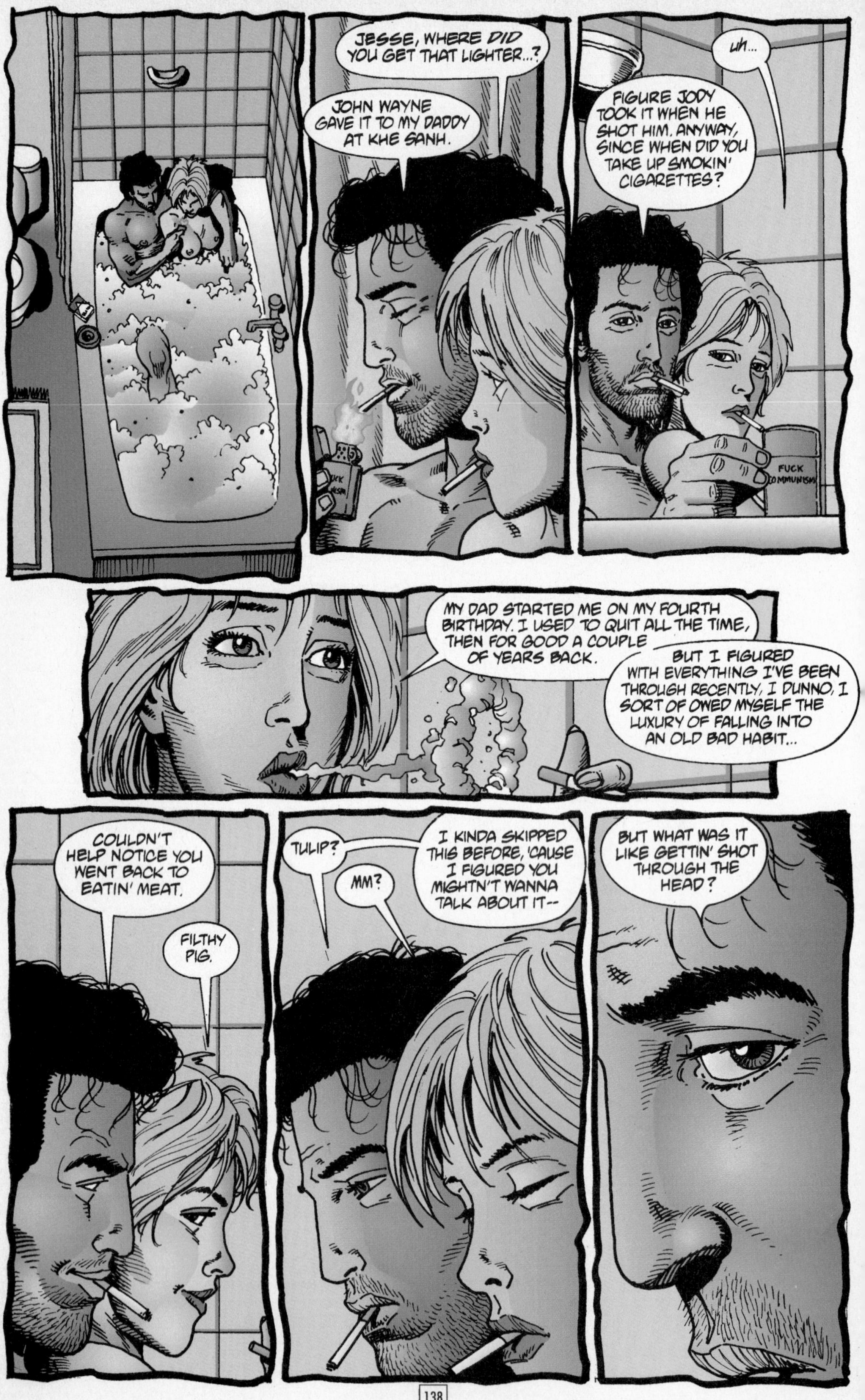
JESSE, WHERE DID YOU GET THAT LIGHTER...?
JOHN WAYNE GAVE IT TO MY DADDY AT KHE SANH.
uh...
FIGURE JODY TOOK IT WHEN HE SHOT HIM. ANYWAY, SINCE WHEN DID YOU TAKE UP SMOKIN' CIGARETTES?
MY DAD STARTED ME ON MY FOURTH BIRTHDAY. I USED TO QUIT ALL THE TIME, THEN FOR GOOD A COUPLE OF YEARS BACK.
BUT I FIGURED WITH EVERYTHING I'VE BEEN THROUGH RECENTLY, I DUNNO, I SORT OF OWED MYSELF THE LUXURY OF FALLING INTO AN OLD BAD HABIT...
COULDN'T HELP NOTICE YOU WENT BACK TO EATIN' MEAT.
FILTHY PIG.
TULIP?
MM?
I KINDA SKIPPED THIS BEFORE, 'CAUSE I FIGURED YOU MIGHTN'T WANNA TALK ABOUT IT--
BUT WHAT WAS IT LIKE GETTIN' SHOT THROUGH THE HEAD?

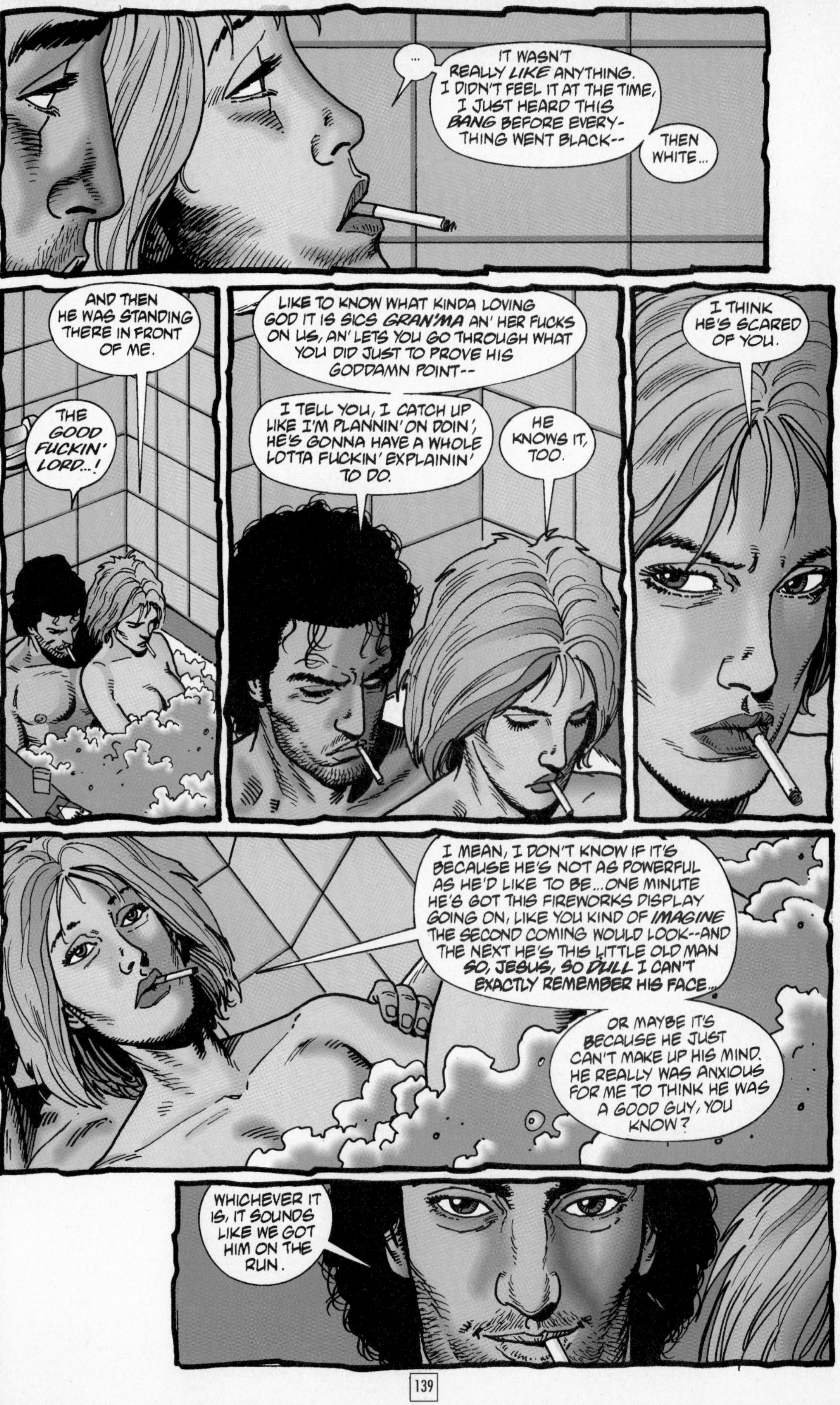
...
IT WASN'T REALLY LIKE ANYTHING. I DIDN'T FEEL IT AT THE TIME, I JUST HEARD THIS BANG BEFORE EVERY-THING WENT BLACK--
THEN WHITE...
AND THEN HE WAS STANDING THERE IN FRONT OF ME.
THE GOOD FUCKIN' LORD...!
LIKE TO KNOW WHAT KINDA LOVING GOD IT IS SICS GRAN'MA AN' HER FUCKS ON US, AN' LETS YOU GO THROUGH WHAT YOU DID JUST TO PROVE HIS GODDAMN POINT--
I TELL YOU, I CATCH UP LIKE I'M PLANNIN' ON DOIN', HE'S GONNA HAVE A WHOLE LOTTA FUCKIN' EXPLAININ' TO DO.
HE KNOWS IT, TOO.
I THINK HE'S SCARED OF YOU.
I MEAN, I DON'T KNOW IF IT'S BECAUSE HE'S NOT AS POWERFUL AS HE'D LIKE TO BE...ONE MINUTE HE'S GOT THIS FIREWORKS DISPLAY GOING ON, LIKE YOU KIND OF IMAGINE THE SECOND COMING WOULD LOOK--AND THE NEXT HE'S THIS LITTLE OLD MAN SO, JESUS, SO DULL I CAN'T EXACTLY REMEMBER HIS FACE...
OR MAYBE IT'S BECAUSE HE JUST CAN'T MAKE UP HIS MIND. HE REALLY WAS ANXIOUS FOR ME TO THINK HE WAS A GOOD GUY, YOU KNOW?
WHICHEVER IT IS, IT SOUNDS LIKE WE GOT HIM ON THE RUN.

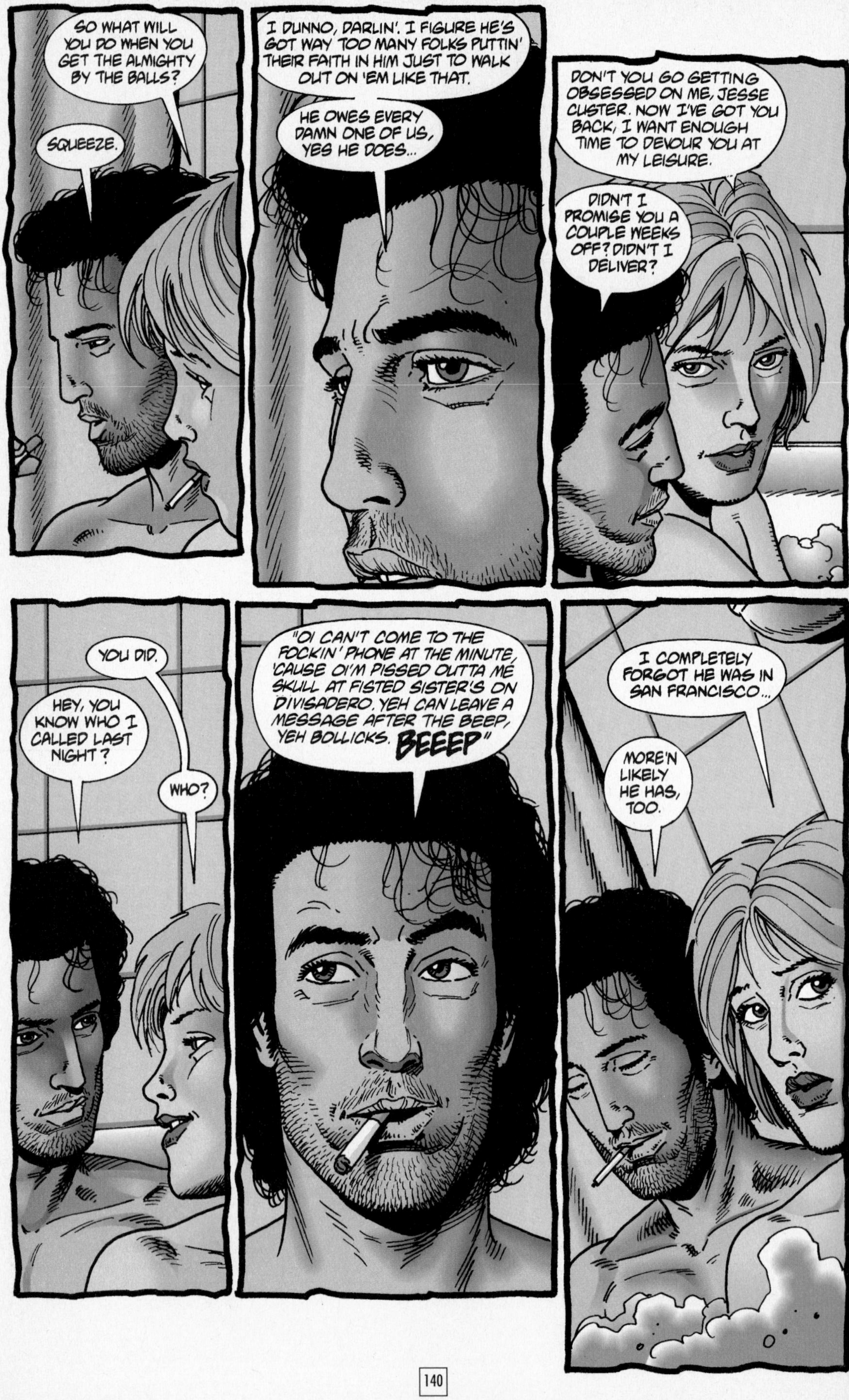
SO WHAT WILL YOU DO WHEN YOU GET THE ALMIGHTY BY THE BALLS?
SQUEEZE.
I DUNNO, DARLIN'. I FIGURE HE'S GOT WAY TOO MANY FOLKS PUTTIN' THEIR FAITH IN HIM JUST TO WALK OUT ON 'EM LIKE THAT.
HE OWES EVERY DAMN ONE OF US, YES HE DOES...
DON'T YOU GO GETTING OBSESSED ON ME, JESSE CUSTER. NOW I'VE GOT YOU BACK, I WANT ENOUGH TIME TO DEVOUR YOU AT MY LEISURE.
DIDN'T I PROMISE YOU A COUPLE WEEKS OFF? DIDN'T I DELIVER?
YOU DID.
HEY, YOU KNOW WHO I CALLED LAST NIGHT?
WHO?
"OI CAN'T COME TO THE FOCKIN' PHONE AT THE MINUTE, 'CAUSE OI'M PISSED OUTTA ME SKULL AT FISTED SISTER'S ON DIVISADERO. YEH CAN LEAVE A MESSAGE AFTER THE BEEP, YEH BOLLICKS. BEEEP"
I COMPLETELY FORGOT HE WAS IN SAN FRANCISCO...
MORE'N LIKELY HE HAS, TOO.

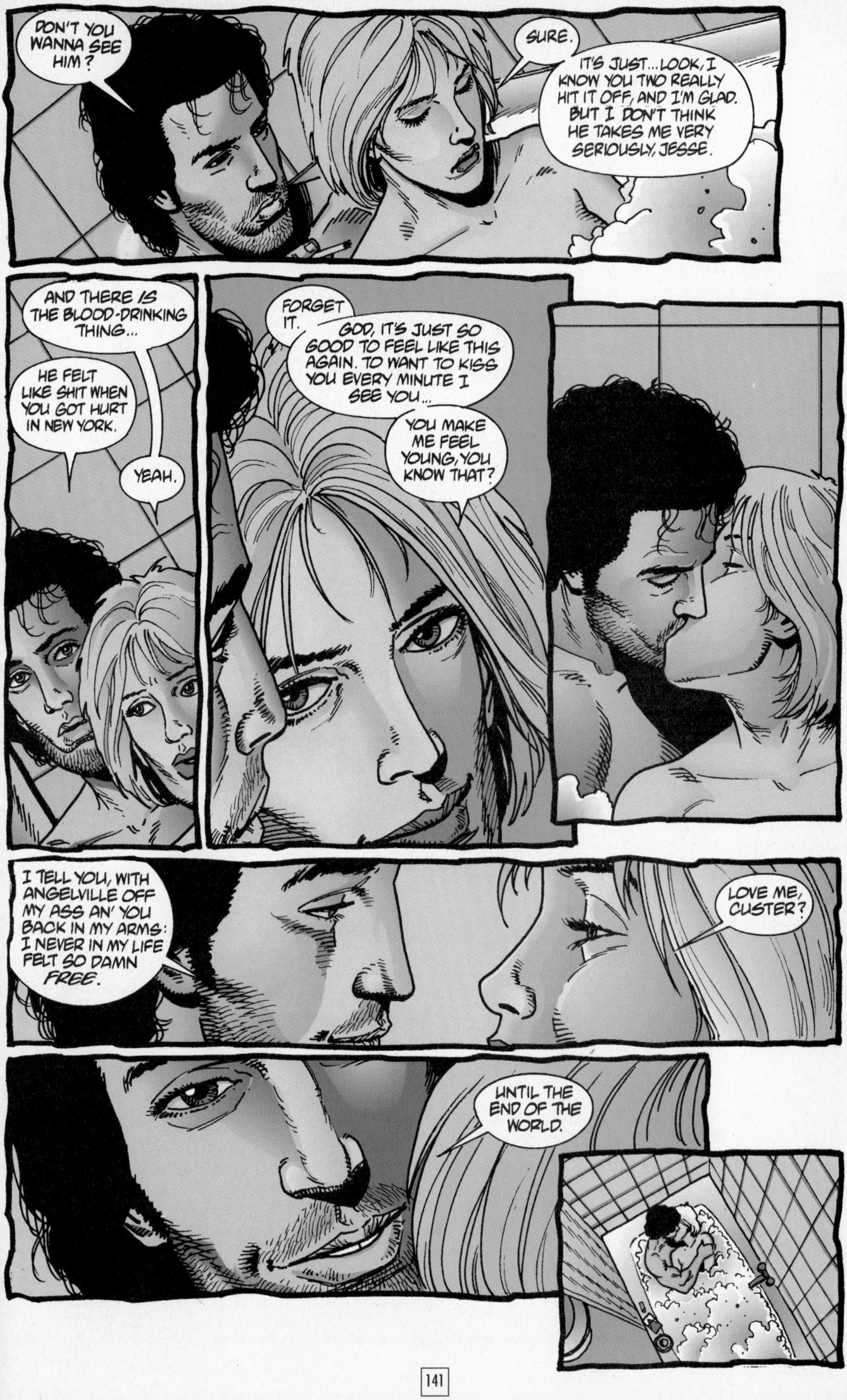
DON'T YOU WANNA SEE HIM?
SURE.
IT'S JUST... LOOK, I KNOW YOU TWO REALLY HIT IT OFF, AND I'M GLAD. BUT I DON'T THINK HE TAKES ME VERY SERIOUSLY, JESSE.
AND THERE IS THE BLOOD-DRINKING THING...
HE FELT LIKE SHIT WHEN YOU GOT HURT IN NEW YORK.
YEAH.
FORGET IT.
GOD, IT'S JUST SO GOOD TO FEEL LIKE THIS AGAIN. TO WANT TO KISS YOU EVERY MINUTE I SEE YOU...
YOU MAKE ME FEEL YOUNG, YOU KNOW THAT?
I TELL YOU, WITH ANGELVILLE OFF MY ASS AN' YOU BACK IN MY ARMS: I NEVER IN MY LIFE FELT SO DAMN FREE.
LOVE ME, CUSTER?
UNTIL THE END OF THE WORLD.

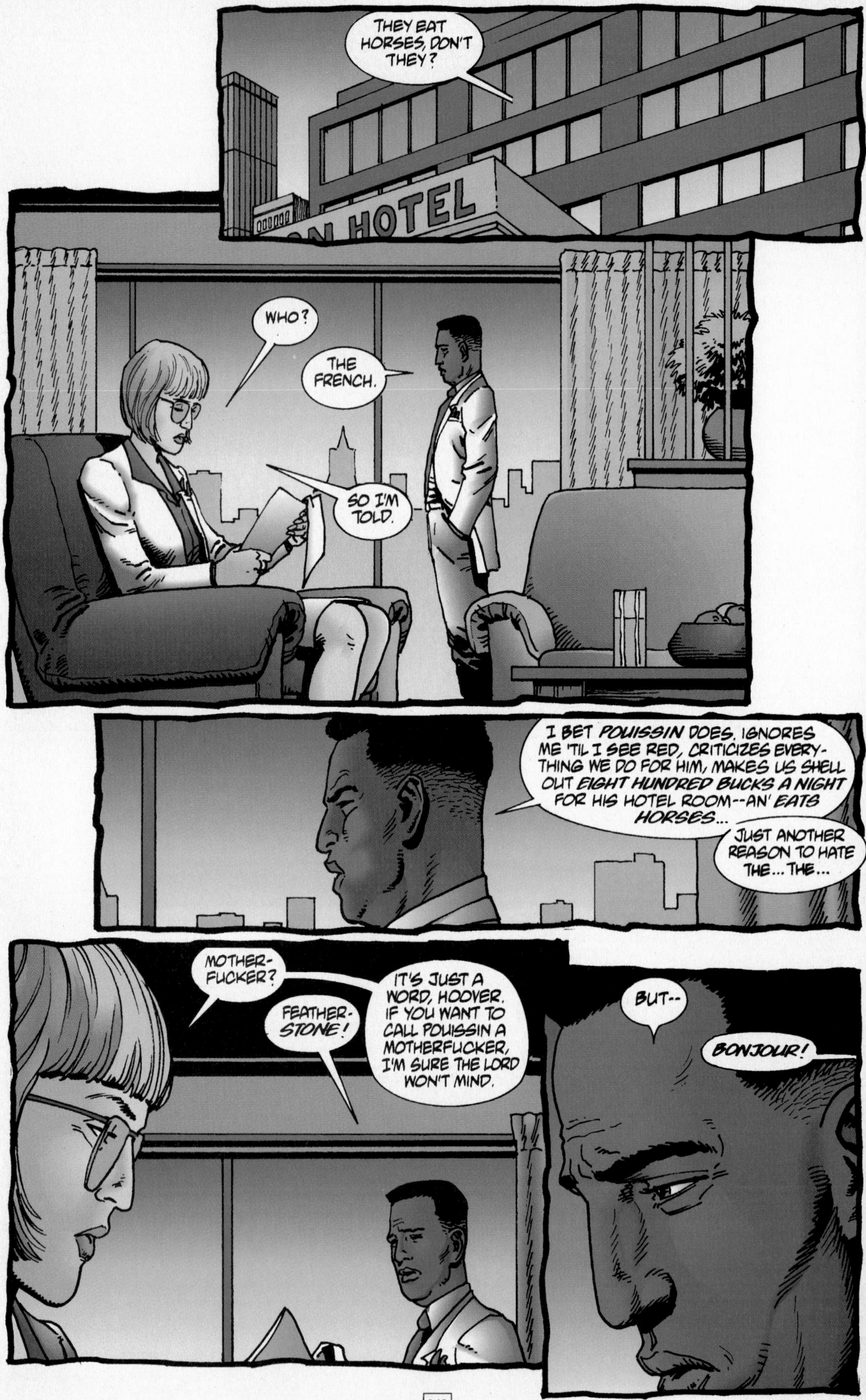
ON HOTEL
THEY EAT HORSES, DON'T THEY?
WHO?
THE FRENCH.
SO I'M TOLD.
I BET POUISSIN DOES. IGNORES ME 'TIL I SEE RED, CRITICIZES EVERYTHING WE DO FOR HIM, MAKES US SHELL OUT EIGHT HUNDRED BUCKS A NIGHT FOR HIS HOTEL ROOM--AN' EATS HORSES...
JUST ANOTHER REASON TO HATE THE... THE...
MOTHER-FUCKER?
FEATHER-STONE!
IT'S JUST A WORD, HOOVER. IF YOU WANT TO CALL POUISSIN A MOTHERFUCKER, I'M SURE THE LORD WON'T MIND.
BUT--
BONJOUR!

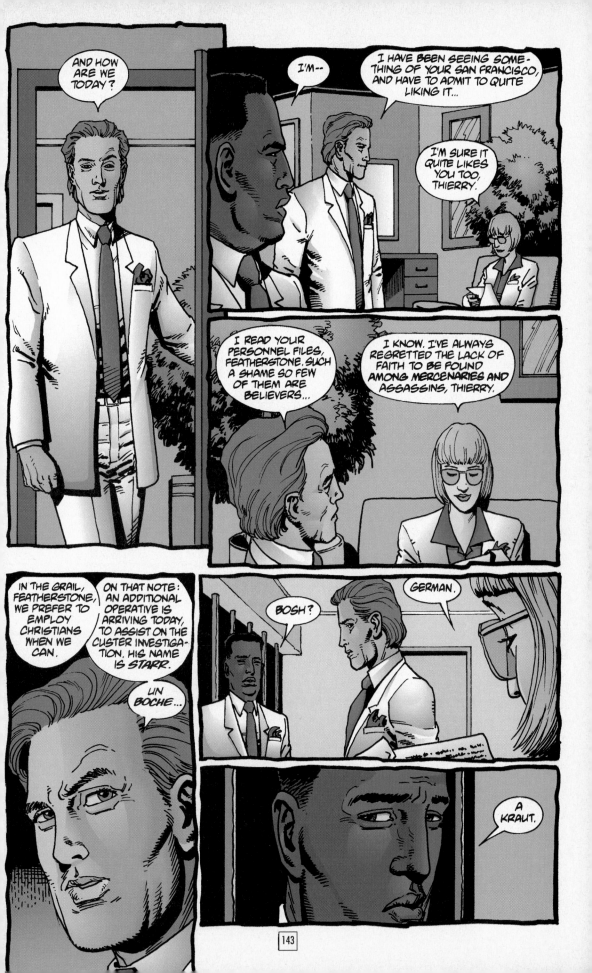

AND HOW ARE WE TODAY?

I'M--

I HAVE BEEN SEEING SOMETHING OF YOUR SAN FRANCISCO, AND HAVE TO ADMIT TO QUITE LIKING IT...

I'M SURE IT QUITE LIKES YOU TOO, THIERRY.

I READ YOUR PERSONNEL FILES, FEATHERSTONE. SUCH A SHAME SO FEW OF THEM ARE BELIEVERS...

I KNOW. I'VE ALWAYS REGRETTED THE LACK OF FAITH TO BE FOUND AMONG MERCENARIES AND ASSASSINS, THIERRY.

IN THE GRAIL, FEATHERSTONE, WE PREFER TO EMPLOY CHRISTIANS WHEN WE CAN.

ON THAT NOTE: AN ADDITIONAL OPERATIVE IS ARRIVING TODAY, TO ASSIST ON THE CUSTER INVESTIGATION. HIS NAME IS STARR.

UN BOCHE...

BOSH?

GERMAN.

A KRAUT.

143

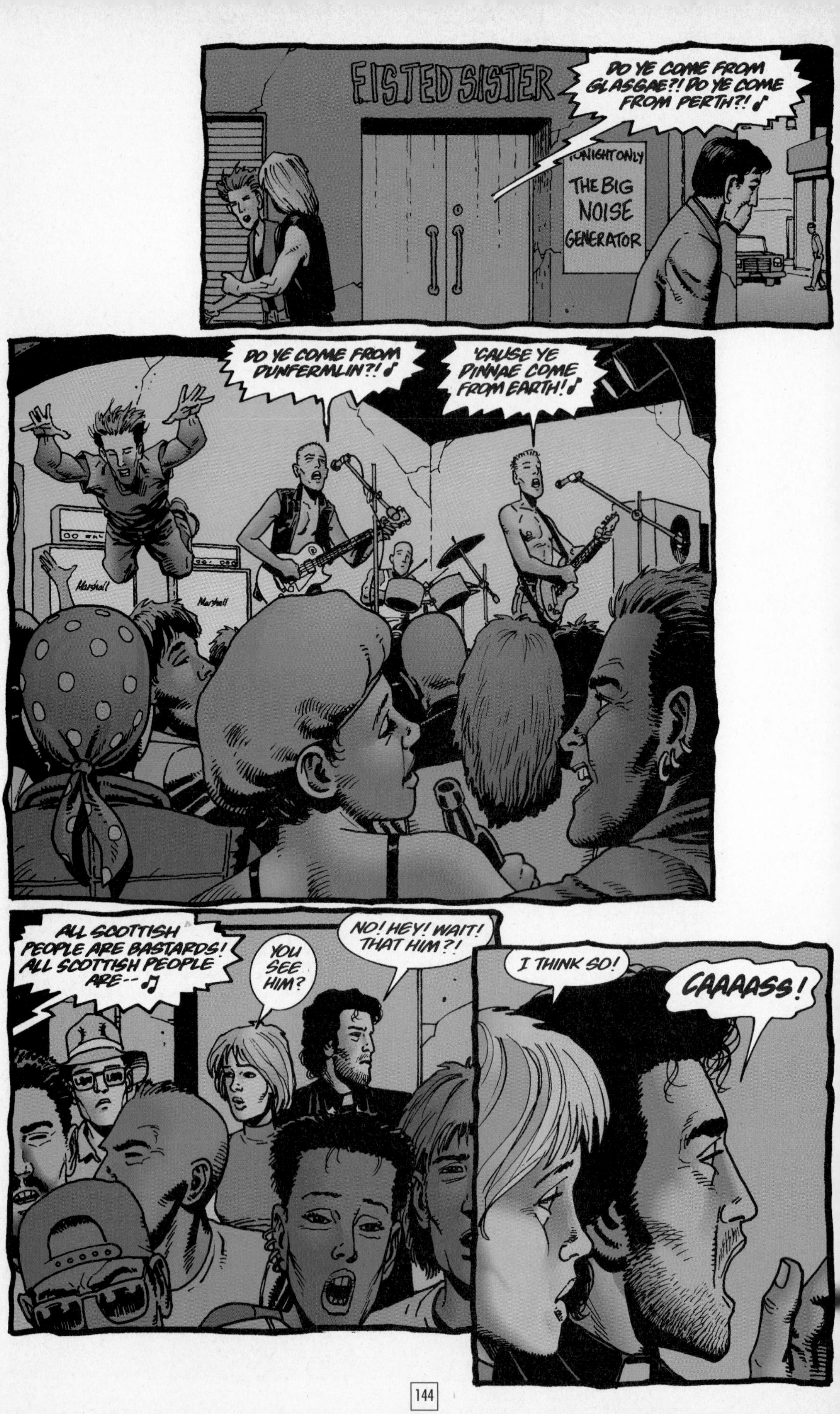
FISTED SISTER
DO YE COME FROM GLASGAE?! DO YE COME FROM PERTH?! ♪
TONIGHT ONLY
THE BIG NOISE GENERATOR
DO YE COME FROM DUNFERMLIN?! ♪
'CAUSE YE DINNAE COME FROM EARTH! ♪
Marshall
Marshall
ALL SCOTTISH PEOPLE ARE BASTARDS! ALL SCOTTISH PEOPLE ARE-- ♫
YOU SEE HIM?
NO! HEY! WAIT! THAT HIM?!
I THINK SO!
CAAAASS!

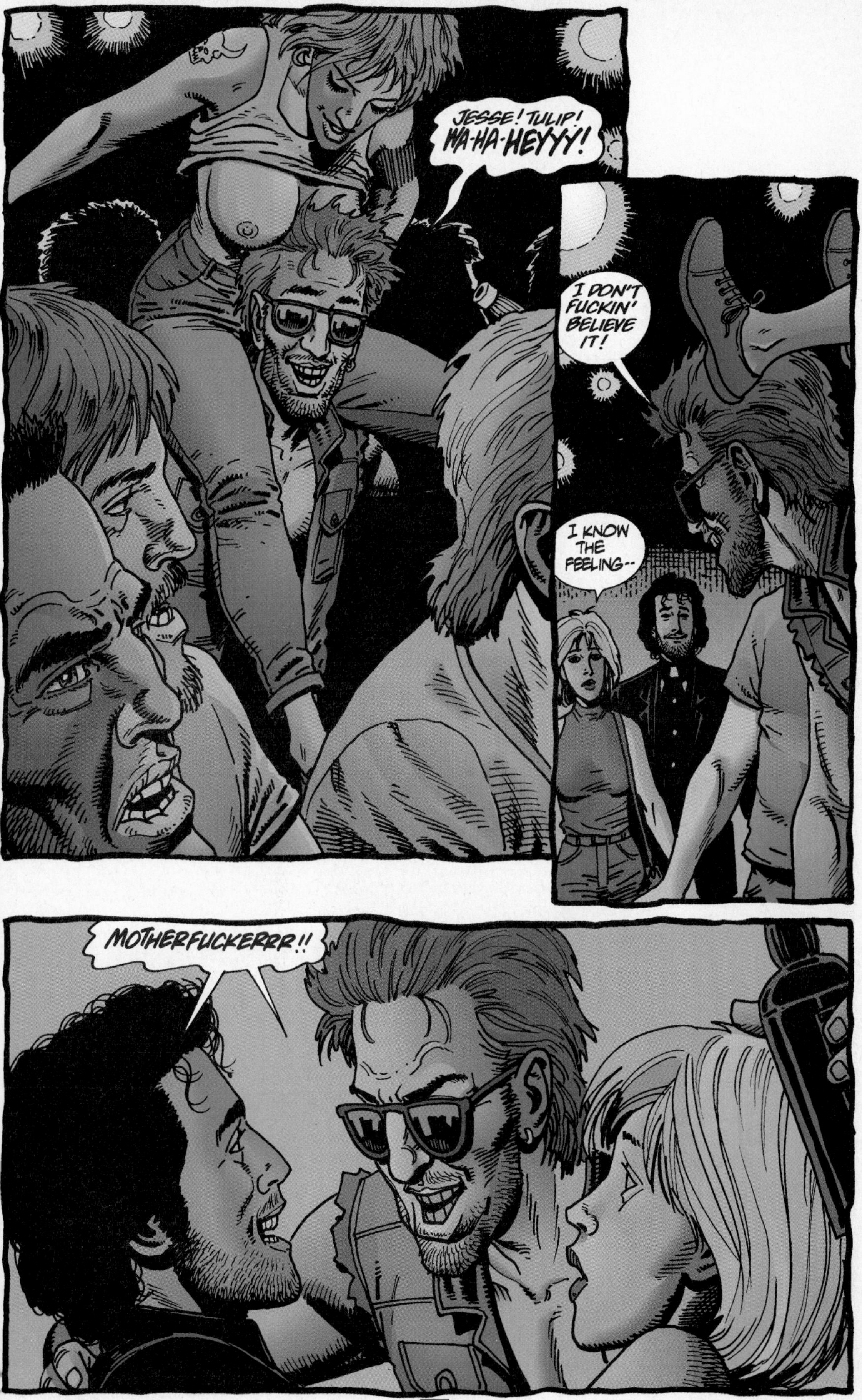
JESSE! TULIP! WA-HA-HEYYY!
I DON'T FUCKIN' BELIEVE IT!
I KNOW THE FEELING--
MOTHERFUCKERRR!!

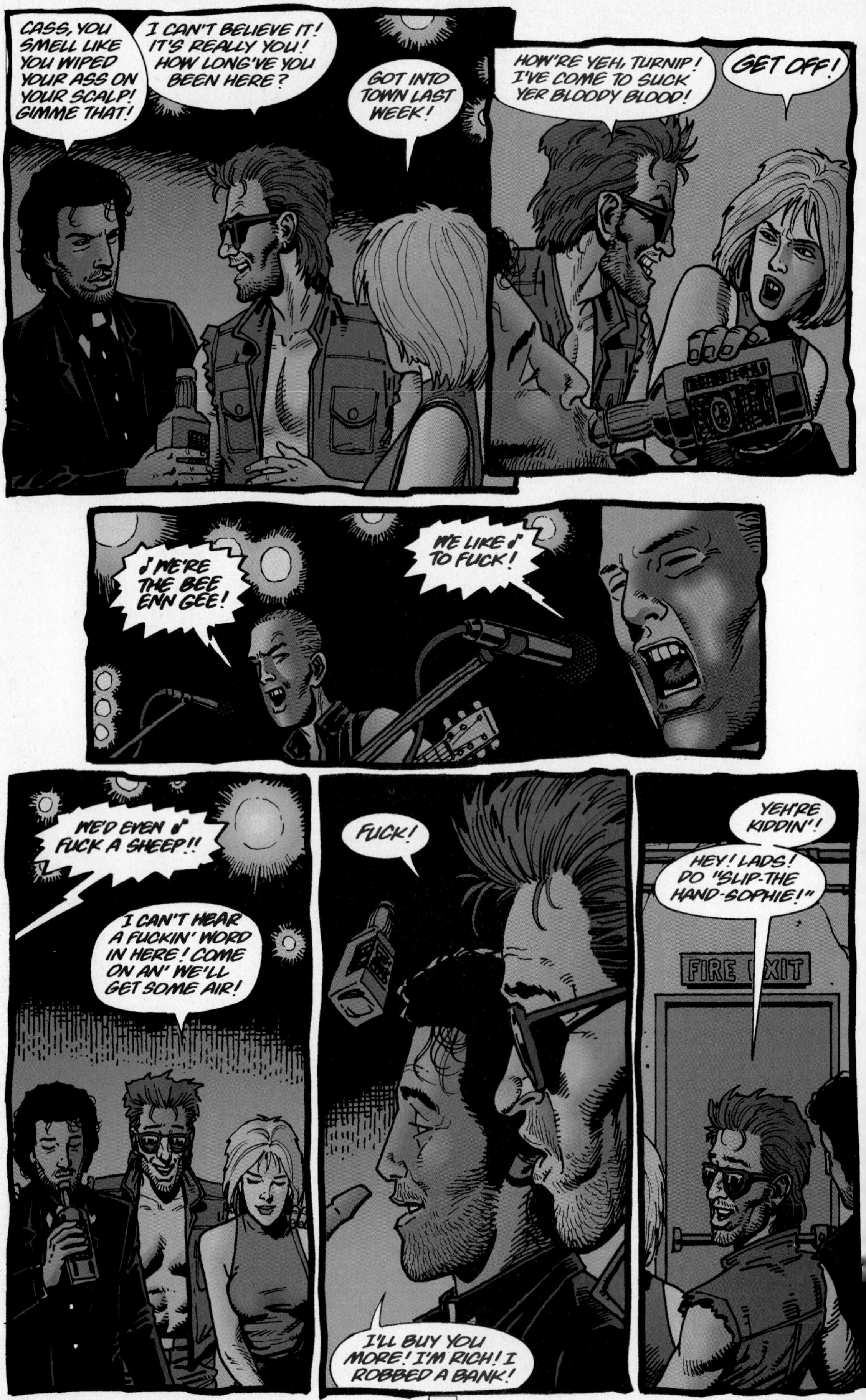
CASS, YOU SMELL LIKE YOU WIPED YOUR ASS ON YOUR SCALP! GIMME THAT!
I CAN'T BELIEVE IT! IT'S REALLY YOU! HOW LONG'VE YOU BEEN HERE?
GOT INTO TOWN LAST WEEK!
HOW'RE YEH, TURNIP! I'VE COME TO SUCK YER BLOODY BLOOD!
GET OFF!
♪ WE'RE THE BEE ENN GEE!
WE LIKE ♪ TO FUCK!
WE'D EVEN ♪ FUCK A SHEEP!!
I CAN'T HEAR A FUCKIN' WORD IN HERE! COME ON AN' WE'LL GET SOME AIR!
FUCK!
I'LL BUY YOU MORE! I'M RICH! I ROBBED A BANK!
YEH'RE KIDDIN'!
HEY! LADS! DO "SLIP-THE HAND-SOPHIE!"

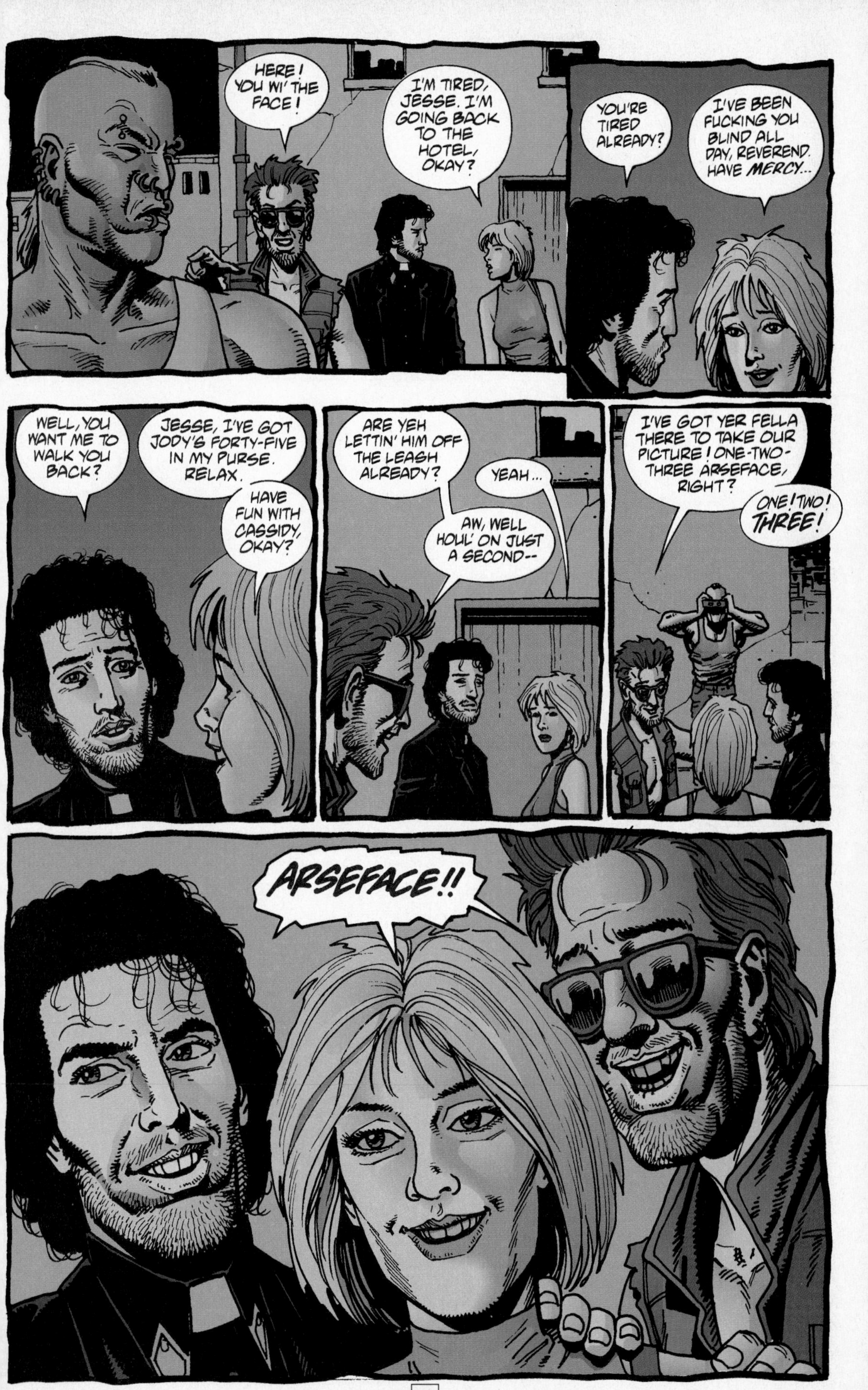

HERE! YOU WI' THE FACE!
I'M TIRED, JESSE. I'M GOING BACK TO THE HOTEL, OKAY?
YOU'RE TIRED ALREADY?
I'VE BEEN FUCKING YOU BLIND ALL DAY, REVEREND. HAVE MERCY...
WELL, YOU WANT ME TO WALK YOU BACK?
JESSE, I'VE GOT JODY'S FORTY-FIVE IN MY PURSE. RELAX.
HAVE FUN WITH CASSIDY, OKAY?
ARE YEH LETTIN' HIM OFF THE LEASH ALREADY?
YEAH...
AW, WELL HOUL' ON JUST A SECOND--
I'VE GOT YER FELLA THERE TO TAKE OUR PICTURE! ONE-TWO-THREE ARSEFACE, RIGHT?
ONE! TWO! THREE!
ARSEFACE!!

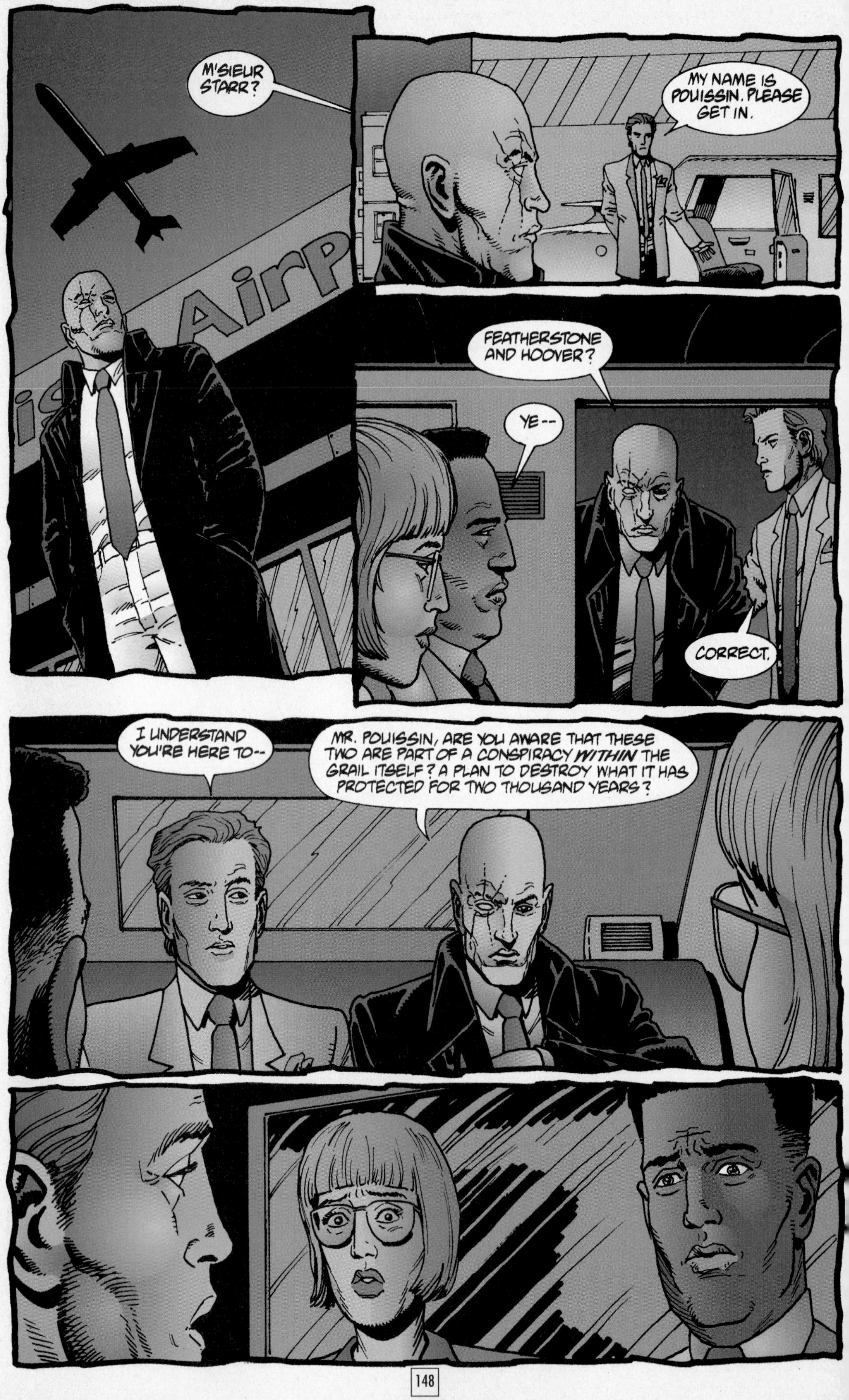
M'SIEUR STARR?
MY NAME IS POUISSIN. PLEASE GET IN.
FEATHERSTONE AND HOOVER?
YE--
CORRECT.
I UNDERSTAND YOU'RE HERE TO--
MR. POUISSIN, ARE YOU AWARE THAT THESE TWO ARE PART OF A CONSPIRACY *WITHIN* THE GRAIL ITSELF? A PLAN TO DESTROY WHAT IT HAS PROTECTED FOR TWO THOUSAND YEARS?

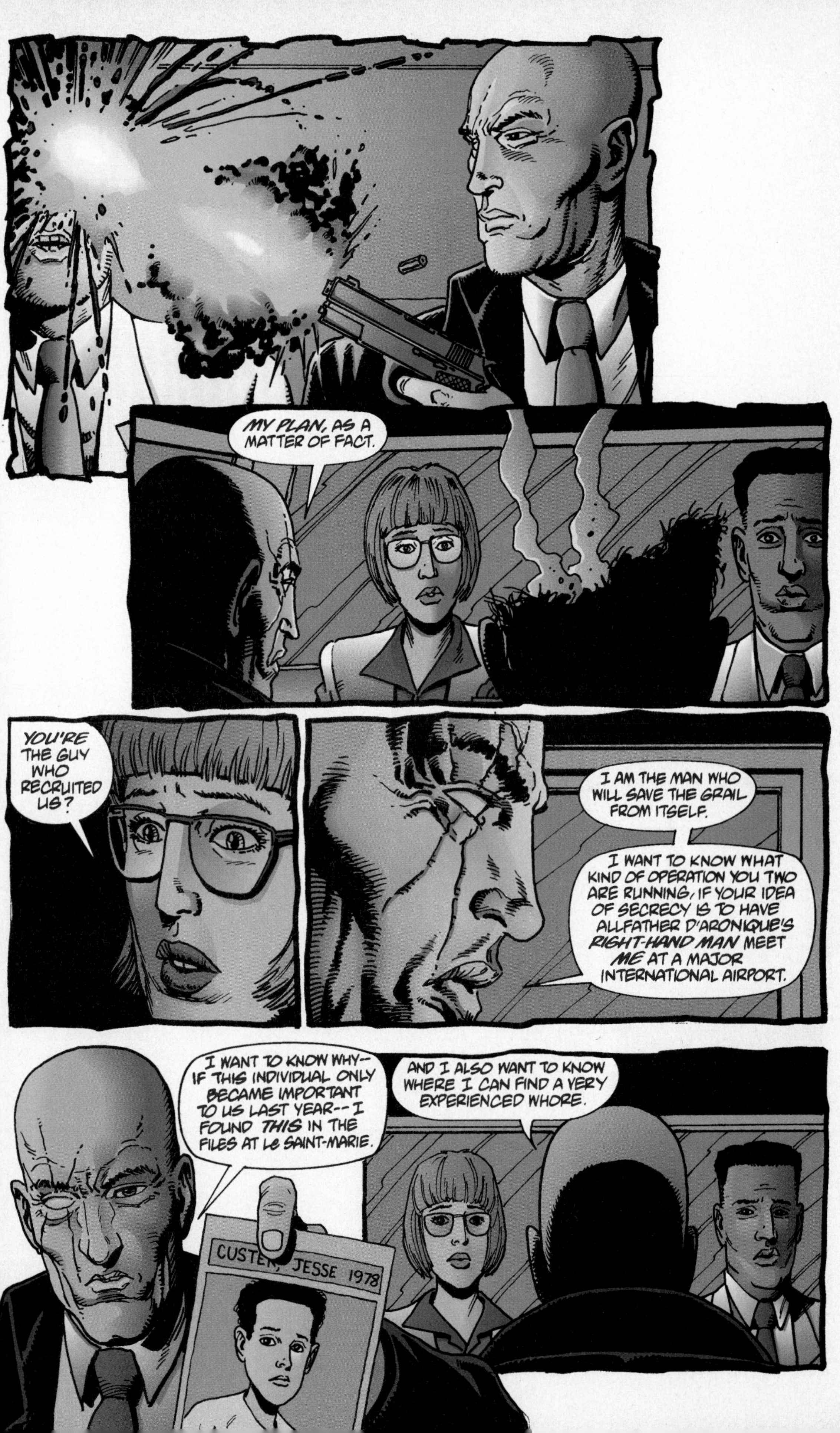

MY PLAN, AS A MATTER OF FACT.
YOU'RE THE GUY WHO RECRUITED US?
I AM THE MAN WHO WILL SAVE THE GRAIL FROM ITSELF.
I WANT TO KNOW WHAT KIND OF OPERATION YOU TWO ARE RUNNING, IF YOUR IDEA OF SECRECY IS TO HAVE ALLFATHER D'ARONIQUE'S RIGHT-HAND MAN MEET ME AT A MAJOR INTERNATIONAL AIRPORT.
I WANT TO KNOW WHY-- IF THIS INDIVIDUAL ONLY BECAME IMPORTANT TO US LAST YEAR-- I FOUND THIS IN THE FILES AT Le SAINT-MARIE.
AND I ALSO WANT TO KNOW WHERE I CAN FIND A VERY EXPERIENCED WHORE.
CUSTER, JESSE 1978

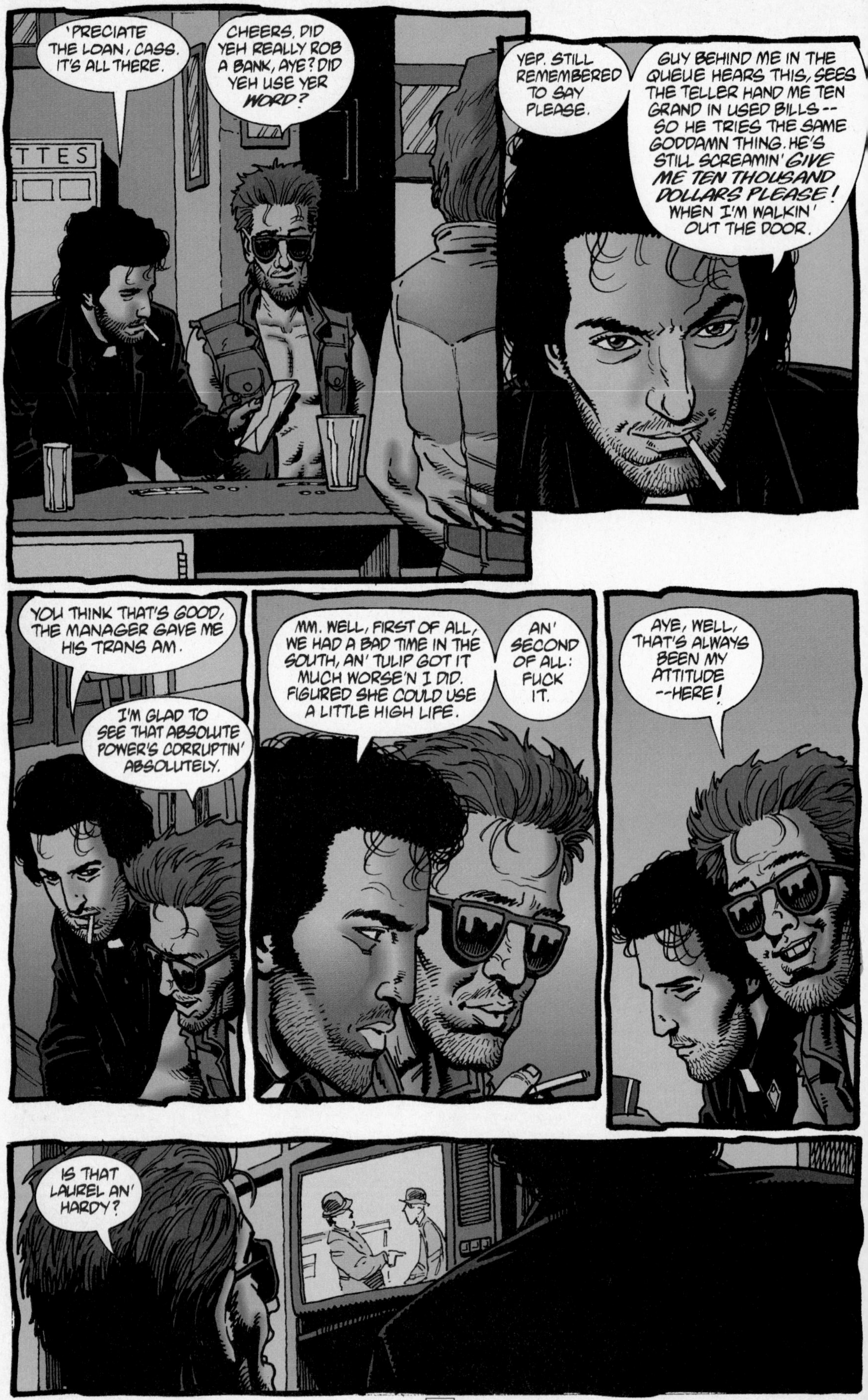
'PRECIATE THE LOAN, CASS. IT'S ALL THERE.
CHEERS. DID YEH REALLY ROB A BANK, AYE? DID YEH USE YER WORD?
TTES
YEP. STILL REMEMBERED TO SAY PLEASE.
GUY BEHIND ME IN THE QUEUE HEARS THIS, SEES THE TELLER HAND ME TEN GRAND IN USED BILLS -- SO HE TRIES THE SAME GODDAMN THING. HE'S STILL SCREAMIN' GIVE ME TEN THOUSAND DOLLARS PLEASE! WHEN I'M WALKIN' OUT THE DOOR.
YOU THINK THAT'S GOOD, THE MANAGER GAVE ME HIS TRANS AM.
I'M GLAD TO SEE THAT ABSOLUTE POWER'S CORRUPTIN' ABSOLUTELY.
MM. WELL, FIRST OF ALL, WE HAD A BAD TIME IN THE SOUTH, AN' TULIP GOT IT MUCH WORSE'N I DID. FIGURED SHE COULD USE A LITTLE HIGH LIFE.
AN' SECOND OF ALL: FUCK IT.
AYE, WELL, THAT'S ALWAYS BEEN MY ATTITUDE --HERE!
IS THAT LAUREL AN' HARDY?

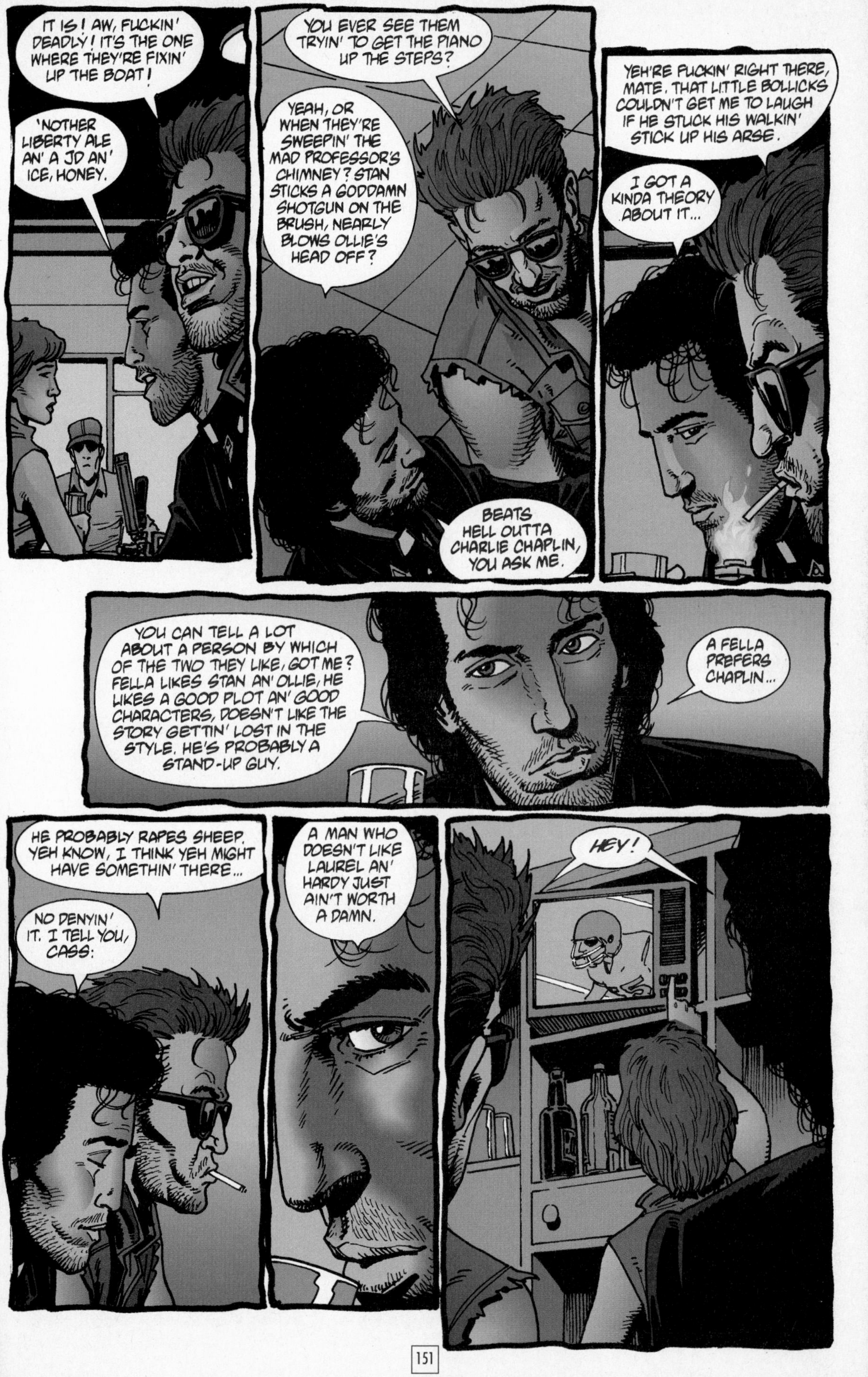
IT IS! AW, FUCKIN' DEADLY! IT'S THE ONE WHERE THEY'RE FIXIN' UP THE BOAT!
'NOTHER LIBERTY ALE AN' A JD AN' ICE, HONEY.
YOU EVER SEE THEM TRYIN' TO GET THE PIANO UP THE STEPS?
YEAH, OR WHEN THEY'RE SWEEPIN' THE MAD PROFESSOR'S CHIMNEY? STAN STICKS A GODDAMN SHOTGUN ON THE BRUSH, NEARLY BLOWS OLLIE'S HEAD OFF?
BEATS HELL OUTTA CHARLIE CHAPLIN, YOU ASK ME.
YEH'RE FUCKIN' RIGHT THERE, MATE. THAT LITTLE BOLLICKS COULDN'T GET ME TO LAUGH IF HE STUCK HIS WALKIN' STICK UP HIS ARSE.
I GOT A KINDA THEORY ABOUT IT...
YOU CAN TELL A LOT ABOUT A PERSON BY WHICH OF THE TWO THEY LIKE, GOT ME? FELLA LIKES STAN AN' OLLIE, HE LIKES A GOOD PLOT AN' GOOD CHARACTERS, DOESN'T LIKE THE STORY GETTIN' LOST IN THE STYLE. HE'S PROBABLY A STAND-UP GUY.
A FELLA PREFERS CHAPLIN...
HE PROBABLY RAPES SHEEP. YEH KNOW, I THINK YEH MIGHT HAVE SOMETHIN' THERE...
NO DENYIN' IT. I TELL YOU, CASS:
A MAN WHO DOESN'T LIKE LAUREL AN' HARDY JUST AIN'T WORTH A DAMN.
HEY!

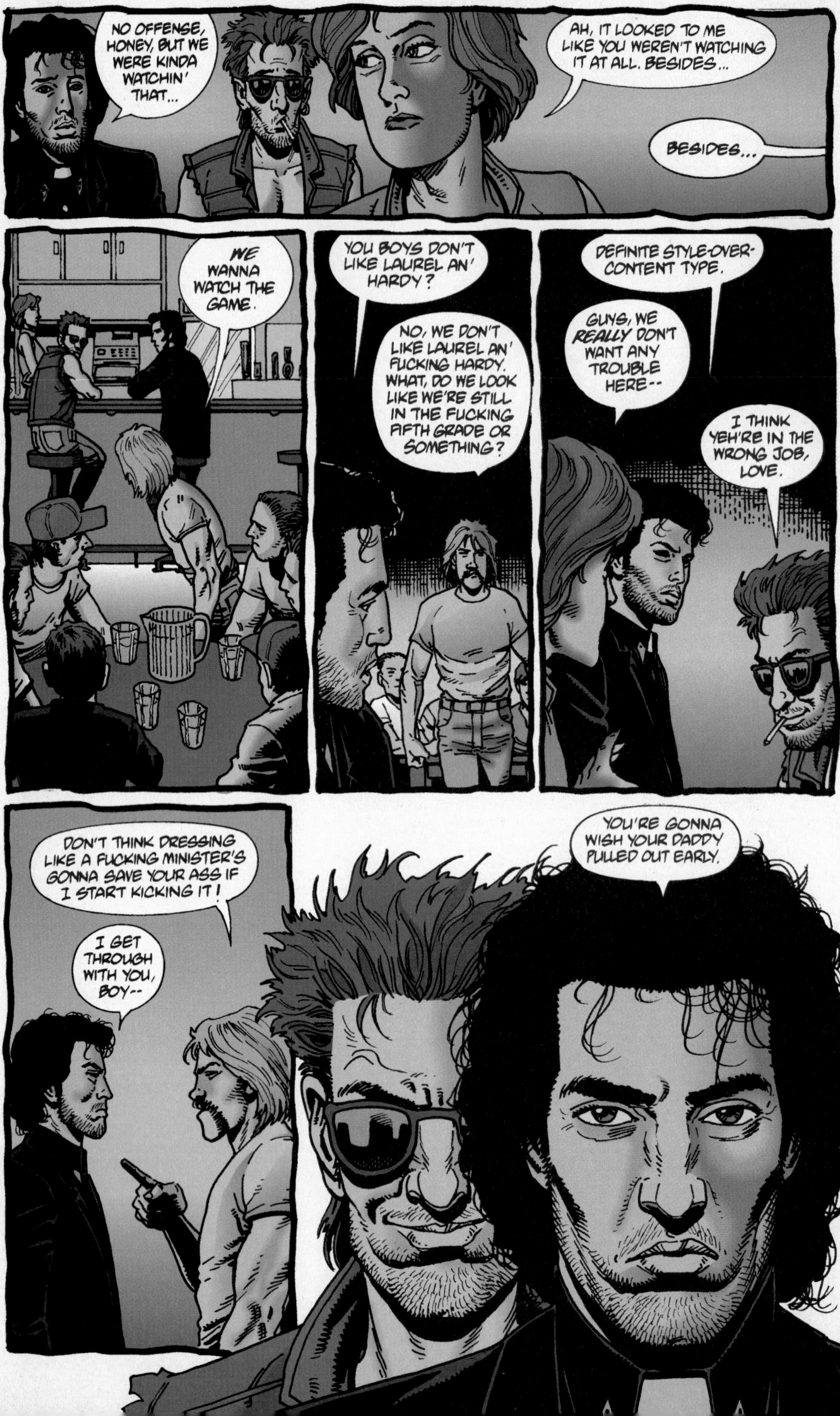
NO OFFENSE, HONEY, BUT WE WERE KINDA WATCHIN' THAT...
AH, IT LOOKED TO ME LIKE YOU WEREN'T WATCHING IT AT ALL. BESIDES...
BESIDES...
WE WANNA WATCH THE GAME.
YOU BOYS DON'T LIKE LAUREL AN' HARDY?
NO, WE DON'T LIKE LAUREL AN' FUCKING HARDY. WHAT, DO WE LOOK LIKE WE'RE STILL IN THE FUCKING FIFTH GRADE OR SOMETHING?
DEFINITE STYLE-OVER-CONTENT TYPE.
GUYS, WE REALLY DON'T WANT ANY TROUBLE HERE--
I THINK YEH'RE IN THE WRONG JOB, LOVE.
DON'T THINK DRESSING LIKE A FUCKING MINISTER'S GONNA SAVE YOUR ASS IF I START KICKING IT!
I GET THROUGH WITH YOU, BOY--
YOU'RE GONNA WISH YOUR DADDY PULLED OUT EARLY.

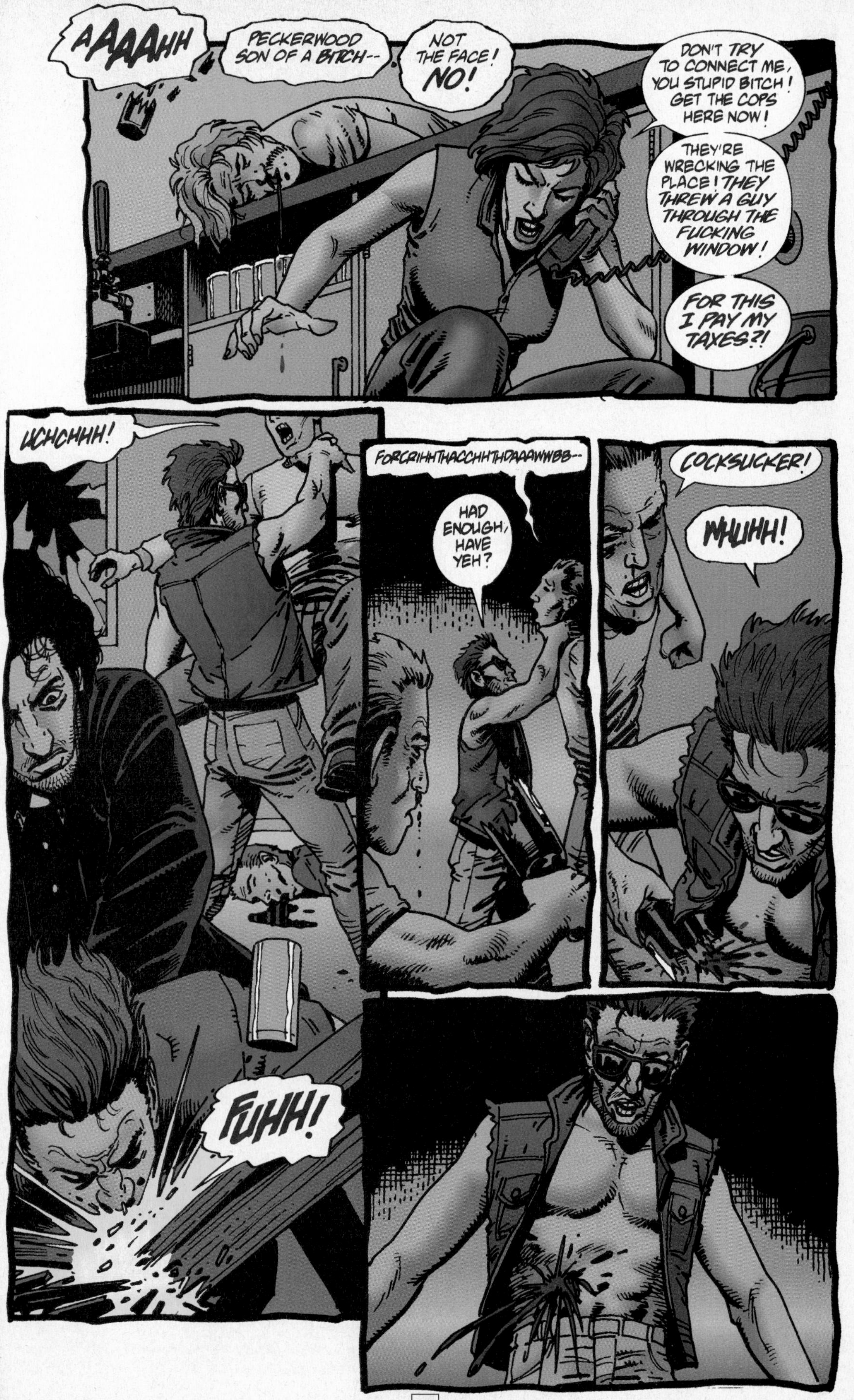

AAAAHH
PECKERWOOD SON OF A BITCH--
NOT THE FACE! NO!
DON'T TRY TO CONNECT ME, YOU STUPID BITCH! GET THE COPS HERE NOW!
THEY'RE WRECKING THE PLACE! THEY THREW A GUY THROUGH THE FUCKING WINDOW!
FOR THIS I PAY MY TAXES?!
UCHCHHH!
FORCRIHHTHACCHHTHDAAAWWBB--
HAD ENOUGH, HAVE YEH?
COCKSUCKER!
WHUHH!
FUHH!

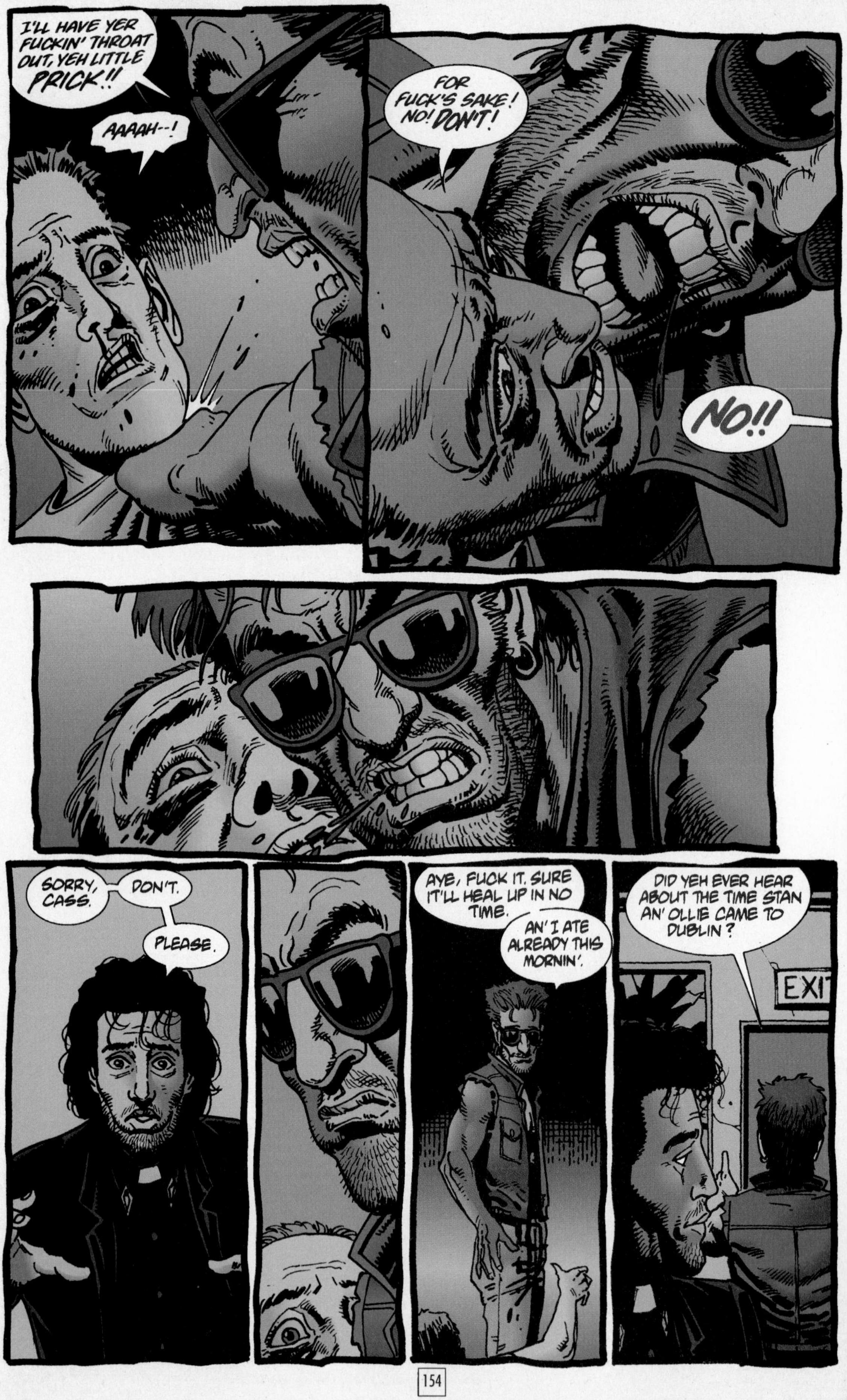
I'LL HAVE YER FUCKIN' THROAT OUT, YEH LITTLE PRICK!!
AAAAH--!
FOR FUCK'S SAKE! NO! DON'T!
NO!!
SORRY, CASS.
DON'T.
PLEASE.
AYE, FUCK IT. SURE IT'LL HEAL UP IN NO TIME.
AN' I ATE ALREADY THIS MORNIN'.
DID YEH EVER HEAR ABOUT THE TIME STAN AN' OLLIE CAME TO DUBLIN?
EXIT

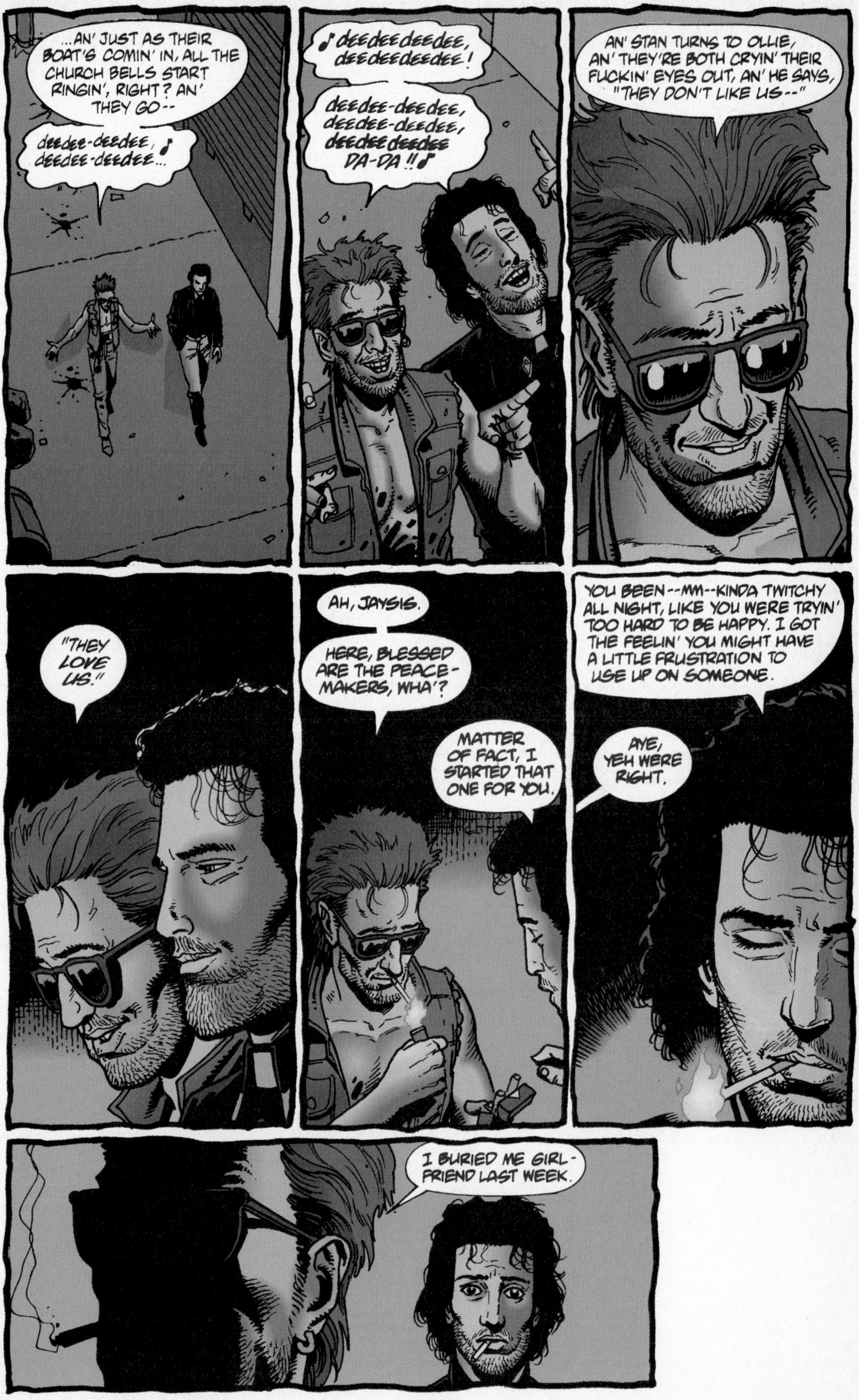

...AN' JUST AS THEIR BOAT'S COMIN' IN, ALL THE CHURCH BELLS START RINGIN', RIGHT? AN' THEY GO--
deedee-deedee, deedee-deedee...
deedeedeedee, deedeedeedee!
deedee-deedee, deedee-deedee, deedeedeedee DA-DA!!
AN' STAN TURNS TO OLLIE, AN' THEY'RE BOTH CRYIN' THEIR FUCKIN' EYES OUT, AN' HE SAYS, "THEY DON'T LIKE US--"
"THEY LOVE US."
AH, JAYSIS.
HERE, BLESSED ARE THE PEACE-MAKERS, WHA'?
MATTER OF FACT, I STARTED THAT ONE FOR YOU.
YOU BEEN--MM--KINDA TWITCHY ALL NIGHT, LIKE YOU WERE TRYIN' TOO HARD TO BE HAPPY. I GOT THE FEELIN' YOU MIGHT HAVE A LITTLE FRUSTRATION TO USE UP ON SOMEONE.
AYE, YEH WERE RIGHT.
I BURIED ME GIRL-FRIEND LAST WEEK.

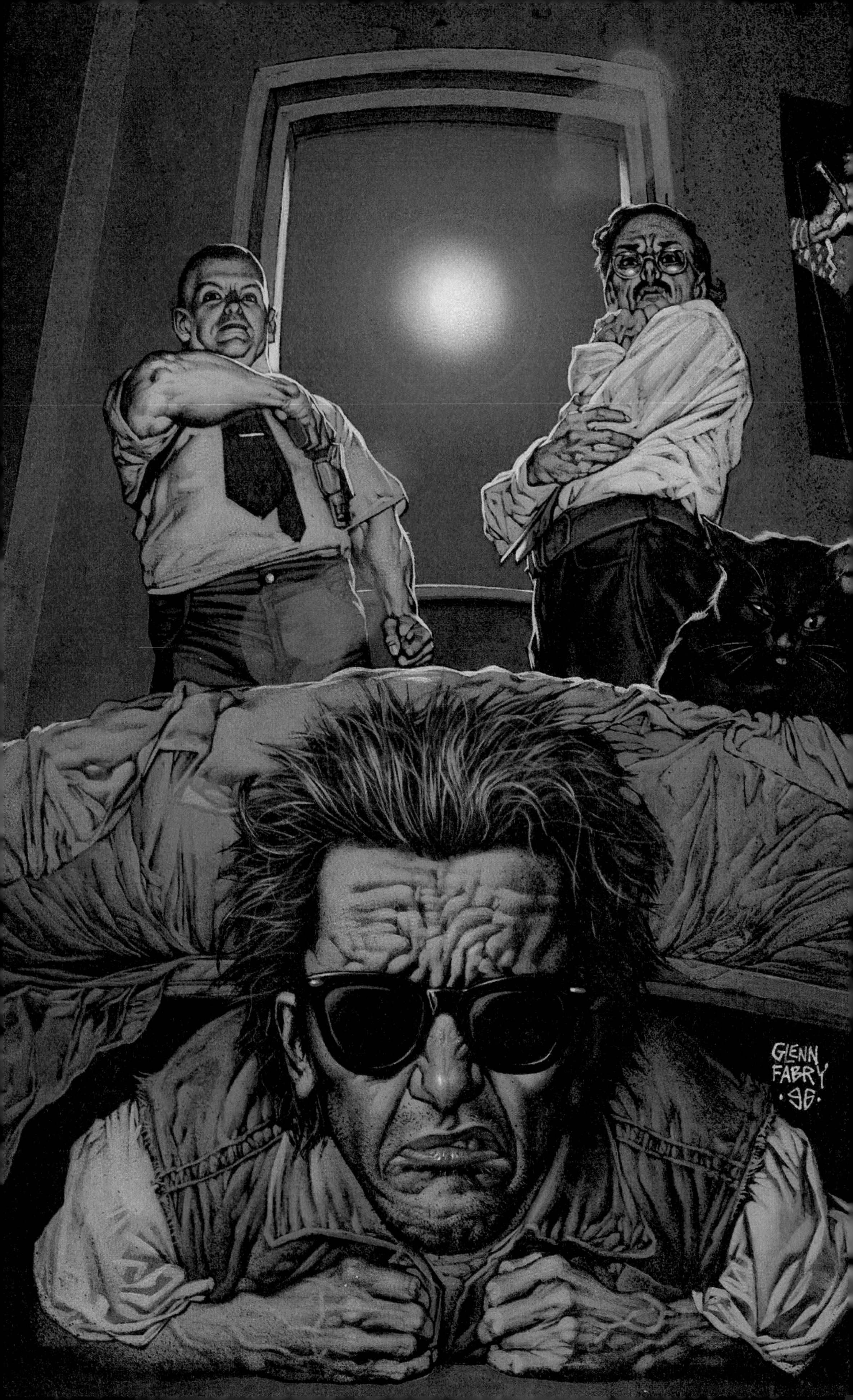
GLENN
FABRY
·96·

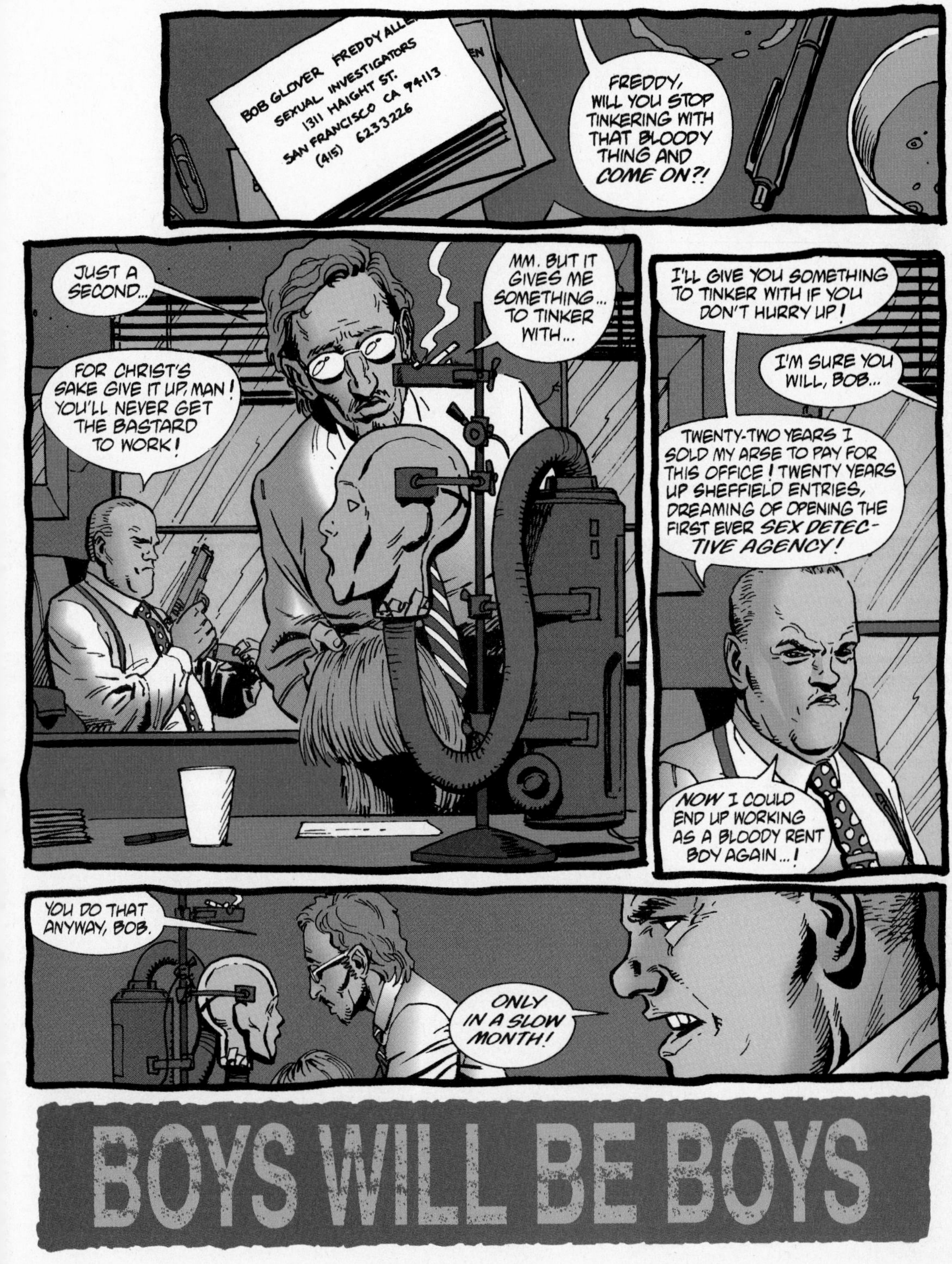
BOB GLOVER FREDDY ALLEN
SEXUAL INVESTIGATORS
1311 HAIGHT ST.
SAN FRANCISCO CA 94113
(415) 6233226
FREDDY, WILL YOU STOP TINKERING WITH THAT BLOODY THING AND COME ON?!
JUST A SECOND...
FOR CHRIST'S SAKE GIVE IT UP, MAN! YOU'LL NEVER GET THE BASTARD TO WORK!
MM. BUT IT GIVES ME SOMETHING... TO TINKER WITH...
I'LL GIVE YOU SOMETHING TO TINKER WITH IF YOU DON'T HURRY UP!
I'M SURE YOU WILL, BOB...
TWENTY-TWO YEARS I SOLD MY ARSE TO PAY FOR THIS OFFICE! TWENTY YEARS UP SHEFFIELD ENTRIES, DREAMING OF OPENING THE FIRST EVER SEX DETECTIVE AGENCY!
NOW I COULD END UP WORKING AS A BLOODY RENT BOY AGAIN...!
YOU DO THAT ANYWAY, BOB.
ONLY IN A SLOW MONTH!

BOYS WILL BE BOYS

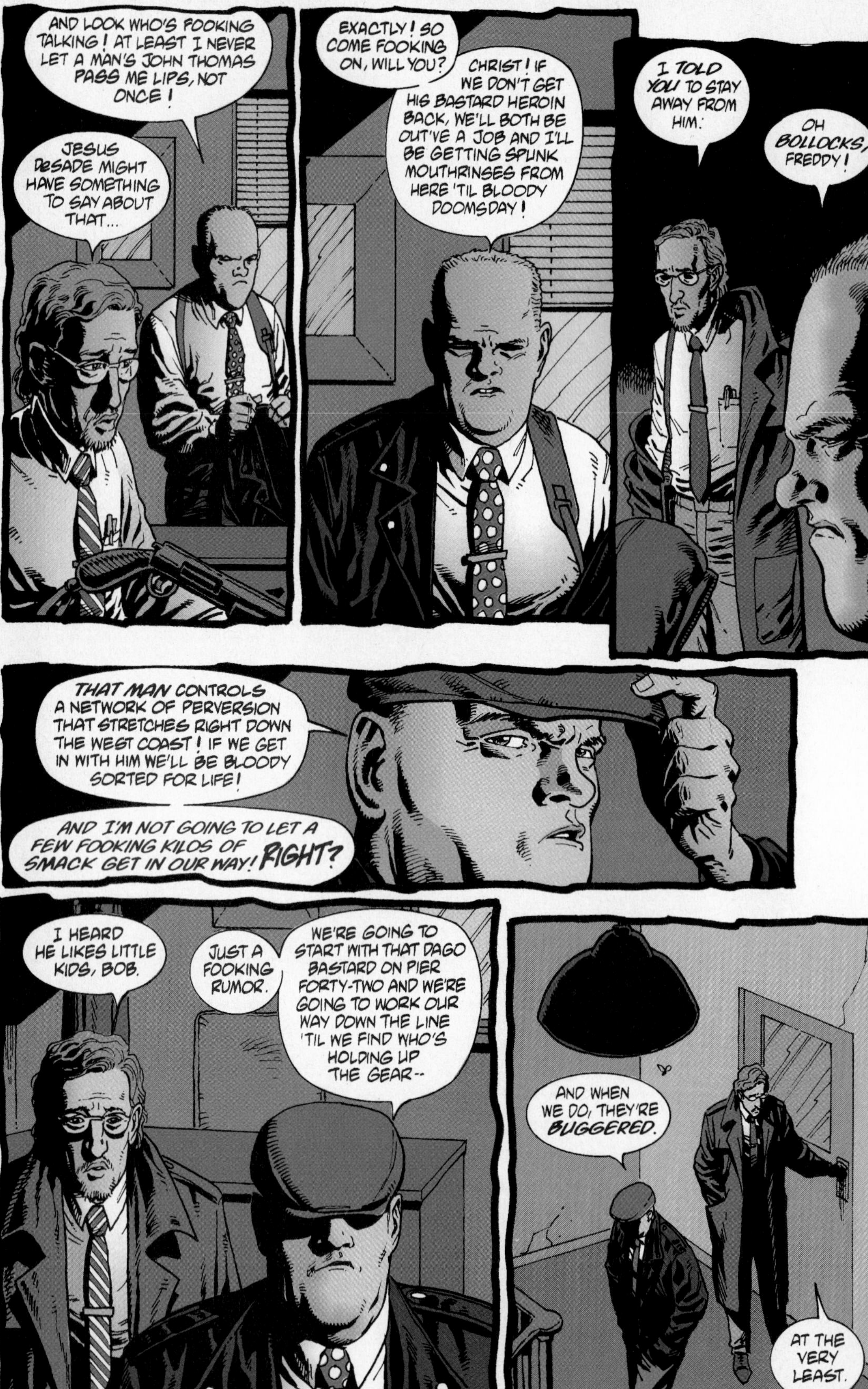
AND LOOK WHO'S FOOKING TALKING! AT LEAST I NEVER LET A MAN'S JOHN THOMAS PASS ME LIPS, NOT ONCE!
JESUS DeSADE MIGHT HAVE SOMETHING TO SAY ABOUT THAT...
EXACTLY! SO COME FOOKING ON, WILL YOU?
CHRIST! IF WE DON'T GET HIS BASTARD HEROIN BACK, WE'LL BOTH BE OUT'VE A JOB AND I'LL BE GETTING SPUNK MOUTHRINSES FROM HERE 'TIL BLOODY DOOMSDAY!
I TOLD YOU TO STAY AWAY FROM HIM.
OH BOLLOCKS, FREDDY!
THAT MAN CONTROLS A NETWORK OF PERVERSION THAT STRETCHES RIGHT DOWN THE WEST COAST! IF WE GET IN WITH HIM WE'LL BE BLOODY SORTED FOR LIFE!
AND I'M NOT GOING TO LET A FEW FOOKING KILOS OF SMACK GET IN OUR WAY! RIGHT?
I HEARD HE LIKES LITTLE KIDS, BOB.
JUST A FOOKING RUMOR.
WE'RE GOING TO START WITH THAT DAGO BASTARD ON PIER FORTY-TWO AND WE'RE GOING TO WORK OUR WAY DOWN THE LINE 'TIL WE FIND WHO'S HOLDING UP THE GEAR--
AND WHEN WE DO, THEY'RE BUGGERED.
AT THE VERY LEAST.

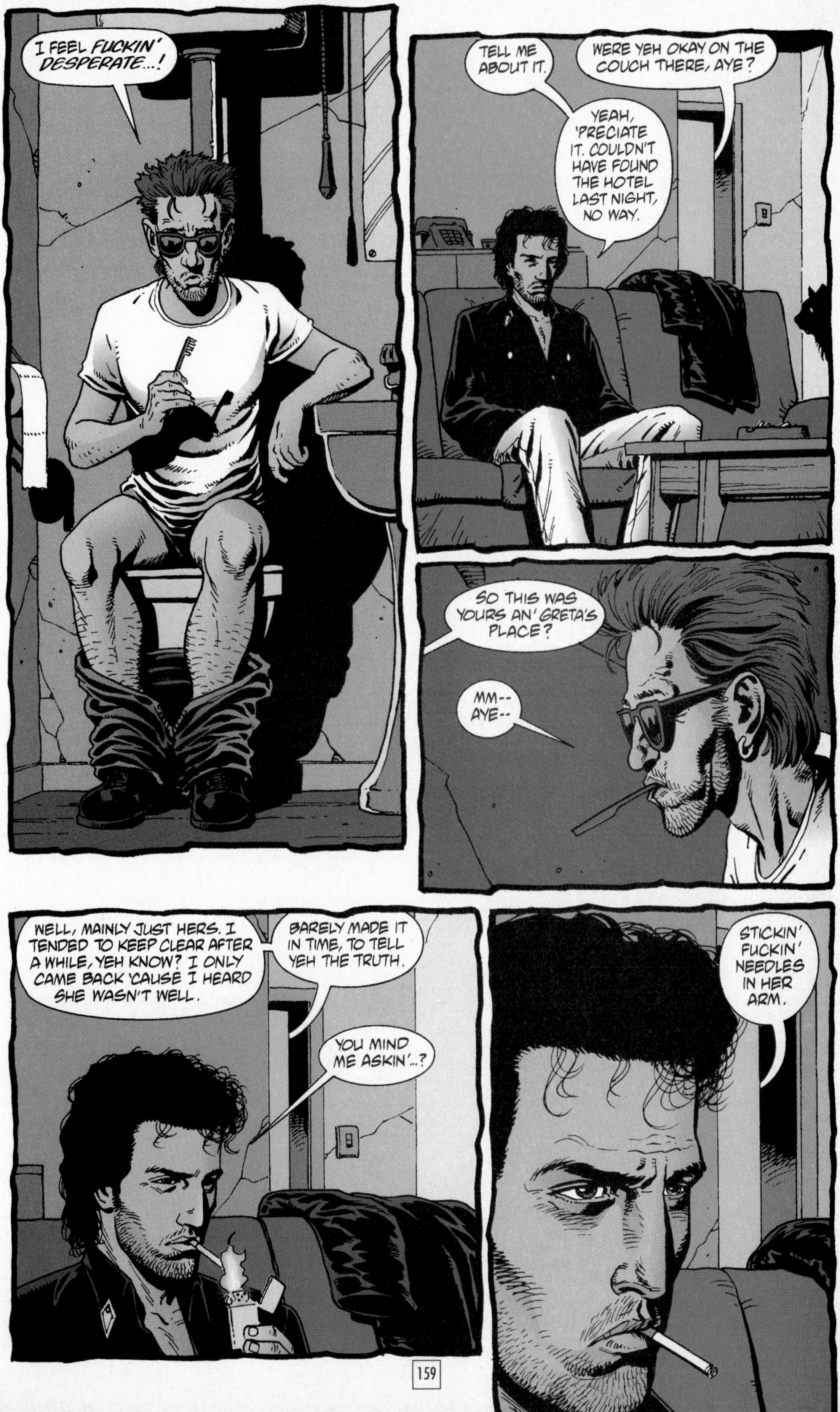
I FEEL *FUCKIN'* *DESPERATE*...!
TELL ME ABOUT IT.
WERE YEH OKAY ON THE COUCH THERE, AYE?
YEAH, 'PRECIATE IT. COULDN'T HAVE FOUND THE HOTEL LAST NIGHT, NO WAY.
SO THIS WAS YOURS AN' GRETA'S PLACE?
MM-- AYE--
WELL, MAINLY JUST HERS. I TENDED TO KEEP CLEAR AFTER A WHILE, YEH KNOW? I ONLY CAME BACK 'CAUSE I HEARD SHE WASN'T WELL.
BARELY MADE IT IN TIME, TO TELL YEH THE TRUTH.
YOU MIND ME ASKIN'...?
STICKIN' FUCKIN' NEEDLES IN HER ARM.

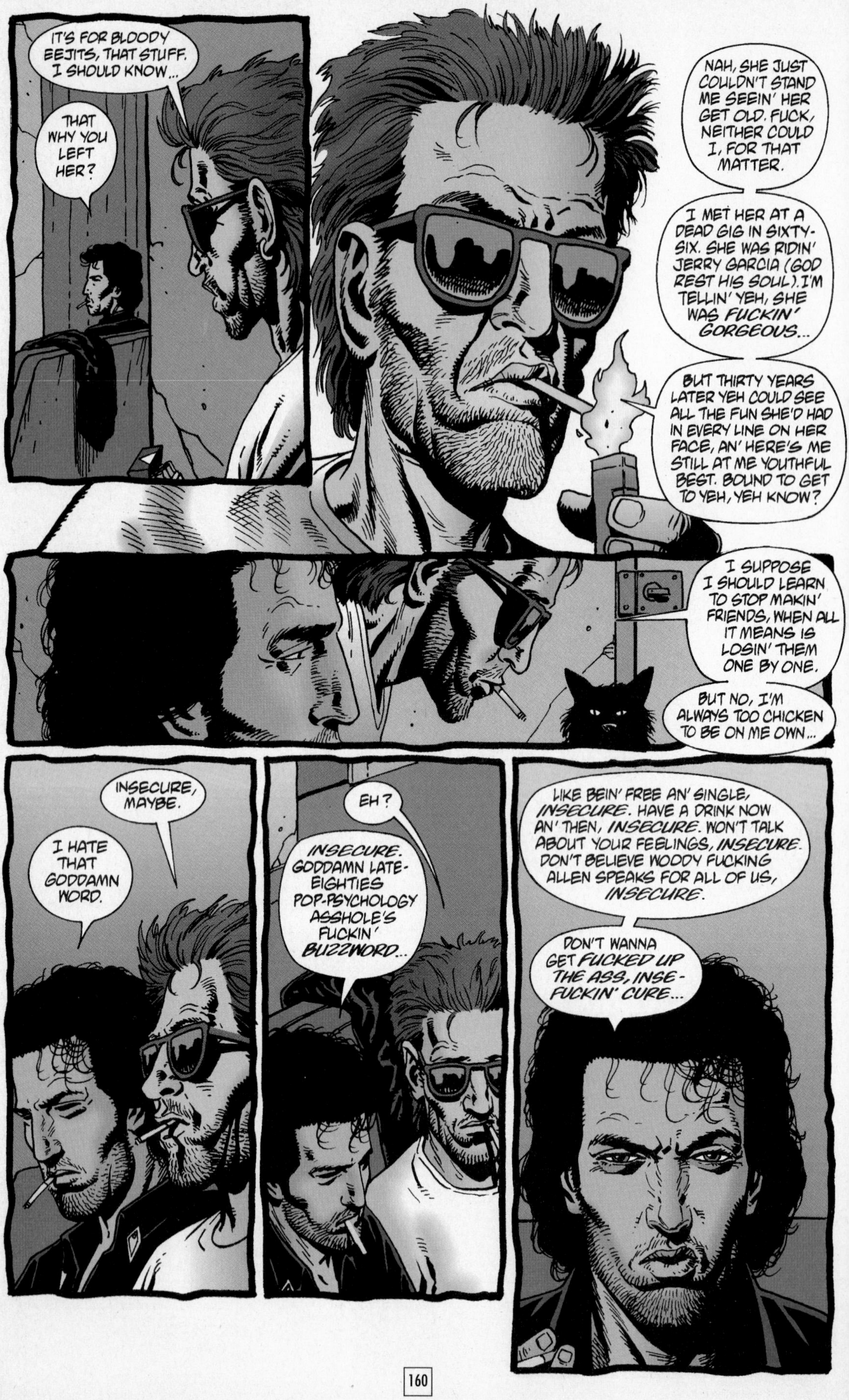
IT'S FOR BLOODY EEJITS, THAT STUFF. I SHOULD KNOW...
THAT WHY YOU LEFT HER?
NAH, SHE JUST COULDN'T STAND ME SEEIN' HER GET OLD. FUCK, NEITHER COULD I, FOR THAT MATTER.
I MET HER AT A DEAD GIG IN SIXTY-SIX. SHE WAS RIDIN' JERRY GARCIA (GOD REST HIS SOUL). I'M TELLIN' YEH, SHE WAS FUCKIN' GORGEOUS...
BUT THIRTY YEARS LATER YEH COULD SEE ALL THE FUN SHE'D HAD IN EVERY LINE ON HER FACE, AN' HERE'S ME STILL AT ME YOUTHFUL BEST. BOUND TO GET TO YEH, YEH KNOW?
I SUPPOSE I SHOULD LEARN TO STOP MAKIN' FRIENDS, WHEN ALL IT MEANS IS LOSIN' THEM ONE BY ONE.
BUT NO, I'M ALWAYS TOO CHICKEN TO BE ON ME OWN...
INSECURE, MAYBE.
I HATE THAT GODDAMN WORD.
EH?
INSECURE. GODDAMN LATE-EIGHTIES POP-PSYCHOLOGY ASSHOLE'S FUCKIN' BUZZWORD...
LIKE BEIN' FREE AN' SINGLE, INSECURE. HAVE A DRINK NOW AN' THEN, INSECURE. WON'T TALK ABOUT YOUR FEELINGS, INSECURE. DON'T BELIEVE WOODY FUCKING ALLEN SPEAKS FOR ALL OF US, INSECURE.
DON'T WANNA GET FUCKED UP THE ASS, INSE-FUCKIN'-CURE...

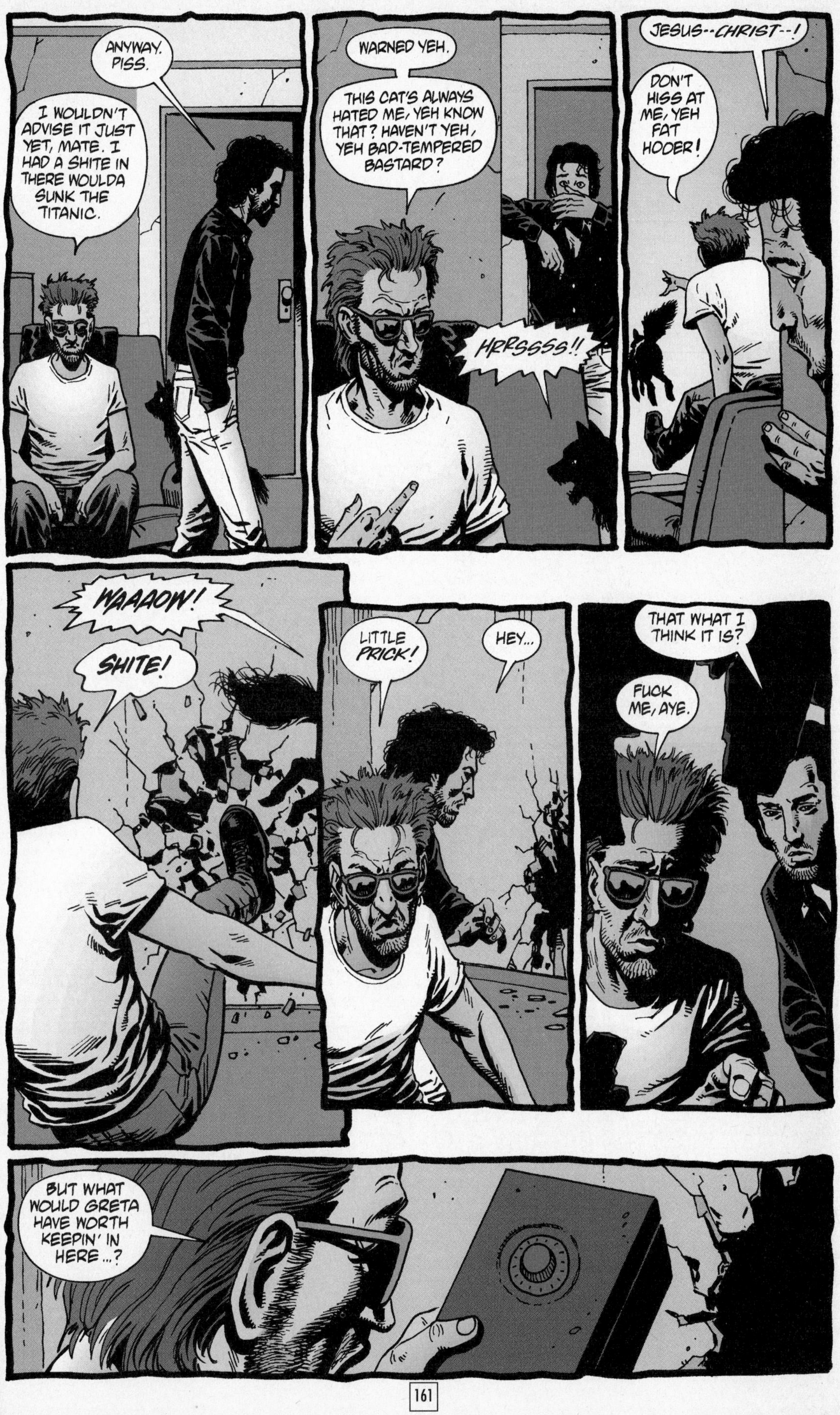
ANYWAY. PISS.
I WOULDN'T ADVISE IT JUST YET, MATE. I HAD A SHITE IN THERE WOULDA SUNK THE TITANIC.
WARNED YEH.
THIS CAT'S ALWAYS HATED ME, YEH KNOW THAT? HAVEN'T YEH, YEH BAD-TEMPERED BASTARD?
HRRSSSS!!
JESUS--CHRIST--!
DON'T HISS AT ME, YEH FAT HODER!
WAAAOW!
SHITE!
LITTLE PRICK!
HEY...
THAT WHAT I THINK IT IS?
FUCK ME, AYE.
BUT WHAT WOULD GRETA HAVE WORTH KEEPIN' IN HERE...?

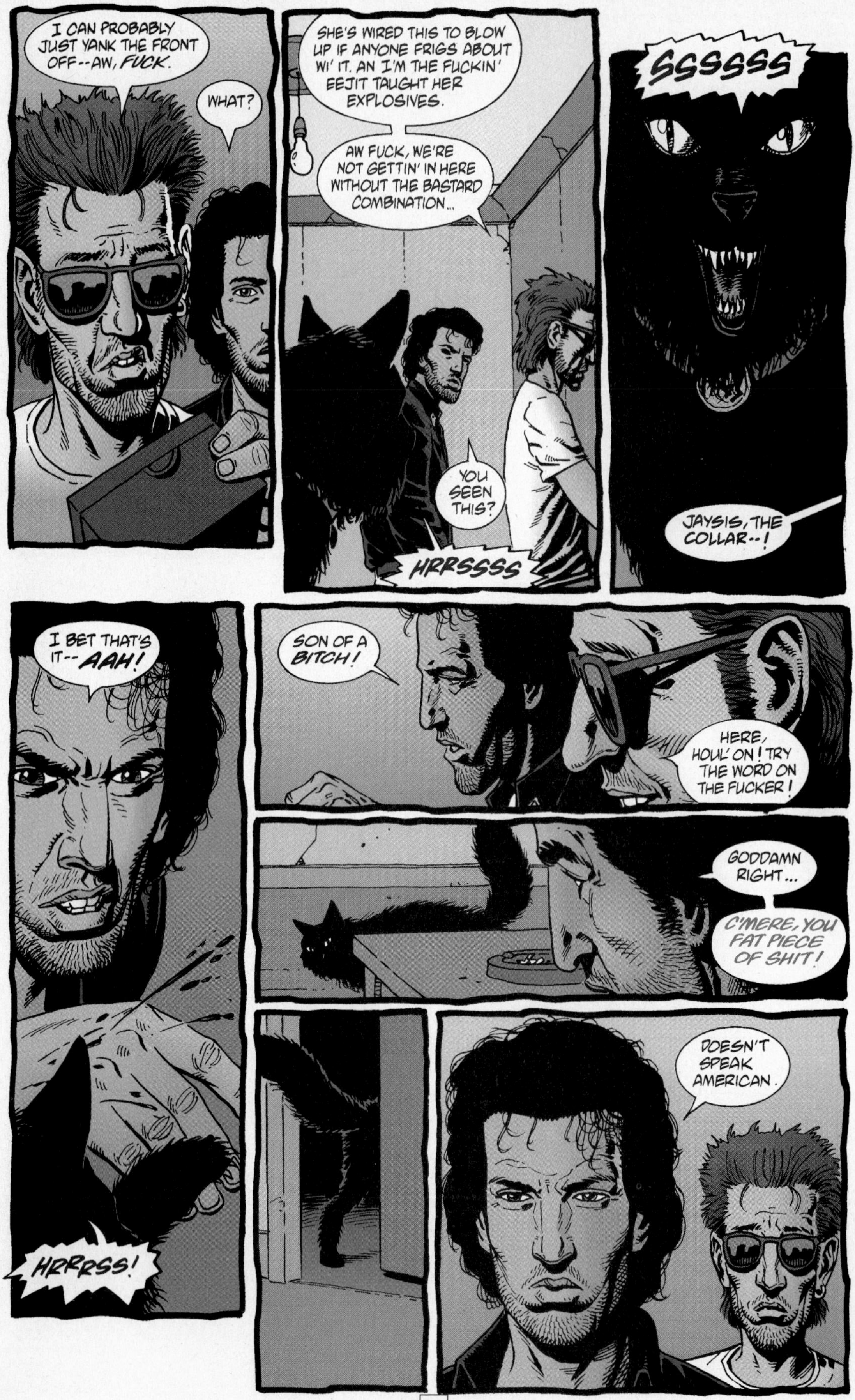
I CAN PROBABLY JUST YANK THE FRONT OFF--AW, *FUCK*.
WHAT?
SHE'S WIRED THIS TO BLOW UP IF ANYONE FRIGS ABOUT WI' IT. AN I'M THE FUCKIN' EEJIT TAUGHT HER EXPLOSIVES.
AW FUCK, WE'RE NOT GETTIN' IN HERE WITHOUT THE BASTARD COMBINATION...
YOU SEEN THIS?
HRRSSSS
SSSSSS
JAYSIS, THE COLLAR--!
I BET THAT'S IT--*AAH!*
HRRRSS!
SON OF A *BITCH!*
HERE, HOUL' ON! TRY THE WORD ON THE FUCKER!
GODDAMN RIGHT...
C'MERE, YOU FAT PIECE OF SHIT!
DOESN'T SPEAK AMERICAN.

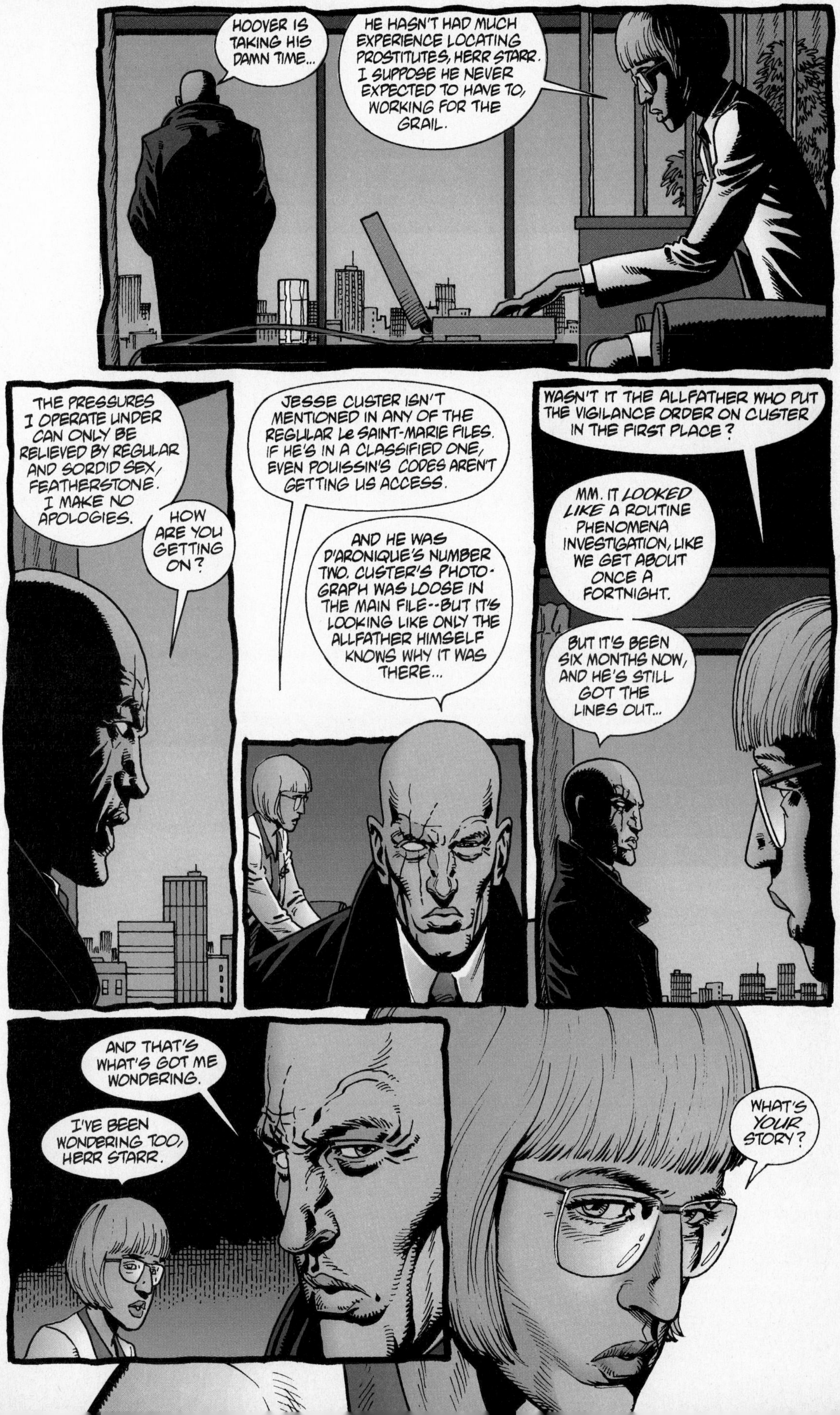
HOOVER IS TAKING HIS DAMN TIME...
HE HASN'T HAD MUCH EXPERIENCE LOCATING PROSTITUTES, HERR STARR. I SUPPOSE HE NEVER EXPECTED TO HAVE TO, WORKING FOR THE GRAIL.
THE PRESSURES I OPERATE UNDER CAN ONLY BE RELIEVED BY REGULAR AND SORDID SEX, FEATHERSTONE. I MAKE NO APOLOGIES.
HOW ARE YOU GETTING ON?
JESSE CUSTER ISN'T MENTIONED IN ANY OF THE REGULAR LE SAINT-MARIE FILES. IF HE'S IN A CLASSIFIED ONE, EVEN POUISSIN'S CODES AREN'T GETTING US ACCESS.
AND HE WAS D'ARONIQUE'S NUMBER TWO. CUSTER'S PHOTOGRAPH WAS LOOSE IN THE MAIN FILE--BUT IT'S LOOKING LIKE ONLY THE ALLFATHER HIMSELF KNOWS WHY IT WAS THERE...
WASN'T IT THE ALLFATHER WHO PUT THE VIGILANCE ORDER ON CUSTER IN THE FIRST PLACE?
MM. IT LOOKED LIKE A ROUTINE PHENOMENA INVESTIGATION, LIKE WE GET ABOUT ONCE A FORTNIGHT.
BUT IT'S BEEN SIX MONTHS NOW, AND HE'S STILL GOT THE LINES OUT...
AND THAT'S WHAT'S GOT ME WONDERING.
I'VE BEEN WONDERING TOO, HERR STARR.
WHAT'S YOUR STORY?

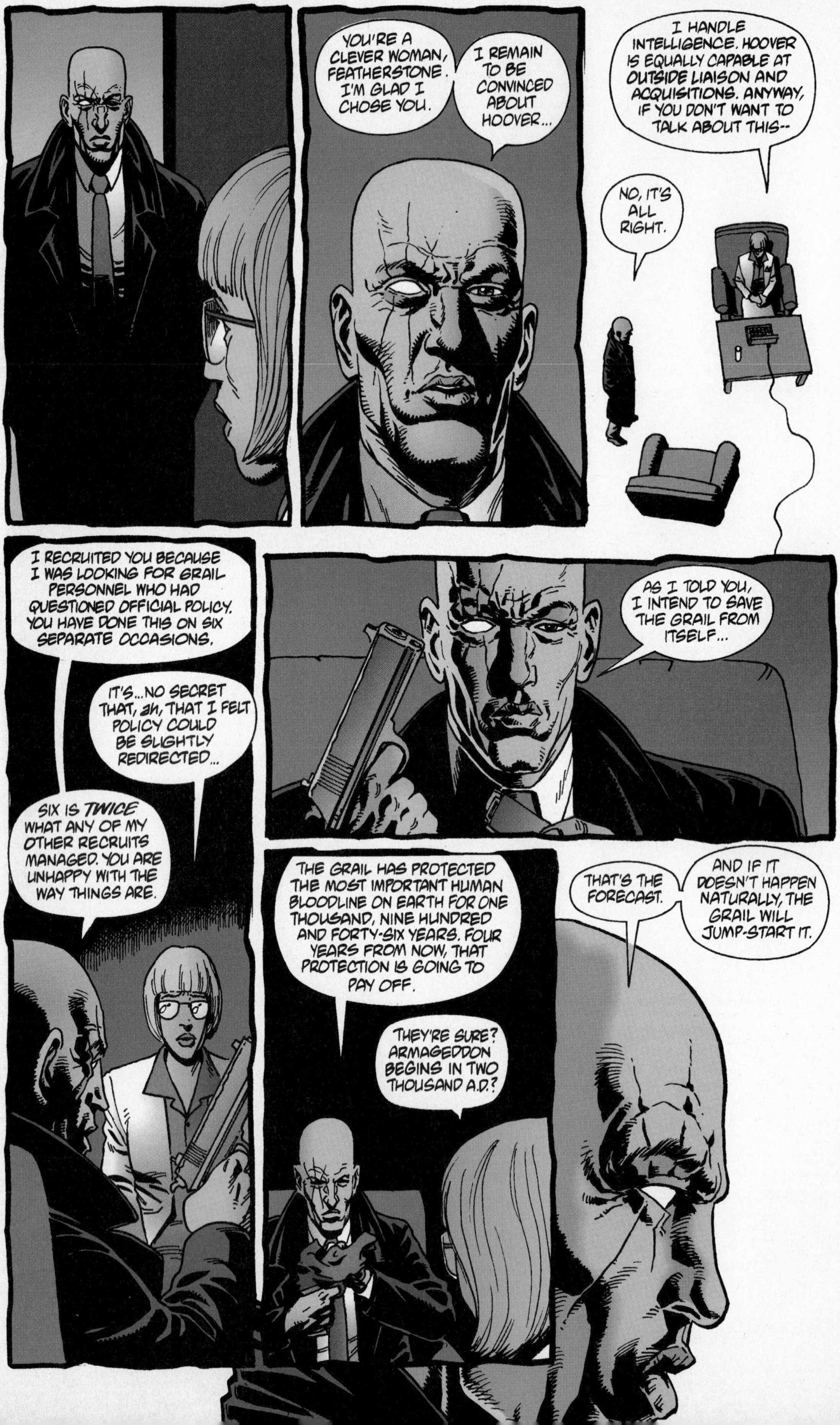
YOU'RE A CLEVER WOMAN, FEATHERSTONE. I'M GLAD I CHOSE YOU.
I REMAIN TO BE CONVINCED ABOUT HOOVER...
I HANDLE INTELLIGENCE. HOOVER IS EQUALLY CAPABLE AT OUTSIDE LIAISON AND ACQUISITIONS. ANYWAY, IF YOU DON'T WANT TO TALK ABOUT THIS--
NO, IT'S ALL RIGHT.
I RECRUITED YOU BECAUSE I WAS LOOKING FOR GRAIL PERSONNEL WHO HAD QUESTIONED OFFICIAL POLICY. YOU HAVE DONE THIS ON SIX SEPARATE OCCASIONS.
IT'S...NO SECRET THAT, ah, THAT I FELT POLICY COULD BE SLIGHTLY REDIRECTED...
SIX IS TWICE WHAT ANY OF MY OTHER RECRUITS MANAGED. YOU ARE UNHAPPY WITH THE WAY THINGS ARE.
AS I TOLD YOU, I INTEND TO SAVE THE GRAIL FROM ITSELF...
THE GRAIL HAS PROTECTED THE MOST IMPORTANT HUMAN BLOODLINE ON EARTH FOR ONE THOUSAND, NINE HUNDRED AND FORTY-SIX YEARS. FOUR YEARS FROM NOW, THAT PROTECTION IS GOING TO PAY OFF.
THEY'RE SURE? ARMAGEDDON BEGINS IN TWO THOUSAND A.D.?
THAT'S THE FORECAST.
AND IF IT DOESN'T HAPPEN NATURALLY, THE GRAIL WILL JUMP-START IT.

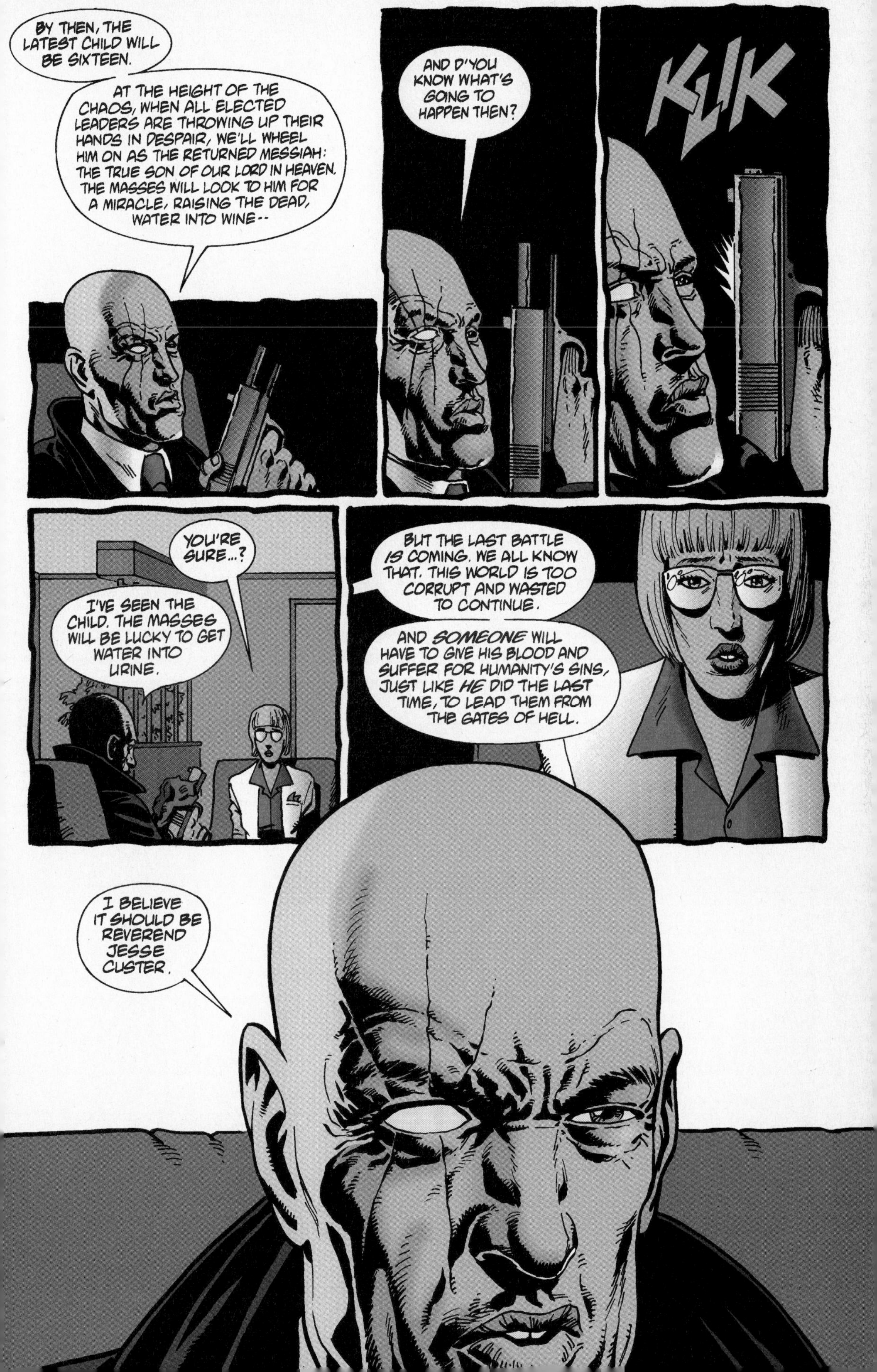

BY THEN, THE LATEST CHILD WILL BE SIXTEEN.
AT THE HEIGHT OF THE CHAOS, WHEN ALL ELECTED LEADERS ARE THROWING UP THEIR HANDS IN DESPAIR, WE'LL WHEEL HIM ON AS THE RETURNED MESSIAH: THE TRUE SON OF OUR LORD IN HEAVEN. THE MASSES WILL LOOK TO HIM FOR A MIRACLE, RAISING THE DEAD, WATER INTO WINE--
AND D'YOU KNOW WHAT'S GOING TO HAPPEN THEN?
KLIK
YOU'RE SURE...?
I'VE SEEN THE CHILD. THE MASSES WILL BE LUCKY TO GET WATER INTO URINE.
BUT THE LAST BATTLE IS COMING. WE ALL KNOW THAT. THIS WORLD IS TOO CORRUPT AND WASTED TO CONTINUE.
AND SOMEONE WILL HAVE TO GIVE HIS BLOOD AND SUFFER FOR HUMANITY'S SINS, JUST LIKE HE DID THE LAST TIME, TO LEAD THEM FROM THE GATES OF HELL.
I BELIEVE IT SHOULD BE REVEREND JESSE CUSTER.

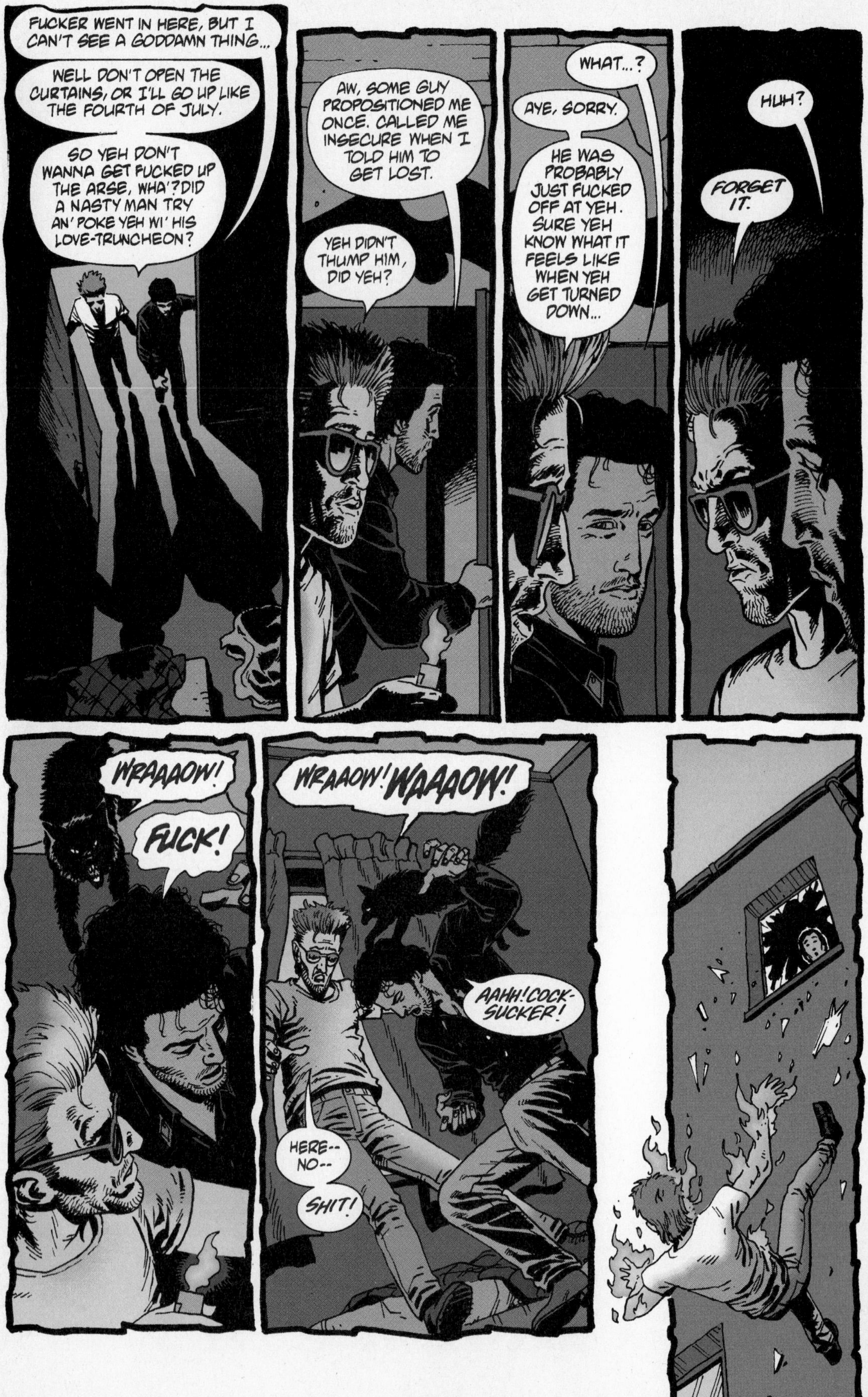
FUCKER WENT IN HERE, BUT I CAN'T SEE A GODDAMN THING...
WELL DON'T OPEN THE CURTAINS, OR I'LL GO UP LIKE THE FOURTH OF JULY.
SO YEH DON'T WANNA GET FUCKED UP THE ARSE, WHA'? DID A NASTY MAN TRY AN' POKE YEH WI' HIS LOVE-TRUNCHEON?
AW, SOME GUY PROPOSITIONED ME ONCE. CALLED ME INSECURE WHEN I TOLD HIM TO GET LOST.
YEH DIDN'T THUMP HIM, DID YEH?
WHAT...?
AYE, SORRY.
HE WAS PROBABLY JUST FUCKED OFF AT YEH. SURE YEH KNOW WHAT IT FEELS LIKE WHEN YEH GET TURNED DOWN...
HUH?
FORGET IT.
WRAAAOW!
FUCK!
WRAAOW! WAAAOW!
AAHH! COCK-SUCKER!
HERE-- NO--
SHIT!

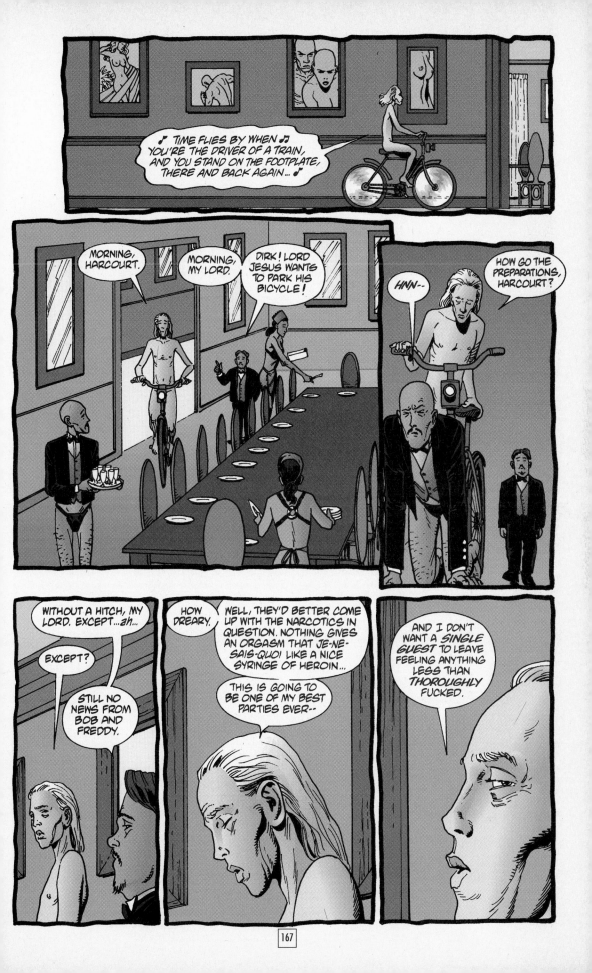

♪ TIME FLIES BY WHEN ♫ YOU'RE THE DRIVER OF A TRAIN, AND YOU STAND ON THE FOOTPLATE, THERE AND BACK AGAIN... ♪

MORNING, HARCOURT.

MORNING, MY LORD.

DIRK! LORD JESUS WANTS TO PARK HIS BICYCLE!

HNN--

HOW GO THE PREPARATIONS, HARCOURT?

WITHOUT A HITCH, MY LORD. EXCEPT...*ah...*

EXCEPT?

STILL NO NEWS FROM BOB AND FREDDY.

HOW DREARY.

WELL, THEY'D BETTER COME UP WITH THE NARCOTICS IN QUESTION. NOTHING GIVES AN ORGASM THAT JE-NE-SAIS-QUOI LIKE A NICE SYRINGE OF HEROIN...

THIS IS GOING TO BE ONE OF MY BEST PARTIES EVER--

AND I DON'T WANT A *SINGLE GUEST* TO LEAVE FEELING ANYTHING LESS THAN *THOROUGHLY* FUCKED.

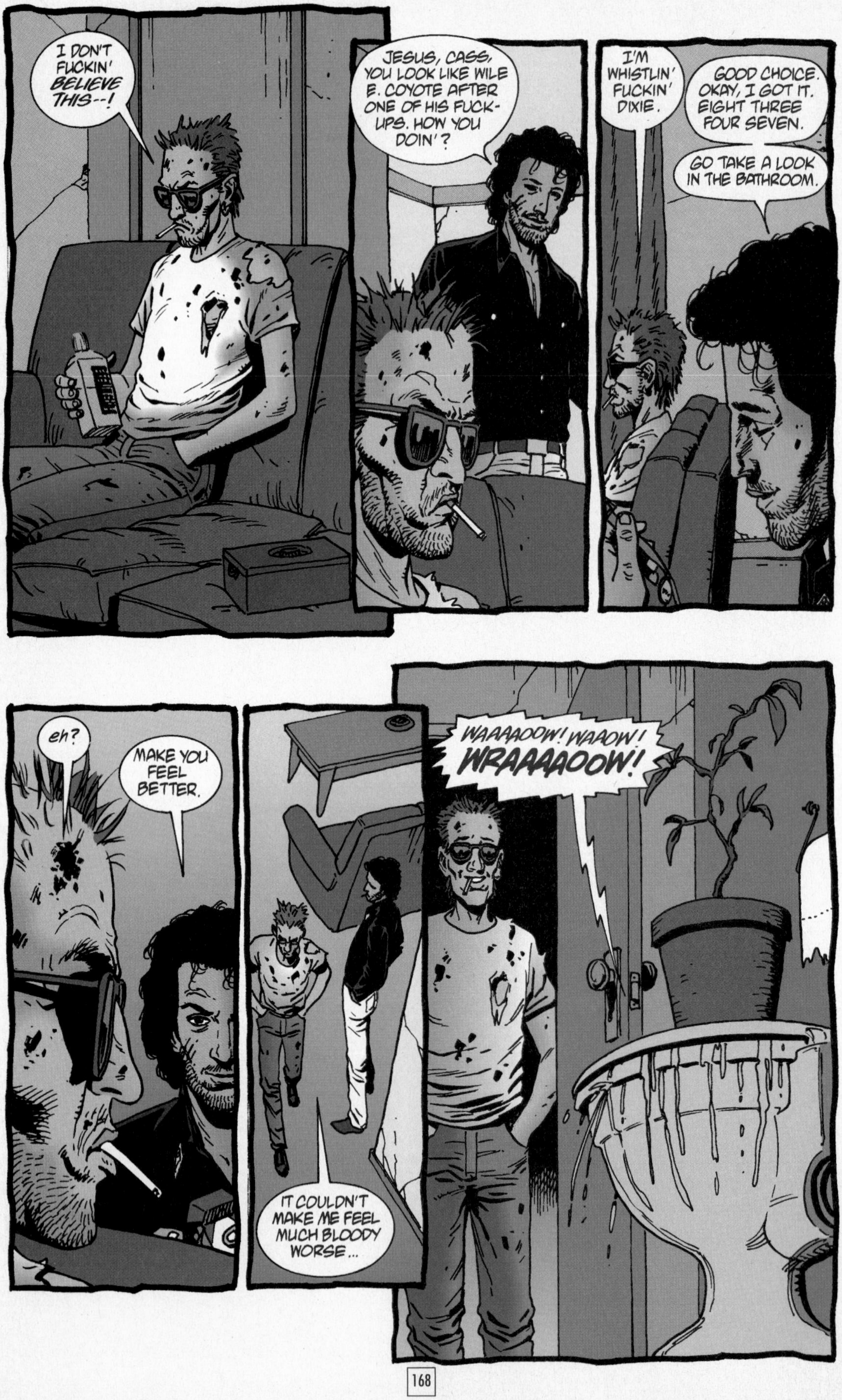
I DON'T FUCKIN' BELIEVE THIS--!
JESUS, CASS, YOU LOOK LIKE WILE E. COYOTE AFTER ONE OF HIS FUCK-UPS. HOW YOU DOIN'?
I'M WHISTLIN' FUCKIN' DIXIE.
GOOD CHOICE. OKAY, I GOT IT. EIGHT THREE FOUR SEVEN.
GO TAKE A LOOK IN THE BATHROOM.
eh?
MAKE YOU FEEL BETTER.
IT COULDN'T MAKE ME FEEL MUCH BLOODY WORSE...
WAAAAOOW! WAAOW! WRAAAAOOW!

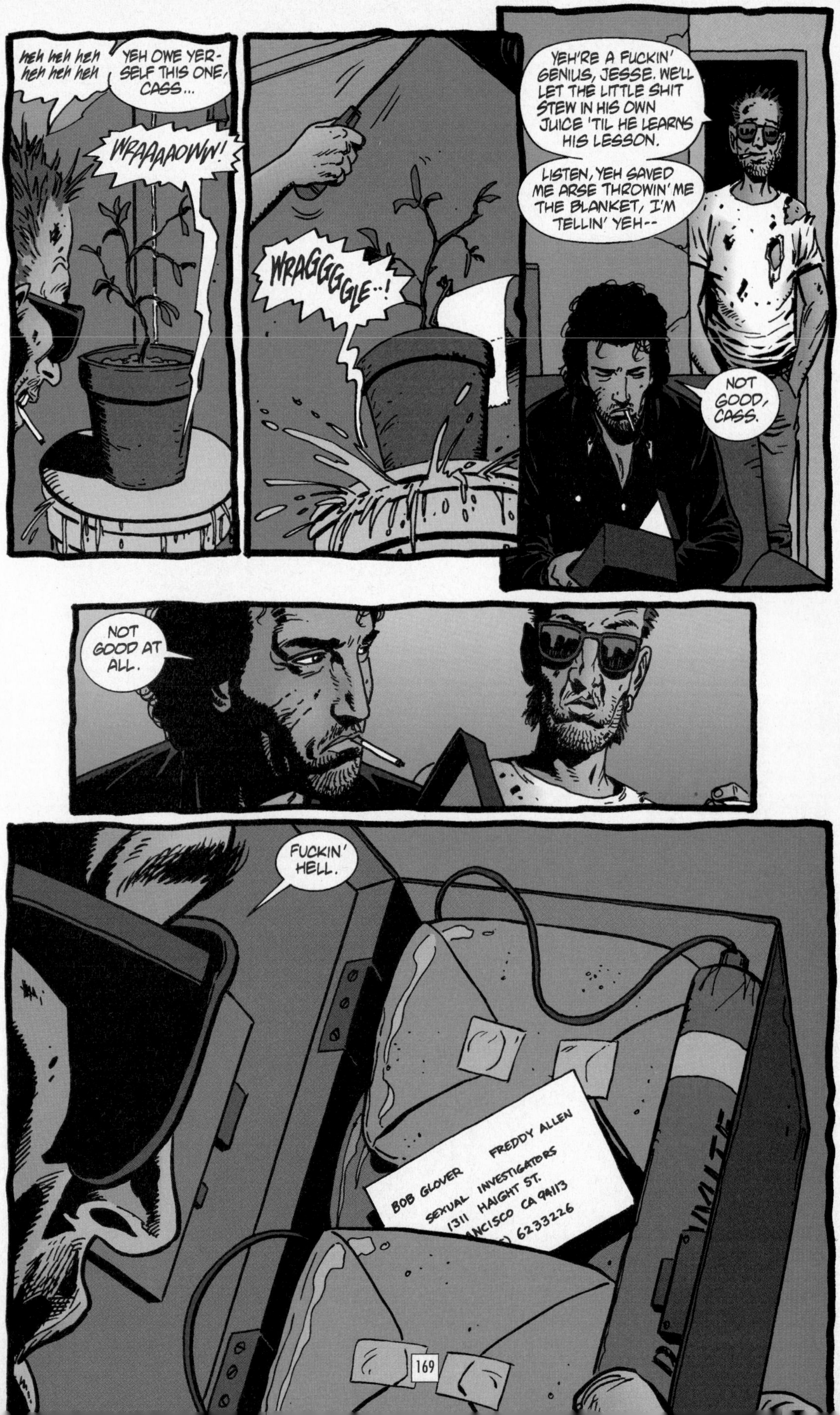
heh heh heh heh heh heh
YEH OWE YER-SELF THIS ONE, CASS...
WRAAAAOWW!
WRAGGGGLE...!
YEH'RE A FUCKIN' GENIUS, JESSE. WE'LL LET THE LITTLE SHIT STEW IN HIS OWN JUICE 'TIL HE LEARNS HIS LESSON.
LISTEN, YEH SAVED ME ARSE THROWIN' ME THE BLANKET, I'M TELLIN' YEH--
NOT GOOD, CASS.
NOT GOOD AT ALL.
FUCKIN' HELL.
BOB GLOVER FREDDY ALLEN
SEXUAL INVESTIGATORS
1311 HAIGHT ST.
ANCISCO CA 94113
) 6233226

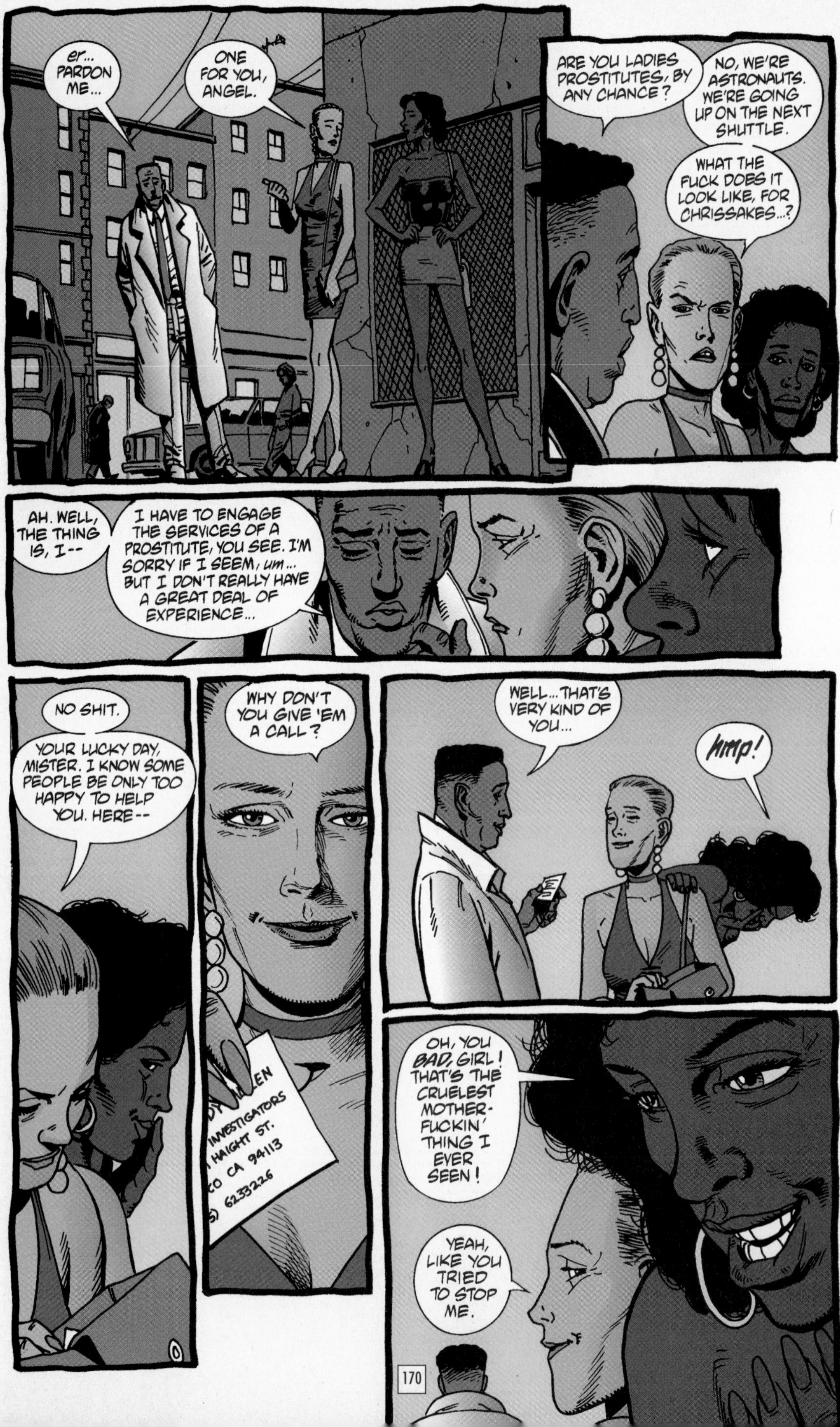
er... PARDON ME...
ONE FOR YOU, ANGEL.
ARE YOU LADIES PROSTITUTES, BY ANY CHANCE?
NO, WE'RE ASTRONAUTS. WE'RE GOING UP ON THE NEXT SHUTTLE.
WHAT THE FUCK DOES IT LOOK LIKE, FOR CHRISSAKES...?
AH. WELL, THE THING IS, I--
I HAVE TO ENGAGE THE SERVICES OF A PROSTITUTE, YOU SEE. I'M SORRY IF I SEEM, um... BUT I DON'T REALLY HAVE A GREAT DEAL OF EXPERIENCE...
NO SHIT.
YOUR LUCKY DAY, MISTER. I KNOW SOME PEOPLE BE ONLY TOO HAPPY TO HELP YOU. HERE--
WHY DON'T YOU GIVE 'EM A CALL?
INVESTIGATORS
HAIGHT ST.
CO CA 94113
6233226
WELL... THAT'S VERY KIND OF YOU...
hmp!
OH, YOU BAD, GIRL! THAT'S THE CRUELEST MOTHER-FUCKIN' THING I EVER SEEN!
YEAH, LIKE YOU TRIED TO STOP ME.

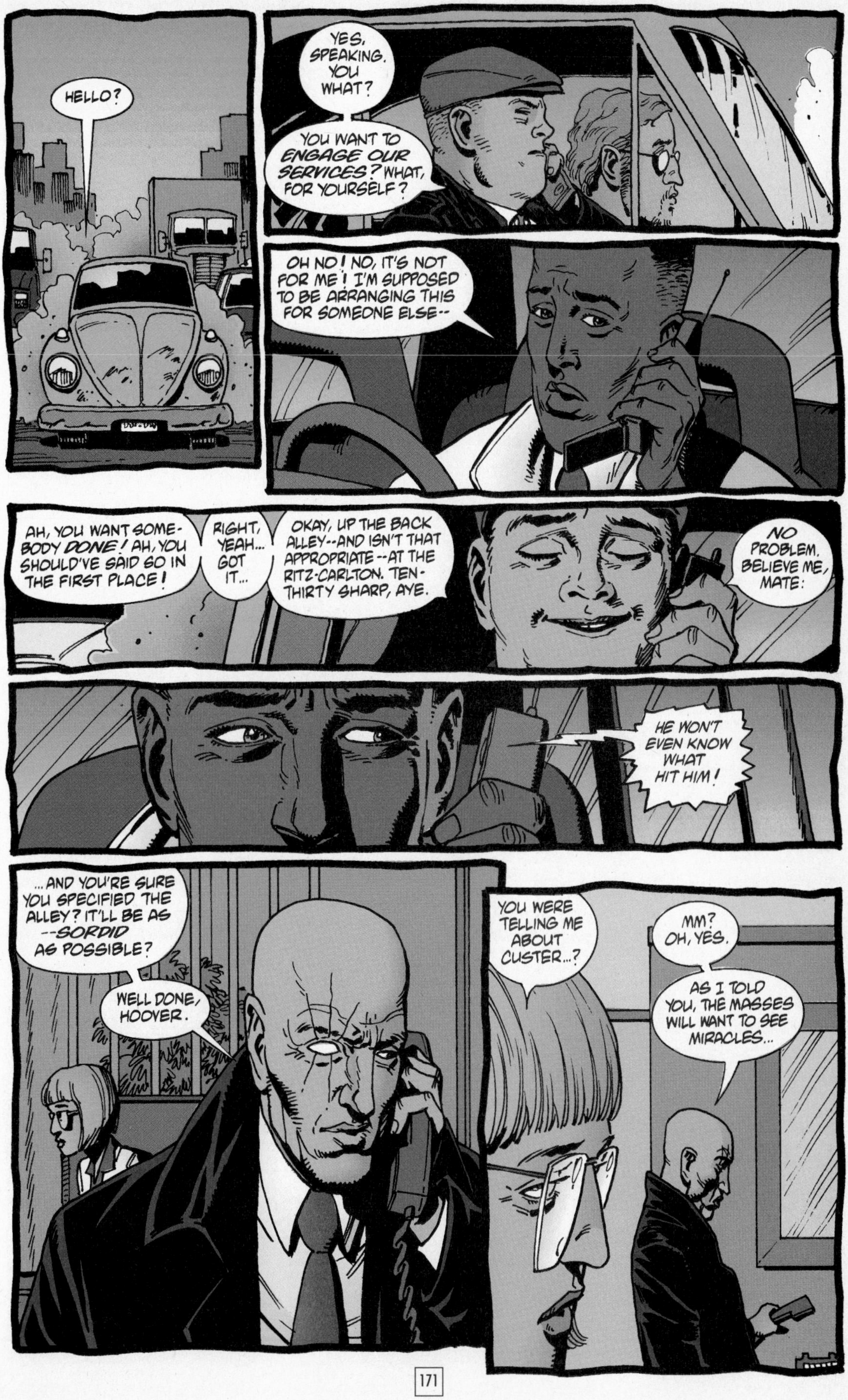
HELLO?
YES, SPEAKING. YOU WHAT?
YOU WANT TO ENGAGE OUR SERVICES? WHAT, FOR YOURSELF?
OH NO! NO, IT'S NOT FOR ME! I'M SUPPOSED TO BE ARRANGING THIS FOR SOMEONE ELSE--
AH, YOU WANT SOMEBODY DONE! AH, YOU SHOULD'VE SAID SO IN THE FIRST PLACE!
RIGHT, YEAH... GOT IT...
OKAY, UP THE BACK ALLEY--AND ISN'T THAT APPROPRIATE--AT THE RITZ-CARLTON. TEN-THIRTY SHARP, AYE.
NO PROBLEM. BELIEVE ME, MATE:
HE WON'T EVEN KNOW WHAT HIT HIM!
...AND YOU'RE SURE YOU SPECIFIED THE ALLEY? IT'LL BE AS --SORDID AS POSSIBLE?
WELL DONE, HOOVER.
YOU WERE TELLING ME ABOUT CUSTER...?
MM? OH, YES.
AS I TOLD YOU, THE MASSES WILL WANT TO SEE MIRACLES...

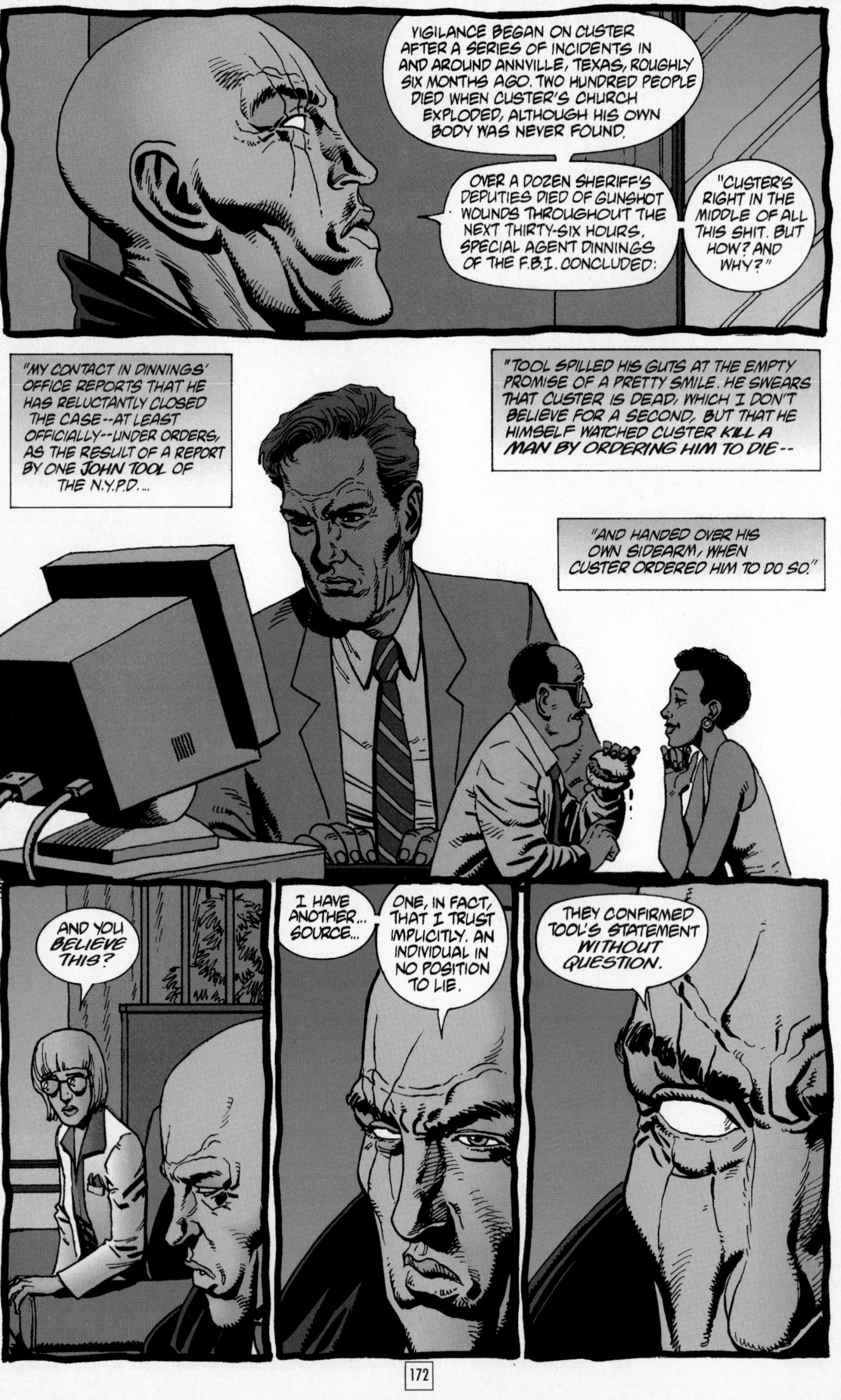
VIGILANCE BEGAN ON CUSTER AFTER A SERIES OF INCIDENTS IN AND AROUND ANNVILLE, TEXAS, ROUGHLY SIX MONTHS AGO. TWO HUNDRED PEOPLE DIED WHEN CUSTER'S CHURCH EXPLODED, ALTHOUGH HIS OWN BODY WAS NEVER FOUND.
OVER A DOZEN SHERIFF'S DEPUTIES DIED OF GUNSHOT WOUNDS THROUGHOUT THE NEXT THIRTY-SIX HOURS. SPECIAL AGENT DINNINGS OF THE F.B.I. CONCLUDED:
"CUSTER'S RIGHT IN THE MIDDLE OF ALL THIS SHIT. BUT HOW? AND WHY?"
"MY CONTACT IN DINNINGS' OFFICE REPORTS THAT HE HAS RELUCTANTLY CLOSED THE CASE--AT LEAST OFFICIALLY--UNDER ORDERS, AS THE RESULT OF A REPORT BY ONE JOHN TOOL OF THE N.Y.P.D....
"TOOL SPILLED HIS GUTS AT THE EMPTY PROMISE OF A PRETTY SMILE. HE SWEARS THAT CUSTER IS DEAD, WHICH I DON'T BELIEVE FOR A SECOND, BUT THAT HE HIMSELF WATCHED CUSTER KILL A MAN BY ORDERING HIM TO DIE--
"AND HANDED OVER HIS OWN SIDEARM, WHEN CUSTER ORDERED HIM TO DO SO."
AND YOU BELIEVE THIS?
I HAVE ANOTHER... SOURCE...
ONE, IN FACT, THAT I TRUST IMPLICITLY. AN INDIVIDUAL IN NO POSITION TO LIE.
THEY CONFIRMED TOOL'S STATEMENT WITHOUT QUESTION.

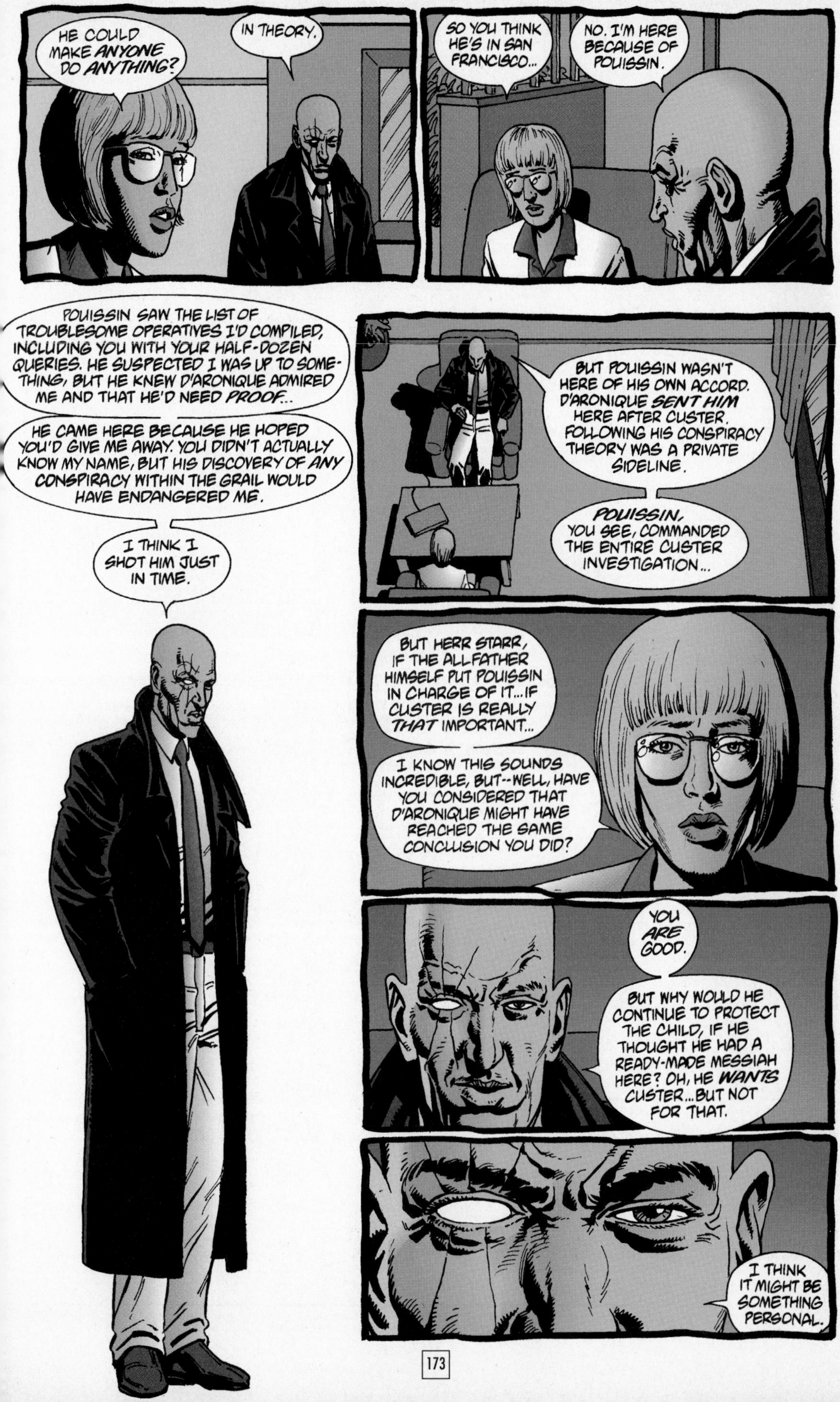
HE COULD MAKE ANYONE DO ANYTHING?
IN THEORY.
SO YOU THINK HE'S IN SAN FRANCISCO...
NO. I'M HERE BECAUSE OF POUISSIN.
POUISSIN SAW THE LIST OF TROUBLESOME OPERATIVES I'D COMPILED, INCLUDING YOU WITH YOUR HALF-DOZEN QUERIES. HE SUSPECTED I WAS UP TO SOMETHING, BUT HE KNEW D'ARONIQUE ADMIRED ME AND THAT HE'D NEED PROOF...
HE CAME HERE BECAUSE HE HOPED YOU'D GIVE ME AWAY. YOU DIDN'T ACTUALLY KNOW MY NAME, BUT HIS DISCOVERY OF ANY CONSPIRACY WITHIN THE GRAIL WOULD HAVE ENDANGERED ME.
I THINK I SHOT HIM JUST IN TIME.
BUT POUISSIN WASN'T HERE OF HIS OWN ACCORD. D'ARONIQUE SENT HIM HERE AFTER CUSTER. FOLLOWING HIS CONSPIRACY THEORY WAS A PRIVATE SIDELINE.
POUISSIN, YOU SEE, COMMANDED THE ENTIRE CUSTER INVESTIGATION...
BUT HERR STARR, IF THE ALLFATHER HIMSELF PUT POUISSIN IN CHARGE OF IT...IF CUSTER IS REALLY THAT IMPORTANT...
I KNOW THIS SOUNDS INCREDIBLE, BUT--WELL, HAVE YOU CONSIDERED THAT D'ARONIQUE MIGHT HAVE REACHED THE SAME CONCLUSION YOU DID?
YOU ARE GOOD.
BUT WHY WOULD HE CONTINUE TO PROTECT THE CHILD, IF HE THOUGHT HE HAD A READY-MADE MESSIAH HERE? OH, HE WANTS CUSTER...BUT NOT FOR THAT.
I THINK IT MIGHT BE SOMETHING PERSONAL.

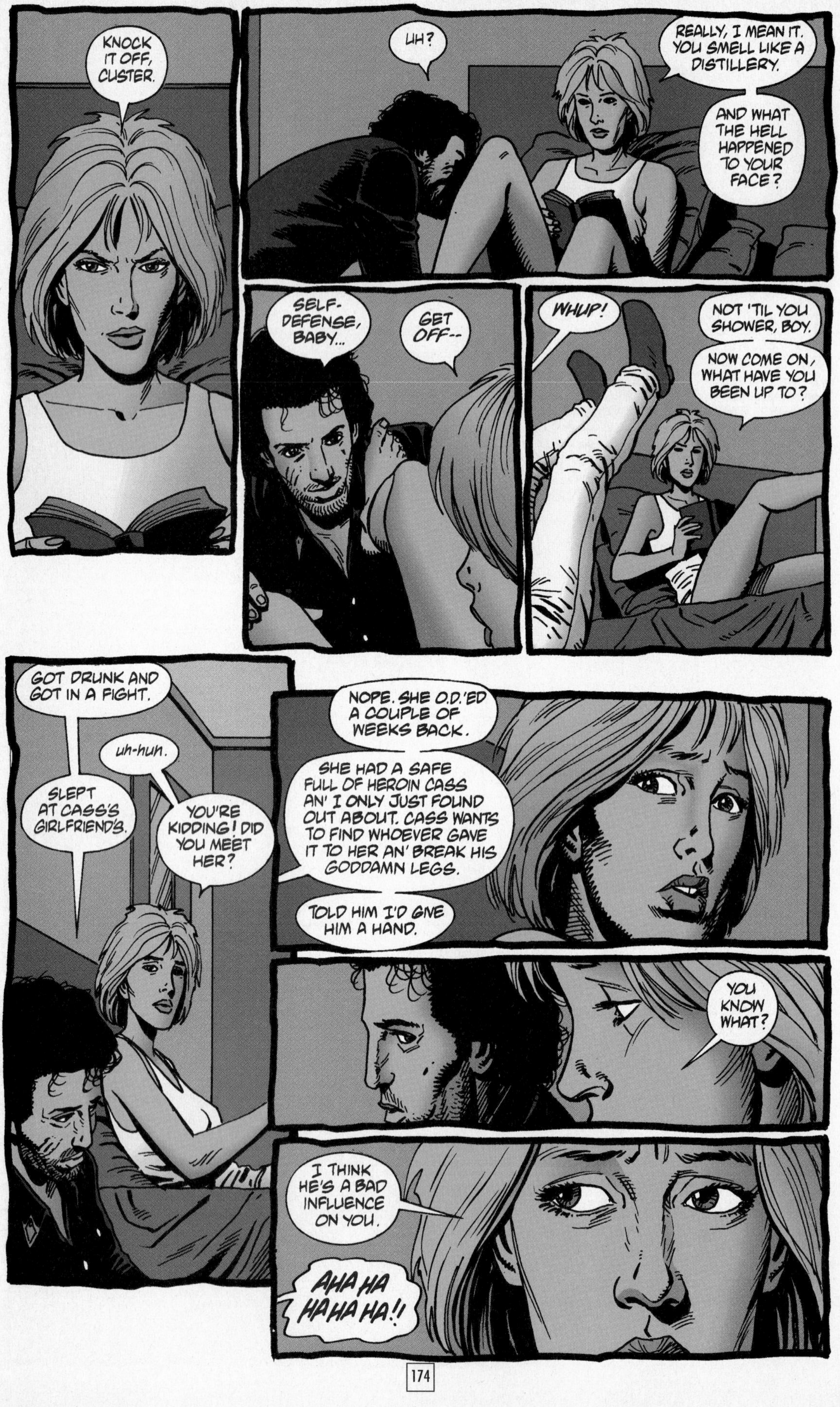

KNOCK IT OFF, CUSTER.
UH?
REALLY, I MEAN IT. YOU SMELL LIKE A DISTILLERY.
AND WHAT THE HELL HAPPENED TO YOUR FACE?
SELF-DEFENSE, BABY...
GET OFF--
WHUP!
NOT 'TIL YOU SHOWER, BOY.
NOW COME ON, WHAT HAVE YOU BEEN UP TO?
GOT DRUNK AND GOT IN A FIGHT.
uh-huh.
SLEPT AT CASS'S GIRLFRIEND'S.
YOU'RE KIDDING! DID YOU MEET HER?
NOPE. SHE O.D.'ED A COUPLE OF WEEKS BACK.
SHE HAD A SAFE FULL OF HEROIN CASS AN' I ONLY JUST FOUND OUT ABOUT. CASS WANTS TO FIND WHOEVER GAVE IT TO HER AN' BREAK HIS GODDAMN LEGS.
TOLD HIM I'D GIVE HIM A HAND.
YOU KNOW WHAT?
I THINK HE'S A BAD INFLUENCE ON YOU.
AHA HA HA HA HA!!

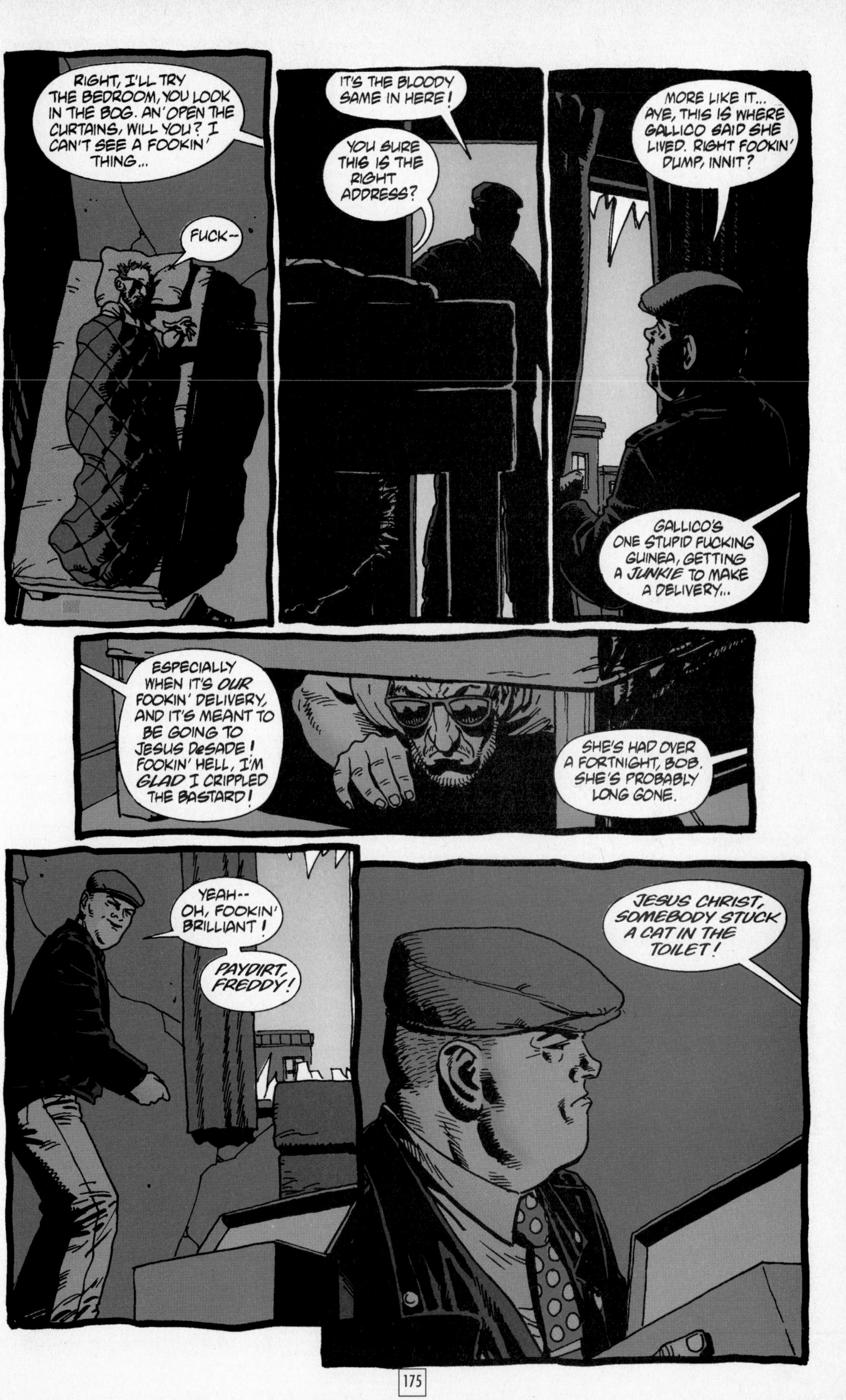
RIGHT, I'LL TRY THE BEDROOM, YOU LOOK IN THE BOG. AN' OPEN THE CURTAINS, WILL YOU? I CAN'T SEE A FOOKIN' THING...
FUCK--
IT'S THE BLOODY SAME IN HERE!
YOU SURE THIS IS THE RIGHT ADDRESS?
MORE LIKE IT... AYE, THIS IS WHERE GALLICO SAID SHE LIVED. RIGHT FOOKIN' DUMP, INNIT?
GALLICO'S ONE STUPID FUCKING GUINEA, GETTING A JUNKIE TO MAKE A DELIVERY...
ESPECIALLY WHEN IT'S OUR FOOKIN' DELIVERY, AND IT'S MEANT TO BE GOING TO JESUS DeSADE! FOOKIN' HELL, I'M GLAD I CRIPPLED THE BASTARD!
SHE'S HAD OVER A FORTNIGHT, BOB. SHE'S PROBABLY LONG GONE.
YEAH-- OH, FOOKIN' BRILLIANT!
PAYDIRT, FREDDY!
JESUS CHRIST, SOMEBODY STUCK A CAT IN THE TOILET!

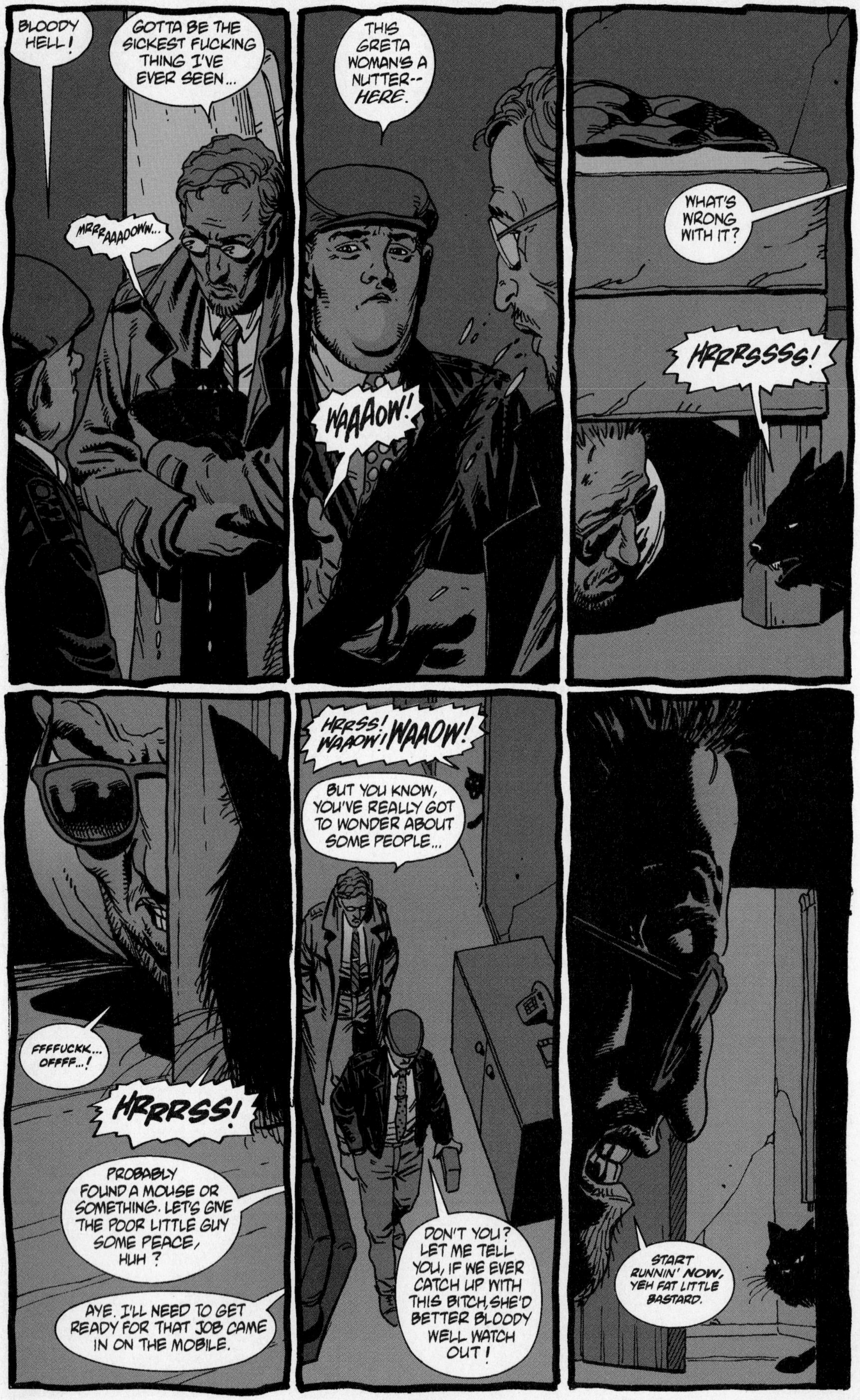
BLOODY HELL!
GOTTA BE THE SICKEST FUCKING THING I'VE EVER SEEN...
MRRRAAADOWN...
THIS GRETA WOMAN'S A NUTTER-- HERE.
WAAAOW!
WHAT'S WRONG WITH IT?
HRRRSSSS!
FFFFUCKK... OFFFF...!
HRRRSS!
PROBABLY FOUND A MOUSE OR SOMETHING. LET'S GIVE THE POOR LITTLE GUY SOME PEACE, HUH?
AYE. I'LL NEED TO GET READY FOR THAT JOB CAME IN ON THE MOBILE.
HRRSS! WAAOW! WAAOW!
BUT YOU KNOW, YOU'VE REALLY GOT TO WONDER ABOUT SOME PEOPLE...
DON'T YOU? LET ME TELL YOU, IF WE EVER CATCH UP WITH THIS BITCH, SHE'D BETTER BLOODY WELL WATCH OUT!
START RUNNIN' NOW, YEH FAT LITTLE BASTARD.

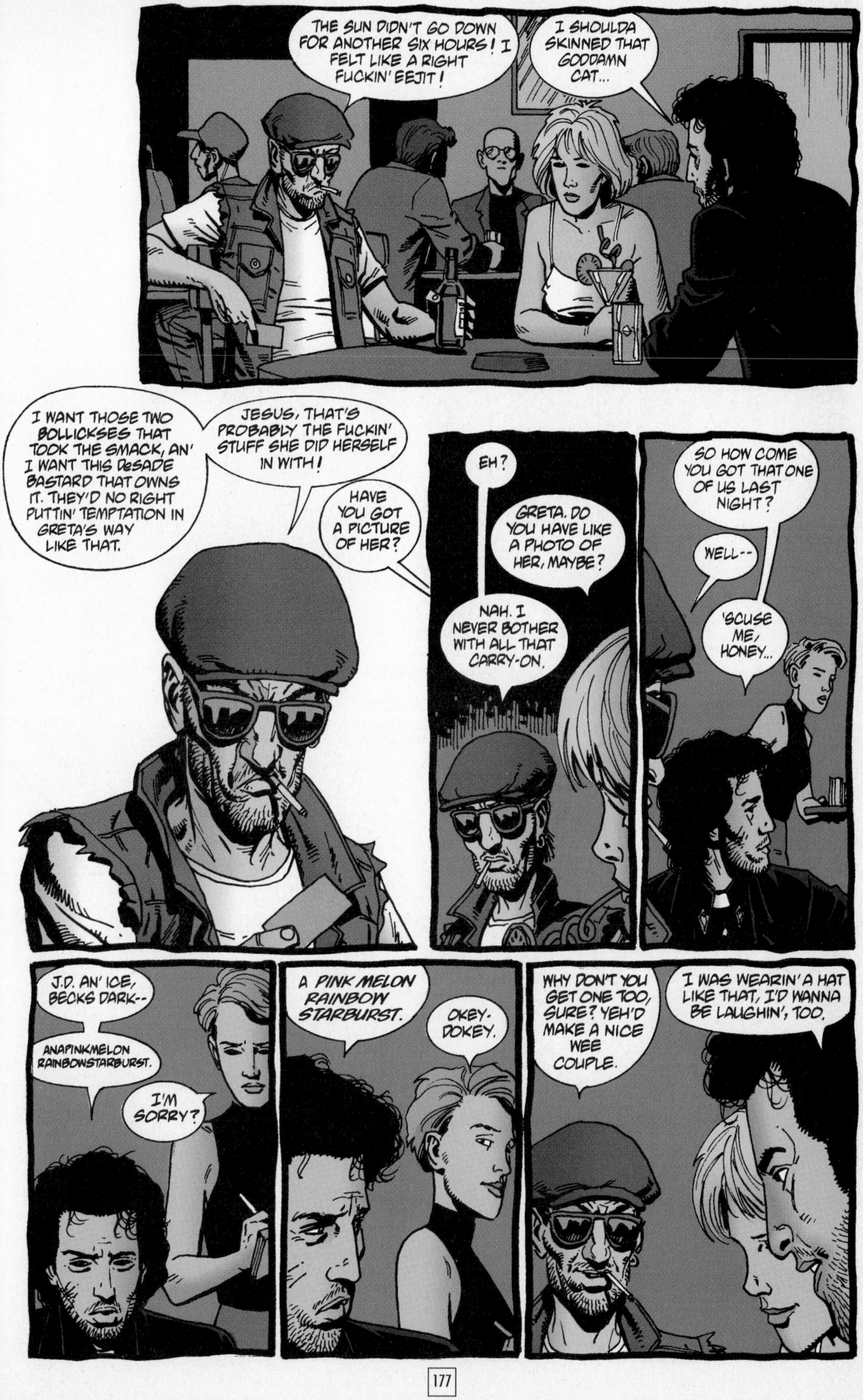

THE SUN DIDN'T GO DOWN FOR ANOTHER SIX HOURS! I FELT LIKE A RIGHT FUCKIN' EEJIT!
I SHOULDA SKINNED THAT GODDAMN CAT...
I WANT THOSE TWO BOLLICKSES THAT TOOK THE SMACK, AN' I WANT THIS DeSADE BASTARD THAT OWNS IT. THEY'D NO RIGHT PUTTIN' TEMPTATION IN GRETA'S WAY LIKE THAT.
JESUS, THAT'S PROBABLY THE FUCKIN' STUFF SHE DID HERSELF IN WITH!
HAVE YOU GOT A PICTURE OF HER?
EH?
GRETA. DO YOU HAVE LIKE A PHOTO OF HER, MAYBE?
NAH. I NEVER BOTHER WITH ALL THAT CARRY-ON.
SO HOW COME YOU GOT THAT ONE OF US LAST NIGHT?
WELL--
'SCUSE ME, HONEY...
J.D. AN' ICE, BECKS DARK--
ANAPINKMELON RAINBOWSTARBURST.
I'M SORRY?
A PINK MELON RAINBOW STARBURST.
OKEY-DOKEY.
WHY DON'T YOU GET ONE TOO, SURE? YEH'D MAKE A NICE WEE COUPLE.
I WAS WEARIN' A HAT LIKE THAT, I'D WANNA BE LAUGHIN', TOO.

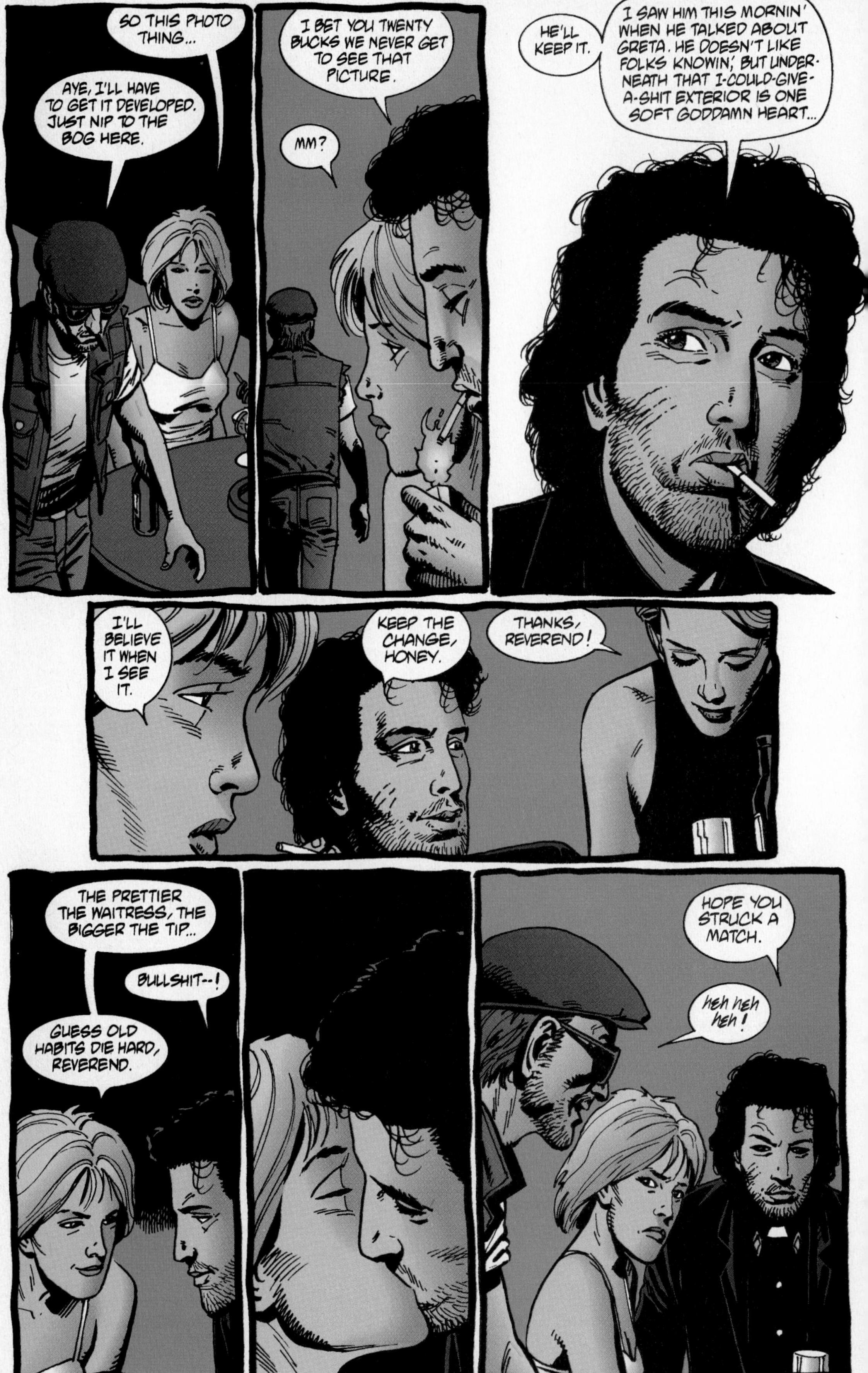
SO THIS PHOTO THING...
AYE, I'LL HAVE TO GET IT DEVELOPED. JUST NIP TO THE BOG HERE.
I BET YOU TWENTY BUCKS WE NEVER GET TO SEE THAT PICTURE.
MM?
HE'LL KEEP IT.
I SAW HIM THIS MORNIN' WHEN HE TALKED ABOUT GRETA. HE DOESN'T LIKE FOLKS KNOWIN', BUT UNDERNEATH THAT I-COULD-GIVE-A-SHIT EXTERIOR IS ONE SOFT GODDAMN HEART...
I'LL BELIEVE IT WHEN I SEE IT.
KEEP THE CHANGE, HONEY.
THANKS, REVEREND!
THE PRETTIER THE WAITRESS, THE BIGGER THE TIP...
BULLSHIT--!
GUESS OLD HABITS DIE HARD, REVEREND.
HOPE YOU STRUCK A MATCH.
heh heh heh!

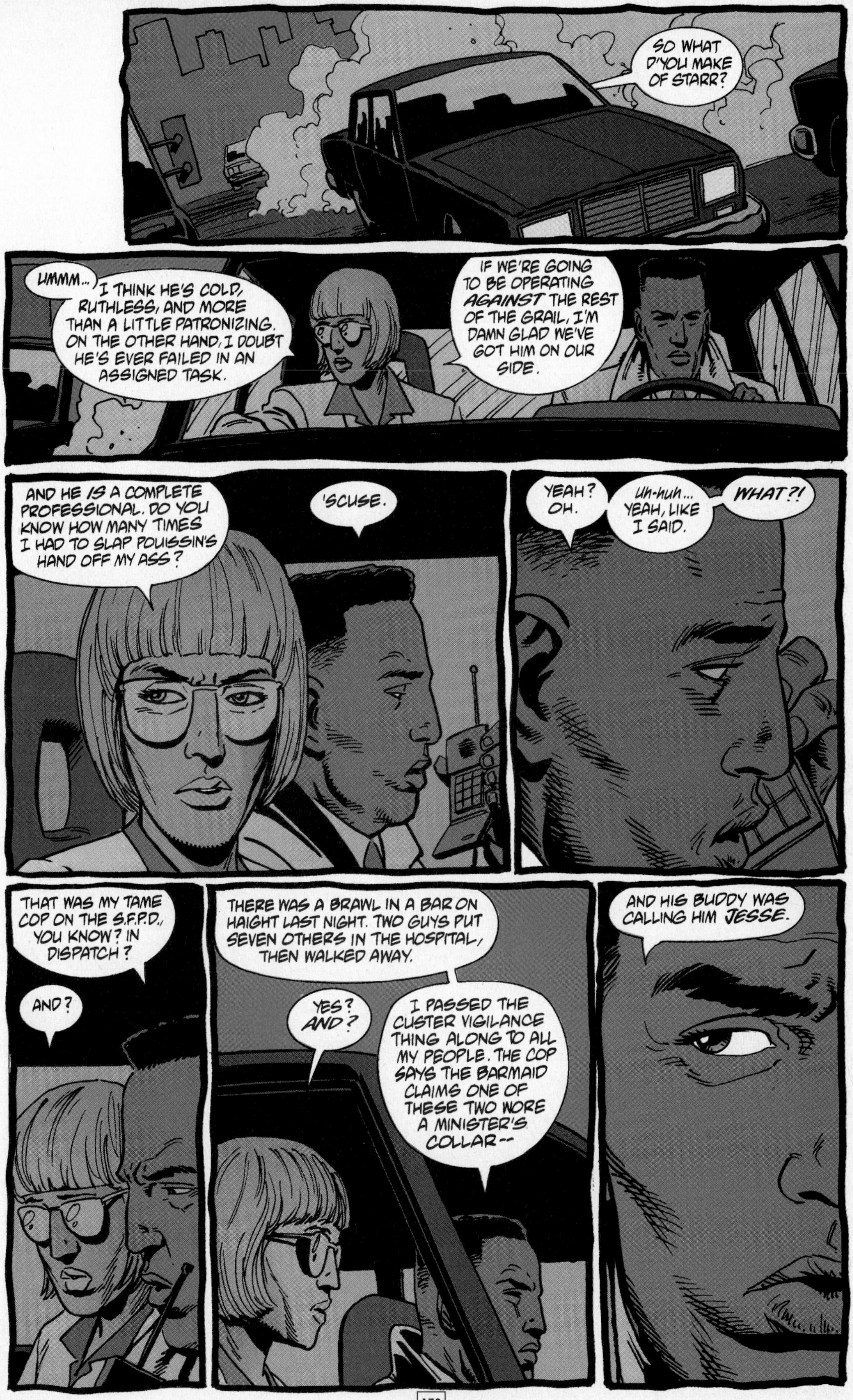
SO WHAT D'YOU MAKE OF STARR?
UMMM...
I THINK HE'S COLD, RUTHLESS, AND MORE THAN A LITTLE PATRONIZING. ON THE OTHER HAND, I DOUBT HE'S EVER FAILED IN AN ASSIGNED TASK.
IF WE'RE GOING TO BE OPERATING AGAINST THE REST OF THE GRAIL, I'M DAMN GLAD WE'VE GOT HIM ON OUR SIDE.
AND HE IS A COMPLETE PROFESSIONAL. DO YOU KNOW HOW MANY TIMES I HAD TO SLAP POUISSIN'S HAND OFF MY ASS?
'SCUSE.
YEAH? OH.
Uh-huh... YEAH, LIKE I SAID.
WHAT?!
THAT WAS MY TAME COP ON THE S.F.P.D., YOU KNOW? IN DISPATCH?
AND?
THERE WAS A BRAWL IN A BAR ON HAIGHT LAST NIGHT. TWO GUYS PUT SEVEN OTHERS IN THE HOSPITAL, THEN WALKED AWAY.
YES? AND?
I PASSED THE CUSTER VIGILANCE THING ALONG TO ALL MY PEOPLE. THE COP SAYS THE BARMAID CLAIMS ONE OF THESE TWO WORE A MINISTER'S COLLAR--
AND HIS BUDDY WAS CALLING HIM JESSE.

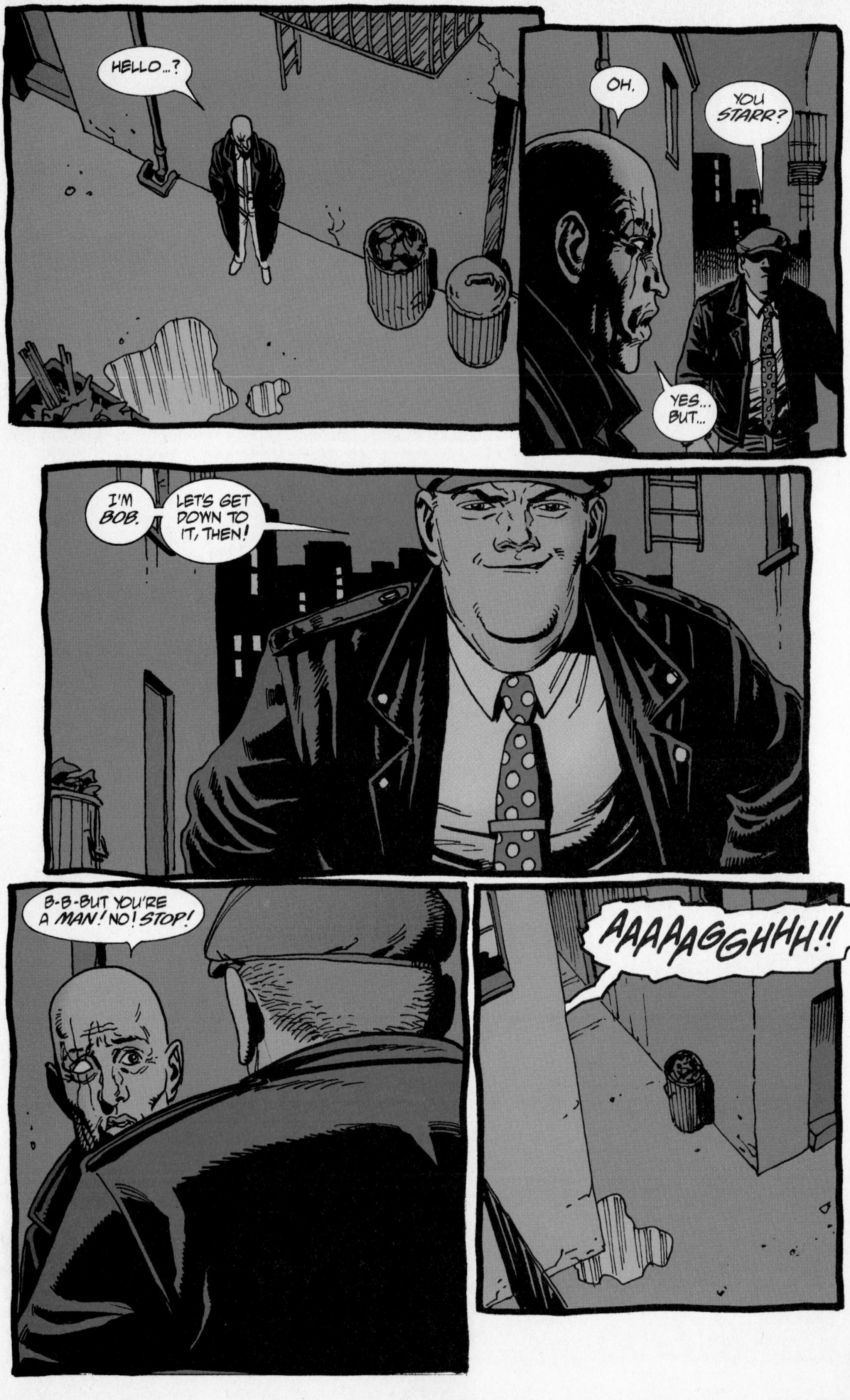
HELLO...?
OH.
YOU STARR?
YES... BUT...
I'M BOB.
LET'S GET DOWN TO IT, THEN!
B-B-BUT YOU'RE A MAN! NO! STOP!
AAAAAGGHHH!!

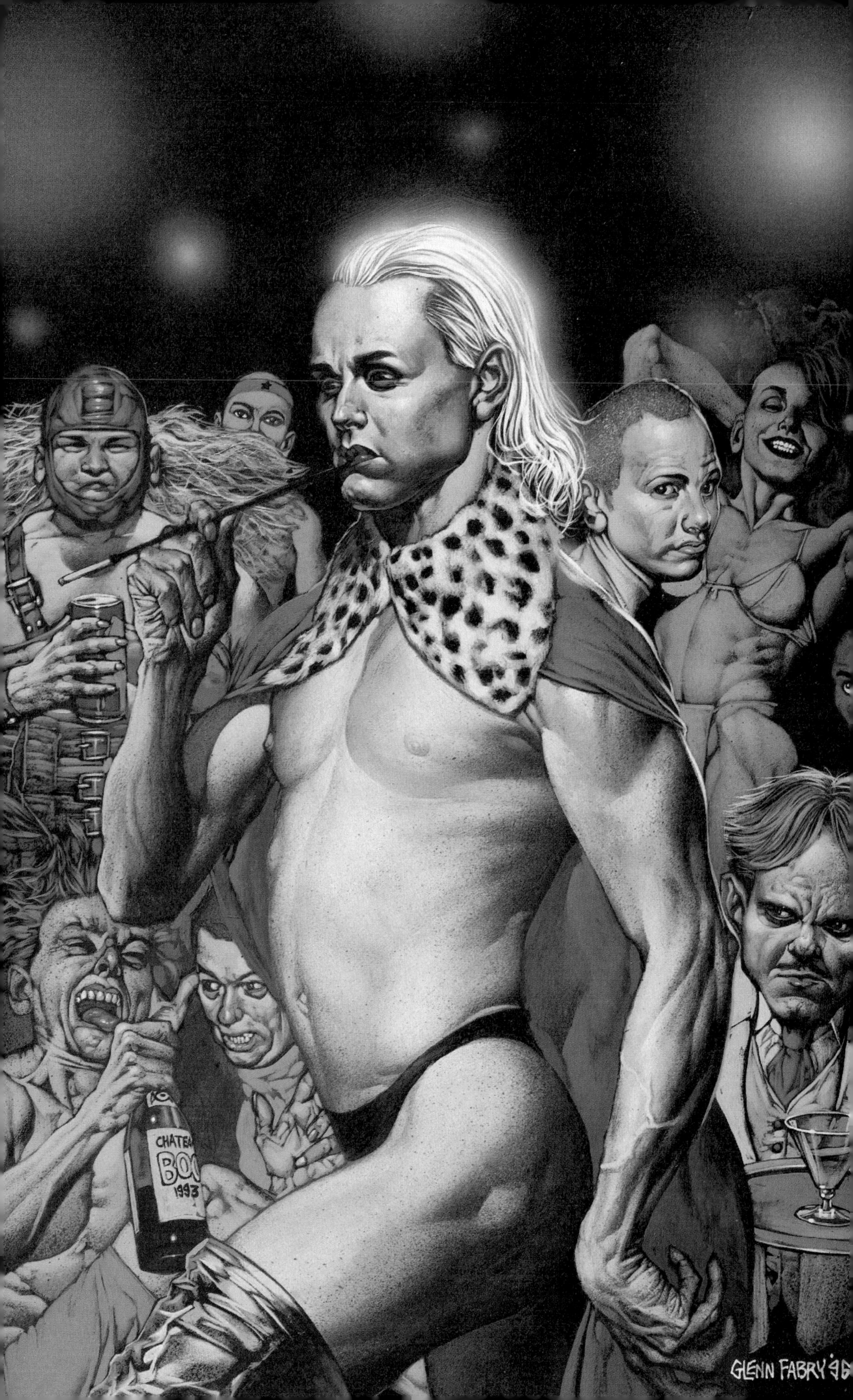
CHATEA
BOO
1993
GLENN FABRY '96

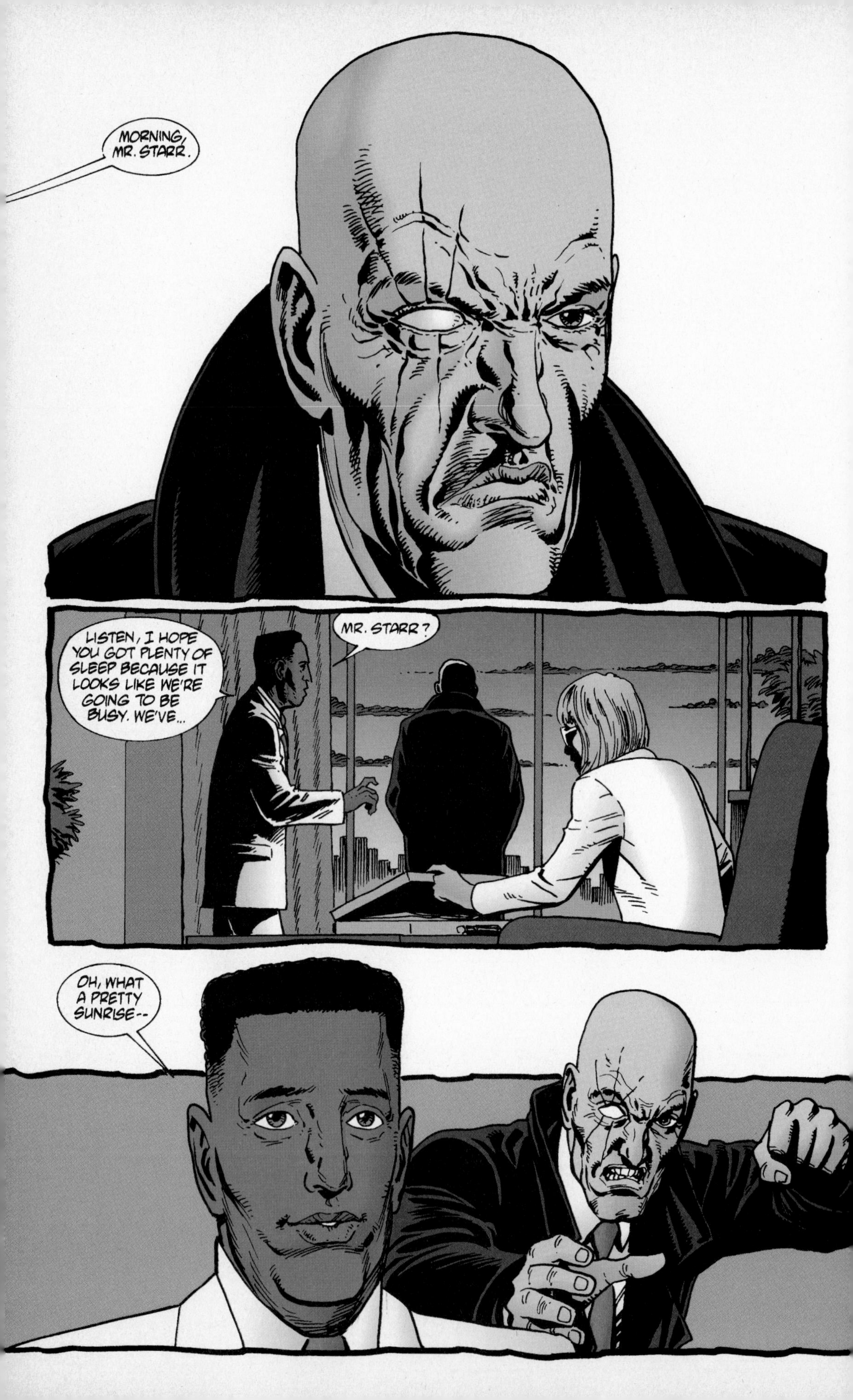
MORNING, MR. STARR.
LISTEN, I HOPE YOU GOT PLENTY OF SLEEP BECAUSE IT LOOKS LIKE WE'RE GOING TO BE BUSY. WE'VE...
MR. STARR?
OH, WHAT A PRETTY SUNRISE--

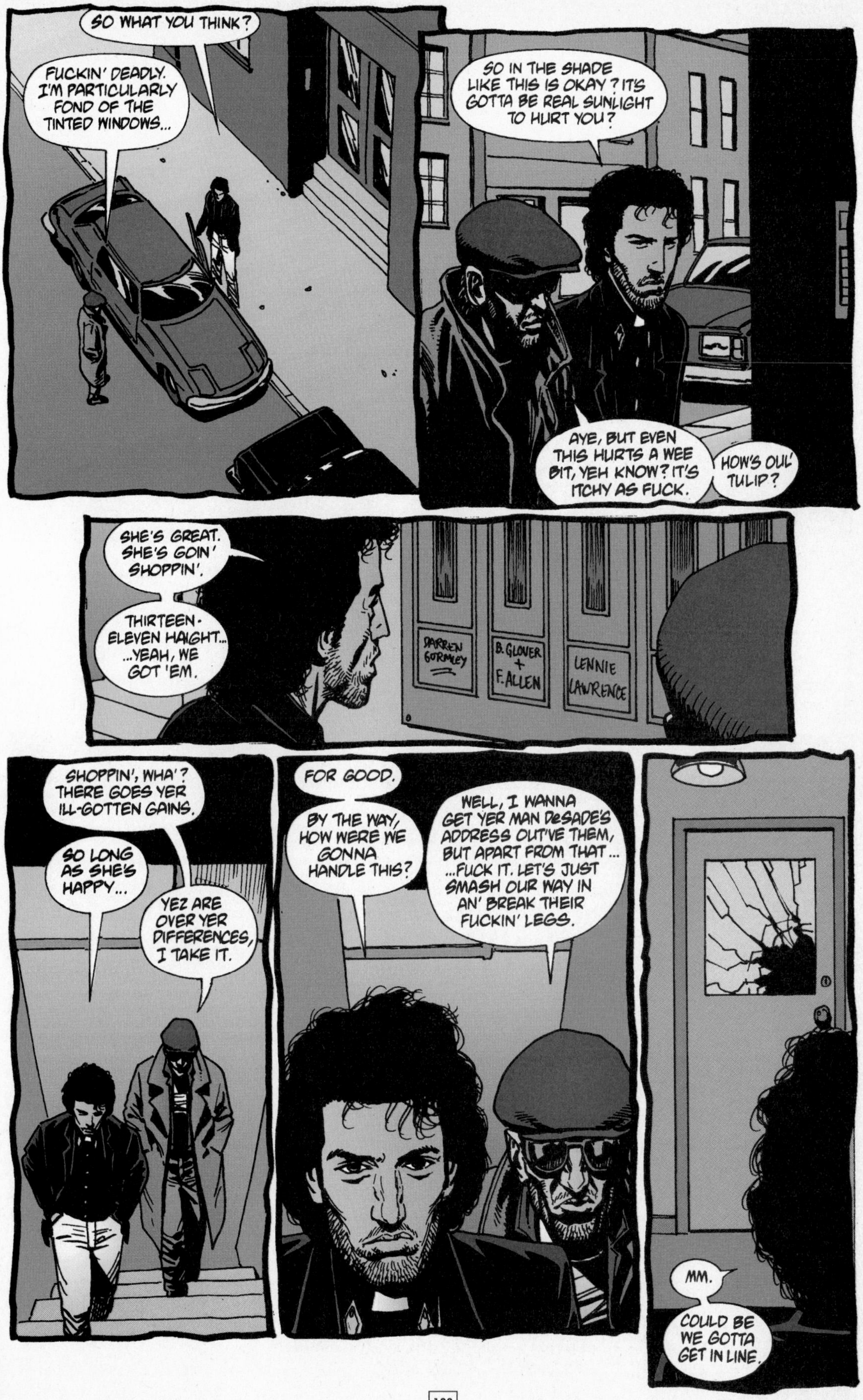

SO WHAT YOU THINK?
FUCKIN' DEADLY. I'M PARTICULARLY FOND OF THE TINTED WINDOWS...
SO IN THE SHADE LIKE THIS IS OKAY? IT'S GOTTA BE REAL SUNLIGHT TO HURT YOU?
AYE, BUT EVEN THIS HURTS A WEE BIT, YEH KNOW? IT'S ITCHY AS FUCK.
HOW'S OUL' TULIP?
SHE'S GREAT. SHE'S GOIN' SHOPPIN'.
THIRTEEN-ELEVEN HAIGHT... ...YEAH, WE GOT 'EM.
DARREN GORMLEY
B. GLOVER + F. ALLEN
LENNIE LAWRENCE
SHOPPIN', WHA'? THERE GOES YER ILL-GOTTEN GAINS.
SO LONG AS SHE'S HAPPY...
YEZ ARE OVER YER DIFFERENCES, I TAKE IT.
FOR GOOD.
BY THE WAY, HOW WERE WE GONNA HANDLE THIS?
WELL, I WANNA GET YER MAN DeSADE'S ADDRESS OUT'VE THEM, BUT APART FROM THAT... ...FUCK IT. LET'S JUST SMASH OUR WAY IN AN' BREAK THEIR FUCKIN' LEGS.
MM.
COULD BE WE GOTTA GET IN LINE.

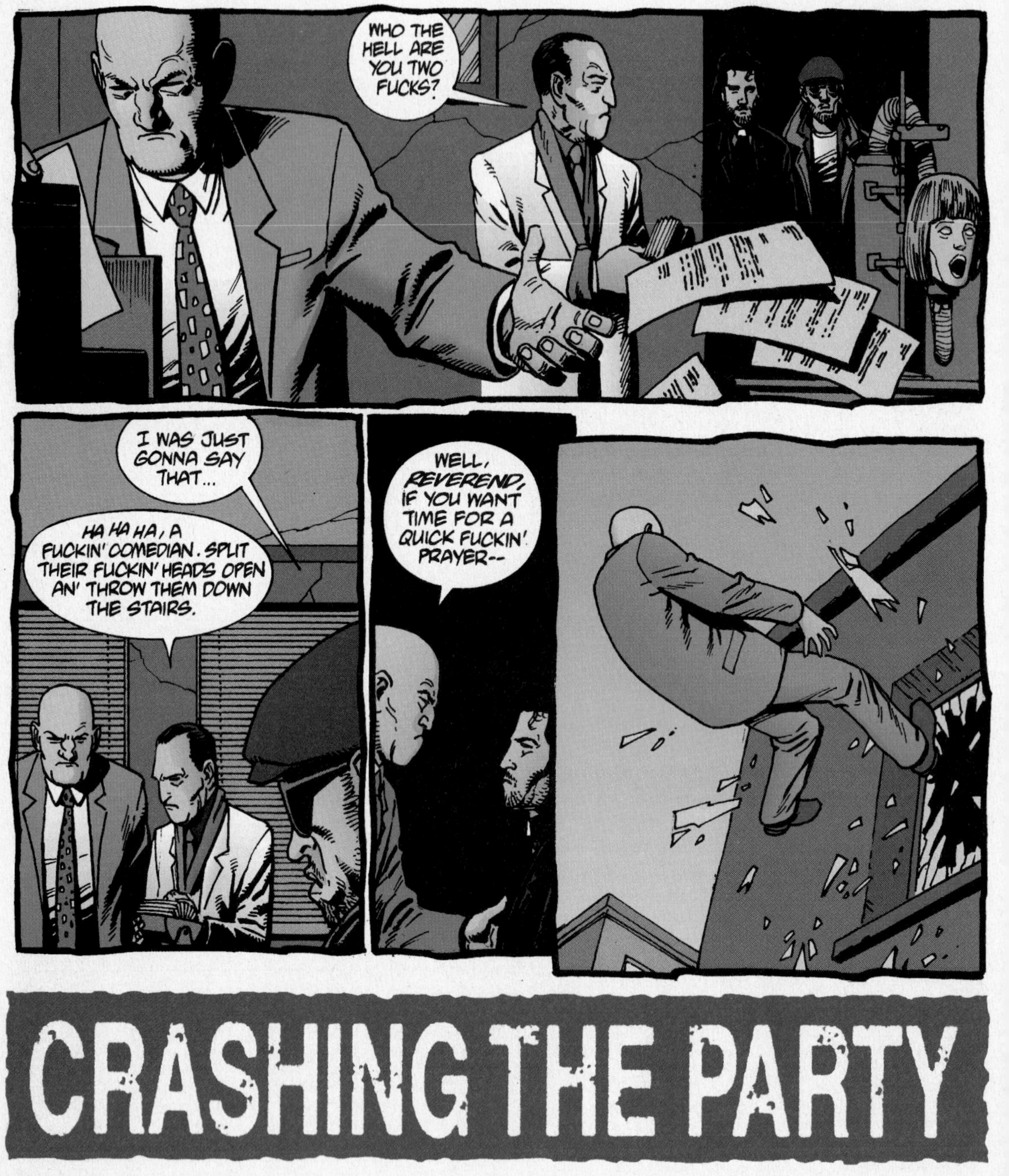
WHO THE HELL ARE YOU TWO FUCKS?
I WAS JUST GONNA SAY THAT...
HA HA HA, A FUCKIN' COMEDIAN. SPLIT THEIR FUCKIN' HEADS OPEN AN' THROW THEM DOWN THE STAIRS.
WELL, *REVEREND*, IF YOU WANT TIME FOR A QUICK FUCKIN' PRAYER--

CRASHING THE PARTY

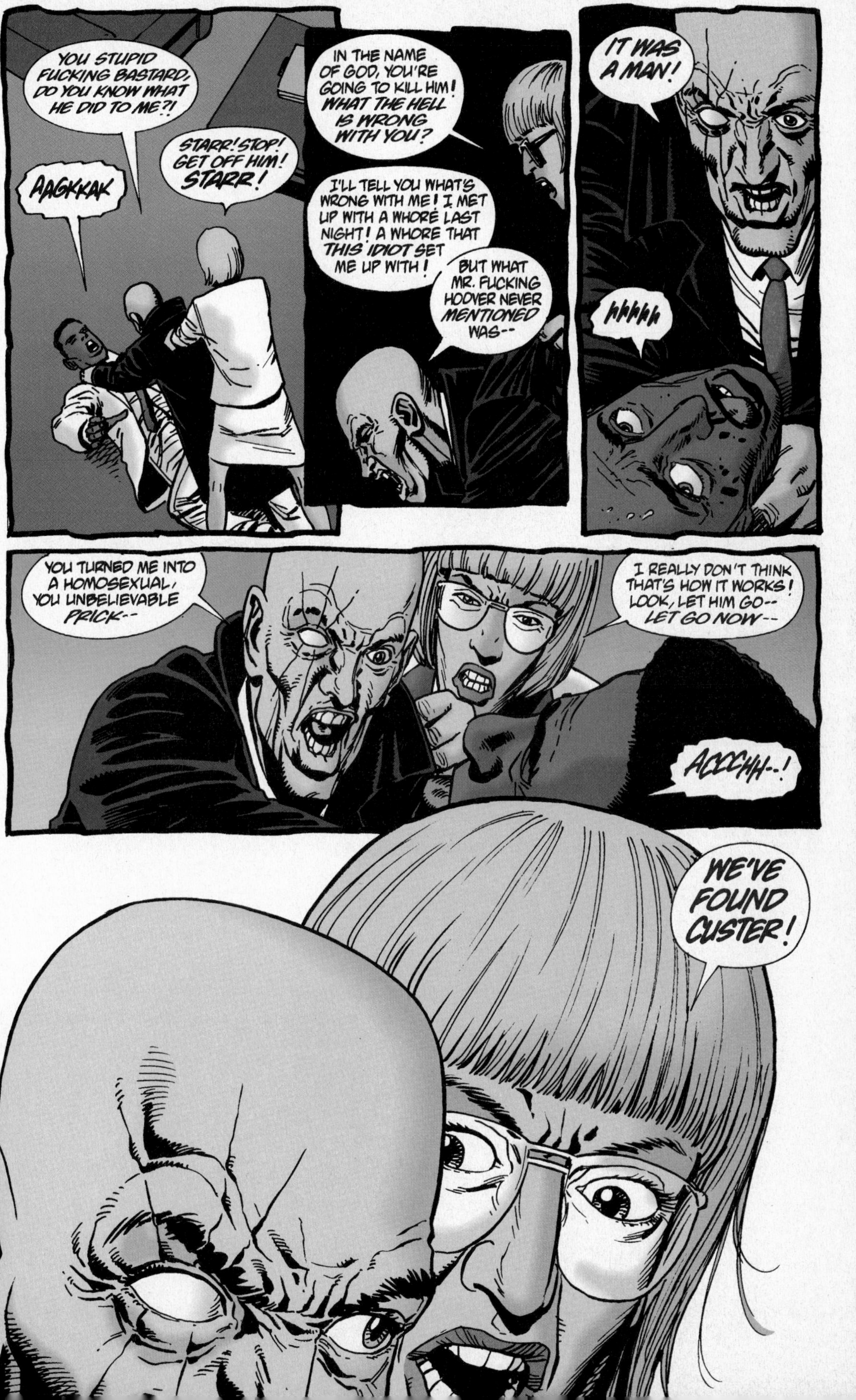

YOU STUPID FUCKING BASTARD, DO YOU KNOW WHAT HE DID TO ME?!
STARR! STOP! GET OFF HIM! STARR!
AAGKKAK
IN THE NAME OF GOD, YOU'RE GOING TO KILL HIM! WHAT THE HELL IS WRONG WITH YOU?
I'LL TELL YOU WHAT'S WRONG WITH ME! I MET UP WITH A WHORE LAST NIGHT! A WHORE THAT THIS IDIOT SET ME UP WITH!
BUT WHAT MR. FUCKING HOOVER NEVER MENTIONED WAS--
IT WAS A MAN!
hhhhh
YOU TURNED ME INTO A HOMOSEXUAL, YOU UNBELIEVABLE PRICK--
I REALLY DON'T THINK THAT'S HOW IT WORKS! LOOK, LET HIM GO-- LET GO NOW--
ACCCHH--!
WE'VE FOUND CUSTER!

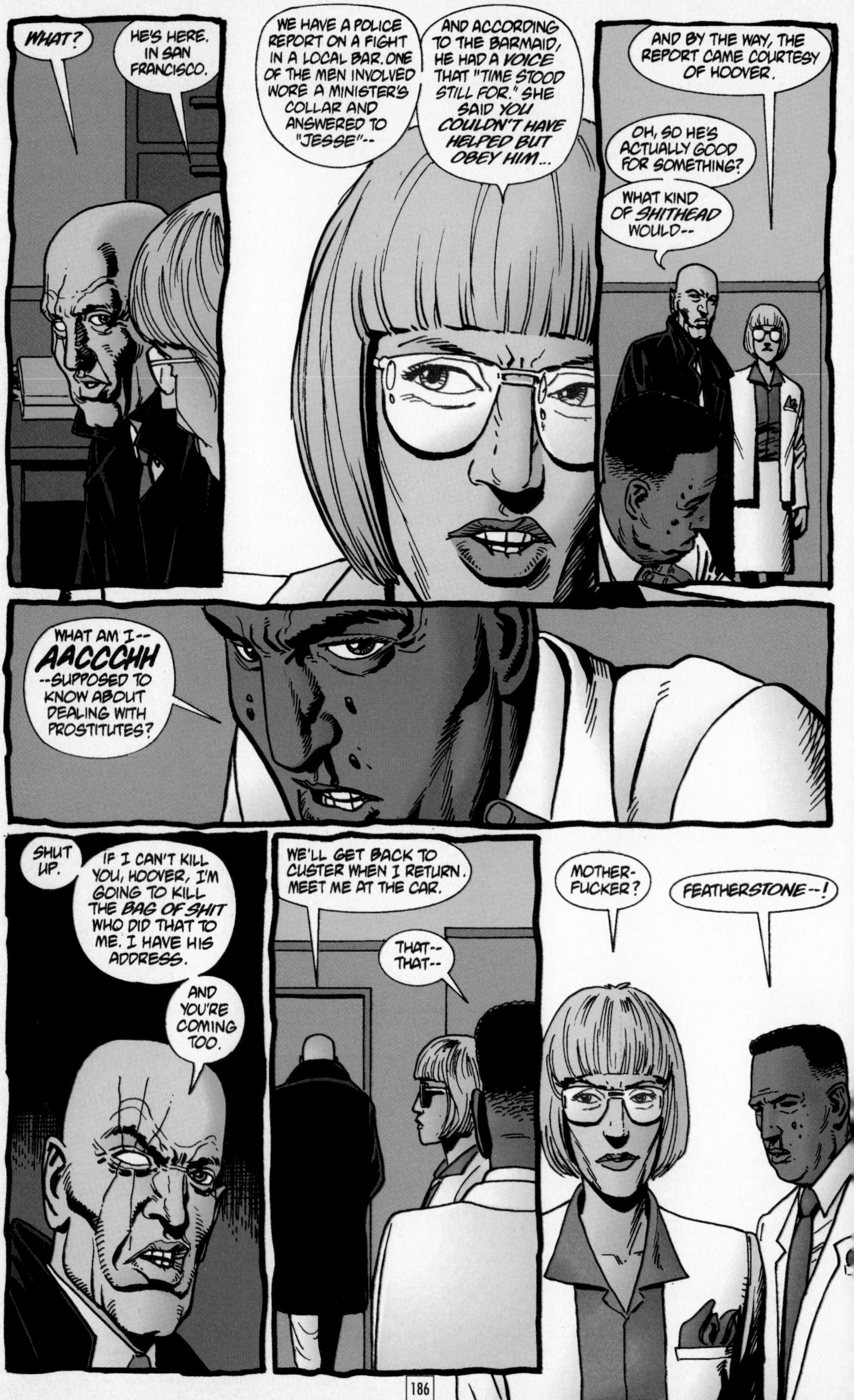
WHAT?
HE'S HERE. IN SAN FRANCISCO.
WE HAVE A POLICE REPORT ON A FIGHT IN A LOCAL BAR. ONE OF THE MEN INVOLVED WORE A MINISTER'S COLLAR AND ANSWERED TO "JESSE"--
AND ACCORDING TO THE BARMAID, HE HAD A *VOICE* THAT "TIME STOOD STILL FOR." SHE SAID *YOU COULDN'T HAVE HELPED BUT OBEY HIM*...
AND BY THE WAY, THE REPORT CAME COURTESY OF HOOVER.
OH, SO HE'S ACTUALLY GOOD FOR SOMETHING?
WHAT KIND OF *SHITHEAD* WOULD--
WHAT AM I-- AACCCHH --SUPPOSED TO KNOW ABOUT DEALING WITH PROSTITUTES?
SHUT UP.
IF I CAN'T KILL YOU, HOOVER, I'M GOING TO KILL THE *BAG OF SHIT* WHO DID THAT TO ME. I HAVE HIS ADDRESS.
AND YOU'RE COMING TOO.
WE'LL GET BACK TO CUSTER WHEN I RETURN. MEET ME AT THE CAR.
THAT-- THAT--
MOTHER-FUCKER?
FEATHERSTONE--!

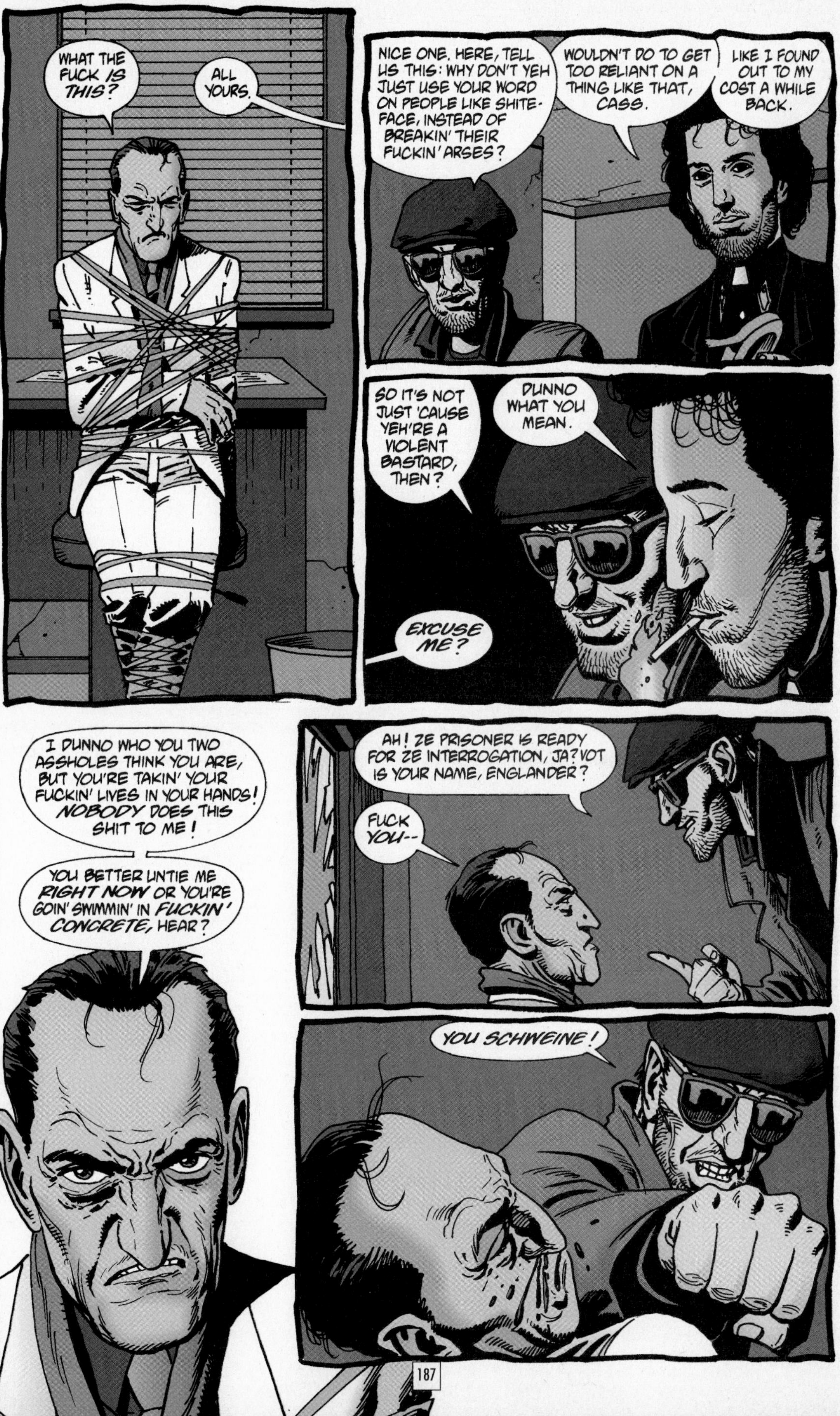
WHAT THE FUCK *IS* *THIS*?
ALL YOURS.
NICE ONE. HERE, TELL US THIS: WHY DON'T YEH JUST USE YOUR WORD ON PEOPLE LIKE SHITE-FACE, INSTEAD OF BREAKIN' THEIR FUCKIN' ARSES?
WOULDN'T DO TO GET TOO RELIANT ON A THING LIKE THAT, CASS.
LIKE I FOUND OUT TO MY COST A WHILE BACK.
SO IT'S NOT JUST 'CAUSE YEH'RE A VIOLENT BASTARD, THEN?
DUNNO WHAT YOU MEAN.
EXCUSE ME?
I DUNNO WHO YOU TWO ASSHOLES THINK YOU ARE, BUT YOU'RE TAKIN' YOUR FUCKIN' LIVES IN YOUR HANDS! *NOBODY* DOES THIS SHIT TO ME!
YOU BETTER UNTIE ME *RIGHT NOW* OR YOU'RE GOIN' SWIMMIN' IN *FUCKIN' CONCRETE*, HEAR?
AH! ZE PRISONER IS READY FOR ZE INTERROGATION, JA? VOT IS YOUR NAME, ENGLANDER?
FUCK *YOU*--
YOU SCHWEINE!

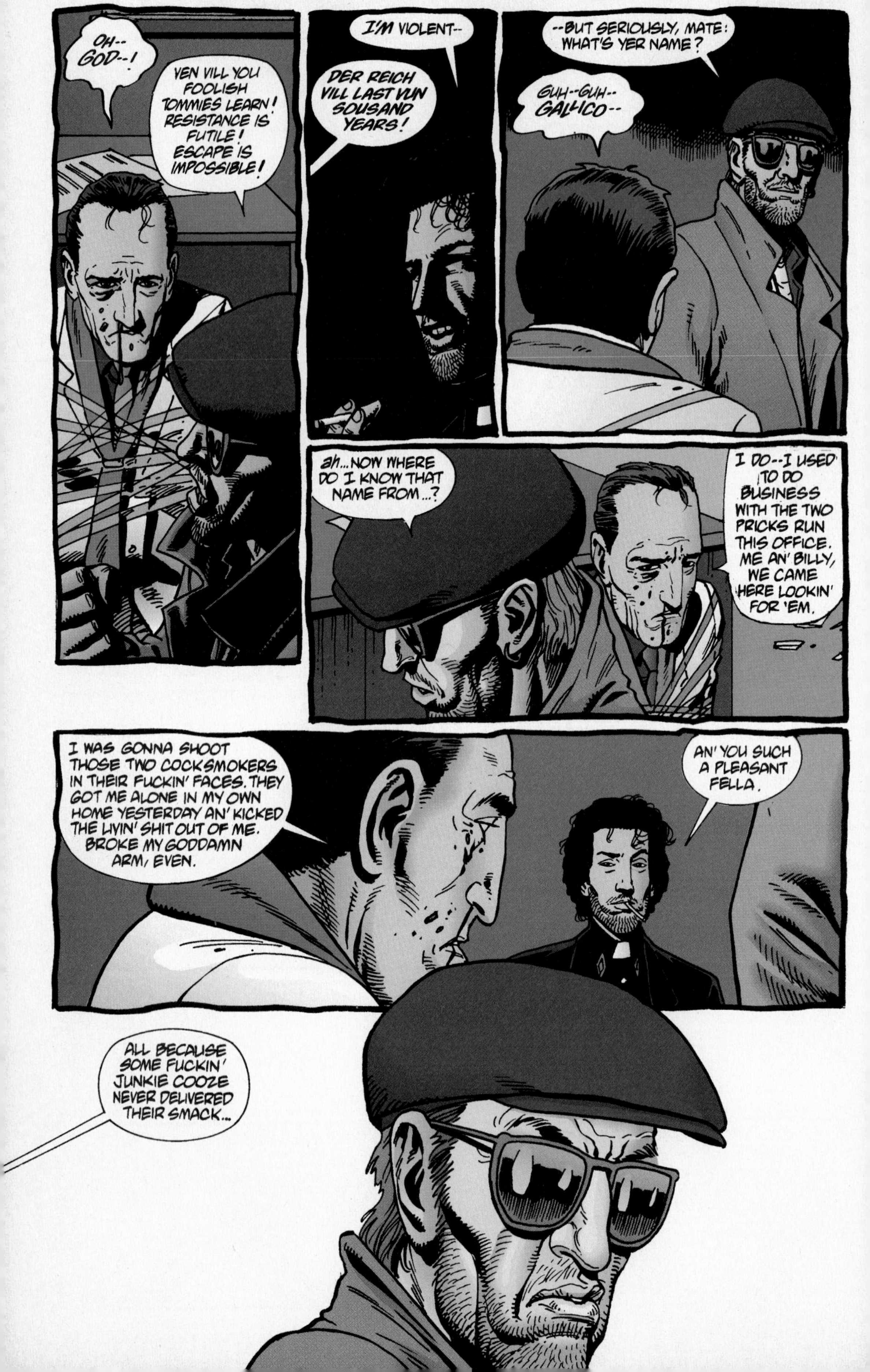
OH-- GOD--!
VEN VILL YOU FOOLISH TOMMIES LEARN! RESISTANCE IS FUTILE! ESCAPE IS IMPOSSIBLE!
I'M VIOLENT--
DER REICH VILL LAST VUN SOUSAND YEARS!
--BUT SERIOUSLY, MATE: WHAT'S YER NAME?
GUH--GUH-- GALLICO--
ah...NOW WHERE DO I KNOW THAT NAME FROM...?
I DO--I USED TO DO BUSINESS WITH THE TWO PRICKS RUN THIS OFFICE. ME AN' BILLY, WE CAME HERE LOOKIN' FOR 'EM.
I WAS GONNA SHOOT THOSE TWO COCKSMOKERS IN THEIR FUCKIN' FACES. THEY GOT ME ALONE IN MY OWN HOME YESTERDAY AN' KICKED THE LIVIN' SHIT OUT OF ME. BROKE MY GODDAMN ARM, EVEN.
AN' YOU SUCH A PLEASANT FELLA.
ALL BECAUSE SOME FUCKIN' JUNKIE COOZE NEVER DELIVERED THEIR SMACK...

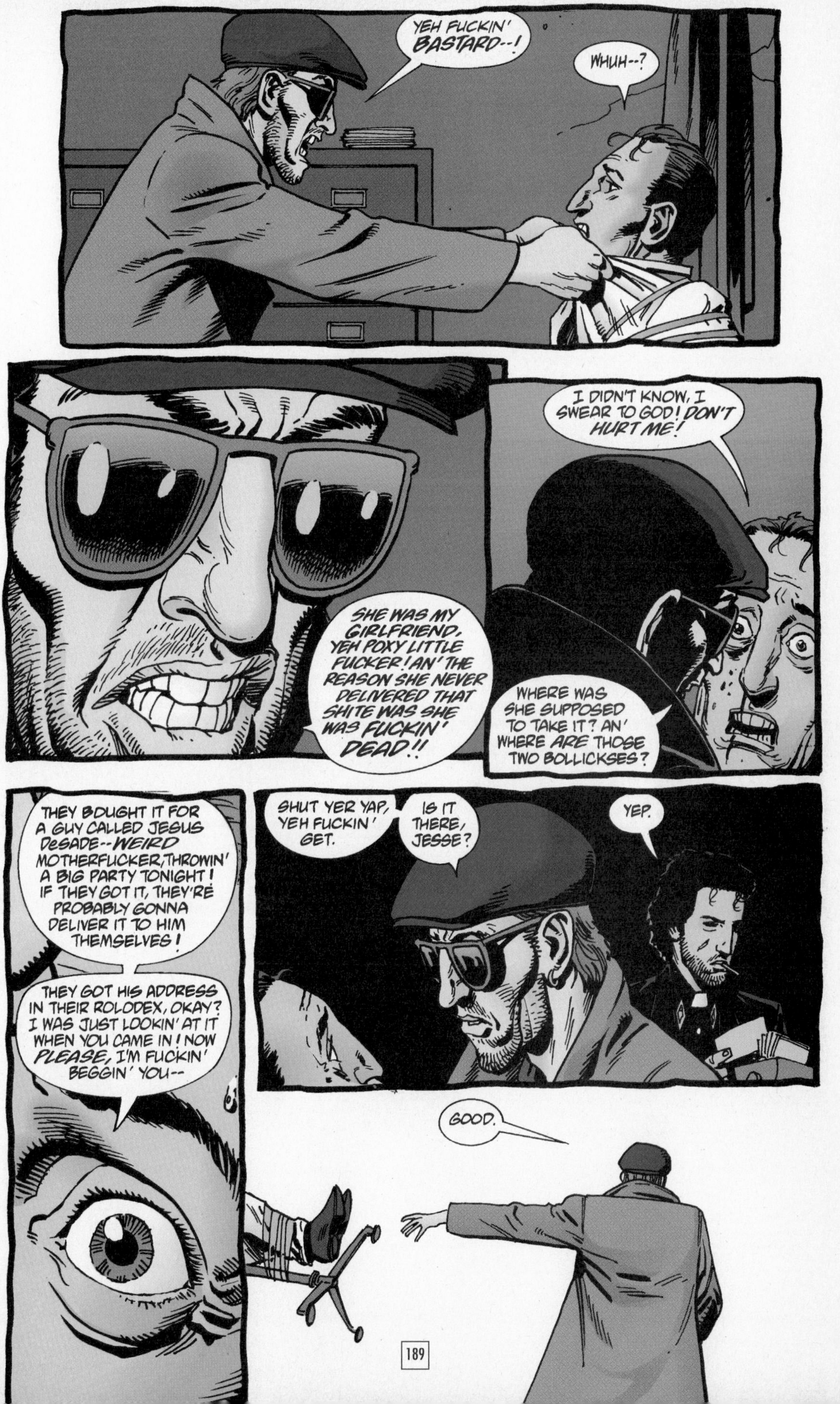
YEH FUCKIN' BASTARD--!
WHUH--?
I DIDN'T KNOW, I SWEAR TO GOD! DON'T HURT ME!
SHE WAS MY GIRLFRIEND, YEH POXY LITTLE FUCKER! AN' THE REASON SHE NEVER DELIVERED THAT SHITE WAS SHE WAS FUCKIN' DEAD!!
WHERE WAS SHE SUPPOSED TO TAKE IT? AN' WHERE ARE THOSE TWO BOLLICKSES?
THEY BOUGHT IT FOR A GUY CALLED JESUS DeSADE--WEIRD MOTHERFUCKER, THROWIN' A BIG PARTY TONIGHT! IF THEY GOT IT, THEY'RE PROBABLY GONNA DELIVER IT TO HIM THEMSELVES!
THEY GOT HIS ADDRESS IN THEIR ROLODEX, OKAY? I WAS JUST LOOKIN' AT IT WHEN YOU CAME IN! NOW PLEASE, I'M FUCKIN' BEGGIN' YOU--
SHUT YER YAP, YEH FUCKIN' GET.
IS IT THERE, JESSE?
YEP.
GOOD.

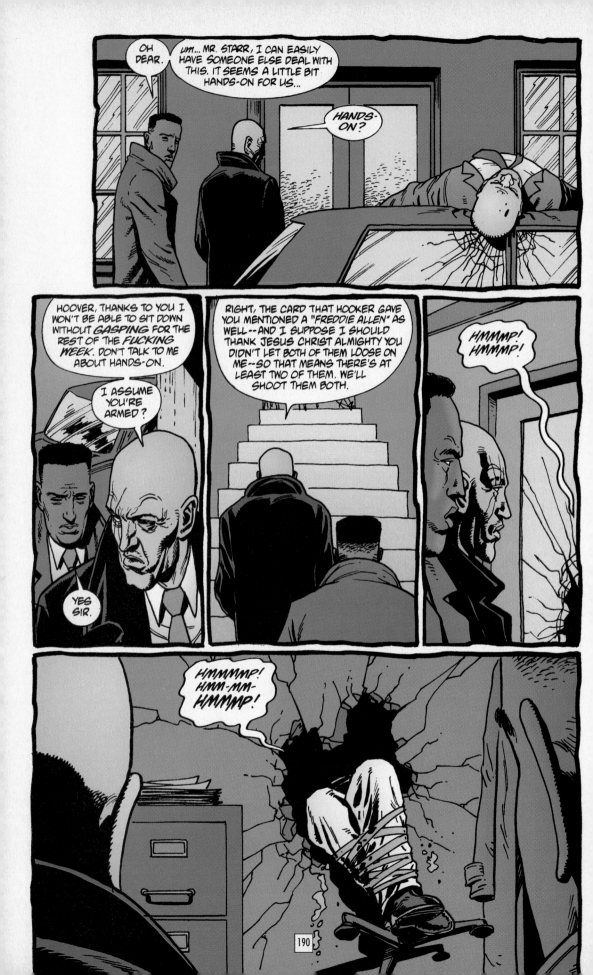

OH DEAR.

UM... MR. STARR, I CAN EASILY HAVE SOMEONE ELSE DEAL WITH THIS. IT SEEMS A LITTLE BIT HANDS-ON FOR US...

HANDS-ON?

HOOVER, THANKS TO YOU I WON'T BE ABLE TO SIT DOWN WITHOUT *GASPING* FOR THE REST OF THE *FUCKING WEEK.* DON'T TALK TO ME ABOUT HANDS-ON.

I ASSUME YOU'RE ARMED?

YES SIR.

RIGHT, THE CARD THAT HOOKER GAVE YOU MENTIONED A "FREDDIE ALLEN" AS WELL--AND I SUPPOSE I SHOULD THANK JESUS CHRIST ALMIGHTY YOU DIDN'T LET BOTH OF THEM LOOSE ON ME--SO THAT MEANS THERE'S AT LEAST TWO OF THEM. WE'LL SHOOT THEM BOTH.

HMMMP! HMMMP!

HMMMMP! HMM-MM-HMMMP!

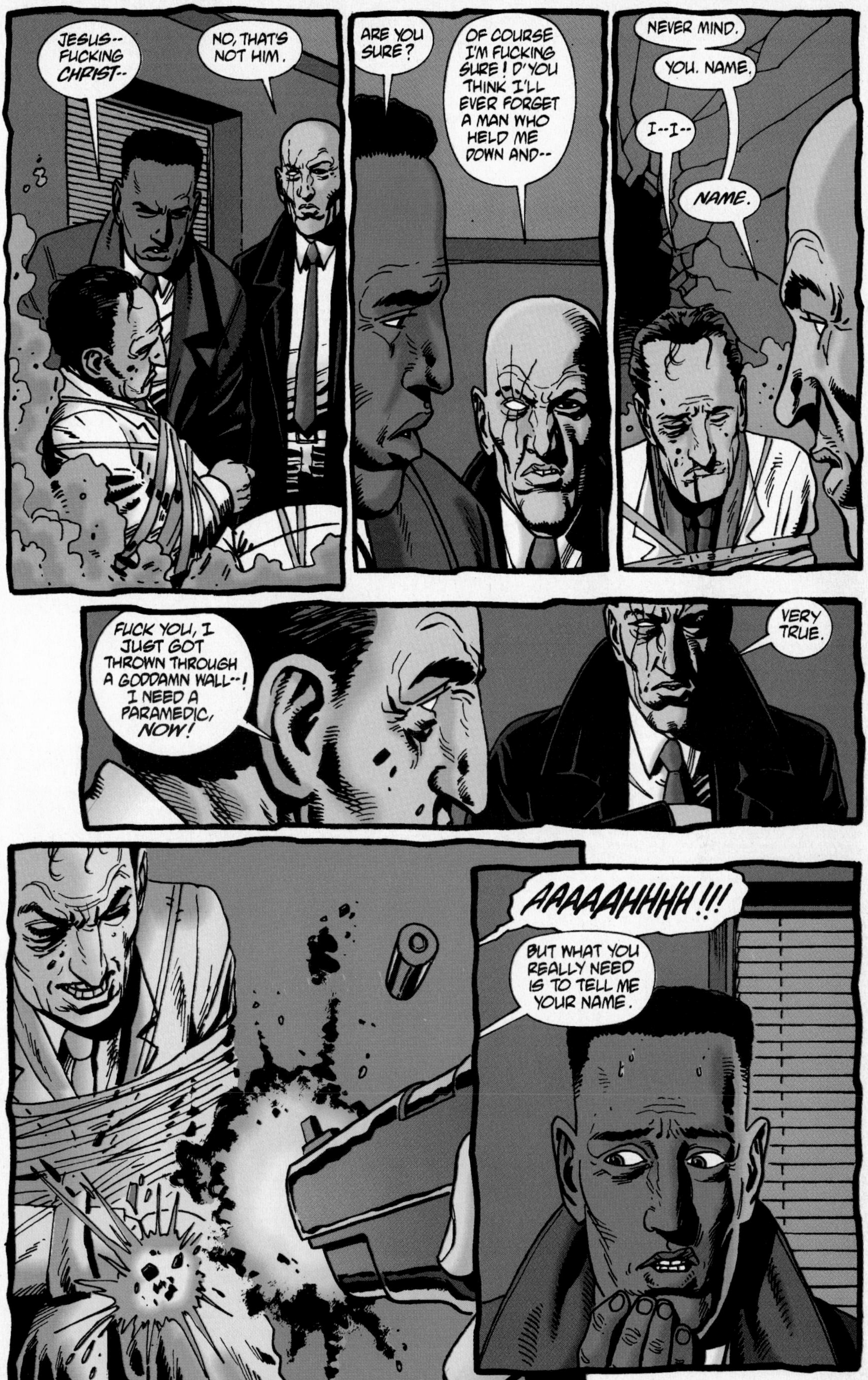
JESUS--
FUCKING
CHRIST--
NO, THAT'S NOT HIM.
ARE YOU SURE?
OF COURSE I'M FUCKING SURE! D'YOU THINK I'LL EVER FORGET A MAN WHO HELD ME DOWN AND--
NEVER MIND.
YOU. NAME.
I--I--
NAME.
FUCK YOU, I JUST GOT THROWN THROUGH A GODDAMN WALL--! I NEED A PARAMEDIC, NOW!
VERY TRUE.
AAAAAHHHH!!!
BUT WHAT YOU REALLY NEED IS TO TELL ME YOUR NAME.

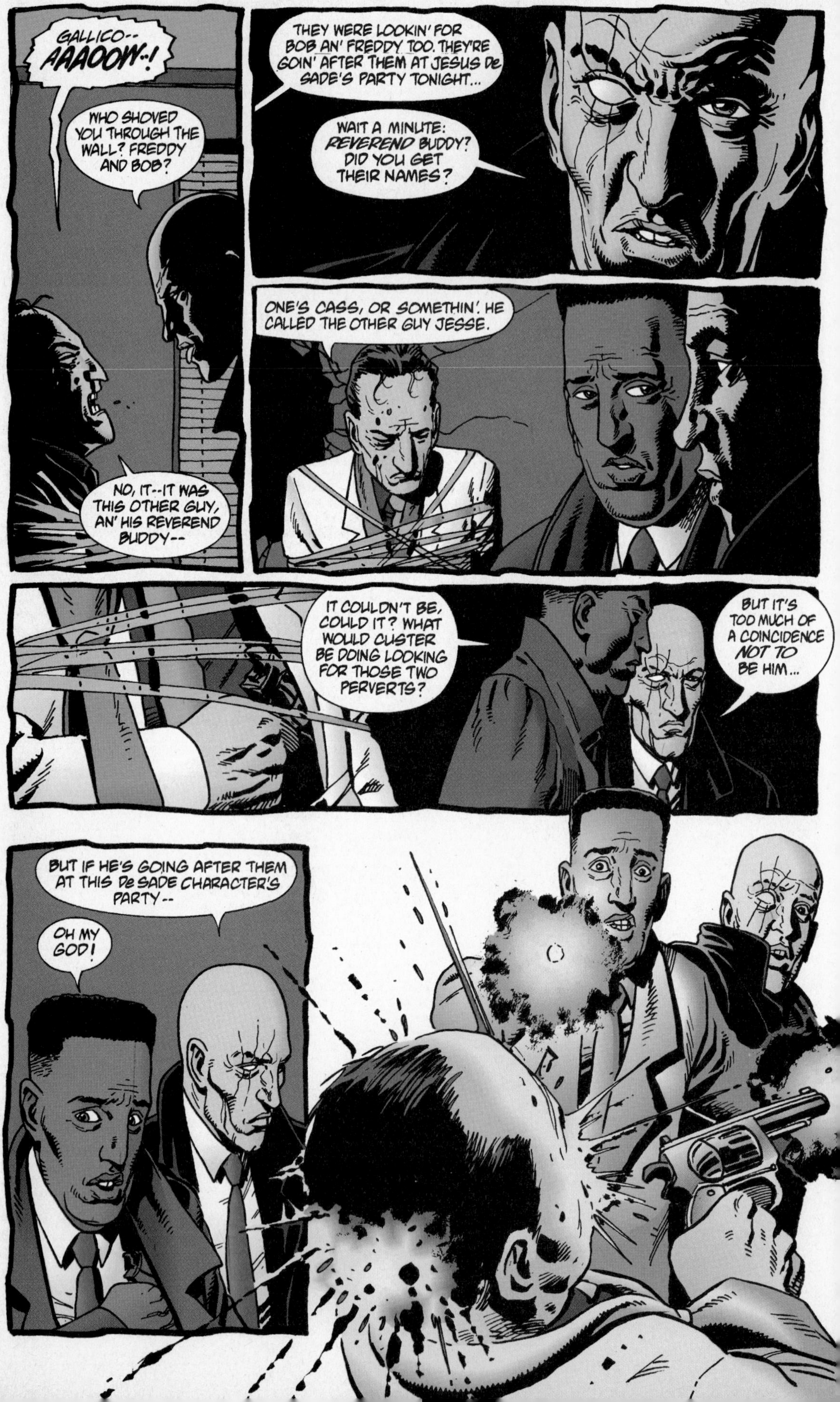
GALLICO--
AAAOOW--!
WHO SHOVED YOU THROUGH THE WALL? FREDDY AND BOB?
NO, IT--IT WAS THIS OTHER GUY, AN' HIS REVEREND BUDDY--
THEY WERE LOOKIN' FOR BOB AN' FREDDY TOO. THEY'RE GOIN' AFTER THEM AT JESUS De SADE'S PARTY TONIGHT...
WAIT A MINUTE: REVEREND BUDDY? DID YOU GET THEIR NAMES?
ONE'S CASS, OR SOMETHIN'. HE CALLED THE OTHER GUY JESSE.
IT COULDN'T BE, COULD IT? WHAT WOULD CUSTER BE DOING LOOKING FOR THOSE TWO PERVERTS?
BUT IT'S TOO MUCH OF A COINCIDENCE NOT TO BE HIM...
BUT IF HE'S GOING AFTER THEM AT THIS De SADE CHARACTER'S PARTY--
OH MY GOD!

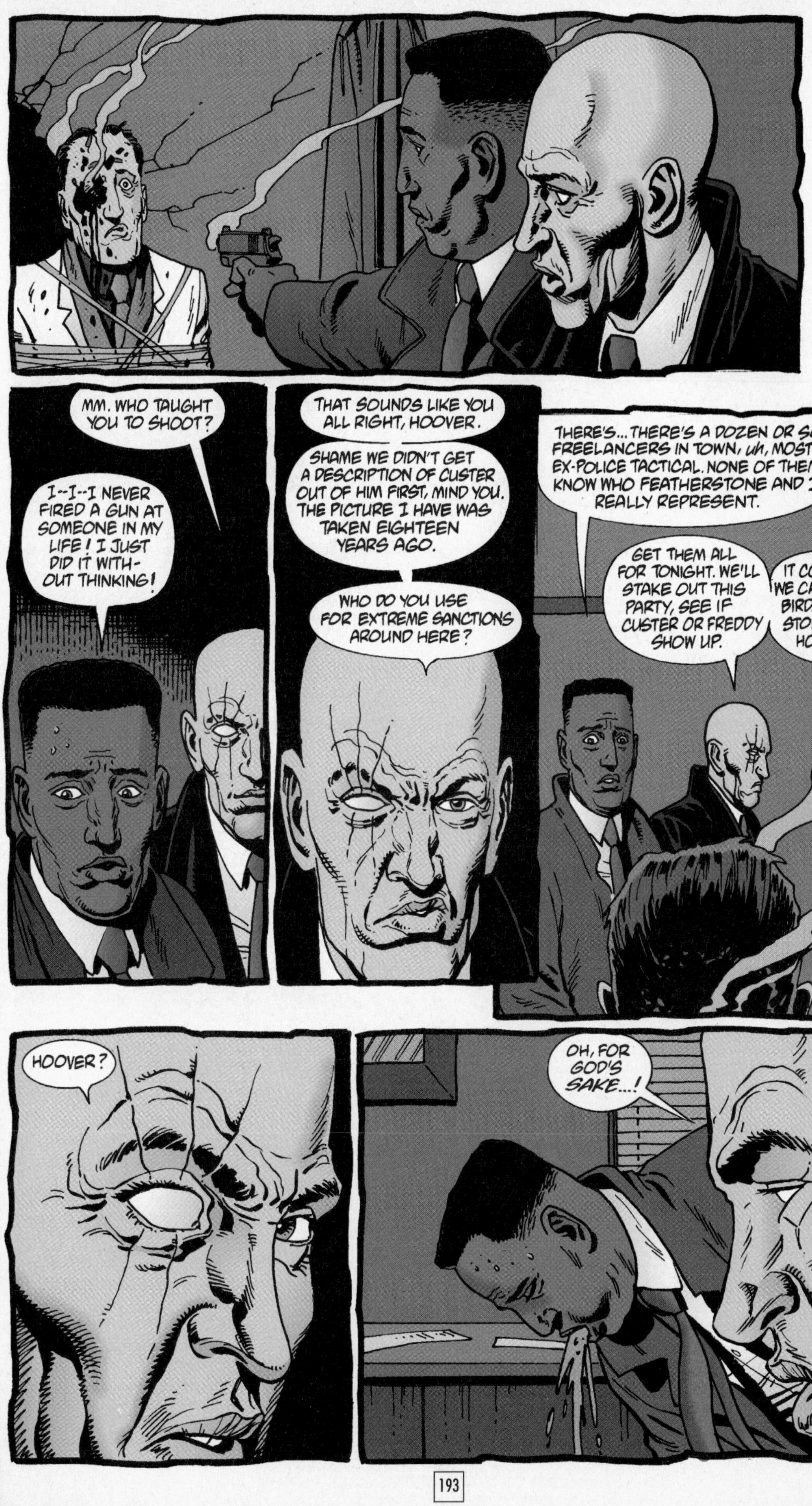

MM. WHO TAUGHT YOU TO SHOOT?
I--I--I NEVER FIRED A GUN AT SOMEONE IN MY LIFE! I JUST DID IT WITH-OUT THINKING!
THAT SOUNDS LIKE YOU ALL RIGHT, HOOVER.
SHAME WE DIDN'T GET A DESCRIPTION OF CUSTER OUT OF HIM FIRST, MIND YOU. THE PICTURE I HAVE WAS TAKEN EIGHTEEN YEARS AGO.
WHO DO YOU USE FOR EXTREME SANCTIONS AROUND HERE?
THERE'S... THERE'S A DOZEN OR SO FREELANCERS IN TOWN, *uh*, MOSTLY EX-POLICE TACTICAL. NONE OF THEM KNOW WHO FEATHERSTONE AND I REALLY REPRESENT.
GET THEM ALL FOR TONIGHT. WE'LL STAKE OUT THIS PARTY, SEE IF CUSTER OR FREDDY SHOW UP.
IT COULD BE WE CAN KILL TWO BIRDS WITH ONE STONE HERE, HOOVER...
HOOVER?
OH, FOR GOD'S *SAKE*...!

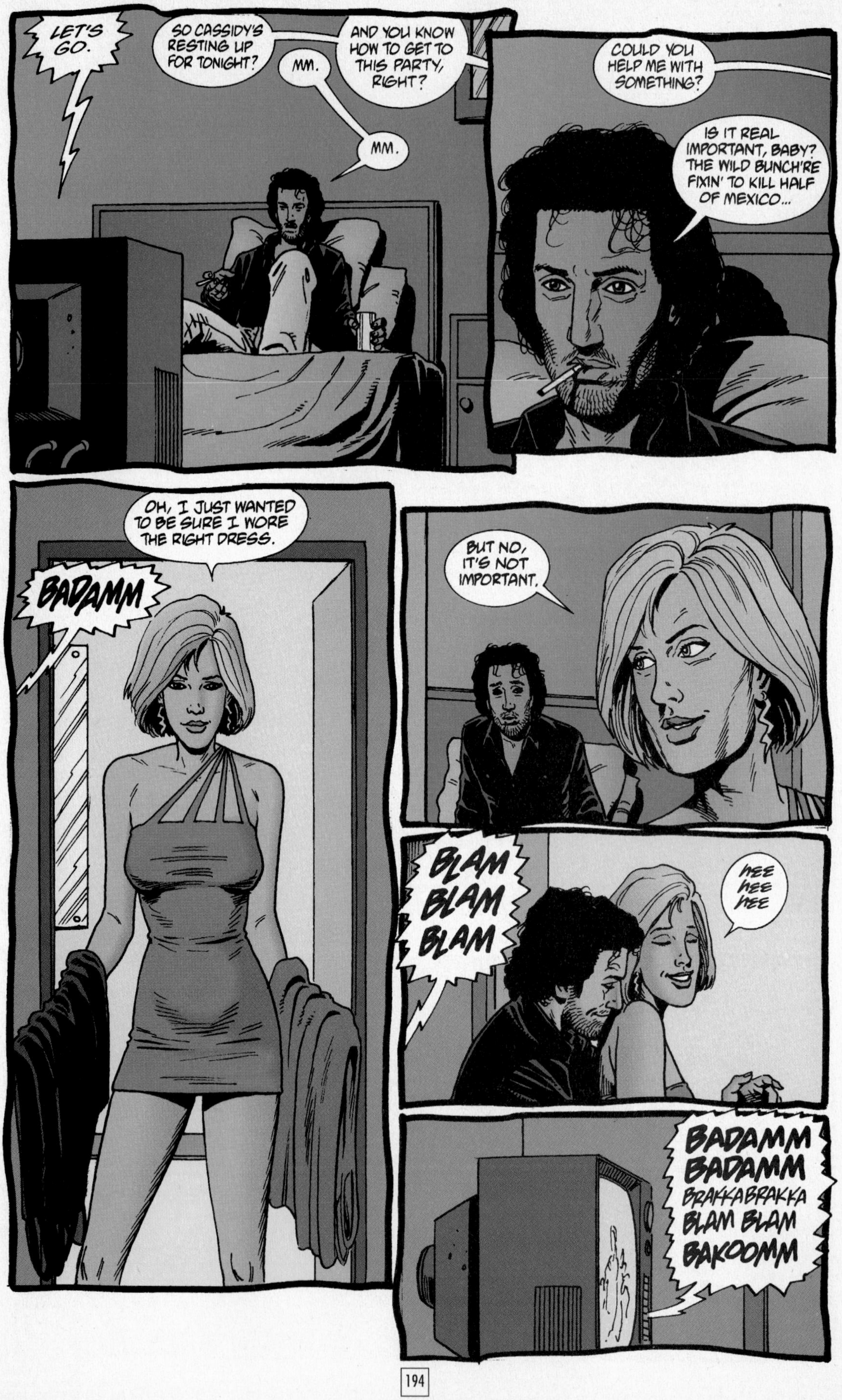
LET'S GO.
SO CASSIDY'S RESTING UP FOR TONIGHT?
MM.
AND YOU KNOW HOW TO GET TO THIS PARTY, RIGHT?
MM.
COULD YOU HELP ME WITH SOMETHING?
IS IT REAL IMPORTANT, BABY? THE WILD BUNCH'RE FIXIN' TO KILL HALF OF MEXICO...
OH, I JUST WANTED TO BE SURE I WORE THE RIGHT DRESS.
BADAMM
BUT NO, IT'S NOT IMPORTANT.
BLAM BLAM BLAM
HEE HEE HEE
BADAMM BADAMM BRAKKABRAKKA BLAM BLAM BAKOOMM

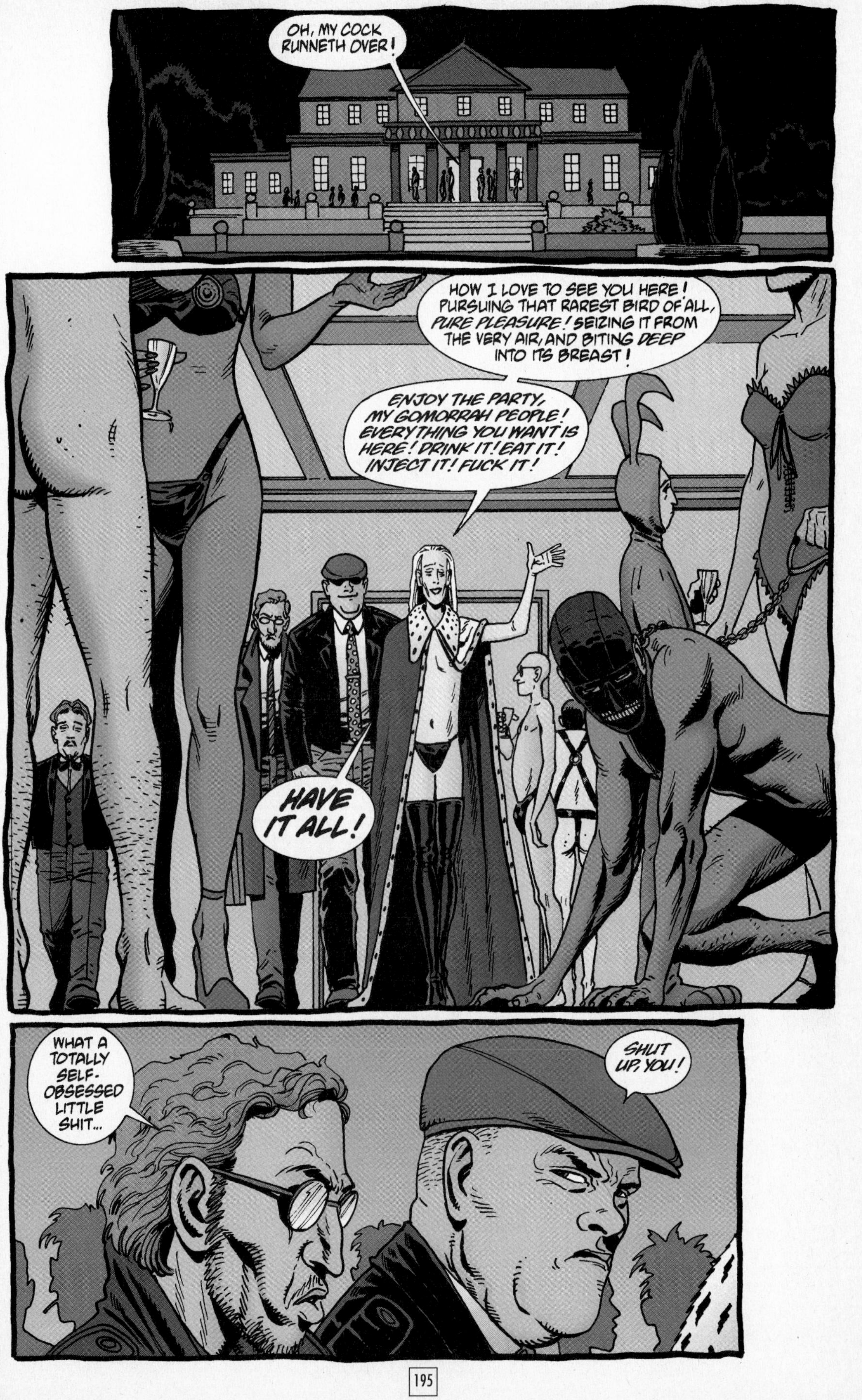
OH, MY COCK RUNNETH OVER!
HOW I LOVE TO SEE YOU HERE! PURSUING THAT RAREST BIRD OF ALL, PURE PLEASURE! SEIZING IT FROM THE VERY AIR, AND BITING DEEP INTO ITS BREAST!
ENJOY THE PARTY, MY GOMORRAH PEOPLE! EVERYTHING YOU WANT IS HERE! DRINK IT! EAT IT! INJECT IT! FUCK IT!
HAVE IT ALL!
WHAT A TOTALLY SELF-OBSESSED LITTLE SHIT...
SHUT UP, YOU!

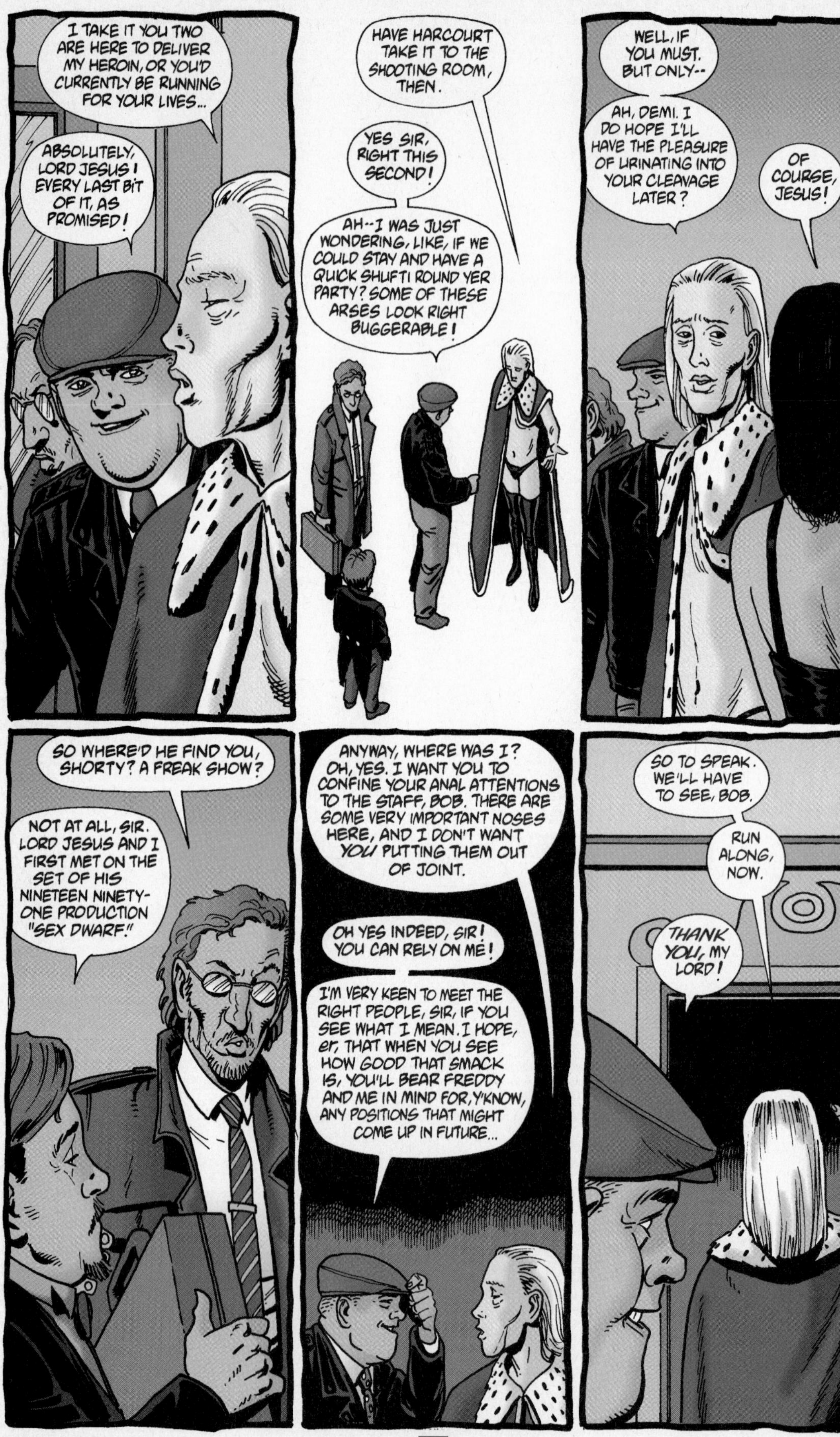
I TAKE IT YOU TWO ARE HERE TO DELIVER MY HEROIN, OR YOU'D CURRENTLY BE RUNNING FOR YOUR LIVES...
ABSOLUTELY, LORD JESUS! EVERY LAST BIT OF IT, AS PROMISED!
HAVE HARCOURT TAKE IT TO THE SHOOTING ROOM, THEN.
YES SIR, RIGHT THIS SECOND!
AH--I WAS JUST WONDERING, LIKE, IF WE COULD STAY AND HAVE A QUICK SHUFTI ROUND YER PARTY? SOME OF THESE ARSES LOOK RIGHT BUGGERABLE!
WELL, IF YOU MUST. BUT ONLY--
AH, DEMI. I DO HOPE I'LL HAVE THE PLEASURE OF URINATING INTO YOUR CLEAVAGE LATER?
OF COURSE, JESUS!
SO WHERE'D HE FIND YOU, SHORTY? A FREAK SHOW?
NOT AT ALL, SIR. LORD JESUS AND I FIRST MET ON THE SET OF HIS NINETEEN NINETY-ONE PRODUCTION "SEX DWARF."
ANYWAY, WHERE WAS I? OH, YES. I WANT YOU TO CONFINE YOUR ANAL ATTENTIONS TO THE STAFF, BOB. THERE ARE SOME VERY IMPORTANT NOSES HERE, AND I DON'T WANT *YOU* PUTTING THEM OUT OF JOINT.
OH YES INDEED, SIR! YOU CAN RELY ON ME!
I'M VERY KEEN TO MEET THE RIGHT PEOPLE, SIR, IF YOU SEE WHAT I MEAN. I HOPE, *er*, THAT WHEN YOU SEE HOW *GOOD* THAT SMACK IS, YOU'LL BEAR FREDDY AND ME IN MIND FOR, Y'KNOW, ANY POSITIONS THAT MIGHT COME UP IN FUTURE...
SO TO SPEAK. WE'LL HAVE TO SEE, BOB.
RUN ALONG, NOW.
THANK YOU, MY LORD!

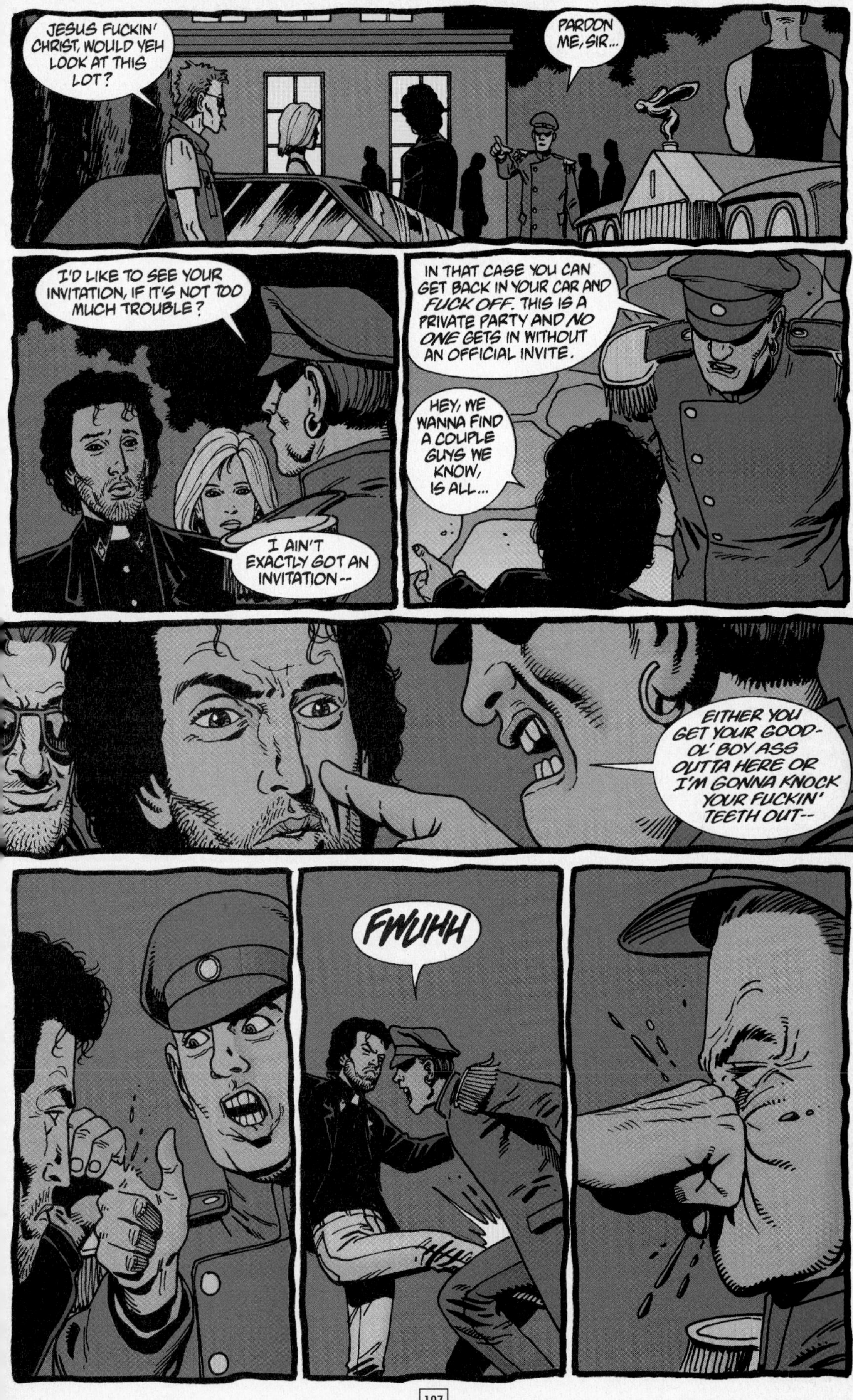
JESUS FUCKIN' CHRIST, WOULD YEH LOOK AT THIS LOT?
PARDON ME, SIR...
I'D LIKE TO SEE YOUR INVITATION, IF IT'S NOT TOO MUCH TROUBLE?
I AIN'T EXACTLY GOT AN INVITATION--
IN THAT CASE YOU CAN GET BACK IN YOUR CAR AND FUCK OFF. THIS IS A PRIVATE PARTY AND NO ONE GETS IN WITHOUT AN OFFICIAL INVITE.
HEY, WE WANNA FIND A COUPLE GUYS WE KNOW, IS ALL...
EITHER YOU GET YOUR GOOD-OL' BOY ASS OUTTA HERE OR I'M GONNA KNOCK YOUR FUCKIN' TEETH OUT--
FWUHH

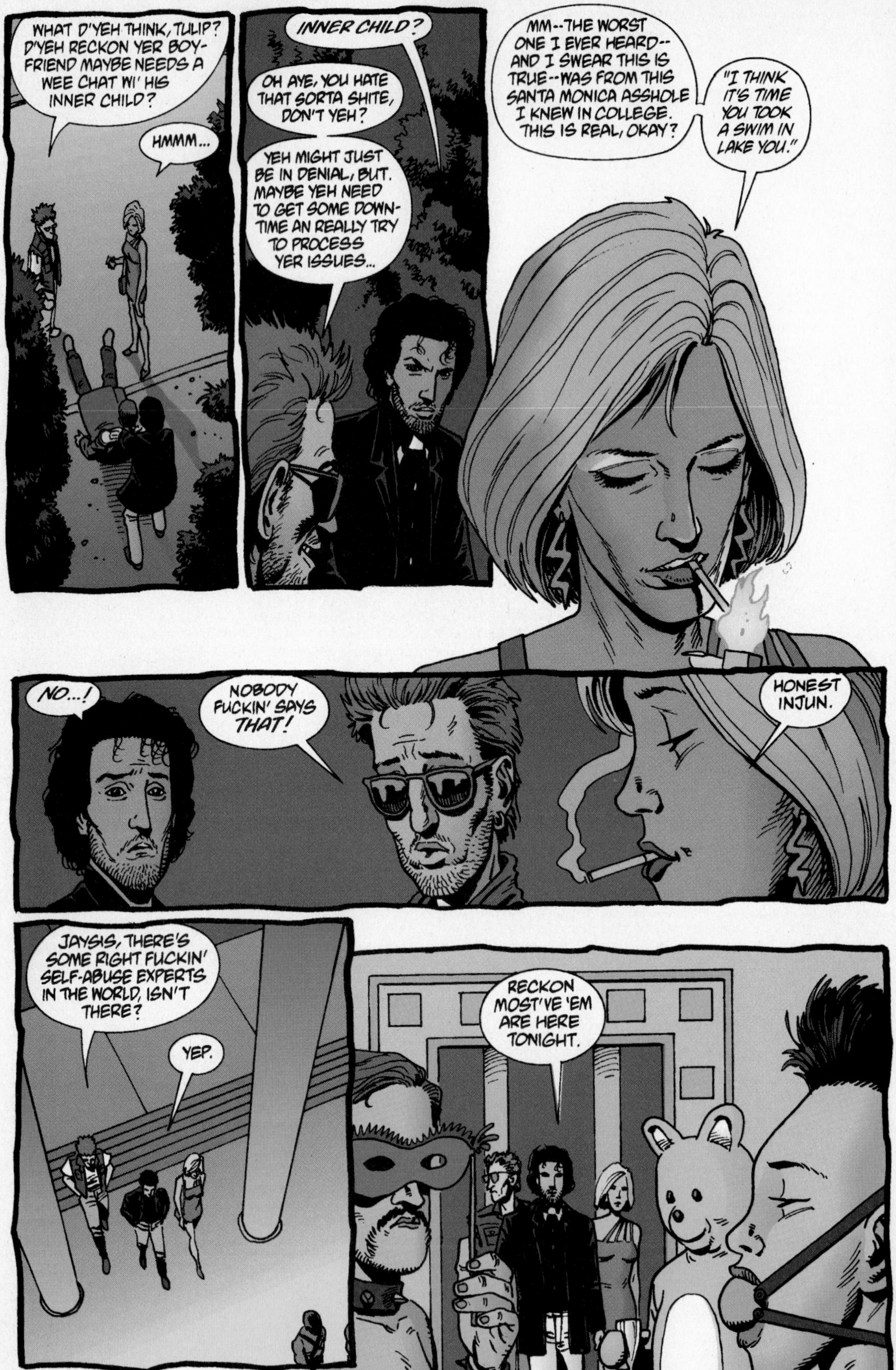
WHAT D'YEH THINK, TULIP? D'YEH RECKON YER BOY-FRIEND MAYBE NEEDS A WEE CHAT WI' HIS INNER CHILD?
HMMM...
INNER CHILD?
OH AYE, YOU HATE THAT SORTA SHITE, DON'T YEH?
YEH MIGHT JUST BE IN DENIAL, BUT. MAYBE YEH NEED TO GET SOME DOWN-TIME AN REALLY TRY TO PROCESS YER ISSUES...
MM--THE WORST ONE I EVER HEARD--AND I SWEAR THIS IS TRUE--WAS FROM THIS SANTA MONICA ASSHOLE I KNEW IN COLLEGE. THIS IS REAL, OKAY?
"I THINK IT'S TIME YOU TOOK A SWIM IN LAKE YOU."
NO...!
NOBODY FUCKIN' SAYS THAT!
HONEST INJUN.
JAYSIS, THERE'S SOME RIGHT FUCKIN' SELF-ABUSE EXPERTS IN THE WORLD, ISN'T THERE?
YEP.
RECKON MOST'VE 'EM ARE HERE TONIGHT.

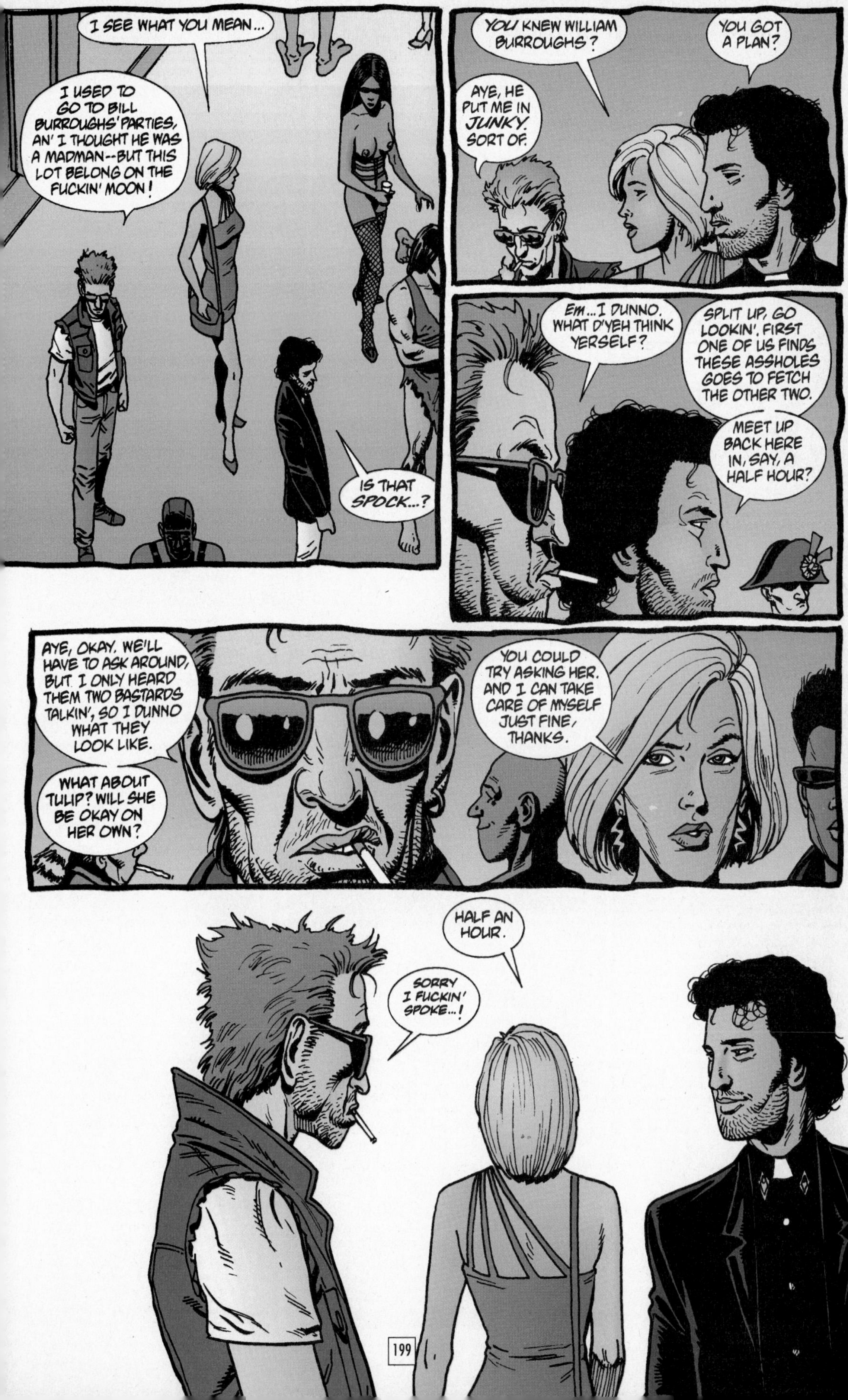
I SEE WHAT YOU MEAN...
I USED TO GO TO BILL BURROUGHS' PARTIES, AN' I THOUGHT HE WAS A MADMAN--BUT THIS LOT BELONG ON THE FUCKIN' MOON!
IS THAT SPOCK...?
YOU KNEW WILLIAM BURROUGHS?
AYE, HE PUT ME IN JUNKY. SORT OF.
YOU GOT A PLAN?
EM...I DUNNO. WHAT D'YEH THINK YERSELF?
SPLIT UP, GO LOOKIN'. FIRST ONE OF US FINDS THESE ASSHOLES GOES TO FETCH THE OTHER TWO.
MEET UP BACK HERE IN, SAY, A HALF HOUR?
AYE, OKAY. WE'LL HAVE TO ASK AROUND, BUT. I ONLY HEARD THEM TWO BASTARDS TALKIN', SO I DUNNO WHAT THEY LOOK LIKE.
WHAT ABOUT TULIP? WILL SHE BE OKAY ON HER OWN?
YOU COULD TRY ASKING HER. AND I CAN TAKE CARE OF MYSELF JUST FINE, THANKS.
HALF AN HOUR.
SORRY I FUCKIN' SPOKE...!

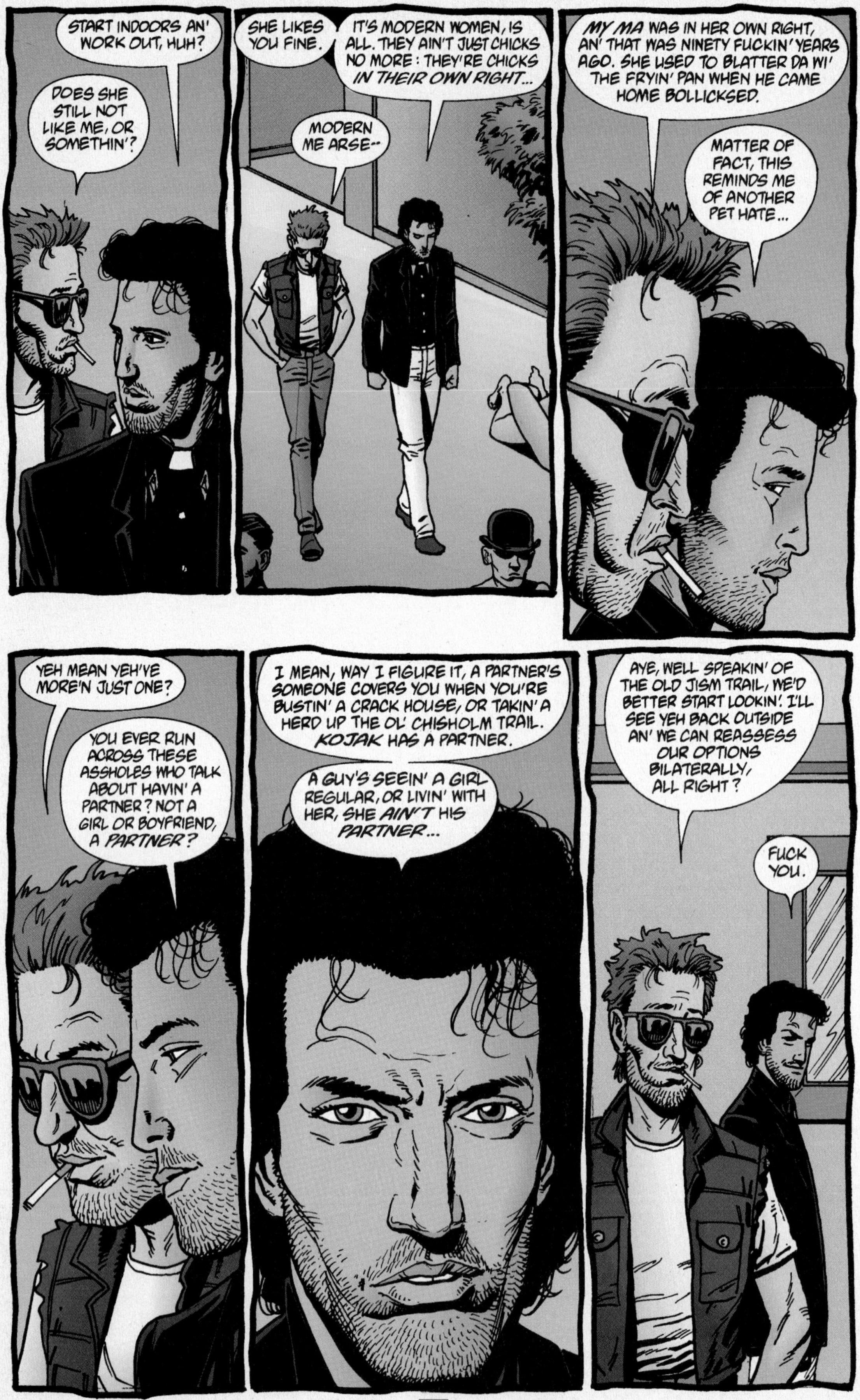
START INDOORS AN' WORK OUT, HUH?
DOES SHE STILL NOT LIKE ME, OR SOMETHIN'?
SHE LIKES YOU FINE.
IT'S MODERN WOMEN, IS ALL. THEY AIN'T JUST CHICKS NO MORE: THEY'RE CHICKS *IN THEIR OWN RIGHT*...
MODERN ME ARSE--
MY MA WAS IN HER OWN RIGHT, AN' THAT WAS NINETY FUCKIN' YEARS AGO. SHE USED TO BLATTER DA WI' THE FRYIN' PAN WHEN HE CAME HOME BOLLICKSED.
MATTER OF FACT, THIS REMINDS ME OF ANOTHER PET HATE...
YEH MEAN YEH'VE MORE'N JUST ONE?
YOU EVER RUN ACROSS THESE ASSHOLES WHO TALK ABOUT HAVIN' A PARTNER? NOT A GIRL OR BOYFRIEND, A *PARTNER*?
I MEAN, WAY I FIGURE IT, A PARTNER'S SOMEONE COVERS YOU WHEN YOU'RE BUSTIN' A CRACK HOUSE, OR TAKIN' A HERD UP THE OL' CHISHOLM TRAIL. *KOJAK* HAS A PARTNER.
A GUY'S SEEIN' A GIRL REGULAR, OR LIVIN' WITH HER, SHE *AIN'T* HIS *PARTNER*...
AYE, WELL SPEAKIN' OF THE OLD JISM TRAIL, WE'D BETTER START LOOKIN'. I'LL SEE YEH BACK OUTSIDE AN' WE CAN REASSESS OUR OPTIONS BILATERALLY, ALL RIGHT?
FUCK YOU.

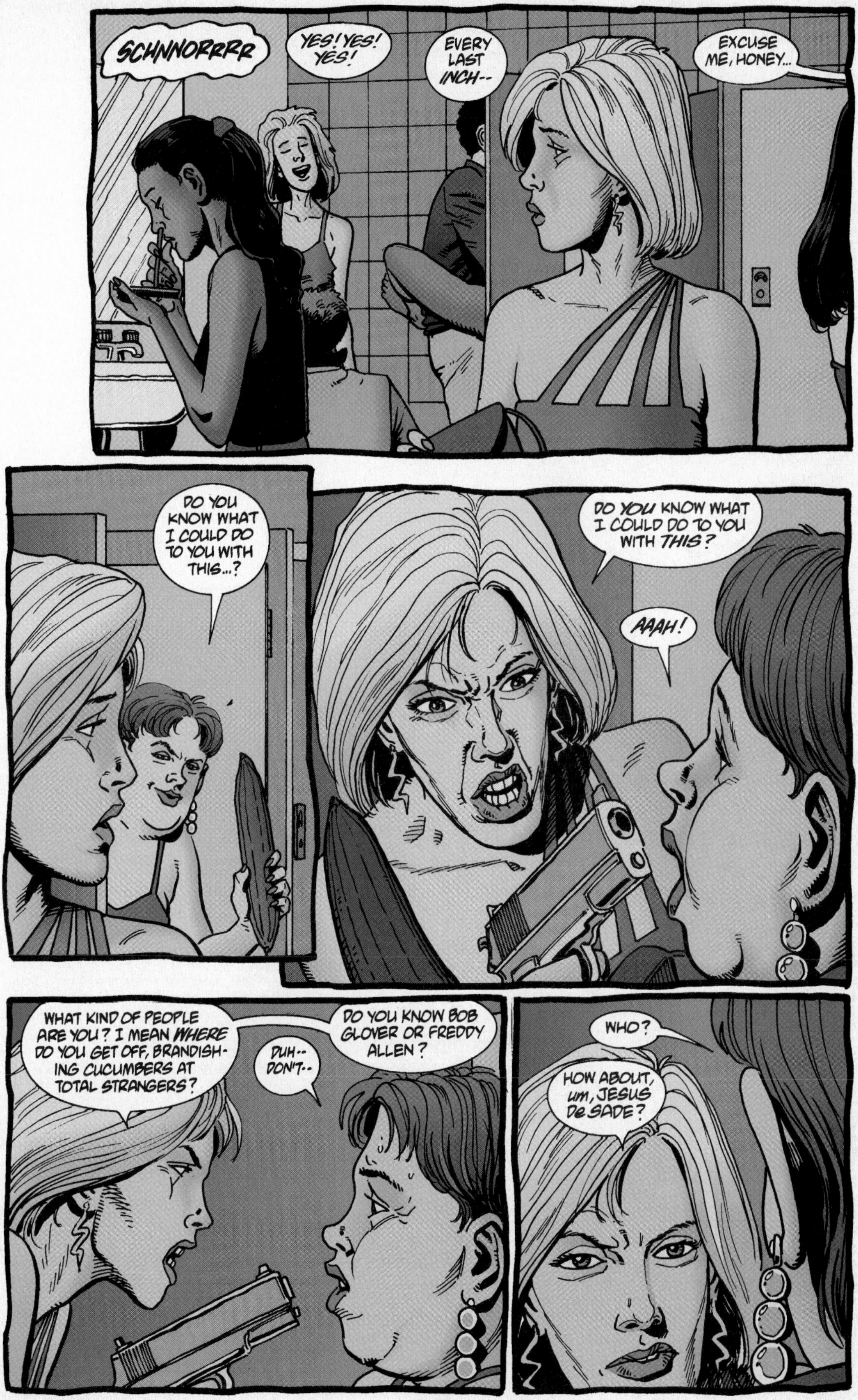
SCHNNORRRR
YES! YES! YES!
EVERY LAST INCH--
EXCUSE ME, HONEY...
DO YOU KNOW WHAT I COULD DO TO YOU WITH THIS...?
DO YOU KNOW WHAT I COULD DO TO YOU WITH THIS?
AAAH!
WHAT KIND OF PEOPLE ARE YOU? I MEAN WHERE DO YOU GET OFF, BRANDISH-ING CUCUMBERS AT TOTAL STRANGERS?
DUH-- DON'T--
DO YOU KNOW BOB GLOVER OR FREDDY ALLEN?
WHO?
HOW ABOUT, UM, JESUS De SADE?

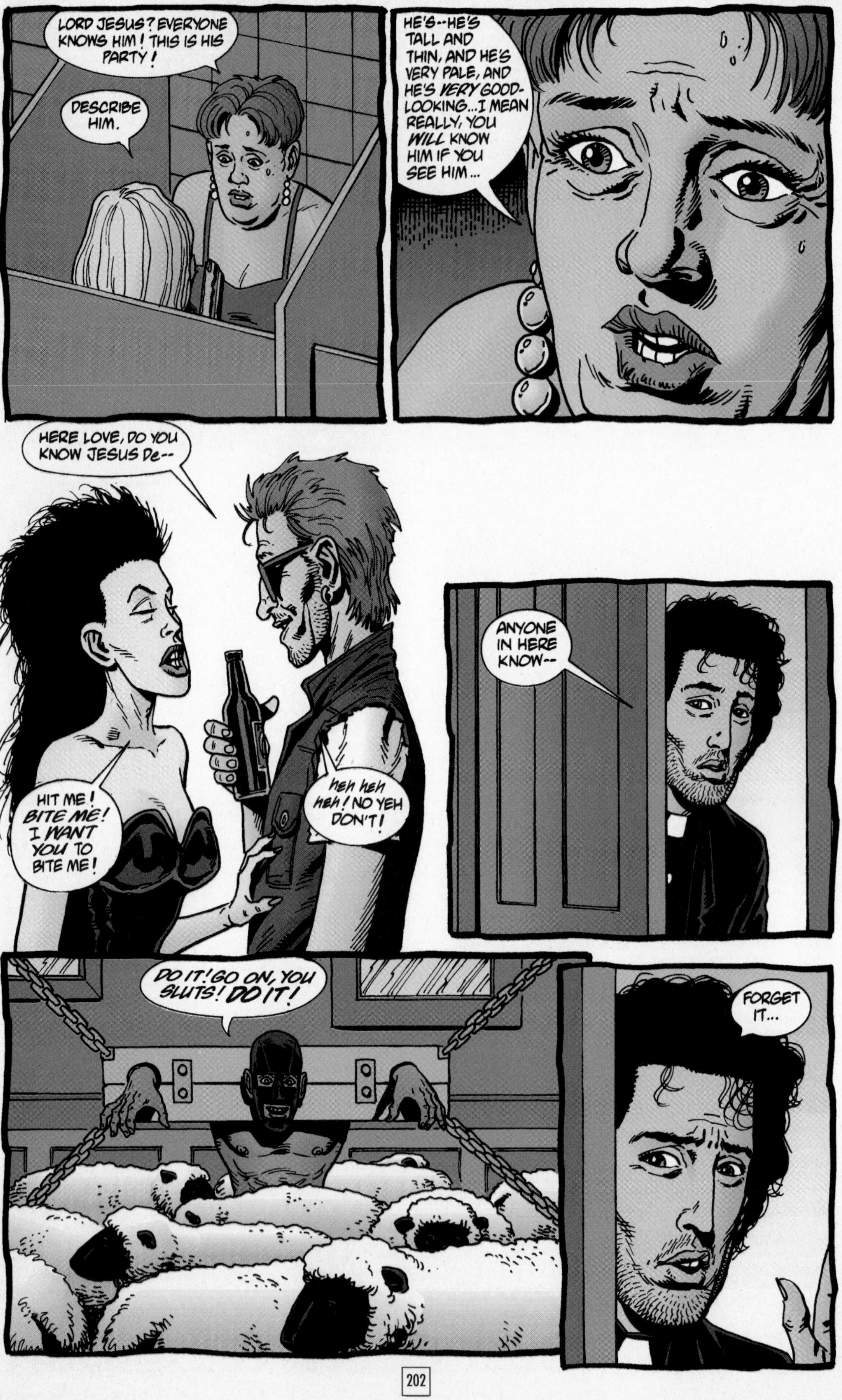
LORD JESUS? EVERYONE KNOWS HIM! THIS IS HIS PARTY!
DESCRIBE HIM.
HE'S--HE'S TALL AND THIN, AND HE'S VERY PALE, AND HE'S VERY GOOD-LOOKING...I MEAN REALLY, YOU WILL KNOW HIM IF YOU SEE HIM...
HERE LOVE, DO YOU KNOW JESUS De--
HIT ME! BITE ME! I WANT YOU TO BITE ME!
heh heh heh! NO YEH DON'T!
ANYONE IN HERE KNOW--
DO IT! GO ON, YOU SLUTS! DO IT!
FORGET IT...

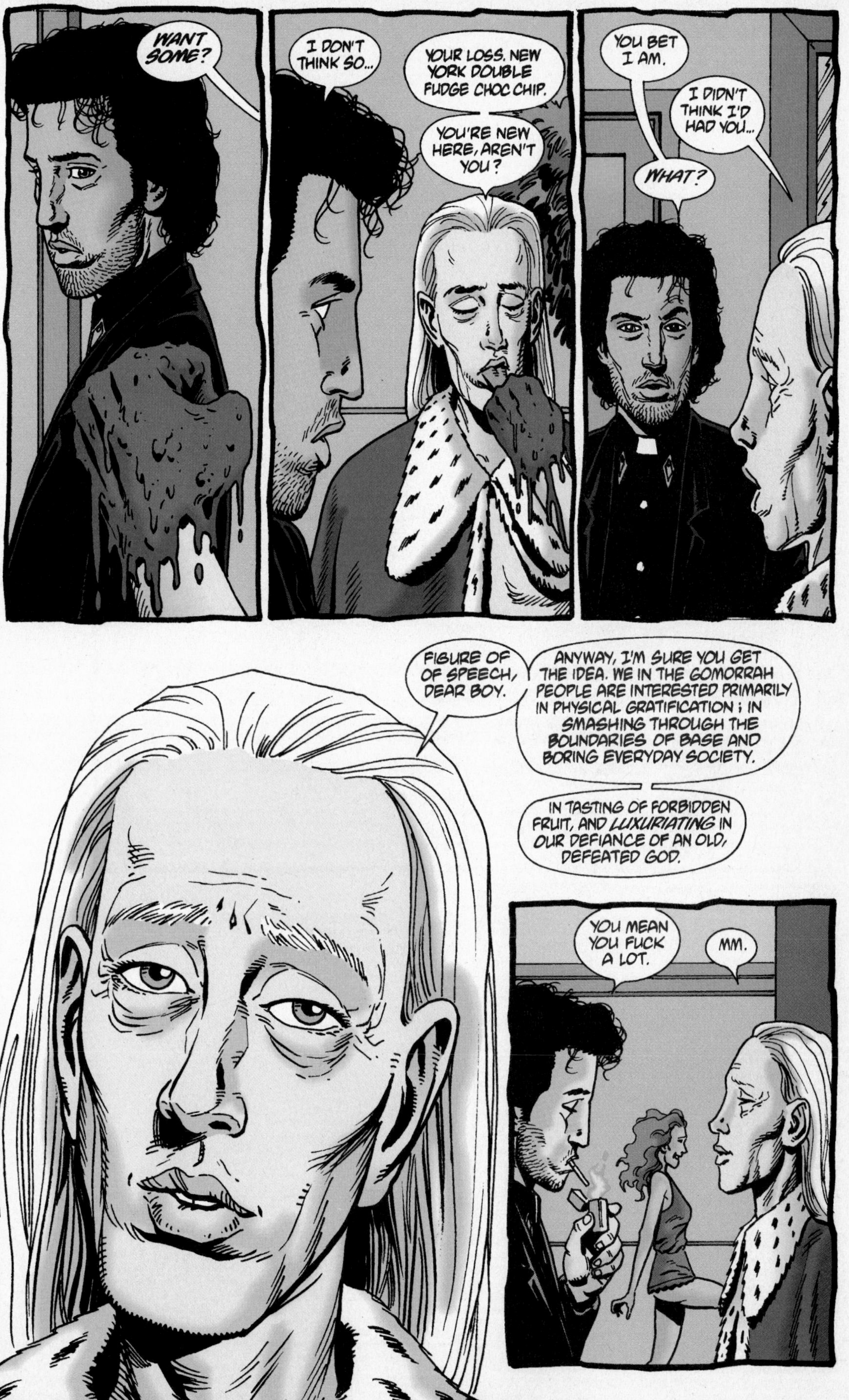
WANT SOME?
I DON'T THINK SO...
YOUR LOSS. NEW YORK DOUBLE FUDGE CHOC CHIP.
YOU'RE NEW HERE, AREN'T YOU?
YOU BET I AM.
WHAT?
I DIDN'T THINK I'D HAD YOU...
FIGURE OF SPEECH, DEAR BOY.
ANYWAY, I'M SURE YOU GET THE IDEA. WE IN THE GOMORRAH PEOPLE ARE INTERESTED PRIMARILY IN PHYSICAL GRATIFICATION ; IN SMASHING THROUGH THE BOUNDARIES OF BASE AND BORING EVERYDAY SOCIETY.
IN TASTING OF FORBIDDEN FRUIT, AND LUXURIATING IN OUR DEFIANCE OF AN OLD, DEFEATED GOD.
YOU MEAN YOU FUCK A LOT.
MM.

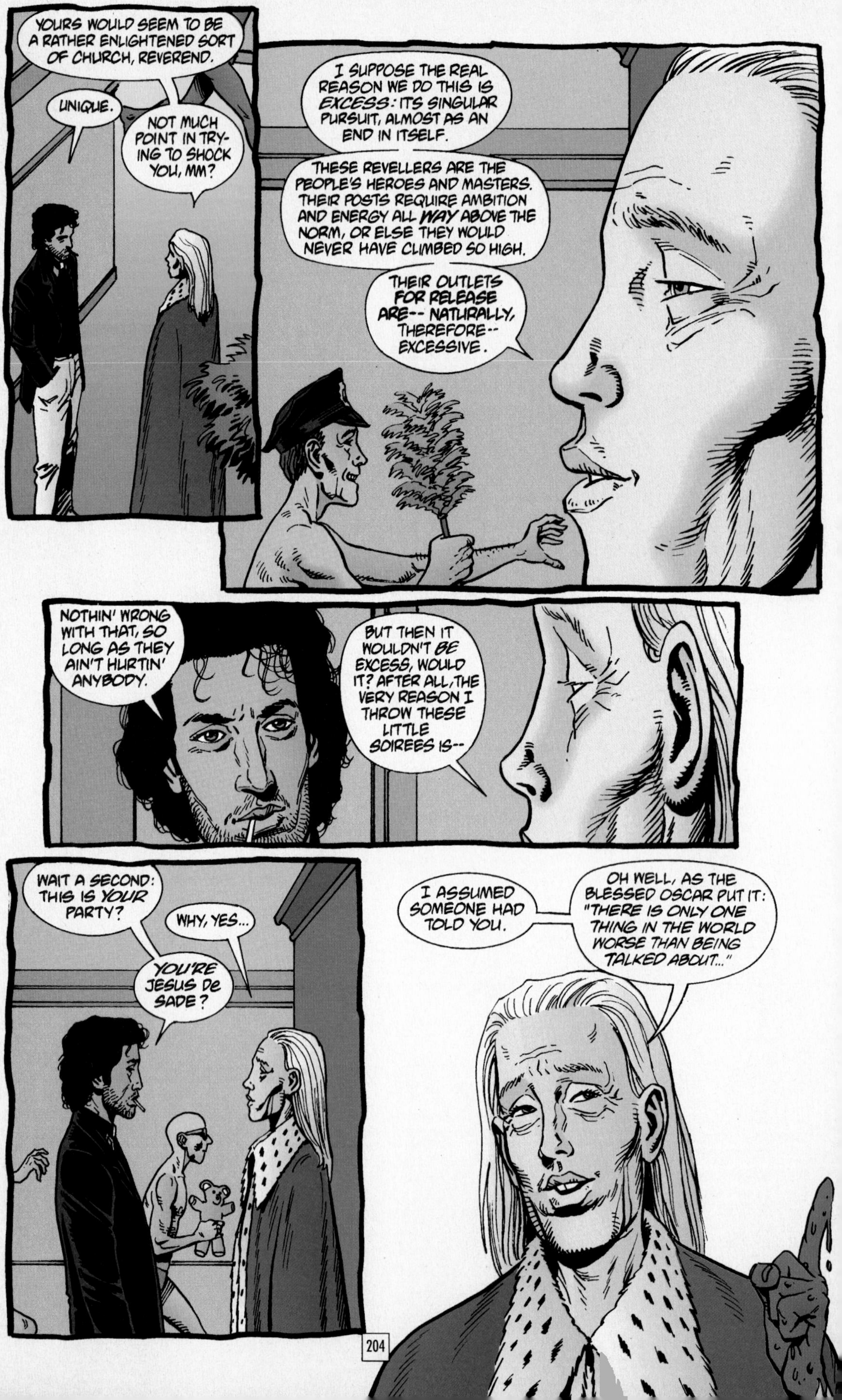

YOURS WOULD SEEM TO BE A RATHER ENLIGHTENED SORT OF CHURCH, REVEREND.
UNIQUE.
NOT MUCH POINT IN TRYING TO SHOCK YOU, MM?
I SUPPOSE THE REAL REASON WE DO THIS IS *EXCESS*: ITS SINGULAR PURSUIT, ALMOST AS AN END IN ITSELF.
THESE REVELLERS ARE THE PEOPLE'S HEROES AND MASTERS. THEIR POSTS REQUIRE AMBITION AND ENERGY ALL *WAY* ABOVE THE NORM, OR ELSE THEY WOULD NEVER HAVE CLIMBED SO HIGH.
THEIR OUTLETS **FOR RELEASE** ARE-- NATURALLY, THEREFORE-- EXCESSIVE.
NOTHIN' WRONG WITH THAT, SO LONG AS THEY AIN'T HURTIN' ANYBODY.
BUT THEN IT WOULDN'T *BE* EXCESS, WOULD IT? AFTER ALL, THE VERY REASON I THROW THESE LITTLE SOIREES IS--
WAIT A SECOND: THIS IS *YOUR* PARTY?
WHY, YES...
YOU'RE JESUS DE SADE?
I ASSUMED SOMEONE HAD TOLD YOU.
OH WELL, AS THE BLESSED OSCAR PUT IT: *"THERE IS ONLY ONE THING IN THE WORLD WORSE THAN BEING TALKED ABOUT..."*

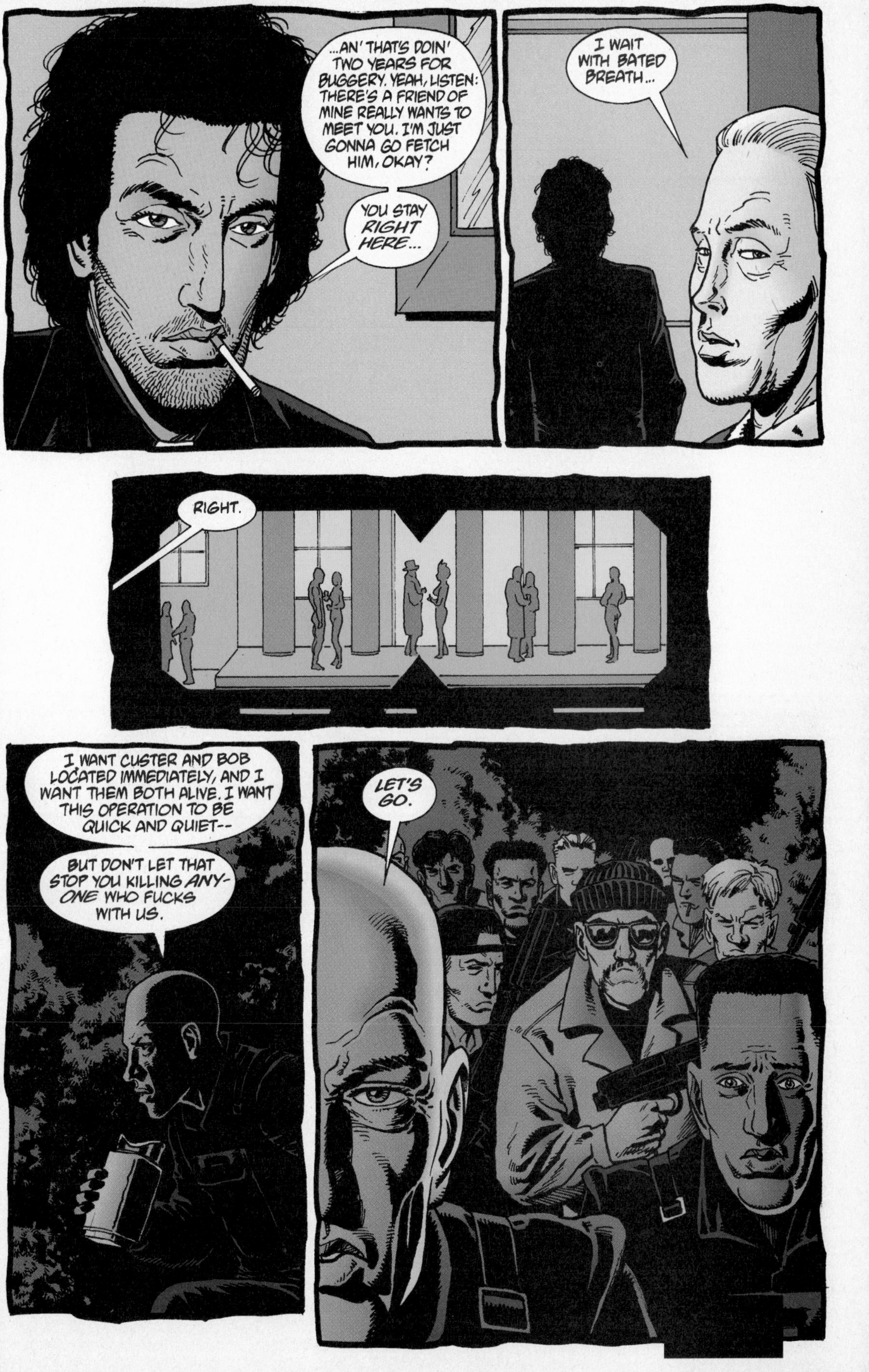
...AN' THAT'S DOIN' TWO YEARS FOR BUGGERY. YEAH, LISTEN: THERE'S A FRIEND OF MINE REALLY WANTS TO MEET YOU. I'M JUST GONNA GO FETCH HIM, OKAY?
YOU STAY *RIGHT HERE*...
I WAIT WITH BATED BREATH...
RIGHT.
I WANT CUSTER AND BOB LOCATED IMMEDIATELY, AND I WANT THEM BOTH ALIVE. I WANT THIS OPERATION TO BE QUICK AND QUIET--
BUT DON'T LET THAT STOP YOU KILLING *ANYONE* WHO FUCKS WITH US.
LET'S GO.

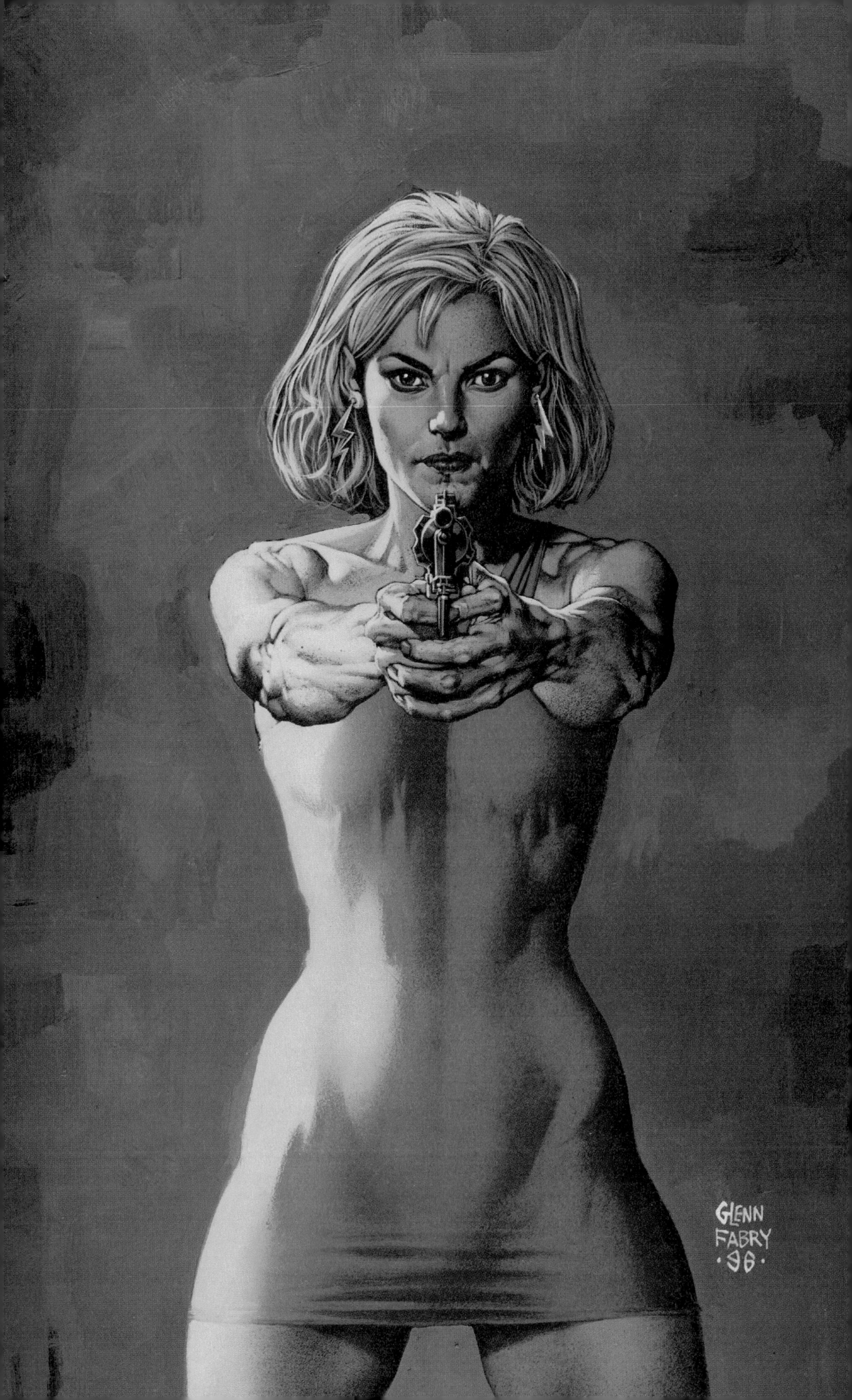
GLENN
FABRY
·96·

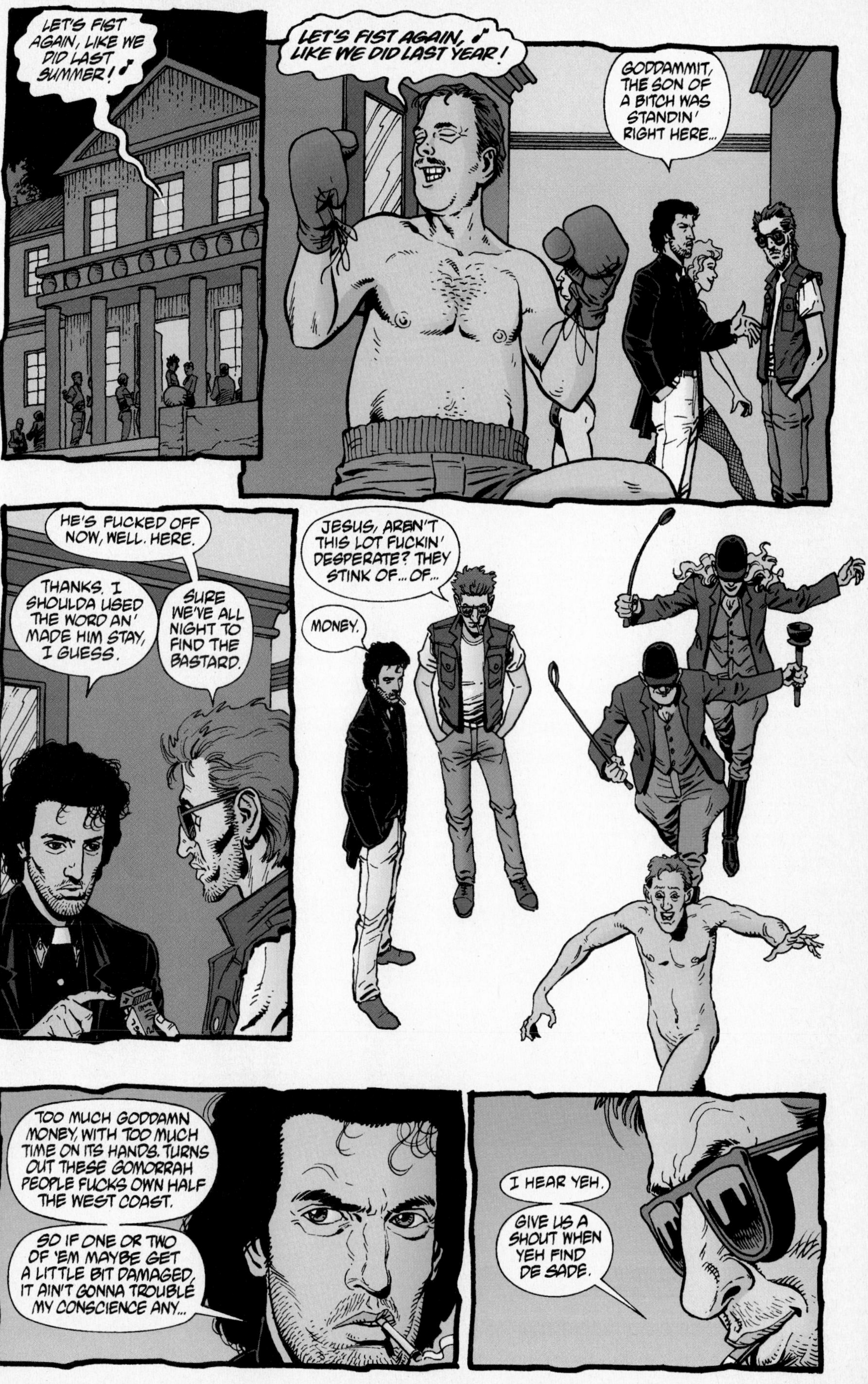
LET'S FIST AGAIN, LIKE WE DID LAST SUMMER!
LET'S FIST AGAIN, LIKE WE DID LAST YEAR!
GODDAMMIT, THE SON OF A BITCH WAS STANDIN' RIGHT HERE...
HE'S FUCKED OFF NOW, WELL. HERE.
THANKS. I SHOULDA USED THE WORD AN' MADE HIM STAY, I GUESS.
SURE WE'VE ALL NIGHT TO FIND THE BASTARD.
JESUS, AREN'T THIS LOT FUCKIN' DESPERATE? THEY STINK OF... OF...
MONEY.
TOO MUCH GODDAMN MONEY, WITH TOO MUCH TIME ON ITS HANDS. TURNS OUT THESE GOMORRAH PEOPLE FUCKS OWN HALF THE WEST COAST.
SO IF ONE OR TWO OF 'EM MAYBE GET A LITTLE BIT DAMAGED, IT AIN'T GONNA TROUBLE MY CONSCIENCE ANY...
I HEAR YEH.
GIVE US A SHOUT WHEN YEH FIND DE SADE.

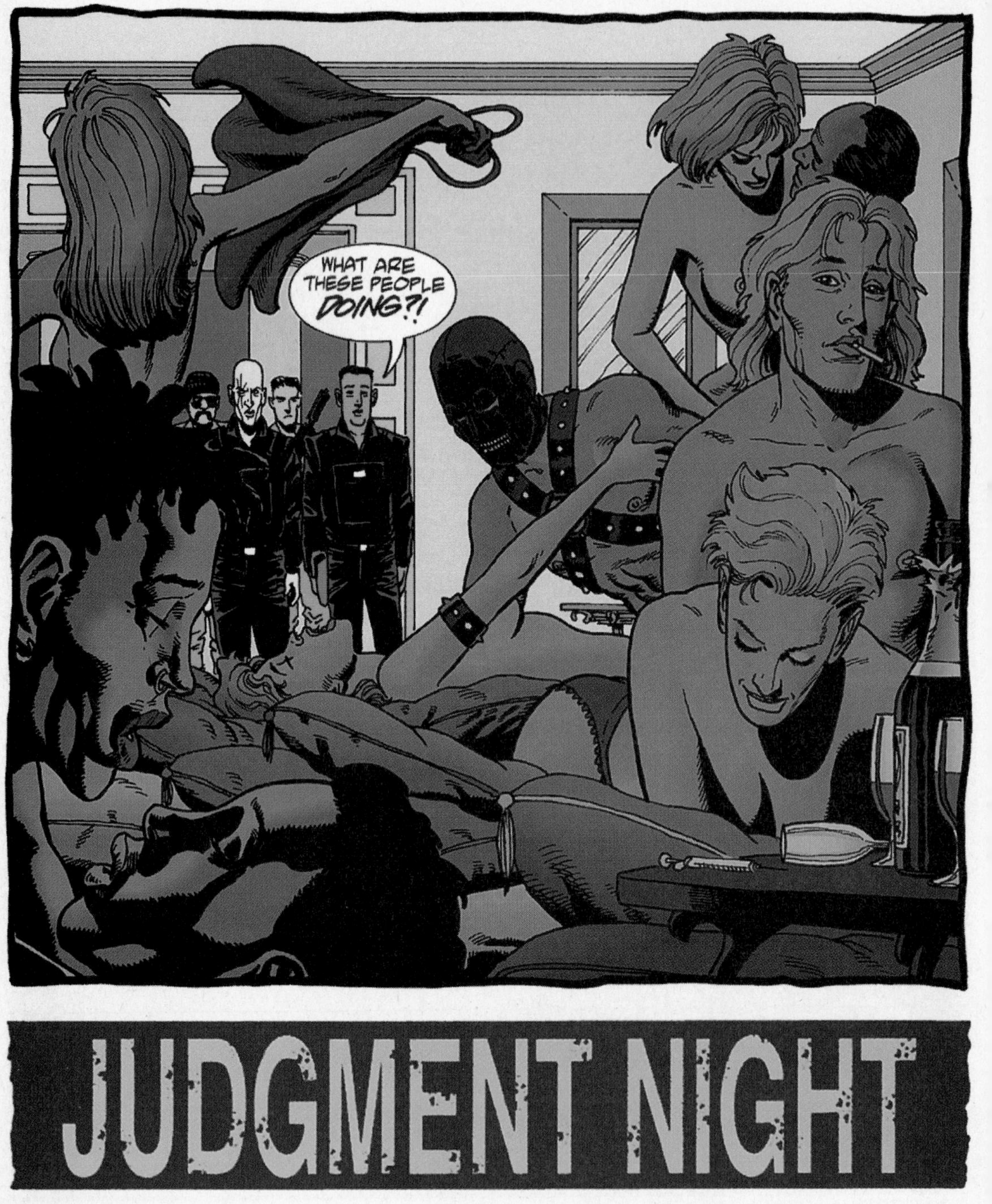
WHAT ARE THESE PEOPLE DOING?!

JUDGMENT NIGHT

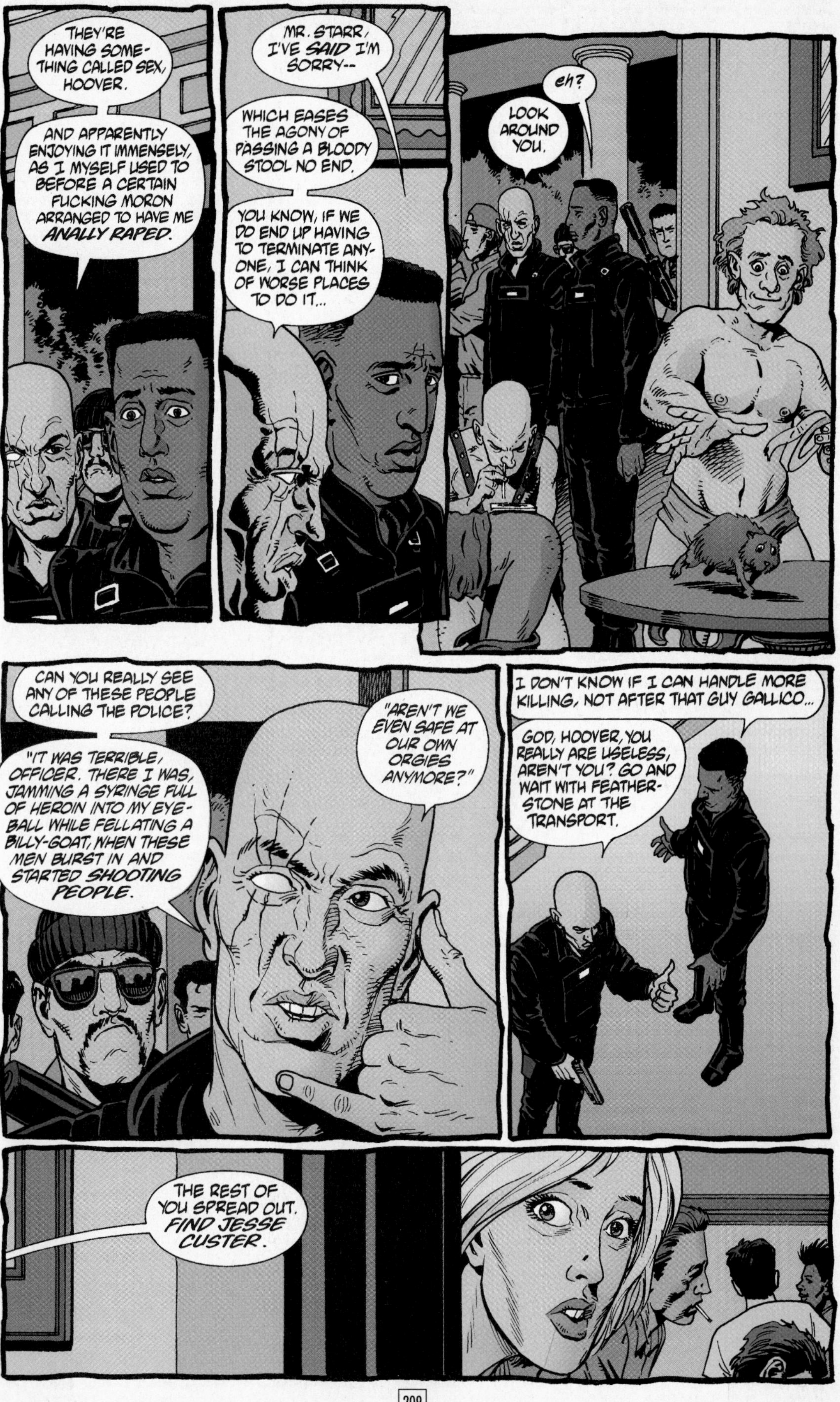
THEY'RE HAVING SOME-THING CALLED SEX, HOOVER.
AND APPARENTLY ENJOYING IT IMMENSELY, AS I MYSELF USED TO BEFORE A CERTAIN FUCKING MORON ARRANGED TO HAVE ME ANALLY RAPED.
MR. STARR, I'VE SAID I'M SORRY--
WHICH EASES THE AGONY OF PASSING A BLOODY STOOL NO END.
YOU KNOW, IF WE DO END UP HAVING TO TERMINATE ANY-ONE, I CAN THINK OF WORSE PLACES TO DO IT...
eh?
LOOK AROUND YOU.
CAN YOU REALLY SEE ANY OF THESE PEOPLE CALLING THE POLICE?
"IT WAS TERRIBLE, OFFICER. THERE I WAS, JAMMING A SYRINGE FULL OF HEROIN INTO MY EYE-BALL WHILE FELLATING A BILLY-GOAT, WHEN THESE MEN BURST IN AND STARTED SHOOTING PEOPLE.
"AREN'T WE EVEN SAFE AT OUR OWN ORGIES ANYMORE?"
I DON'T KNOW IF I CAN HANDLE MORE KILLING, NOT AFTER THAT GUY GALLICO...
GOD, HOOVER, YOU REALLY ARE USELESS, AREN'T YOU? GO AND WAIT WITH FEATHER-STONE AT THE TRANSPORT.
THE REST OF YOU SPREAD OUT. FIND JESSE CUSTER.

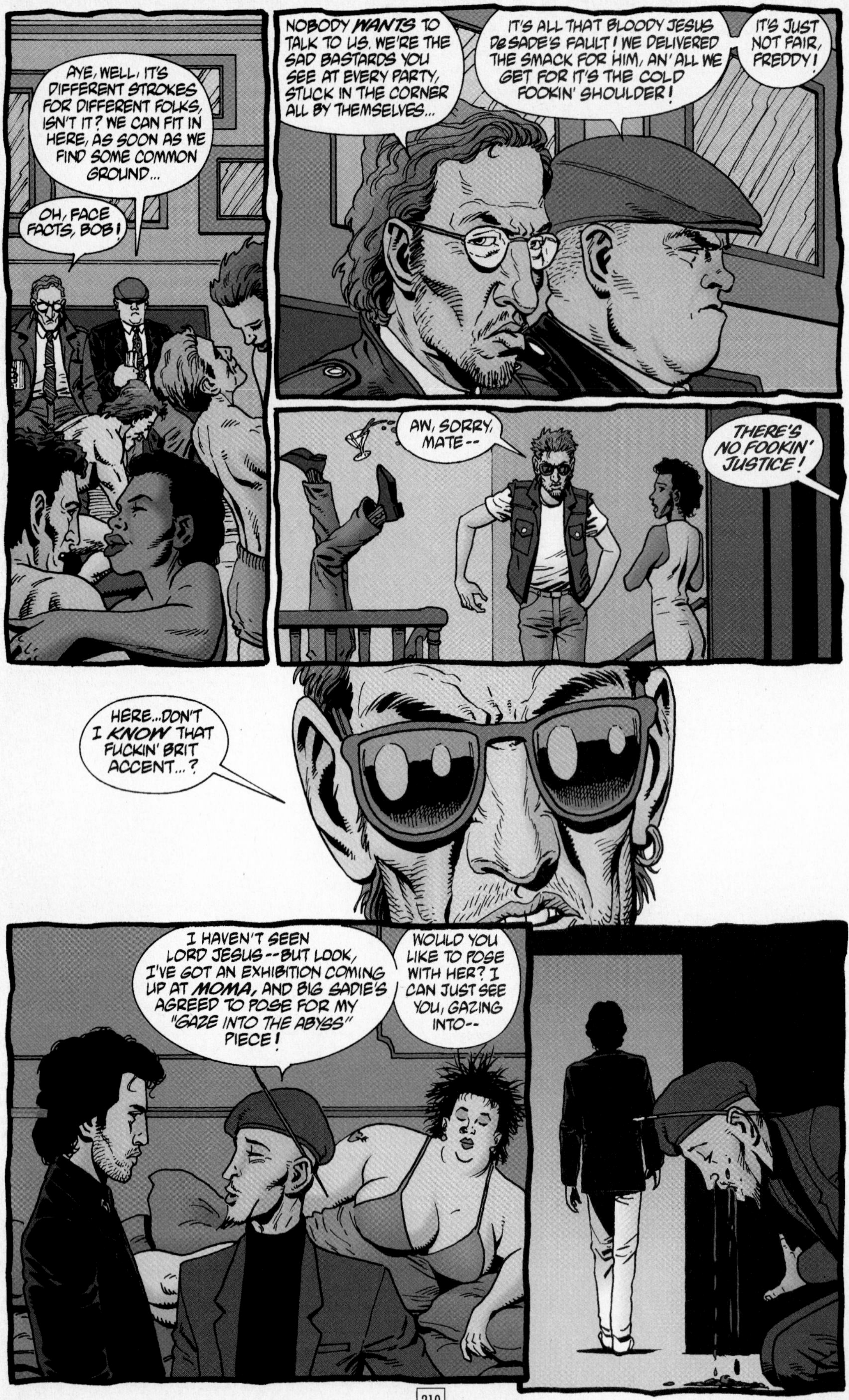
AYE, WELL, IT'S DIFFERENT STROKES FOR DIFFERENT FOLKS, ISN'T IT? WE CAN FIT IN HERE, AS SOON AS WE FIND SOME COMMON GROUND...
OH, FACE FACTS, BOB!
NOBODY WANTS TO TALK TO US. WE'RE THE SAD BASTARDS YOU SEE AT EVERY PARTY, STUCK IN THE CORNER ALL BY THEMSELVES...
IT'S ALL THAT BLOODY JESUS DeSADE'S FAULT! WE DELIVERED THE SMACK FOR HIM, AN' ALL WE GET FOR IT'S THE COLD FOOKIN' SHOULDER!
IT'S JUST NOT FAIR, FREDDY!
AW, SORRY, MATE--
THERE'S NO FOOKIN' JUSTICE!
HERE...DON'T I KNOW THAT FUCKIN' BRIT ACCENT...?
I HAVEN'T SEEN LORD JESUS--BUT LOOK, I'VE GOT AN EXHIBITION COMING UP AT MOMA, AND BIG SADIE'S AGREED TO POSE FOR MY "GAZE INTO THE ABYSS" PIECE!
WOULD YOU LIKE TO POSE WITH HER? I CAN JUST SEE YOU, GAZING INTO--

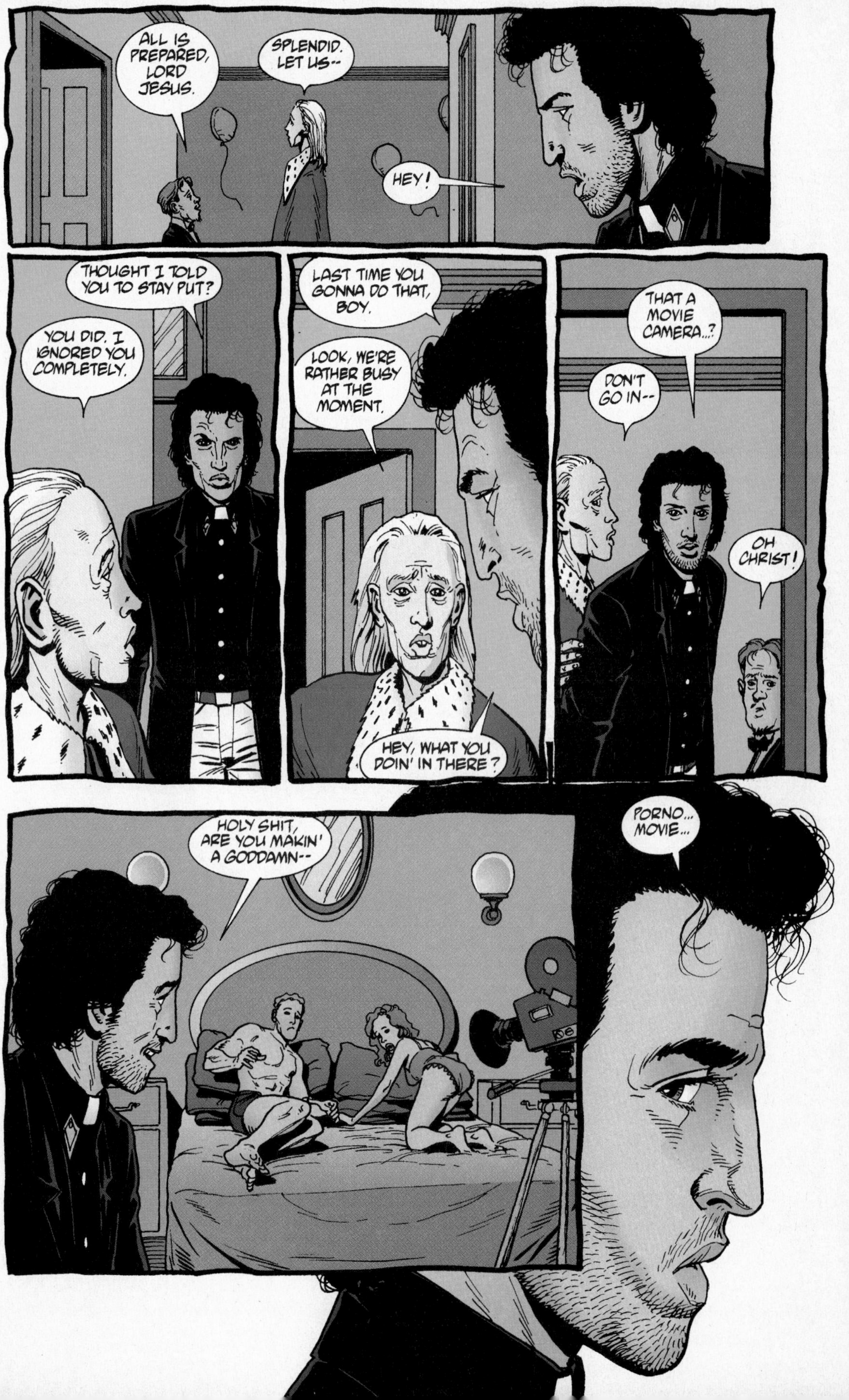
ALL IS PREPARED, LORD JESUS.
SPLENDID. LET US--
HEY!
THOUGHT I TOLD YOU TO STAY PUT?
YOU DID. I IGNORED YOU COMPLETELY.
LAST TIME YOU GONNA DO THAT, BOY.
LOOK, WE'RE RATHER BUSY AT THE MOMENT.
HEY, WHAT YOU DOIN' IN THERE?
THAT A MOVIE CAMERA..?
DON'T GO IN--
OH CHRIST!
HOLY SHIT, ARE YOU MAKIN' A GODDAMN--
PORNO... MOVIE...

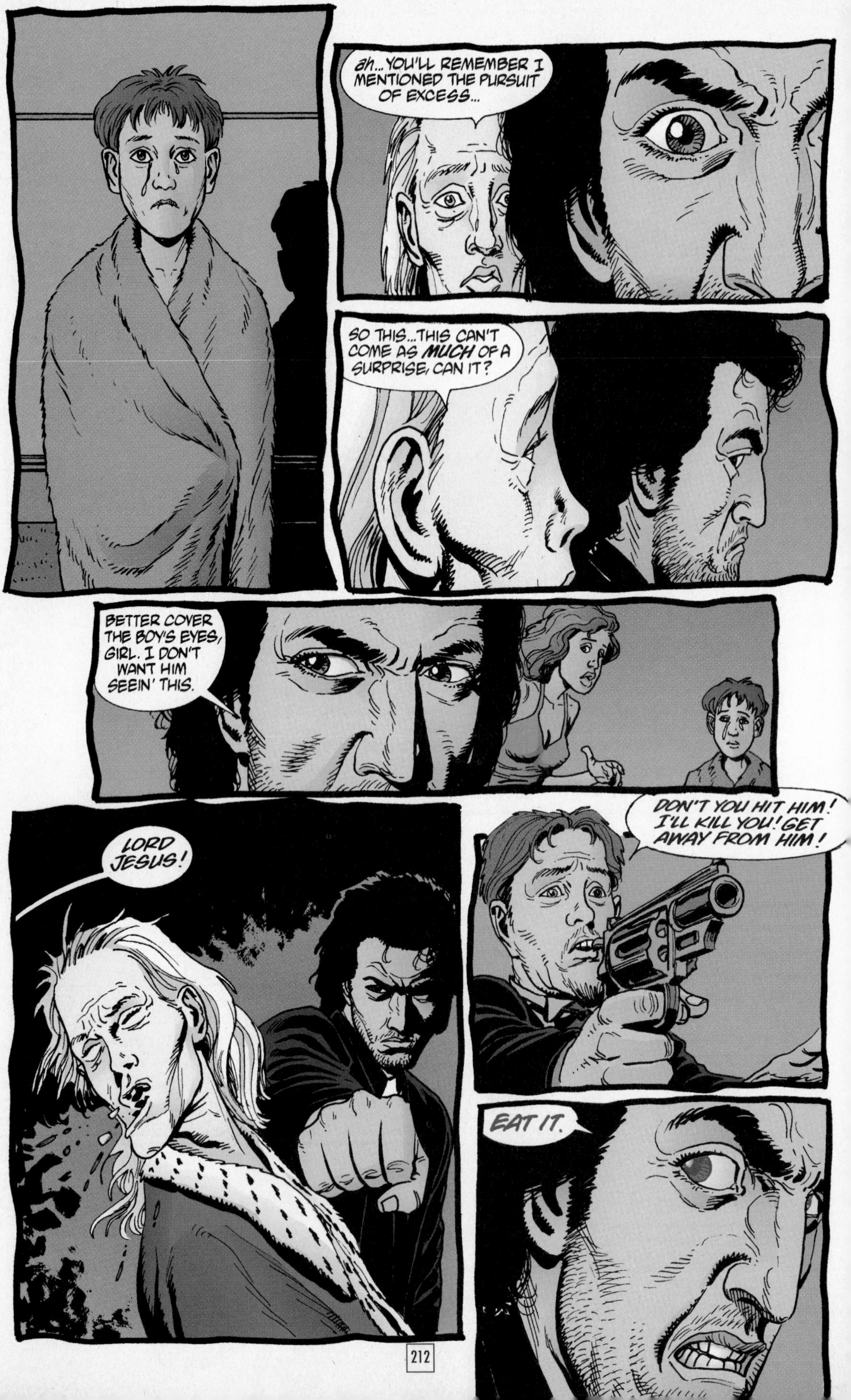
ah... YOU'LL REMEMBER I MENTIONED THE PURSUIT OF EXCESS...
SO THIS...THIS CAN'T COME AS MUCH OF A SURPRISE, CAN IT?
BETTER COVER THE BOY'S EYES, GIRL. I DON'T WANT HIM SEEIN' THIS.
LORD JESUS!
DON'T YOU HIT HIM! I'LL KILL YOU! GET AWAY FROM HIM!
EAT IT.

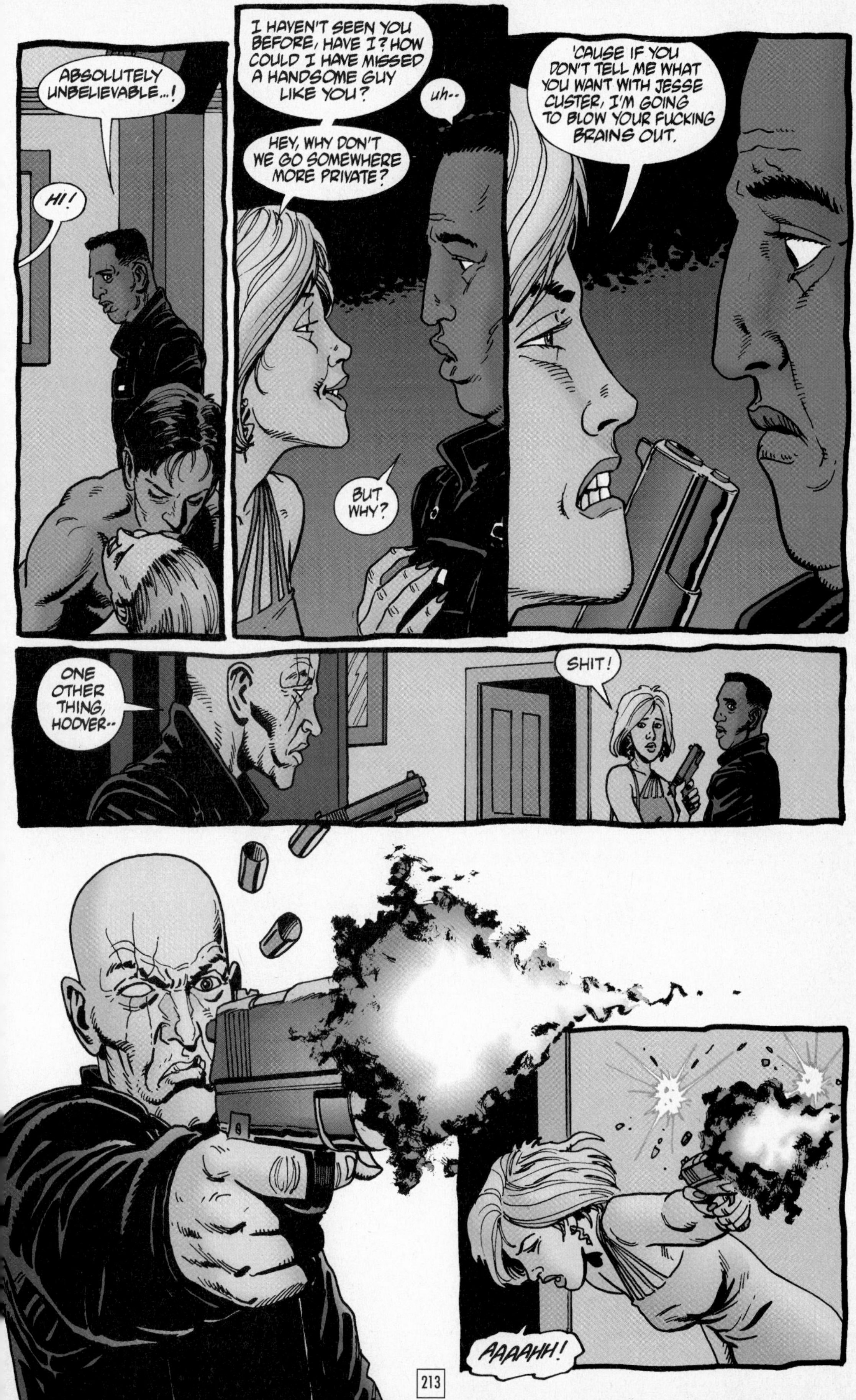
ABSOLUTELY UNBELIEVABLE...!
HI!
I HAVEN'T SEEN YOU BEFORE, HAVE I? HOW COULD I HAVE MISSED A HANDSOME GUY LIKE YOU?
uh--
HEY, WHY DON'T WE GO SOMEWHERE MORE PRIVATE?
BUT WHY?
'CAUSE IF YOU DON'T TELL ME WHAT YOU WANT WITH JESSE CUSTER, I'M GOING TO BLOW YOUR FUCKING BRAINS OUT.
ONE OTHER THING, HOOVER--
SHIT!
AAAAHH!

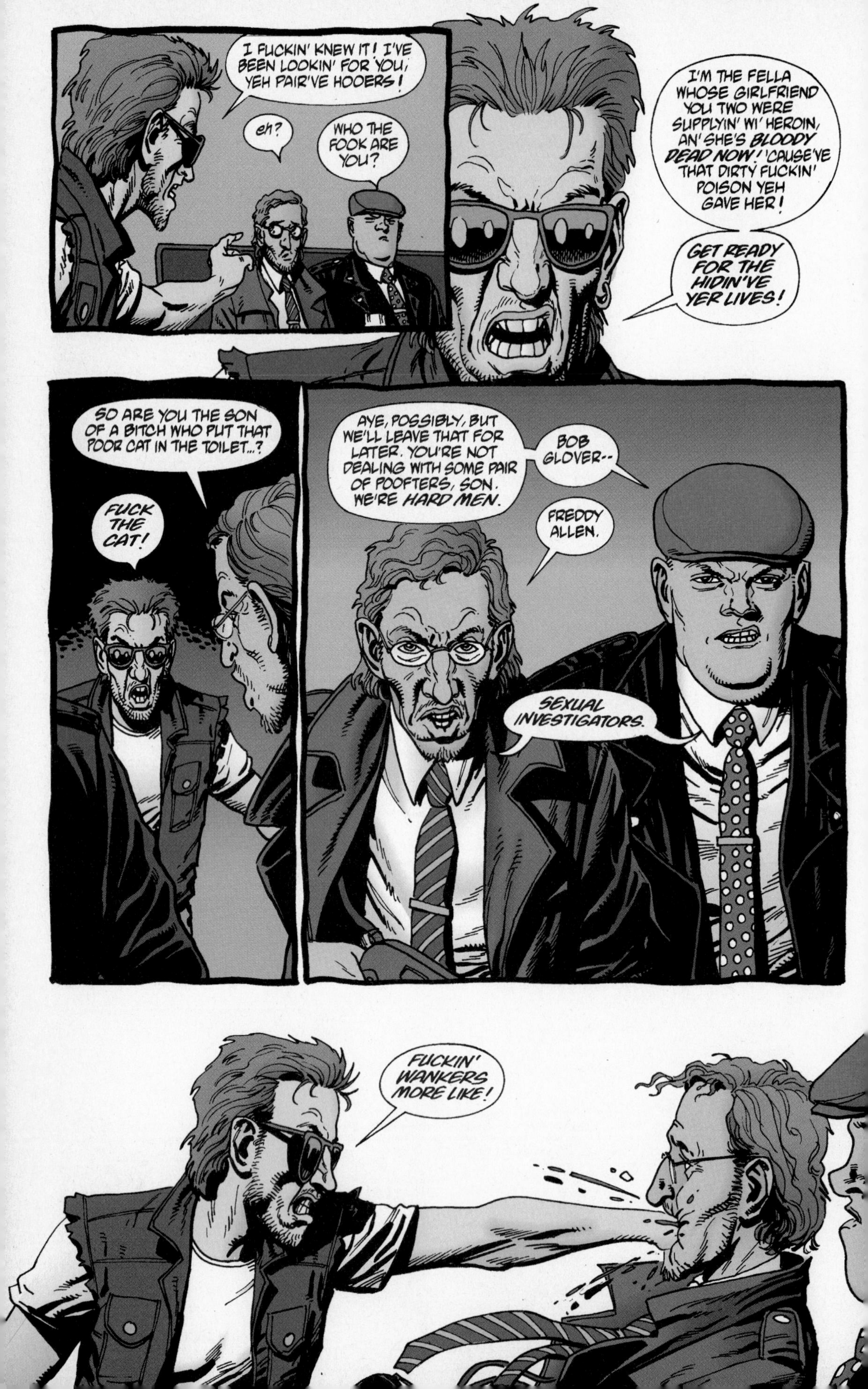
I FUCKIN' KNEW IT! I'VE BEEN LOOKIN' FOR YOU, YEH PAIR'VE HOOERS!
eh?
WHO THE FOOK ARE YOU?
I'M THE FELLA WHOSE GIRLFRIEND YOU TWO WERE SUPPLYIN' WI' HEROIN, AN' SHE'S BLOODY DEAD NOW! 'CAUSE'VE THAT DIRTY FUCKIN' POISON YEH GAVE HER!
GET READY FOR THE HIDIN'VE YER LIVES!
SO ARE YOU THE SON OF A BITCH WHO PUT THAT POOR CAT IN THE TOILET...?
FUCK THE CAT!
AYE, POSSIBLY, BUT WE'LL LEAVE THAT FOR LATER. YOU'RE NOT DEALING WITH SOME PAIR OF POOFTERS, SON. WE'RE HARD MEN.
BOB GLOVER--
FREDDY ALLEN.
SEXUAL INVESTIGATORS.
FUCKIN' WANKERS MORE LIKE!

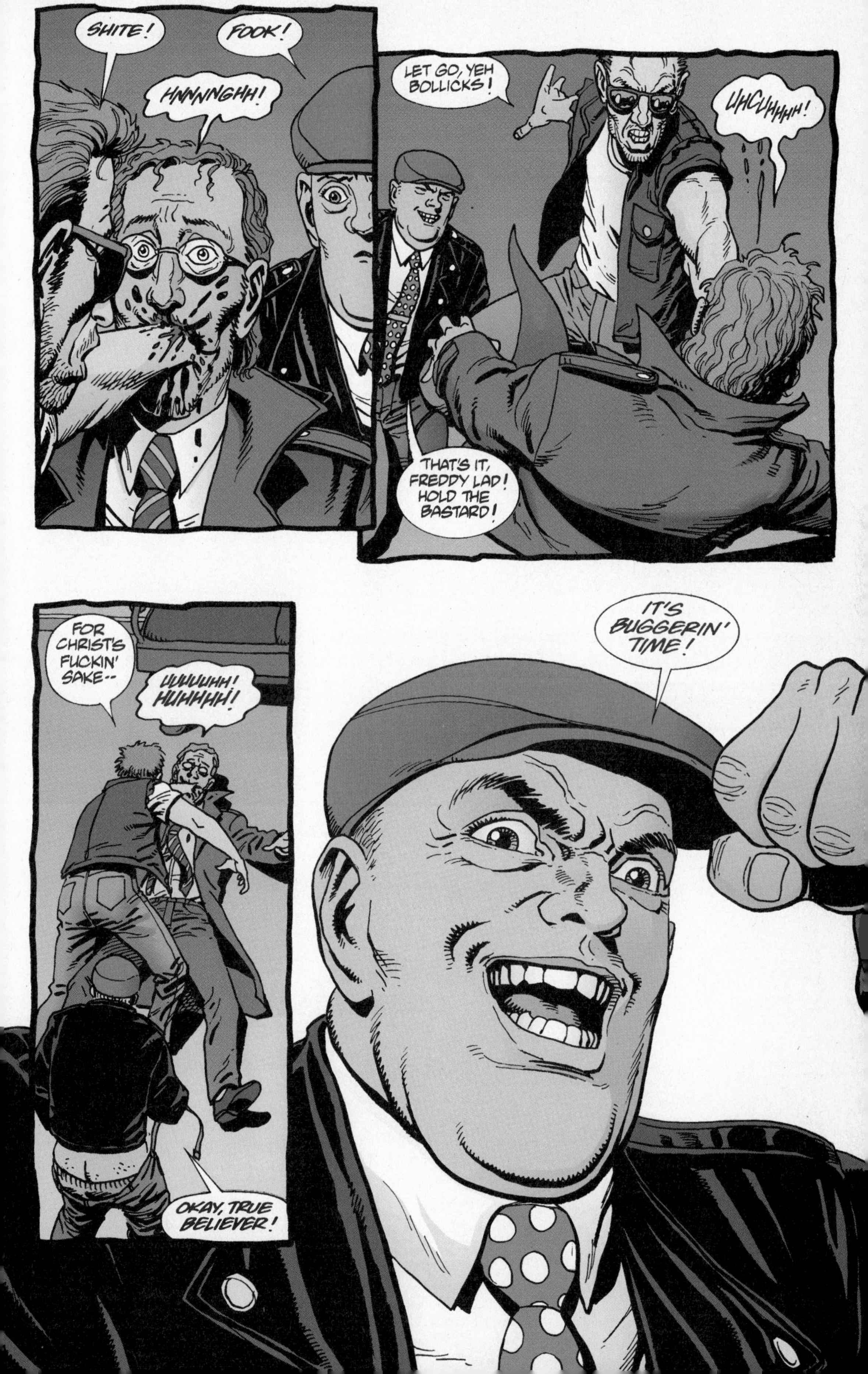
SHITE!
FOOK!
HNNNNGHH!
LET GO, YEH BOLLICKS!
UHCUHHHH!
THAT'S IT, FREDDY LAD! HOLD THE BASTARD!
FOR CHRIST'S FUCKIN' SAKE--
UUUUUHH! HUHHHH!
OKAY, TRUE BELIEVER!
IT'S BUGGERIN' TIME!

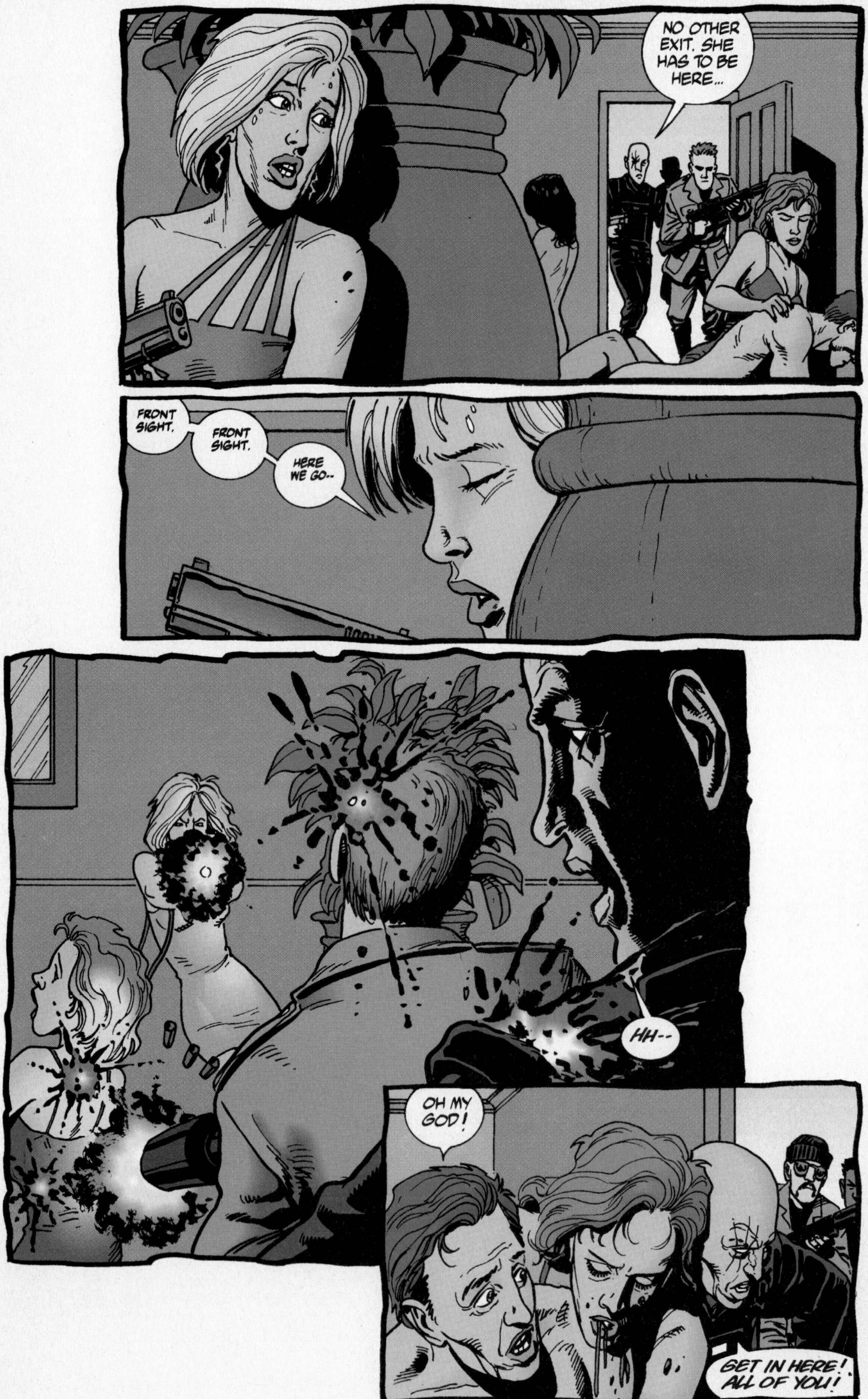
NO OTHER EXIT. SHE HAS TO BE HERE...
FRONT SIGHT.
FRONT SIGHT.
HERE WE GO..
HH--
OH MY GOD!
GET IN HERE! ALL OF YOU!

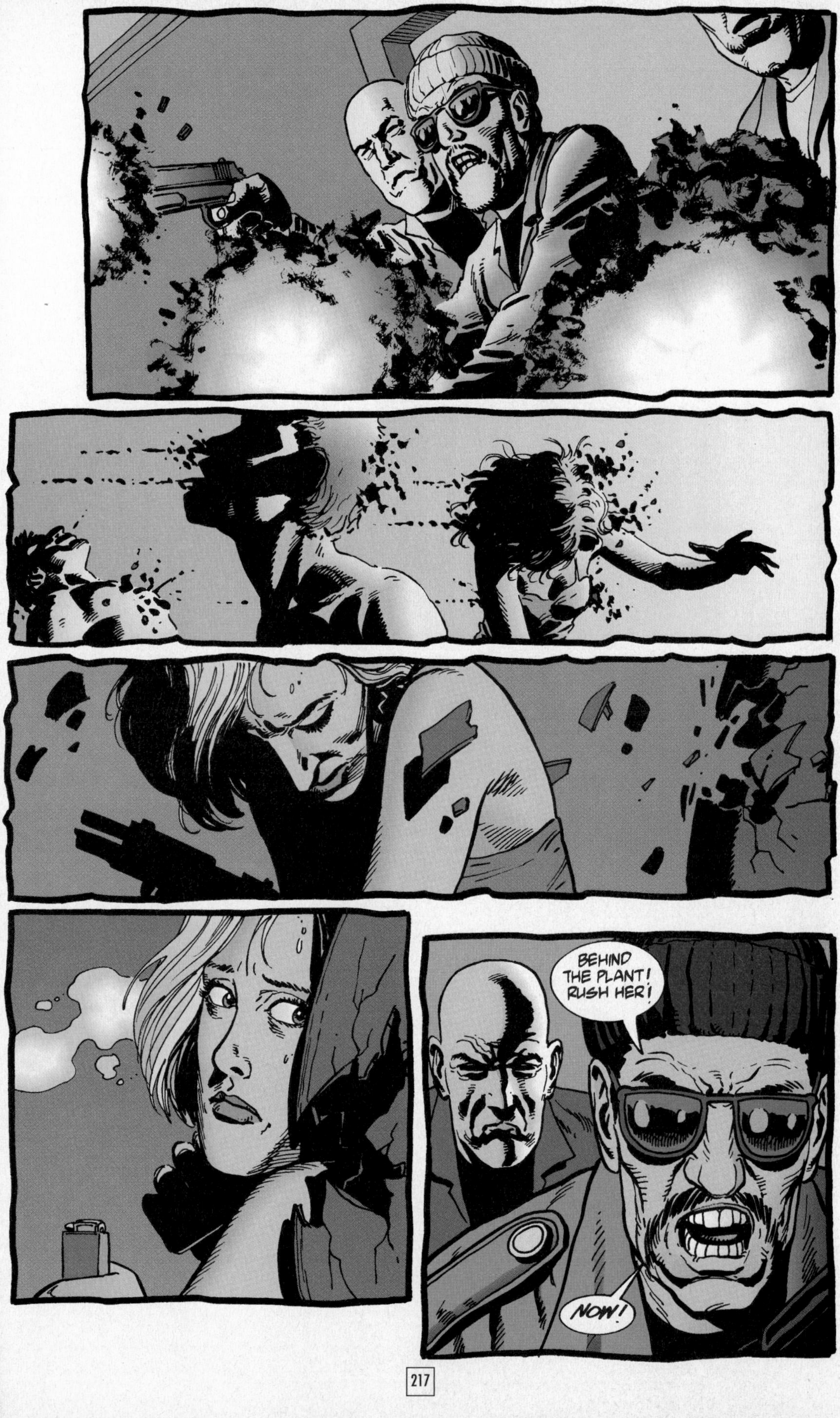
BEHIND THE PLANT! RUSH HER!
NOW!

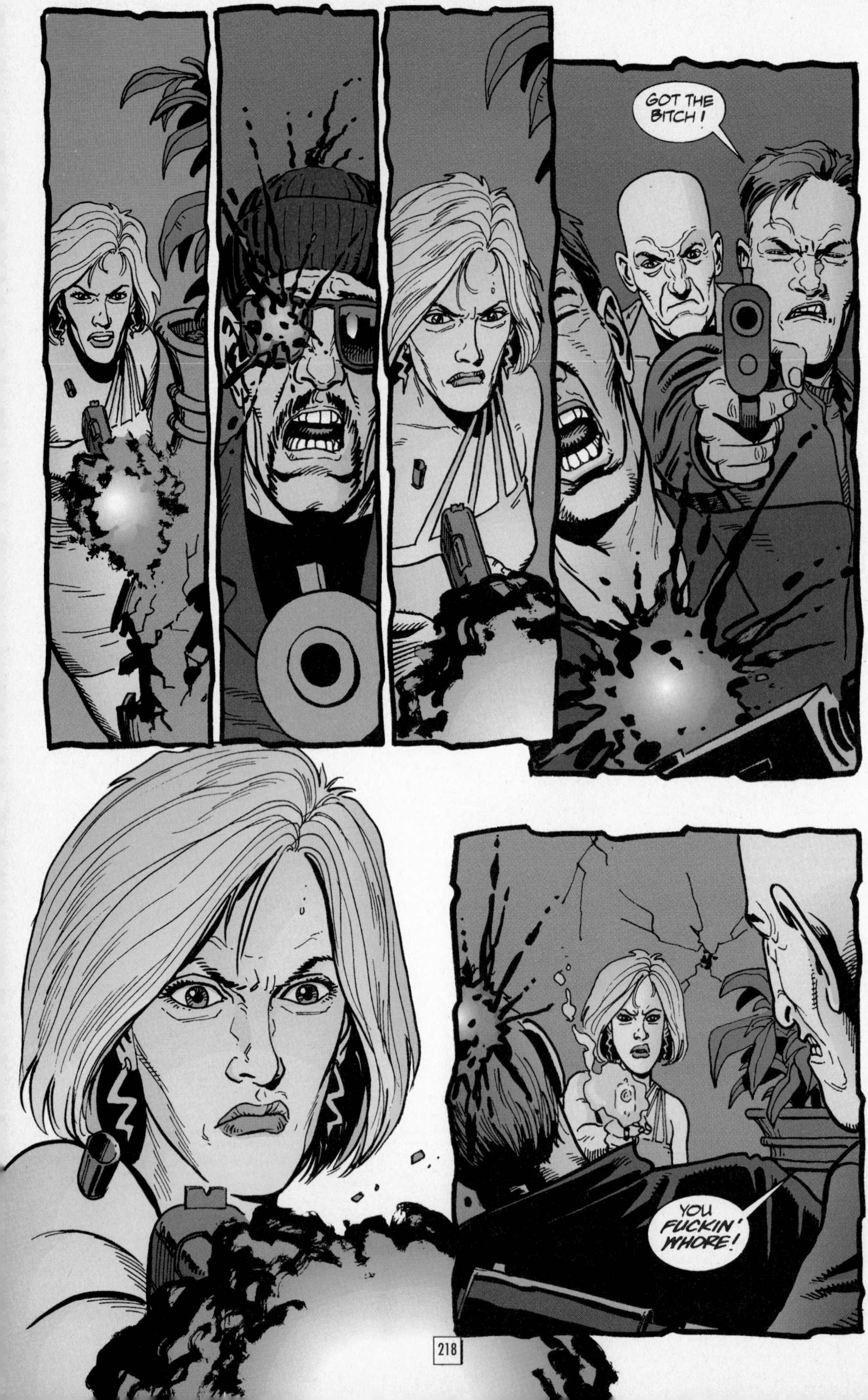
GOT THE BITCH!
YOU FUCKIN' WHORE!

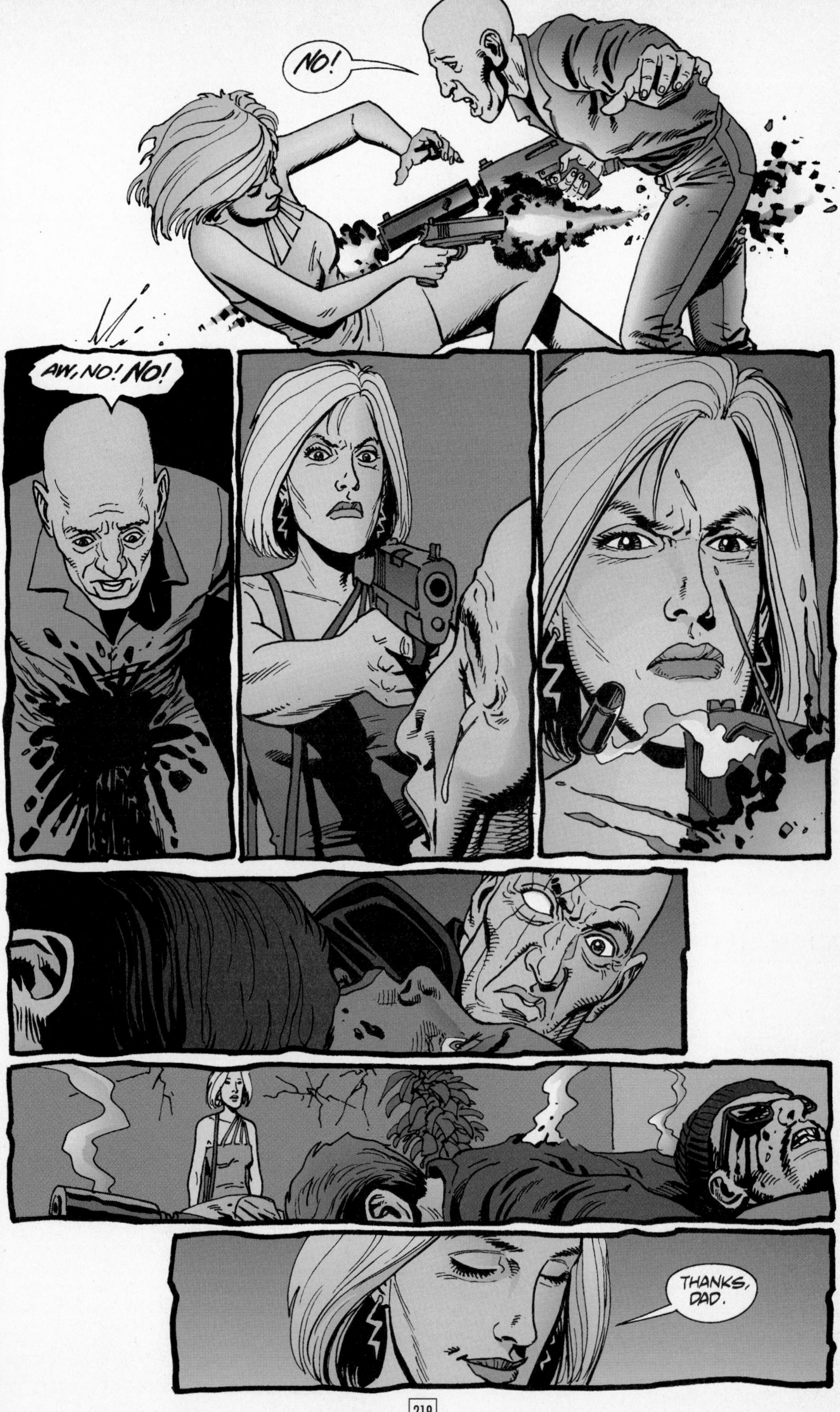
NO!
AW, NO! NO!
THANKS, DAD.

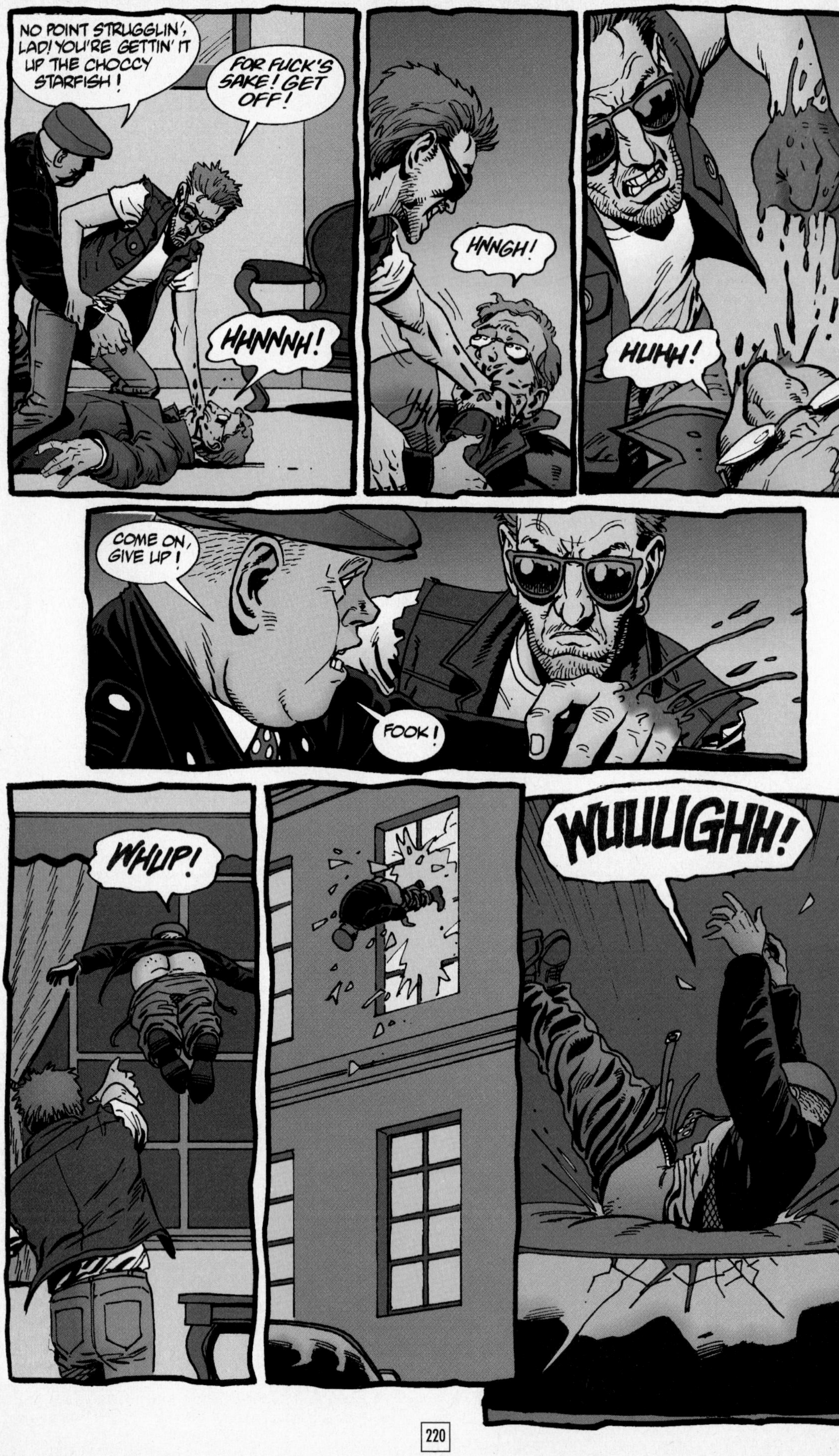

NO POINT STRUGGLIN', LAD! YOU'RE GETTIN' IT UP THE CHOCCY STARFISH!
FOR FUCK'S SAKE! GET OFF!
HHNNNH!
HNNGH!
HUHH!
COME ON, GIVE UP!
FOOK!
WHUP!
WUUUGHH!

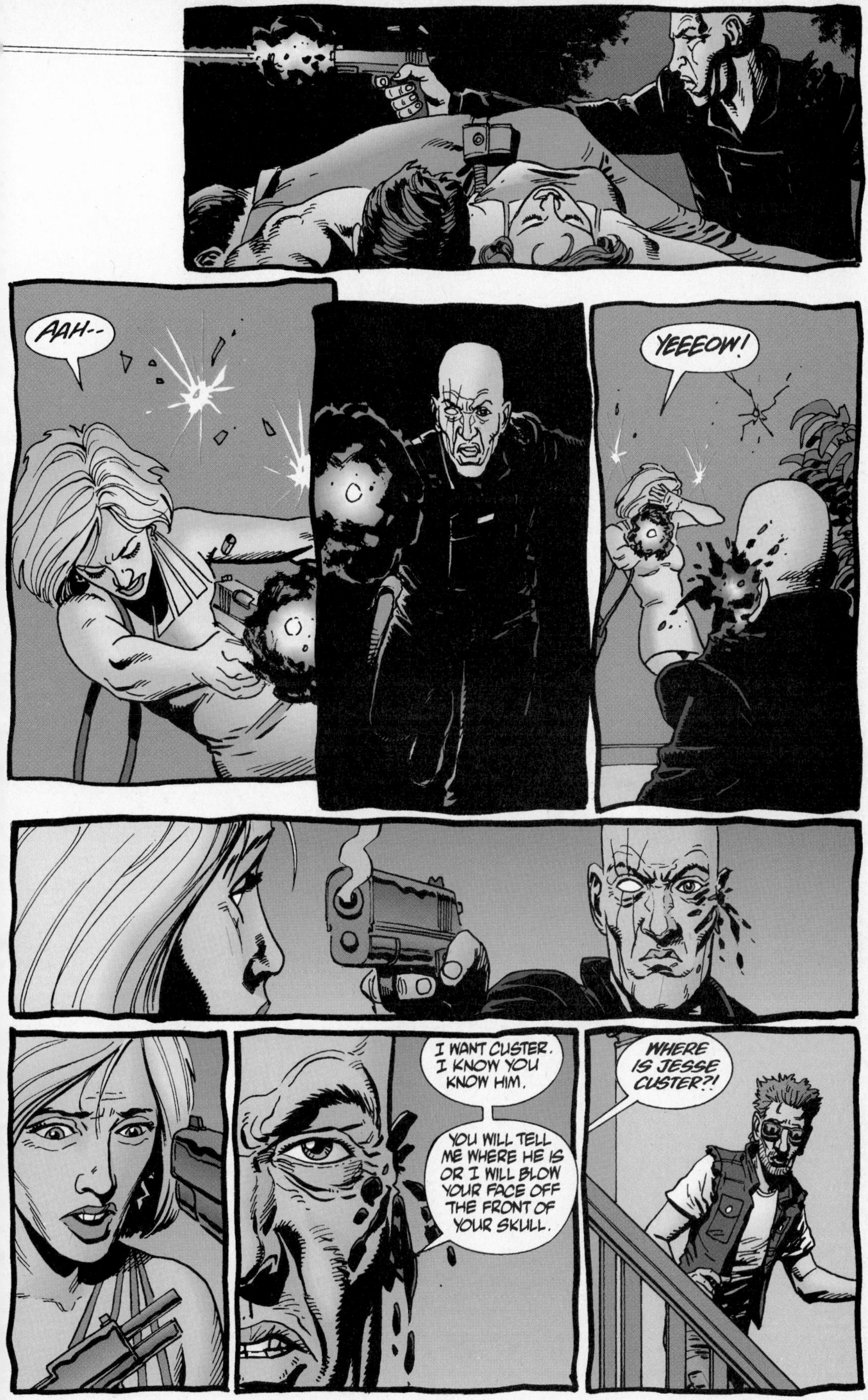
AAH--
YEEEOW!
I WANT CUSTER. I KNOW YOU KNOW HIM.
YOU WILL TELL ME WHERE HE IS OR I WILL BLOW YOUR FACE OFF THE FRONT OF YOUR SKULL.
WHERE IS JESSE CUSTER?!

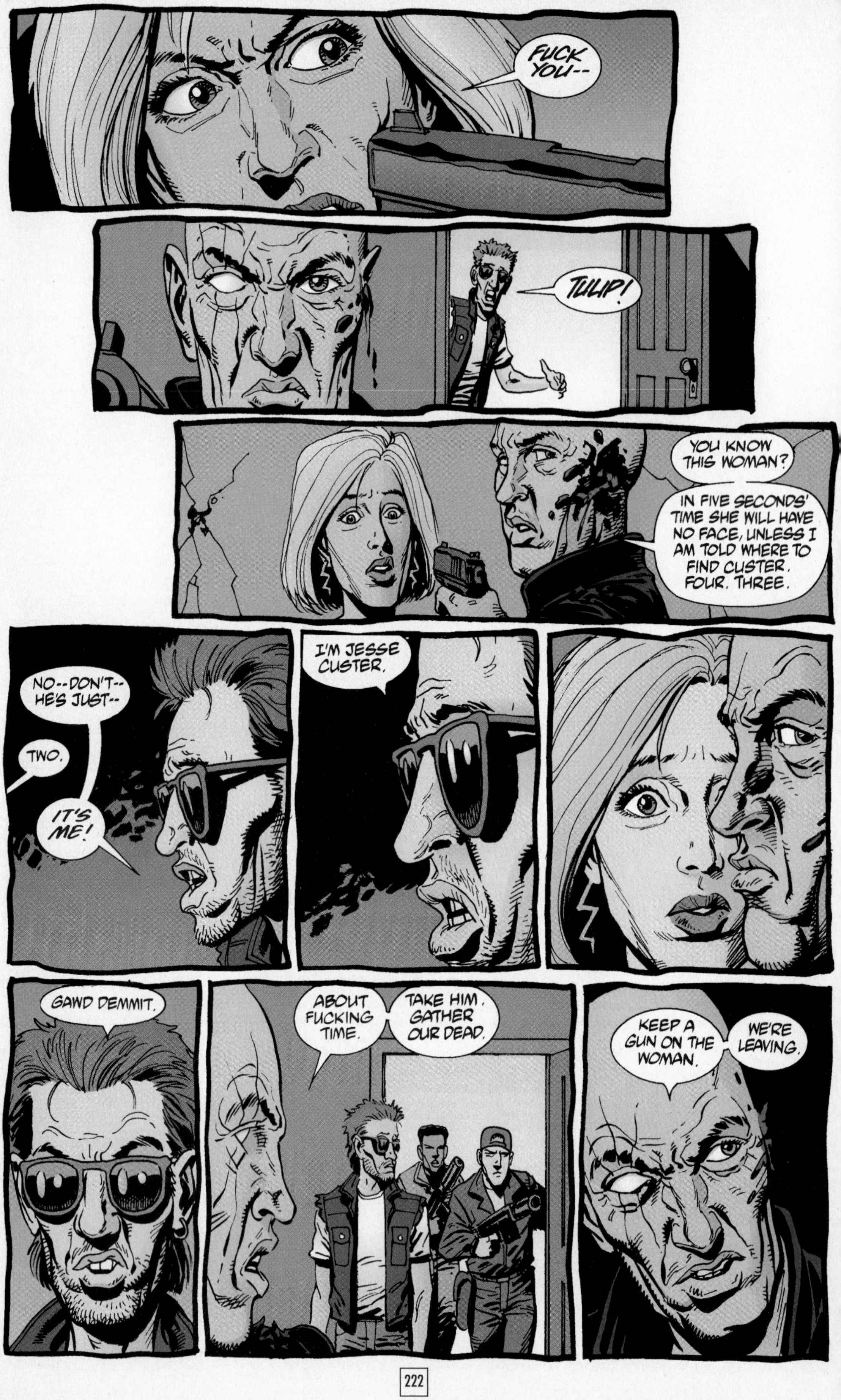
FUCK YOU--
TULIP!
YOU KNOW THIS WOMAN?
IN FIVE SECONDS' TIME SHE WILL HAVE NO FACE, UNLESS I AM TOLD WHERE TO FIND CUSTER. FOUR. THREE.
NO--DON'T--HE'S JUST--
TWO.
IT'S ME!
I'M JESSE CUSTER.
GAWD DEMMIT.
ABOUT FUCKING TIME.
TAKE HIM. GATHER OUR DEAD.
KEEP A GUN ON THE WOMAN.
WE'RE LEAVING.

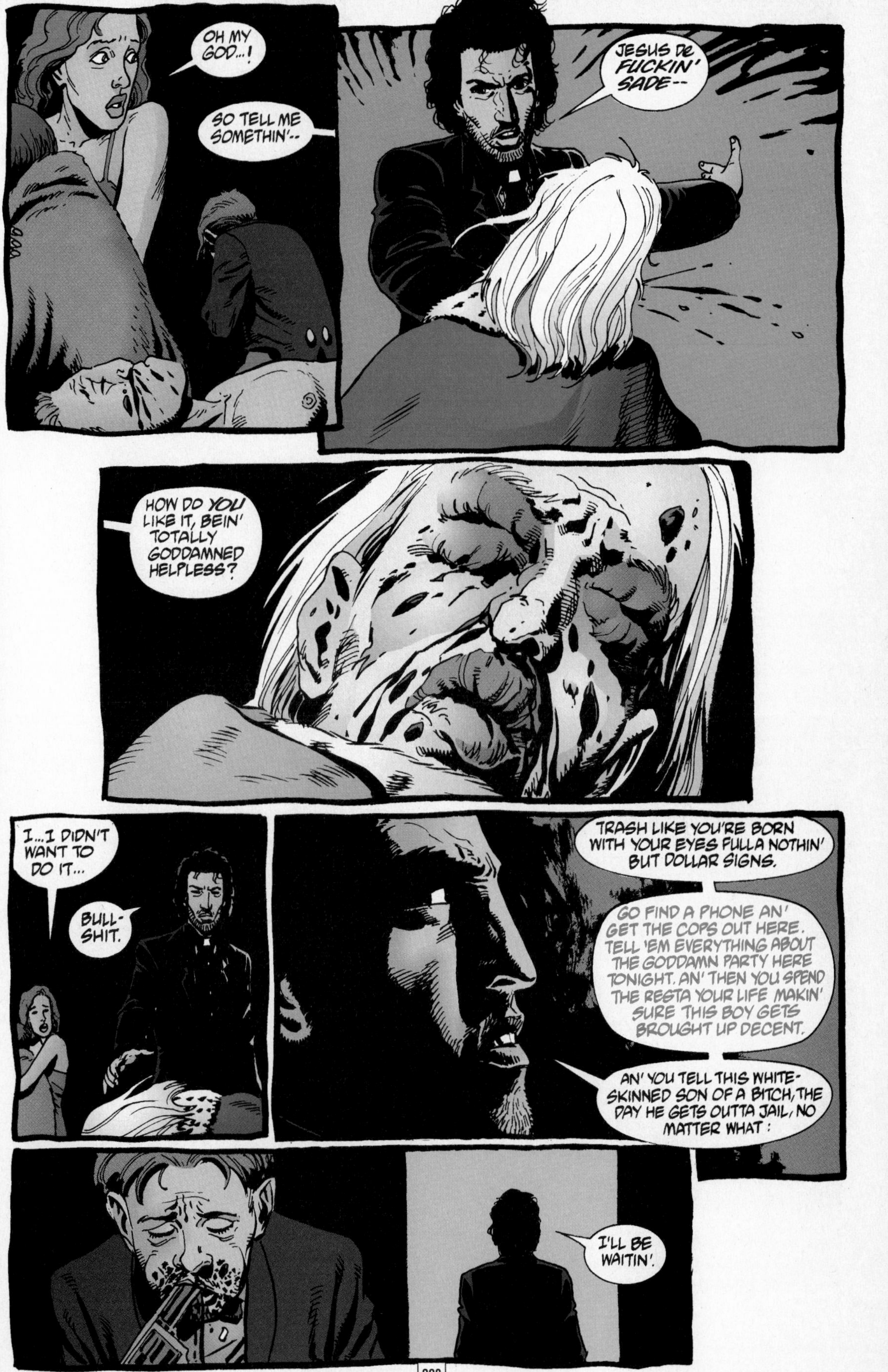
OH MY GOD...!
SO TELL ME SOMETHIN'--
JESUS DE FUCKIN' SADE--
HOW DO YOU LIKE IT, BEIN' TOTALLY GODDAMNED HELPLESS?
I...I DIDN'T WANT TO DO IT...
BULL-SHIT.
TRASH LIKE YOU'RE BORN WITH YOUR EYES FULLA NOTHIN' BUT DOLLAR SIGNS.
GO FIND A PHONE AN' GET THE COPS OUT HERE. TELL 'EM EVERYTHING ABOUT THE GODDAMN PARTY HERE TONIGHT. AN' THEN YOU SPEND THE RESTA YOUR LIFE MAKIN' SURE THIS BOY GETS BROUGHT UP DECENT.
AN' YOU TELL THIS WHITE-SKINNED SON OF A BITCH, THE DAY HE GETS OUTTA JAIL, NO MATTER WHAT :
I'LL BE WAITIN'.

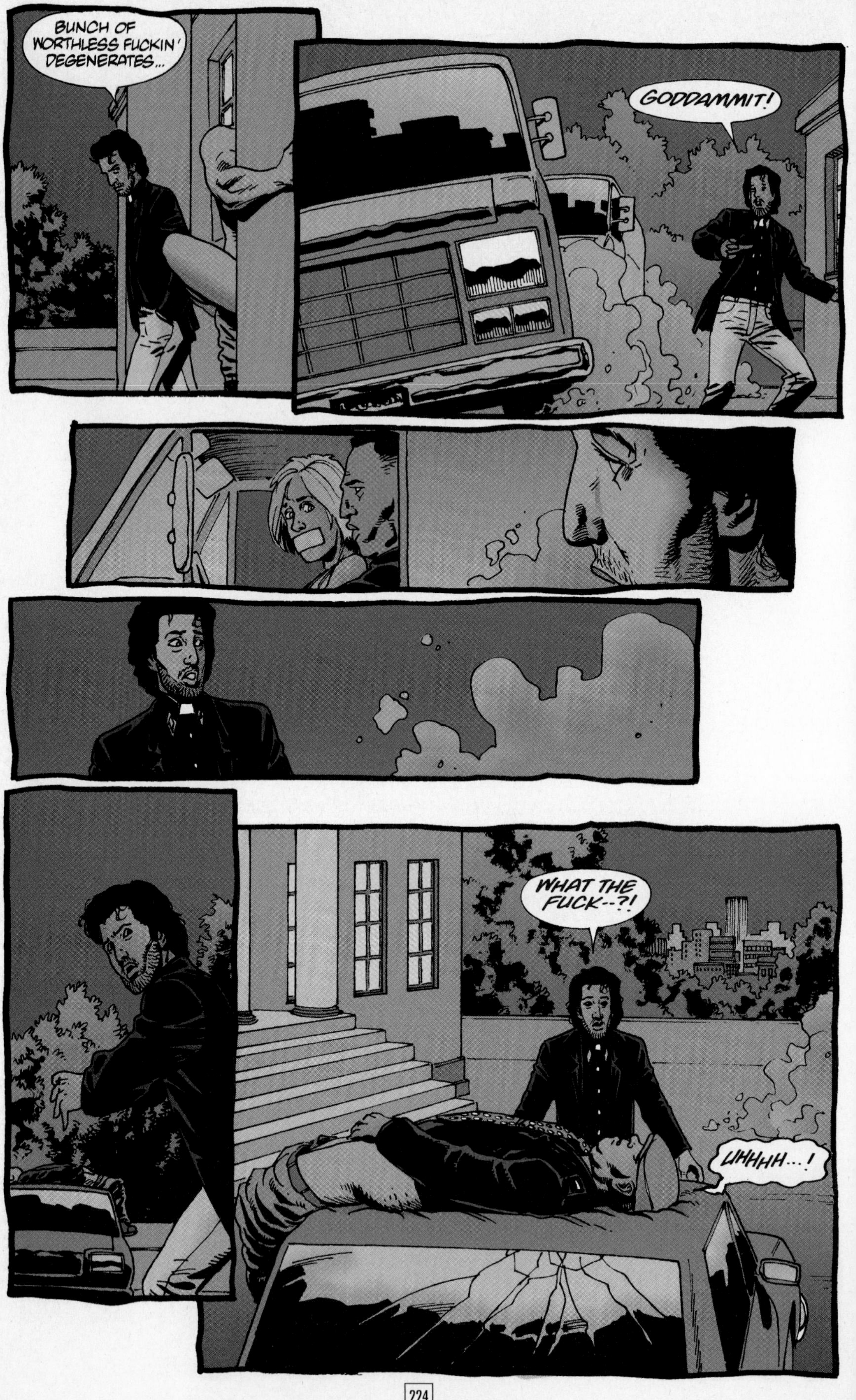
BUNCH OF WORTHLESS FUCKIN' DEGENERATES...
GODDAMMIT!
WHAT THE FUCK--?!
UHHHH...!

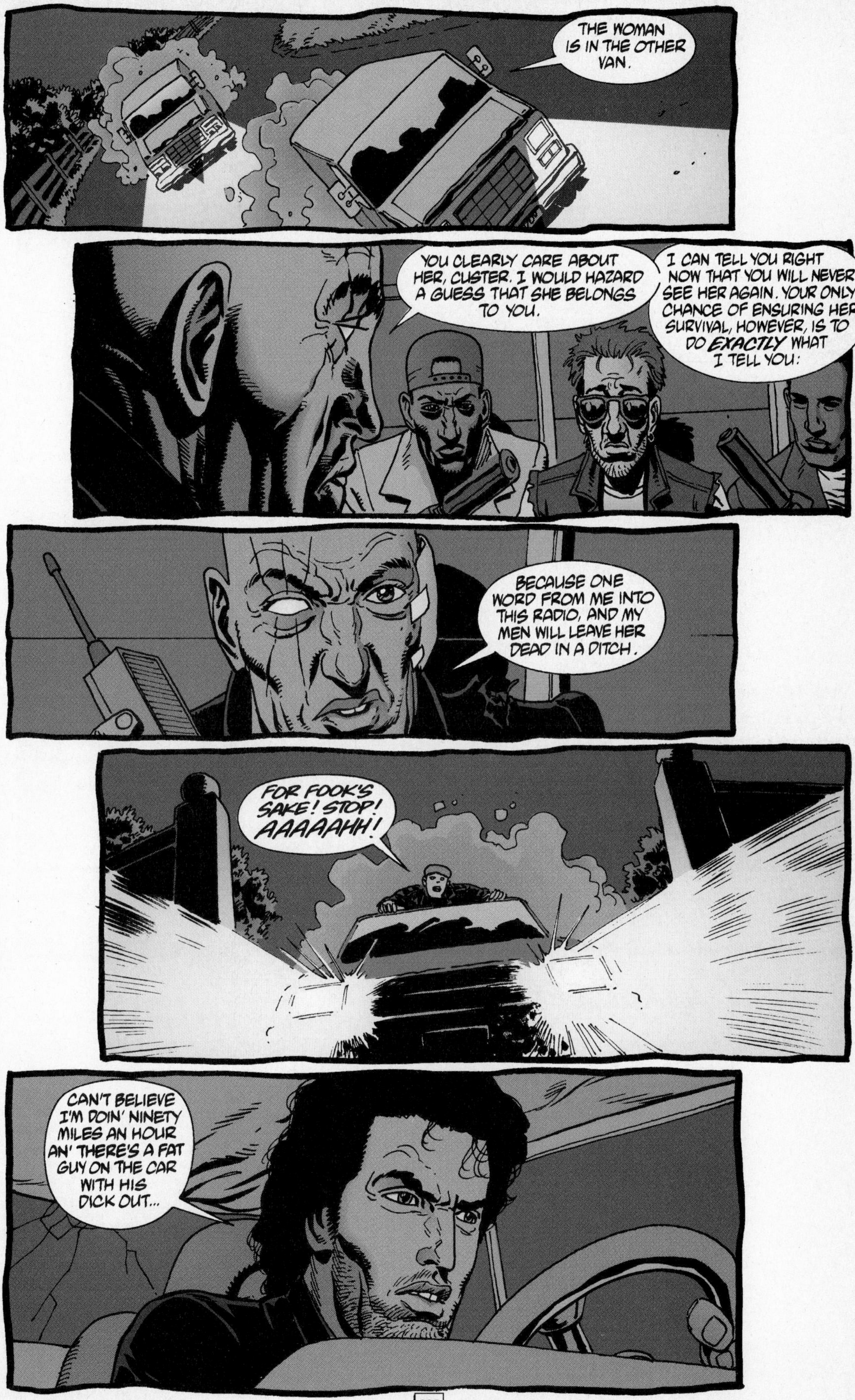
THE WOMAN IS IN THE OTHER VAN.
YOU CLEARLY CARE ABOUT HER, CUSTER. I WOULD HAZARD A GUESS THAT SHE BELONGS TO YOU.
I CAN TELL YOU RIGHT NOW THAT YOU WILL NEVER SEE HER AGAIN. YOUR ONLY CHANCE OF ENSURING HER SURVIVAL, HOWEVER, IS TO DO EXACTLY WHAT I TELL YOU:
BECAUSE ONE WORD FROM ME INTO THIS RADIO, AND MY MEN WILL LEAVE HER DEAD IN A DITCH.
FOR FOOK'S SAKE! STOP! AAAAAHH!
CAN'T BELIEVE I'M DOIN' NINETY MILES AN HOUR AN' THERE'S A FAT GUY ON THE CAR WITH HIS DICK OUT...

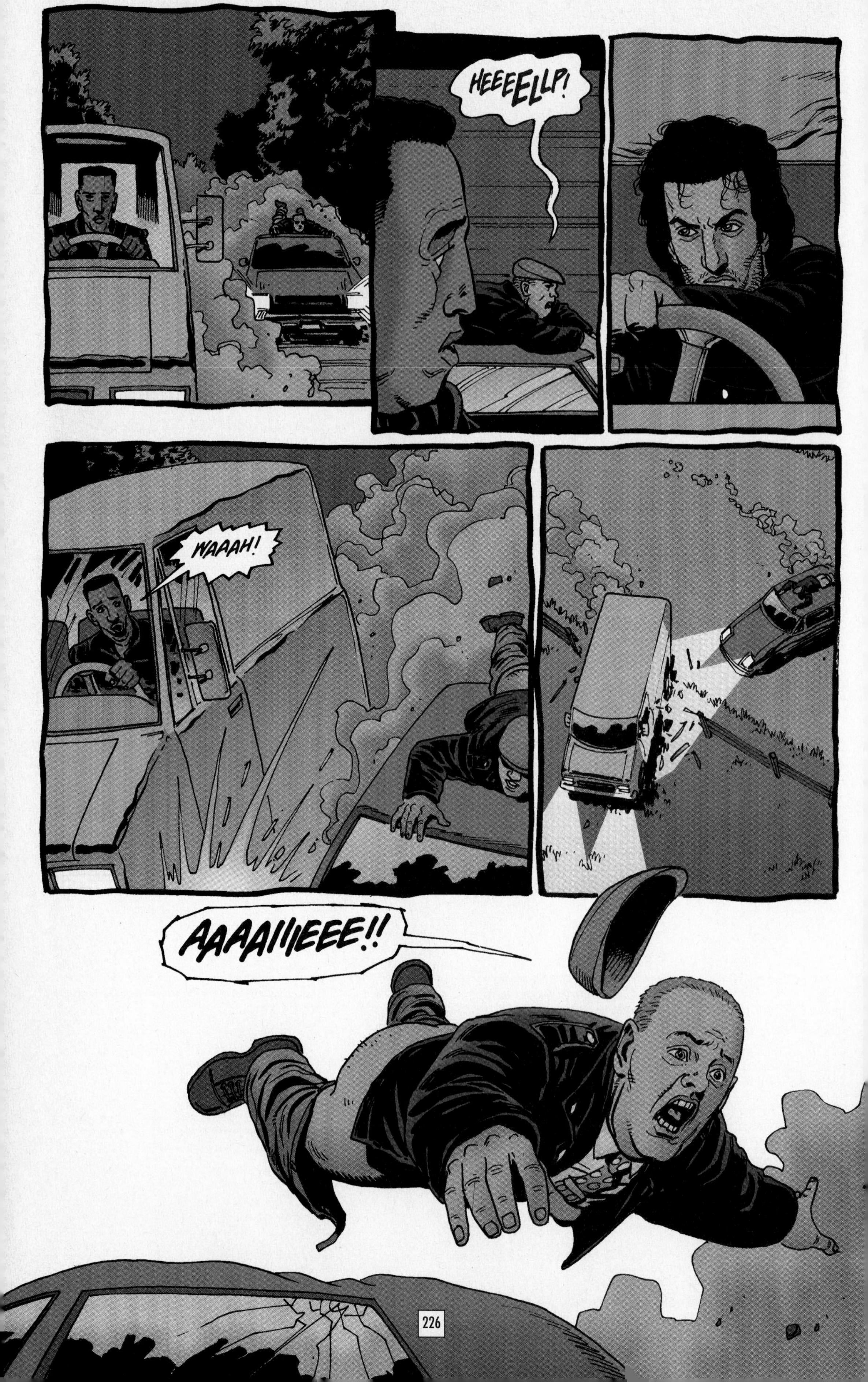
HEEEELLLP!
WAAAH!
AAAAIIIEEE!!

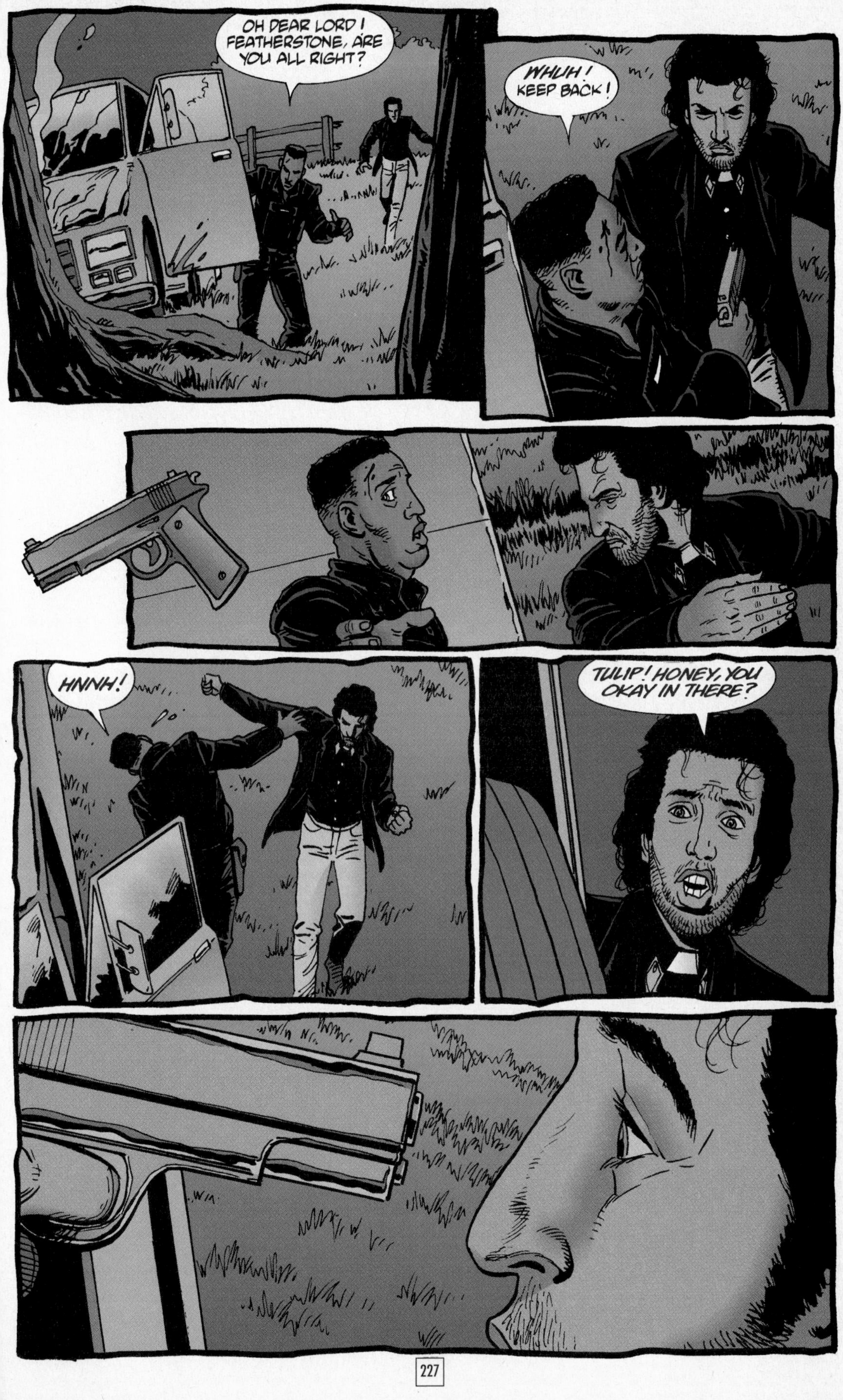
OH DEAR LORD! FEATHERSTONE, ARE YOU ALL RIGHT?
WHUH! KEEP BACK!
HNNH!
TULIP! HONEY, YOU OKAY IN THERE?

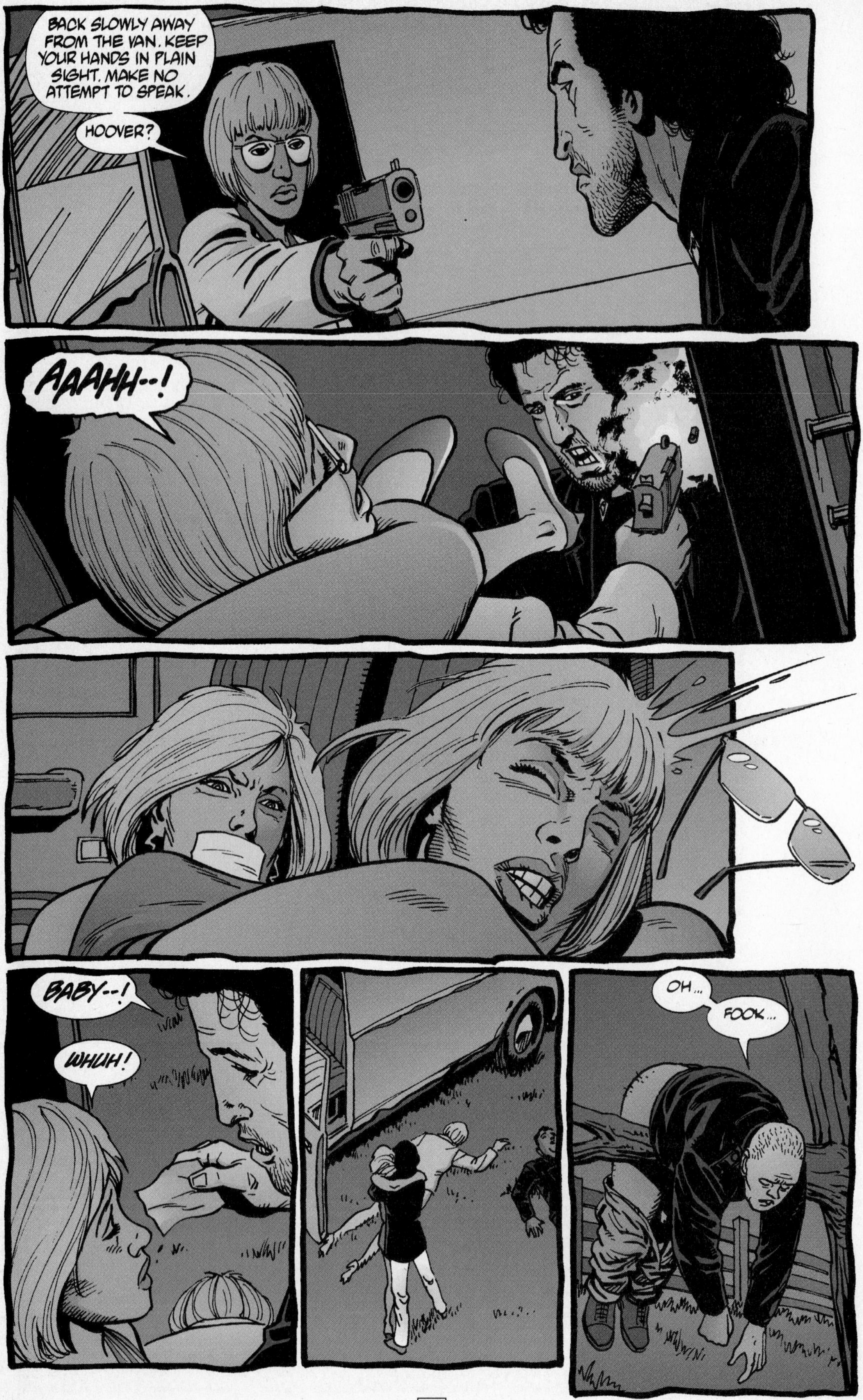
BACK SLOWLY AWAY FROM THE VAN. KEEP YOUR HANDS IN PLAIN SIGHT. MAKE NO ATTEMPT TO SPEAK.
HOOVER?
AAAHH--!
BABY--!
WHUH!
OH...
FOOK...

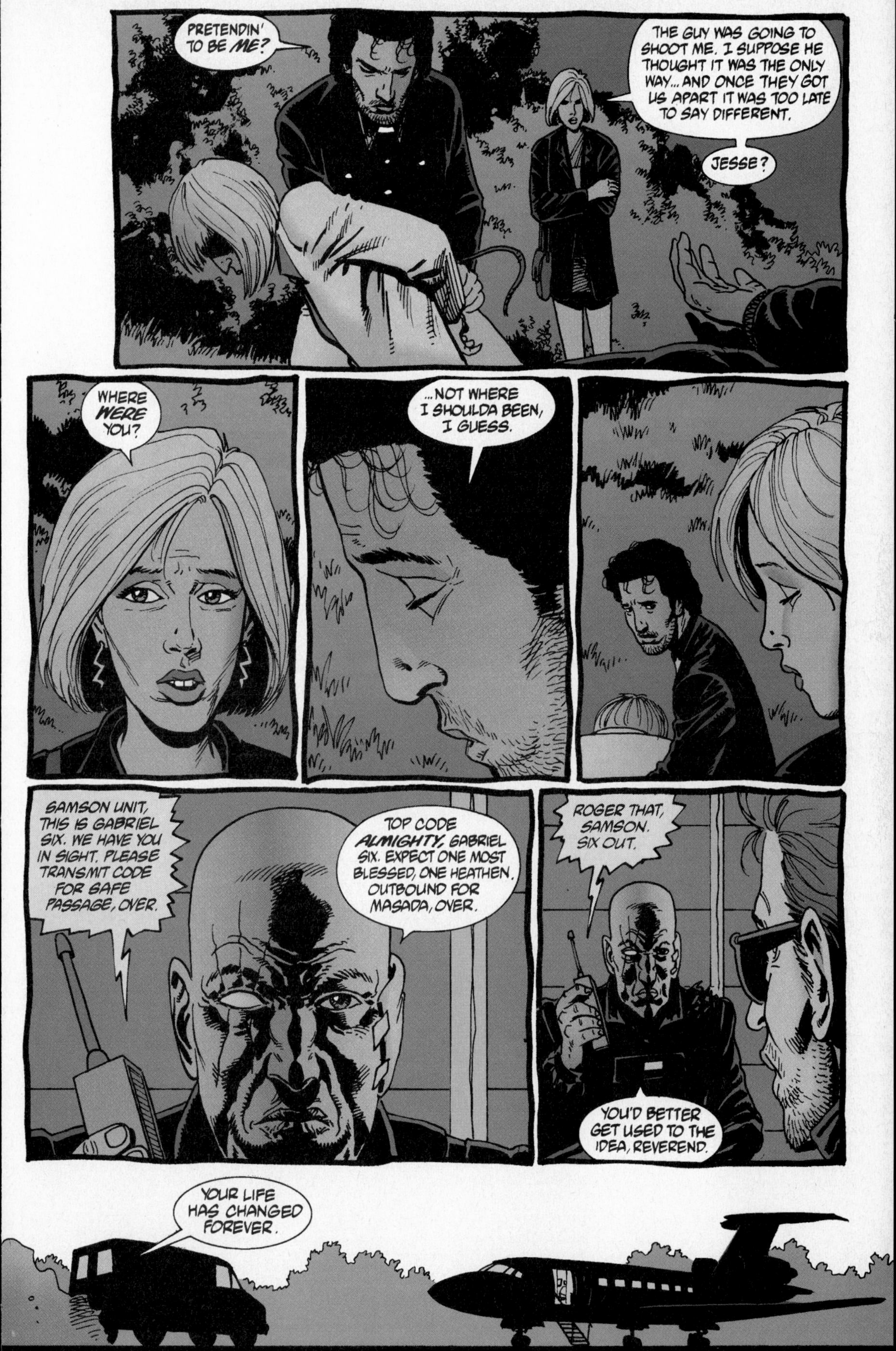
PRETENDIN' TO BE *ME*?
THE GUY WAS GOING TO SHOOT ME. I SUPPOSE HE THOUGHT IT WAS THE ONLY WAY... AND ONCE THEY GOT US APART IT WAS TOO LATE TO SAY DIFFERENT.
JESSE?
WHERE *WERE* YOU?
...NOT WHERE I SHOULDA BEEN, I GUESS.
SAMSON UNIT, THIS IS GABRIEL SIX. WE HAVE YOU IN SIGHT. PLEASE TRANSMIT CODE FOR SAFE PASSAGE, OVER.
TOP CODE *ALMIGHTY,* GABRIEL SIX. EXPECT ONE MOST BLESSED, ONE HEATHEN, OUTBOUND FOR MASADA, OVER.
ROGER THAT, SAMSON. SIX OUT.
YOU'D BETTER GET USED TO THE IDEA, REVEREND.
YOUR LIFE HAS CHANGED FOREVER.

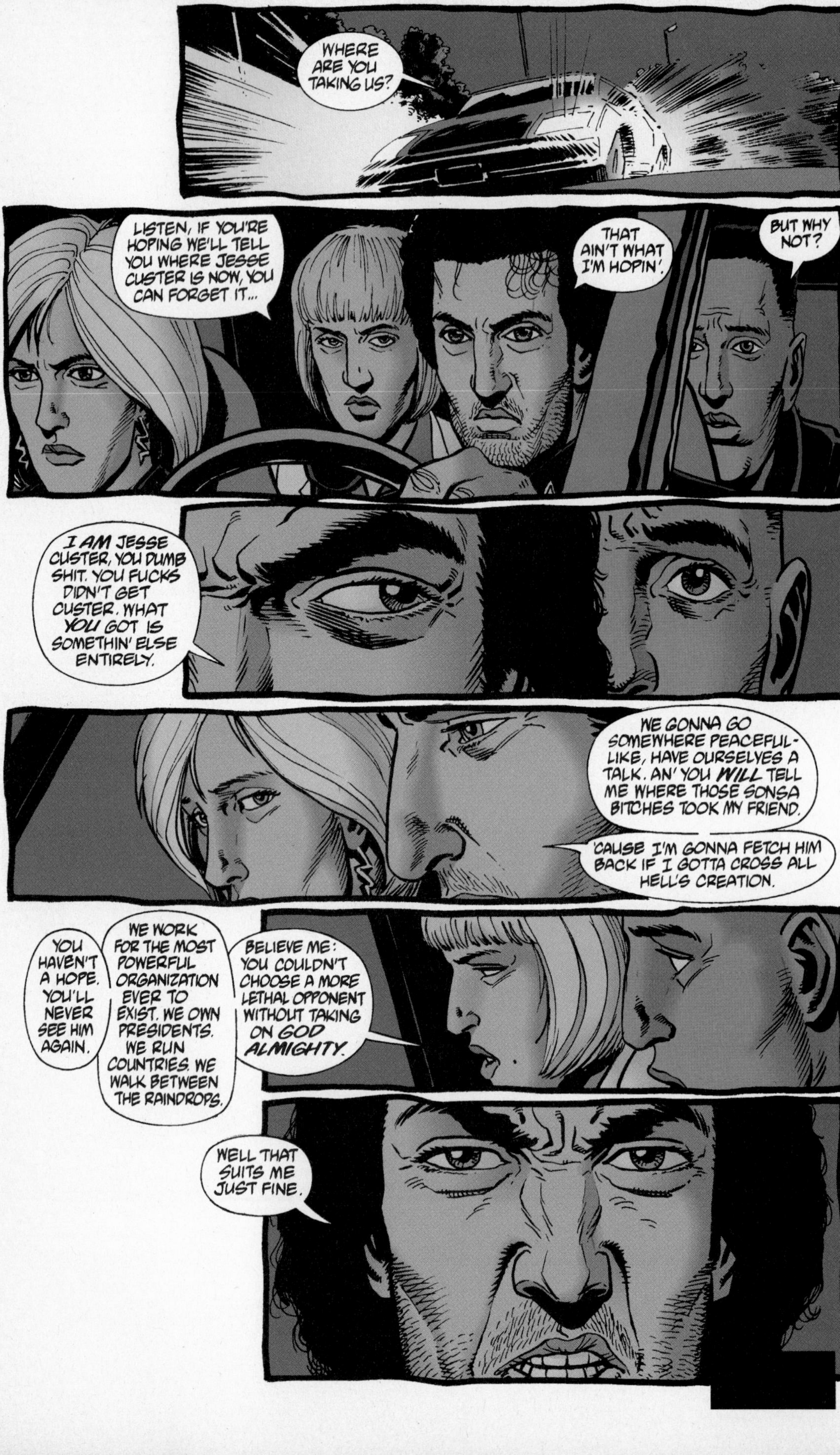
WHERE ARE YOU TAKING US?
LISTEN, IF YOU'RE HOPING WE'LL TELL YOU WHERE JESSE CUSTER IS NOW, YOU CAN FORGET IT...
THAT AIN'T WHAT I'M HOPIN'.
BUT WHY NOT?
I AM JESSE CUSTER, YOU DUMB SHIT. YOU FUCKS DIDN'T GET CUSTER. WHAT YOU GOT IS SOMETHIN' ELSE ENTIRELY.
WE GONNA GO SOMEWHERE PEACEFUL-LIKE, HAVE OURSELVES A TALK. AN' YOU WILL TELL ME WHERE THOSE SONSA BITCHES TOOK MY FRIEND.
'CAUSE I'M GONNA FETCH HIM BACK IF I GOTTA CROSS ALL HELL'S CREATION.
YOU HAVEN'T A HOPE. YOU'LL NEVER SEE HIM AGAIN.
WE WORK FOR THE MOST POWERFUL ORGANIZATION EVER TO EXIST. WE OWN PRESIDENTS. WE RUN COUNTRIES. WE WALK BETWEEN THE RAINDROPS.
BELIEVE ME: YOU COULDN'T CHOOSE A MORE LETHAL OPPONENT WITHOUT TAKING ON GOD ALMIGHTY.
WELL THAT SUITS ME JUST FINE.

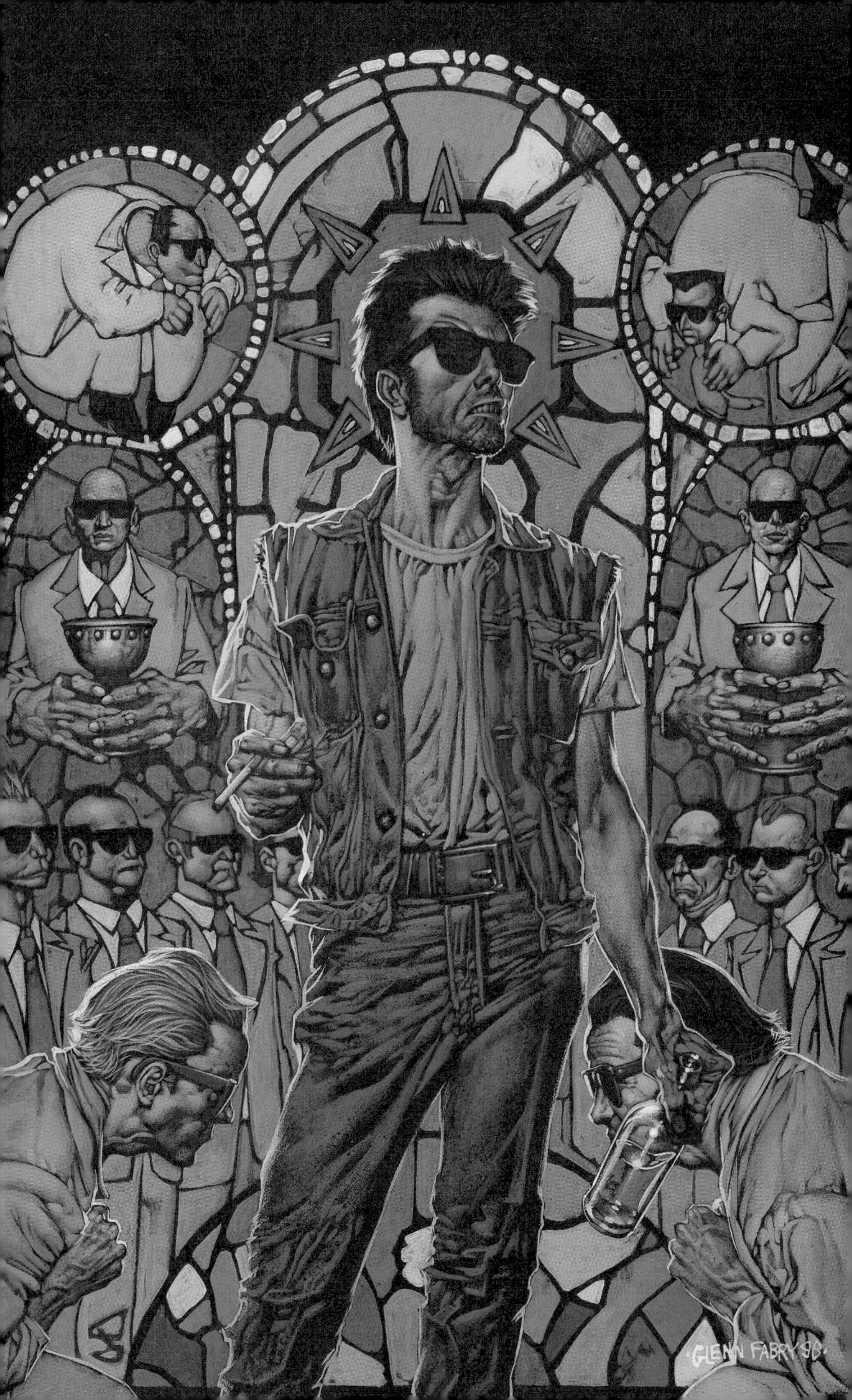
GLENN FABRY 96

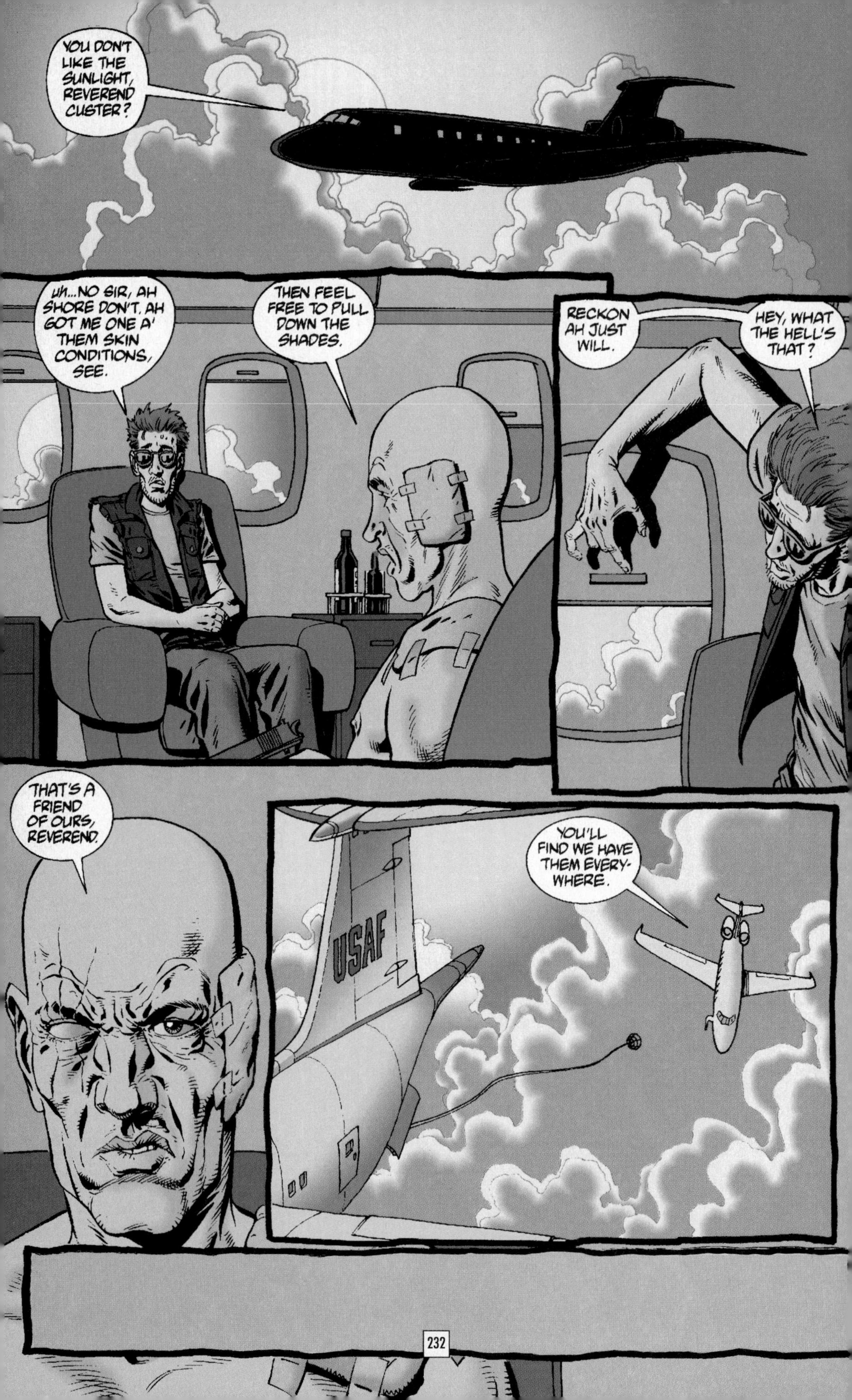
YOU DON'T LIKE THE SUNLIGHT, REVEREND CUSTER?
uh...NO SIR, AH SHORE DON'T. AH GOT ME ONE A' THEM SKIN CONDITIONS, SEE.
THEN FEEL FREE TO PULL DOWN THE SHADES.
RECKON AH JUST WILL.
HEY, WHAT THE HELL'S THAT?
THAT'S A FRIEND OF OURS, REVEREND.
YOU'LL FIND WE HAVE THEM EVERY-WHERE.
USAF

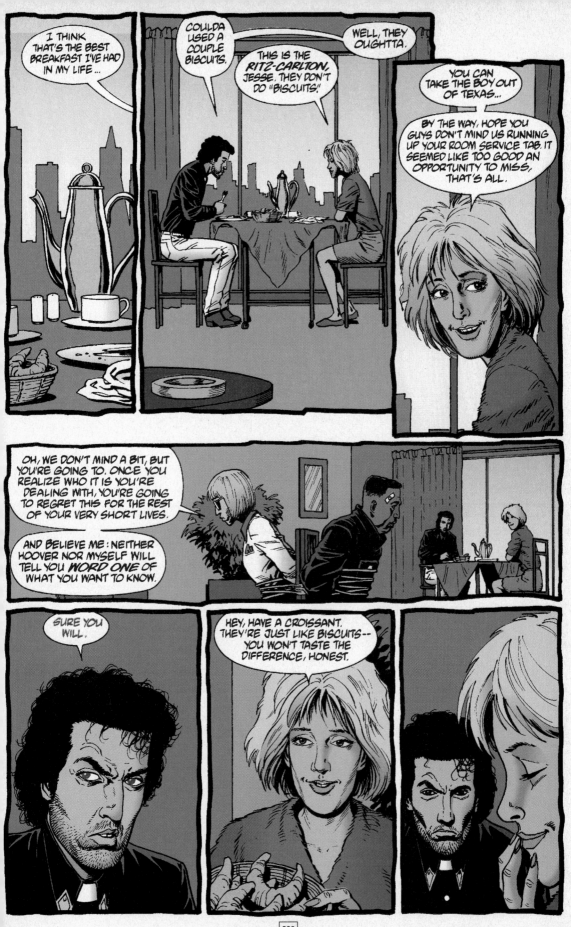

I THINK THAT'S THE BEST BREAKFAST I'VE HAD IN MY LIFE...

COULDA USED A COUPLE BISCUITS.

THIS IS THE *RITZ-CARLTON,* JESSE. THEY DON'T DO "BISCUITS."

WELL, THEY OUGHTTA.

YOU CAN TAKE THE BOY OUT OF TEXAS...

BY THE WAY, HOPE YOU GUYS DON'T MIND US RUNNING UP YOUR ROOM SERVICE TAB. IT SEEMED LIKE TOO GOOD AN OPPORTUNITY TO MISS, THAT'S ALL.

OH, WE DON'T MIND A BIT, BUT YOU'RE GOING TO. ONCE YOU REALIZE WHO IT IS YOU'RE DEALING WITH, YOU'RE GOING TO REGRET THIS FOR THE REST OF YOUR VERY SHORT LIVES.

AND BELIEVE ME: NEITHER HOOVER NOR MYSELF WILL TELL YOU *WORD ONE* OF WHAT YOU WANT TO KNOW.

SURE YOU WILL.

HEY, HAVE A CROISSANT. THEY'RE JUST LIKE BISCUITS-- YOU WON'T TASTE THE DIFFERENCE, HONEST.

MIRACLE MAN

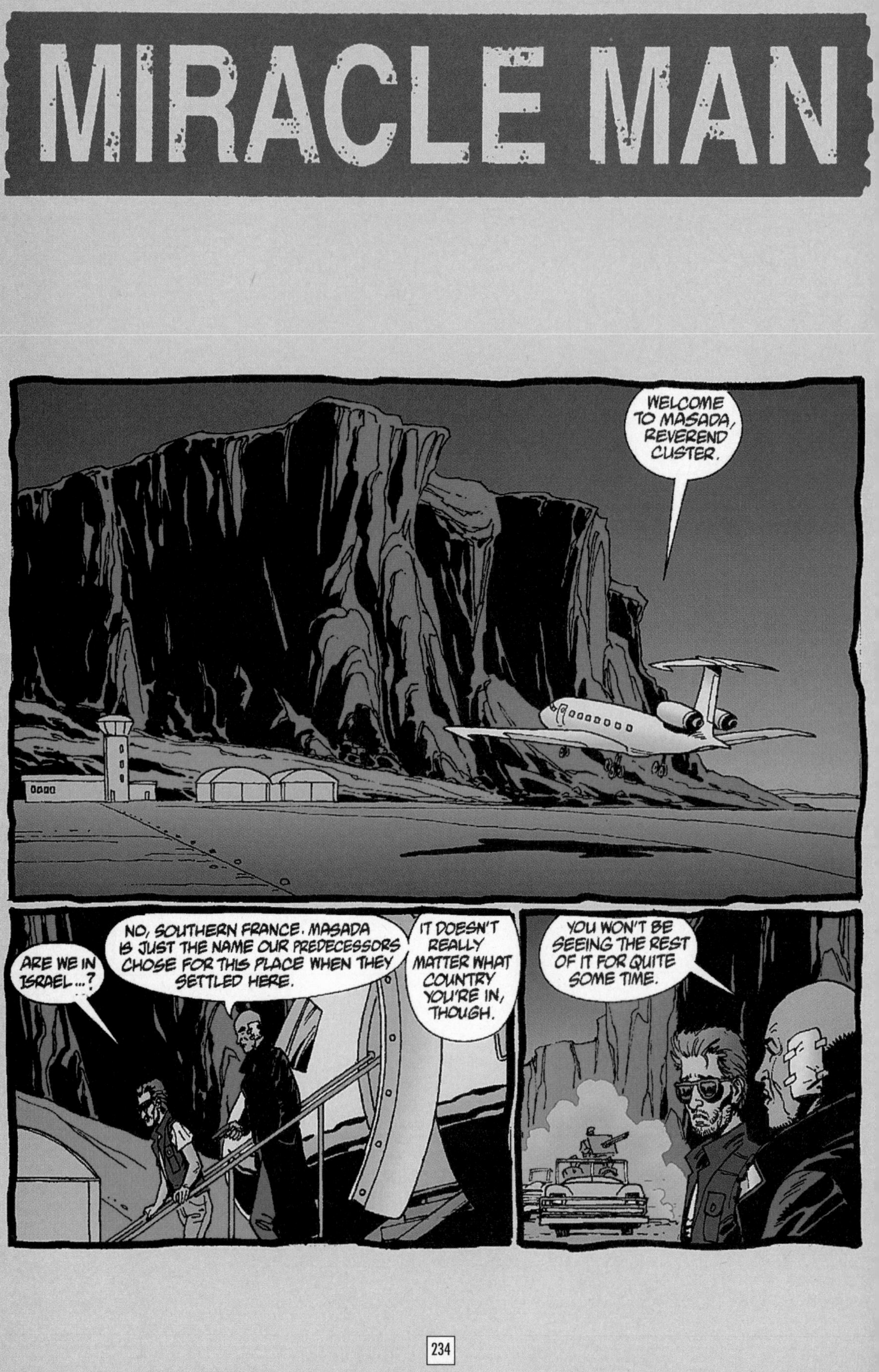
WELCOME TO MASADA, REVEREND CUSTER.
ARE WE IN ISRAEL...?
NO, SOUTHERN FRANCE. MASADA IS JUST THE NAME OUR PREDECESSORS CHOSE FOR THIS PLACE WHEN THEY SETTLED HERE.
IT DOESN'T REALLY MATTER WHAT COUNTRY YOU'RE IN, THOUGH.
YOU WON'T BE SEEING THE REST OF IT FOR QUITE SOME TIME.

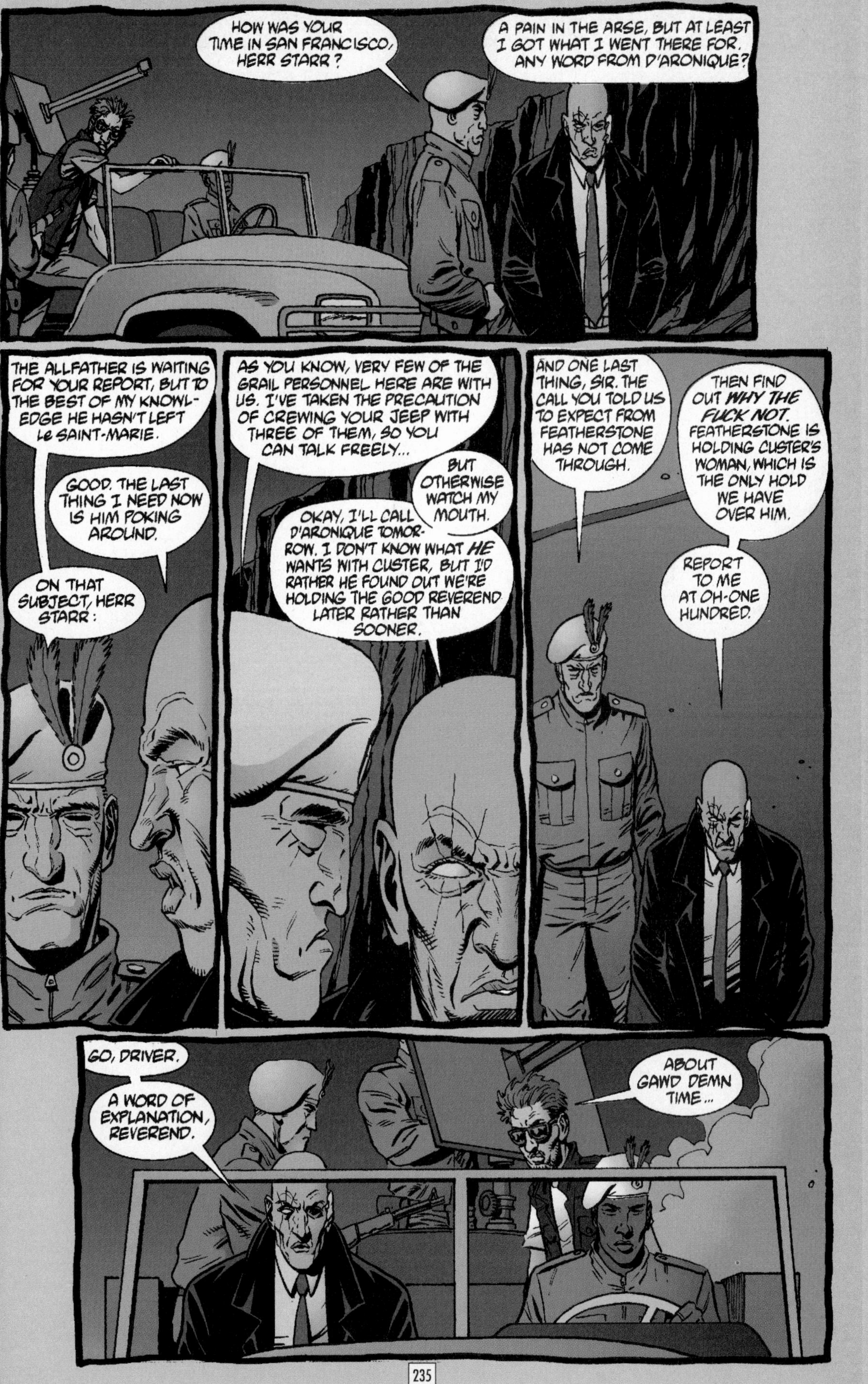
HOW WAS YOUR TIME IN SAN FRANCISCO, HERR STARR?
A PAIN IN THE ARSE, BUT AT LEAST I GOT WHAT I WENT THERE FOR. ANY WORD FROM D'ARONIQUE?
THE ALLFATHER IS WAITING FOR YOUR REPORT, BUT TO THE BEST OF MY KNOWLEDGE HE HASN'T LEFT le SAINT-MARIE.
GOOD. THE LAST THING I NEED NOW IS HIM POKING AROUND.
ON THAT SUBJECT, HERR STARR:
AS YOU KNOW, VERY FEW OF THE GRAIL PERSONNEL HERE ARE WITH US. I'VE TAKEN THE PRECAUTION OF CREWING YOUR JEEP WITH THREE OF THEM, SO YOU CAN TALK FREELY...
BUT OTHERWISE WATCH MY MOUTH.
OKAY, I'LL CALL D'ARONIQUE TOMORROW. I DON'T KNOW WHAT HE WANTS WITH CUSTER, BUT I'D RATHER HE FOUND OUT WE'RE HOLDING THE GOOD REVEREND LATER RATHER THAN SOONER.
AND ONE LAST THING, SIR. THE CALL YOU TOLD US TO EXPECT FROM FEATHERSTONE HAS NOT COME THROUGH.
THEN FIND OUT WHY THE FUCK NOT. FEATHERSTONE IS HOLDING CUSTER'S WOMAN, WHICH IS THE ONLY HOLD WE HAVE OVER HIM.
REPORT TO ME AT OH-ONE HUNDRED.
GO, DRIVER.
A WORD OF EXPLANATION, REVEREND.
ABOUT GAWD DEMN TIME...

A TIME IS COMING WHEN WE MAY HAVE TO MOVE VERY QUICKLY INDEED, SO I WANT YOU TO FULLY UNDERSTAND YOUR PART IN THINGS.

YOU MAY BE FAMILIAR WITH THE FIRST PART OF THIS STORY.

ALMOST TWO THOUSAND YEARS AGO, THREE MEN WERE CRUCIFIED ON A HILL ABOVE JERUSALEM. TWO WERE THIEVES, AND DIED AS SUCH. THE THIRD WAS NOT, AND DID NOT DIE.

UH... YEAH, AH THINK AH HEARD THAT'N BEFORE...

WHAT YOU WON'T HAVE HEARD IS THAT HE DID NOT DIE EVEN IN A PHYSICAL SENSE. HAVING PAID OFF THE LOCAL AUTHORITIES, HIS FOLLOWERS DRUGGED HIM INTO A COMA WITH A SOPORIFIC WHILE HE WAS STILL ON THE CROSS. THREE DAYS LATER--WHEN THE DRUG WORE OFF--HE "ROSE FROM THE DEAD."

HE TOOK A WIFE CALLED MARY, HAD SEVERAL CHILDREN, AND WAS RUN OVER AND KILLED BY AN OFFAL CART AT THE AGE OF FORTY-EIGHT.

WHOSE GAWD DEMN TESTAMENT IS THAT? WEEKLY WORLD NEWS?

THAT IS THE LEGEND OF THE GRAIL.

THOSE CHILDREN HE HAD WERE BORN OF THE MOST SACRED, MOST BLESSED LINEAGE THIS WORLD HAS EVER SEEN.

THE FOUNDERS OF THE GRAIL TOOK THEM TO A SECRET PLACE IN THE DESERT, WHERE THEY WERE ALLOWED TO BREED ONLY WITH EACH OTHER. WHEN THE GRAIL MOVED TO EUROPE IN THE SIXTH CENTURY, THEY BROUGHT THE CHILDREN'S DESCENDANTS WITH THEM.

AND TO THIS DAY, REVEREND, WE KEEP THE BLOODLINE SAFE AND PURE.

WE GUARD THE BLOOD OF THE LAMB.

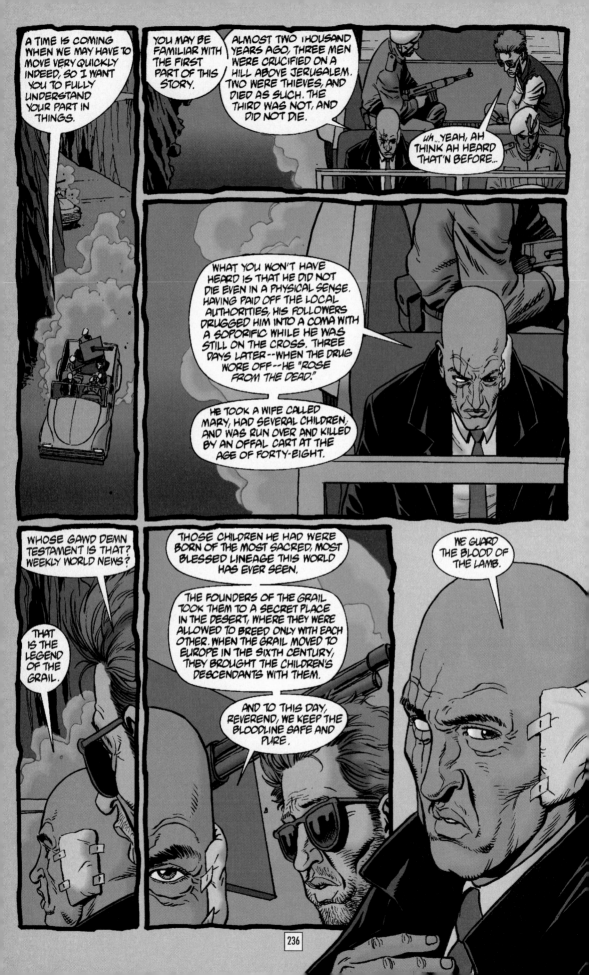

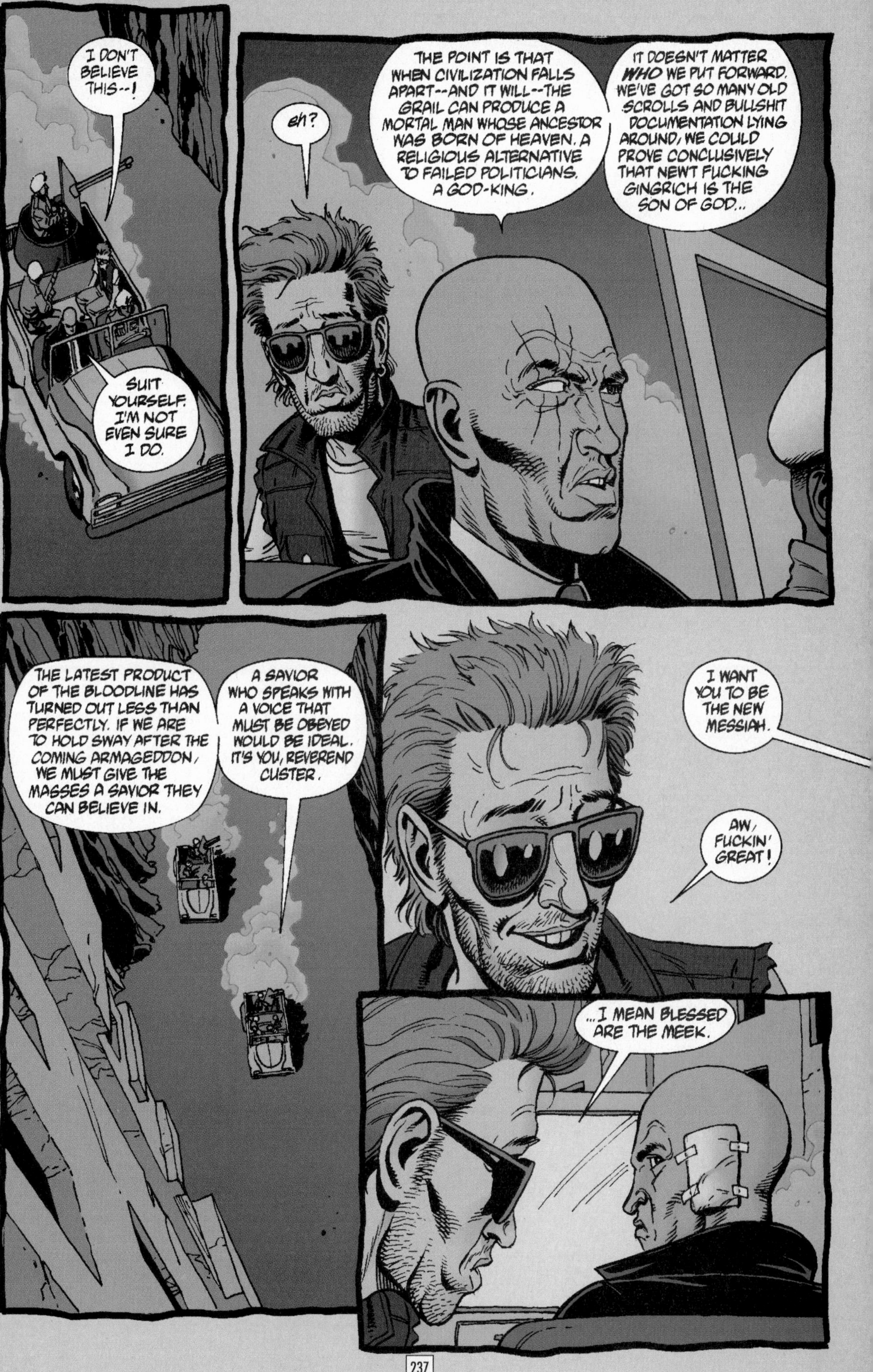
I DON'T BELIEVE THIS--!
SUIT YOURSELF. I'M NOT EVEN SURE I DO.
eh?
THE POINT IS THAT WHEN CIVILIZATION FALLS APART--AND IT WILL--THE GRAIL CAN PRODUCE A MORTAL MAN WHOSE ANCESTOR WAS BORN OF HEAVEN. A RELIGIOUS ALTERNATIVE TO FAILED POLITICIANS. A GOD-KING.
IT DOESN'T MATTER WHO WE PUT FORWARD. WE'VE GOT SO MANY OLD SCROLLS AND BULLSHIT DOCUMENTATION LYING AROUND, WE COULD PROVE CONCLUSIVELY THAT NEWT FUCKING GINGRICH IS THE SON OF GOD...
THE LATEST PRODUCT OF THE BLOODLINE HAS TURNED OUT LESS THAN PERFECTLY. IF WE ARE TO HOLD SWAY AFTER THE COMING ARMAGEDDON, WE MUST GIVE THE MASSES A SAVIOR THEY CAN BELIEVE IN.
A SAVIOR WHO SPEAKS WITH A VOICE THAT MUST BE OBEYED WOULD BE IDEAL. IT'S YOU, REVEREND CUSTER.
I WANT YOU TO BE THE NEW MESSIAH.
AW, FUCKIN' GREAT!
...I MEAN BLESSED ARE THE MEEK.

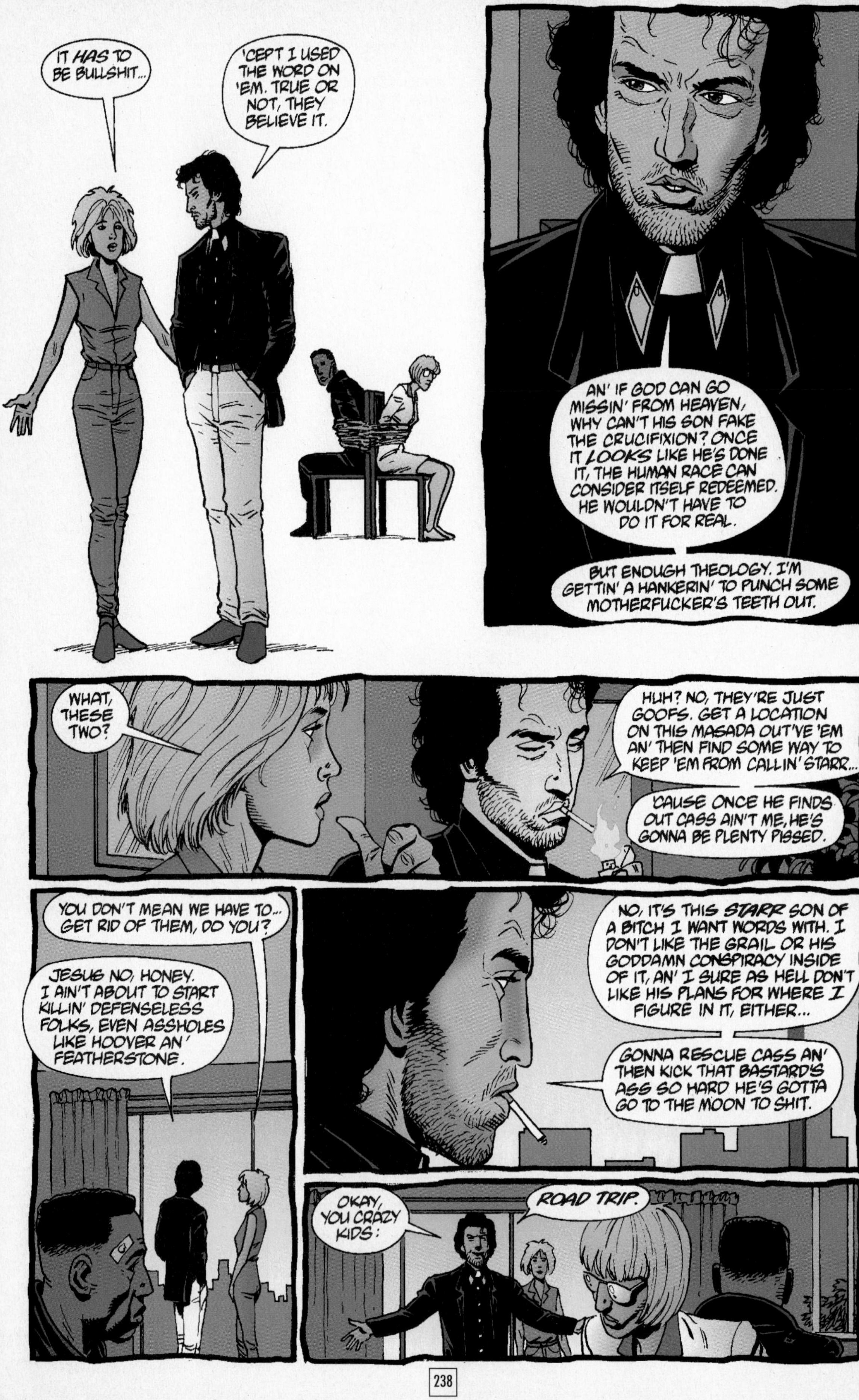
IT HAS TO BE BULLSHIT...
'CEPT I USED THE WORD ON 'EM. TRUE OR NOT, THEY BELIEVE IT.
AN' IF GOD CAN GO MISSIN' FROM HEAVEN, WHY CAN'T HIS SON FAKE THE CRUCIFIXION? ONCE IT LOOKS LIKE HE'S DONE IT, THE HUMAN RACE CAN CONSIDER ITSELF REDEEMED. HE WOULDN'T HAVE TO DO IT FOR REAL.
BUT ENOUGH THEOLOGY. I'M GETTIN' A HANKERIN' TO PUNCH SOME MOTHERFUCKER'S TEETH OUT.
WHAT, THESE TWO?
HUH? NO, THEY'RE JUST GOOFS. GET A LOCATION ON THIS MASADA OUT'VE 'EM AN' THEN FIND SOME WAY TO KEEP 'EM FROM CALLIN' STARR...
'CAUSE ONCE HE FINDS OUT CASS AIN'T ME, HE'S GONNA BE PLENTY PISSED.
YOU DON'T MEAN WE HAVE TO... GET RID OF THEM, DO YOU?
JESUS NO, HONEY. I AIN'T ABOUT TO START KILLIN' DEFENSELESS FOLKS, EVEN ASSHOLES LIKE HOOVER AN' FEATHERSTONE.
NO, IT'S THIS STARR SON OF A BITCH I WANT WORDS WITH. I DON'T LIKE THE GRAIL OR HIS GODDAMN CONSPIRACY INSIDE OF IT, AN' I SURE AS HELL DON'T LIKE HIS PLANS FOR WHERE I FIGURE IN IT, EITHER...
GONNA RESCUE CASS AN' THEN KICK THAT BASTARD'S ASS SO HARD HE'S GOTTA GO TO THE MOON TO SHIT.
OKAY, YOU CRAZY KIDS:
ROAD TRIP.

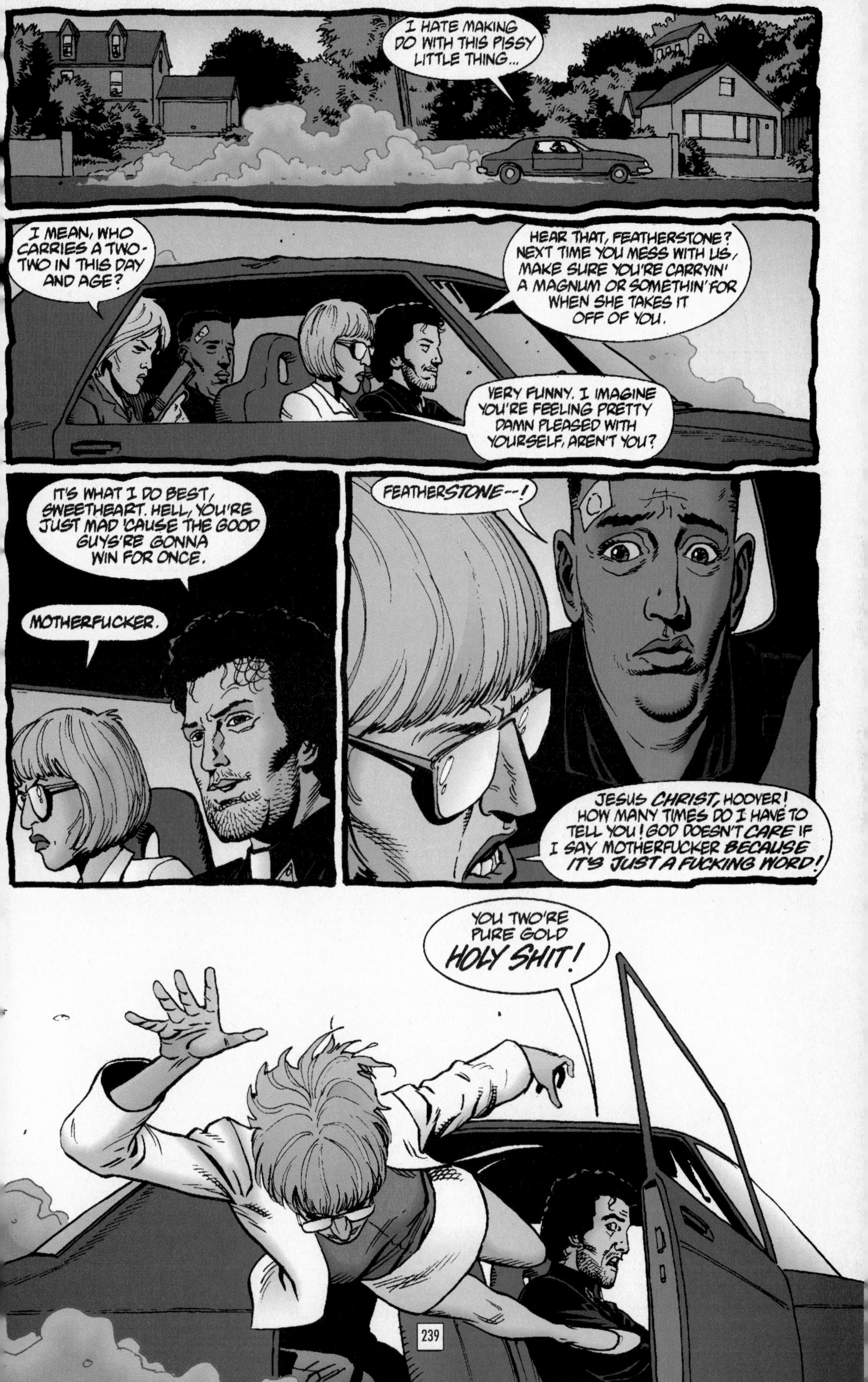
I HATE MAKING DO WITH THIS PISSY LITTLE THING...
I MEAN, WHO CARRIES A TWO-TWO IN THIS DAY AND AGE?
HEAR THAT, FEATHERSTONE? NEXT TIME YOU MESS WITH US, MAKE SURE YOU'RE CARRYIN' A MAGNUM OR SOMETHIN' FOR WHEN SHE TAKES IT OFF OF YOU.
VERY FUNNY. I IMAGINE YOU'RE FEELING PRETTY DAMN PLEASED WITH YOURSELF, AREN'T YOU?
IT'S WHAT I DO BEST, SWEETHEART. HELL, YOU'RE JUST MAD 'CAUSE THE GOOD GUYS'RE GONNA WIN FOR ONCE.
MOTHERFUCKER.
FEATHERSTONE--!
JESUS CHRIST, HOOVER! HOW MANY TIMES DO I HAVE TO TELL YOU! GOD DOESN'T CARE IF I SAY MOTHERFUCKER BECAUSE IT'S JUST A FUCKING WORD!
YOU TWO'RE PURE GOLD
HOLY SHIT!

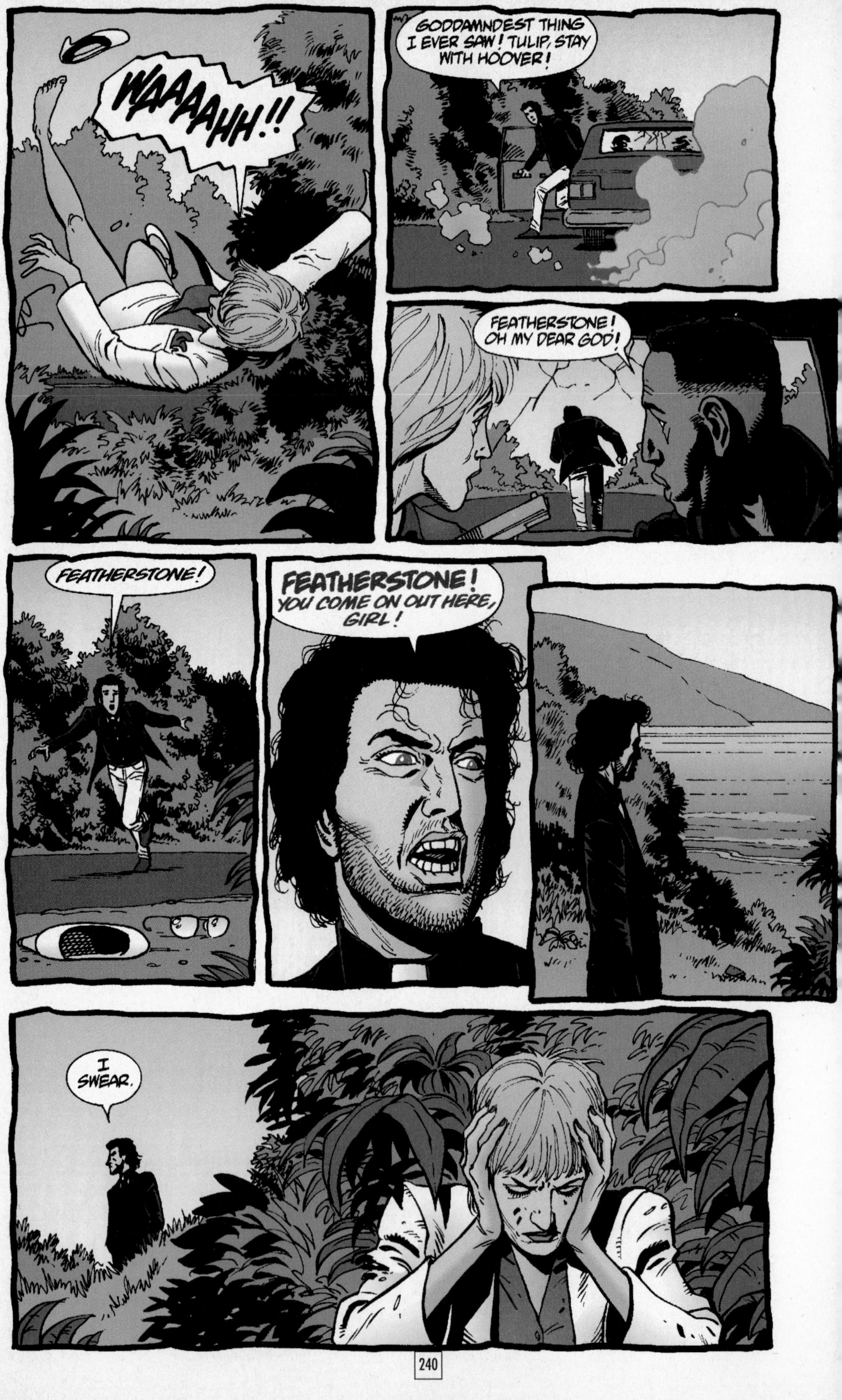
WAAAAAHH!!
GODDAMNDEST THING I EVER SAW! TULIP, STAY WITH HOOVER!
FEATHERSTONE! OH MY DEAR GOD!
FEATHERSTONE!
FEATHERSTONE! YOU COME ON OUT HERE, GIRL!
I SWEAR.

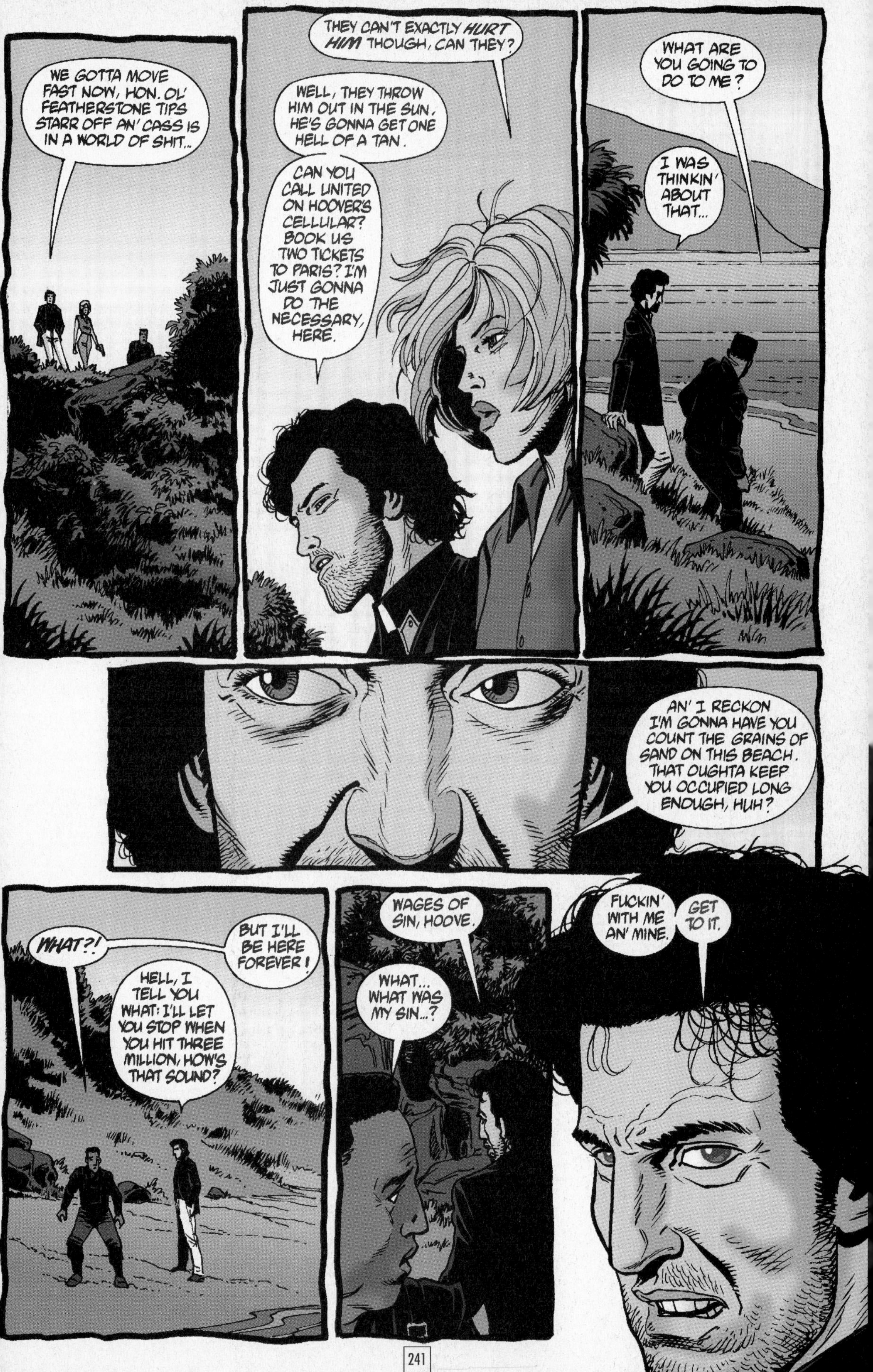
WE GOTTA MOVE FAST NOW, HON. OL' FEATHERSTONE TIPS STARR OFF AN' CASS IS IN A WORLD OF SHIT...
THEY CAN'T EXACTLY HURT HIM THOUGH, CAN THEY?
WELL, THEY THROW HIM OUT IN THE SUN, HE'S GONNA GET ONE HELL OF A TAN.
CAN YOU CALL UNITED ON HOOVER'S CELLULAR? BOOK US TWO TICKETS TO PARIS? I'M JUST GONNA DO THE NECESSARY, HERE.
WHAT ARE YOU GOING TO DO TO ME?
I WAS THINKIN' ABOUT THAT...
AN' I RECKON I'M GONNA HAVE YOU COUNT THE GRAINS OF SAND ON THIS BEACH. THAT OUGHTA KEEP YOU OCCUPIED LONG ENOUGH, HUH?
WHAT?!
BUT I'LL BE HERE FOREVER!
HELL, I TELL YOU WHAT: I'LL LET YOU STOP WHEN YOU HIT THREE MILLION, HOW'S THAT SOUND?
WAGES OF SIN, HOOVE.
WHAT... WHAT WAS MY SIN...?
FUCKIN' WITH ME AN' MINE.
GET TO IT.

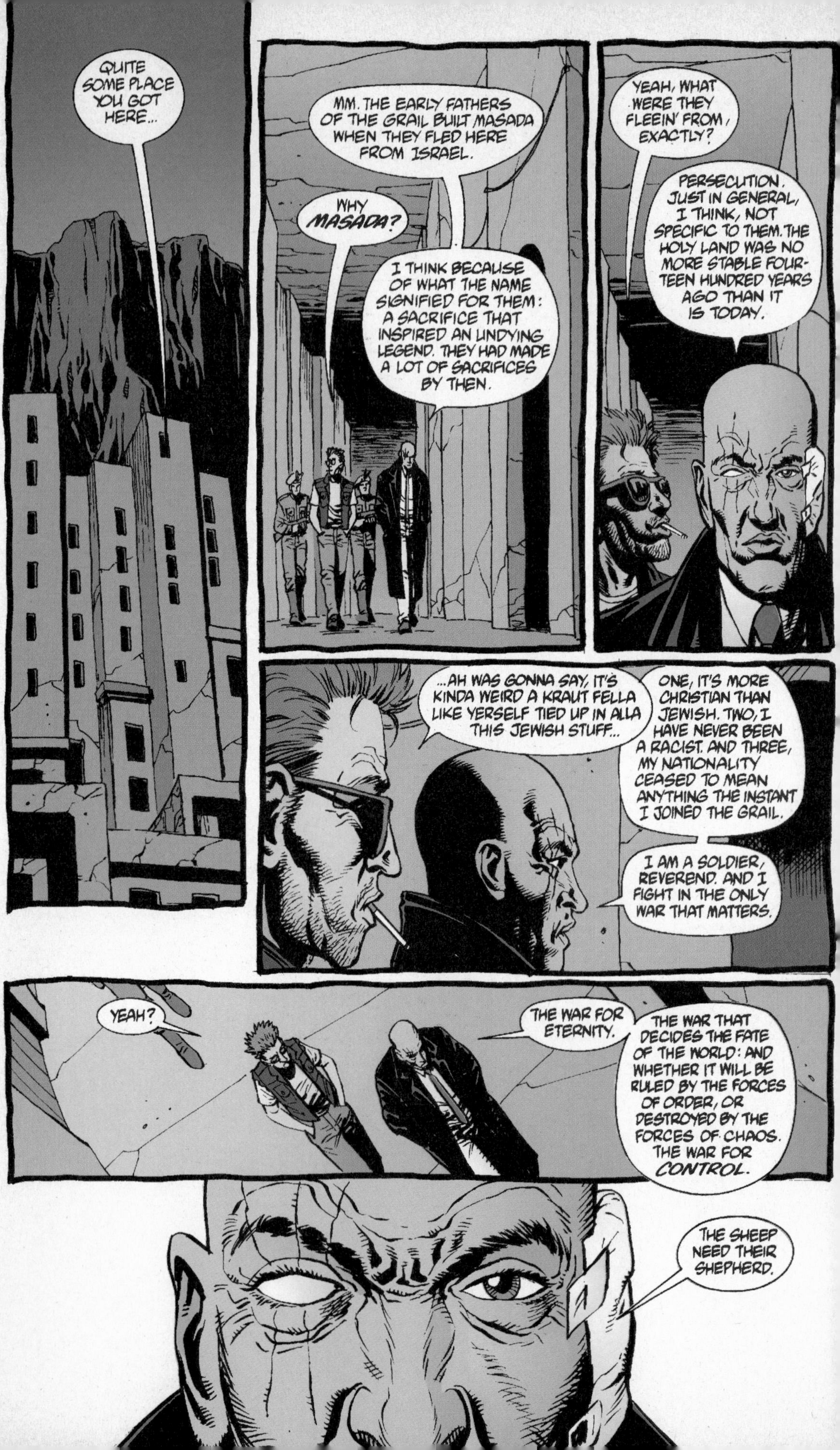
QUITE SOME PLACE YOU GOT HERE...
MM. THE EARLY FATHERS OF THE GRAIL BUILT MASADA WHEN THEY FLED HERE FROM ISRAEL.
WHY MASADA?
I THINK BECAUSE OF WHAT THE NAME SIGNIFIED FOR THEM: A SACRIFICE THAT INSPIRED AN UNDYING LEGEND. THEY HAD MADE A LOT OF SACRIFICES BY THEN.
YEAH, WHAT WERE THEY FLEEIN' FROM, EXACTLY?
PERSECUTION. JUST IN GENERAL, I THINK, NOT SPECIFIC TO THEM. THE HOLY LAND WAS NO MORE STABLE FOURTEEN HUNDRED YEARS AGO THAN IT IS TODAY.
...AH WAS GONNA SAY, IT'S KINDA WEIRD A KRAUT FELLA LIKE YERSELF TIED UP IN ALLA THIS JEWISH STUFF...
ONE, IT'S MORE CHRISTIAN THAN JEWISH. TWO, I HAVE NEVER BEEN A RACIST. AND THREE, MY NATIONALITY CEASED TO MEAN ANYTHING THE INSTANT I JOINED THE GRAIL.
I AM A SOLDIER, REVEREND. AND I FIGHT IN THE ONLY WAR THAT MATTERS.
YEAH?
THE WAR FOR ETERNITY.
THE WAR THAT DECIDES THE FATE OF THE WORLD: AND WHETHER IT WILL BE RULED BY THE FORCES OF ORDER, OR DESTROYED BY THE FORCES OF CHAOS. THE WAR FOR CONTROL.
THE SHEEP NEED THEIR SHEPHERD.

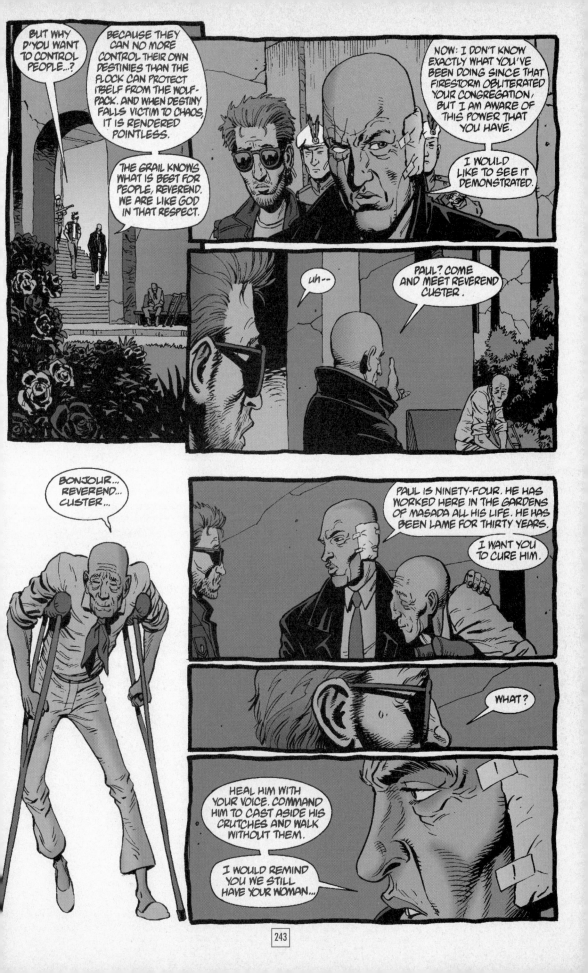

BUT WHY D'YOU WANT TO CONTROL PEOPLE...?

BECAUSE THEY CAN NO MORE CONTROL THEIR OWN DESTINIES THAN THE FLOCK CAN PROTECT ITSELF FROM THE WOLF-PACK. AND WHEN DESTINY FALLS VICTIM TO CHAOS, IT IS RENDERED POINTLESS.

THE GRAIL KNOWS WHAT IS BEST FOR PEOPLE, REVEREND. WE ARE LIKE GOD IN THAT RESPECT.

NOW: I DON'T KNOW EXACTLY WHAT YOU'VE BEEN DOING SINCE THAT FIRESTORM OBLITERATED YOUR CONGREGATION, BUT I AM AWARE OF THIS POWER THAT YOU HAVE.

I WOULD LIKE TO SEE IT DEMONSTRATED.

uh--

PAUL? COME AND MEET REVEREND CUSTER.

BONJOUR... REVEREND... CUSTER...

PAUL IS NINETY-FOUR. HE HAS WORKED HERE IN THE GARDENS OF MASADA ALL HIS LIFE. HE HAS BEEN LAME FOR THIRTY YEARS.

I WANT YOU TO CURE HIM.

WHAT?

HEAL HIM WITH YOUR VOICE. COMMAND HIM TO CAST ASIDE HIS CRUTCHES AND WALK WITHOUT THEM.

I WOULD REMIND YOU WE STILL HAVE YOUR WOMAN...

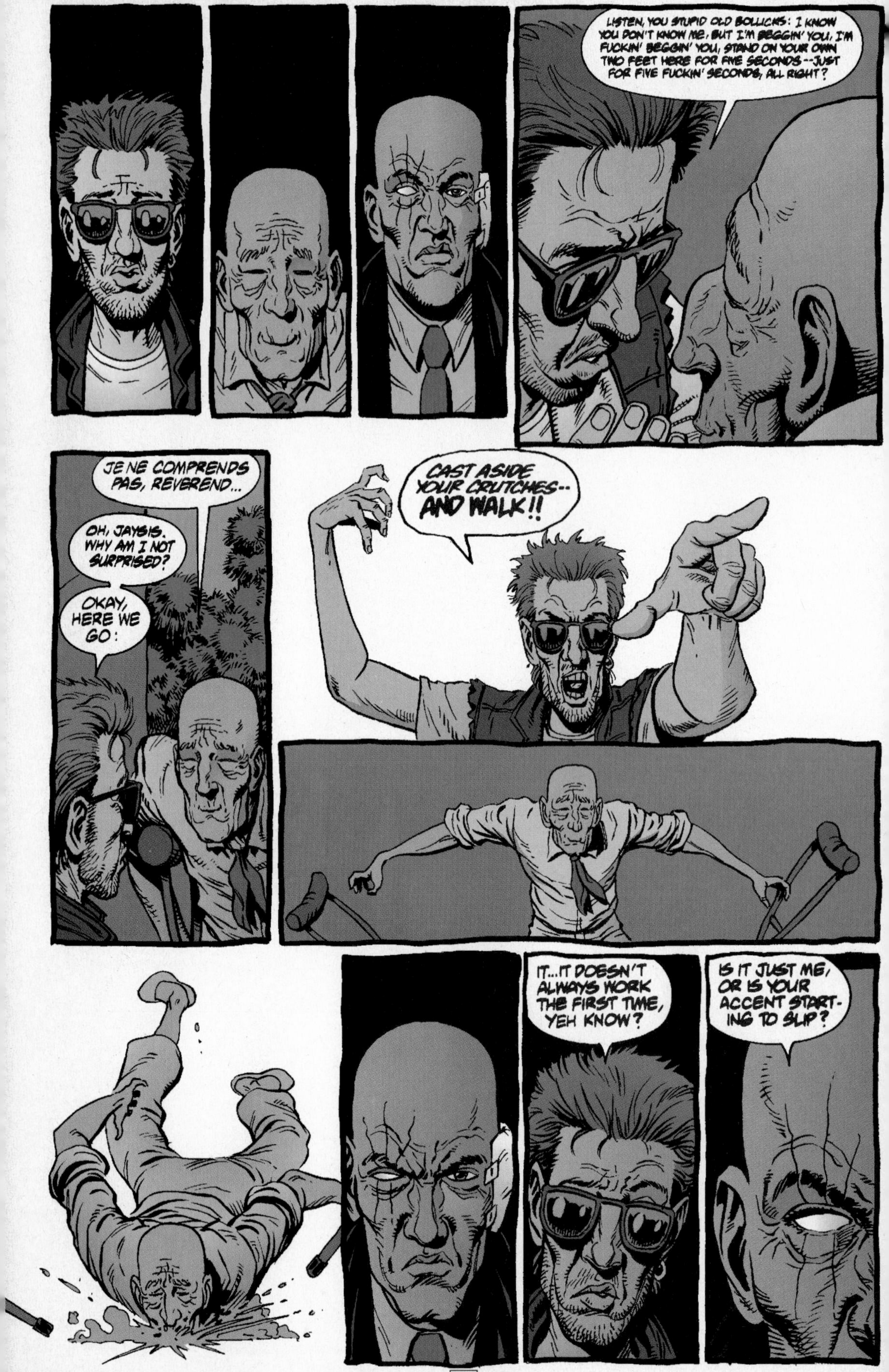
LISTEN, YOU STUPID OLD BOLLICKS: I KNOW YOU DON'T KNOW ME, BUT I'M BEGGIN' YOU, I'M FUCKIN' BEGGIN' YOU, STAND ON YOUR OWN TWO FEET HERE FOR FIVE SECONDS--JUST FOR FIVE FUCKIN' SECONDS, ALL RIGHT?
JE NE COMPRENDS PAS, REVEREND...
OH, JAYSIS. WHY AM I NOT SURPRISED?
OKAY, HERE WE GO:
CAST ASIDE YOUR CRUTCHES--AND WALK!!
IT...IT DOESN'T ALWAYS WORK THE FIRST TIME, YEH KNOW?
IS IT JUST ME, OR IS YOUR ACCENT STARTING TO SLIP?

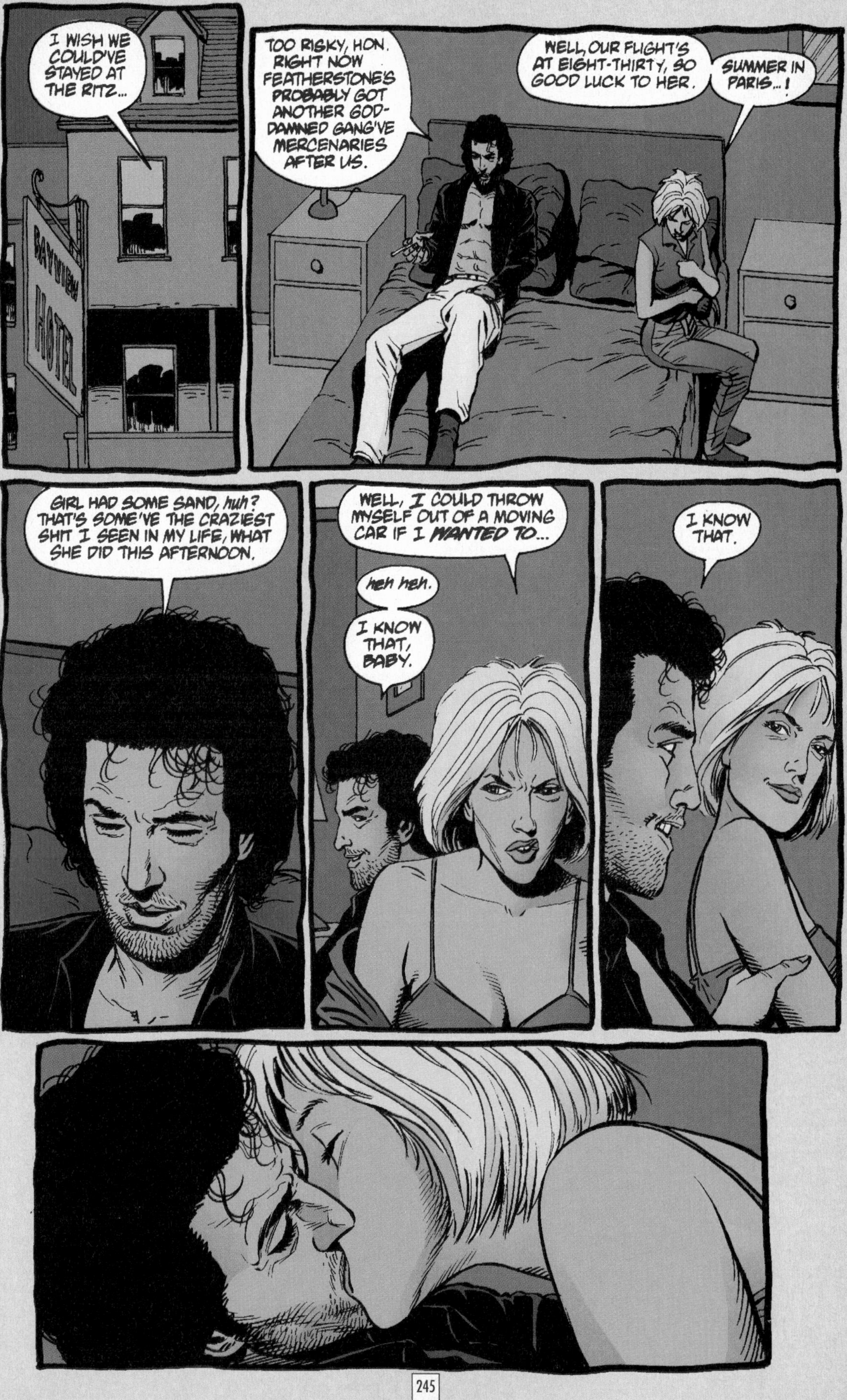

I WISH WE COULD'VE STAYED AT THE RITZ...
TOO RISKY, HON. RIGHT NOW FEATHERSTONE'S PROBABLY GOT ANOTHER GOD-DAMNED GANG'VE MERCENARIES AFTER US.
WELL, OUR FLIGHT'S AT EIGHT-THIRTY, SO GOOD LUCK TO HER.
SUMMER IN PARIS...!
GIRL HAD SOME SAND, *huh*? THAT'S SOME'VE THE CRAZIEST SHIT I SEEN IN MY LIFE, WHAT SHE DID THIS AFTERNOON.
WELL, I COULD THROW MYSELF OUT OF A MOVING CAR IF I *WANTED TO*...
heh heh.
I KNOW THAT, BABY.
I KNOW THAT.

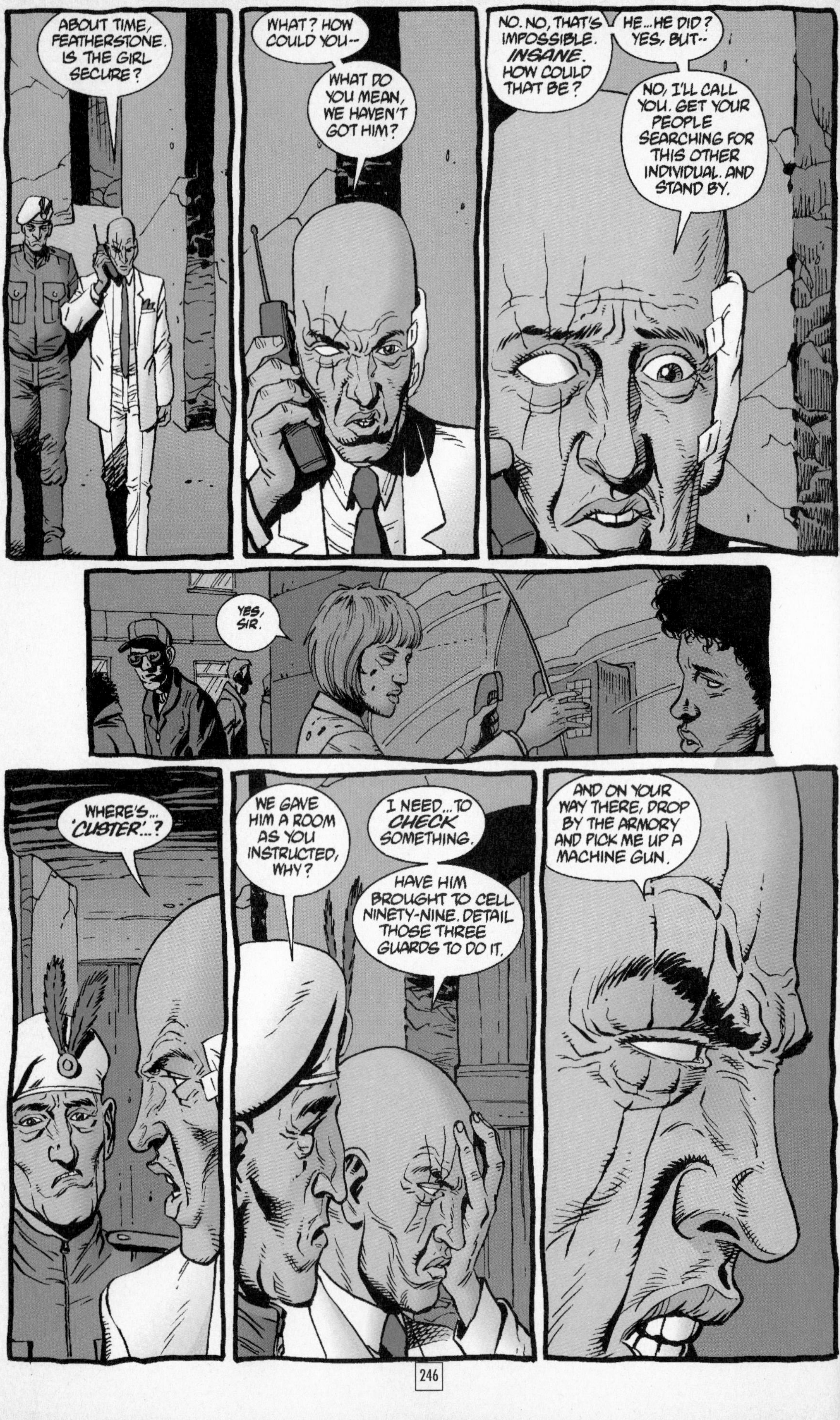
ABOUT TIME, FEATHERSTONE. IS THE GIRL SECURE?
WHAT? HOW COULD YOU--
WHAT DO YOU MEAN, WE HAVEN'T GOT HIM?
NO. NO, THAT'S IMPOSSIBLE. INSANE. HOW COULD THAT BE?
HE...HE DID? YES, BUT--
NO, I'LL CALL YOU. GET YOUR PEOPLE SEARCHING FOR THIS OTHER INDIVIDUAL. AND STAND BY.
YES, SIR.
WHERE'S... 'CUSTER'...?
WE GAVE HIM A ROOM AS YOU INSTRUCTED, WHY?
I NEED... TO CHECK SOMETHING.
HAVE HIM BROUGHT TO CELL NINETY-NINE. DETAIL THOSE THREE GUARDS TO DO IT.
AND ON YOUR WAY THERE, DROP BY THE ARMORY AND PICK ME UP A MACHINE GUN.

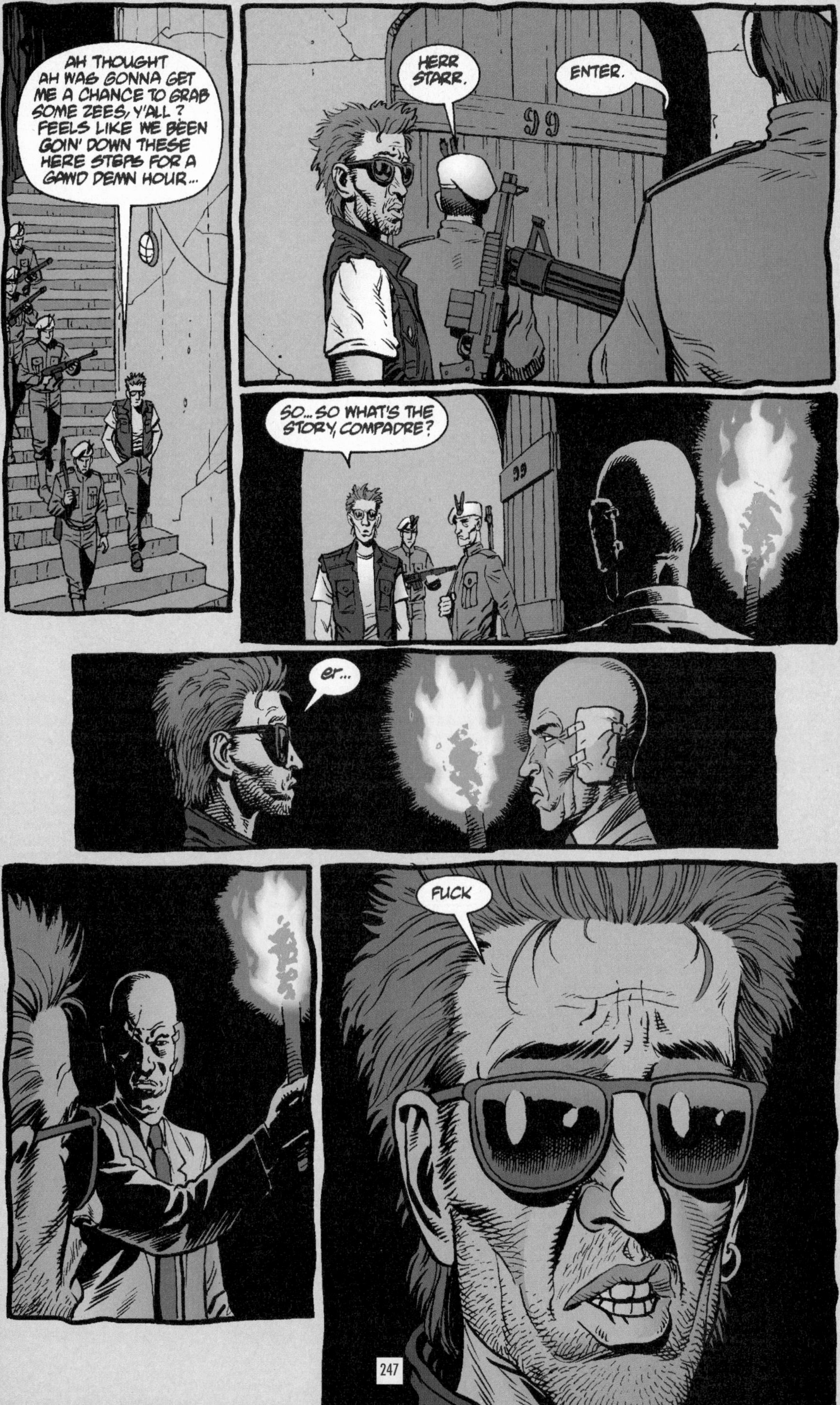
AH THOUGHT AH WAS GONNA GET ME A CHANCE TO GRAB SOME ZEES, Y'ALL? FEELS LIKE WE BEEN GOIN' DOWN THESE HERE STEPS FOR A GAWD DEMN HOUR...
HERR STARR.
ENTER.
99
SO... SO WHAT'S THE STORY, COMPADRE?
er...
FUCK

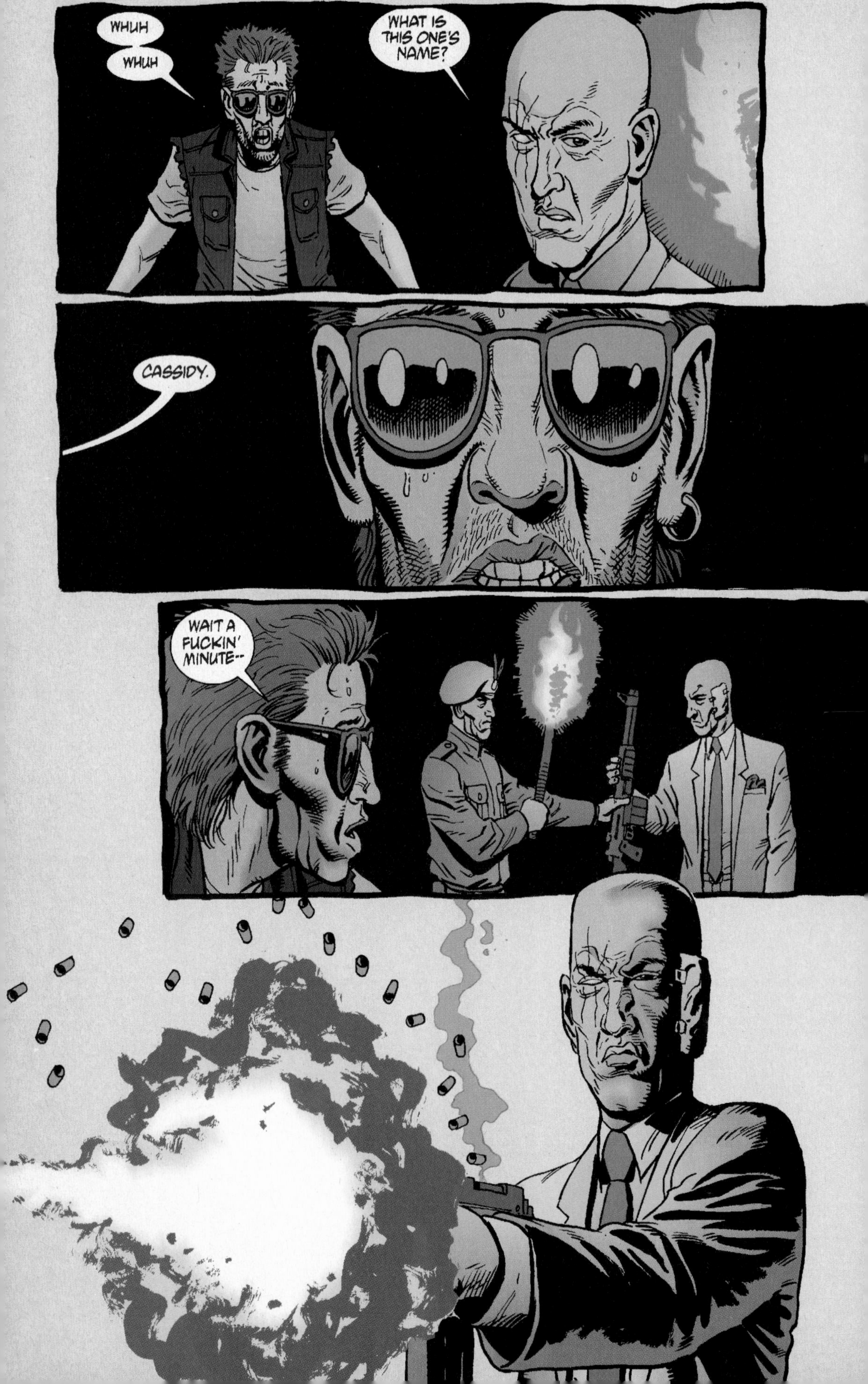
WHUH
WHUH
WHAT IS THIS ONE'S NAME?
CASSIDY.
WAIT A FUCKIN' MINUTE--

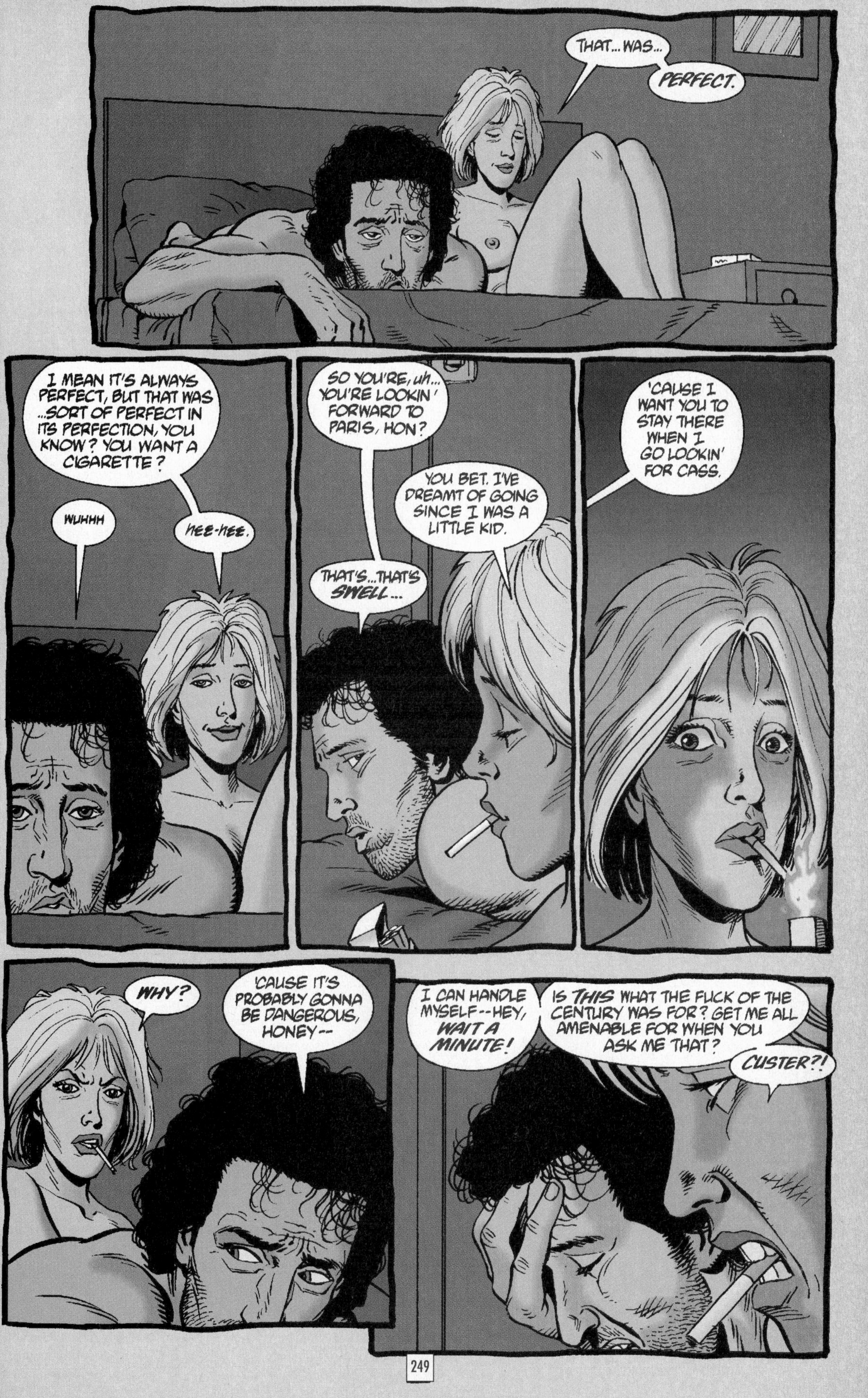
THAT... WAS... PERFECT.
I MEAN IT'S ALWAYS PERFECT, BUT THAT WAS ...SORT OF PERFECT IN ITS PERFECTION, YOU KNOW? YOU WANT A CIGARETTE?
WUHHH
hee-hee.
SO YOU'RE, uh... YOU'RE LOOKIN' FORWARD TO PARIS, HON?
YOU BET. I'VE DREAMT OF GOING SINCE I WAS A LITTLE KID.
THAT'S...THAT'S SWELL...
'CAUSE I WANT YOU TO STAY THERE WHEN I GO LOOKIN' FOR CASS.
WHY?
'CAUSE IT'S PROBABLY GONNA BE DANGEROUS, HONEY--
I CAN HANDLE MYSELF--HEY, WAIT A MINUTE!
IS THIS WHAT THE FUCK OF THE CENTURY WAS FOR? GET ME ALL AMENABLE FOR WHEN YOU ASK ME THAT?
CUSTER?!

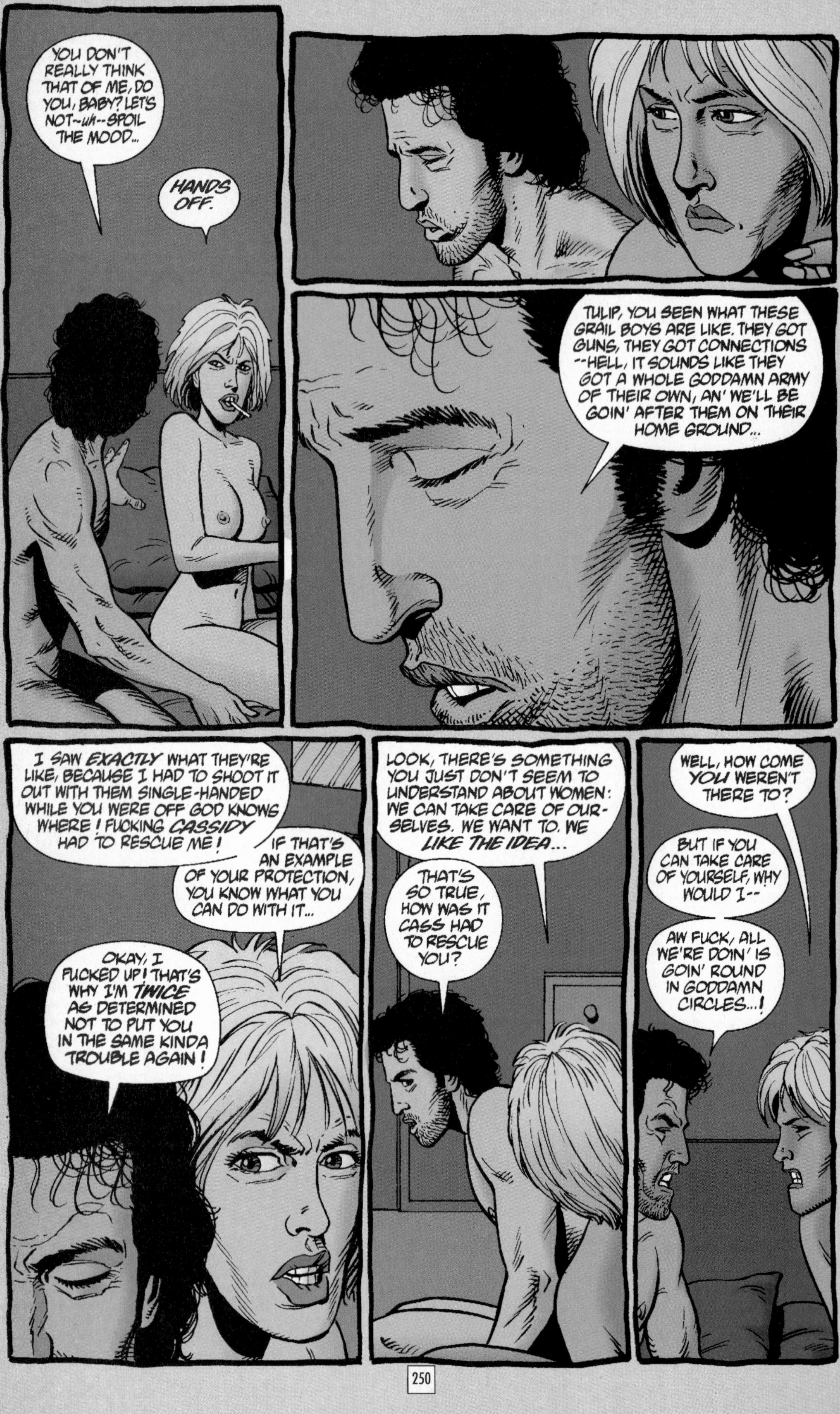
YOU DON'T REALLY THINK THAT OF ME, DO YOU, BABY? LET'S NOT--uh--SPOIL THE MOOD...
HANDS OFF.
TULIP, YOU SEEN WHAT THESE GRAIL BOYS ARE LIKE. THEY GOT GUNS, THEY GOT CONNECTIONS --HELL, IT SOUNDS LIKE THEY GOT A WHOLE GODDAMN ARMY OF THEIR OWN, AN' WE'LL BE GOIN' AFTER THEM ON THEIR HOME GROUND...
I SAW EXACTLY WHAT THEY'RE LIKE, BECAUSE I HAD TO SHOOT IT OUT WITH THEM SINGLE-HANDED WHILE YOU WERE OFF GOD KNOWS WHERE! FUCKING CASSIDY HAD TO RESCUE ME!
IF THAT'S AN EXAMPLE OF YOUR PROTECTION, YOU KNOW WHAT YOU CAN DO WITH IT...
OKAY, I FUCKED UP! THAT'S WHY I'M TWICE AS DETERMINED NOT TO PUT YOU IN THE SAME KINDA TROUBLE AGAIN!
LOOK, THERE'S SOMETHING YOU JUST DON'T SEEM TO UNDERSTAND ABOUT WOMEN: WE CAN TAKE CARE OF OURSELVES. WE WANT TO. WE LIKE THE IDEA...
THAT'S SO TRUE, HOW WAS IT CASS HAD TO RESCUE YOU?
WELL, HOW COME YOU WEREN'T THERE TO?
BUT IF YOU CAN TAKE CARE OF YOURSELF, WHY WOULD I--
AW FUCK, ALL WE'RE DOIN' IS GOIN' ROUND IN GODDAMN CIRCLES...!

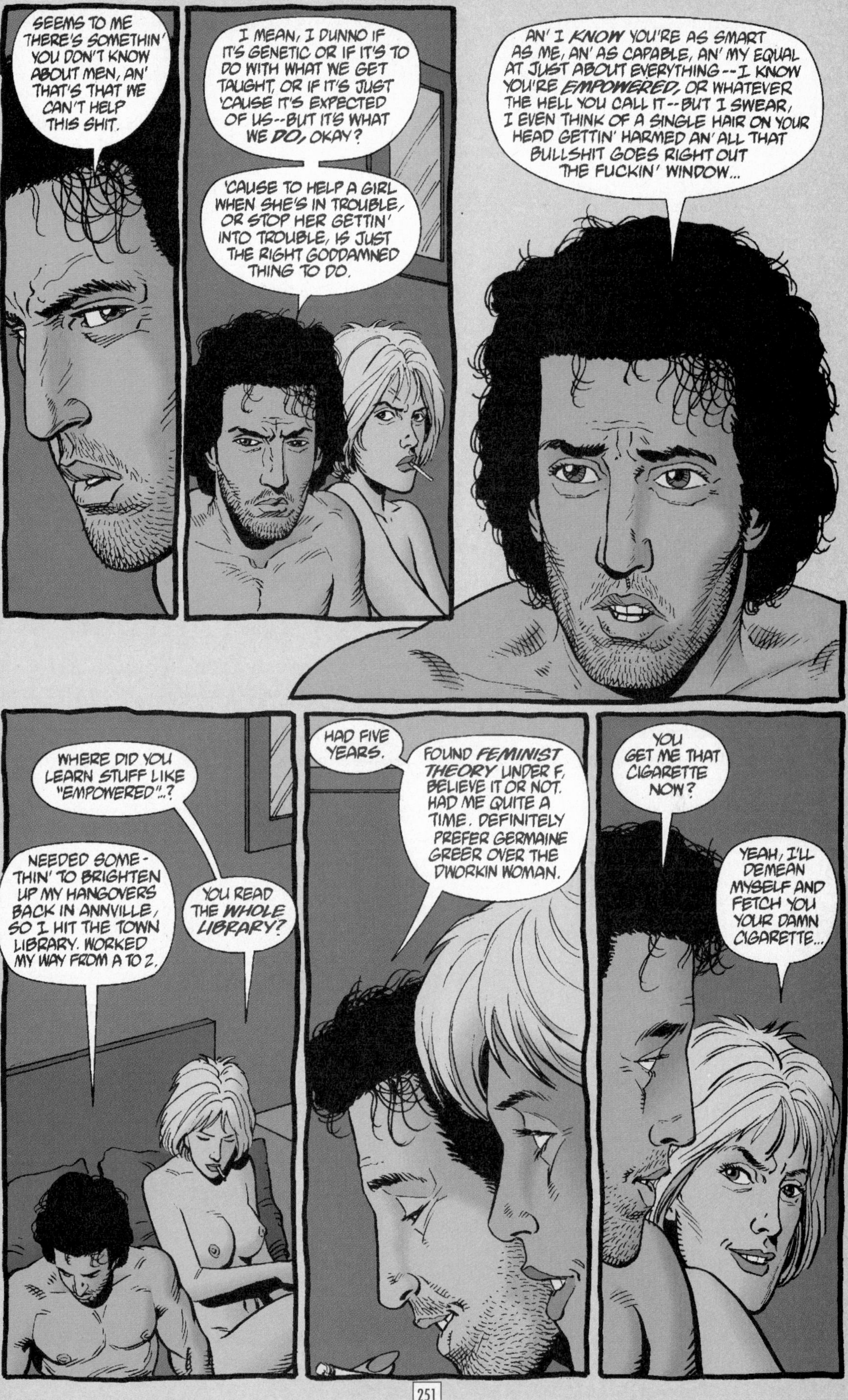
SEEMS TO ME THERE'S SOMETHIN' YOU DON'T KNOW ABOUT MEN, AN' THAT'S THAT WE CAN'T HELP THIS SHIT.
I MEAN, I DUNNO IF IT'S GENETIC OR IF IT'S TO DO WITH WHAT WE GET TAUGHT, OR IF IT'S JUST 'CAUSE IT'S EXPECTED OF US--BUT IT'S WHAT WE DO, OKAY?
'CAUSE TO HELP A GIRL WHEN SHE'S IN TROUBLE, OR STOP HER GETTIN' INTO TROUBLE, IS JUST THE RIGHT GODDAMNED THING TO DO.
AN' I KNOW YOU'RE AS SMART AS ME, AN' AS CAPABLE, AN' MY EQUAL AT JUST ABOUT EVERYTHING--I KNOW YOU'RE EMPOWERED, OR WHATEVER THE HELL YOU CALL IT--BUT I SWEAR, I EVEN THINK OF A SINGLE HAIR ON YOUR HEAD GETTIN' HARMED AN' ALL THAT BULLSHIT GOES RIGHT OUT THE FUCKIN' WINDOW...
WHERE DID YOU LEARN STUFF LIKE "EMPOWERED"...?
NEEDED SOMETHIN' TO BRIGHTEN UP MY HANGOVERS BACK IN ANNVILLE, SO I HIT THE TOWN LIBRARY. WORKED MY WAY FROM A TO Z.
YOU READ THE WHOLE LIBRARY?
HAD FIVE YEARS.
FOUND FEMINIST THEORY UNDER F, BELIEVE IT OR NOT. HAD ME QUITE A TIME. DEFINITELY PREFER GERMAINE GREER OVER THE DWORKIN WOMAN.
YOU GET ME THAT CIGARETTE NOW?
YEAH, I'LL DEMEAN MYSELF AND FETCH YOU YOUR DAMN CIGARETTE...

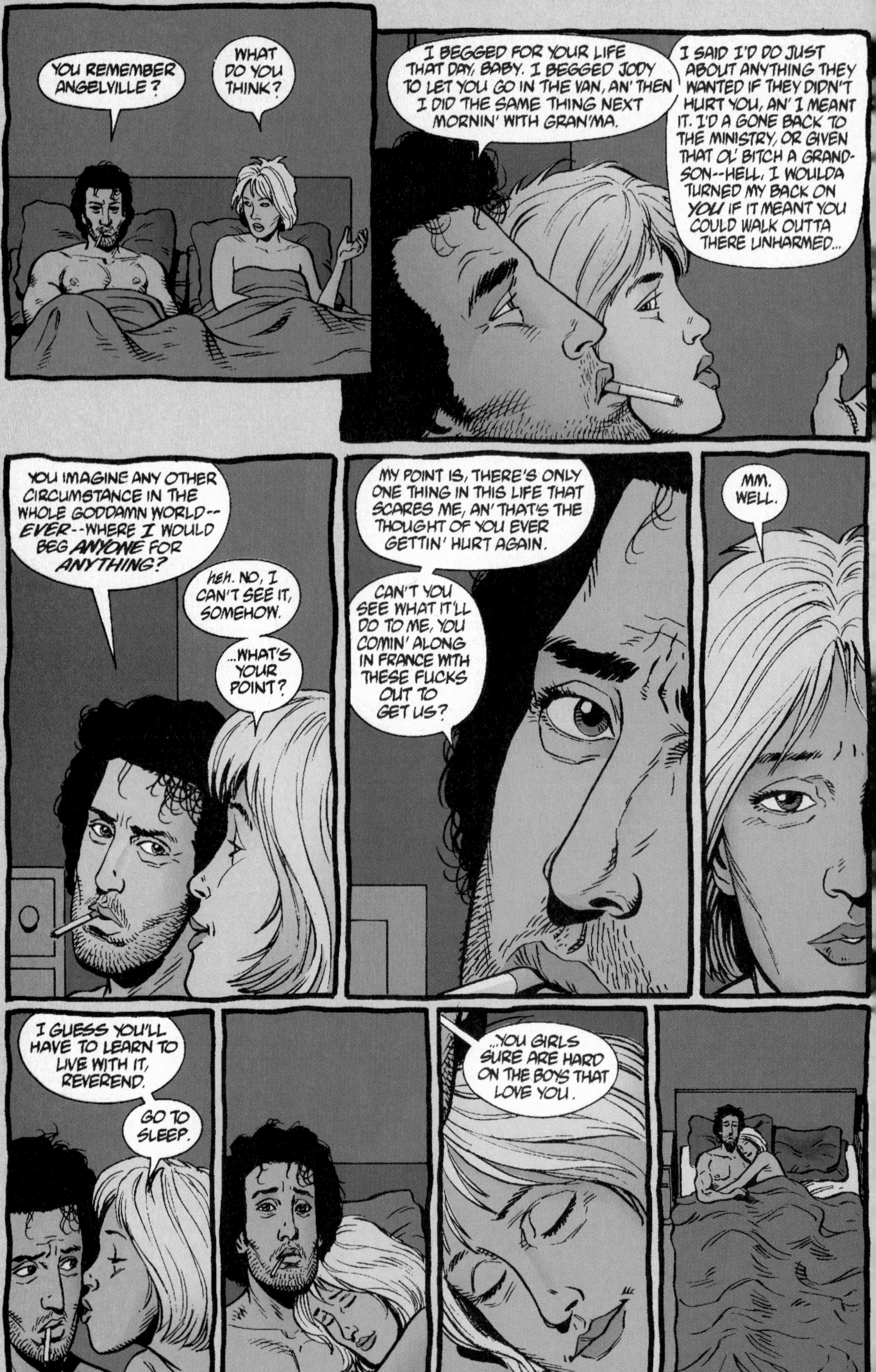
YOU REMEMBER ANGELVILLE?
WHAT DO YOU THINK?
I BEGGED FOR YOUR LIFE THAT DAY, BABY. I BEGGED JODY TO LET YOU GO IN THE VAN, AN' THEN I DID THE SAME THING NEXT MORNIN' WITH GRAN'MA.
I SAID I'D DO JUST ABOUT ANYTHING THEY WANTED IF THEY DIDN'T HURT YOU, AN' I MEANT IT. I'D A GONE BACK TO THE MINISTRY, OR GIVEN THAT OL' BITCH A GRANDSON--HELL, I WOULDA TURNED MY BACK ON YOU IF IT MEANT YOU COULD WALK OUTTA THERE UNHARMED...
YOU IMAGINE ANY OTHER CIRCUMSTANCE IN THE WHOLE GODDAMN WORLD--EVER--WHERE I WOULD BEG ANYONE FOR ANYTHING?
heh. NO, I CAN'T SEE IT, SOMEHOW.
...WHAT'S YOUR POINT?
MY POINT IS, THERE'S ONLY ONE THING IN THIS LIFE THAT SCARES ME, AN' THAT'S THE THOUGHT OF YOU EVER GETTIN' HURT AGAIN.
CAN'T YOU SEE WHAT IT'LL DO TO ME, YOU COMIN' ALONG IN FRANCE WITH THESE FUCKS OUT TO GET US?
MM. WELL.
I GUESS YOU'LL HAVE TO LEARN TO LIVE WITH IT, REVEREND.
GO TO SLEEP.
...YOU GIRLS SURE ARE HARD ON THE BOYS THAT LOVE YOU.

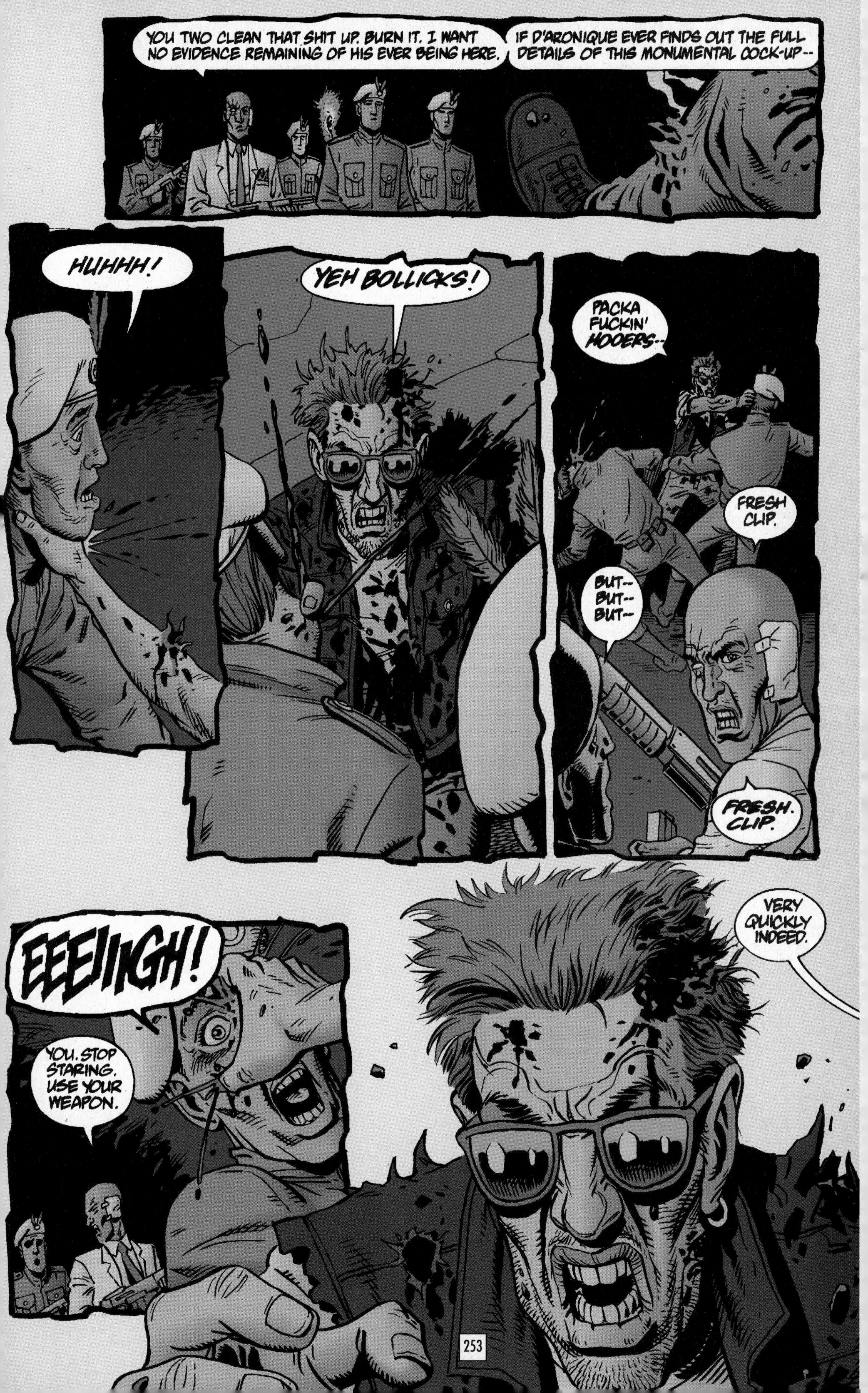

YOU TWO CLEAN THAT SHIT UP. BURN IT. I WANT NO EVIDENCE REMAINING OF HIS EVER BEING HERE.
IF D'ARONIQUE EVER FINDS OUT THE FULL DETAILS OF THIS MONUMENTAL COCK-UP--
HUHHH!
YEH BOLLICKS!
PACKA FUCKIN' HOOERS--
FRESH CLIP.
BUT-- BUT-- BUT--
FRESH. CLIP.
EEEIIIIGH!
VERY QUICKLY INDEED.
YOU. STOP STARING. USE YOUR WEAPON.

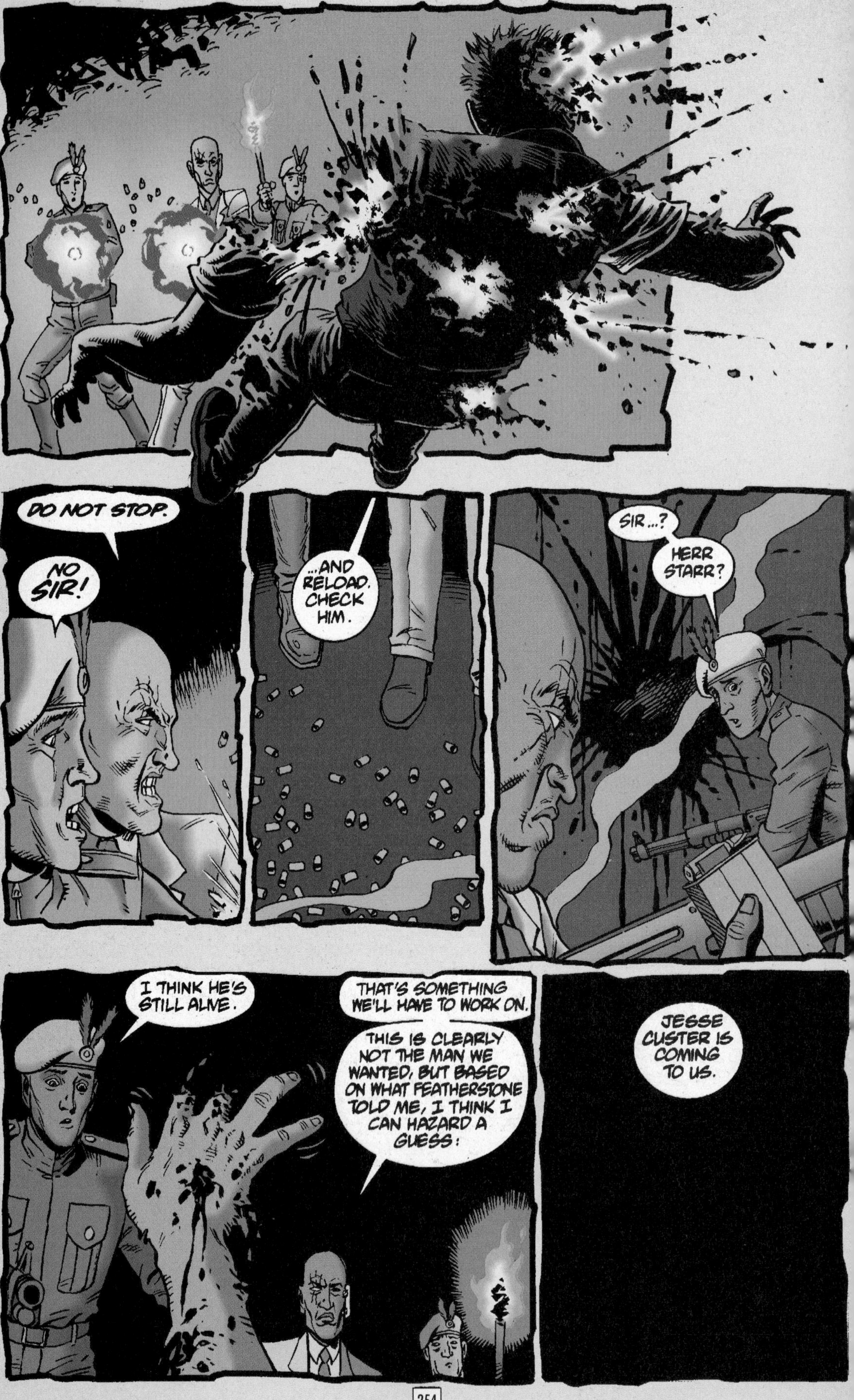
DO NOT STOP.
NO SIR!
...AND RELOAD. CHECK HIM.
SIR...?
HERR STARR?
I THINK HE'S STILL ALIVE.
THAT'S SOMETHING WE'LL HAVE TO WORK ON.
THIS IS CLEARLY NOT THE MAN WE WANTED, BUT BASED ON WHAT FEATHERSTONE TOLD ME, I THINK I CAN HAZARD A GUESS:
JESSE CUSTER IS COMING TO US.

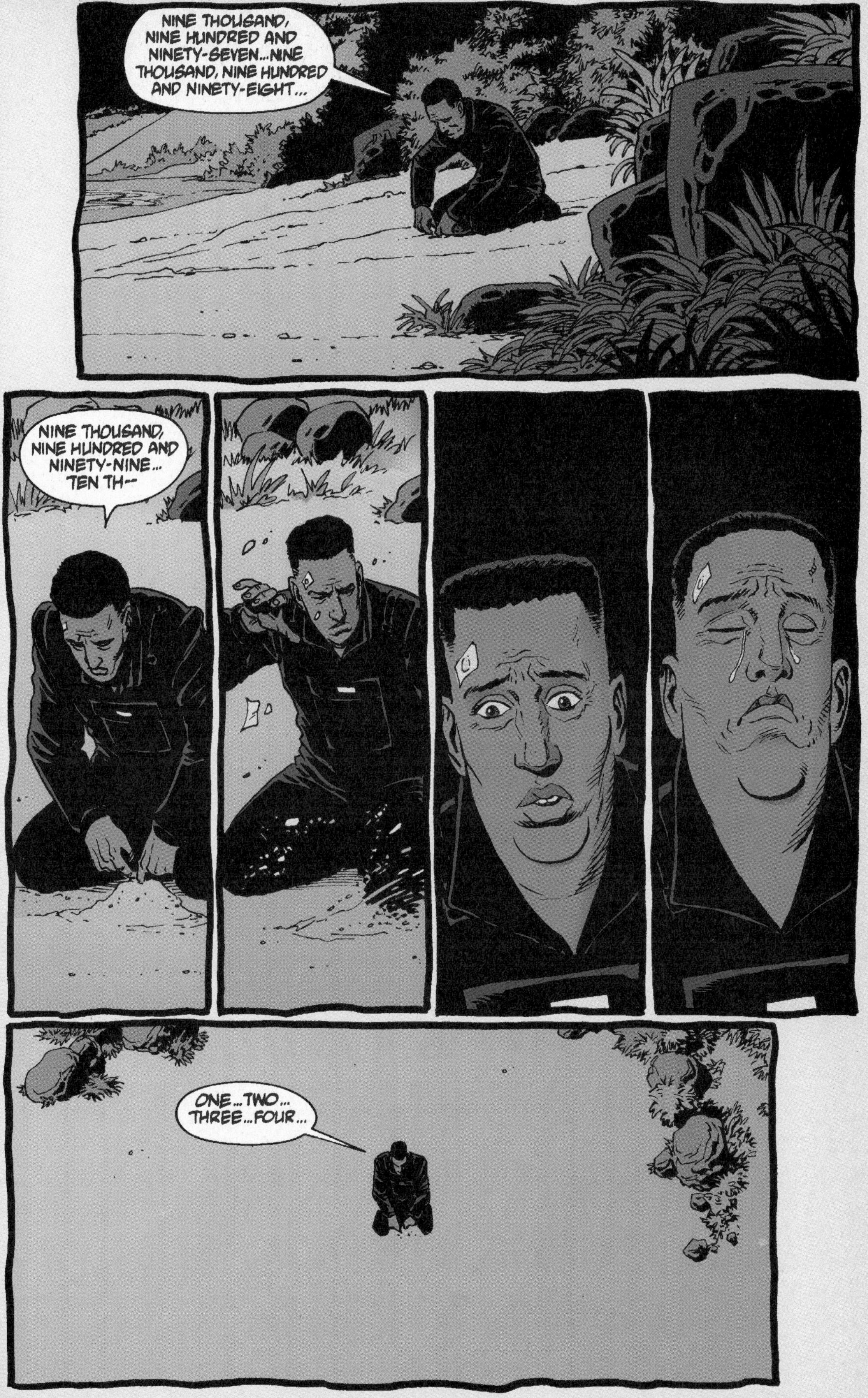
NINE THOUSAND, NINE HUNDRED AND NINETY-SEVEN...NINE THOUSAND, NINE HUNDRED AND NINETY-EIGHT...
NINE THOUSAND, NINE HUNDRED AND NINETY-NINE... TEN TH--
ONE...TWO... THREE...FOUR...

Look for these other Vertigo books:

All Vertigo titles are Suggested for Mature Readers

graphic novels

I DIE AT MIDNIGHT
Kyle Baker

KILL YOUR BOYFRIEND
Grant Morrison/Philip Bond/D'Israeli

MENZ INSANA
Christopher Fowler/John Bolton

MR. PUNCH
Neil Gaiman/Dave McKean

MYSTERY PLAY
Grant Morrison/Jon J Muth

TELL ME, DARK
Karl Edward Wagner/Kent Williams/
John Ney Rieber

TOXIC GUMBO
Lydia Lunch/Ted McKeever

VEILS
P. McGreal/S.J. Phillips/
J. Villarrubia/R. Guay

WHY I HATE SATURN
Kyle Baker

YOU ARE HERE
Kyle Baker

collections

100 BULLETS: FIRST SHOT, LAST CALL
Brian Azzarello/Eduardo Risso

BLACK ORCHID
Neil Gaiman/Dave McKean

THE BOOKS OF FAERIE
Bronwyn Carlton/John Ney Rieber/
Peter Gross

THE BOOKS OF FAERIE: AUBERON'S TALE
B. Carlton/J.N. Rieber/ P. Gross/
M. Buckingham/various

THE BOOKS OF MAGIC
N. Gaiman/J. Bolton/S. Hampton/
C. Vess/P. Johnson

THE BOOKS OF MAGIC: BINDINGS
John Ney Rieber/Gary Amaro/
Peter Gross

THE BOOKS OF MAGIC: SUMMONINGS
J.N. Rieber/P. Gross/P. Snejbjerg/
G. Amaro/D. Giordano

THE BOOKS OF MAGIC: RECKONINGS
J.N. Rieber/P. Snejbjerg/P. Gross/
J. Ridgway

THE BOOKS OF MAGIC: TRANSFORMATIONS
John Ney Rieber/Peter Gross

THE BOOKS OF MAGIC: GIRL IN THE BOX
John Ney Rieber/Peter Gross/
Peter Snejbjerg

BREATHTAKER
Mark Wheatley/Marc Hempel

THE COMPLEAT MOONSHADOW
J.M. DeMatteis/Jon J Muth

DEATH: THE HIGH COST OF LIVING
Neil Gaiman/Chris Bachalo/
Mark Buckingham

DEATH: THE TIME OF YOUR LIFE
N. Gaiman/C. Bachalo/M. Buckingham/
M. Pennington

DOG MOON
Robert Hunter/Timothy Truman

DOOM PATROL: CRAWLING FROM THE WRECKAGE
Grant Morrison/Richard Case/various

THE DREAMING: BEYOND THE SHORES OF NIGHT
Various writers and artists

THE DREAMING: THROUGH THE GATES OF HORN AND IVORY
Various writers and artists

ENIGMA
Peter Milligan/Duncan Fegredo

HELLBLAZER: ORIGINAL SINS
Jamie Delano/John Ridgway/various

HELLBLAZER: DANGEROUS HABITS
Garth Ennis/William Simpson/various

HELLBLAZER: FEAR AND LOATHING
Garth Ennis/Steve Dillon

HELLBLAZER: TAINTED LOVE
Garth Ennis/Steve Dillon

HELLBLAZER: DAMNATION'S FLAME
G. Ennis/S. Dillon/W. Simpson/
P. Snejbjerg

HOUSE OF SECRETS: FOUNDATIONS
Steven T. Seagle/Teddy Kristiansen

THE INVISIBLES: BLOODY HELL IN AMERICA
Grant Morrison/Phil Jimenez/
John Stokes

THE INVISIBLES: COUNTING TO NONE
Grant Morrison/Phil Jimenez/
John Stokes

THE INVISIBLES: SAY YOU WANT A REVOLUTION
G. Morrison/S. Yeowell/J. Thompson/
D. Cramer

THE INVISIBLES: KISSING MR. QUIMPER
G. Morrison/C. Weston/I. Reis/various

MICHAEL MOORCOCK'S MULTIVERSE
M. Moorcock/W. Simonson/J. Ridgway/
M. Reeve

MERCY
J.M. DeMatteis/Paul Johnson

NEIL GAIMAN & CHARLES VESS' STARDUST
Neil Gaiman/Charles Vess

NEIL GAIMAN'S MIDNIGHT DAYS
N. Gaiman/T. Kristiansen/S. Bissette/
J. Totleben/M. Mignola/various

NEVADA
S. Gerber/P. Winslade/S. Leialoha/
D. Giordano

PREACHER: GONE TO TEXAS
Garth Ennis/Steve Dillon

PREACHER: UNTIL THE END OF THE WORLD
Garth Ennis/Steve Dillon

PREACHER: PROUD AMERICANS
Garth Ennis/Steve Dillon

PREACHER: ANCIENT HISTORY
G. Ennis/S. Pugh/C. Ezquerra/R. Case

PREACHER: DIXIE FRIED
Garth Ennis/Steve Dillon

PREACHER: SALVATION
Garth Ennis/Steve Dillon

PREACHER: WAR IN THE SUN
Garth Ennis/Steve Dillon/
Peter Snejbjerg

THE SYSTEM
Peter Kuper

SWAMP THING: SAGA OF THE SWAMP THING
Alan Moore/Steve Bissette/
John Totleben

SWAMP THING: LOVE AND DEATH
A. Moore/S. Bissette/J. Totleben/
S. McManus

SWAMP THING: ROOTS
Jon J Muth

TERMINAL CITY
Dean Motter/Michael Lark

TRANSMETROPOLITAN: BACK ON THE STREET
Warren Ellis/Darick Robertson/various

TRANSMETROPOLITAN: LUST FOR LIFE
Warren Ellis/Darick Robertson/various

TRANSMETROPOLITAN: YEAR OF THE BASTARD
Warren Ellis/Darick Robertson/
Rodney Ramos

TRUE FAITH
Garth Ennis/Warren Pleece

UNCLE SAM
Steve Darnall/Alex Ross

UNKNOWN SOLDIER
Garth Ennis/Kilian Plunkett

V FOR VENDETTA
Alan Moore/David Lloyd

VAMPS
Elaine Lee/William Simpson

WITCHCRAFT
J. Robinson/P. Snejbjerg/M. Zulli/
S. Yeowell/T. Kristiansen

the Sandman library

THE SANDMAN: PRELUDES & NOCTURNES
N. Gaiman/S. Kieth/M. Dringenberg/
M. Jones

THE SANDMAN: THE DOLL'S HOUSE
N. Gaiman/M. Dringenberg/M. Jones/
C. Bachalo/M. Zulli/S. Parkhouse

THE SANDMAN: DREAM COUNTRY
N. Gaiman/K. Jones/C. Vess/
C. Doran/M. Jones

THE SANDMAN: THE DREAM HUNTERS
Neil Gaiman/Yoshitaka Amano

THE SANDMAN: SEASON OF MISTS
N. Gaiman/K. Jones/M. Dringenberg/
M. Jones/various

THE SANDMAN: A GAME OF YOU
Neil Gaiman/Shawn McManus/various

THE SANDMAN: FABLES AND REFLECTIONS
Neil Gaiman/various

THE SANDMAN: BRIEF LIVES
Neil Gaiman/Jill Thompson/Vince Locke

THE SANDMAN: WORLDS' END
Neil Gaiman/various

THE SANDMAN: THE KINDLY ONES
N. Gaiman/M. Hempel/R. Case/various

THE SANDMAN: THE WAKE
N. Gaiman/M. Zulli/J. Muth/C. Vess

DUSTCOVERS- THE COLLECTED SANDMAN COVERS 1989 - 1997
Dave McKean/Neil Gaiman

THE SANDMAN COMPANION
Hy Bender

To find more collected editions and monthly comic books from DC Comics,
call 1-888-COMIC BOOK for the nearest comics shop or go to your local book store.

Visit us at www.dccomics.com

VER0011